BVR's Guide to Physician Practice Valuation

Mark O. Dietrich, CPA/ABV
Editor

BVR
What It's Worth
1000 SW Broadway, Suite 1200, Portland, OR 97205
(503) 291-7963 • www.bvresources.com

BVR
What It's Worth

Publisher: Sarah Andersen

Managing Editor: Janice Prescott

Chair and CEO: David Foster

President: Lucretia Lyons

Vice President of Sales: Lexie Gross

Customer Service Manager: Jasmine Pearsall

ISBN: 978-1-62150-001-8

Library of Congress Control Number: 2012936144

Table of Contents

Introduction

The new edition of BVR's *Guide to Physician Practice Valuation* is the essential resource for understanding the complexities inherent in physician practice valuation, whether for sale to a hospital, private equity firm, another physician, or for marital dissolution or other litigation. This second edition contains nine additional chapters and revisions to six existing chapters. The guide opens with a detailed analysis of the healthcare economy and healthcare markets, updated to reflect the increasing recognition in the trade press and general media of the role that local market forces play. Among the new chapters is one addressing traditional practice buy-ins and buyouts as well as how the presence of noncompete agreements affects value. Another deals with the actual valuation of noncompete agreements and personal goodwill, the key to many litigation engagements as well as to tax planning associated with conversion of C corporations to S corporations or to tax-exempt status. A sample table of contents for a detailed valuation report provides a roadmap for the valuation analyst to approach the engagement.

The application of the anti-kickback statute and Stark Law to valuation practice is explored in a completely updated chapter. A related new chapter devoted to the *Bradford Regional* case analyzes the risks to the valuation analyst of being unfamiliar with the regulatory construct as does another new chapter on measuring intangible value in physician practices, the latter co-authored by the industry's most experienced healthcare valuation experts. An entire chapter is devoted to the leading Tax Court case on valuation of a practice for sale to a tax-exempt entity. Various other chapters explore the not-so-subtle nuances of valuing a physician practice, including coding analysis, ancillary technical component revenue, "incident to" billing for midlevel providers, valuing accounts receivable, and benchmarking and normalization of expense. The most common reason for a medical practice valuation is a divorce, and two chapters on the unique issues of divorce valuation are provided with relevant case law listed.

Practical guidance coupled with adherence to professional and regulatory standards define the 2012 *Guide to Physician Practice Valuation*. I am sure you will find it to be a valuable component of your valuation library.

Mark O. Dietrich
CPA/ABV

About the Authors

ABOUT THE EDITOR

Mark O. Dietrich, CPA/ABV, is editor, technical editor, and contributing author to the Business Valuation Resources/American Health Lawyers' Association *Guide to Healthcare Valuation 3rd Edition* (2012), editor and principal author of Business Valuation Resources' *Guide to Physician Practice Valuation* (2nd Edition, due in 2012), and co-author with Gregory Anderson, CPA, CVA, of *The Financial Professional's Guide to Healthcare Reform* to be published by John Wiley & Sons in 2012. Mark is also author of the *Medical Practice Valuation Guidebook* and co-author of PPC's *Guide to Healthcare Consulting*, along with more than 100 articles on valuation, taxation, managed care, and the healthcare regulatory environment. Mark's career experience includes serving as partner-in-charge of the annual audit of an 80 physician tax-exempt faculty group practice, representation of tax-exempt and taxable entities in Internal Revenue Service field audits, participation in the development of a 250-physician independent network and negotiation of its managed care and Medicare Advantage contracts, and more than 200 valuation engagements in the healthcare industry.

A regular speaker at national conferences on healthcare valuation and other topics, Mark also lectured in the United Kingdom during 2009 and 2011 on managed care, healthcare valuation, and valuation of medical practices to Her Majesty's Revenue and Customs and has been invited to Scotland and Northern Ireland in 2012. He is a member of the editorial board of *Financial Valuation and Litigation Expert* and the AICPA's National Healthcare Industry Conference Committee and will chair that conference in 2012. Mark has also served on the AICPA's ABV Credential Committee and ABV Exam Review Course Task Force.

CONTRIBUTING AUTHORS

Gregory D. Anderson, CPA/ABV, CVA, is a partner in the Health Care Practice Group of HORNE LLP, a CPA and business advisory firm headquartered in the southeastern United States. He concentrates his practice in the design and valuation of hospital-physician employment and other compensation arrangements; income distribution plans of physician group practices; and valuation of medical practices, hospitals, and other healthcare facilities. He serves as the firm's healthcare valuation services director and writes and lectures on fair market value, physician compensation, and Stark lawmatters.

Steven Andes, Ph.D., CPA is the American Osteopathic Association's director of physician information and professor and research assistant at the University of Illinois at Chicago. He attended University of Illinois at Urbana-Champaign, DePaul University, and Loyola University of Chicago.

Carol W. Carden, CPA/ABV, ASA, CFE, is a principal with PYA and provides business valuation and related consulting services to a wide variety of business organizations, primarily in the healthcare industry. Ms. Carden's primary areas of expertise are in finance, valuation, managed care, and revenue cycle operations for healthcare organizations. She has performed appraisals of businesses and securities for a wide variety of purposes such as mergers, acquisitions, joint ventures, management service agreements, and other intangible assets. She is also a nationally recognized speaker and writer on healthcare valuation topics. She is the chair of the Business Valuation Committee for the AICPA, was chair of the 2010 National AICPA Business Valuation Conference, and was on the planning committee for the 2011 AICPA National Healthcare Conference.

Frank Cohen, CMPA is principal and senior analyst for The Frank Cohen Group, LLC and a certified Master Black Belt in Lean Six Sigma. As a consultant and researcher, his areas of expertise include data mining, predictive analytics, applied statistics, process improvement, and evidence-based decision support. Mr. Cohen is the author of several books, including his newest, *Lean Six Sigma for the Medical Practice: Improving Profits by Improving Processes*. He has participated in and published numerous articles and studies and trained thousands of physicians, administrators, CPAs, and other healthcare professionals in all areas of healthcare analytics. He spent eight years as a physician assistant in the Navy and as a civilian, as well as a clinic administrator and hospital CEO. His clients include hospitals, medical practices, medical associations, legal and accounting professionals, government agencies, and other healthcare professionals.

J. Gregory Endicott, CPA/ABV, ASA, MBA, is the managing director of Strategic Value Group LLC, a firm that provides business valuation and related consulting services primarily in the areas of healthcare and financial reporting. Mr. Endicott's primary areas of expertise are in valuations for transactional, compliance, and financial reporting purposes. He has performed appraisals of businesses, intangible assets, compensation arrangements, and other agreements for a variety of purposes and is a nationally recognized speaker.

David Fein, MBA, is the CEO and president of ValuSource, which for over 20 years has been the leading provider of business valuation software, data and report writers for CPAs, mergers and acquisitions professionals, and business owners. Since 1997, Mr. Fein has partnered with the Medical Group Management Association (MGMA) to develop its interactive survey CD-ROMs, which provide data and benchmarking tools on physicians' compensation, business costs, and coding practices. ValuSource has crucial technology and data for anyone that needs to benchmark or value a medical practice.

Gregory S. Feltenberger, MBA, CACMPE, FACHE, CPHIMS, has over 16 years of operational health care experience. He is the chief of information project management at the Office of the Air Force Surgeon General, Air Force Medical Support Agency, Decision Support Branch, in Falls Church, Va. Greg has been a chief information officer, chief of information management, and group practice manager. In addition, Greg completed a 10-month fellowship in survey development, analysis, and performance measurement at the MGMA. He is a Ph.D. student at Old Dominion University in the health services research program. He is a fellow in the American College of Medical Practice Executives (ACMPE), the standard-setting and certification body of the MGMA; a fellow in the American College of Healthcare Executives; a certified medical practice executive in the American College of Medical Practice Executives; and a certified professional in healthcare information and management systems in the Healthcare Information and Management Systems Society. Greg is principal and co-founder of SmHart Inc. (www.SmHart.net), an education, training, and organizational improvement consulting firm. Finally, Greg co-authored a book titled, *Benchmarking Success: The Essential Guide for Medical Practices* with David N. Gans, published by the MGMA in 2008.

Ronald D. Finkelstein, CPA/ABV, is a principal in the accounting and tax services department at Morrison, Brown, Argiz & Farra LLC (MBAF), where he directs the firm's Health Care Services Group. Ron has extensive experience in assisting healthcare providers with merger and acquisition transactions. Ron has been a frequent lecturer both locally and nationally on a wide variety of healthcare accounting and practice management topics. Clients include ambulatory surgery centers, imaging centers, anatomic and clinical laboratories, health maintenance organizations, home health providers, hospitals, and physician group practices. A contributing editor to the quarterly publication *Practice Management Advisor,* Ron is a former member of the Steering Committee of the AICPA National Healthcare Industry Conference and past president of the National CPA Health Care Advisor's Association. In addition, Ron is a member of the Healthcare Financial Management Association, the MGMA, and the American Health Lawyers Association.

David N. Gans, MSHA, FACMPE, administers research and development at MGMA-ACMPE and its research affiliate, the MGMA Center for Research in Englewood, Col. He is an educational program speaker, author of a monthly column in *MGMA Connexion,* and he provides technical assistance to the association's staff and members on topic areas of benchmarking, use of survey data, financial management, cost-efficiency, physician compensation and productivity, managerial compensation, the resource-based relative value scale, employee staffing, cost accounting, medical group organization, and emergency preparedness. He is a retired colonel in the United States Army Reserve. He is a fellow in the American College of Medical Practice Executives and a certified medical practice executive in the American College of Medical Practice Executives.

Lydia M. Glatz, CPA, is a senior manager at Morrison, Brown, Argiz & Farra LLC (MBAF). She focuses on providing tax, accounting, and consulting services to clients in the healthcare industry. Her experience in the healthcare due diligence area has helped numerous buyers and sellers reach successful M&A transactions. Her clients include ambulatory surgery centers, physician practice management companies, and physician group practices in the primary care; ear, nose and throat; obstetrics and gynecology; radiology; and anesthesia specialties. Lydia has written several articles on issues affecting physicians and the healthcare industry. She is past president of the Broward chapter of the Florida Institute of Certified Public Accountants and has a B.S. in accounting from Florida Atlantic University.

Matthew D. Jenkins, JD, is a partner in the Richmond, Va., office of Hunton & Williams LLP and heads the firm's Health Law Group. He has worked extensively with hospitals and multihospital systems on regulatory, corporate, governance, and transactional matters. He has led a number of nonprofit entities through conversion transactions resulting in the creation of substantial community foundations. His work also involves legislative matters and practice before administrative agencies. Mr. Jenkins is a member of the American Bar Association's Health Law Section, where he serves as a vice-chair of the Transactional & Business Interest Group. He served two terms as a governor's appointee on the Special Advisory Commission on Mandated Health Insurance Benefits for the Commonwealth of Virginia. He is a past chair of the Health Law Section of the Virginia State Bar. Mr. Jenkins earned his J.D. in 1984 from the University of Virginia.

Tracy Farryl Katz, Esq., CPA, is a partner at Gursey Schneider LLP in the firm's Litigation Support Department, specializing in the area of forensic accounting in family law and civil litigation matters. She has performed a wide range of litigation accounting services including: business appraisals, determination of gross cash flow available for support, determination of celebrity goodwill, net spendable evaluations, pension plan allocations, stock option apportionments, characterization of assets, analysis of reimbursement claims, lifestyle analyses, and contract and royalty analyses in the film, television, and music industries. She graduated from the Southwestern School of Law in Los Angeles.

W. James Lloyd, CPA/ABV, ASA, CBA, CFE, is a senior member of the valuation, transaction advisory, and litigation consulting practice of Pershing Yoakley & Associates P.C. (PYA), a certified public accounting and healthcare consulting firm based in Knoxville, Tenn. Mr. Lloyd provides business valuation, fair market value compensation, economic damages analysis, and related consulting services to a wide range of business organizations, primarily in the healthcare industry. Mr. Lloyd has valued hundreds of healthcare organizations, intangible assets, and various economic relationships between hospitals and physicians. Mr. Lloyd is the chair of the AICPA's ABV Credential Committee and is a frequent speaker at various national and regional conferences.

James M. Pinna, Esq., is an attorney in the Richmond, Va., office of Hunton & Williams LLP and practices with the firm's Health Law Group. He works primarily with hospitals, multihospital systems, and other healthcare providers on regulatory, transactional, corporate governance, and compliance matters. He is a vice chair of the Business & Transactions Interest Group of the American Bar Association's Health Law Section and a member of the American Health Lawyers Association. Previously, he worked in business development for National Nephrology Associates, a privately held dialysis company based in Nashville. Mr. Pinna earned his J.D. from the University of Virginia.

Todd J. Sorensen, MBA, AVA, is a partner with VMG Health. He specializes in providing valuation and transaction advisory services to the firm's healthcare clients. He has acted as financial advisor in transactions with physician groups, acute care hospitals, health maintenance organizations, preferred provider organizations, diagnostic centers, ambulatory surgery centers, home health agencies, physical and operational therapy centers, institutional pharmacies, retail pharmacies and rural health clinics. Mr. Sorensen received his MBA from Baylor University.

Reed Tinsley, CPA, CVA, CFP, CHBC, is the owner of Reed Tinsley, CPA. He is a certified valuation analyst and certified healthcare business consultant. Reed has published numerous articles in national and regional publications and is frequently asked to speak on a variety of health care topics, including valuation, operational management, revenue enhancement, and financial oversight. He has also written *Medical Practice Management Handbook for CPAs,* originally published by Harcourt Brace. He attended the University of Texas at Austin and the University of Texas at Austin—The Red McCombs School of Business.

Stacey D. Udell, CPA/ABV/CFF, ASA, CVA, a partner in the public accounting firm of Gold Gocial Gerstein LLC. Ms. Udell specializes in business valuation, forensic accounting, economic damages, and litigation support for a wide range of businesses and professional practices for purposes such as estate and gift tax planning and compliance, divorce, business succession planning, mergers and acquisitions, shareholder litigation, and bankruptcy proceedings. Ms. Udell is a contributing author to the *Family Law Services Handbook,* published by John Wiley & Sons.

Kathie L. Wilson, CPA, CVA, maintains a consulting practice, assisting accountants and attorneys in the areas of medical practice accounting and valuation and family law litigation in the San Francisco Bay Area. She holds a Masters in Taxation from Bentley College and a B.A. in business administration from the University of Washington.

Chapter 1

The Healthcare Economy

By Mark O. Dietrich, CPA/ABV

The following material is based upon data from the Centers for Medicaid and Medicare Office of the Actuary released in September 2011. That office historically prepared annual projections of national health expenditures (NHE) released in February of each year using an established model that incorporates three separate factors: actuarial, econometric, and judgmental. The February 2010 NHE release was made in September 2010 to reflect the reform, and the most recent update was then released in September 2011. The projections go through 2020.[1]

The September 2010 projection described the impact of the Patient Protection and Affordable Care Act (Affordable Care Act):

> Growth in National Health Expenditures (NHE) in the United States over the coming decade is expected to be slightly higher as a result of the implementation of the Patient Protection and Affordable Care Act (Affordable Care Act), as well as other relevant legislative and regulatory changes since the publication of our February 2010 projections. Average annual growth in NHE for 2009 through 2019 is expected to be 6.3%, 0.2 percentage points faster than pre-reform estimates. NHE as a share of gross domestic product (GDP) is expected to be 19.6% by 2019, or 0.3 percentage points higher than projected before reform.
>
> Many of the major Affordable Care Act's provisions go into effect in 2014, resulting in substantive differences in projected growth of NHE compared to estimates made pre-reform. An expansion of Medicaid coverage (to all persons under age 65 in households

1 A detailed description of the methodology is located at www.cms.hhs.gov/NationalHealthExpendData/downloads/projections-methodology-2006.pdf and the data are at www.cms.hhs.gov/NationalHealthExpendData/03_NationalHealthAccountsProjected.asp.

> with incomes less than 138% of the federal poverty level), combined with the advent of state-level health insurance exchanges, is expected to result in NHE growth of 9.2% in 2014 (2.6 percentage points higher than projected before reform was passed).
>
> Over the latter stages of the projection period (2015 through 2019), the impact of the Affordable Care Act on health coverage is anticipated to continue as more people acquire, or shift, into new or different coverage. By 2019, 92.7% of the U.S. population is expected to have health insurance (an increase of 10 percentage points) driven, in part, by growth in Medicaid, which when combined with the Children's Health Insurance Program (CHIP), is projected to cover 82 million persons. Also by 2019, 30.6 million people are expected to be enrolled in health insurance exchange plans.
>
> [Post-reform] Principally due to the expansion of Medicaid eligibility and additional CHIP funding in 2014, Medicaid and CHIP enrollment is expected to increase by 21.8 million people, with total spending projected to grow 17.4% (11.1 percentage points faster than the pre-reform projection). The federal government is expected to finance most of the care for the new Medicaid beneficiaries through a 100% federal medical assistance percentage, which will phase down to 90% in 2020 and thereafter.
>
> Provisions of the Affordable Care Act are projected to result in a lower average annual Medicare spending growth rate for 2012 through 2019 (6.2%), 1.3 percentage points lower than pre-reform estimates. The relatively lower projected Medicare expenditure growth rate reflects reduced annual payment updates for most Medicare services, substantial reductions to managed care plan payments, and the creation of the Independent Payment Advisory Board.

The September 2011 forecast for the decade through 2020 is as follows, with healthcare spending reaching 19.6% of GDP by that time, driven in part by a large jump in the GDP-share in 2009 due to the recession, as modified by the Affordable Care Act:

> In 2010, NHE is projected to have reached $2.6 trillion and grown 3.9%, down from 4.0% in 2009. Estimated spending growth in 2010 was slow due to continuing declines in employment and private health insurance coverage associated with the recent recession. GDP growth is projected to have been 3.8% in 2010, nearly the same rate of growth as NHE. The health share of GDP is expected to have remained constant between 2009 and 2010, at 17.6%.
>
> Between 2011 and 2013, health spending is projected to grow faster due to expected improvements in the economy, reaching a rate of 5.5% by 2013. Private health insurance and out-of-pocket spending are both projected to grow faster over this period. Private health insurance spending is projected to grow 4.8% in 2013, up from 2.6% in 2010, as employer-sponsored insurance enrollment is expected to increase with gains in employment. Out-of-pocket spending is projected to grow 3.9% in 2013, up from 1.8% in 2010, as growth in household incomes is expected to lead to more healthcare

spending and as employers are anticipated to increase cost-sharing requirements in employer-sponsored insurance plans.

In 2014, health spending is projected to grow 8.3%. This projected acceleration in the growth rate, up from 5.5% in 2013, is primarily the result of the Affordable Care Act's coverage-related expansions. Medicaid eligibility is set to increase to persons under age 65 in families with income up to 138% of the federal poverty level in 2014. As a result, Medicaid enrollment is expected to increase by 19.5 million people and spending is projected to grow 20.3%. The new health insurance exchanges are expected to cover 13.9 million people in 2014 and contribute to 9.4% growth in private health insurance spending. Because people gaining coverage through the Medicaid expansion and the exchanges are expected to be younger and in better health than currently insured persons, on average, it is anticipated that a relatively higher share of their new costs would go toward physician and clinical services and prescription drugs and a lower share toward hospital and long-term care services.

Over the projection period (2010-2020), average annual health spending growth (5.8%) is anticipated to outpace average annual growth in the overall economy by 1.1 percentage points (4.7%). By 2020, national health spending is expected to reach $4.6 trillion and comprise 19.8% of GDP. The government-sponsored share of health spending is projected to increase from 45% in 2010 to about 50% by 2020, driven by expected robust Medicare enrollment growth, Medicaid coverage expansions, and exchange plan premium and cost-sharing subsidies."

Medicare spending is expected to have slowed in 2010 due to the reform's cutbacks in Medicare Advantage payments. The statement below regarding slower growth due to physician fee schedules cuts appears annually, but those cuts never take place.

Medicare spending is estimated to have been $525 billion in 2010 as growth slowed to 4.5%, down from 7.9% in 2009, due in part to an across-the-board reduction in the rate of growth for payments to Medicare's private health plans by 3.4% . Medicare is projected to grow 5.9% in 2011, but only 1.7% in 2012; the slow growth in 2012 is driven by a 29.4% reduction in physician payment rates required under the Medicare sustainable growth rate (SGR) formula.[2] (Under an alternative scenario where physician payment rate updates are based on growth in the Medicare Economic Index (MEI), Medicare spending growth is projected to accelerate to 6.6% in 2012.) Average annual Medicare spending growth is anticipated to be 6.3% for 2013 through 2020, reflecting increasing enrollment (as the oldest baby boomers become eligible for Medicare) that will drive up spending, and provisions of the Affordable Care Act that call for reduced fee-for-service provider payment updates and lower payments to private plans.

2 Such "required" cuts have been consistently overturned by Congress for many years.

Hospital spending trends were described as follows. The reform legislation contemplates paying for the expansion in significant part through cutbacks in hospital spending; however, the chief actuary of CMS[3] does not believe many of those savings can be realized:

> Hospital spending growth is estimated to have slowed by half a percentage point, to 4.6% in 2010, and to reach $794.3 billion, with slower growth in spending by private health insurance plans and Medicare. For 2011 through 2013, growth in hospital spending is projected to accelerate, reaching 5.3% by 2013, as private health insurance spending growth rates increase with a rebound in enrollment and Medicare growth increases as the oldest baby boomers start to enroll. Hospital spending growth is projected to accelerate to 7.2% in 2014. This faster growth rate reflects increases in service use due to the coverage expansions under Medicaid and private insurance, partially offset by lower Medicare payment rate increases for hospitals mandated by the Affordable Care Act. Hospital spending is projected to grow 6.2% per year during the period 2015 to 2020, with Medicare spending growth generally outpacing private health insurance spending growth, reflecting the shift of baby boomers onto Medicare.

The government researchers found that physician spending growth increased only 2.4% in 2010. Although recent history suggests otherwise, the physician spending growth rate was forecast to decline in 2010 due to projected cuts under both Medicare's sustainable growth rate formula (see discussion infra) and whether that formula is suspended by Congressional action. The alternative growth calculation without those cuts is 4.5 percentage points.

> Physician and clinical services spending growth is estimated to have slowed to a historically low rate of 2.4% in 2010, with spending of $517.8 billion, driven by a reduction in visits related to the recession and a less severe flu season than in 2009. Spending growth is expected to accelerate to 4% in 2011 and then slow to 0.8% in 2012, due to the 29.4% Medicare physician payment rate cut under Medicare's SGR formula. (If the payment rate update was based on the growth rate of the MEI, physician and clinical spending would be projected to grow 4.5% in 2012.) In 2014, physician and clinical services spending is projected to grow 8.9%, related to the Medicaid and exchange coverage expansions. Physician and clinical services spending is projected to grow at an average rate of 5.6% between 2015 and 2020, with Medicaid and Medicare spending growth generally outpacing private health insurance spending growth.

One of the principal drivers of the increase in health expenditures is prescription drug costs. It is important to understand the underlying components of the increase because the general growth rate in health expenditures will not serve as a valid proxy for the industry's individual subsets, which often have different rates of growth.

3 s3.amazonaws.com/thf_media/2010/pdf/OACT-Memo-FinImpactofPPACA-Enacted.pdf.

> Prescription drug spending is projected to have grown 3.5% in 2010, to $258.6 billion, with continued slow growth in the use of drugs and an increasing share of prescriptions being filled with generic drugs. While growth between 2011 and 2013 is projected to be faster (at an average rate of 5.7% annually), the loss of patent protection of several of the best-selling brand-name drugs in 2011 limits growth. In 2014, prescription drug spending is expected to grow faster, at a rate of 10.7%, driven by a substantial increase in the use of drugs by newly insured persons in Medicaid and the exchange plans. Prescription drug spending growth is expected to average 7.2% from 2015 through 2020, reflecting slower increases in generic drugs' share of the market and the costs of new drugs becoming available during these years.

Exhibit 1 plots the increase in total national expenditures (left axis) using projected data for the years 2006 to 2020 against those for prescription drugs (right axis). Note that there was a flattening of prescription growth commencing in 2006 followed by an upturn in the rate of increase commencing in 2009. Factors contributing to this rapid increase in prescription drug spending include consumer advertising and new product development, along with increased reliance on clinical pharmacology.

Exhibit 1. National Health Expenditures and Prescription Drugs

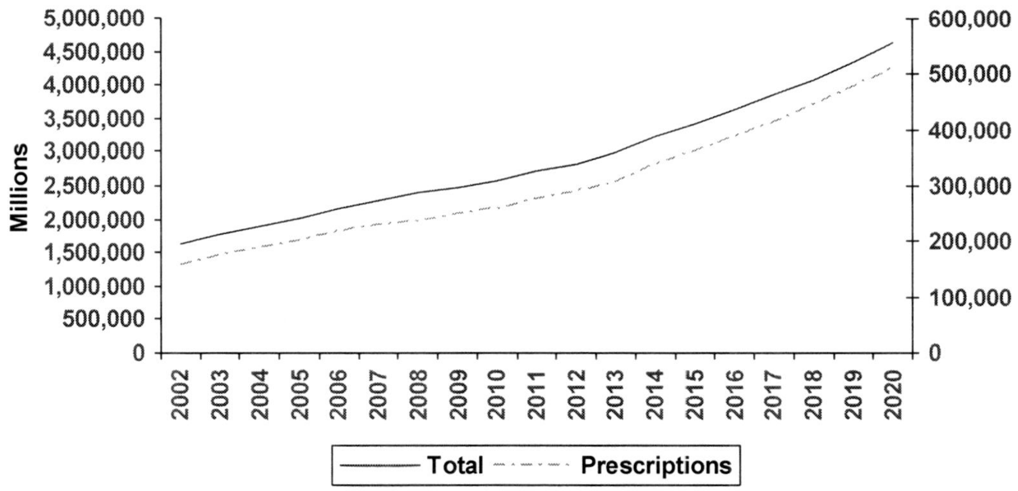

Each year, coincident with the release of the annual projections of national health expenditures, members of the CMS Office of the Actuary publish an article in the journal *Health Affairs* on the projections. The 2011 projections initially appeared in the January, 2011 edition.[4] Data contained in that article based on the NHE indicate that pharmaceutical spending increases continue to outstrip all other sectors except home health,

4 Anne Martin, David Lassman, Lekha Whittle, Aaron Catlin and the National Health Expenditure Accounts Team: "Recession Contributes to Slowest Annual Rate of Increase in Health Spending in Five Decades," *Health Affairs*, 30, no.1 (2011): 11-22.

rising at 5.3%, compared to 4% for physician services. Home health spending is exploding due to the aging population and a push by government and private insurers to move care for the elderly out of more expensive nursing home settings, as shown in Exhibit 2.

Exhibit 2. Annual Increase by Category

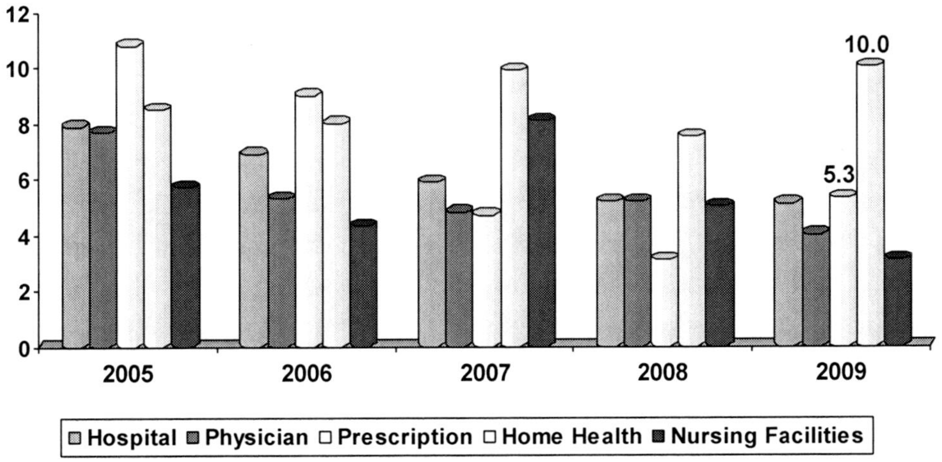

The trend can be seen comparatively with other components in Exhibit 3 based on the 2011 Milliman Medical Index, with pharmacy spending having slowed relative to other sectors except for physicians as indicated in Exhibit 2.[5]

Exhibit 3. Annual Increase by Category

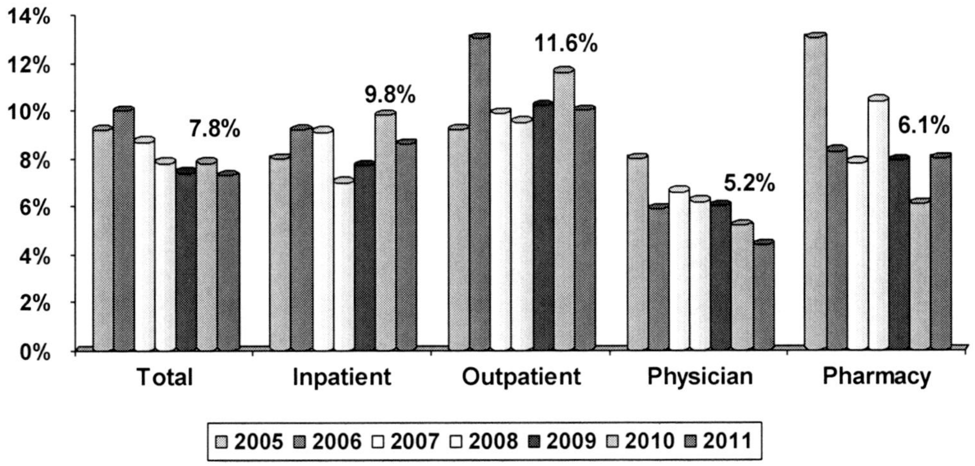

5 publications.milliman.com/periodicals/mmi/pdfs/milliman-medical-index-2011.pdf, May 11, 2011.

Prescription drug spending is important for a variety of reasons. Physicians and mental health professionals increasingly rely upon pharmaceuticals to treat various conditions, often as a substitute for surgery or other procedures (e.g., coronary artery disease). The new Medicare prescription drug benefit was effective in 2006.

In contrast to prescription drugs, Medicare spending (Exhibit 4, right axis, purple line) was increasing at slightly more than the overall national rate before Part D. Note the extraordinary effect that the new Medicare drug benefit has on Medicare spending by comparing the current projection to the prior projection as reflected in the red line. Shifting prescription drug spending to Medicare has caused the rate of growth in Medicare and overall spending to come close together. [The decline from 1997 to 2000 reflects the success of the Balanced Budget Act (BBA) of 1997 in slowing Medicare spending increases, which was cited by the chief actuary of CMS in his analysis of the healthcare reform legislation.] As noted above, projected Medicare spending post-reform is budgeted to grow more slowly than pre-reform, based upon a variety of factors, including limits in the annual hospital market basket updates for payments discussed infra. However, the chief actuary questions whether such changes will occur.

Medicaid (Exhibit 5) is a program shared between the federal and state government that covers the poor and, historically more significant, nursing home costs for lower-income seniors. Program spending slows in 2006 due to the advent of the Medicare prescription drug benefit as described above and then resumes growth at a higher rate. This pattern is also reflective of the aging population, slower economic growth post-Sept. 11, the continuation of the recession that began in 2008, and immigration patterns. Where Medicaid spending was expected to outstrip Medicare spending in 2005, the Medicare drug benefit had changed that, until the coming explosion in Medicaid spending as a result of the reform legislation. Medicaid is one of,[6] if not the, principal deficit

Exhibit 4. National Health Expenditures and Medicare

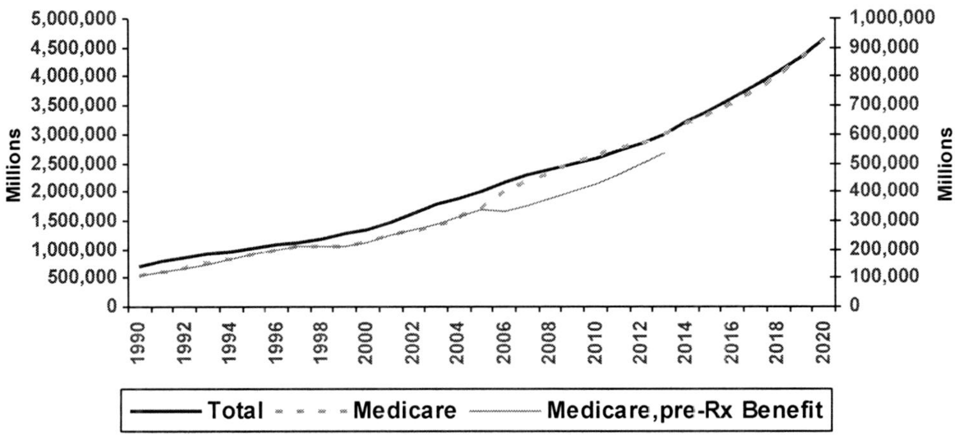

6 Unionized state employee pensions and benefits being the principal other one.

driver in state budgets and generally speaking is the largest line item in those budgets. Post-reform, Medicaid is expected to grow dramatically, as more than 50% of the newly insured are supposed to be covered by Medicaid.

Exhibit 5. National Health Expenditures and Medicaid

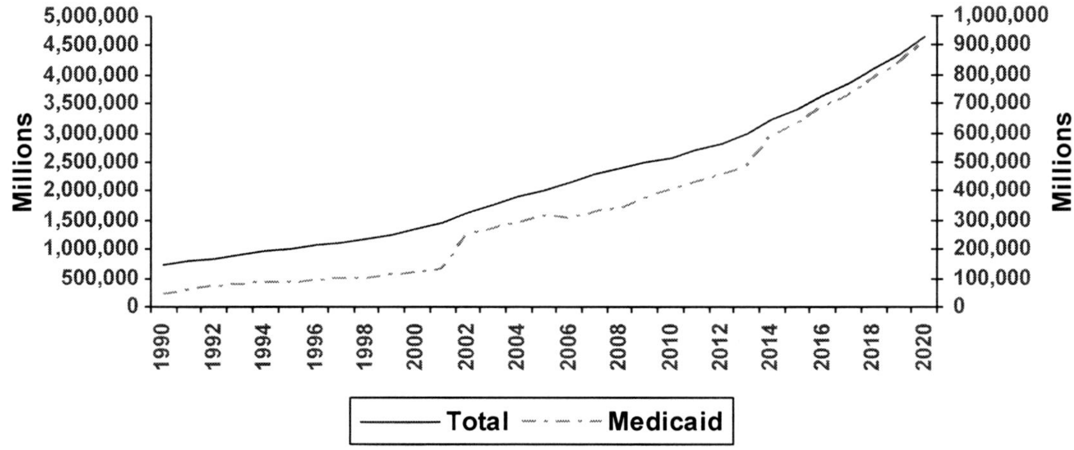

Finally, the actual and projected trends for hospital and physician expenditures are plotted (Exhibit 6, right axis) against national health expenditures. As noted elsewhere in this report, physician expenditures are projected to grow more slowly for a variety of reasons, including present Medicare reimbursement limitations.

Exhibit 6. National Health Expenditure, Hospital and Physician Costs

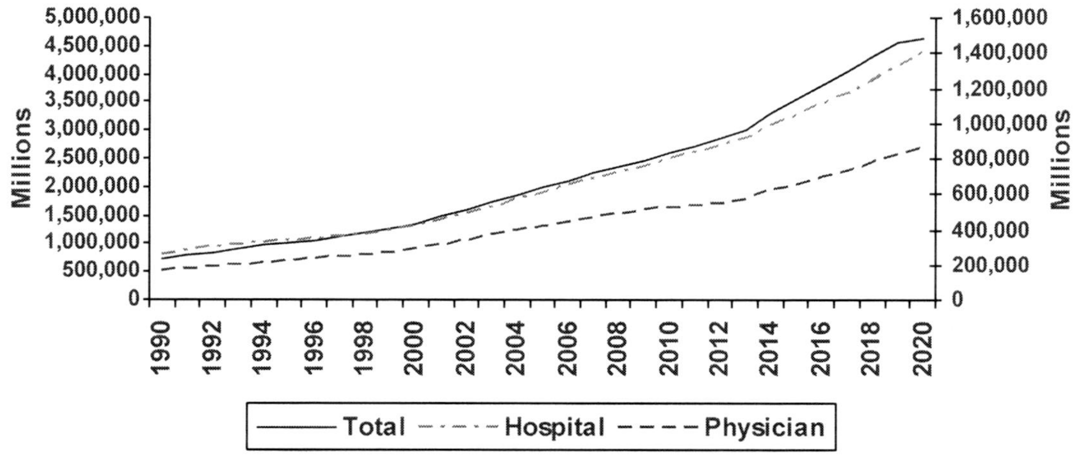

Healthcare spending is expected to continue to outstrip growth in GDP, exacerbated in the recession, as shown in Exhibit 7 from MedPAC's *2010 Report to Congress*.

Exhibit 7. Health Care Spending Growth

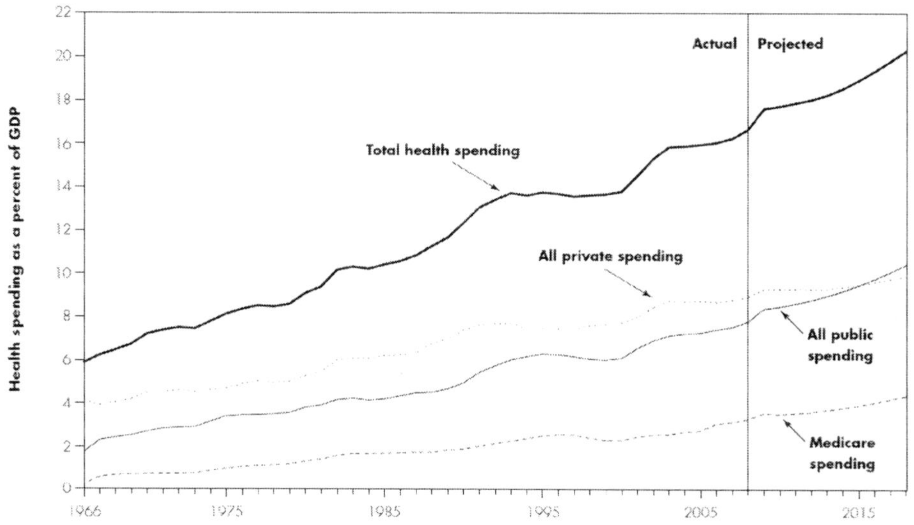

There are five principal sponsors of sources for the payment of health expenditures, as shown in Exhibit 8.[7]

Exhibit 8. 2009 National Health Expenditures, by Sponsor

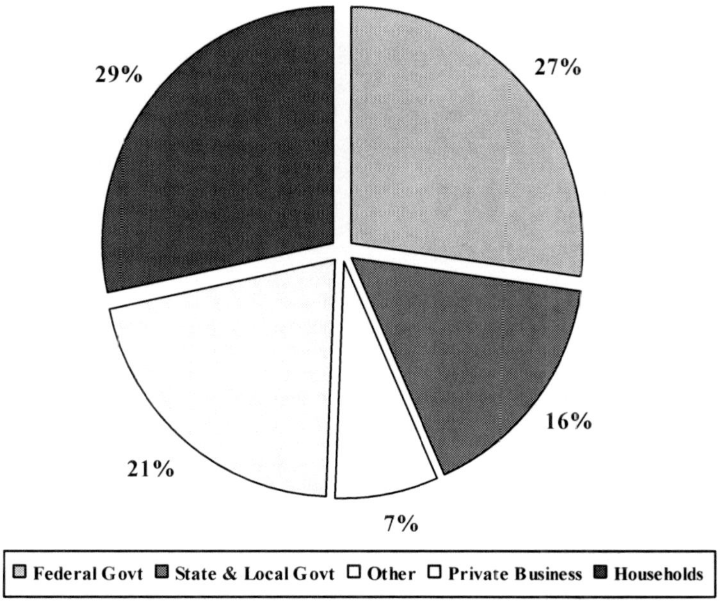

7 Ibid. "Recession Contributes to Slowest Annual Rate of Increase in Health Spending in Five Decades," *Health Affairs*, 30, no.1 (2011):11-22.

Healthcare Indicators

Utilization

Overall, inpatient admissions (or discharges) for the over-age-65 (Medicare) population continue to grow, based upon data from MedPAC's *2011 Report to Congress,* even though the *rate* of inpatient admissions per 1,000 population has grown less dramatically. (See Exhibit 9.) More services take place in the outpatient department of hospitals as well. This type of analysis is significant in valuing medical practices that have material earnings from hospital services. This would include the surgical specialties and consultative medical specialties, such as cardiology and particularly invasive cardiology. It also is connected to the trend to move surgical cases to ambulatory surgery centers, one of the most significant trends of the last decade.

A contributing factor to the loss of inpatient hospital revenue for nonsurgical physicians is the increasing presence of hospitalists, specially trained internists who typically work for a hospital and follow a patient throughout the course of their hospitalization. Many times, physicians who would prefer to follow their own patients while in-hospital are pressured into allowing the employed hospitalists to handle the care—and take the corresponding revenue stream.

Exhibit 9. Hospital Discharge and Admissions Trend[8]

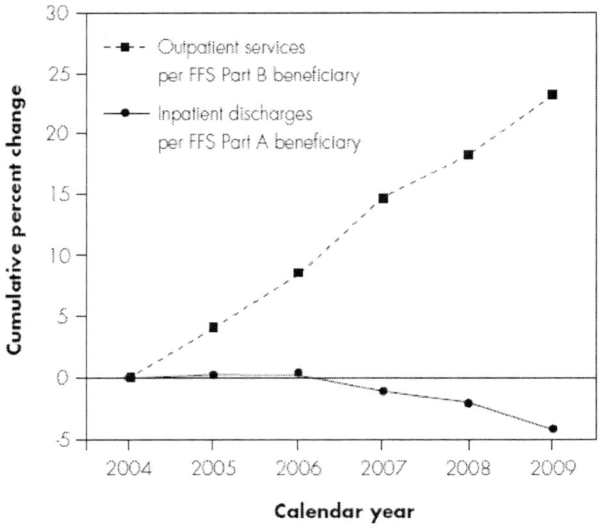

Note: FFS (fee-for-service). Data are for short-term general and surgical hospitals, including critical access and children's hospitals.

Source: MedPAC analysis of MedPAR and hospital outpatient claims data from CMS.

8 *2011 Report to Congress,* Medicare Payment Advisory Commission.

Costs

Costs per inpatient admission had increased relatively slowly before 2001. This pattern is consistent with other data discussed herein indicating that hospitals are seeing large revenue increases after years of pricing pressure. Overall data (Exhibit 10) on hospital costs per day show a steady increase each year.

Exhibit 10. Inpatient Cost Trend[9]

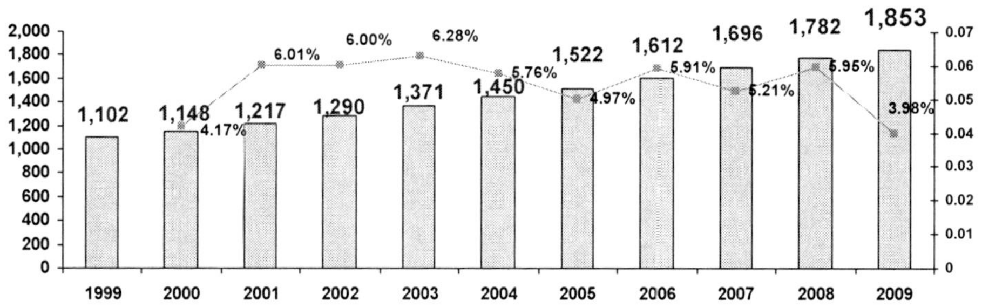

In contrast to hospital inpatient costs, outpatient visit costs have been increasing at a steadier rate as shown in Exhibits 11 and 12 from MedPac's 2011 *Report to Congress*. Hospitals have been progressively moving volume toward, and expanding the services of, outpatient settings where the government had historically been less successful in controlling utilization and price. Hospital inpatient services have for several decades been paid a fixed rate per *discharge* diagnosis (DRG) (known as a prospective payment system—PPS[10]) that varies principally based upon the number of admissions, rather than the number of days, in the hospital. Until comparatively recently, *outpatient* services were not paid under a PPS. This was changed by the BBA and implemented in August 2000. Such changes, of course, are very forecasting long-term growth trends.

Exhibit 11. Cost Growth in 2009

	Annual cost growth			
Cost measure	**2006**	**2007**	**2008**	**2009**
Inpatient costs per discharge	5.1%	4.2%	5.5%	3.0%
Outpatient costs per service	2.6	5.6	5.1	4.8
Weighted average	4.6	4.5	5.4	3.3
Input price inflation	4.2	3.4	4.3	2.6

Note: Cost growth numbers are not adjusted for reported changes in case mix. Analysis excludes critical access hospitals and Maryland hospitals. The weighted average is based on hospitals' inpatient and outpatient Medicare costs.

Source: MedPAC analysis of Medicare Cost Report and claims files from CMS.

9 http://www.statehealthfacts.kff.org/comparemaptable.jsp?ind=273&cat=5, 2009 data.
10 www.cms.gov/providers/.

Exhibit 12. Medicare Growth in 2009

Hospital services	2004	2008	2009	Mean annual change 2004–2009	Change 2008–2009
Inpatient services					
Total FFS payments (in billions)	$100	$110	$114	2.7%	3.7%
Payments per FFS enrollee	2,831	3,202	3,337	3.6	4.2
Outpatient services					
Total FFS payments (in billions)	24	31	34	8.6	11.2
Payments per FFS enrollee	723	988	1,104	10.6	11.7
Inpatient and outpatient services					
Total FFS payments (in billions)	124	140	148	3.8	5.3
Payments per FFS enrollee	3,554	4,191	4,441	5.0	6.0

Note: FFS (fee-for-service). Reported hospital spending includes all hospitals covered by Medicare's inpatient prospective payment system along with critical access hospitals. Maryland hospitals are excluded. Fiscal year 2009 payments include partial imputation to account for hospitals that typically do not submit their cost reports to CMS before CMS makes the most recent year available to the public. Although the number of Medicare beneficiaries grew significantly from 2004 to 2009, the number of FFS beneficiaries declined over that time due to the shift of beneficiaries to the Medicare Advantage program. For the purposes of calculating payments per FFS beneficiary, we identified populations of FFS beneficiaries eligible for inpatient (Part A) and outpatient (Part B) coverage and excluded enrollees in Maryland. Due to rounding, totals may not equal the sum of their parts.

Source: MedPAC analysis of CMS hospital cost reports and MedPAR files.

Finally, outpatient visit growth continues to increase, while actual inpatient days per 1,000 continue to decline.[11]

Exhibit 13. Hospital Outpatient and Inpatient Volume

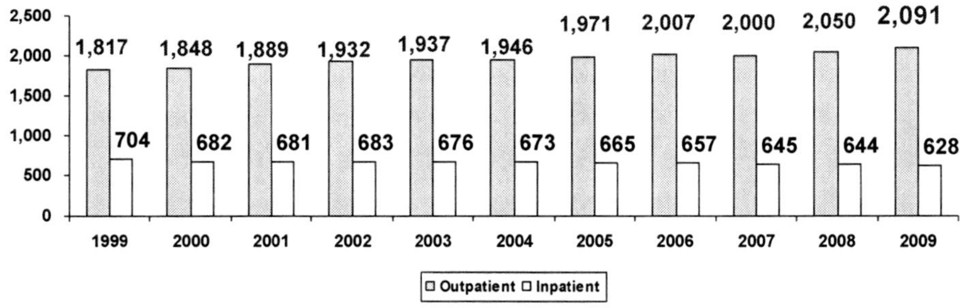

Medical expense inflation continues to outstrip the overall CPI, with hospital inflation leading the way, consistent with the inpatient costs per admission in Exhibit 13. Physician costs, in contrast, are increasing at a rate less than that of the medical CPI and significantly less than hospital costs and GDP (Exhibit 14). Hospital costs before 2000 and then again after 2008 had risen at a rate slightly less than GDP, reflecting the downward pressure on costs and utilization from HMOs and limited government payment increases. As the economy entered recession in 2008, healthcare expenditures continued to increase, even increasing during 2009, when the GDP and CPI otherwise declined, leading to concerns about deflation elsewhere in the economy. Once again, the healthcare segment proved to be more or less indifferent to the broad economy,

11 www.statehealthfacts.kff.org/comparemaptable.jsp?ind=390&cat=8, 2009 data.

an important factor to consider when conducting the valuation of healthcare entities because growth is rarely negative, even in a recession. [12,13]

Exhibit 14. % Change: CPI-All, GDP and Various CPI-Healthcare

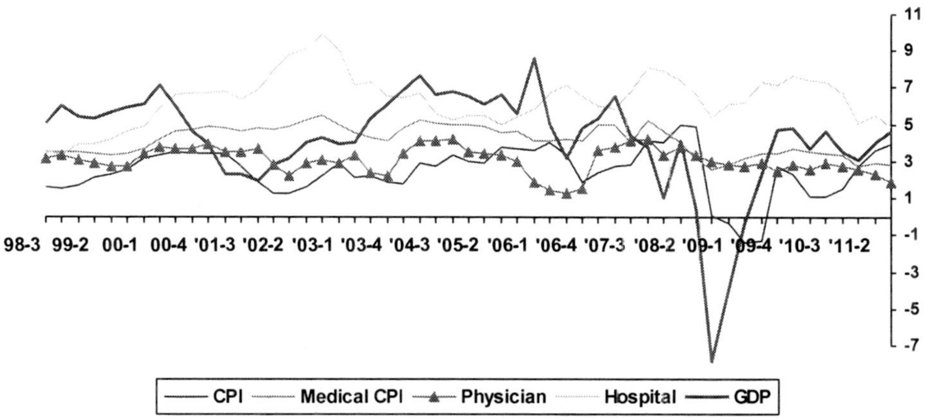

(Rates shown in Exhibit 14 represent the percent change from same period of previous year.)

A comparison of the CPI and medical care CPI with a trend line for medical care is shown in Exhibit 15. The recession has flattened the cost trend in the medical CPI.

Exhibit 15. CPI and CPI Healthcare

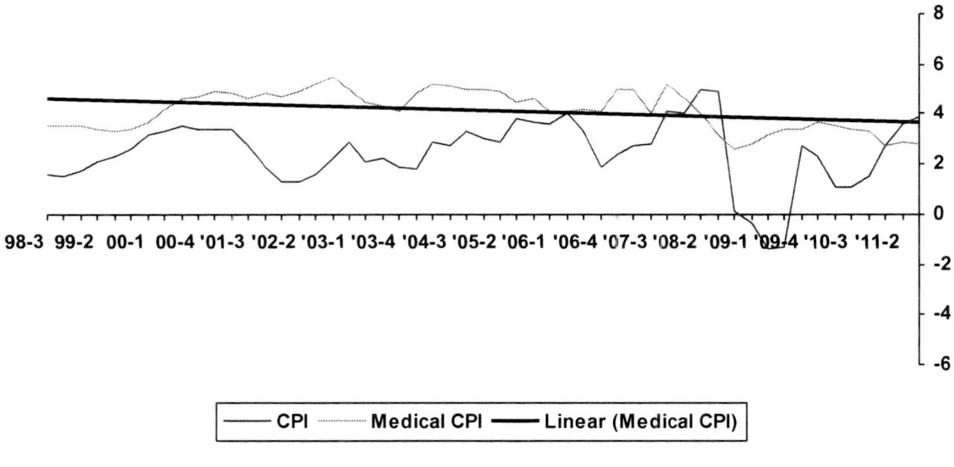

More telling, perhaps, is the CPI for medical care services (physicians and hospitals) versus that of physicians and hospitals taken alone, indicating that hospital costs are the main driver of healthcare inflation (Exhibit 16).

12 www.bls.gov/cpi/#tables, Nov. 22, 2011.
13 www.bea.gov/newsreleases/national/gdp/gdpnewsrelease.htm, Table 1, Current Dollar.

Exhibit 16. CPI Healthcare[14]

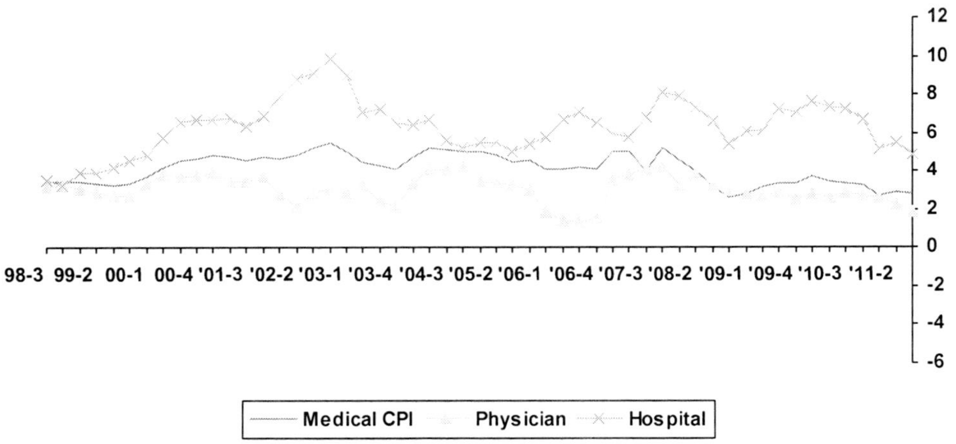

The data indicate that physician practice expenses were increasing at a higher rate than physician earnings, including fringe benefits,[15] although both are less than the medical CPI as shown in Exhibit 17. Data on physician wages and salaries are no longer presented, although they showed considerably lower growth then the reported earnings number through the last data point, in 2004, before subsequent revisions to the data. Benefit growth accounts for a significant part of the reported increase. Importantly, the values are also *productivity adjusted* using Bureau of Labor Statistics nonfarm multifactor productivity, a generic workforce measure that does not reflect physician practices. Historically, both reports and projections of practice expense growth being less than the rate of earnings growth do not, in fact, materialize; however, they continue to appear in the forecast! The year 2007 represents an exception due to the significant rate increases for physicians, offsetting years of accelerating costs without increases in per unit fees.

CMS forecasts of physician earnings typically reflect the threat of significant cuts due to failure to repeal the sustainable growth rate formula discussed elsewhere herein in the absence of legislative change, unless those cuts have been legislatively deferred, such as was the case in 2005 through 2011. This is a result of the artificial constraints placed upon increases in physician reimbursement by the Medicare program, which are not present for any other class of provider (e.g., hospitals or home health care), although the reform legislation imposes certain productivity targets on hospitals for the first time. However, the reform legislation imposes requirements for productivity gains on hospitals, which, notably, the chief actuary of CMS says are likely unobtainable.

14 www.cms.hhs.gov/MedicareProgramRatesStats/03_HlthCrInds.asp#TopOfPage.
15 www.cms.hhs.gov/MedicareProgramRatesStats/04_MarketBasketData.asp.

Exhibit 17. MD Earnings and Practice Expense Trend[16, 17]

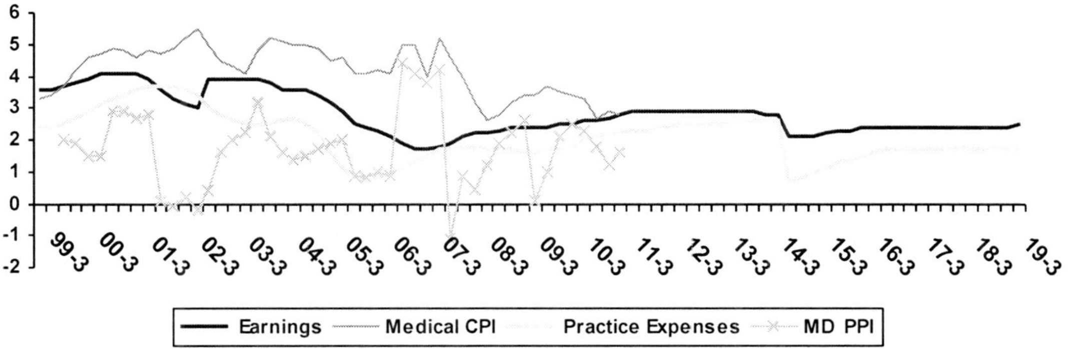

This PPI for physicians has steadily maintained a compound rate of growth of approximately 2%, although the year-to-year changes are quite volatile, particularly in 2007. In fact, the *compound* rate of growth in physician fees during this 15-year period was only 1.96% (Exhibit 18).

Exhibit 18. Producer Price Index, Physician Services

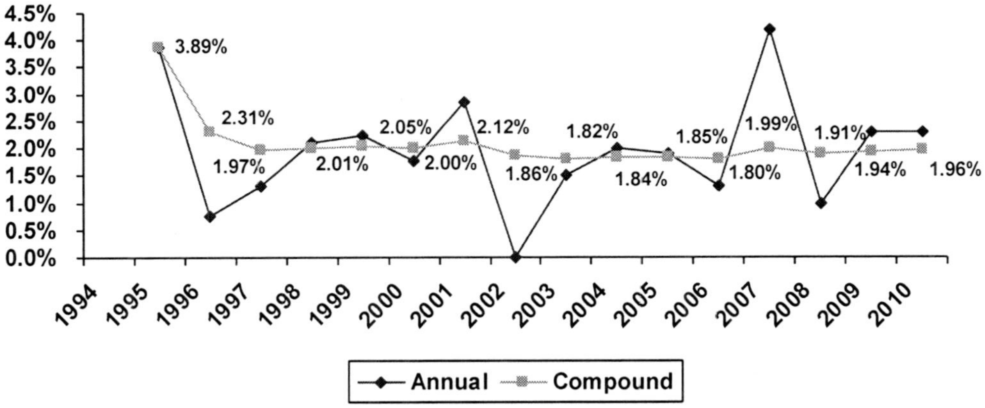

Trends in Physician Supply and Demand and Utilization

Exhibit 19 illustrates the breakdown of patient office visits by individual physician specialties from the National Center for Health Statistics.[18] General and family practice, internal medicine, and pediatrics accounted for 50.61% of all patient office visits in 2007, down from 51% in 2006.

16 www.bls.gov/schedule/archives/ppi_nr.htm, Nov. 22, 2011.

17 www.bls.gov/cpi/#tables.

18 National Health Statistics 2007 NAMCS micro-data file documentation. Note that not all of the possible physician specialties were separately tracked in the NCHS study.

Exhibit 19. Patent Office Visits by Individual Physician Specialties

Specialty	2007 % of visits	2006 % of visits	2005 % of visits	2004 % of visits	2003 % of visits	2002 % of visits	2001 % of visits	2000 % of visits
General practice/ family practice	22.9%	23.1%	22.4%	22.8%	24.6%	24.2%	23.9%	24.1%
Internal medicine	14.5	13.9	17.4	16.1	15.6	17.6	15.3	15.2
Pediatrics	13.2	13.6	13.4	12.8	10.4	13.5	12.6	12.6
All others	10.6	13.0	12.1	13.5	13.1	11.7	11.0	11.7
Obstetrics/gynecology	7.4	7.7	6.7	7.2	8.8	7.9	7.9	7.9
Ophthalmology	5.9	6.4	6.1	5.2	5.4	5.6	6.1	5.2
Orthopedic surgery	5.1	5.3	4.8	4.8	4.8	4.3	5.3	5.6
Dermatology	4.5	2.8	3.4	3.7	3.3	3.6	4.3	4.2
Cardiovascular	3.3	2.9	2.8	2.5	2.8	2.3	3.2	2.6
Psychiatry	3.3	2.8	2.9	3.4	3.2	2.4	3.1	3.5
General surgery	2.0	1.6	2.5	2.1	2.2	1.9	2.2	2.1
Otolaryngology	2.0	1.9	2.3	2.2	2.4	1.9	2.0	2.0
Urology	1.9	2.0	2.0	2.0	2.0	1.9	1.9	2.3
Neurology	1.7	1.4	1.4	1.6	1.4	1.1	1.2	1.0

Data from the *2007 National Ambulatory Medical Care Survey*[19] show the shift from small practices to larger practices over the last 10 years in Exhibit 20.

Exhibit 20. Shift From Larger Practices to Smaller Practices

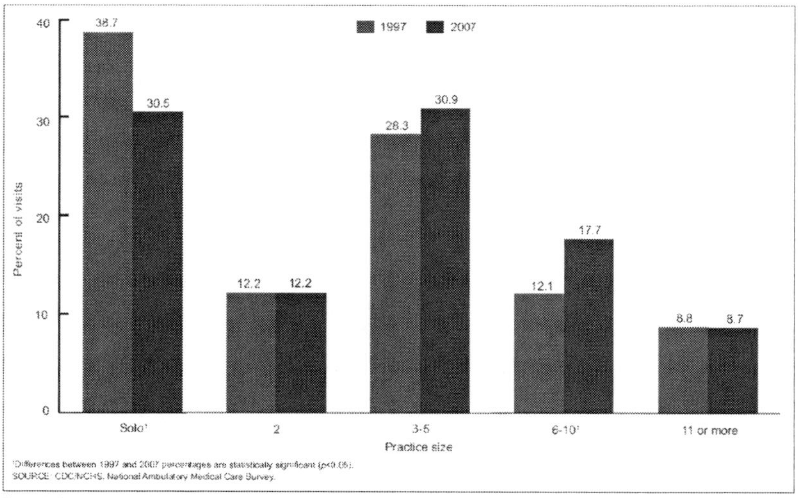

Figure 1. Percentage of office visits by practice size: United States, 1997 and 2007

19 *National Ambulatory Medical Care Survey: 2007 Summary*, Nov. 3, 2010 www.cdc.gov/nchs/data/nhsr/nhsr027.pdf.

Exhibit 21 shows expected office visits per patient per year from the same NCHS data[20] and is valuable for estimating patient volume in an office setting, particularly where capitation may be involved.

Exhibit 21. Total Office Visits Per Patient Per Year for All Physician Specialties[21]

Age	All	Female	Male
<1	7.316		
1–4	3.413		
5–14	1.998		
<15	1.966	3.838	2.855
15–24	2.488	2.646	1.411
25–44	3.733	2.533	1.621
45–64	7.124	3.339	3.183
65–74	6.689	4.252	6.609
>75	7.610	6.756	8.014
Total	7.316	7.347	2.855

Exhibit 22 takes the data from Exhibit 21 and depicts all specialties accounting for more than 4% of patient visits. It is important to note that these specialties are predominantly primary care, or specialties such as ophthalmology and ob/gyn that have primary care-like features, i.e., the need to be seen by many patients regularly. Only orthopedics and ophthalmology among the non-primary care specialties have significant patient volume.

Exhibit 22. Concentration of Visits/Physicians by Specialty

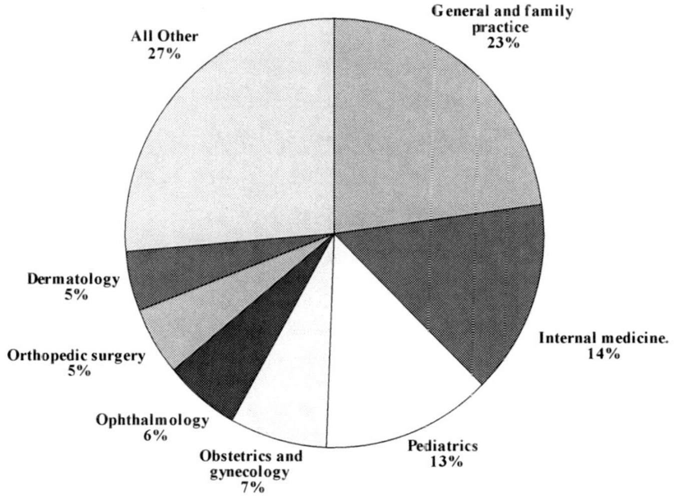

20 *National Ambulatory Medical Care Survey: 2007 Summary*, Nov. 3, 2010 www.cdc.gov/nchs/data/nhsr/nhsr027.pdf.
21 *National Ambulatory Medical Care Survey: 2007 Summary*, Nov. 3, 2010 www.cdc.gov/nchs/data/nhsr/nhsr027.pdf.

The Kaiser Family Foundation breaks down Primary Care Physicians in 2008 in Exhibit 23.

Exhibit 23. Breakdown of Primary Care Physicians

United States	Percent	0% - 100%
Internal Medicine	35%	
Family Practice	29%	
Pediatrics	18%	
Obstetrics/Gynecology	12%	
General Practice	6%	
Total Primary Care	100%	

In interpreting the relative number of *office* visits among the various specialties illustrated, readers should bear in mind that the surgical specialties in particular perform many of their services in *hospital* settings. In addition, the medical specialties, such as cardiology and nephrology, for example, have many encounters in the hospital as well, such as for consultations requested by other physicians.[22]

The physician recruiting firm Merritt Hawkins released its annual report in May 2011. Data on annual recruiting engagements indicate that the specialties in highest demand include family medicine, internal medicine, hospitalist, orthopedic surgery, ob/gyn, and cardiology. Hospitals or existing practices looking to recruit such physicians typically find the starting salary very high and the structure of a future buy-in on the table from the outset.

Primary care physicians in internal medicine and family practice are in high demand, bucking the specialist trend, making it difficult or impossible in many markets to sell an interest in a practice at a significant price. Some speculate that the shortage of specialists is driving the demand for internists and family practitioners, who may provide higher-level adult medical care when specialists such as cardiologists are not available.

A serious shortage of physicians and particularly primary care (generalist) physicians is expected in the next several decades. This has negative implications for practice value because the ease of entry into the market for new suppliers is enhanced when demand for services is unmet and in excess.[23]

22 www.cdc.gov/nchs/fastats/docvisit.htm.

23 "Will Generalist Physician Supply Meet Demands of an Increasing and Aging Population?" Jack M. Colwill, James M. Cultice, and Robin L. Kruse; *Health Affairs*, 29 April 2008.

Medicare-participating physicians by specialty and region are shown in Exhibits 24 and 25 from the publication *2009 CMS Statistics*.[24] The regional data is of particular note, given the differing concentrations of physicians per 100,000 population around the country.

Exhibit 24. Part B Practicioners/CMS Region

	Active practitioners	Practitioners per 100,000 population
All regions	1,245,003 [1]	413
Boston	96,484	676
New York	147,395	527
Philadelphia	133,101	459
Atlanta	221,727	374
Chicago	211,442	410
Dallas	118,319	323
Kansas City	62,890	469
Denver	46,248	444
San Francisco	151,680	325
Seattle	55,717	449

[1] Includes non-Federal physicians, limited licensed and non-physician practitioners. Practitioners with multi-State practices are duplicated in the enumeration for each State in which they operate.

NOTES: Physicians as of July 2007. Civilian population as of July 1, 2007. Resident population for outlying areas and the Virgin Islands are not available.

SOURCES: CMS, ORDI, and the Bureau of the Census.

Exhibit 25. Part B Practitioners Active in Patient Care/Selected Years

	July 2007	
	Number	Percent
All Part B Practitioners	1,087,845	100.0
Physician Specialties	667,340	61.3
Primary Care	246,314	22.6
Medical Specialties	108,694	10.0
Surgical Specialties	108,031	9.9
Emergency Medicine	36,644	3.4
Anesthesiology	38,358	3.5
Radiology	37,595	3.5
Pathology	13,984	1.3
Obstetrics/Gynecology	38,515	3.5
Psychiatry	38,921	3.6
Other and Unknown	284	0.0
Limited Licensed Practitioners	126,006	11.6
Non-physician Practitioners	294,499	27.1

NOTES: Specialty code is self-reported and may not correspond to actual board certification. Totals do not necessarily equal the sum of rounded components. Reflect unduplicated counts.

SOURCE: CMS, Office of Research, Development, and Information.

24 www.cms.gov/ResearchGenInfo/02_CMSStatistics.asp.

2010 CMS Statistics[25] suggest there are considerably fewer practitioners today than there were three years ago (see Exhibit 26).

Exhibit 26. Medicare Participating and Nonparticipating Physicians and Practitioners

	Calendar Year 2010
All Part B Practitioners	973,299
Physician Specialties	616,749
Internal Medicine[1]	103,840
Family Practice	82,242
Emergency Medicine	40,066
Anesthesiology	38,300
Radiology[2]	36,034
Obstetrics/Gynecology	32,367
Psychiatry[3]	28,739
Cardiology	24,590
Orthopedic Surgery	22,765
Other and Unknown	207,806
Limited Licensed Practitioners	96,004
Non-physician Practitioners	260,546

[1] Includes the Internal Medicine, Endocrinology, and Medical Oncology.
[2] Includes Radiology, Nuclear Medicine, and Interventional Radiology.
[3] Includes Psychiatry and Neuropsychiatry.

NOTE: Top 9 specialties presented, in terms of total counts.

SOURCE: CMS, Office of Financial Management.

Trends in Health Insurance Coverage

According to the Census Bureau's 2011 survey:[26] "in 2010, the percentage of people without health insurance, 16.3%, was not statistically different from the rate in 2009. The number of uninsured people increased to 49.9 million in 2010 from 49 million in 2009. The percentage of people with health insurance in 2010 was not statistically different from 2009, while the number of insured increased to 256.2 million in 2010 from 255.3 million in 2009. The percentage of people covered by private health insurance decreased in 2010, to 64%, while the number of people covered by private health insurance was not statistically different from 2009, at 195.9 million. The percentage of people covered by private health insurance has been decreasing since 2001. The percentage and number of people covered by government health insurance increased to 31% and 95 million in 2010 from 30.6% and 93.2 million in 2009. The percentage of people covered by employment-based health insurance decreased to 55.3% in 2010 from 56.1% in 2009. The number of people covered by employment-based health insurance decreased to 169.3 million from 170.8 million. The percentage and number of people covered by Medicaid in 2010, 15.9% and 48.6 million, were not statistically different from 2009 estimates (Exhibit 27). The

25 www.cms.gov/ResearchGenInfo/02_CMSStatistics.asp.
26 www.census.gov/prod/2011pubs/p60-239.pdf, issued September 2011.

percentage and number of people covered by Medicare increased in 2010, to 14.5% and 44.3 million."

Exhibit 27 indicates the percentages of the United States population covered by insurance during 2009 and 2010. The figures in the accompanying table add to more than 100% because some individuals were covered by more than one form of insurance during the year.

Exhibit 27. Coverage by Type of Health Insurance: 2009 and 2010

(People as of March of the following year. For information on confidentiality protection, sampling error, nonsampling error, and definitions, see *www.census.gov/apsd/techdoc/cps/cpsmar11.pdf*)

Coverage type	2009	2010
Any private plan[1]	64.5	*64.0
Any private plan alone[2]	53.3	*52.7
Employment-based[1]	56.1	*55.3
Employment-based alone[2]	46.6	*45.8
Direct-purchase[1]	9.6	*9.8
Direct-purchase alone[2]	3.7	3.7
Any government plan[1]	30.6	*31.0
Any government plan alone[2]	19.4	19.7
Medicare[1]	14.3	*14.5
Medicare alone[2]	4.5	*4.7
Medicaid[1]	15.7	15.9
Medicaid alone[2]	11.2	11.2
Military health care[1,3]	4.1	4.2
Military health care alone[2,3]	1.3	1.3
Uninsured	16.1	16.3

*Statistically different from zero at the 90 percent confidence level.

[1]The estimates by type of coverage are *not* mutually exclusive; people can be covered by more than one type of health insurance during the year.

[2]The estimates by type of coverage are mutually exclusive; people did not have any other type of health insurance during the year.

[3]Military health care includes Tricare and CHAMPVA (Civilian Health and Medical Program of the Department of Veteran Affairs), as well as care provided by the Department of Veterans Affairs and the military.

Source: U.S. Census Bureau, Current Population Survey, 2010 and 2011 Annual Social and Economic Supplements.

Summary

The preceding review indicates that healthcare spending is advancing at a rate in excess of that of inflation and exceeds GDP growth. The success of managed care in controlling medical costs has long since come to an end, resulting in a focus on new insurance products that are putting the consumer at increased risk for their decisions, something the reform legislation purports to reinforce. *Overall* trends in healthcare spending, however, are neither indicative nor predictive of trends in specific subsectors of the industry. Physician incomes generally are increasing at a rate less than the medical CPI, even as their operating expenses increase at a greater rate. Hospital expenses have consistently grown faster than the CPI and recently, at a rate faster than GDP, particularly in the recession. This latter trend reflects increases in both utilization and unit prices.

Concentration of Market Share

As can be seen in Exhibit 28, based upon a Government Accountability Office study, the provision of health insurance is significantly state-specific. Most markets are

Exhibit 28. Provision of Health Insurance, by State

	Number of Licensed Carriers	Largest Carrier	Market Share of Largest Carrier	Market Share of 5 Largest Carriers	Rank of Largest BCBS carrier	Market Share of all BCBS carriers
Alabama	NA	BCBS of Alabama	78.0%	NA	1	NA
Alaska	12	Premera Blue Cross	66.0	100.0%	1	66.0%
Arizona	53	United of Arizona	29.0	66.0	2	19.0
Colorado	27	United	24.0	72.0	3	13.0
Connecticut	25	Anthem BCBS of Connecticut	NA	NA	1	NA
Delaware	16	BCBS of Delaware	58.0	99.0	1	58.0
District of Columbia	13	Group H&M BCBS	43.0	97.0	1	65.0
Florida	29	United of Florida	22.0	78.0	3	31.0
Georgia	75	BCBS of Georgia	27.0	65.0	1	41.0
Idaho	16	BCBS of Idaho	45.0	97.0	1	87.0
Illinois	51	NA	NA	NA	NA	NA
Iowa	60	Wellmark BCBS	56.0	91.0	1	68.0
Kansas	28	BCBS of Kansas	NA	NA	1	NA
Kentucky	10	Anthem BCBS	43.0	93.0	1	43.0
Louisiana	35	Louisiana BCBS	29.0	85.0	1	54.0
Maine	12	Anthem BCBS	48.0	98.0	1	63.0
Maryland	16	CareFirst	43.0	90.0	1	59.0
Massachusetts	25	BCBS of Massachusetts	32.0	86.0	1	39.0
Michigan	45	BCBS of Michigan	62.0	78.0	1	69.0
Minnesota	11	BCBSM	45.0	98.0	1	45.0
Missouri	38	Health Alliance Life	46.0	87.0	3	8.0
Montana	13	BCBS of Montana	36.0	85.0	1	36.0
Nevada	35	Health Plan of Nevada	NA	NA	NA	NA
New Jersey	16	Aetna Health	37.0	86.0	2	27.0
New York	29	Oxford	21.0	63.0	2	36.0
North Carolina	32	BCBS of North Carolina	54.0	89.0	1	54.0
North Dakota	9	Noridian/BCBS	93.0	99.0	1	93.0
Ohio	63	Community BCBS	32.0	79.0	1	32.0
Oklahoma	36	Group Health BCBS	30.0	71.0	1	49.0
Oregon	12	Lifewise (Premera)	25.0	79.0	5	14.0
Rhode Island	3	BCBS of Rhode Island	NA	NA	1	NA
South Carolina	29	BCBS of South Carolina	49.0	87.0	1	49.0
Tennessee	41	BCBS of Tennessee	49.0	85.0	1	49.0
Texas	58	United	19.0	59.0	3	17.0
Utah	22	Regence BCBS	40.0	93.0	1	40.0
Vermont	12	BCBS of Vermont	73.0	100.0	1	84.0
Virginia	45	Anthem BCBS	NA	NA	1	NA
Washington	12	Premera Blue Cross	57.0	92.0	1	85.0
West Virginia	33	BCBS	43.0	77.0	1	43.0
Wisconsin	50	United of Wisconsin	20.0	49.0	3	6.0
Wyoming	15	BCBS of Wyoming	40.0	74.0	1	38.0
Average	29.05		43.3	83.7	1	46.5
(Source: *GAO Private Health Insurance Study*)						

dominated by a few insurance companies; many are dominated by a *single* company. This fact results in strikingly different market conditions from state to state and virtual oligopolistic or monopolistic valuation of physician services.

Reflective of the GAO study, an independent study was conducted in January 2008 by Mark Dietrich[27] (published in the Summer 2008 edition of *Business Valuation Review*) of the distribution of for-profit and nonprofit health insurers and providers in a number of specific markets in the United States. The findings are summarized as follows.

The degree of revenue and profit for healthcare provider entities varies significantly from state to state and even within different regions of individual states. As a threshold matter, areas with high healthcare spending and particularly high Medicare[28] spending tend to offer the greatest opportunity for profit. The elderly, of course, receive the bulk of medical care. Given that high localized spending is the primary driver of profit, the other factors contributing to the pattern of location of larger for-profit providers include:

- The presence and market strength of Blue Cross plans,
- The degree of market strength of local nonprofit hospitals versus for-profit hospitals,
- The degree of market strength of local nonprofit health insurers versus for-profit health insurers,
- Certificate of need laws, and
- Other local demographic and economic factors including:
    - Income levels of population;
    - Health insurance coverage statistics, including coverage by Medicaid;
    - Hospital spending per capita and in total; and
    - Physician spending per capita and in total.

Healthcare markets are highly localized and use of out-of-market data because the valuation of a healthcare business requires a detailed analysis of conditions in the source market as well as the subject market. Regulatory restrictions on the use of market data

27 "Healthcare Market Structure and Its Implication for Valuation of Privately Held Provider Entities: An Empirical Analysis," *Business Valuation Review*, Summer 2008.
28 Medicare spending varies considerably from region to region with states such as Florida, Texas, California, and Tennessee having high per capita and total dollar spending and many for-profit providers.

in the Stark laws cannot be dismissed because there are fundamental economic reasons for those restrictions as well as professional standards that require they be respected. Markets in which larger for-profit provider entities are present will have transactions that reflect not only the local market conditions but also the revenue and earnings growth inherent in the motivation of public companies. Public healthcare providers such as AMSG are consolidators driven by acquisition growth. Even those nonprofit markets where healthcare spending and insurer concentration are otherwise similar to for-profit markets may have very different values for local entities than are indicated by consolidator-driven multiples. Thus, methods under the market approach have to be used with considerable skill and intensive analysis.[29]

Large for-profit providers of this type pay prices for healthcare businesses that reflect the actions of the stock market, as described in the following quote. Nonprofit providers that dominate healthcare delivery in Connecticut do not have an economic basis to pay multiples driven by the stock market. The following quote is also taken from the article:

> Growth potential in the form of acquisition growth is typically only available to publicly traded companies whose stock prices are in large part driven by expected growth rates. High growth rates typically result in high valuation multiples due to low capitalization rates. Economies of scale from acquisitions that affect future "same store" profit growth also contribute to localized valuation differences. As such, all things being equal, a growth-driven public company is able to pay a higher value for a given business because the stock market rewards growth.[30]

Based on this analysis, larger for-profit providers—publicly traded or private equity funded—are primarily located south of the Mason-Dixon Line, where labor unions have historically been less prevalent. Primary locations for these large providers include Florida, Texas, Tennessee, and California. As such, transactions engaged in by these companies are not deemed relevant for valuation purposes in Connecticut since they do not do business here and therefore, would not be part of the universe of hypothetical buyers.

The State of Managed Care

As noted elsewhere herein, one of the most significant issues affecting the healthcare economy and therefore, the forecast of future cash flow is the underwriting cycle. In part, that cycle of premium increases and decreases reflects the relationship between

29 "Healthcare Market Structure and Its Implication for Valuation of Privately Held Provider Entities: An Empirical Analysis"; *Business Valuation Review*, Summer 2008.

30 See also "Understanding the Difference Between Strategic Value and Fair Market Value in Consolidating Industries" *Business Valuation Review*, June 2002, by Mark O. Dietrich.

the costs of provider payments and the premium charged. Exhibit 29 reflects both seasonality as well as overall decreases.

Exhibit 29. Premium and Cost Trends[31]

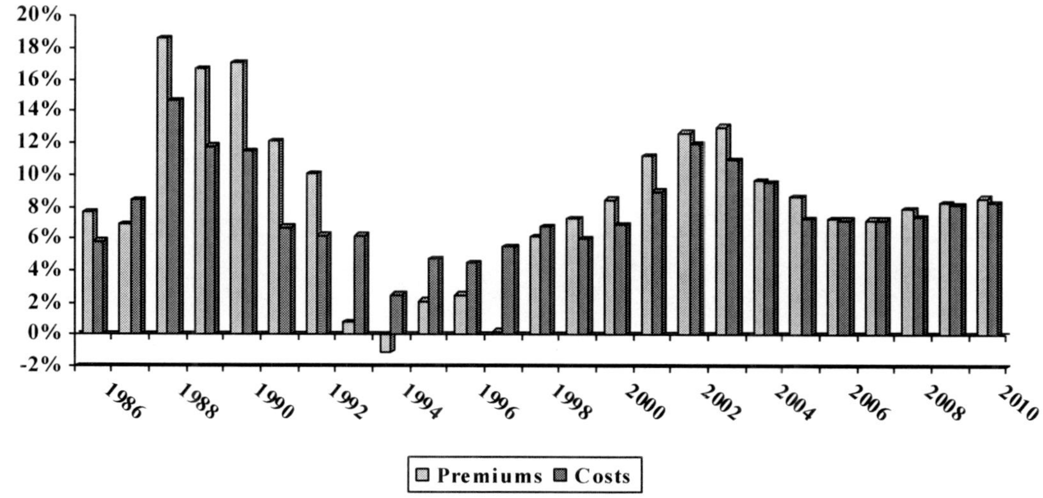

An important trend influencing health insurance premium growth is the use of so-called "buy-downs," or cost shifting to employees via cost-sharing for premiums, deductibles, and co-pays for care. To elaborate, "cost-sharing of premiums" refers to the practice of having the employer pay less than 100% of the cost of insurance. "Deductible" refers to the practice of requiring the employee to pay a certain amount, say $1,000, out-of-pocket before insurance takes over. A "co-pay" refers to the amount that an employee must pay for each medical encounter, such as $25 for an office visit or $250 per hospital visit. Another increasingly common buy-down is to charge a higher co-pay on prescriptions for name-brand drugs versus generics (referred to as a tiered formulary). Clearly, cost sharing by the consumers of their health care substantially influences the volume of consumption.

Each of these devices reduces the premium charged by the health insurer for coverage and also reduces the health insurers' medical costs. Thus, when we read that premiums are increasing by 12%, the overall cost of medical care—including that now borne by the consumer—is likely increasing at a higher rate. This is also reflected in the fact that before the recession, most health insurers were experiencing a decrease in their medical costs (the medical loss ratio—MLR). This cyclical phenomenon was a major contributor to reform's mandating minimum MLRs

31 Based on *Health Care- Managed Care*, Jan. 7, 2010, Barclays Capital, sourced from Milliman, CMS, and company documents.

The historical pattern in the aggregate MLR for various companies in the industry are shown in Exhibit 30. As the MLR declines, profits are likely to increase.

Exhibit 30. Trend in MLR

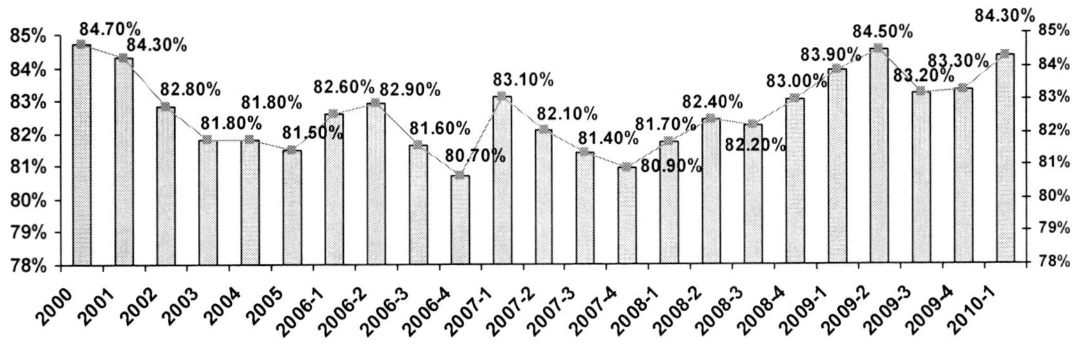

Medical costs included in the MLR consist of four distinct components: inpatient, outpatient, physician, and pharmacy. Inpatient costs refer to hospital and other facilities, while outpatient includes ambulatory surgery, imaging, and lab work.

Managed care insurers at one time were actually engaged in taking risk for the cost of care of their insureds. Due to the catastrophic losses of the 1990s, which forced many, particularly smaller, competitors out of business, the industry has increasingly turned to providing *self-funded* or *self-insured* plans to employers. Under these arrangements, the insurer acts as the administrator[32] on behalf of the employer, and the employer (and its employees via any cost-sharing) assume the risk of their care. The insurer charges a fee for providing access to its provider network, paying claims, and providing "stop-loss," or excess limits, coverage.[33] Typical stop-loss levels vary with the size of the insured group and the resultant actuarial risk but may be as little as $10,000 or as high as $100,000 or more. Self-insured plans also escaped many of reform's more burdensome provisions, and reform is likely to accelerate the trend toward self-insuring for those employers large enough to consider it. Although newly self-insured groups will not escape reforms to the underlying benefit requirements, they will avoid the enormous cost increases associated with merging the small group and individual markets contemplated by the legislation as happened in Massachusetts, the model for reform.

Premium Trend

The increase in medical insurance premiums exploded again in 2011, in significant part due to the federal reform legislation, which exposes insurers to significant additional risk and cost from coverage of previously uninsured and likely unhealthier individuals. In

32 Also known as ASO or administrative services only business.

33 See the Glossary at the end of this report.

addition, the legislation contains a "jawboning" provision requiring insurers to defend increases in excess of 10% to the federal Department of Health and Human Services (HHS), but not permitting HHS to do anything about it. Not surprisingly, most insurers raised premiums just under that level!

According to the Kaiser Family Foundation and Health Research and Educational Trust (HRET) *2011 Employer Health Benefits Survey* released in September 2011:

> The key findings from the 2011 survey, conducted from January 2011 through May 2011, include increases in the average single and family premiums, as well higher enrollment in high deductible health plans with savings options (HDHP/SOs). The 2011 survey includes new questions on the percentage of firms with grandfathered health plans, changes in benefits for preventive care, enrollment of adult children due to the new health reform law, and the use of stop-loss coverage by firms with self-funded plans.
>
> The average annual premiums for employer-sponsored health insurance in 2011 are $5,429 for single coverage and $15,073 for family coverage. Compared to 2010, premiums for single coverage are 8% higher and premiums for family coverage are 9% higher. The 9% growth rate in family premiums for 2011 is significantly higher than the 3% growth rate in 2010. Since 2001, average premiums for family coverage have increased 113% (Exhibit 31). Average premiums for family coverage are lower for workers in small firms (those with three to 199 workers) than for workers in large firms, those with 200 workers or more ($14,098 versus $15,520), shown in Exhibit 32. Average premiums for HDHP/SOs are lower than the overall average for all plan types for both single and family coverage.

Exhibit 31. Average Annual Premiums for Single and Family Coverage, 1999-2011

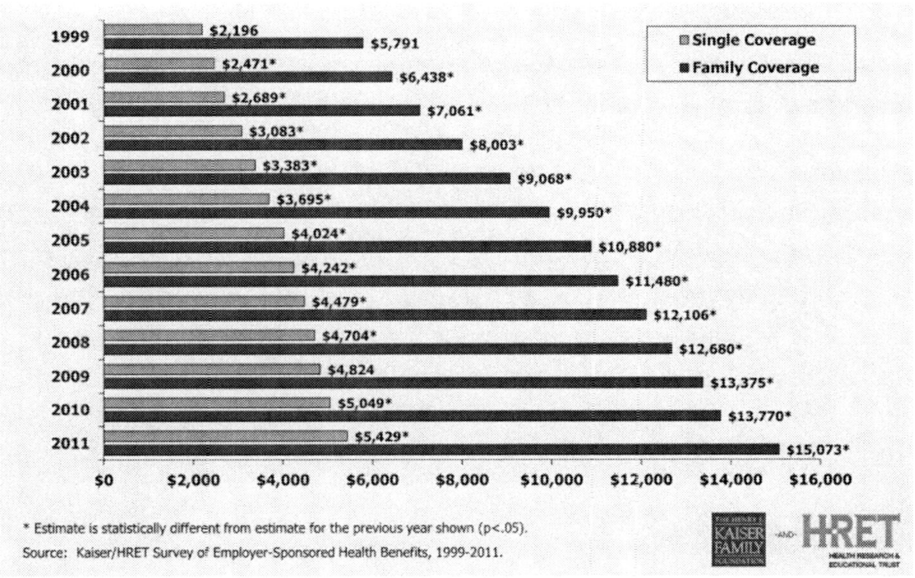

There is significant variation around the average annual premiums as a result of factors such as benefits, cost sharing, and geographic cost differences. Nineteen percent of covered workers are in plans with an annual total premium for family coverage of at least $18,087 (120% of the average family premium), while 21% of covered workers are in plans where the family premium is less than $12,058 (80% of the average premium). [34]

Exhibit 32. Average Annual Worker Premium Contributions Paid by Covered Workers for Single and Family Coverage, 1999- 2011

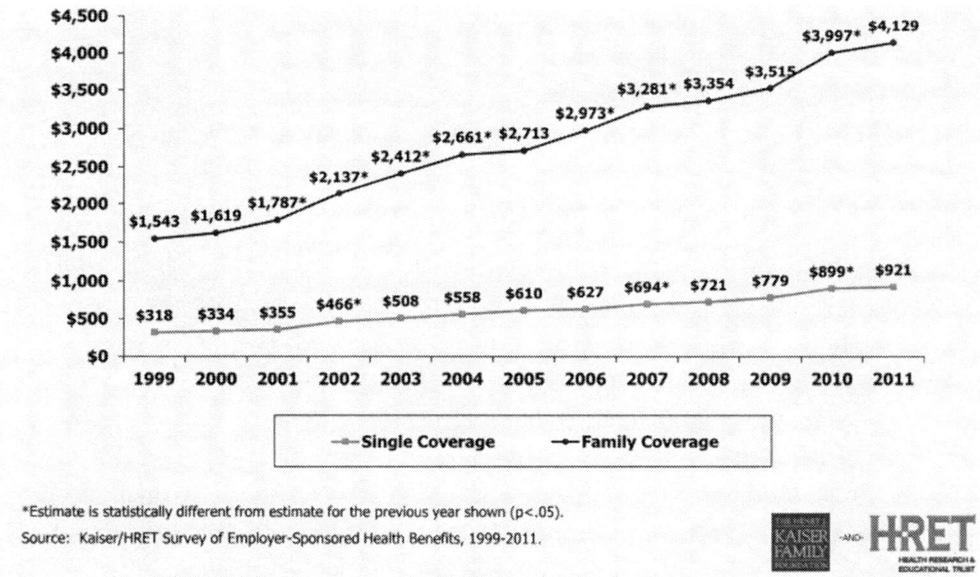

As suggested by the first sentence in the last quoted paragraph above, comparison of premiums without knowledge of underlying benefit and cost-sharing *is not possible.*

In addition to the significant increases in overall costs, the portion of that cost borne by the employee has grown significantly, especially for family plans.

Product Trend

Another significant trend is the move away from HMO (tightly restricted) products and into PPO (preferred provider organization) and POS (point of service) products. In a PPO,[35] insureds pay lower costs when seeing a provider who is "in-network," while deductibles, co-pays, and even overall benefit limits may apply when seeing out-of-network providers. A curious but critical result of the movement away from HMOs is the contribution of the *unmanaged* forms of insurance to the cost spiral! The ability of patients insured by PPOs to self-refer and the general lack of data from insurers to

34 ehbs.kff.org/ 2011 Report.
35 See the Glossary at the end of this report.

the provider community on those patients preclude the type of clinical management shown to improve health and reduce cost.

A POS plan is one in which the insured typically has to choose an in-network primary care physician but may be allowed to self-refer to specialists (in or out of network), again with deductibles, co-pays, and perhaps overall benefit limits. In some cases, insurers have attempted to place capitated provider groups at-risk for out-of-network care in POS plans. (This is perhaps the best analogy to the accountable care organization model that would place providers at-risk for the cost of care to unmanaged, fee-for-service Medicare beneficiaries.)

The dramatic shift away from HMO products in the managed care business in recent years is indicated in Exhibit 33. It is important to note that managed care companies referred to generically as "HMOs" may in fact offer PPO and POS products. This is certainly true of Blue Cross/Blue Shield plans, Aetna/US Healthcare, and United Health, to name a few.

The *2011 Kaiser Family Foundation/HRET Survey* found that HMO enrollment continued to decline, and at a faster pace than previous years, with PPOs holding the largest market share by a considerable margin and high deductible plans showing a significant spike.

Exhibit 33. Distribution of Health Play Enrollment for Covered Workers, by Plan Type, 1988-2011[36]

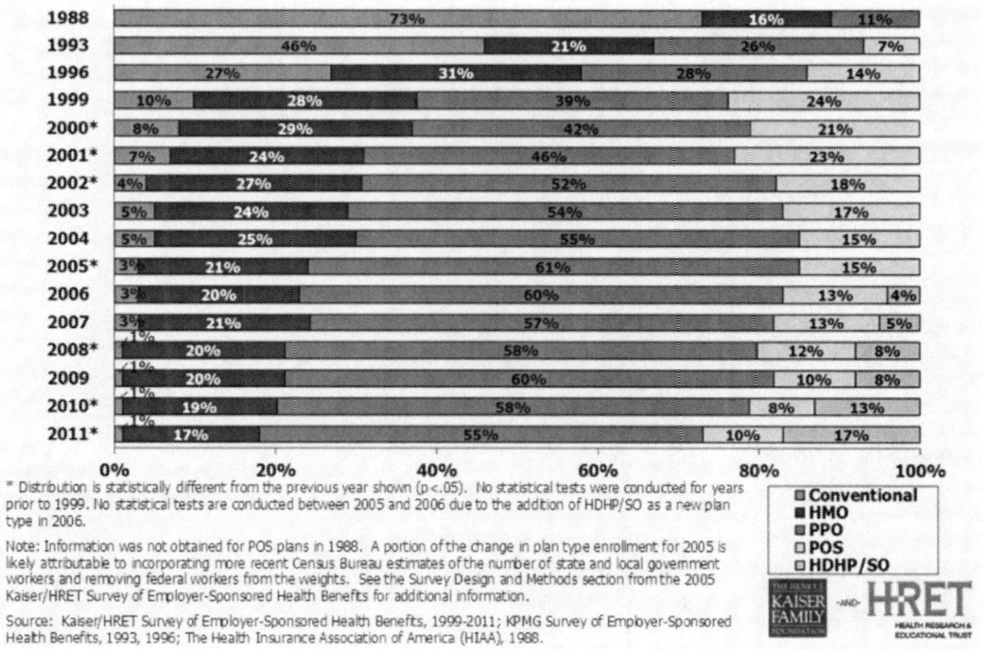

36 PPO (preferred provider organization), POS (point of service plan), HDHP (high deductible health plan).

Regional Differences

Exhibit 34, from the *Kaiser/HRET Survey*, indicates the substantial differences between the various regions of the country, something that apparently was completely ignored in the reform legislation and particularly the so-called Cadillac tax on health insurance plans. Plans in high-cost states such as Massachusetts in the Northeast will reach the Cadillac-plan level in 2018, while plans in lower-cost areas may never reach it.

Exhibit 34. Average Monthly and Annual Premiums for Covered Workers, by Plan Type and Region

	Monthly		Annual	
	Single Coverage	*Family Coverage*	*Single Coverage*	*Family Coverage*
HMO				
Northeast	$486*	$1,332	$5,826*	$15,981
Midwest	472	1,322	5,659	15,861
South	428	1,273	5,131	15,279
West	428	1,229	5,131	14,743
ALL REGIONS	**$446**	**$1,274**	**$5,350**	**$15,288**
PPO				
Northeast	$496*	$1,375*	$5,948*	$16,503*
Midwest	485	1,337	5,824	16,042
South	426*	1,175*	5,118*	14,104*
West	491	1,350	5,892	16,200
ALL REGIONS	**$465**	**$1,284**	**$5,584**	**$15,404**
POS				
Northeast	$537	$1,438	$6,442	$17,253
Midwest	464	1,229	5,569	14,746
South	450	1,210	5,403	14,519
West	506	1,268	6,067	15,211
ALL REGIONS	**$487**	**$1,272**	**$5,841**	**$15,260**
HDHP/SO				
Northeast	$398	$1,139	$4,781	$13,673
Midwest	390	1,137	4,675	13,640
South	409	1,201	4,902	14,407
West	404	1,072	4,846	12,865
ALL REGIONS	**$399**	**$1,142**	**$4,793**	**$13,704**
ALL PLANS				
Northeast	$482*	$1,334*	$5,785*	$16,013*
Midwest	458	1,276	5,497	15,310
South	426*	1,194*	5,110*	14,329*
West	460	1,259	5,514	15,103
ALL REGIONS	**$452**	**$1,256**	**$5,429**	**$15,073**

* Estimate is statistically different within plan and coverage types from estimate for all firms not in the indicated region (p<.05).

Source: Kaiser/HRET Survey of Employer-Sponsored Health Benefits, 2011.

Firm Size Differences

More compelling is the significant difference in the out of pocket cost of health insurance coverage to small firm employees versus large firm employees, a critical failure of the Massachusetts reform legislation that the federal legislation is modeled on. (See Exhibits 35 and 36.)

Exhibit 35. Percentage of Covered Workers Enrolled in a Plan With a General Annual Deductible of $1,000 or More for Single Coverage, by Firm Size

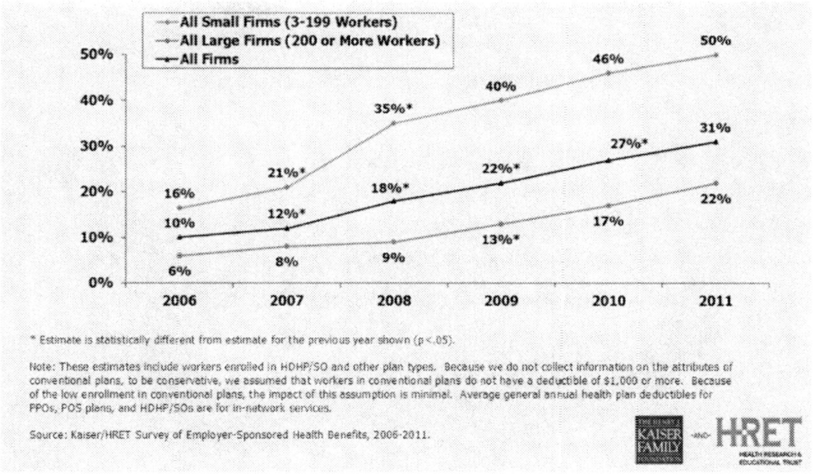

Exhibit 36. Percentage of Covered Workers Enrolled in a Plan With a General Annual Deductible of $2,000 or More for Single Coverage, by Firm Size

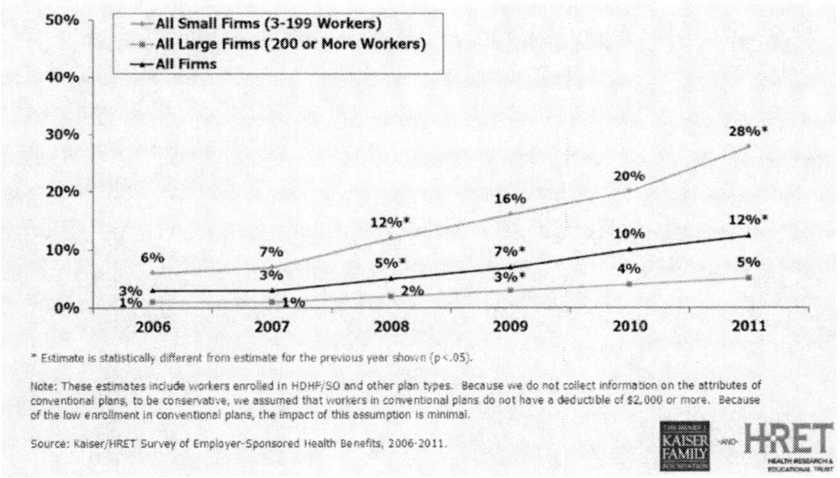

Decline in HMOs

As a result of the major financial losses of the 1990s, there has been both a reduction in the number of managed care companies and greater enrollment growth in those who survived, as insureds were forced to find solvent insurers. CMS reports that the number of HMOs has declined from a peak of 652 in 1997 to 490 in 2002, with further losses in 2003 and 2004. The Kaiser Family Foundation[37] indicates the number of HMOs in July 2008 was 577 (see Exhibit 37), down from 602 in the previous year. By July 2010,

37 www.statehealthfacts.org/.

the count had declined to only 452. This has resulted in growth in enrollment and premiums for the *major* players, despite an overall *decrease* in the number of individuals covered by managed care products, as noted above in *Trends in Health Insurance Coverage.*

Exhibit 37. Number of HMOs by State

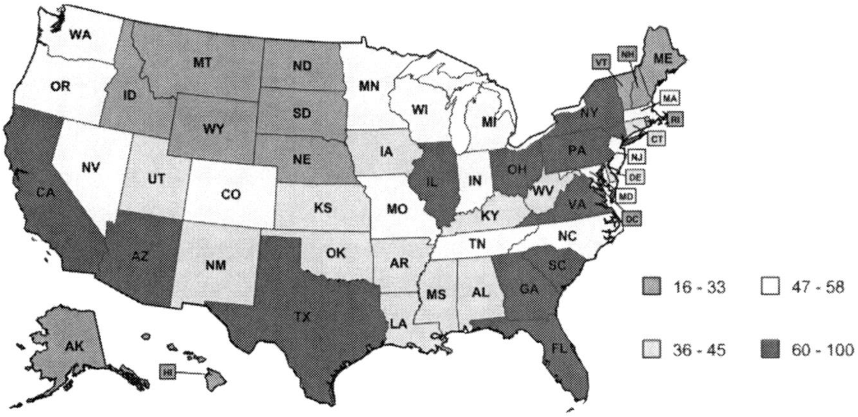

Perhaps a more significant trend in markets dominated by the national health insurance companies is the move to consumer-directed health plans (CDHPs). Rather than simply making the consumption of healthcare services more costly and therefore painful, CDHPs seek to change the attitude of the consumer about healthcare spending, focusing on cost-effective purchasing. These types of plans are based upon the consumer having a budget for healthcare and choosing how that budget is to be spent. For example, a $5,000 budget from an employer may be used for health insurance premiums, uninsured medical expenses, or even health club memberships. Health savings accounts (HSAs) are one variant of this type of plan.

Summary

Managed care plans are in a period of significant change brought about by the combined uncertainty of the recession and the reform legislation. Employers are shifting more of the costs of healthcare onto employees via benefit buy-downs. The backlash against the tightly managed care characteristic of HMOs has resulted in a rapid growth of PPO and POS plans, both of which feature higher consumer costs and drive overall costs higher as well due to the fundamental lack of clinical control over spending in those products. Current indications are that CDHPs, including HSAs, are likely to be the growth product in the foreseeable future. The federal reform legislation will exacerbate the growing disparity between the high cost of benefits in the small employer market and the lower cost in the large employer market.

Acute Care Hospitals: Average Length of Stay

Medicare patients ALOS

Average length of stay (ALOS) is a measurement of the average number of days a patient stays in the hospital for each discharge. Earlier in this report, it was noted that the number of admission and discharges is showing an uptrend. In contrast, ALOS had steadily declined from 1992 until 2004 (Exhibit 38 presents the most recent year for which data are available). The 2007 and 2008 ALOS, however, was the same, and declines appear to have bottomed out.[38]

This trend is very significant for hospitals, which, as noted earlier, are paid a *fixed amount per discharge*. Under such a payment system, there is a financial incentive to get the patient out of the hospital sooner, because *costs* tend to be correlated with days in the hospital and revenues are *fixed* based on the admission and discharge (and its character). Therefore, the hospital is likely to lose money on a long stay, and make money on a short stay. The inability to drive length of stay down still farther accounts in part for the strong adverse reaction from the hospital industry to cuts mandated by the BBA and later mitigated by the Balanced Budget Revision Act of 1999 and the Benefits Improvement and Protection Act of 2000.

Exhibit 38. Average Length of Stay, by Year

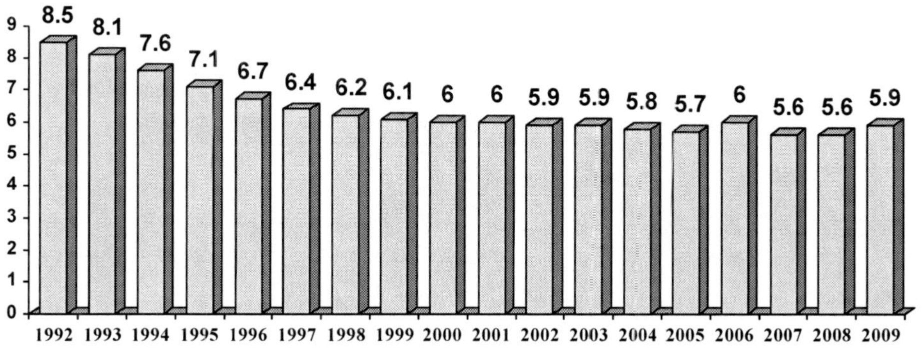

All patients ALOS

ALOS is one of the key factors for evaluating the cost-adjusted clinical efficiency of hospital-based treatment. *The 2007 and 2006 Hospital Discharge Survey* from the Centers for Disease Control[39] (released in December 2010 and July 2008, respectively) found that hospitalization ALOS for the population taken as a whole was 4.8 days, identical to the 2006 survey result. Males had an average length of stay of 5.2 days, compared with 4.5 days for females, also identical to the 2006 results. ALOS per admission in 2007 was

38 www.cms.hhs.gov/MedicareFeeforSvcPartsAB/03_MEDPAR.asp#TopOfPage, last updated September, 2011.
39 www.cdc.gov/nchs/nhds.htm July 30, 2008; released December 2010: rates per 10,000 unchanged in report from 2006.

highest in the Northeast, at 5.3 days; followed by the South, at 4.9; the West, at 4.6 days; and Midwest, at 4.2, which are identical to 2006 (see Exhibits 39 and 40). This data are for all admissions, as opposed to the Medicare data, which are for Medicare patients only.

Exhibit 39. Data by Region

	2006 Rate per 10,000	2006 ALOS	2006 Days/1,000	2007 Rate per 10,000	2007 ALOS	2007 Days/1,000
N. East	1,330.7	5.3	705.3	1,330.7	5.3	703.2
Midwest	1,202.3	4.2	505.0	1,202.3	4.2	507.8
South	1,212.0	4.9	593.9	1,212.0	4.9	594.7
West	940.2	4.6	432.5	940.2	4.6	432.3
Total	1,168.7	4.8	561.0	1,168.7	4.8	557.8

Exhibit 40. Graph of Regional Data

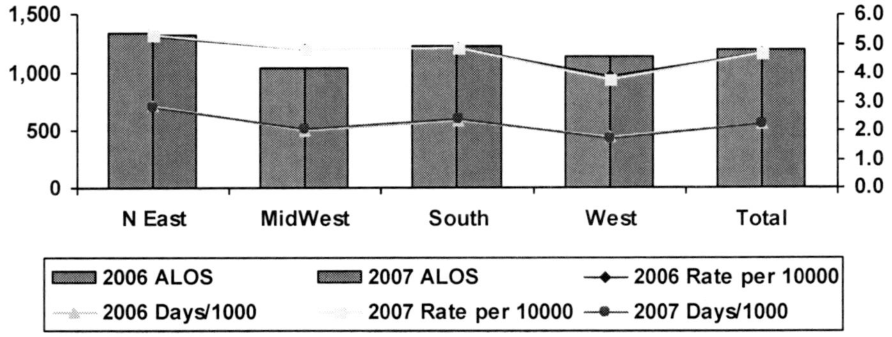

The comparison of data by age group (or cohort) for 2007 and 2006 shows virtually no change, with ALOS holding steady (see Exhibits 41 and 42).

Exhibit 41. Data by Age Cohort

	2006 Rate per 10,000	2006 ALOS	2006 Days/1,000	2007 Rate per 10,000	2007 ALOS	2007 Days/1,000
<15	378.2	4.8	181.5	378.0	4.8	180.9
15-44	861.2	3.7	318.6	861.0	3.7	322.9
45-64	1,161.2	5.0	580.6	1,161.0	5.0	579.3
65	3,507.9	5.5	1,929.3	3,507.0	5.5	1,919.7

Exhibit 42. Graph of Age Data

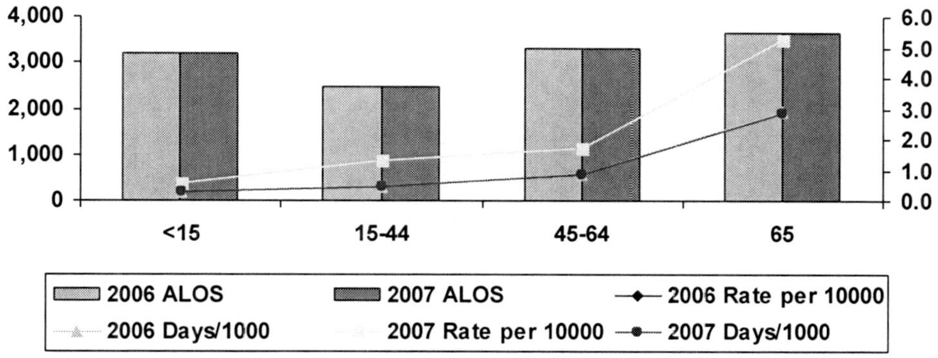

Principal Reason for Admission

Heart disease diagnoses represent 22% of all 18,482 admissions for males, with cardiac catheterization the most frequent procedure, and 11% of 27,482 for females. Thus, coronary artery bypass surgery, cardiac catheterization, and angioplasty are main revenue drivers in acute care hospitals, followed by digestive procedures of the type principally done by general surgeons (see Exhibit 43).

Exhibit 43. Principal Category of Admission and Discharge

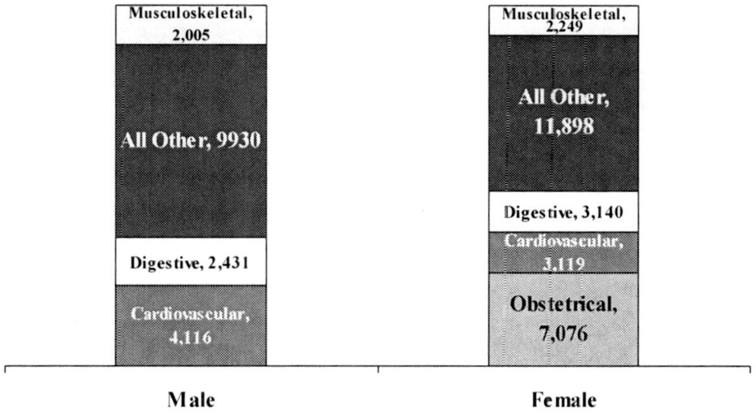

Source: Table 32. Number of all-listed procedures for discharges from short-stay hospitals, by sex and procedure category: United States, 2006

Costs per stay

Hospital costs vary significantly from state to state, reflecting differences in wage scales, living costs, and real estate, to name a few. Representative data for 2008 and 2007 from the American Hospital Association find that costs are generally highest on the coasts, lowest in the mountain states, and increasing almost everywhere (see Exhibit 44); data for 50 states are shown in Exhibit 45.[40]

40 www.statehealthfacts.kff.org/cgi-bin/healthfacts.cgi?action=profile, 2007 data.

Exhibit 44. Cost Per Inpatient Hospital Day

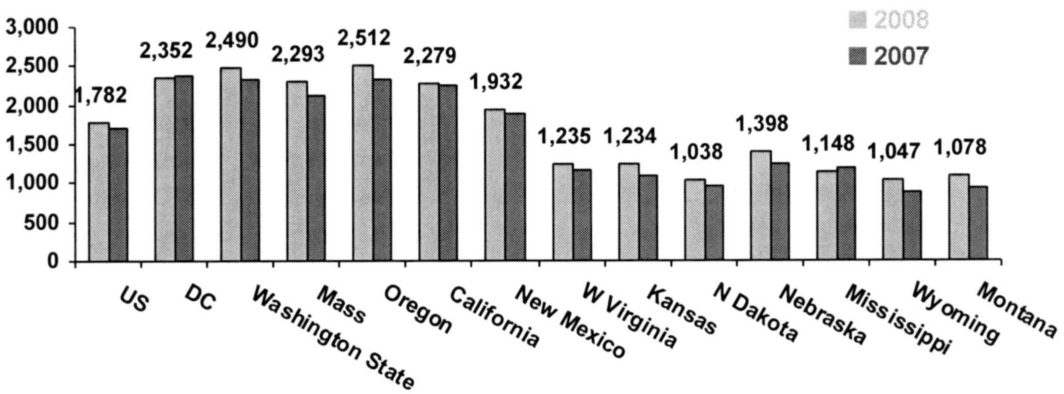

Exhibit 45. Hospital Costs by State

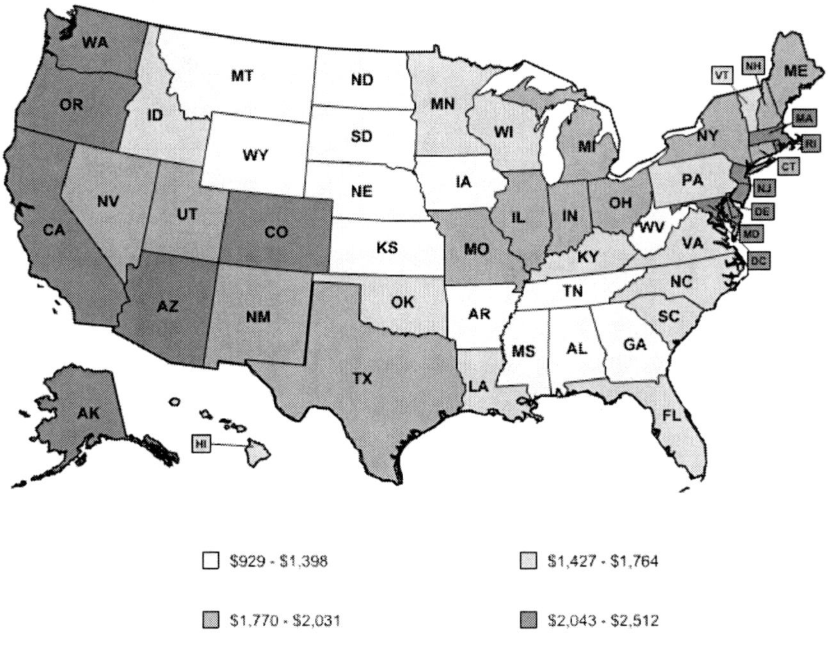

Acute Care Hospital Payments

Medicare inpatient hospital payments from the federal government are based upon a statutory formula pegged to a "market basket" of economic inputs. The actual update is usually less than the market basket for budgetary reasons.[41] Exhibit 46 shows the history for hospitals since 1988, with the substantial declines after the Balanced Budget Act of 1997. The 2011 increase is 2.6% for those hospitals that submit quality data, reduced by

41 A CMS explanation of the Medicare inpatient and other payment formulas is located at www.cms.gov/reports/hcimu/hcimu_04292002_append.pdf.

the 0.25% mandated by the healthcare reform legislation, for a net of 2.35%. Hospitals not submitting quality data receive only 0.35%. There is a separate adjustment for coding intensity of 2.9%, making the true adjustment a negative (0.55%). CMS estimated the effect of the 2012 final rule at a 1% increase.[42]

The 2010 increase is described as follows:

> The Centers for Medicare & Medicaid Services (CMS) today announced that acute care hospitals will receive an inflation update in their payment rates of 2.1% in fiscal year 2010. Earlier this year, CMS had proposed to reduce payments to account for the effect of increases in aggregate payments due to changes in hospital coding practices that do not reflect increases in patient's severity of illness.[43]

Exhibit 46. Inpatient PPS Update—Urban

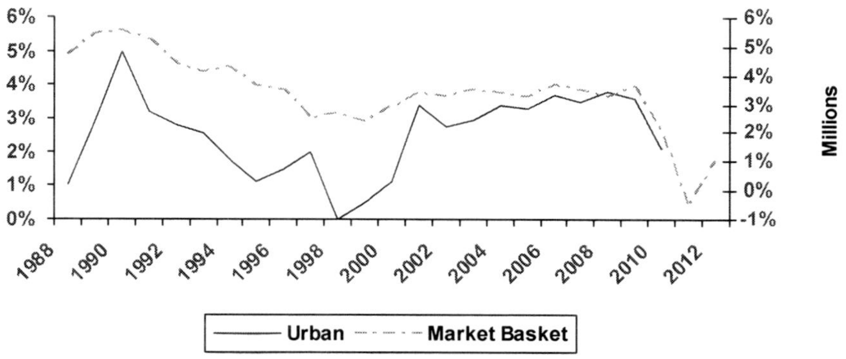

One of the key financial components of paying for the new federal healthcare reform legislation is a cutback in the market basket update, in part through required adjustments for productivity using a 10-year moving average of economywide private, nonfarm productivity gains, somewhat analogous to one element of the physician sustainable growth rate calculation discussed elsewhere herein.

The market basket update for 2009 was 3.6%. "In this final [2009] rule, CMS completes the transition so that its payment rates are 100% cost-based. In addition, CMS is making changes to hospital cost reports that will allow Medicare to distinguish between high- and low-cost supplies and devices and to further refine and improve our cost-based payments." [44]

> The final rule updates IPPS rates by a market basket of 3.6% for inflation (1.6% for hospitals that do not submit quality data). However, CMS estimates that the new

42 Medicare's FY 2012 Hospital Inpatient Prospective Payment System final rule, Fact Sheet, August 2011.
43 Ibid.
44 www.cms.hhs.gov/apps/media/press/factsheet.asp?Counter=3223.

> MS-DRGs will result in improvements in coding and documentation that increase spending without a real change in patient severity of illness. CMS estimates that Medicare spending for inpatient hospital services in FY 2009 will increase 1.8% as a result of changes in coding and documentation. However, rather than reducing IPPS rates by 1.8% in FY 2009 for budget neutrality, the law requires CMS to reduce the IPPS rates by 0.9% for FY 2009. If based on a retrospective review of FY 2008 and FY 2009 claims, CMS determines that improvements in documentation and coding from adopting the MS-DRGs led to an increase in total Medicare spending for inpatient hospital services, the law requires CMS to apply further adjustments to Medicare's IPPS rates in FY 2010 and later years to recoup this increased spending.[45]

For 2008, most hospitals saw an increase of 3.5%, although changes (moving toward hospital costs rather than charges) being made gradually by CMS to the DRG system could result in some hospitals seeing actual decreases.

> Payments to all hospitals will increase by an estimated average of 3.5% for FY 2008 when all provisions of the rule are taken into account, primarily as a result of the 3.3% market basket increase. Payments to specific hospitals may increase more or less than this amount depending on the patients they serve. For instance, urban hospitals generally treat more severely ill patients and are estimated to receive a 3.8% increase in payments.[46]

Hospitals with a large percentage of Medicare admissions are confronted with revenues rising at less than operating costs, the latter reflected in the market basket. Principal areas for rising costs include prescription drugs, labor (including a severe shortage of nursing staff), and liability insurance. The principal factors driving hospital revenue, besides the Medicare market basket, include the aging population's demand for more services, increase in market share, and the success of negotiations with insurers.

THE MEDICARE PROGRAM AND PHYSICIANS

> The Medicare program has two components. Hospital insurance (HI), or Medicare Part A, helps pay for hospital, home health, skilled nursing facility, and hospice care for the aged and disabled. Supplementary medical insurance (SMI) consists of Medicare Part B and Part D. Part B helps pay for physician, outpatient hospital, home health, and other services for the aged and disabled who have voluntarily enrolled. Part D provides subsidized access to drug insurance coverage on a voluntary basis for all beneficiaries and premium and cost-sharing subsidies for low-income enrollees. Medicare also has a Part C, which serves as an alternative to traditional Part A and Part B coverage. Under this option, beneficiaries can choose to enroll in and receive

45 www.cms.hhs.gov/apps/media/press/factsheet.asp?Counter=3223.
46 www.cms.hhs.gov/apps/media/press/release.asp?Counter=2335.

care from private Medicare Advantage and certain other health insurance plans that contract with Medicare. The costs for such beneficiaries are generally paid on a prospective, capitated basis from the HI and SMI Part B trust fund accounts.[47]

When Medicare began on July 1, 1966, approximately 19 million people enrolled. In 2009, almost 46 million people are enrolled in one or both of Parts A and B of the Medicare program, and almost 11 million of them have chosen to participate in a Medicare Advantage plan (see Exhibit 47).[48]

Exhibit 47. Total Medicare Private Health Enrollment[49]

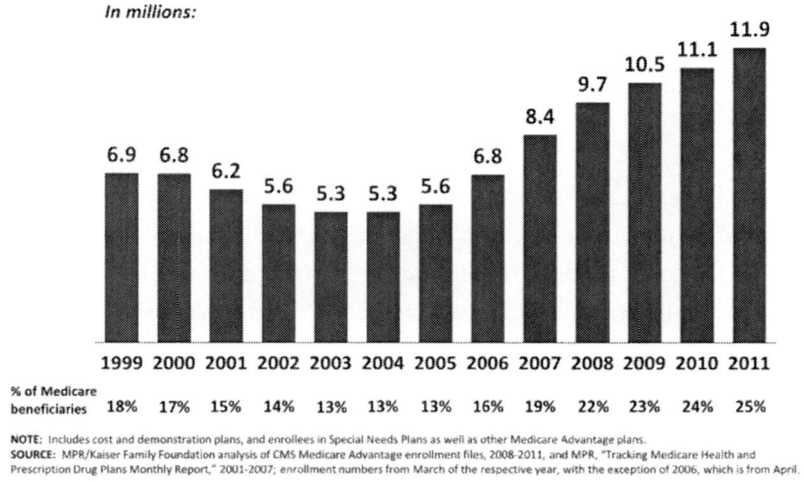

Part A is generally provided automatically and free of premiums to persons age 65 or over who are eligible for Social Security or railroad retirement benefits, whether they have claimed these monthly cash benefits or not. Also, workers and their spouses with a sufficient period of Medicare-only coverage in federal, state, or local government employment are eligible beginning at age 65. Similarly, individuals who have been entitled to Social Security or railroad retirement disability benefits for at least 24 months and government employees with Medicare-only coverage who have been disabled for more than 29 months are entitled to Part A benefits. (As noted previously, the waiting period is waived for persons with Lou Gehrig's Disease. It should also be noted that, over the years, certain liberalizations have been made to both the waiting period requirement and the limit on earnings allowed for entitlement to Medicare coverage based on disability.)

47 2010 Medicare Trustees' Report.

48 Office of the Actuary Summary as of Nov. 1, 2009, www.cms.hhs.gov/MedicareProgramRatesStats/02_SummaryMedicareMedicaid.asp.

49 Medicare Advantage Enrollment Market Update, Kaiser Family Foundation, September 2011, www.kff.org/medicare/.

Part A coverage is also provided to insured workers with ESRD (and to insured workers' spouses and children with ESRD), as well as to some otherwise ineligible aged and disabled beneficiaries who voluntarily pay a monthly premium for their coverage. In 2008, Part A provided protection against the costs of hospital and specific other medical care to about 45 million people (37.5 million aged and 7.4 million disabled enrollees). Part A benefit payments totaled $232.3 billion in 2008.[50]

Medicare originally consisted of two parts: HI, also known as Part A, and SMI, which in the past, was also known simply as Part B. Part A helps pay for inpatient hospital, home health, skilled nursing facility, and hospice care. Part A is provided free of premiums to most eligible people; certain otherwise ineligible people may voluntarily pay a monthly premium for coverage. Part B helps pay for physician, outpatient hospital, home health, and other services. To be covered by Part B, all eligible people must pay a monthly premium."[51]

The Balanced Budget Act of 1997 (BBA) made a number of significant changes in the Medicare program, many of which are phased in over multiple years. These changes are significant to the providers affected by them and in many cases, may mean lower revenues from the Medicare program. Exceptions to this were physicians who perform primarily cognitive services rather than procedures; they actually received significantly improved reimbursement.

Subsequent modifications in the dramatic changes wrought by the BBA by the Balanced Budget Revision Act of 1999 (BBRA) and the Benefits Improvements Act of 2000 (BIPA) primarily affected hospitals, skilled nursing facilities, Medicare+ Choice Plans, and other nonphysician providers. In November 2003, a comprehensive revision of the Medicare+ Choice program was legislated in the Medicare Modernization Act. After 2004, the new Medicare Advantage private plans' capitation rates grow at the same rate as fee-for-service Medicare, although the reported high rate of profits to insurers caused Congress to implement cutbacks in the Medicare Advantage Plan payments as part of the healthcare reform legislation.

Physician Reimbursement

Medicare pays physicians under the resource-based relative value scale (RBRVS) where each current procedural terminology code (CPT) is assigned a certain number of relative value units (RVUs). These RVUs are then multiplied by a conversion factor to set the fee Medicare pays. Prior to the BBA, there were three such conversion factors: one for surgery, one for primary care and one for other nonsurgical services. The

50 Office of the Actuary Summary, ibid .

51 Office of the Actuary Summary, ibid.

BBA substituted a single conversion factor based upon the primary care factor for the three prior conversion factors. The effect has been a broad cutback in reimbursement for surgical services.

Resource-Based Relative Value Scale

The number of RVUs is based upon the consumption of three types of resources in the delivery of physician services:

Physician Work

The principal factors comprising this component are time, technical skill and physical effort, mental effort and judgment, and the stress on the physician of certain patient risk factors.

Practice Costs

This component looks at the cost of delivering services by physician type, for example, family medicine versus cardiac surgery. Physician practice costs per dollar of revenue tend to be much higher in primary care than surgery.

Malpractice Insurance Cost

Surgical specialties, particularly obstetrics, neurosurgery, and cardiac surgery, tend to have the highest malpractice insurance. This is the least important of the three components.

Geographic Adjustment

There is an additional adjustment for the geographic location of the practice based upon various government studies, including the census, HUD data, and others.[52]

The changeover to RBRVS mandated by the BBA resulted in a substantial increase in the RVUs assigned to office-based CPT codes. A significant portion was related to the practice expenses component described above, due to the fact that office-based physicians have higher operating costs per dollar of revenue than do hospital-based physicians. In addition, HCFA (CMS) believed that the prior reimbursement system overcompensated hospital-based surgeons and similar physicians because the Medicare program paid the hospital separately for the cost of its facilities, which had been used by the surgeons.

52 The fee schedule for each geographic area can be located at www.cms.gov/providers/pufdownload/carrcrst.asp.

The Evaluation and Management Codes

In the office-based specialties, primary care, and consultative medicine, RBRVS is particularly significant in how office visits and other evaluation and management services are to be coded and reimbursed. RBRVS requires that physicians code according to a three-factor test:

1. *History* of the patient and complaint;
2. *Examination* of the patient necessary, and
3. *Complexity* of medical decision making.

Each of these three factors has four levels of intensity associated with it. For example, a Level III office examination, or CPT 99213, requires the second level of intensity in each of the history, exam, and decision making components. A Level IV exam, or CPT 99214, requires the third level of intensity in two of the three components. Under RBRVS reimbursement systems, such as Medicare, the patient's chart *must document the level of service for each component.*[53]

Exhibit 48, using the pre-BBA 1997 schedule and the 2011 National Physician Fee Schedule, demonstrates how increasing levels of service, as reflected in the CPT codes, result in increasing levels of payment under Medicare RBRVS, as well as the cumulative effect in reimbursement of the changes described herein.[54]

Exhibit 48. Comparative Fees for Established Patient Sick Visits

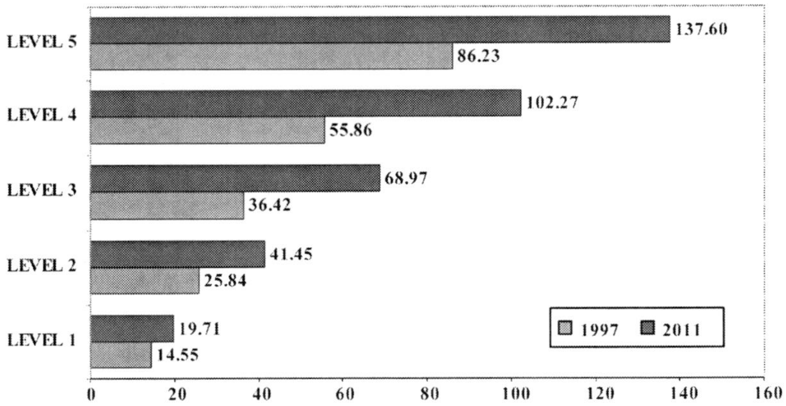

RBRVS is also typically used by HMOs, which therefore tend to pay higher rates for primary care services, since such services are key to the provision of healthcare to members.

53 Various versions of the documentation guidelines can be located at www.cms.gov/medlearn/emdoc.asp.
54 The National Physician Fee Schedule is at www.cms.gov/PhysicianFeeSched/PFSNPAF/list.asp?filterType=none&filterByDID=-99&sortByDID=2&sortOrder=descending&intNumPerPage=10.

There has been a marked shift in the use of these five codes over the last 12 years as indicated in Exhibit 49 based on data taken from CMS.[55]

Exhibit 49. Shift in the Use of Five Codes

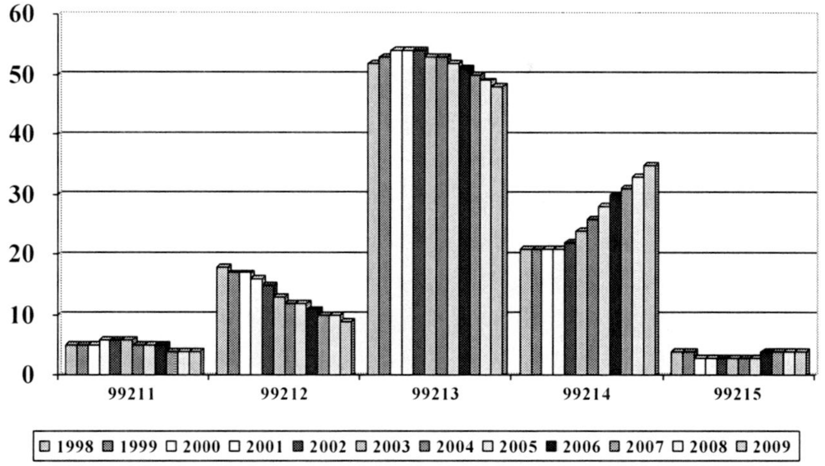

2007 Increases in the Value of E&M Services

In the June 29, 2006 *Federal Register*, CMS announced its intent to increase the relative values of evaluation and management (E&M) services in 2007, following closely on the heels of a suggestion by MedPAC in its March 2006 report that these services had declined in value, in large part to the benefit of high-tech imaging services. The final rule was released Nov. 2, 2006 and adopted the proposed rule in large part.

> The work component for RVUs associated with an intermediate office visit [99213], the most commonly billed physician's service, will increase by 37%. The work component for RVUs for an office visit requiring moderately complex decision making and for a hospital visit also requiring moderately complex decision making will increase by 29% and 31%, respectively. Both of these services rank in the top 10 most frequently billed physicians' services out of more than 7,000 types of services paid under the physician fee schedule.

The 99213 code presently has a fully implemented work RVU value of 0.67. Under the final rule, the value rises to 0.92 RVUs. This represents an increase in the value of nearly 18%. Significantly, because of the budget neutrality provisions of the existing Part B system, the increased cost associated with the increased RVUs has to come from reduction in the value of other services, and CMS reduced all work RVUs by 10.1% to meet the budget neutrality provisions. CMS is also changing the practice expense component of the RVUs to be phased in over four years through 2010.

55 e.g., www.cms.gov/apps/ama/license.asp?file=/MedicareFeeforSvcPartsAB/Downloads/Level1SERV07.pdf.

The following discussion tracks the history of changes in physician reimbursement since the enactment of the BBA and demonstrates the significant and often unpredictable changes.

Medicare Conversion Factor

Overview of the Problem

In March of each year, CMS releases its preliminary estimate (the final calculation is released in September) of the SGR and the conversion factor for the following year. For example, the annual computation *had* estimated that Medicare physician reimbursement would *drop* by 5.7% in 2003, as a result of two errors in 1998 and 1999 that affected the statutory limit on allowed expenditures for physician services. These errors carried forward to all future years, resulting in a lower overall limit on physician spending of approximately 6.4%. The compound rate of increase in the annual physician fee schedule update from 1998 through 2005 was only ***0.3%***! The Consolidated Appropriations Resolution of 2003 permitted CMS to correct the 1998 and 1999 errors, resulting in an *increase* in the fee schedule for 2003 rather than the prior decrease. Annual declines in the vicinity of 4% to 5% are generally expected under existing law. The Medicare Modernization Act of November 2003 overrode the scheduled decreases in the 2004 and 2005 conversion factors with 1.5% increases.

The pattern since 2006 has been for Congress to belatedly suspend the statutory cutbacks in the conversion factor. The 2007 conversion factor of $35.9848 initially reflected a decrease of 5% and was subsequently overturned by Congress and left equal to the 2006 factor. The 2008 factor was scheduled to drop by 10.1% until the end of December 2007, when the Medicare, Medicaid, and SCHIP Extension Act of 2007 legislation updated the conversion factor by 0.5%, to $38.0870. In July 2008, Congress extended the $38.09 conversion factor for the balance of 2008 over the president's veto and put a 1.1% increase in place for 2009. As of November 2009, Congress had not acted to repeal the scheduled cut for 2010. *Note:* See the discussion regarding the calculation of the 2010 and 2009 later herein as Exhibit 50 cannot be understood absent that discussion.

Exhibit 51 traces the growth rate in *real* GDP (in 1996 dollars) and the Medicare SGR, MEI, and the actual conversion factor update. CMS made critical mistakes in computing the 2000 and 2001 conversion factors resulting in excess payments that were being paid back prior to the February 2003 legislative change. Note that the two regain parity in 2005.[56] The red line plots what spending *would have been* based upon inflation in

56 Data from www.cms.hhs.gov/NationalHealthExpendData/Downloads/proj2007.pdf and www.cms.hhs.gov/SustainableGRatesConFact/01_overview.asp.

physician practice expenses, similar to that used to set fees for other sectors of the healthcare industry, such as hospitals.

Exhibit 52 demonstrates that despite the SGR attempt to limit growth in physician spending, actual spending is considerably higher.

Exhibit 50. Medicare Conversion Factor

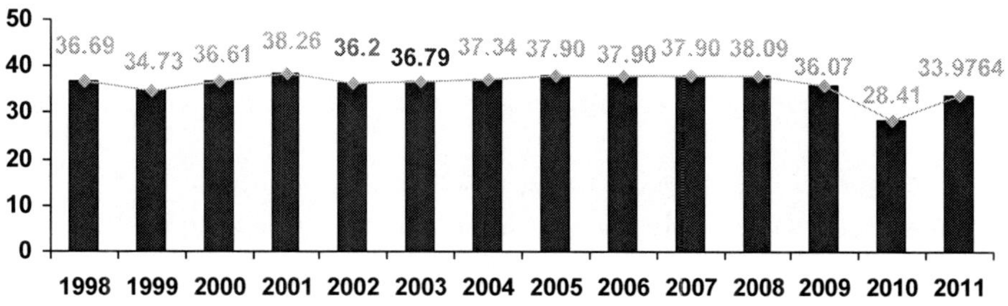

Exhibit 51. Percent Change in Real GDP and Physician Spending

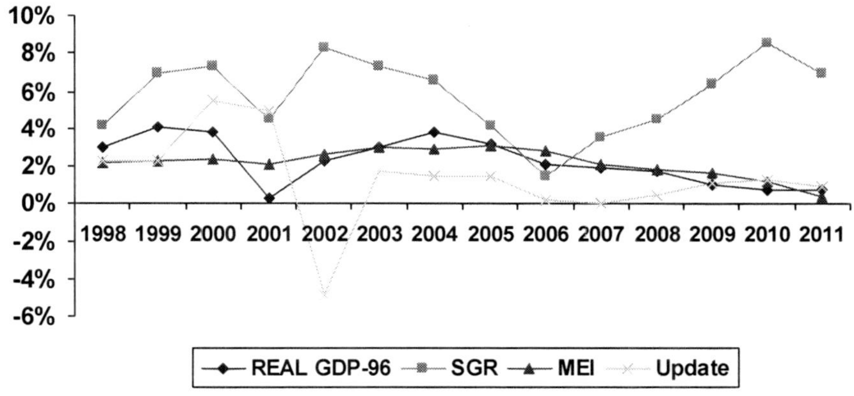

Exhibit 52. Quarterly SGR "Allowed" Versus Actual Expenditures

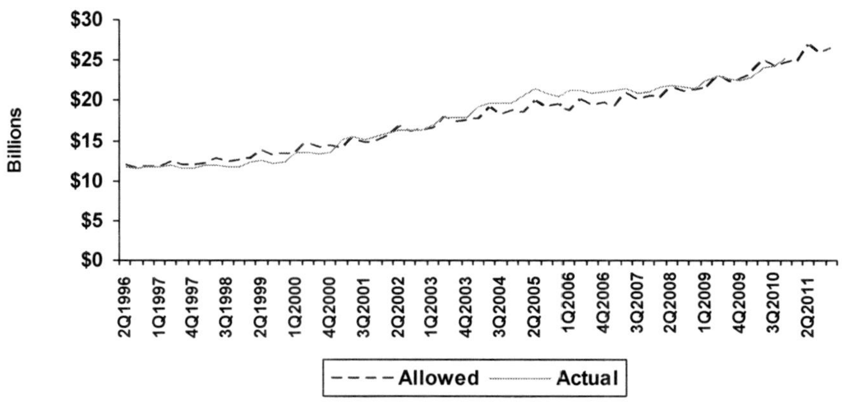

Determining the Conversion Factor

CMS first determines the MEI, which measures the weighted average price change for various inputs involved with producing physicians' services. The MEI is then multiplied by the update adjustment factor, which is based upon a statutory formula that limits annual expenditures for physician services (see SGR above). The MEI is similar in concept to the market basket update for hospitals described elsewhere herein.

> The MEI is a fixed-weight input price index, with an adjustment for the change in economywide labor productivity. This index, which has 1996 base weights, is comprised of two broad categories: physician's own time and physician's practice expense.[57]

A review of these factors for 2003 as a representative year illuminates in part the underlying mathematical rationale. For example, the increase in nonphysician salaries and benefits was computed at 4.2% and given a weight in the overall computation of 16.8%. In effect, the MEI is an inflation adjustment factor for the cost of delivering physician services, including the estimated effect of productivity growth based on broad factors in the economy—not in physician offices. The update is equal to the product of one plus the percentage increase in the MEI (divided by 100) and one plus the update adjustment factor.

The update adjustment factor is designed "to reflect success or failure in meeting the expenditure target that the law refers to as 'allowed expenditures.'" Allowed expenditures are equal to actual expenditures in a base period updated each year by the SGR.

The SGR is based upon the following:

1. The estimated change in fees for physicians' services.

2. The estimated change in the average number of Medicare fee-for-service beneficiaries.

3. The estimated projected growth in real GDP per capita, which CMS estimated at 2.8% for 2004. The Medicare Modernization Act changed the GDP factor to a 10-year average growth, but it had little effect on the computation of the conversion factor, and in fact, due to the rapid growth of the economy in the last two years before the 2008 recession, has actually made the situation worse rather than better!

4. The estimated change in expenditures due to changes in law or regulations.

57 *Federal Register* Vol. 66, No. 212, Nov. 1, 2001.

The base period allowed expenditures to roll forward from an initial fiscal year ending March 31, 1997. The formula reduces or increases for the current and future years by any excess or deficient expenditure in prior years. This is the critical point that a valuator or consultant must understand: Physician expenses under the Medicare program cannot exceed a limit established by a pre-determined, statutory formula, built off of historical expenditures and real GDP.

Recap of the annual computation

To recap, the MEI is basically an inflation factor based upon physician compensation and physician office expenses; the annual allowed expenditures are based upon FY March 1997 expenditures increased by the SGR; and the update adjustment factor, which forces the projected expenditures for the upcoming year to be no more than a predetermined limit.

Overview of Year-by-Year Changes in the Conversion Factor

Commencing with the phase-in of the changes mandated by the BBA, 1998 saw substantial increases in fee-for-service revenue for physicians in office-based medical specialties such as internal medicine, family medicine, and cardiology. Much of this rise stemmed from increases in the relative value of the evaluation and management codes. Radiology and pathology also saw significant increases.

In contrast, hospital-based surgical specialties such as orthopedics and cardiac surgery saw dramatic reductions in reimbursement.

CMS continued to refine its implementation of the BBA changes. The 1999 change generally provided moderate increases for the office-based medical specialties, ranging from 2% for internal medicine to 7% for family practice. The variability in the level of increase can be explained by the different utilization of individual CPT codes among the various specialties.

Cardiac surgery and neurosurgery received significant cutbacks from the 1999 changes, and radiology suffered a cut of 10%, undoing the increase received under the 1998 changes. Similarly, pathology reimbursement was cut by 13%. Cardiology practices saw reimbursement cut by 9% as fees for invasive procedures such as cardiac catheterization and balloon angioplasty received significant cuts. The conversion factor was set at $34.73, a significant decrease (5.3%) from the 1998 factor of $36.69.

As a result of intensive lobbying by the profession, CMS undertook a major revision in the assessment of the *practice expense component* of the RBRVS in 2000. The conversion factor was set at $36.6137, an increase over 1999 of 5.4%, which basically recaptured the 1999 decrease of 5.3%. Some of the practice specialties that had previously received dramatic cuts found those cuts mitigated, while others found no such relief.

Notably, a highly successful lobbying effort by its trade association resulted in a dramatic turnaround for pathology, with reimbursement increases of 9% over three years partially offsetting the prior year's 13% decline.

The changes in the practice expenses component of services provided by the various specialties must be *revenue neutral* under the law. As such, to the extent that any specialty received more reimbursement, other specialties received less. Cardiology, cardiac surgery, and gastroenterology received reimbursement cuts, primarily due to decreases in the RVUs associated with procedures performed by these physicians, such as echocardiography.

In November 2000, CMS issued the scheduled updates to the RBRVS for 2001. The update reflected changes mandated by the BBA and subsequent legislation. The 2001 physician fee schedule conversion factor was $38.2581 per RVU, an increase of 4.5% over the 2000 factor of $36.6137.

Changes in 2002 basically followed the legislative formula, with the RVU changes of the BBA now phased in fully. The 2002 physician fee schedule conversion factor was *$36.1992, a 5.4% decrease from the 2000 factor of $38.2581 per RVU.* This reflected primarily decreased growth in per capita GDP as well as the cumulative effect of various errors made in prior computations of the SGR that resulted in it being set at too high a level.

The annual physician fee schedule update is difficult to predict with any certainty until the annual measurement date (September 1) occurs. After a cut in the 2003 conversion factor of 4.4% was announced belatedly at the end of 2002, Congress modified the conversion factor in mid-February to eliminate the cumulative effect of prior errors that had overstated earlier conversion factors.

"For CY 2002, the MEI is equal to 3% (1.030). The update adjustment factor is equal to –1.1% (0.989) … The act requires an additional 0.2% (0.998) reduction to the update for 2003. Thus, the product of the MEI (1.030), the update adjustment factor (0.989), and the statutory adjustment factor (0.998) equals the CY 2003 update of 1.0166 [1.6%]."

Applying the 1.0162 factor (adjusted for budget neutrality) to the 2002 conversion factor of $36.1992 results in the 2003 conversion factor of *$36.7856.*

Prior to yet another legislative "fix" in the Medicare Modernization Act (Act) of 2003, the 2004 update was to be equal to the following: the product of one plus the percentage increase in the MEI (divided by 100) and one plus the update adjustment factor (UAF). For CY 2004, the MEI is equal to 2.9% (1.029). The UAF is –7% (0.930). Section 1848(d)(4)(F) of the act requires an additional 0.2% (0.998) reduction to the update for 2004. Thus, the product of the MEI (1.029), the UAF (0.930), and the statutory adjustment factor

(0.998) would have resulted in a CY 2004 update of –4.5% (0.9551). The calculation for 2005 would have produced an update of approximately –3.3%. The act set the increase at 1.5% for 2004 as well as 2005. Thus, the 2004 physician fee schedule conversion factor will be *$37.3374* and the 2005 conversion factor is *$37.8975.*

As of Nov, 2, 2005, CMS announced the final rule for the conversion factor in 2006 of *$36.1770,* a decrease of 4.4%, which was subsequently revised in February 2006 by the Deficit Reduction Act to maintain the 2005 conversion factor is *$37.8975.* The 2007 conversion factor—*$37.8975*—is identical to 2006 as a result of the repeal of the scheduled decrease in the Tax Relief and Health Care Act of 2006, thus there was no increase for three years. A 10.1% cut was due to be implemented in 2008, but was (again) suspended at the last minute by Congress and an increase of 0.5% (one-half of one percent) was adopted, or *$38.09.* The 2009 Medicare physician fee schedule final rule on Oct. 30, 2008 provides for the statutorily mandated 1.1% update for calendar year 2009; *however,* the budget neutrality adjustment to the conversion factor associated with the review and reallocation of RVUs was -6.41%, resulting in a rate of *$36.07.*

2011 Changes

The CMS issued the 2011 Medicare physician fee schedule final rule on Nov, 2, 2010, which provided for the statutorily mandated negative update for calendar year 2011, resulting in a conversion factor of $25.5217; subsequently, Congress overturned the cut yet again, resulting in a conversion factor of $33.9764.

Exhibit 53, taken from the final rule, shows the changes in expected payments for each of the various physician specialties based upon revisions in the RVUs for the various CPT codes billed to Medicare by each of those specialties. The principal changes affecting payments to the various specialties are in the practice expense (PE) RVUs, while less significant changes are in the work (physician effort) RVUs. The "full" and "tran" refer to the phase-in of the RVU changes over four years; the "tran" represents the effect in 2011, which is the second year of the phase-in period. "Full" represents what the impact would look like in 2013.

2010 Changes

The CMS issued the 2010 Medicare physician fee schedule final rule on Oct. 30, 2009, which provides for the statutorily mandated -21.2% update for calendar year 2010; *however,* the budget neutrality adjustment is included in the conversion factor now where historically it was applied to a reduction of RVUs for each CPT code. This makes the apparent conversion factor lower than it might otherwise have been. As noted elsewhere herein, the cut in the conversion factor has not been implemented as of May 2010 and was in fact repealed in June 2010. Even though that cut was not implemented, the practice expense RVU changes shown in Exhibits 54 and 55 do take effect.

Exhibit 53. 2011 Summary of Changes by Principal Affected Practice Specialty

Specialty	Allowed Charges (mil)	Impact of Work and	Impact of PE RVU and MPPR Changes		Impact of MEI	Combined Impact	
			Full	Tran		Full	Tran
TOTAL	$81,980	0%	0%	0%	0%	0%	0%
ALLERGY/IMMUNOLOGY	$181	0%	0%	1%	4%	4%	5%
ANESTHESIOLOGY	$1,793	0%	4%	2%	-3%	2%	-1%
CARDIAC SURGERY	$382	0%	-1%	0%	0%	-1%	0%
CARDIOLOGY	$6,951	0%	-5%	-2%	1%	-5%	-2%
COLON AND RECTAL SURGERY	$138	0%	4%	2%	0%	5%	3%
CRITICAL CARE	$240	0%	3%	2%	-2%	1%	0%
DERMATOLOGY	$2,749	0%	2%	2%	3%	5%	4%
EMERGENCY MEDICINE	$2,600	0%	2%	1%	-3%	-2%	-3%
ENDOCRINOLOGY	$395	1%	4%	2%	0%	4%	2%
FAMILY PRACTICE	$5,512	0%	4%	2%	0%	4%	2%
GASTROENTEROLOGY	$1,800	0%	3%	1%	-1%	2%	1%
GENERAL PRACTICE	$728	0%	3%	1%	0%	3%	1%
GENERAL SURGERY	$2,286	0%	3%	1%	0%	3%	1%
GERIATRICS	$188	0%	5%	2%	-2%	4%	1%
HAND SURGERY	$103	0%	4%	2%	2%	6%	4%
HEMATOLOGY/ONCOLOGY	$1,912	0%	-4%	-2%	2%	-2%	0%
INFECTIOUS DISEASE	$584	0%	4%	2%	-2%	3%	0%
INTERNAL MEDICINE	$10,696	0%	3%	2%	-1%	3%	1%
INTERVENTIONAL PAIN MGMT	$390	-1%	3%	1%	1%	2%	0%
INTERVENTIONAL RADIOLOGY	$224	-2%	-8%	-4%	0%	-9%	-5%
MULTISPECIALTY CLINIC/OTHER	$46	0%	-7%	-5%	1%	-5%	-4%
NEPHROLOGY	$1,946	1%	1%	1%	-1%	1%	1%
NEUROLOGY	$1,457	0%	5%	2%	0%	5%	2%
NEUROSURGERY	$642	-2%	1%	0%	1%	0%	-1%
NUCLEAR MEDICINE	$59	0%	-7%	-4%	0%	-6%	-4%
OBSTETRICS/GYNECOLOGY	$670	0%	1%	1%	1%	2%	2%
OPHTHALMOLOGY	$5,287	-1%	4%	0%	1%	4%	0%
ORTHOPEDIC SURGERY	$3,432	0%	3%	1%	1%	4%	3%
OTOLARNGOLOGY	$941	0%	3%	2%	1%	5%	3%
PATHOLOGY	$1,069	-1%	-1%	0%	0%	-2%	-1%
PEDIATRICS	$68	0%	2%	1%	0%	2%	1%
PHYSICAL MEDICINE	$895	0%	4%	2%	-1%	4%	1%
PLASTIC SURGERY	$317	0%	4%	2%	1%	5%	3%
PSYCHIATRY	$1,149	1%	2%	1%	-3%	0%	-1%
PULMONARY DISEASE	$1,786	-1%	2%	1%	-1%	1%	-1%
RADIATION ONCOLOGY	$1,939	-2%	-9%	-3%	4%	-7%	-1%
RADIOLOGY	$5,052	-2%	-12%	-7%	-1%	-14%	-10%
RHEUMATOLOGY	$511	0%	1%	0%	2%	2%	2%
THORACIC SURGERY	$398	0%	-1%	0%	0%	-1%	0%
UROLOGY	$1,950	-1%	-6%	-3%	1%	-7%	-3%
VASCULAR SURGERY	$708	-1%	-3%	-2%	0%	-4%	-2%
AUDIOLOGIST	$54	0%	-6%	-1%	2%	-5%	0%
CHIROPRACTOR	$756	0%	4%	2%	-2%	2%	0%
CLINICAL PSYCHOLOGIST	$577	0%	-6%	-2%	-4%	-10%	-6%
CLINICAL SOCIAL WORKER	$390	0%	-5%	-2%	-4%	-9%	-5%
DIAGNOSTIC TESTING FACILITY	$909	0%	-27%	-16%	2%	-23%	-15%
INDEPENDENT LABORATORY	$1,039	-1%	-7%	-3%	5%	-4%	1%
NURSE ANES / ANES ASST	$726	0%	4%	2%	-4%	1%	-1%
NURSE PRACTITIONER	$1,212	0%	4%	2%	-1%	4%	1%
OPTOMETRY	$970	0%	4%	1%	1%	6%	2%
ORAL/MAXILLOFACIAL SURGERY	$40	0%	5%	3%	2%	7%	5%
PHYSICAL/OCCUPATIONAL THERA	$2,204	0%	0%	-3%	-2%	-1%	-5%
PHYSICIAN ASSISTANT	$893	0%	3%	2%	0%	3%	1%
PODIATRY	$1,801	0%	6%	3%	1%	7%	4%
PORTABLE X-RAY	$94	0%	2%	0%	6%	7%	6%
RADIATION THERAPY CENTERS	$71	0%	-13%	-5%	8%	-6%	3%
OTHER	$69	2%	3%	1%	0%	5%	3%

Exhibit 54. 2010 Changes in Individual CPT Code Reimbursement

CPT[1]/ HCPCS	MOD	Description	Facility			Non-facility		
			2009 ($)	2010 ($)	Percent Change	2009 ($)	2010 ($)	Percent Change
11721		Debride nail, 6 or more	27.77	20.74	-25%	40.39	31.25	-23%
17000		Destruct premalg lesion	48.69	40.90	-16%	69.97	57.95	-17%
27130		Total hip arthroplasty	1359.71	1082.84	-20%	NA	NA	NA
27244		Treat thigh fracture	1144.39	917.52	-20%	NA	NA	NA
27447		Total knee arthroplasty	1456.37	1158.40	-20%	NA	NA	NA
33533		CABG, arterial, single	1892.05	1534.21	-19%	NA	NA	NA
35301		Rechanneling of artery	1067.93	868.66	-19%	NA	NA	NA
43239		Upper GI endoscopy, biopsy	165.55	134.08	-19%	323.16	257.08	-20%
66821		After cataract laser surgery	251.38	216.45	-14%	266.53	228.67	-14%
66984		Cataract surg w/iol, 1 stage	638.74	549.09	-14%	NA	NA	NA
67210		Treatment of retinal lesion	561.56	478.93	-15%	580.67	493.98	-15%
71010		Chest x-ray	NA	NA	NA	24.16	18.18	-25%
71010	26	Chest x-ray	9.02	7.10	-21%	9.02	7.10	-21%
77056		Mammogram, both breasts	NA	NA	NA	107.48	82.95	-23%
77056	26	Mammogram, both breasts	44.36	34.66	-22%	44.36	34.66	-22%
77057		Mammogram, screening	NA	NA	NA	81.15	61.64	-24%
77057	26	Mammogram, screening	35.71	27.84	-22%	35.71	27.84	-22%
77427		Radiation tx management, x5	188.27	153.11	-19%	188.27	153.11	-19%
78465	26	Heart image (3d), multiple	78.99	62.21	-21%	78.99	62.21	-21%
88305	26	Tissue exam by pathologist	37.15	28.97	-22%	37.15	28.97	-22%
90801		Psy dx interview	128.04	100.27	-22%	152.92	121.01	-21%
90862		Medication management	45.08	35.79	-21%	55.18	44.31	-20%
90935		Hemodialysis, one evaluation	66.36	53.12	-20%	NA	NA	NA
92012		Eye exam established pat	45.80	38.35	-16%	70.69	58.80	-17%
92014		Eye exam & treatment	70.33	58.80	-16%	103.15	85.79	-17%
92980		Insert intracoronary stent	847.93	644.53	-24%	NA	NA	NA
93000		Electrocardiogram, complete	20.92	NA	NA	20.92	15.62	-25%
93010		Electrocardiogram report	9.02	7.10	-21%	9.02	7.10	-21%
93015		Cardiovascular stress test	100.27	73.00	-27%	100.27	73.00	-27%
93307	26	Echo exam of heart	49.77	38.35	-23%	49.77	38.35	-23%

continued

Exhibit 54. 2010 Changes in Individual CPT Code Reimbursement, Continued

CPT[1]/ HCPCS	MOD	Description	Facility			Non-facility		
			2009 ($)	2010 ($)	Percent Change	2009 ($)	2010 ($)	Percent Change
93510	26	Left heart catheterization	248.86	185.21	-26%	248.86	185.21	-26%
98941		Chiropractic manipulation	30.30	24.15	-20%	33.90	27.27	-20%
99203		Office/outpatient visit, new	68.17	57.38	-16%	91.97	76.98	-16%
99213		Office/outpatient visit, est	44.72	38.06	-15%	61.31	51.70	-16%
99214		Office/outpatient visit, est	69.25	58.80	-15%	92.33	77.55	-16%
99222		Initial hospital care	122.63	100.27	-18%	NA	NA	NA
99223		Initial hospital care	180.33	147.14	-18%	NA	NA	NA
99231		Subsequent hospital care	37.15	30.11	-19%	NA	NA	NA
99232		Subsequent hospital care	66.72	54.26	-19%	NA	NA	NA
99233		Subsequent hospital care	95.58	77.83	-19%	NA	NA	NA
99236		Observ/hosp same date	207.38	166.18	-20%	NA	NA	NA
99239		Hospital discharge day	96.30	77.83	-19%	NA	NA	NA
99243		Office consultation	97.38	Discontinued	Discontinued	124.79	Discontinued	Discontinued
99244		Office consultation	154.00	Discontinued	Discontinued	184.30	Discontinued	Discontinued
99253		Inpatient consultation	114.69	Discontinued	Discontinued	NA	NA	NA
99254		Inpatient consultation	165.55	Discontinued	Discontinued	NA	NA	NA
99283		Emergency dept visit	61.31	48.57	-21%	NA	NA	NA
99284		Emergency dept visit	114.33	91.18	-20%	NA	NA	NA

Exhibit 55. 2010 Summary of Changes by Principal Affected Practice Specialty

	(A)	(B)	(C)	(D)	(E)	(F)	(G)	(H)
		Allowed Charges	Impact of Work RVU	Impact of PE RVU Changes**		Impact of MP RVU	Combined Impact	
	Specialty	(mil $)	Changes	Full	Tran	Changes	Full	Tran
1	TOTAL	77,796	0%	0%	0%	0%	0%	0%
2	ALLERGY/IMMUNOLOGY	173	0%	-1%	0%	0%	-2%	0%
3	ANESTHESIOLOGY	1,744	0%	4%	1%	0%	3%	0%
4	CARDIAC SURGERY	373	-1%	-1%	0%	2%	1%	1%
5	CARDIOLOGY	7,158	-1%	-10%	-5%	-1%	-13%	-8%
6	COLON AND RECTAL SURGERY	130	-1%	4%	1%	1%	4%	1%
7	CRITICAL CARE	223	-1%	2%	1%	1%	3%	1%
8	DERMATOLOGY	2,520	1%	1%	1%	1%	3%	3%
9	EMERGENCY MEDICINE	2,416	0%	2%	1%	0%	3%	1%
10	ENDOCRINOLOGY	374	-1%	3%	0%	0%	2%	0%
11	FAMILY PRACTICE	5,094	2%	5%	2%	1%	7%	4%
12	GASTROENTEROLOGY	1,792	-2%	0%	0%	1%	0%	-1%
13	GENERAL PRACTICE	727	1%	4%	1%	0%	6%	3%
14	GENERAL SURGERY	2,227	-1%	3%	1%	1%	4%	1%
15	GERIATRICS	170	1%	6%	2%	1%	8%	3%
16	HAND SURGERY	89	-1%	3%	1%	-1%	2%	-1%
17	HEMATOLOGY/ONCOLOGY	1,897	0%	-5%	-1%	0%	-6%	-1%
18	INFECTIOUS DISEASE	554	-1%	3%	0%	1%	3%	0%
19	INTERNAL MEDICINE	10,133	1%	4%	1%	1%	5%	2%
20	INTERVENTIONAL PAIN MANAGE.	356	-2%	3%	-1%	0%	0%	-3%
21	INTERVENTIONAL RADIOLOGY	225	-1%	-9%	-2%	0%	-10%	-3%
22	NEPHROLOGY	1,803	-1%	2%	0%	1%	2%	1%
23	NEUROLOGY	1,414	-3%	4%	1%	0%	1%	-2%
24	NEUROSURGERY	591	-1%	2%	0%	0%	1%	-1%
25	NUCLEAR MEDICINE	74	-5%	-15%	-10%	-2%	-23%	-18%
26	OBSTETRICS/GYNECOLOGY	624	0%	0%	-1%	0%	0%	-1%
27	OPHTHALMOLOGY	4,758	0%	11%	3%	2%	13%	5%
28	ORTHOPEDIC SURGERY	3,261	0%	3%	1%	-1%	2%	0%
29	OTOLARNGOLOGY	933	-1%	1%	-1%	0%	0%	-2%
30	PATHOLOGY	994	0%	-1%	1%	-1%	-3%	-1%
31	PEDIATRICS	65	1%	3%	1%	0%	4%	2%
32	PHYSICAL MEDICINE	824	-1%	6%	2%	0%	5%	1%
33	PLASTIC SURGERY	284	0%	4%	1%	1%	5%	2%
34	PSYCHIATRY	1,095	0%	2%	1%	1%	3%	2%
35	PULMONARY DISEASE	1,765	-1%	2%	0%	1%	2%	0%
36	RADIATION ONCOLOGY	1,809	0%	-3%	0%	-2%	-5%	-1%
37	RADIOLOGY	5,056	0%	-14%	-3%	-2%	-16%	-5%
38	RHEUMATOLOGY	493	0%	-1%	0%	0%	-2%	-1%
39	THORACIC SURGERY	389	-1%	0%	0%	2%	1%	1%
40	UROLOGY	1,993	-1%	-8%	-3%	0%	-10%	-4%
41	VASCULAR SURGERY	656	-1%	-3%	-2%	0%	-3%	-2%
42	AUDIOLOGIST	36	-1%	-16%	-9%	-7%	-23%	-17%
43	CHIROPRACTOR	713	0%	3%	1%	1%	4%	2%
44	CLINICAL PSYCHOLOGIST	544	0%	-8%	-2%	0%	-8%	-2%
45	CLINICAL SOCIAL WORKER	362	0%	-7%	-1%	0%	-7%	-1%
46	NURSE ANESTHETIST	681	0%	4%	1%	0%	4%	1%
47	NURSE PRACTITIONER	1,018	1%	5%	1%	1%	6%	3%
48	OPTOMETRY	848	1%	10%	3%	1%	12%	5%
49	ORAL/MAXILLOFACIAL SURGERY	36	-1%	4%	1%	0%	3%	0%
50	PHYSICAL/OCCUPATIONAL THERAPY	1,883	0%	9%	3%	-1%	8%	2%
51	PHYSICIAN ASSISTANT	757	0%	4%	1%	0%	5%	2%
52	PODIATRY	1,682	1%	6%	2%	-1%	6%	2%
53	DIAGNOSTIC TESTING FACILITY	923	-1%	-29%	-7%	-4%	-34%	-12%
54	INDEPENDENT LABORATORY	970	0%	-5%	0%	-1%	-7%	-1%
55	PORTABLE X-RAY SUPPLIER	87	0%	8%	3%	-1%	7%	2%

2009 Changes

The CMS issued the 2009 Medicare physician fee schedule final rule on Oct. 30, 2008, which provides for the statutorily mandated 1.1% update for calendar year 2009 (see Exhibit 56); *however*, the budget neutrality adjustment to the conversion factor associated with the review and reallocation of RVUs was -6.41%, resulting in a rate of $36.07 (last year, the budget neutrality adjustment was accomplished by applying an across-the-board reduction to work RVUs of 10%). As described below, *an additional 4% in payment incentives* for adopting electronic prescribing and reporting on certain quality measures was part of the final rule; thus, any forecast of 2009 and subsequent cash flows would have to consider the likelihood of qualifying for the incentive.

> … the reporting period for the 2009 PQRI [Physician Quality Reporting Initiative] is defined as the entire year, or Jan. 1, 2009 through Dec. 31, 2009. Therefore, for the 2009 PQRI, eligible professionals who satisfactorily report data on quality measures for covered professional services furnished between Jan. 1, 2009 through Dec. 31, 2009 will receive an incentive payment equal to 2% of the total estimated allowed charges submitted by no later than Feb. 28, 2010 for all covered professional services furnished between Jan. 1, 2009 and Dec. 31, 2009.
>
> Specifically, for 2009, in accordance with Section 1848(m)(2) of the act, as added by Section 132(a) of the MIPPA, a "successful electronic prescriber" as defined by MIPPA and further discussed below, is eligible to receive an incentive payment equal to 2% of the total estimated allowed charges submitted not later than two months after the end of the reporting period for all covered professional services furnished during the 2009 reporting period. This new E-Prescribing Incentive Program is separate from and in addition to any incentive payment that eligible professionals may earn through the PQRI program discussed above.[58]

Exhibit 56. Percent Change From 2008 to 2009

			Facility (e.g., HOPD)			Non-Facility (MD Office)		
CODE	MOD	DESCRIPTION	2008	2009	Change	2008	2009	Change
11721		Debride nail, 6 or more	$27.42	$27.77	1%	$39.61	$40.39	2%
17000		Destruct premalg. lesion	46.47	48.69	5	67.41	69.97	4
27130		Total hip arthroplasty	1,336.09	1,359.71	2	NA	NA	NA
27244		Treat thigh fracture	1,077.10	1,144.39	6	NA	NA	NA
27447		Total knee arthroplasty	1,435.12	1,456.37	1	NA	NA	NA
33533		CABG, arterial, single	1,854.84	1,892.05	2	NA	NA	NA
35301		Rechanneling of artery	1,045.11	1,067.93	2	NA	NA	NA
43239		Upper GI endoscopy, biopsy	156.92	165.55	5	329.07	323.16	-2
66821		After cataract laser surgery	253.53	222.81	-12	270.97	237.80	-12
66821		After cataract laser surgery	249.47	251.38	1	266.23	266.53	0

continued

58 CMS-1403-FC

Exhibit 56. Percent Change From 2008 to 2009, Continued

			Facility (e.g., HOPD)			Non-Facility (MD Office)		
CODE	MOD	DESCRIPTION	2008	2009	Change	2008	2009	Change
66984		Cataract surg. w/iol, 1 stage	626.15	638.74	2	NA	NA	NA
67210		Treatment of retinal lesion	545.79	561.56	3	567.88	580.67	2
71010		Chest X-ray	NA	NA	NA	25.52	24.16	-5
71010	26	Chest X-ray	$8.76	$9.02	3%	$8.76	$9.02	3%
77056		Mammogram, both breasts	NA	NA	NA	104.74	107.48	3
77056	26	Mammogram, both breasts	41.9	44.36	6	41.9	44.36	6
77057		Mammogram, screening	NA	NA	NA	82.65	81.15	-2
77057	26	Mammogram, screening	33.9	35.71	5	33.9	35.71	5
77427		Radiation tx management, x5	177.1	188.27	6	177.1	188.27	6
78465	26	Heart image (3d), multiple	74.27	78.99	6	74.27	78.99	6
88305	26	Tissue exam by pathologist	36.18	37.15	3	36.18	37.15	3
90801		Psy. dx interview	125.31	128.04	2	147.02	152.92	4
90862		Medication management	43.8	45.08	3	52.18	55.18	6
90935		Hemodialysis, one evaluation	65.13	66.36	2	NA	NA	NA
92012		Eye exam established pat.	43.04	45.80	6	70.08	70.69	1%
92014		Eye exam and treatment	66.27	70.33	6	101.69	103.15	1
92980		Insert intracoronary stent	806.3	847.93	5	NA	NA	NA
93010		Electrocardiogram report	8.38	9.02	8	8.38	9.02	8
93015		Cardiovascular stress test	103.98	100.27	-4	103.98	100.27	-4
93307	26	Echo exam of heart	47.23	49.77	5	47.23	49.77	5
93510	26	Left heart catheterization	241.09	248.86	3	241.09	248.86	3
98941		Chiropractic manipulation	28.57	30.30	6	33.14	33.9	2
99203		Office/outpatient visit, new	65.51	68.17	4	91.03	91.97	1
99213		Office/outpatient visit, est.	41.9	44.72	7	59.8	61.31	3
99214		Office/outpatient visit, est.	65.51	69.25	6	89.89	92.33	3
99223		Initial hospital care	171.77	180.33	5	NA	NA	NA
99231		Subsequent hospital care	35.42	37.15	5	NA	NA	NA
99232		Subsequent hospital care	63.22	66.72	6	NA	NA	NA
99233		Subsequent hospital care	90.65	95.58	5	NA	NA	NA
99236		Observ./hosp. same date	200.34	207.38	4	NA	NA	NA
99239		Hospital discharge day	92.93	96.30	4	NA	NA	NA
99243		Office consultation	92.93	97.38	5	122.26	124.79	2
99244		Office consultation	145.49	154.00	6	179.01	184.3	3
99253		Inpatient consultation	108.55	114.69	6	NA	NA	NA
99254		Inpatient consultation	156.54	165.55	6	NA	NA	NA
99283		Emergency dept. visit	59.03	61.31	4	NA	NA	NA
99284		Emergency dept. visit	108.93	114.33	5	NA	NA	NA
99291		Critical care, first hour	204.15	212.07	4	250.99	253.91	1
99292		Critical care, add'l 30 min.	102.45	106.04	3	111.98	114.69	2%
99348		Home visit, est. patient	NA	NA	NA	76.17	79.35	4
99350		Home visit, est. patient	NA	NA	NA	155.78	160.86	3
G0008		Admin. influenza virus vac.	NA	NA	NA	20.57	20.92	2
G0317		ESRD related svs 4+mo 20+yrs	$283.09	$245.29	-13%	$283.09	$245.29	-13

2009 Changes in Individual CPT Code Reimbursement

Despite the apparent cut in the 2009 conversion factor, the increase in RVUs for many office-based procedures results in a fairly significant increase for the two most commonly used codes, 99213 and 99214, as well as the consultation codes and hospital inpatient codes. As seen in Exhibit 57, those increases are being paid for by diagnostic imaging providers.

2009 Summary of Changes by Principal Affected Practice Specialty

Exhibit 57 shows CMS's estimate of the impact on payments in **2009** from ***both*** the Work and Practice Expense RVU changes described in the previous section ***and*** the Conversion Factor. Note that imaging providers are primarily bearing the brunt of the changes in RVUs.

Exhibit 57. Increases for 99213, 99214, Consultation Codes, and Hospital Inpatient Codes

Specialty	Allowed Charges -mil	RVU Changes*	Budget Neutrality	Statutory 1.1%	Total***
Total	$81,669	0%	0%	1%	1%
Allergy/immunology	184	1	-3	1	-1
Anesthesiology	$1,966	-1%	3%	1%	3%
Cardiac surgery	400	0	1	1	2
Cardiology	7,775	-2	-1	1	-2
Colon and rectal surgery	136	0	1	1	2
Critical care	224	0	2	1	3
Dermatology	2,557	2	-2	1	1
Emergency medicine	2,451	0	3	1	4
Endocrinology	385	0	0	1	2
Family practice	5,354	0	0	1	2
Gastroenterology	1,883	2	1	1	3
General practice	842	0	0	1	2
General surgery	2,408	1	1	1	3
Geriatrics	175	0	2	1	3
Hand surgery	88	-1	-1	1	-1
Hematology/oncology	2,019	-1	-2	1	-1
Infectious disease	561	1	2	1	4
Internal medicine	10,662	0	1	1	2
Interventional radiology	228	-1	0	1	0
Nephrology	1,840	-1	1	1	2
Neurology	1,489	0	0	1	1

continued

Exhibit 57. Increases for 99213, 99214, Consultation Codes, and Hospital Inpatient Codes, Continued

Specialty	Allowed Charges -mil	RVU Changes*	Budget Neutrality	Statutory 1.1%	Total***
Neurosurgery	620	-1	0	1	0
Nuclear medicine	79	-1	-2	1	-1
Obstetrics/gynecology	654	0	0	1	0
Ophthalmology	5,026	0	0	1	0
Orthopedic surgery	3,454	0	0	1	0
Otolarngology	984	-1	-1	1	-1
Pathology	1,007	0	0	1	1
Pediatrics	72	1	0	1	2
Physical medicine	850	0	1	1	1
Plastic surgery	288	0	0	1	1
Psychiatry	1,169	1	2	1	4
Pulmonary disease	1,828	1	1	1	3
Radiation oncology	1,854	-1	-3	1	-3
Radiology	5,554	0	-1	1	0
Rheumatology	521	0	-1	1	-1
Thoracic surgery	431	0	1	1	2
Urology	2,146	0	-1	1	0
Vascular surgery	685	0	-1	1	1
Audiologist	33	-9	-2	1	-10
Chiropractor	768	-1	2	1	2
Clinical psychologist	571	-2	3	1	2
Clinical social worker	378	-1	3	1	3
Nurse anesthetist	846	0	4	1	5
Nurse practitioner	963	1	1	1	3
Optometry	867	0	-1	1	0
Oral/maxillofacial surgery	38	1	-1	1	1
Physical/occupational Therapy	1,772	2	0	1	3
Physician assistant	711	0	1	1	2
Podiatry	1,727	1	-1	1	1
Diagnostic testing facility	1,186	-2	-5	1	-6
Independent laboratory	878	5	-4	1	2
Portable X-ray supplier	$87	2%	-4%	1%	-2%

* PE changes are CY 2009 third-year transition changes. For fully implemented CY 2010 PE changes, see CMS-1403-FC.
** Prior to the application of the OPPS imaging caps under DRA 5102.
***Components may not sum to total due to rounding.

Note: Exhibit 58 reflects CMS calculation of fee schedule changes[59] *before* the repeal of the 10.1% cut in the 2008 conversion factor; a revised table was not issued. You can *estimate* the changes for each code by adding 0.5% to the 2007 numbers shown in conjunction with Exhibit 58.

Exhibit 58. 2008 Changes in Individual CPT Code Reimbursement

			Facility (e.g., HOPD)			Non-Facility (MD Office)		
CODE	MOD	DESCRIPTION	2007	2008	Change	2007	2009	Change
11721		Debride nail, 6 or more	$28.80	$24.53	-15%	$39.03	$35.43	-9%
17000		Destruct premalg. lesion	44.72	41.56	-7	63.29	60.30	-5
27130		Total hip arthroplasty	1,360.52	1,194.77	-12	NA	NA	NA
27244		Treat thigh fracture	1,100.92	963.11	-13	NA	NA	NA
27447		Total knee arthroplasty	1,464.74	1,283.35	-12	NA	NA	NA
33533		CABG, arterial, single	1,908.52	1,658.44	-13	NA	NA	NA
35301		Rechanneling of artery	1,071.74	934.49	-13	NA	NA	NA
43239		Upper GI endoscopy, biopsy	155.00	140.36	-9	325.16	294.01	-10
66821		After cataract laser surgery	253.53	222.81	-12	270.97	237.80	-12
66984		Cataract surg. w/iol, 1 stage	641.98	560.08	-13	NA	NA	NA
67210		Treatment of retinal lesion	556.34	487.86	-12	580.59	507.96	-13
71010		Chest X-ray	NA	NA	NA	26.15	22.83	-13
71010	26	Chest X-ray	8.72	7.84	-10	8.72	7.84	-10
77056		Mammogram, both breasts	NA	NA	NA	97.40	93.35	-4
77056	26	Mammogram, both breasts	41.31	37.48	-9	41.31	37.48	-9
77057		Mammogram, screening	NA	NA	NA	81.86	73.93	-10
77057	26	Mammogram, screening	33.35	30.32	-9	33.35	30.32	-9
77427		Radiation tx management, x5	176.22	158.42	-10	176.22	158.42	-10
78465	26	Heart image (3d), multiple	73.14	66.43	-9	73.14	66.43	-9
88305	26	Tissue exam by pathologist	37.90	32.36	-15	37.90	32.36	-15
90801		Psy. dx interview	129.99	112.08	-14	145.15	131.50	-9
90862		Medication management	44.72	39.18	-12	50.40	46.67	-7
90935		Hemodialysis, one evaluation	67.46	58.26	-14	NA	NA	NA
92012		Eye exam established pat.	34.11	38.50	13	61.77	62.69	1
92014		Eye exam and treatment	55.71	59.28	6	91.33	90.96	0
92980		Insert intracoronary stent	795.85	720.88	-9	NA	NA	NA
93000		Electrocardiogram, complete	24.63	20.78	-16	24.63	20.78	-16
93010		Electrocardiogram report	8.34	7.50	-10	8.34	7.50	-10

continued

59 CMS-1385-FC.pdf, http://www.cms.hhs.gov/PhysicianFeeSched/

Exhibit 58. 2008 Changes in Individual CPT Code Reimbursement, Continued

			Facility (e.g., HOPD)			Non-Facility (MD Office)		
CODE	MOD	DESCRIPTION	2007	2008	Change	2007	2009	Change
93015		Cardiovascular stress test	104.22	93.01	-11	104.22	93.01	-11
93307	26	Echo exam of heart	46.99	42.24	-10	46.99	42.24	-10
93510	26	Left heart catheterization	242.92	215.31	-11	242.92	215.31	-11
98941		Chiropractic manipulation	28.80	25.55	-11	33.35	29.64	-11
99203		Office/outpatient visit, new	67.08	58.60	-13	91.71	81.42	-11
99213		Office/outpatient visit, est.	42.07	37.48	-11	59.50	53.15	-11
99214		Office/outpatient visit, est.	66.32	58.60	-12	90.20	80.40	-11
99222		Initial hospital	119.00	104.59	-12	NA	NA	NA
99223		Initial hospital	173.57	153.65	-11	NA	NA	NA
99231		Subsequent hospital care	35.62	31.68	-11	NA	NA	NA
99232		Subsequent hospital care	63.67	56.55	-11	NA	NA	NA
99233		Subsequent hospital care	90.95	81.08	-11	NA	NA	NA
99236		Observ/hosp. same date	205.40	179.20	-13	NA	NA	NA
99239		Hospital discharge day	94.74	83.13	-12	NA	NA	NA
99243		Office consultation	93.23	83.13	-11	122.41	109.36	-11
99244		Office consultation	145.91	130.14	-11	179.26	160.12	-11
99253		Inpatient consultation	108.77	97.09	-11	NA	NA	NA
99254		Inpatient consultation	156.52	140.02	-11	NA	NA	NA
99283		Emergency dept. visit	60.64	52.81	-13	NA	NA	NA
99284		Emergency dept. visit	110.28	97.44	-12	NA	NA	NA
99291		Critical care, first hour	208.82	182.61	-13	256.19	224.17	-12
99292		Critical care, add'l 30 min.	104.60	91.64	-12	114.45	100.16	-12
99348		Home visit, est. patient	NA	NA	NA	66.32	68.14	2
99350		Home visit, est. patient	NA	NA	NA	150.83	139.34	-8
G0008		Admin. influenza virus vac.	NA	NA	NA	18.95	18.40	-3
G0317		ESRD related svs 4+mo 20+yrs	283.09	245.29	-13	283.09	245.29	-13

2008 Summary of *RVU* Changes by Principal Affected Practice Specialty

Exhibit 59 shows CMS's estimate of the impact on payments in 2008 from *only* the work and PE RVU changes described in the previous section *without* either the suspended cut in the conversion factor *or* the 0.5% increase. It should offer a rough estimate of the relative positions of the specialties for 2008. Note the winners and losers, particularly anesthesiology.

Exhibit 59. CMS's Estimate of Impact on Payments in 2008

Specialty	Percent Change
Total	0%
Allergy/immunology	2
Anesthesiology	14
Cardiac surgery	-2
Cardiology	-2
Colon and rectal surgery	0
Critical care	-1
Dermatology	2
Emergency medicine	-2
Endocrinology	-1
Family practice	0
Gastroenterology	0
General practice	0
General surgery	-1
Geriatrics	3
Hand surgery	-2
Hematology/oncology	-1
Infectious disease	-1

Specialty	Percent Change
Internal medicine	0
Interventional radiology	-2
Nephrology	-3
Neurology	-1
Neurosurgery	-2
Nuclear medicine	4
Obstetrics/gynecology	-1
Ophthalmology	1
Orthopedic surgery	-1
Otolaryngology	1
Pathology	-2
Pediatrics	0
Physical medicine	-1
Plastic surgery	-1
Psychiatry	0
Pulmonary disease	-1
Radiation oncology	0
Radiology	0

Specialty	Percent Change
Rheumatology	-1
Thoracic surgery	-2
Urology	-1
Vascular surgery	-1
Audiologist	12
Chiropractor	-2
Clinical psychologist	-3
Clinical social worker	-3
Nurse anesthetist	22
Nurse practitioner	2
Optometry	4
Oral/maxillofacial surgery	-1
Physical/occupational therapy	0
Physicians assistant	2
Podiatry	0
Diagnostic testing facility	3
Independent laboratory	2
Portable X-ray supplier	0

Chapter 2

Healthcare Market Structure and Its Implication for Valuation of Privately Held Provider Entities—An Empirical Analysis

By Mark O. Dietrich, CPA/ABV

Author's Note

I originally conducted this study in early 2008 to see if I could confirm my hypothesis and experience that there were underlying structural reasons that existed in local markets that would explain—and convince my colleagues of—the vast differences in reimbursement, profitability, and market participants that I had encountered in my appraisal and consulting practice and seminar presentations. As the research demonstrated, there *were* longstanding, historical reasons for these differences. The results first appeared in the Summer 2008 edition of *Business Valuation Review* and the information is reprinted with permission.

Subsequent to my research, a variety of other studies appeared, including one by the Government Accountability Office (GAO), another in the journal *Health Affairs*, one by the Center for Studying Health System Change, and one by KQED National Public Radio reporter Sarah Varney.[1] A series of annual studies titled "National Insurer Report Card" by the American Medical Association of concentration of insurer market share also bears out the findings in this article.

The GAO report *Nonprofit Hospitals: Variation in Standards and Guidance Limits Comparison of How Hospitals Meet Community Benefit Requirements* was released in September 2008. Figure 1 is taken from that report and shows a concentration of nonprofit hospitals consistent with my research.

1 www.npr.org/2010/11/18/131410569/big-hospital-chains-use-clout-to-dictate-premiums, November 2010.

Figure 1. Geographic Distributions of Nonprofit Hospitals in 2006

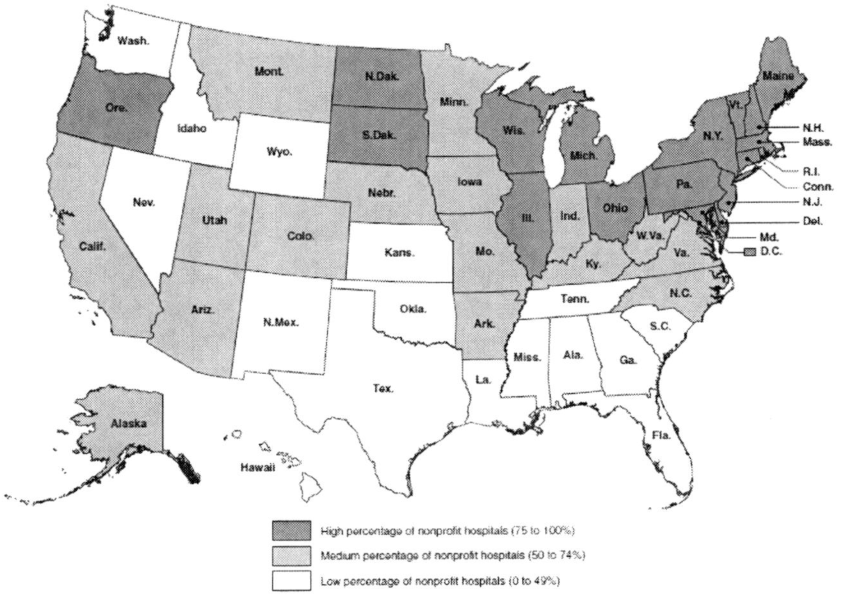

Sources: GAO analysis of 2006 CMS data; Map Resources (map).

Note: Hospitals include nonfederal, acute care, general hospitals.

The *Health Affairs* study "The Increased Concentration of Health Plan Markets Can Benefit Consumers Through Lower Hospital Prices"[2] found that markets in which insurers held the upper hand in terms of market power had lower hospital prices by approximately 12%, while most markets had high concentrations of hospital market power and this latter condition led to higher hospital prices.

Research Brief No. 16 from the Center for Studying Health System Change, "Wide Variation in Hospital and Physician Payment Rates Evidence of Provider Market Power," looked at eight specific healthcare markets—Cleveland; Indianapolis; Los Angeles; Miami; Milwaukee; Richmond, Va.; San Francisco; and rural Wisconsin—and found dramatic differences in inpatient hospital rates consistent with local market power of insurers and providers.

Finally, Greg Anderson and I documented much of my earlier work as well as our joint work elsewhere herein ("Evaluating RVU-Based Compensation Arrangements") in our 2012 book *The Financial Professional's Guide to Healthcare Reform*. Timothy Smith's work in this third edition of the *Healthcare Guide* expands on and emphasizes Greg's and my seminal work on market differences in RVU payment rates and the resultant limitations on generic market data.

2 Glenn A. Melnick, Yu-Chu Shen and Vivian Yaling Wu, *Health Affairs*, 30, no.9 (2011):1728-1733.

Results of Original Study

The explosion in healthcare transactions after a 10-year hiatus has created a booming market for appraisal and valuation services. One of the peculiar aspects of the healthcare industry is that many if not most transactions must be supported by an independent appraisal due to governmental regulatory concerns. As such, failure of appraisers or valuation analysts to understand healthcare markets and government regulations can lead to transactions taking place at prices inconsistent with both economic reality and, as discussed later herein, regulatory parameters. These transactions can then find their way into databases relied upon by other appraisers resulting in further transactions based upon suspect opinions of value.

The degree of revenue and profit for healthcare provider entities varies significantly from state to state and even within different regions of individual states. As a threshold matter, areas with high healthcare spending and particularly high Medicare[3] spending tend to offer the greatest opportunity for profit. The elderly, of course, receive the bulk of medical care. Given that high localized spending is the primary driver of profit, what other factors contribute to the pattern of location of larger for-profit providers?

- The presence and market strength of Blue Cross plans;
- The degree of market strength of local nonprofit hospitals versus for-profit hospitals;
- The degree of market strength of local nonprofit health insurers versus for-profit health insurers;
- Certificate of need laws; and
- Other local demographic and economic factors.

As discussed later herein with respect to Blue Cross plans and nonprofit hospitals, these primary indicators reflect prevailing attitudes in different areas of the nation about the appropriateness of "profit" motivation in the provision of health care. In turn, the presence or lack thereof of these larger for-profit providers and insurers has a substantial impact on the acquisition and sales value of provider entities. This impact can be traced to at least two specific factors: the likelihood that for-profit entities will be acquirers of providers in a given area and the revenue and profit growth potential inherent in such acquisitions.

3 Medicare is a federal program primarily for the elderly and is distinct from Medicaid, a state-determined program for the poor that is funded 50% by federal funds and 50% by state funds.

Growth potential in the form of acquisition growth is typically only available to publicly traded companies whose stock prices are in large part driven by expected growth rates. High growth rates typically result in high valuation multiples due to low capitalization rates. Economies of scale from acquisitions that affect future "same store" profit growth also contribute to localized valuation differences. As such, all things being equal, a growth-driven public company is able to pay a higher value for a given business because the stock market rewards growth.[4]

The Stark laws contain restrictions on the use of "comparable" market data, much of which are pegged to local market conditions. As far back as 1994, published statements of the Internal Revenue Service focused on local factors that determined the character of a market. The factors discussed in this chapter suggest that the government agencies' views of fair market value should be seriously considered by appraisers and analysts in their own opinions of fair market value.

This study offers appraisers and valuation analysts a foundation for comparing market conditions in different areas of the country. In turn, it provides a basis for determining whether market data in the form of merged and acquired companies or guideline companies is comparable to a given subject company that is being valuated.

Data Sources and Impact on Analysis

Sources of data utilized in this study include that maintained by The Kaiser Family Foundation (KFF). KFF maintains data on the breakdown of for-profit and not-for-profit hospitals for each of the 50 states, along with Medicare and Medicaid enrollment, spending, length of stay, and other detailed statistical data, some of which are described and utilized in this article. Detail of the market share of each state's health maintenance organization (HMO) and preferred provider organization (PPO) enrollment is available from each state's division or department of insurance or, for example, from Lehman Brothers' *Managed Care Guidebook*.[5] Often states will provide detail at the county level as well. Data on local Medicare spending from the Centers for Medicare and Medicaid (CMS) were also utilized, along with information taken directly from the Securities and Exchange Commission (SEC) filings of the public companies discussed.

Local market conditions can lead to dramatic differences in provider revenue, profitability, and related acquisition demand. This affects both the relevance of transaction data in determining fair market value as well as the perceived risk of provider entities

4 See "Understanding the Difference Between Strategic Value and Fair Market Value in Consolidating Industries" *Business Valuation Review*, June 2002, by the author.

5 Used in this study's market analysis.

in a given market area, which in turn affects the discount rate and value determined under the income approach.

As will be seen from the analysis throughout this chapter, for-profit public companies engaged in the healthcare industry tend to concentrate their activities in certain states, notably Texas and Florida, which have specific characteristics discernible from the data sources. The analysis considers presence and dominance of the following companies and certain of their competitors:

- Ambulatory surgery: AmSurg (AMSG);
- Hospitals: HCA, Tenet, HMA, Vanguard;
- Health insurers: United Healthcare (United), as well as Aetna, Cigna, Humana and Health Net, collectively referred to later as "other public"; and
- Imaging: Radnet.

Public Healthcare Insurers

One key to understanding the strategy of provider entities such as AMSG discussed later is to examine the presence of the for-profit health insurers in a given state as well as the concentration of market power by those companies along with Blue Cross plans and local HMOs. The more concentrated a market is in terms of health insurers, the less likely a healthcare services provider will be able to negotiate favorable contracts. This is because market control over pricing is then held by those few insurers.[6] That, of course, leads to an expectation of lower profits.

A number of large publicly traded companies are engaged in providing health insurance, primarily in a managed-care format. These include United Healthcare, Aetna, Cigna, Humana, and Health Net.[7] There has been a spate of consolidation in the industry stemming back to the late 1990s, when a number of smaller entities got burned at the bottom of the so-called "underwriting cycle."[8] Aggressive setting of premiums over multiyear contracts to build market share resulted in bankruptcy or near-bankruptcy for such companies as Oxford when the costs increased more rapidly than expected. The consolidation trend continues today, driven in part by Medicare Advantage contracts as reflected in the acquisition of PacifiCare—the originator of Secure Horizons, the oldest Medicare HMO in the country—by United. Given the present backlash against

6 The Federal Trade Commission and Department of Justice Anti-Trust Division favor insurers over providers.

7 Wellpoint is a large public company; however, it owns Blue Cross plans, including Anthem, which are otherwise addressed.

8 This is the business cycle for the insurance industry and refers generally to the annual gap between premium increases and cost increases and the medical loss ratio, that portion of the premium expended on medical costs.

managed care, Medicare HMOs are the principal source of growth for these public health insurers.

For purpose of this analysis, using data from Lehman Brothers' *2007 Managed Care Guidebook*, the market shares of each of the 50 states were divided into subgroupings based upon 1) Blue Cross plans; 2) United (the largest public health insurer); 3) Aetna, Cigna, Health Net, and Humana; and 4) local HMOs with strong market presence, e.g., Harvard Pilgrim and Tufts in Massachusetts. After eliminating states[9] where for-profit insurers had small market share, where for-profit providers had little or no market presence, and rural states, 35 states were left in the sample.

The remaining states were then ranked by the concentration of market power in the hands of those insurers as well as by the number of insurers[10] operating in each market. Concentration percentages were as high as 98% in Alaska, where the Blue Cross plan had a 49% share and the named public companies collectively had a 49% share as well. Rhode Island's market consolidation ratio was 97%, with 58% in the Blue Cross plan and 26% in United. The lowest concentrations were in Wisconsin and Kansas. The latter market is highly stratified, however, as described later herein.

Market Share

Exhibits 1, 2, and 3 summarize the analysis for eight states, divided into those where public for-profit providers are principally present (Florida, Texas, California, and Tennessee) and those where they have little or no presence (New York, North Carolina, Massachusetts, and Michigan). Market concentration is defined here as the total market share of the Blue Cross plans, public health insurers, and large local health insurers. Average is the market concentration divided by the number of insurers included in the market concentration total. Blue Cross Plans are discussed in the next section.

Exhibit 1 lists the above larger states where for profit providers are prevalent. Although market concentration varies, these states generally have smaller Blue Cross plans and a large market presence of for-profit health insurers (shown as United and other public). Tennessee is the only state in the top half of market concentration[11] where for-profit providers are prevalent—and it is the location of the headquarters of many of those companies.

9 Hawaii, Idaho, Iowa, Maine, Montana, Nebraska, Nevada, New Mexico, North Dakota, Oklahoma, South Dakota, Utah, Vermont, West Virginia.

10 For example, New York has multiple Blue Cross plans.

11 The median is 85% versus 86% for Tennessee.

Exhibit 1. Insurance Market Concentration in States Where For-Profit Providers are Prevalent

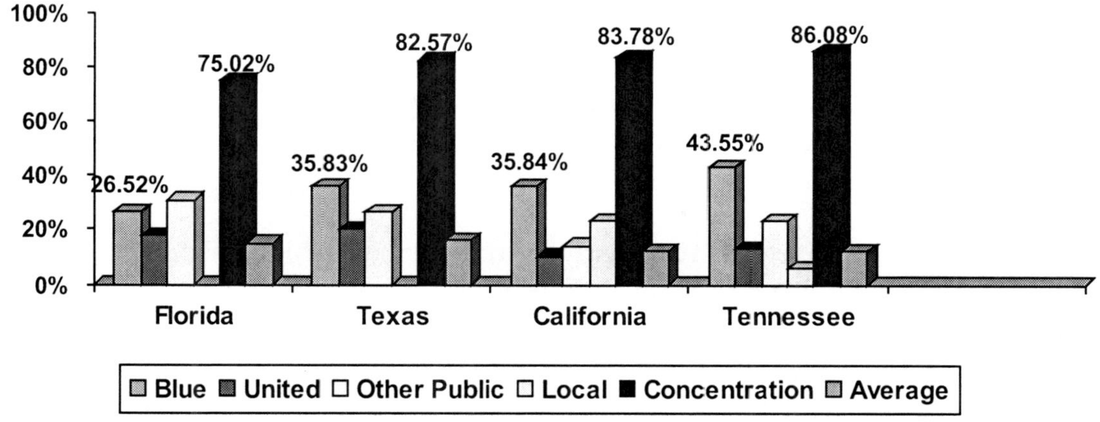

Exhibit 2 is of representative larger states where for profit providers are not prevalent. Although market concentration again varies, these states generally have very large Blue Cross plans and a small market presence of for-profit health insurers.

Exhibit 2. Insurance Market Concentration States Where For-Profit Providers are not Prevalent

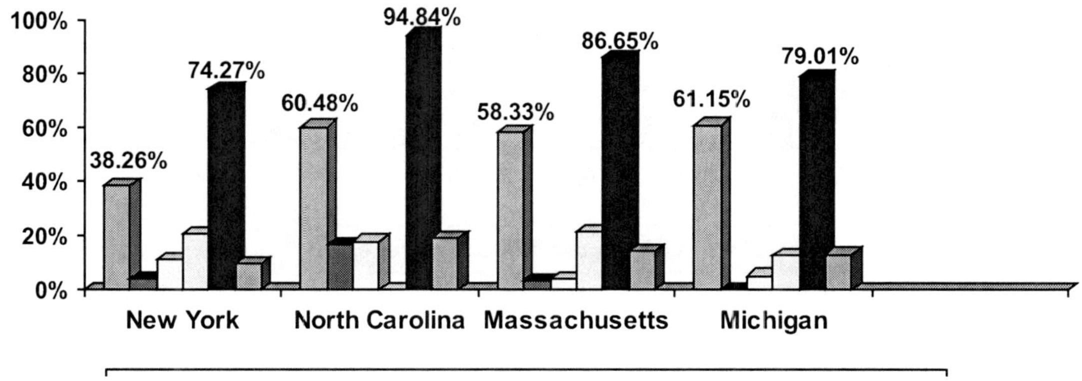

History of Blue Cross Plans

The history of Blue Cross plans plays an important part in the structure of today's health insurance and provider markets. Blue Cross plans expanded rapidly during the Second World War's period of wage and price controls as union sought enhanced benefits to supplement their members' limited incomes. At one point, there were more than 100 Blue Cross plans, the majority of which were located in the industrialized states primarily north of the Mason-Dixon Line in what is sometimes called the Rust Belt. Certain plans refused to contract with for-profit hospitals, thus serving as an effective barrier to market entry. Blue Cross plans also enjoyed a tax-exempt status[12] for many years and protection from anti-trust action in many states.

12 Repealed in the Tax Reform Act of 1986.

As will be seen below, this type of insurance market analysis is one critical element in understanding why public healthcare companies locate in some states and not others. In turn, the acquisition transactions of those public companies are likely only relevant in such states. Further, if an analyst or appraiser is considering the guideline publicly trade company method, it is likely only relevant in those states where the purported guideline companies are active.

Exhibit 3 combines the earlier two charts to compare Blue Cross, for-profit (the combined United and other public companies' share), and market concentration. In markets where for-profit insurers are prevalent (Florida, Texas, California, and Tennessee), Blue Cross plans are less so and for-profit hospitals also tend to be more prevalent, as seen in the next section.

Exhibit 3. Comparative Insurance Market Consolidation

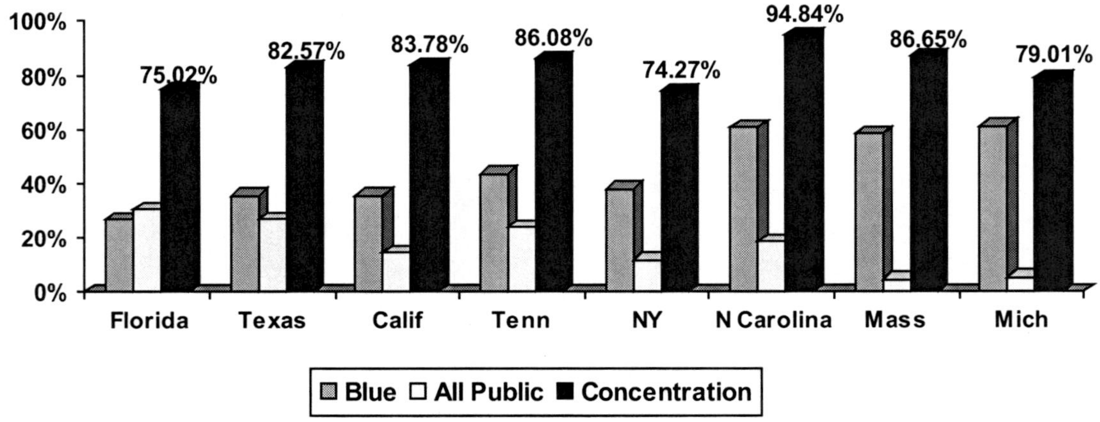

Public Hospital Companies

As a basis for the analysis of four[13] public, for-profit hospital providers, extracts from their 2006 Form 10-Ks follow below. From these extracts, the primary state locations and the extent of concentration can be observed as well as the rationale for locating there (see Tenet and Vanguard Health below). Two other hospital chains not discussed below are LifePoint and Community Health. LifePoint,[14] based in Brentwood, Tenn., has operations primarily in the rural South and border states including Alabama, Louisiana, Kentucky, and Virginia. Community Health,[15] based in Franklin, Tenn., has many of its facilities in Texas, Alabama, Tennessee, northeastern Illinois, and southeastern Pennsylvania.

13 HCA has since been taken private in one of the largest leveraged buy outs ever.

14 LifePoint Hospitals operated 50 hospitals in 19 states as of May 2007.

15 As of Dec. 31, 2006, it owned, leased, or operated 77 hospitals, with an aggregate of 9,117 licensed beds in 22 states.

HCA (now privately held)

We operated 173 hospitals at Dec. 31, 2006, and 73 of those hospitals are located in Florida and Texas. Our Florida and Texas facilities' combined revenues represented approximately 51% of our consolidated revenues for the year ended Dec. 31, 2006. This concentration makes us particularly sensitive to regulatory, economic, environmental, and competition changes in those states.

Tenet

As of Dec. 31, 2006, the largest concentrations of licensed beds in our general hospitals were in California (23.6%), Florida (22.8%), and Texas (18.3%). Strong concentrations of hospital beds within market areas help us contract more successfully with managed care payers; reduce management, marketing and other expenses; and more efficiently utilize resources. However, such concentrations increase the risk that, should any adverse economic, regulatory, environmental, or other development occur in these areas, our business, financial condition, results of operations or cash flows could be materially adversely affected.

HMA Health Management Associates Inc.

As of Dec. 31, 2006, we operated 60 hospitals, with a total of 8,589 licensed beds. During the year ended Dec. 31, 2006, we operated facilities in Alabama, Arkansas, Florida, Georgia, Kentucky, Mississippi, Missouri, North Carolina, Oklahoma, Pennsylvania, South Carolina, Tennessee, Texas, Virginia, Washington, and West Virginia.

Our facilities are heavily concentrated in Florida and Mississippi, which makes us sensitive to regulatory, economic, and competitive changes in those states, as well as the harmful effects of hurricanes and other severe weather activity in such states. We operated 61 hospitals on Feb. 23, 2007, with 29 of those hospitals in Florida and Mississippi. Such geographic concentration of our hospitals makes us particularly sensitive to regulatory, economic, environmental, and competitive changes in those states. Any material changes therein in Florida or Mississippi could have a disproportionate effect on our business.

Vanguard Health

Our ability to negotiate favorable contracts with health maintenance organizations, insurers offering preferred provider arrangements and other managed care plans significantly affects the revenues and operating results of our hospitals. Revenues derived from health maintenance organizations, insurers offering preferred provider arrangements and other managed care plans, including Medicare and Medicaid managed care plans, accounted for approximately 52% of our net patient revenues for the year ended June 30, 2007. Managed care organizations offering prepaid and discounted

> medical services packages represent an increasing portion of our admissions, a general trend in the industry which has limited hospital revenue growth nationwide and a trend that may continue if the Medicare Modernization Act increases enrollment in Medicare managed care plans. In addition, private payers are increasingly attempting to control healthcare costs through direct contracting with hospitals to provide services on a discounted basis, increased utilization review, including the use of hospitalists, and greater enrollment in managed care programs such as health maintenance organizations and preferred provider organizations. Additionally, the trend toward consolidation among private managed care payers tends to increase their bargaining prices over fee structures.
>
> Approximately 35% of our net patient revenues for the year ended June 30, 2007 came from Medicare and Medicaid programs, excluding Medicare and Medicaid managed plans. In recent years, federal and state governments have made significant changes in the Medicare and Medicaid programs. Some of those changes adversely affect the reimbursement we receive for certain services. In addition, due to budget deficits in many states, significant decreases in state funding for Medicaid programs have occurred or are being proposed.
>
> Historically, we have concentrated our operations in markets with high population growth and median income in excess of the national average.

At first glance, Vanguard may represent a partial anomaly in the public companies discussed herein. Seventeen percent of its hospital beds are located in Massachusetts, with approximately half of those in Framingham and Natick[16] and the other half in Worcester, 20 miles west. The Framingham and Natick facilities were acquired from Tenet after that entity's difficulties stemming from a federal government investigation of its Alvaredo facility in San Diego, Calif.; Tenet had acquired them in 1999 from the predecessor of Hospital Corporation of America (HCA) after that entity encountered regulatory problems leading to a fine of nearly $1 billion. Prior to that, Columbia and HCA acquired the facilities as a result of financial difficulties experienced by the local nonprofit institutions in competing with larger nonprofit entities.

Vanguard is a much smaller entity than either HCA or Tenet as can be seen from Exhibit 4 of the total number of beds each entity has and therefore, is less significant to the analysis. It is clear once again that Florida and Texas are primary locations for for-profit hospital providers.

16 The author lives in Framingham and formerly resided in Natick, a bordering community located in Middlesex county, which has the 19th highest total Medicare spending in the nation.

Exhibit 4. Number of Beds by State

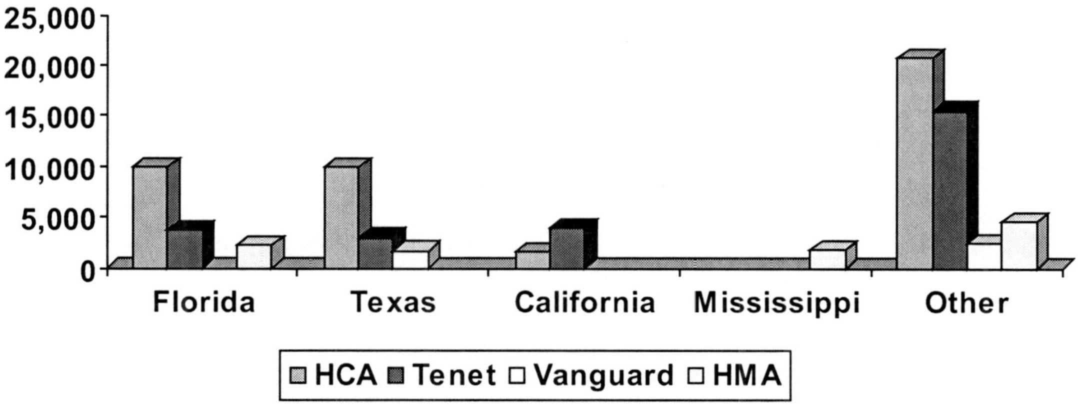

On a percentage basis, HCA and Tenet each have more than 40% of their hospital beds in Florida and Texas (see Exhibit 5).

Exhibit 5. Percent of Beds by Company by State

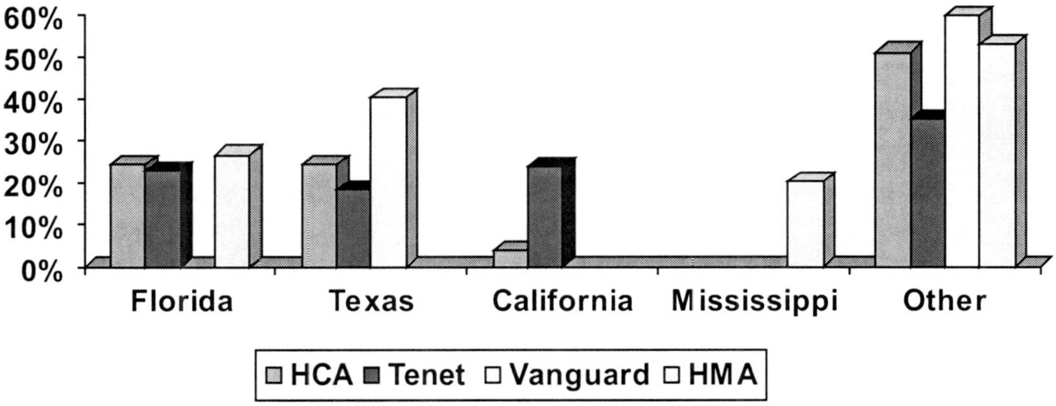

For the valuation of an individual hospital in a state other than Florida, Texas, or California, what is the relevance of transactions by one of these publicly traded entities? As the author and Reed Tinsley, CPA, CVA noted in a co-authored article in the December 2006 American Bar Association's *The Heath Lawyer*:

> What does [out of market] transaction data say or reveal about the value of a hospital with EBITDA of $1 million located in North Carolina? Does it tell a valuator that it could be worth the median [multiple] value of $5 million or the [average multiple] value of $7.5 million—the average being 50% greater than the median? Could it be worth [the highest multiple value of] $18.2 million? Given the Stark regulations requirement that comparable transactions be in a particular market at the time of acquisition, can any of these [out-of-market] multiples be used?

Medicare Part A Spending

Medicare divides providers into two general groupings: Part A hospital insurance, which is paid for by the combined employer-employee 2.9% Medicare tax, and Part B physician insurance, which is paid for out of general federal revenues, after a nominal premium contribution by beneficiaries withheld from Social Security checks. Medicare Advantage, the risk-based Medicare HMO program, publishes per-capita rates county by county across the country split into Part A and Part B components. There are more than 3,200 counties, including Puerto Rico and Guam, with published rates. Because these rates are one proxy for local county Medicare spending,[17] they provide useful insight into a public healthcare provider's location strategy.

Medicare spending is driven by two principal factors: utilization or volume of service, typically expressed in per-beneficiary measures, and price or rate per unit of service. Although beyond the scope of this article, utilization data are readily available from such sources as the Medicare Payment Advisory Commission's (MedPAC) 2007 report *Assessing Alternatives to SGR*.[18] While price or rate is a function of statutory formulas and local cost of service differences, utilization is a function of medical practice styles. The differences in utilization are dramatic and warrant study by an appraiser looking to use out-of-market valuation multiples.

The previous sections discussion on location of for-profit hospitals is consistent with high levels of Medicare spending. Of the top 50 counties, five are in Florida (which has nine of the top 100), four in Texas (which has 15 of the top 100 and another 22 in the next 200) and one in California (which also has nine of the top 100). Two of the top 10 counties (Dade and Okeechobee) are in Florida. The location of individual facilities in other states, such as Louisiana, is typically driven by high localized spending as reflected in Medicare Part A or B statistics.

For total Medicare spending, both Part A and Part B, the pattern is similar but more dramatic for Florida and California as shown in Exhibits 6 and 7.

The counties shown in Exhibit 8 have the largest total dollar Medicare spending. Two counties—Maricopa County, Ariz. and Middlesex County, Mass.—which appear elsewhere in the article where the presence of public for-profit providers was not explained by other factors are clearly explained in this chart. Despite the high levels of Medicare spending, no significant for-profit hospitals are present in Cook County (Chicago) or the various boroughs of New York City,[19] for example. These are counties where unions have historically been very strong.

17 At least for the high-cost counties; low-cost counties have artificially higher rates than their fee-for-service equivalents as a means of inducing Medicare Advantage Plans to offer coverage.

18 Utilization and utilization growth is very high in Florida, for example, and low in mature managed care markets such as San Francisco and Portland, Ore.

19 Less than 3.2 % and 1% of hospital beds in Illinois and New York, respectively, are for-profit according to the Kaiser Family Foundation.

Exhibit 6. # of Top 200 Counties for Part A Per Capita Spending

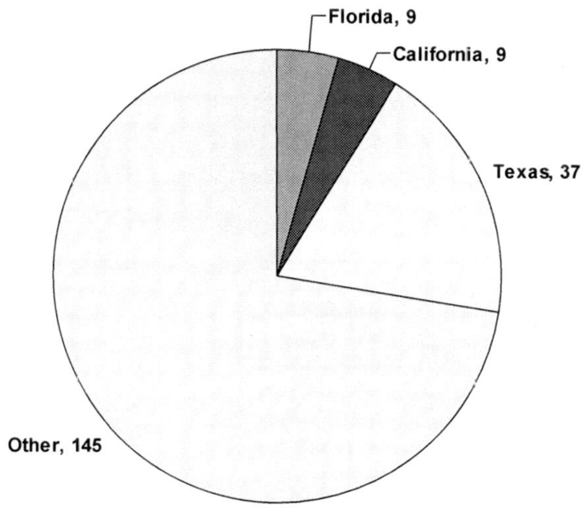

Exhibit 7. # of Top 200 Counties for Part A&B Total Spending

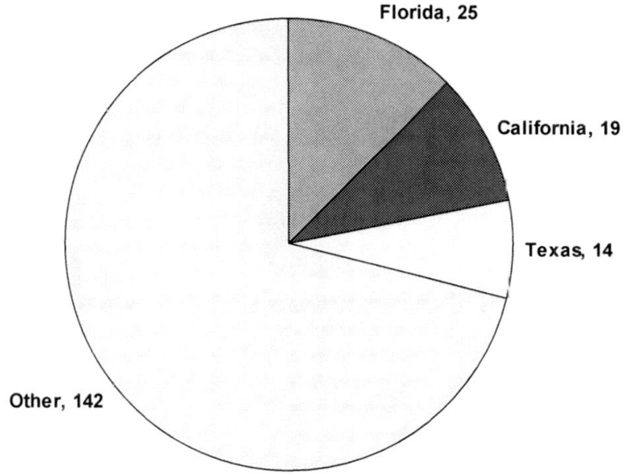

Exhibit 8. 20 Largest Counties for 2005 Medicare Spending ($Billions)

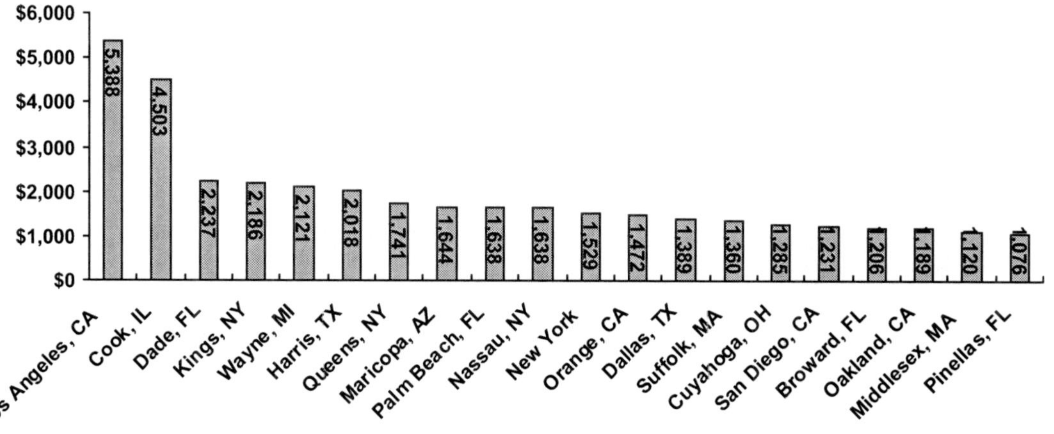

Other Hospital Market Factors

Perhaps the most difficult factor to quantify without local market knowledge or study is the presence of not-for-profit hospitals, particularly large, wealthy teaching hospitals. These institutions tend to be present in large urban markets. Examples include the Harvard-Affiliated Partners Health System in Boston, which includes the Massachusetts General and Brigham & Women's Hospitals; Baylor Health Care System in Dallas;[20] Yale-New Haven Hospital in New Haven, Conn.; any number of institutions in New York City, including Mount Sinai Hospital, Beth Israel Medical Center, and NYU Medical Center; The University of Chicago Health System and Northwestern Memorial Hospital and Health System in Chicago; and Johns Hopkins Hospital and Health System in Baltimore. These institutions frequently have market power not only in terms of hospital volume, but also in terms of physician affiliations, managed care contracts, and political influence.

Another example of nonprofit hospitals are the multistate religious health systems, such as Ascension Health. Many times these institutions are located in underserved areas where access to healthcare is limited by income considerations. They may also be small institutions located in rural areas where providing multidiscipline and emergency care is unprofitable and requires charitable support.

There is nothing that precludes the reporting of acquisitions by not-for-profit hospitals of other hospitals, physician practices, surgery centers, and the like. However, there is often no requirement of reporting, and it is certainly less common than reporting by the public for-profit companies described herein.[21] Some transactions may warrant reporting under generally accepted accounting principles (GAAP) and generally accepted auditing standards (GAAS) and many states require not-for-profits to file financial statements with the state Attorney General's office; fairness opinions may also be required. Analysts and appraisers need to keep in mind that single-state or single-locale not-for-profit transactions[22] likewise reflect only that local market's considerations and are equally suspect as value indicators in other markets.

Valuation Imperative

Appraisers and analysts should bear in mind that in addition to the Stark laws and anti-kickback statutes that apply to all healthcare providers, nonprofit and tax-exempt providers are subject to the requirements of the Internal Revenue Code, including anti-inurement and intermediate sanctions provisions.

20 A highly competitive market with both for-profit and nonprofit hospitals.

21 For competitive reasons and regulatory fear, among others.

22 For example, North and South Carolina not-for-profit integrated healthcare system Novant Health's acquisition of imaging provider MQ Associates.

Example

One common business strategy that hospitals utilize in acquiring physician-owned entities such as ambulatory surgery centers and imaging centers include converting them to hospital outpatient billing or so-called "provider-based billing."[23] This typically results in a higher revenue stream for the same services as both government and nongovernment insurers frequently have different payment levels for the same service based upon the type of provider submitting the bill, i.e., higher revenue for hospital entities than physician entities. Notwithstanding the business strategy, including the enhanced revenue in a valuation where the standard is fair market value raises serious if not fatal concerns. Since physicians cannot access this billing routine when they own the entity outright, including the enhanced revenue available to a hospital owner creates issues under both the Stark law and anti-kickback statute as well as anti-inurement issues for tax-exempt entities.

Surgery Centers

After medical practice purchases, surgery center transaction are perhaps the most common form of healthcare transaction. As a result of private equity deals, AmSurg (AMSG) is one of the few remaining public companies in this line of business. Due to the importance of acquisitions to the value of this company and to the valuation of individual surgery centers, the article addresses AMSG in detail. Although the primary location of its facilities is Florida, followed by Tennessee and California, it does, in fact, have locations in many other states, which make it a particularly interesting subject for analysis. A number of these other locations are examined for consistency with the factors discussed elsewhere herein.

A review of AMSG's Dec. 31, 2006 10-K filing with the SEC revealed the following statements:

> Practice-based [ambulatory surgery centers] ASCs, such as those in which we own a majority interest, depend upon third-party reimbursement programs, including governmental and private insurance programs, to pay for services rendered to patients. We derived approximately 35%, 35%, and 37% of our revenues in the years ended Dec. 31, 2006, 2005, and 2004, respectively, from governmental healthcare programs, primarily Medicare. The Medicare program currently pays ASCs and physicians in accordance with predetermined fee schedules.
>
> At Dec. 31, 2006, 30 of the 156 surgery centers we operated were located in the state of Florida. This concentration makes us particularly sensitive to adverse weather conditions and other factors that affect the state of Florida.

23 Medicare requires eligible healthcare providers to bill services in two parts: one for the facility or technical fee to the hospital or facility for owning the building and equipment and employing nonphysician staff and one for physicians for interpreting and performing the test or procedure known as the professional fee; a hospital-owned facility may be able to bill under higher hospital rates.

> Ninety-two percent of our centers specialize in gastroenterology or ophthalmology procedures. These specialties have a higher concentration of older patients than other specialties, such as orthopedic or [gastro]enterology. We believe the aging demographics of the U.S. population will be a source of procedure growth for these specialties. We target these medical specialties because they generally involve a high volume of lower-risk procedures that can be performed in an outpatient setting on a safe and cost-effective basis.
>
> We begin our acquisition process with a due diligence review of the target center and its market. We use experienced teams of operations and financial personnel to conduct a thorough review of all aspects of the center's operations, including the following:
>
> - market position of the center and the physicians affiliated with the center;
> - payor and case mix;
> - growth opportunities;
> - staffing and supply review; and
> - equipment assessment.
>
> In presenting the advantages to physicians of developing a new practice-based ASC in partnership with us, our development staff emphasizes the proximity of a practice-based surgery center to a physician's office, the simplified administrative procedures, the ability to schedule consecutive cases without preemption by inpatient or emergency procedures, the rapid turnaround time between cases, the high technical competency of the center's clinical staff that performs only a limited number of specialized procedures and the state-of-the-art surgical equipment. We also focus on our expertise in developing and operating centers. In addition, as part of our role as the manager of our surgery center limited partnerships and limited liability companies, we market the centers to third-party payors.

The 10-K also reveals that 105 of the 156 centers are gastroenterology, four multispecialty, 40 ophthalmic, and seven orthopedic. Appraisers and analysts should consider the prospects for these service lines versus other (*non*gastroenterology—also called endoscopy—or ophthalmology) medical service lines when contemplating using AMSG acquisition multiples. It is critical to understand precisely what types of procedures a facility is performing as part of the assessment of market data's relevance.

Exhibit 9 displays AMSG's historical cumulative acquisitions of surgery centers (103, or 66% of the total), and Exhibit 10 shows its cumulative total centers (156) to emphasize the importance of acquisition growth to the value of the company.

Exhibit 9. AMSG Cumulative Acquisitions

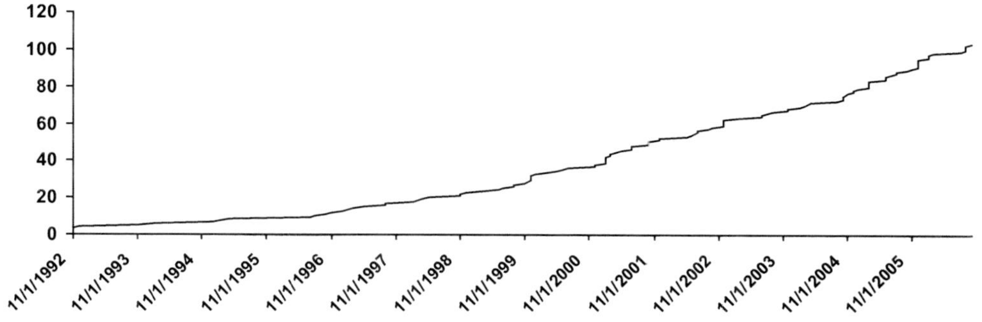

Exhibit 10. AMSG Cumulative Centers

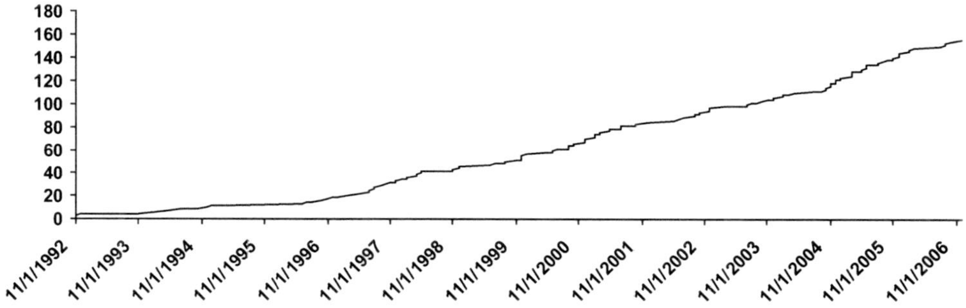

Exhibit 11 shows the location of AMSG's operating rooms (ORs) by state for purposes of the later analysis of the reason for locating in certain states and not others.

Exhibit 11. AMSG ORs by State

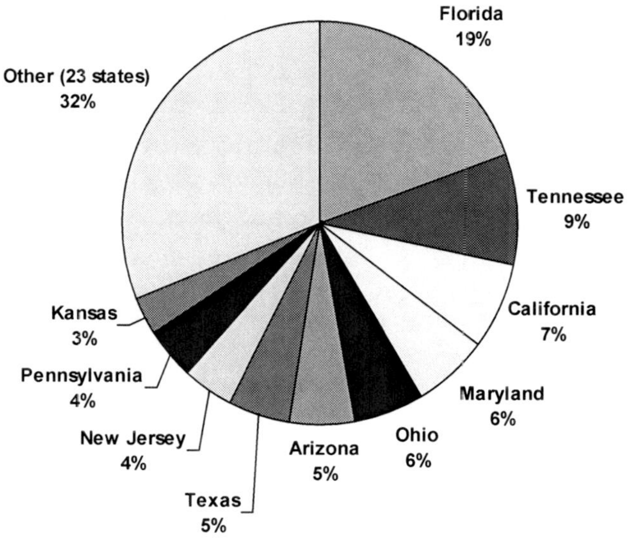

Medicare Part B Spending

The states in which AMSG is located consistently have the highest rates for Part B physician spending—and that is where such transactions are or may be relevant depending upon further analysis. Of the 200 counties with the highest Part B Medicare Advantage rates, half (101) are located in the 10 states in which AMSG has most of its facilities. Of the top 50 counties, five are in Florida, four in Texas (which has 15 of the top 100 and another 22 in the next 200) and six in New Jersey. Two of the top 10 counties (Dade and Okeechobee) are in Florida. Only Arizona does not appear in the top 200 (see Exhibit 12).

Exhibit 12. # of Top 200 Counties for Part B Per Capita Spending

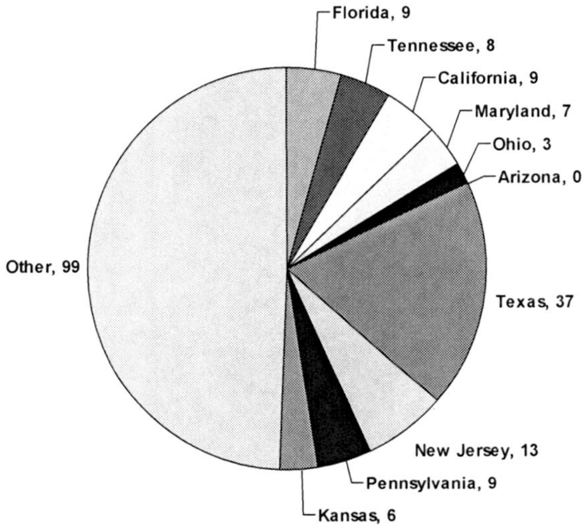

Prevalence of For Profit Hospitals

Earlier, the presence of for-profit hospitals and health insurers was examined. Exhibit 13 shows the percentage of for-profit hospitals[24] for each of the 10 states where AMSG has the largest number of ORs, with the largest states at the left. Florida, Tennessee, and California have 35% of AMSG's capacity. Florida has the second highest percentage of for-profit hospitals in the country, with Tennessee seventh.

Pennsylvania is below the national average, but the activity in this state could be explained in part by a strong state government commitment to rating outpatient surgery facilities, including going so far as to require extensive financial disclosure[25] on top of clinical quality.

Another manner to evaluate for-profit presence is by the number of hospital beds (see Exhibit 14) as opposed to the number of hospitals. Both data sets are relevant because a

24 Kaiser Family Foundation State Health Facts, www.statehealthfacts.kff.org/.

25 Pennsylvania Health Care Cost Containment Council, www.phc4.org.

Exhibit 13. Prevalence of For Profit Hospitals For AMSG's Major States

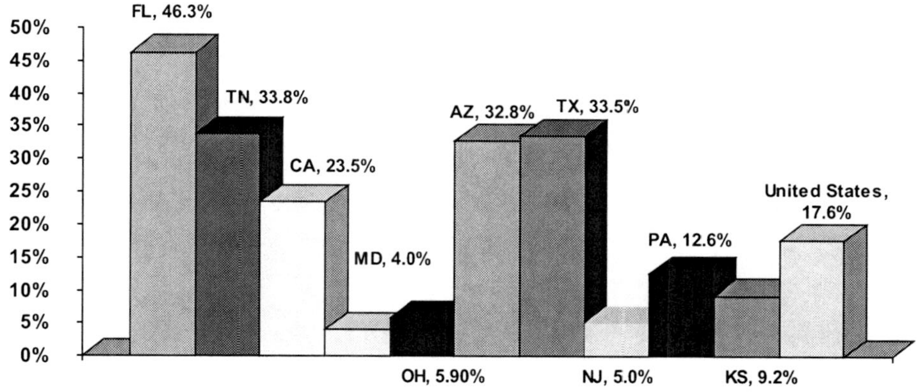

number of specialty hospitals, such as cardiac and orthopedic, may have relatively few beds but extremely high profitability. Cardiac and orthopedic care is at the core of most hospitals' profitability. Appraisers seeking to value a hospital should be certain to understand the underlying case mix of both the purported comparables and the subject. A specialty orthopedic hospital transaction is likely of little use in valuing a general hospital.

Exhibit 14. Prevalence of For Profit Beds For AMSG's Major States

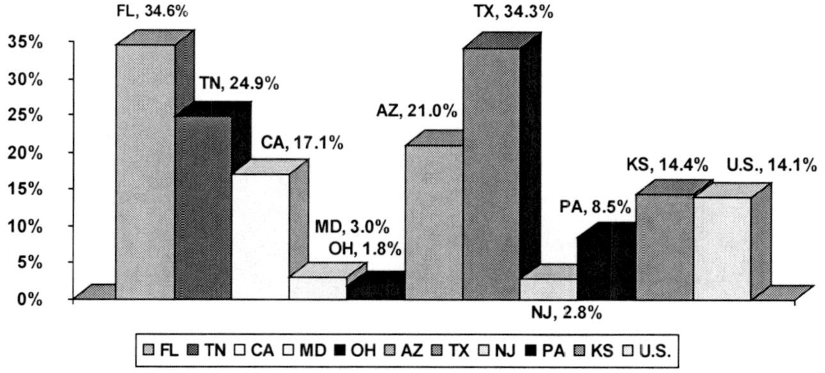

Exhibit 15 summarizes criteria that impact the desirability of locating a surgery center in a given state based upon the 10 states above. Bold items are those that appear partially determinative. For example, Florida has the third highest number of for-profit hospital beds in the country, is ranked 4th in overall healthcare spending, 6th in the concentration of population in metropolitan areas, 9th in spending on physician services, and 19th in per-capita healthcare spending. The percentage of overall spending in the state on physician services is more than 3% greater than the national average.

For certain of the principal states in which AMSG does business, the listed factors do not appear to readily explain the desirability. For example, Kansas is ranked 8th in overall physician spending as a percentage (31.5%) of healthcare expenses but otherwise does not appear attractive based on the criteria. This is where individual local market conditions become important.

Kansas is a largely rural state with population centers in larger cities. The following is the location of the AMSG facilities:

- Hutchinson, Kan.
- Overland Park, Kan.
- Shawnee, Kan.
- Topeka, Kan.
- Wichita, Kan.

Overland Park and Shawnee are part of suburban Kansas City (the metropolitan area includes the larger Kansas City, Mo.), while Hutchinson is a suburb of Wichita. Thus, the ranking of Kansas as a rural state is misleading with respect to the location of the AMSG facilities.

Similarly, Arizona has only high total spending for health care as a positive criteria in the analysis. Arizona, however, has a very high percentage of Medicare-eligible retirees and as noted earlier, Medicare is a key source of revenue for AMSG. Below is a listing of AMSG's Arizona locations.

- Mesa, Ariz.
- Peoria, Ariz.
- Phoenix, Ariz.
- Sun City, Ariz.
- Yuma, Ariz.

Sun City, Mesa, and Peoria are part of greater Phoenix (Maricopa County, described earlier herein), one of the fastest growing metropolitan areas in the nation, with Sun City a prime locale for retirees. Maricopa County has the third highest total Medicare spending in the country at *$1.64 billion*. Yuma is near the Mexican border, and an even more localized market analysis would be in order.

New Jersey is a particularly interesting case in point where the criteria do not appear to explain the presence of AMSG. Fortunately, the Center for Studying Health System Change,[26] which tracks development in 12 markets nationally includes Northern New Jersey, where three of the faculties are located. This is an area where specialist physicians—which would include gastroenterology and ophthalmology—have been terminating provider agreements with insurers to compel higher fees as out-of-network providers. Ambulatory surgery centers are being developed as part of this strategy to shift revenue from hospitals to physicians.

26 www.hschange.org.

Exhibit 15. Criteria That Impact the Desirability of Locating a Surgery Center in a Given State

			RANKINGS				
Top 10 AMSG States	**For-Profit Beds %**	**MD Spending%**	**For-Profit Beds**	**Total Healthcare Spending**	**Metropolitan Pop**	**MD Spending**	**Per Capita**
Florida	**34.6%**	31.5%	**3**	**4**	**6**	**9**	19
Tennessee	**24.9%**	31.4%	**10**	15	26	**10**	21
California	**17.1%**	33.4%	18	**1**	**2**	**3**	44
Maryland	**3.0%**	28.7%	34	19	**7**	20	18
Ohio	1.8%	26.8%	39	7	25	35	15
Arizona	**21.0%**	33.0%	15	21	14	**5**	50
Texas	**34.3%**	30.8%	**4**	**3**	**11**	**11**	45
New Jersey	2.8%	28.2%	35	**9**	**1**	27	13
Pennsylvania	8.5%	26.6%	28	**5**	22	38	11
Kansas	14.4%	31.5%	22	31	35	**8**	24
United States	14.1%	28.2%	NA	NA	NA	NA	

Explanations
For-Profit Beds %: The percentage of all hospitals beds owned by for-profit hospitals.
MD Spending %: The portion of the state's healthcare spending that goes to physician services.
Rankings
For-Profit Beds: The rank based on total for-profit beds, with 1 being highest,
Total Healthcare Spending: The rank based upon total dollars spent.
Metropolitan Population: The rank based upon the percentage of the states population located in metropolitan areas (as opposed to rural).
MD Spending: The rank based upon total dollars spent.
Per Capita: The rank based upon per capita income.

Characteristics of areas with no AMSG locations

AMSG has no facilities in Vermont, Massachusetts, Maine, New Hampshire, and Rhode Island and a single one in Connecticut. Thus, the New England area, for example, would not appear to be a target market. These states have comparatively few for-profit beds (Rhode Island and Vermont have none) and high market concentration of insurers (see Exhibit 16). Maine, New Hampshire, Connecticut, and Vermont have more than 94% market concentration as defined earlier herein, and the largest insurer in each market is a Blue Cross plan, with 67%, 38%, 33%, and 60% market share, respectively.

Valuation Imperative

An appraiser or analyst should also consider the requirement or lack thereof for a certificate of need (CON) in each state[27] where a purported comparable operates and

27 www.ncsl.org/programs/health/cert-need.htm, a CON is basically a form of state-issued license.

Exhibit 16. For Profit Beds in AMSG's No Facility States

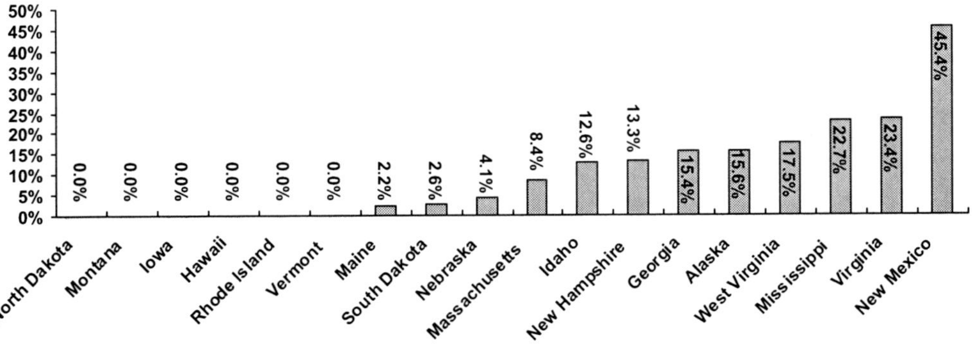

in the state where the valuation subject is located. Florida, Texas, Pennsylvania, and California do not require a CON for an ASC! Lack of a CON makes it easier to establish an ASC—although actually having a difficult-to-obtain CON in a state that requires them is generally deemed to be a valuation positive, assuming the CON is transferable. Some states waive a CON for expenditures below a specified level, e.g., $1 million for an MRI in Missouri.

Radnet

The one large publicly traded[28] provider of fixed location imaging services, Radnet—which acquired its principal competitor Radiologix in the fall of 2006—has the majority of its facilities in three of the same states (California, Maryland, and Florida) listed above, with a concentration in California.

Exhibit 17 reflects total units of equipment (e.g., MRI, CT, and so on).

Certainly, a substantive argument could be made that the multiples paid by Radnet for imaging centers in California would be relevant to the valuation of an imaging center located in California (see Exhibit 18). It seems questionable, particularly in light of regulatory considerations, that those transactions would be relevant in New Mexico or Georgia, for example. At best, the multiples might provide some insight, especially if the effect of acquisition growth could be eliminated.

Acquisition Versus Same Store Growth

One of the most important and fundamental differences between a single location valuation subject and a large multilocation, multimarket alleged comparable is the availability of acquisition growth to enhance value through the earnings or cash flow

28 Alliance is the other with primarily mobile imaging and locations in many states. It has recently turned its attention to development of PET and CT. The revenue prospects for different types of imaging can vary dramatically.

Exhibit 17. Radnet, Units by State

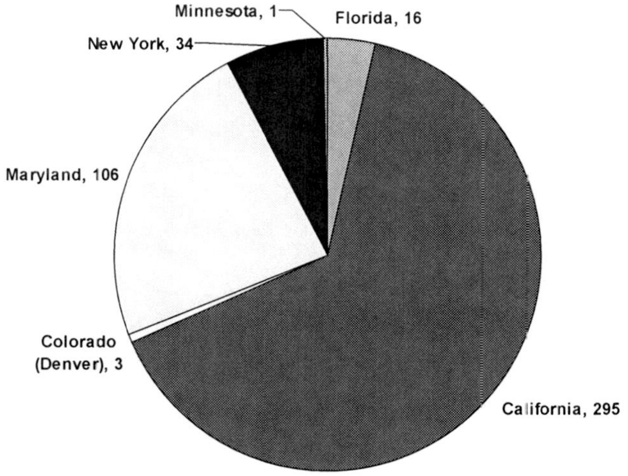

Exhibit 18. Radnet, California Units

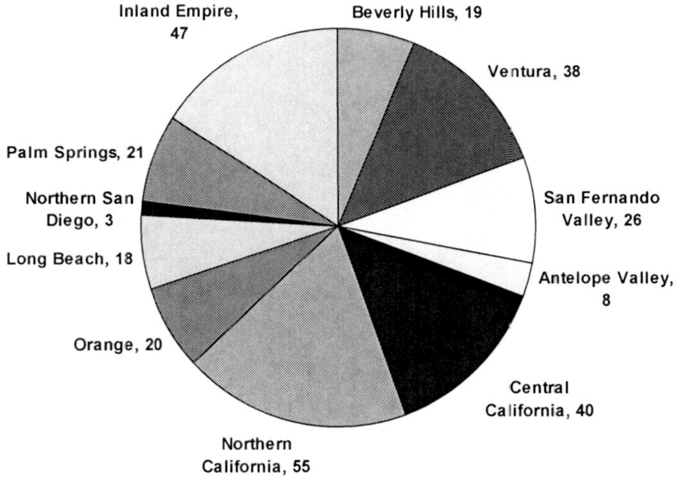

capitalization rate[29] or to offset a decline in same-store revenue and profit growth. Consider the following statement from Lehman Brothers analyst Adam Feinstein about AMSG in anticipation of the announcement of the final rule by the Centers for Medicare and Medicaid with respect to the adoption of a new revenue model for ASCs that would contain significant cutbacks for endoscopy:

> In regards to an LBO, AMSG has noted that it believes that the overhang created by the proposed changes in Medicare reimbursement (with a final rule expected sometime this summer [*2007*] and the changes expected to take effect on Jan. 1, 2008) reduces the likelihood that a financial sponsor would be interested in acquiring the

29 Defined as the discount rate less the long-term or perpetual growth rate.

company (due to the anticipated negative impact in 2008 and 2009). In addition, we get the sense that the company is not interested in going private since *the company has noted that it believes it needs to undertake 12 to 15 acquisitions per year in 2008 and 2009 in order to generate the same cash flow in those years as it will in 2007 (with the anticipated negative impact from the changes in Medicare reimbursement being offset by the cash flow the company acquires).*[30] (*Emphasis added*)

Valuation Imperative

One observation about the valuation implication of AMSG's statement regarding new acquisitions is that for those acquisitions to be accretive to earnings—a necessity if the stock price is to be maintained—acquisition multiples are likely to drop! This is a key test that the appraiser or analyst should employ as part of the reality check for an ultimate valuation conclusion if the merged and acquired company method is being used: Would the acquisition be accretive to earnings?

Another observation is that a single-location endoscopy center, for example, is unlikely to be in a position to respond to per-unit revenue cutbacks by acquiring other endoscopy centers; at best, it might hope to attract additional providers to its facility assuming it had excess capacity.

How would the plan by a public surgery center consolidator to offset per-unit revenue declines impact the transaction price for a single-location provider? Unless that provider is located in a state that the consolidator is active in or likely to become active in, there would be no impact. The universe of hypothetical buyers under the fair market value standard or even for strategic value does not include buyers who are not present in the market. Exhibit 19 presents AMSG's 35 most recent centers by state.

Exhibit 19. New Centers: 2005-2006

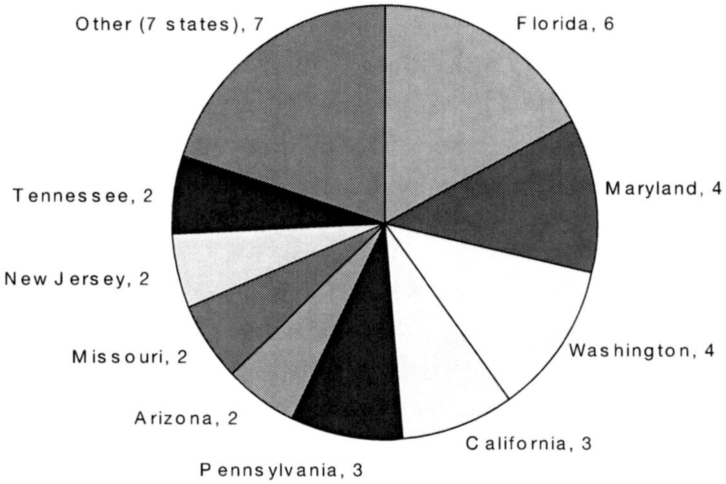

30 Lehman Brothers Health Care Facilities: March Quarter Review: "Buyouts Rule the Day", May 18, 2007.

Implications for Valuation of Private Healthcare Providers

Follow the Money

The old adage "follow the money" is employed in many professions. As the analysis in this article demonstrates, to some extent you can find large for-profit providers by looking at high local rates of healthcare spending. Or perhaps it is more accurate to say you will *not* find those providers where there is low healthcare spending. Factors in addition to total and per-capita spending play a significant role in the desirability of a particular location for larger for-profit entities and highlight the importance of understanding local market conditions, including:

- Income levels of population;
- Health insurance coverage statistics, including coverage by Medicaid;
- Hospital spending per capita and in total;
- Physician spending per capita and in total;
- Competing nonprofit providers, including whether the entities have established integrated healthcare networks;
- Identity and market share of health insurers; in large states, regional market concentration should be considered along with statewide data; HMO penetration (reported by KFF) versus indemnity and other types of health insurance should also be considered; and
- Competing for-profit local providers, e.g., Shields MRI in Massachusetts.

All Healthcare is Local

Healthcare markets are highly localized. When seeking to apply comparable transactions under the merged and acquired company method or the guideline publicly traded company method, it is incumbent on the appraiser or analyst to establish that an acquirer or public company is likely to be active in the market of the valuation subject. Failure to establish that limits the usefulness of the market data and may, in fact, lead to an erroneous conclusion of value.

Other relevant local market factors:

- The concentration of the population in urban versus rural areas; urban areas provide easier access;
- In rural areas, the extent and quality of road systems enabling access to healthcare providers; barriers to access such as bridges or ferries from

peninsula or island communities; and

- Age distribution of population.

Earlier, portions of public hospital company 10-Ks were cited that described the economies of scale and negotiating leverage with managed care insurers that were obtained through concentrating activities in a given state. It stands to reason that acquisition multiples in that state could properly reflect the inherent value from the economies of scale, but it is difficult to see how that acquisition multiple could be applied to a valuation subject in another state.

Another element to consider is localized supply and demand for a particular healthcare provider. Hospitals often compete to acquire physician practices, seeking to increase or defensively maintain inpatient admissions and referrals for tests. Nonetheless, there are regulatory prohibitions against considering such admissions and referrals in the purchase price and any demand-driven increase in value is limited to factors not precluded by law. Many times, it is difficult to appropriately include even factors such as reduced cost of capital or economies of scale due to the need to rely upon the fair market value standard.

Other Uses of Market Data

There is an arbitrage effect when private company cash flows are moved into the public markets via acquisition, as described earlier with respect to evaluating whether a particular acquisition would be accretive to earnings. If possible, an appraiser or analyst might attempt to extract acquisition growth from valuation multiples to obtain an indication of market value when acquisition-driven market data are used to value a subject in a market where no such buyer is present. This would require analyzing the out-of-market acquirer's stock and EBITDA valuation multiples and extracting that portion representing acquisition-driven growth. A fundamental analysis can also be performed on the subject to derive discounts from the public company's value for size and growth, for example.[31]

Valuation Imperative

Of course, not all transaction data represents activity of publicly traded companies. However, it is reasonable to believe that privately held or nonprofit buyers of healthcare entities in markets dominated by public for-profits find acquisition prices driven by what the public for-profit is willing to pay, *even if* the nonprofit cannot match the

31 See, e.g., Goeldner, "Adjusting Market Multiples of Public Guideline Companies for the Closely Held Business," ASA 18th Annual BV Conference, October 1999.

growth rate. There are many policy and economic implications beyond the scope of this article with respect to the availability of tax-exempt bonds to lower a nonprofit's cost of capital.

Regulatory Issues

At the outset of the article, it was stated "that the government agencies' views of 'fair market value' should be seriously considered by appraisers and analysts in their own opinions of fair market value." The core of the Stark regulations limitations on use of market data in establishing fair market value can be found in the following extract:

> Usually the fair market price is the price at which bona fide sales have been consummated for assets of like type, quality, and quantity in a particular market at the time of acquisition. . . .[32]

The presence of this statement, drafted at the Department of Health and Human Services, which operates the Medicare program, likely reflects that agency's intimate familiarity with differences in local healthcare spending and providers.

Appraisers conforming to uniform standards of professional appraisal practice (USPAP) and other standards frequently cite those standards as the basis for employing certain methods even in the face of apparent government rejection, typically in tax court or other tax-oriented proceedings. For example, USPAP Standards Rule 9-4 provides in part that

> An appraiser must, when necessary for credible assignment results, analyze the effect on value, if any, of: ... sales of capital stock or other ownership interests in similar business enterprises.

However, the Jurisdictional Exception Rule provides

> If any part of USPAP is contrary to the law or public policy of any jurisdiction, only that part shall be void and of no force or effect in that jurisdiction.

Appraisers and analysts should not assume that government's views of fair market value are inconsistent with the usage of that term in the appraisal profession and do well to remember that the law always trumps professional standards. Improper use of market data in the face of the above regulation could result in unlawful conduct.

Conclusion

The results of this study are important to appraisers and analysts working in the healthcare industry. Healthcare markets are highly localized and use of out-of-market data for

32 420 CFR 411.351.

the valuation of a healthcare business requires a detailed analysis of conditions in the source market as well as the subject market (see Exhibit 20 on next page). Regulatory restrictions on the use market data in the Stark laws cannot be dismissed because there are fundamental economic reasons for those restrictions as well as professional standards that require they be respected.

Markets in which larger for-profit provider entities are present will have transactions that reflect not only the local market conditions, but also the revenue and earnings growth inherent in the motivation of public companies. Public healthcare providers, such as AMSG, are consolidators driven by acquisition growth. Even those nonprofit markets where healthcare spending and insurer concentration are *otherwise* similar to for-profit markets may have very different values for local entities than is indicated by consolidator-driven multiples. Thus, methods under the market approach have to be used with considerable skill and intensive analysis.

There are few absolutes in valuation in general and healthcare valuation in particular. However, terms such as "north," "south," "Rust Belt," and "Mason-Dixon Line" seem to have consequential importance. Finally, there is an abundance of readily available and often free data on local healthcare markets that enable the appraiser or analyst to accomplish the tasks necessary for the appropriate application and weighting of the market approach.

My thanks to Barry Sziklay, James Rigby, Michael Crain, Nancy Fannon, Don Barbo, Kevin Yeanoplos, and Carol Carden who contributed to the review of this paper but may or may not agree with its conclusions.

Exhibit 20. Factors to Consider When Evaluating Out of Market Transactions

Factor	Subject Market	Comparable Market	Data * Source(s)
Economic and demographic factors			
Medicare Part A spending total and per capita			1, 2
Medicare Part B spending total and per capita			1, 2
Pending or anticipated per unit revenue changes			3, 4
Hospital spending per capita and in total			1
Physician spending per capita and in total			1
Per capita income levels of population			1
Age distribution of population			1
The concentration of the population in urban versus rural areas			1
In rural areas, the extent and quality of road systems enabling access to healthcare providers; barriers to access such as bridges or ferries from peninsula or island communities			

continued

Factor	Subject Market	Comparable Market	Data * Source(s)
Health insurance coverage statistics, including coverage by Medicaid			1
Presence of Medicare Advantage plans			2
Medicaid spending and crisis status (Medicaid is typically the single largest line item in a state budget)			1
Health insurer factors			
Identity and market share of health insurers; in large states, regional market concentration should be considered along with statewide data; HMO penetration versus indemnity and other types of health insurance should also be considered			1, 5, 6, 7
Whether or not insurers use network fee schedules or individually negotiated fee schedules			
Utilization factors			
Hospital length of stay			1
Hospital days per 1,000			1
Hospital cost per day			1
Imaging per capita, rate of increase			3
Inpatient versus outpatient surgery			1
Market competition factors			
Presence of publicly held provider entities			6
Competing for-profit local providers			
Competing not-for-profit providers			
The percentage of all hospitals beds owned by for-profit hospitals			1
The rank by state based on total for-profit beds			1
Presence of integrated hospital systems			
Presence of integrated delivery systems with physician networks			
Potential economies of scale resulting from multiple locations in terms of costs, negotiating strength, marketing, etc.			
Whether or not insurers use network fee schedules or individually negotiated fee schedules (again)			
Intensity of market competition for acquisitions			6
Impact of acquisition growth on stock price			
Legal factors			
For physician practices, enforceability of noncompete laws including judicial precedent			
Certificate of need laws for various provider entities			8
Federal regulatory status			9
Anti-kickback Stark laws False Claims Act CMS administrative sanctions Enforcement trends, e.g., big pharmaceutical companies are current target			

continued

Exhibit 20. Factors to Consider When Evaluating Out of Market Transactions, Continued

Factor	Subject Market	Comparable Market	Data * Source(s)
State regulatory status			
Political factors			
Lobby strength of state hospital association, medical society, imaging, ASC, chiropractic, etc.			
Board representation on provider entities, particularly exempt hospitals and teaching hospitals			

*Data Sources:
1. www.statehealthfacts.org/.
2. www.cms.hhs.gov/MedicareAdvtgSpecRateStats/.
3. www.medpac.gov.
4. Centers for Medicare & Medicaid generally.
5. Lehman Brothers analysis.
6. SEC filings.
7. State Insurance Commissioner.
8. www.ncsl.org/programs/health/cert-need.htm.
9. www.cms.hhs.gov/home/regsguidance.asp.

Chapter 3

The Anti-Kickback Statute and Stark Law: Avoiding Valuation of Referrals

By James M. Pinna, Esq. and Matthew D. Jenkins, JD

The federal anti-kickback statute, 42 U.S.C. § 1320a-7b(b), sets forth the general principle that healthcare providers cannot exchange remuneration in return for referrals of federal healthcare program business. The federal physician self-referral law or Stark Law, 42 U.S.C. § 1395nn, incorporates a similar principle by prohibiting certain physician referrals to entities that physicians have compensation arrangements with unless the arrangement meets an applicable exception by, among other things, not providing compensation based on the volume or value of referrals by the physician. The fundamental prohibition on providing remuneration in return for referrals exemplified in these two statutes has important consequences in the valuation context and requires that healthcare providers and their advisors be careful to avoid ascribing value to prior or anticipated referrals when structuring transactions involving healthcare providers. This chapter explores the framework created by the anti-kickback statute and the Stark Law and some of the specific valuation contexts in which healthcare providers and their advisors should be attentive to avoiding the attribution of value to referrals.

The Anti-Kickback Statute

The anti-kickback statute prohibits the knowing and willful offer, payment, solicitation, or receipt of "any remuneration (including any kickback, bribe, or rebate) directly or indirectly, overtly or covertly, in cash or in kind," to induce or reward referrals of items or services reimbursable by a federal healthcare program.[1] In addition to criminal

1 42 U.S.C. § 1320a-7b(b). A "federal healthcare program" includes any plan or program that provides health benefits, whether directly, through insurance, or otherwise, which are funded directly, in whole, or in part by the

penalties, violations of the anti-kickback statute can lead to the imposition of civil sanctions and administrative exclusion from participation in federal healthcare programs (which carries a lower burden of proof than that which is required to sustain a criminal conviction). To prove a violation of the anti-kickback statute, the government must show that an entity: "(a) knowingly and willfully; and (b) with the intent to induce the referral of federal healthcare program business solicited, received, offered, or paid remuneration."[2] Courts have interpreted the anti-kickback statute to prohibit arrangements if one purpose of the arrangement is the inducement of referrals of federal healthcare program patients, regardless of whether there are other appropriate purposes for the arrangement.[3]

Investment and compensation arrangements between healthcare providers should be structured in a manner that does not ascribe value to referrals of federal healthcare program business to avoid implicating the anti-kickback statute. Several courts, as well as the Office of Inspector General of the Department of health and Human Services (OIG), have indicated that certain facts and circumstances in such arrangements, such as paying greater than fair market value for services or items, can support an inference that improper remuneration is being paid to induce referrals.[4] When structuring and valuing investment and compensation arrangements, healthcare providers and their advisors should look to guidance provided by the OIG and court decisions to identify what could be considered improper remuneration for referrals and how to structure their arrangements to avoid problematic remuneration.

federal government. 42 U.S.C. § 1320a-7b(f).

2 *Hanlester Network v. Shalala*, 51 F.3d 1390, 1397-1400 (9th Cir. 1995).

3 *United States v. Greber*, 760 F.2d 68 (3d Cir. 1985), cert. denied, 474 U.S. 988 (1985).

4 See *United States v. Lipkis*, 770 F.2d 1447 (9th Cir. 1985) (Noting that the fair market value of services provided under an arrangement was substantially less than the compensation received, and there is no question that there was payment for the referrals as well as the described services); *United States ex rel. Constantino Perales v. St. Margaret's Hospital*, 243 F. Supp. 2d 843, 851 (C.D. Ill. 2003) (Indicating that payment in excess of fair market value for a physician practice may create an inference of improper remuneration); *United States ex rel. Obert-Hong v. Advocate Health Care*, 211 F. Supp. 2d 1045, 1049 (N.D. Ill. 2002) (Indicating that payment in excess of fair market value for a physician practice may create an inference of improper remuneration); *OIG Special Fraud Alert: "Arrangements for the Provision of Clinical Laboratory Services"* (Issued October 1994), republished at 59 Fed. Reg. 65372 (Dec. 19, 1994) (Whenever a laboratory offers or gives to a source of referrals anything of value not paid for at fair market value, the inference may be made that the thing of value is offered to induce the referral of business. The same is true whenever a referral source solicits or receives anything of value from the laboratory. By "fair market value," we mean value for general commercial purposes. However, fair market value must reflect an arms-length transaction that has not been adjusted to include the additional value that one or both of the parties has attributed to the referral of business between them); Letter from D. McCarty Thornton, Associate General Counsel, OIG to T.J. Sullivan, Technical Assistant, Office of the Associate Chief Counsel, Employee Benefits and Exempt Organizations dated December 22, 1992 (available at oig.hhs.gov/fraud/docs/safeharborregulations/acquisition122292.htm) (Indicating that payment in excess of fair market value may create an inference of improper remuneration); *OIG Supplemental Compliance Program Guidance for Hospitals*, 70 Fed. Reg. 4858, 4866 (Jan. 31, 2005) (Arrangements under which hospitals (a) provide physicians with items or services for free or less than fair market value; (2) relieve physicians of financial obligations they would otherwise incur; or (3) inflate compensation paid to physicians for items or services pose significant risk. In such circumstances, an inference arises that the remuneration may be in exchange for generating business).

Remuneration. Health care providers and their advisors should first understand what could be considered improper remuneration under the anti-kickback statute. In plain English, the term "remunerate" is defined as "to pay an equivalent for."[5] Congress used the term "any remuneration" in the anti-kickback statute to more broadly capture various forms of value that may be traded in exchange for referrals to strengthen the capability of the government to detect, prosecute, and punish fraudulent activities under the Medicare and Medicaid programs.[6] The language "directly or indirectly, overtly or covertly, in cash or in kind" makes clear that the form or manner of remuneration can include indirect, covert, and in-kind transactions. Courts have held that remuneration encompasses both traditional kickback payments, where no actual service was performed, as well as payments for which some service was performed.[7] The fact that Congress included a specific exception for discounts under the anti-kickback statute demonstrates that it otherwise extends even to arrangements where there is no direct payment at all from the party receiving referrals.

Even the mere opportunity to earn profits can constitute improper remuneration to induce referrals. For instance, giving a person the opportunity to generate consulting or service fees, even if those fees are the result of actual services provided, could potentially constitute improper remuneration if coupled with an improper intent to induce referrals.[8] The ability to generate a fee could also potentially constitute improper remuneration when an existing supplier of a healthcare service (e.g., a lab company or radiation therapy center) contracts to supply those services to a provider in a position to refer business (e.g., a physician group) that can then bill and

5 Merriam-Webster Online Dictionary (2011).

6 See H.R. Rep. No. 95-393, Pt. II, 95th Cong., 1st Sess. 53 *reprinted in* 1977 U.S.C.C.A.N. 3039, 3056; *Medicare and State Health Care Programs: Fraud and Abuse; OIG Anti-Kickback Provisions,* 56 Fed. Reg. 35952, 35958 (July 29, 1991) (Congress' intent in placing the term "remuneration" in the statute in 1977 was to cover the transferring of anything of value in any form or manner whatsoever. The statute's language makes clear that illegal payments are prohibited beyond merely "bribes," "kickbacks," and "rebates," which were the three terms used in the original 1972 statute); Hanlester Network, 51 F.3d at 1398 (Noting that the phrase "any remuneration" was intended to broaden the reach of the law that previously referred only to kickbacks, bribes, and rebates); Greber, 760 F.2d at 71 (Indicating that Congress included "any remuneration" to make it clear that even if the transaction was not considered to be a "kickback" for which no service had been rendered, payment could nevertheless violate the statute).

7 *Greber,* 760 F.2d at 71; *United States v. Bay State Ambulance and Hospital Rental Service, Inc.,* 874 F.2d 20, 30 (1st Cir. 1989).

8 See *Bay State Ambulance,* 874 F.2d at 29 (Court acknowledged that opportunity to earn consulting fees could constitute improper remuneration, rejecting defendant's argument that consulting fees had to be of substantially more value than services performed to constitute illegal remuneration and upholding jury instruction indicating that payments could be illegal remuneration if they were made with improper purpose); *Medicare and State Health Care Programs: Fraud and Abuse; Clarification of the Initial OIG Safe Harbor Provisions and Establishment of Additional Safe Harbor Provisions Under the Anti-Kickback Statute,* 64 Fed. Reg. 63518, 63548 (Nov. 19, 1999) (Noting that the opportunity to split a global fee may constitute something of value to a referring party apart from any payment for the referral, such as where an optometrist and ophthalmologist network refers patients for cataract surgery only to ophthalmologists who agree to split the global surgical fee by referring patients back to the optometrist for post-operative care).

collect fees for business typically provided by the existing supplier.[9] Additionally, the OIG has taken the position that the mere opportunity to invest in a joint venture (and consequently receive profit distributions) may in certain circumstances constitute improper remuneration if offered in exchange for past or anticipated referrals.[10]

As indicated by the examples discussed above, healthcare providers should bear in mind that potentially problematic remuneration may take many forms, including: (a) payments or kickbacks for referrals where no services are performed in return; (b) payments for which some services or items was were provided in return; (c) discounts or rebates off the price of an item or service received; or (d) the opportunity to earn profits by generating fees for services or receiving distributions from an investment.

Fair Market Value. One of the primary means to ensure there is no remuneration for referrals in an arrangement is to make sure that the parties pay or receive fair market value in exchange for the items or services provided. Some of the most commonly cited instances of potentially improper remuneration are where a party provides items or services to another party for more or less than fair market value or provides an inappropriate discount or premium to the fair market value purchase price of an investment interest. For example, in the context of purchasing physician practices, courts have held that "to the extent that a payment exceeds the fair market value of the practice, or the value of the services, it can be inferred that the excess amount paid over fair market value is intended as payment for the referral of program-related business."[11] Conversely, it can be argued that when the amount paid for services, items, or investment interests is fair market value, there is a presumption that there is no remuneration in exchange for referrals because the amount paid is solely attributable to the service, item, or investment interest provided.[12] Note, however, that the OIG has not chosen to provide

9 *OIG Special Advisory Bulletin on Contractual Joint Ventures*, 68 Fed. Reg. 23148 (April 30, 2003); see also OIG Advisory Opinion No. 04-17 (Dec. 10, 2004); OIG Advisory Opinion No. 08-10 (Aug. 19, 2008) (Noting that arrangement where intensity-modulated radiation therapy facility block leases time to urologists who then bill Medicare for the professional and technical components could potentially result in problematic remuneration to the urologists in the form of the difference between the fees collected and the fixed amounts to be paid to the facility under the block lease arrangement).

10 OIG Advisory Opinion No. 98-19 (Dec. 14, 1998); OIG Advisory Opinion No. 97-5 (Oct. 6, 1997).

11 *Perales*, 243 F. Supp. 2d at 849; Obert-Hong, 211 F. Supp. 2d at 1049.

12 See Letter from D. McCarty Thornton (Noting the importance of fair market value in the context of physician practice acquisitions and stating that "it is necessary to consider the amounts paid for the practice or as compensation to determine whether they reasonably reflect the fair market value of the practice or the services rendered, to determine whether such items in reality constitute remuneration for referrals"); *United States ex rel. Goodstein v. McLaren*, 202 F. Supp. 2d 671 (E.D. Mich. 2002) (Holding that a lease for medical office space was based on fair market value and not remuneration for referrals of Medicaid patients to the defendant based on applying the statutory allowances for lessee and lessor relationships); U.S. ex rel. Obert-Hong, 211 F. Supp.2d at 1049 (Holding that "the Anti-Kickback Act does not prohibit hospitals from acquiring medical practices, nor does it preclude the seller-doctor from making future referrals to the buyer-hospital, provided there are no economic inducements for those referrals. To comply with the statute, the hospital must simply pay fair market value for the

safe harbor protection to all arrangements that are consistent with fair market value, but rather only a small subset of such arrangements, and the OIG has taken the position that fair market value alone will not insulate an arrangement from violating the anti-kickback statute.[13]

When considering the question of fair market value in the context of healthcare transactions, traditional methods of economic valuation may not always comport with the proscriptions of the anti-kickback statute. For example, parties unfamiliar with the limitations imposed by the anti-kickback statute might normally expect the purchase price for a physician practice acquisition by a hospital to account for potential revenues from anticipated referrals by the selling physician to the hospital for nonphysician services. However, the anti-kickback statute dictates that anticipated referrals to the hospital must be excluded from the calculation of a fair market value purchase price.[14] The safe harbor regulations under the anti-kickback statute also dictate that for purposes of determining the value of space or equipment rentals, "fair market value" is specifically defined to exclude the additional value one party would attribute to the property or equipment as a result of its proximity or convenience to sources of referrals (such as the added value a hospital places on having referring physicians located in a medical building the hospital owns on its property).[15] Additionally, parties should be careful in evaluating comparable market data in healthcare transactions. Merely because another buyer is willing to pay a particular price does not mean the price is fair market value especially if the price offered attributes value to referrals expected to result from the arrangement. Thus, in a market where physician practice acquisition activity is strong, those involved in structuring a transaction should be alert to the risks posed by relying on uninformed pronouncements of the "going rate" as a reliable indication of fair market value in the context of the anti-kickback statute.

Investment Arrangements. The OIG has provided guidance as to appropriate structures for investment arrangements by creating safe harbors that protect certain types of investment interests and provide that the distributions related to such investment interests will not constitute "remuneration" under the anti-kickback statute when all of the safe harbor requirements are satisfied.[16] These safe harbors contain two common requirements that are important to consider in the valuation context: (a) terms on which an investment interest is offered to an investor must not be related to previous or expected volume of referrals, and (b) payment to an investor in return for the

practice's assets").

13 70 Fed. Reg. at 4864 (Neither a legitimate business purpose for the arrangement, nor a fair market value payment, will legitimize a payment if there is also an illegal purpose to induce federal healthcare program business).

14 *Obert-Hong*, 211 F. Supp.2d at 1049.

15 42 C.F.R. § 1001.952(b) and (c); 56 Fed. Reg. at 35971-73.

16 42 C.F.R. § 1001.952(a) and (r).

investment interest must be directly proportional to the capital investment of that investor.[17]

The OIG has provided further guidance on investment arrangements in its Special Fraud Alerts identifying problematic features that could result in a business arrangement that violates the anti-kickback statute.[18] In the OIG's view, these improper investment arrangements are not intended "to raise investment capital legitimately to start a business, but to lock up a stream of referrals from the physician investors and to compensate them indirectly for these referrals."[19] Two of the "questionable features" identified by the OIG as potential indicators of a "suspect joint venture" are: (a) the amount of capital invested by the physician is "disproportionately small" and the returns on investment may be "disproportionately large" when compared to a typical investment in a new business enterprise; and (b) investors may be paid what the OIG terms "extraordinary returns" on the investment in comparison with the risk involved, often well over "50% to 100% per year."[20]

One of the key principles in the guidance on investment arrangements from the OIG is that the amount of payment to each investor must be directly proportional to capital invested. The OIG has issued two separate advisory opinions related to investment in surgery centers that have created some confusion as to what the OIG considers to be disproportionate returns to investors and whether valuation of intangible assets could be construed as attributing value to investor referrals.

In Advisory Opinion 07-05, the OIG took the surprising position that a hospital's purchase of ownership interests in an existing surgery center for fair market value from certain physician owners could potentially generate prohibited remuneration under the federal anti-kickback statute.[21] This result turned in part on the fact that the hospital and the physicians would not receive investment returns directly proportional to the dollar amount of their invested capital (although returns would be directly proportional to percentage ownership interests) because the price paid for investment interests by the hospital (as a later investor) would be higher (due to appreciation in value) than price originally paid for investment interests by the physicians.

The position taken by the OIG in Advisory Opinion 07-05 stands in stark contrast to its position in Advisory Opinion 01-21, which concluded that the distribution of profit and losses in direct proportion to each investor's percentage of equity ownership in a

17 *Id.*

18 OIG Special Fraud Alert: Joint Venture Arrangements (Issued August 1989), republished in 59 Fed. Reg. 65372 (Dec. 19, 1994).

19 *Id.*

20 *Id.*

21 OIG Advisory Opinion No. 07-05 (June 12, 2007).

surgery center (as opposed to original capital investment) does not increase the risk of fraud and abuse, even though it does prevent the arrangement from meeting the anti-kickback statute safe harbor for surgery centers.[22] In fact, the OIG explained in Advisory Opinion 01-21 that there was a reasonable basis for different prices paid by later investors, namely, the appreciation in value of the surgery center over time. The sale of ownership interests in an existing surgery center must occur at fair market value to avoid an inference of improper remuneration to the purchaser or seller, and the OIG could not possibly condone a later investor paying the same price as an original investor when such price is below fair market value due to subsequent appreciation in the value of the underlying security. It should also be noted that when the OIG originally established the safe harbor for investment interests, it explained that "to receive protection, dividend payments can only be tied to the number of shares owned by an investor, and not to his or her referrals," an acknowledgment that dividends are tied to shares of ownership interest held rather than the amount of capital invested.[23] Advisory Opinion 07-05 may be distinguished, however, based on the unique concerns raised by the OIG that the investment by the hospital appeared to be intended to allow specific physician investors to realize a gain on their investment, raising the possibility that the hospital's investment was intended to influence the referrals of those selected physicians.

In Advisory Opinion 09-09, the OIG took the position that the independent development of two surgery centers by a hospital and a group of physicians and the merger of those surgery centers into a joint venture could potentially generate prohibited remuneration under the anti-kickback statute because the hospital and the physicians might receive investment returns that were not directly proportional to their invested capital, but that the risk of abuse was low in part because the valuation of the surgery centers contributed to the joint venture was based on a tangible asset valuation.[24] The OIG noted, however, that under certain circumstances it might be concerned if the valuations of the surgery centers included intangible assets by using a cash flow analysis that could potentially include the value of referrals by the parties to their respective surgery center prior to the merger.

Advisory Opinion 09-09 dealt with a unique, multistep transaction that appeared to be structured to avoid state certificate of need restrictions by developing separate single operating room surgery centers (that would not require certificate of need approval) and then merging them together to create a two operating room surgery center (which would have required certificate of need approval if developed on its own). The key distinguishing feature of this transaction was that the contribution of the surgery centers

22 OIG Advisory Opinion No. 01-21 (Nov. 16, 2001).

23 *Medicare and State Health Care Programs: Fraud and Abuse; OIG Anti-Kickback Provisions;* Rule, 56 Fed. Reg. 35952, 35970 (July 29, 1991).

24 OIG Advisory Opinion No. 09-09 (July 22, 2009).

to the joint venture was agreed to ex ante ("before the event") by the parties. Absent certificate of need restrictions, one could reasonably expect that the parties would have taken the more simple approach of making initial capital contributions to the joint venture and having it develop a two operating room surgery center. As a result, it is reasonable for the OIG to view the contributions of the surgery centers as initial capital investments, rather than contributions of going concerns, and using a tangible asset valuation of the surgery centers serves to prevent either party from abusing the agreed-to arrangement by directing referrals to a particular surgery center to increase the value of their capital contribution. In contrast, if either of the surgery centers had been in operation for many years, and the proposed joint venture had not been agreed to ex ante by the parties, then the contribution of the surgery center, or the purchase of ownership interests therein, should not be viewed merely as an initial capital investment. Dictating a tangible asset valuation in such circumstances could actually lead to the very situation that the OIG wants the parties to avoid: improper remuneration that could be related to referrals. For example, if the physicians purchased ownership interests in an existing surgery center owned by the hospital based on a tangible asset valuation of $1 million when the fair market value of the surgery center was actually $5 million (based on the income approach), then the physicians could be viewed as receiving remuneration (in the form of a discounted purchase price) in exchange for referrals.

At first blush, the OIG's position in Advisory Opinion 09-09 appears to create an untenable conflict between the regulatory framework of the anti-kickback statute and business valuation standards that require a valuator to consider all appropriate valuation approaches and which indicate that the income approach may be the preferred approach for businesses with positive cash flow. However, upon further examination of the unique structure of the transaction at issue, the OIG's position proves to be a reasonable one in the specific scenario where the parties agree to contribute the surgery centers to a joint venture ex ante to their development, and these contributions are, in effect, treated as initial capital investments by parties to the joint venture rather than as contributions of going business concerns. Advisory Opinion 09-09 should not be read in any way to discredit valuations based on the income approach, and in many cases the income approach may be absolutely necessary to ensure that none of the parties to a transaction give or receive improper remuneration by transaction at other than fair market value.

Compensation Arrangements. The OIG has provided guidance regarding appropriate structures for compensation arrangements by creating safe harbors that protect certain types of compensation arrangements when all of the safe harbor requirements are satisfied. There is a safe harbor for employment arrangements that protects "any amount paid by an employer to an employee, who has a bona fide employment relationship with such employer, for employment in the furnishing of any item or service for which payment may be made in whole or in part under Medicare, Medicaid or other federal healthcare programs."[25] This safe harbor gives broad protection for compensation paid to employees, regardless of whether such compensation is fair market value or whether it takes into account the volume or value of referrals. However, as discussed below, the Stark Law does require that compensation to physician employees be consistent with fair market value and not take into account the volume or value of referrals.

With respect to other types of compensation arrangements, the safe harbors for space rentals, equipment rentals, and personal services and management contracts generally include the following characteristics: (a) the aggregate compensation paid over the term of the agreement is set in advance, is consistent with fair market value in arms-length transactions, and is not determined in a manner that takes into account the volume or value of any referrals or business otherwise generated between the parties for which payment may be made in whole or in part under a federal healthcare program,; and (b) the aggregate services contracted for do not exceed those that are reasonably necessary to accomplish the commercially reasonable business purpose of the services.[26] The OIG has noted that per patient, per order, per click, and percentage-based compensation arrangements are disfavored under the anti-kickback statute because they inherently vary based on the volume and value of business generated between the parties.[27]

The Stark Law

The Stark Law prohibits physicians having a financial relationship with an entity from referring patients to such entity for certain "designated health services" provided to Medicare beneficiaries, unless such financial relationship meets one of the exceptions enumerated under the statute or the regulations promulgated thereunder.[28] The Stark Law also prohibits entities from billing individuals or Medicare for designated health services furnished pursuant to a prohibited referral, and any payments (including co-payments) received in violation of this prohibition must be refunded. A financial relationship under the Stark Law can take the form of a direct or indirect ownership

25 42 U.S.C. § 1320a-7b(b)(3)(B); 42 C.F.R. § 1001.952(i)

26 42 C.F.R. § 1001.952(b), (c) & (d).

27 See 56 Fed. Reg. at 35973 (noting that percentage or per-unit agreements between healthcare providers in a position to refer Medicare or Medicaid business threaten to violate the statute because the payments in these arrangements are directly tied to the volume of business or amount of revenue generated, providing an improper incentive to refer); OIG Advisory Opinion 03-8 (April 3, 2003) (noting that that "per patient", "per order", "per click" and similar payment arrangements with referral sources are disfavored); OIG Advisory Opinion 06-02 (March 21, 2006) (noting that percentage-based compensation was inherently problematic from a fair market value perspective because the compensation necessarily relates to the volume and value of business generated between the parties).

28 42 U.S.C. § 1395nn. Designated health services include clinical laboratory services; physical therapy, occupational therapy, and speech-language pathology services; radiology and certain other imaging services; radiation therapy services and supplies; durable medical equipment and supplies; parenteral and enteral nutrients, equipment, and supplies; prosthetics, orthotics, and prosthetic devices and supplies; home health services; outpatient prescription drugs; inpatient and outpatient hospital services. 42 U.S.C. § 1395nn(h)(6); 42 C.F.R. § 411.351.

interest or compensation arrangement. The Stark Law and the regulations promulgated thereunder define a referral as the request by a physician for, or ordering of, or the certifying or recertifying of the need for, any designated health service for which payment may be made under Medicare, but not including any designated health service personally performed by the referring physician.[29]

Fair Market Value. For a compensation arrangement between an entity providing designated health services and a referring physician to avoid the prohibitions on physician referrals, the exceptions under the Stark Law generally require that remuneration under such compensation arrangement be: (a) set in advance; (b) consistent with fair market value; and (c) not determined in a manner that takes into account the volume or value of referrals or other business generated.[30] Note that, unlike the employment safe harbor to the anti-kickback statute, the employment exception to the Stark Law does require that compensation paid to physician employees be consistent with fair market value and not determined in a manner that takes into account the volume or value of referrals. The Centers for Medicare and Medicaid Services (CMS) has also noted that the definition of "fair market value" under the Stark Law is qualified in ways that do not necessarily comport with the usage of the term in standard valuation methodologies. In particular, the Stark Law requires that the methodology for analyzing fair market value exclude valuations where the parties to the transactions are at arm's length but in a position to refer to one another.[31]

For purposes of the Stark Law, fair market value is defined as the value in arm's-length transactions, consistent with the "general market value," which means the price that an asset would bring as the result of bona fide bargaining between well-informed buyers and sellers who are not otherwise in a position to generate business for the other party, or the compensation that would be included in a service agreement as the result of bona fide bargaining between well-informed parties to the agreement who are not otherwise in a position to generate business for the other party, on the date of acquisition of the asset or at the time of the service agreement.[32] The Stark Law regulations also note that a "fair market price" is usually the price at which bona fide sales have been consummated for assets of like type, quality, and quantity in a particular market at the time of acquisition, or the compensation that has been included in bona fide service agreements with comparable terms at the time of the agreement, where the price or compensation has not been determined in any manner that takes into account the volume or value

29 42 U.S.C. § 1395nn(h)(5); 42 CFR § 411.351.

30 See 42 C.F.R. § 411.357(a) (rental of office space), (b) (rental of equipment), (c) (employment), (d) (personal services), (f) (isolated transactions), (i) (payments by physician) and (l) (fair market value).

31 *Medicare Program; Physicians' Referrals to Health Care Entities With Which They Have Financial Relationships (Phase II); Interim Final Rule*; 69 Fed. Reg. 16054, 16107 (March 26, 2004).

32 42 C.F.R. § 411.351.

of anticipated or actual referrals.[33] Note that the foregoing language reflects that the particular market in which a transaction occurs is important in assessing the relevance of comparable transactions.

With respect to space and equipment rentals, the Stark Law regulations specifically define fair market value as the value of rental property for general commercial purposes (not taking into account its intended use, provided that costs incurred by the lessor in developing or upgrading the property or maintaining the property or its improvements may be considered), and in the case of a space rental, this value may not be adjusted to reflect the additional value the prospective lessee or lessor would attribute to the proximity or convenience to the lessor when the lessor is a potential source of patient referrals to the lessee.[34]

Per-Unit and Percentage-Based Compensation. The exceptions under the Stark Law permit per-unit and percentage-based compensation in certain limited circumstances. Unlike the safe harbors under the anti-kickback statute, per-unit or percentage-based compensation can meet the Stark Law requirement of being "set in advance" as long as the per-unit of service amount or specific formula for calculating the compensation is (a) set forth in the written agreement between the parties in sufficient detail so that it can be objectively verified; and (b) may not be changed or modified during the course of the agreement in any manner that takes into account the volume or value of referrals or other business generated by the referring physician.[35] Per-unit compensation (but not percentage-based compensation) is also deemed not to take into account "the volume or value of referrals" under the Stark Law if the compensation is fair market value for services or items actually provided and does not vary during the course of the compensation arrangement in any manner that takes into account referrals or other business generated by the referring physician.[36]

Per-unit or percentage-based compensation may not, however, be used in space or equipment rentals if the per-unit charge reflects services provided to patients referred by the lessor to the lessee or the compensation is based on a percentage of revenue raised, earned, billed, collected or otherwise attributable to the services performed or business generated in the rented space or using the leased equipment.[37] Although CMS has not prohibited percentage-based compensation in arrangements involving nonprofessional services (such as management or billing services), it has indicated that it intends to

33 *Id.*
34 *Id.*
35 42 C.F.R. § 411.354(d).
36 *Id.*; See also 69 Fed. Reg. at 16066-70 (Indicating that percentage compensation arrangements can meet the set in advance requirement, but must also meet the volume or value and other business generated requirement).
37 42 C.F.R. § 411.357(a), (b), (l) and (p).

continue to monitor these types of compensation arrangements for potential abuse.[38] CMS has also noted that it does not consider an agreement to be at fair market value if the lessee is paying a physician-owned lessor substantially more for equipment than it would have to pay a non-physician-owned lessor and has serious questions as to the commercial reasonableness of an agreement if the lessee is performing a sufficiently high volume of procedures such that it would be economically feasible to purchase the equipment rather than lease it.[39] In the view of CMS, these types of arrangements raise the question of whether the lessee is paying more than what it would have to pay another lessor (or if the lessee purchased the equipment) to avoid losing referrals from the lessor.[40] Potential issues that can arise when a lessee is paying a physician lessor more for equipment than it would have to pay a third-party lessor are illustrated in the *Bradford* case discussed below.

Valuation Scenarios to Consider

The following examples of valuation contexts are intended to identify particular scenarios in which healthcare providers and their advisors should be attentive to avoiding the attribution of value to referrals of federal healthcare program business when structuring and valuing business arrangements. These examples also draw on lessons that can be learned from OIG advisory opinions and court cases involving healthcare providers engaged in similar business arrangements.

Compensation Arrangements With Physicians. To avoid prohibited referrals under the Stark Law or an inference of improper remuneration for referrals under the anti-kickback statute, compensation arrangements between healthcare providers and referring physicians should be at fair market value for actual items or services furnished and should not take into account, directly or indirectly, the value or volume of any past or anticipated referrals or other business generated by the physician. When structuring compensation arrangements with physicians within the regulatory framework of the Stark Law and anti-kickback statute, it is important to consider both the amount and type of compensation provided.

Compensation that is fixed in advance may more easily fit within a Stark Law exception or safe harbor to the anti-kickback statute because there is no opportunity for compensation to vary during the term of the arrangement based upon referrals. However,

38 See *Medicare Program; Changes to the Hospital Inpatient Prospective Payment Systems and Fiscal Year 2009 Rates*; 73 Fed. Reg. 48434, 48710 (Aug. 19, 2008). Note that in its 2009 Hospital Inpatient Prospective Payment System Proposed Rule, CMS originally proposed to limit percentage compensation arrangement only to personally performed services. *Medicare Program; Proposed Changes to the Hospital Inpatient Prospective Payment Systems and Fiscal Year 2009 Rates*, 73 Fed. Reg. 23528, 23694 (April 30, 2008).

39 See 73 Fed. Reg. at 48714.

40 *Id.*

healthcare providers must be attentive to make sure the fixed compensation amounts are fair market value for the actual services provided. For example, although compensation based on actual hours worked may not be considered fixed compensation, it may more accurately reflect the fair market value of services provided than a fixed monthly payment (particularly if physicians work less than the anticipated time per month). Health care providers should also be careful when resetting fixed compensation amounts under an arrangement to make sure that the compensation is not adjusted in a manner that provides incentives for increases in referrals.

An example of how fixed compensation arrangements can still pose potential problems is the case of *U.S. v. Campbell (2011)*.[41] This case was based on part-time employment contracts between the University of Medicine and Dentistry of New Jersey and local cardiologists serving as clinical assistant professors with fixed salaries ranging from $50,000 to $180,000 that were alleged to have been entered into by the hospital to ensure a sufficient number of cardiac procedures to avoid losing Level 1 Trauma Center accreditation. The hospital entered into a settlement agreement with the government for alleged violations of the False Claims Act related to these contracts and the government then sought damages from an individual cardiologist related to his contract with the hospital. This case illustrates that healthcare providers and their advisors should carefully consider the specific facts and circumstances of compensation arrangements with referring physicians and keep in mind that even fixed salaries may still pose a problem if the salary is not tied to actual services provided by the physician.

Percentage and per-unit based compensation arrangements with physicians are more prone to being viewed as tied to the volume or value of referrals and should be carefully reviewed to ensure they meet all of the applicable requirements under a Stark Law exception and do not involve space or equipment rentals where the rental charge reflects services provided to patients referred by the lessor to the lessee. Even if a per-unit or percentage-based compensation arrangement meets a Stark Law exception, there is no safe harbor protection for such arrangements under the anti-kickback statute. Moreover, while percentage or per-unit based compensation methodologies may be common in certain business arrangements, such methodologies may be disfavored under the anti-kickback statute when they involve physicians. For instance, although management agreements often include fees based on a percentage of revenue, this type of management fee may raise concerns when the manager is owned by physicians in a position to make referrals to the business being managed.

The need for careful attention when structuring compensation arrangements with physicians is illustrated by the case of *U.S. ex rel Drakeford v. Tuomey Healthcare System*,

41 *U.S. v. Campbell*, 2011 WL 43013, No. 08-1951 (D.N.J., Jan. 4, 2011).

Inc. (2010).[42] This was a qui tam case brought by an orthopedic surgeon contending that the hospital's part-time employment of surgeons violated the Stark Law because the compensation was based on the volume or value of referrals from the physicians to the hospital. The part-time employment agreements tied physician compensation to collections for personally performed professional services, which by itself is a fairly common structure and unlikely to raise concerns under the Stark Law because personally performed services are not considered referrals. However, the agreements also had several unusual features, including 10-year terms, only applying to outpatient surgeries (but not inpatient surgeries or work done in the office), imposing significant noncompete covenants requiring all outpatient surgeries to be performed in the hospital's outpatient surgery center and providing total compensation and benefits that were approximately 30% higher than actual collections for professional services. Taken as a whole, the government characterized these part-time employment agreements as an attempt to limit competition from physician-owned surgery centers by providing compensation and benefits that were significantly higher than what the physician could reasonably expect to collect for their professional services. Although the hospital contended it had legal opinions and third-party valuations supporting the appropriateness of the arrangements, the jury found that these part-time employment agreements violated the Stark Law and the hospital had improperly billed Medicare for approximately $45 million in services tied to referrals that were prohibited under the Stark Law. The *Tuomey* case serves as a reminder that even though employment arrangements with physicians may have safe harbor protection under the anti-kickback statute, they are still susceptible to violating the Stark Law and should be evaluated as a whole to ensure that compensation is fair market value, commercially reasonable, and not tied to volume or value of referrals.

Physician Practice Acquisitions. Hospital acquisitions of physician practices are transactions that commonly require the parties to determine the fair market value of the practice being acquired. As mentioned above, hospitals cannot attribute value to prior or anticipated referrals for hospital services by physician owners when calculating the purchase price for a physician practice. When a physician practice is valued on a going concern basis, revenues tied to referrals from physician owners to the hospital for non-physician services must be excluded because they are unrelated to the going concern value of the business being acquired. This does not mean, however, that the hospital has to disregard revenues of the physician practice attributable to (ai) professional services of the physician owners, because these services do not constitute a referral to another person or entity for reimbursable services or items; or (b) other revenue of the practice, to the extent this revenue is reflective of the going concern value of the practice's business. It is also important that the value of a physician practice on a going concern basis incorporate the post-transaction compensation paid to the physicians by

42 *U.S. ex rel. Drakeford v. Tuomey Healthcare System, Inc.*, No. 3:05-CV-02858-MJP (D.C.S.C., March 29, 2010).

the acquiring hospital. This issue was highlighted in the case of *Derby v. Commissioner (2008)*, where the tax court denied a charitable deduction for the intangible value of a medical practice claimed by the physician owners in connection with the acquisition of a health system that included a purchase price tied solely to tangible assets.[43] This case illustrates that intangible value may not exist if post-transaction compensation to physicians eliminates any potential cash flow to the acquirer of the practice.

When substantially all of the cash flows from a physician practice are allocated to physician compensation, thereby eliminating any residual going concern value, it is common for the practice to be valued on a cost approach basis. This approach determines the liquidation value of the individual assets of the practice as opposed to the going concern value of the practice as a whole. While establishing the value of tangible assets such as equipment and furniture under the cost approach may be fairly straight forward, determining what value, if any, can be attributed to other intangible assets of the practice under the cost approach requires careful consideration. Certain types of intangible assets (like goodwill) may not have any value in the absence of any going concern value for the business (i.e., in the absence of positive post-transaction cash flow net of physician compensation).

For an asset to be attributed value in a liquidation scenario, the practice must have a bona fide right of ownership to the asset that it can legally transfer to the buyer.[44] This may require valuators to consider contractual rights and relevant laws governing the right to ownership of such assets (for example, the transferability of a noncompete under an employment contract). For an asset to have quantifiable value under the cost approach, it must also generate some measurable amount of economic benefit to the buyer, whether in the form of an income or cost avoidance.[45] In other words, the buyer must have a need to acquire the asset for its employment of the physicians such that it would otherwise have to go out and incur the cost of acquiring the asset independently. The value of the asset should take into consideration any functional or economic obsolescence as well as any obligations and costs associated with ownership of the asset. For example, costs of storage and retrieval should be considered in the context of placing value on medical records. Similarly, credit for prior years of service granted to nonphysician employees should be considered in analyzing the value of any trained workforce whose employment contracts are transferred to the buyer.

Acquisitions of Physician-Owned Ancillary Businesses. Another type of transaction that often requires careful consideration under the regulatory framework of the

43 *Derby v. Commissioner*, T.C. Memo 2008-45 (2008).
44 See Shannon P. Pratt, Robert F. Reilly & Robert P. Schweihs, *Valuing a Business: The Analysis and Appraisal of Closely Held Companies*, 325 (4th Ed., 2000).
45 *Id.*

Stark Law and anti-kickback statute is the acquisition of physician-owned ancillary businesses. In-office ancillary businesses such as laboratory, imaging, and surgical suites that are operated as part of a physician practice will often derive substantially all of their business from referrals by the physician owners of the practice. As a result, healthcare providers acquiring these in-office ancillary businesses need to be careful to structure the acquisition in a manner that does not improperly attribute value to anticipated referrals by the physician owners of the practice.

Some of the potential pitfalls to consider when structuring acquisitions of physician-owned ancillary business are highlighted in the case of *United States ex rel. Singh v. Bradford Regional Medical Center*, involving a qui tam action brought against a hospital and local physicians relating to a nuclear camera sublease arrangement.[46] The court in this case concluded that the sublease arrangement between the parties created financial relationships that violated the Stark Law and resulted in prohibited referrals by the physicians to the hospital. Central to this conclusion was the court's determination that payments under the sublease, which included substantial amounts attributable to a noncompete agreement, were greater than what would be paid in the absence of the ability of the physicians to generate referrals to the hospital and inflated to compensate the physicians for their ability to generate such referrals. Thus, the court was able to conclude that the noncompete payments were arrived at by taking into account the volume and value of anticipated referrals by the physicians and were therefore not fair market value for purposes of the Stark Law. Although the hospital had obtained a report from an accountant analyzing the noncompete payments under the sublease using the competitive business valuation method and concluding that they were fair market value, in reaching this conclusion, the accountant had improperly taken into account anticipated revenues to the hospital for not only nuclear imaging services but also CT/MRI, inpatient, and outpatient services based on the assumption that the physicians would likely refer this business to the hospital in the absence of a financial interest in their own facilities (although not required to do so by the noncompete).[47]

The *Bradford* case underscores the need for careful attention when structuring acquisitions of physician-owned ancillary businesses and valuing intangible assets (such as noncompetes) in these arrangements. It also emphasizes the need to consider the element of commercial reasonableness in these types of arrangements. One of the problems in the *Bradford* case was that the parties structured what would typically be a business acquisition as an equipment lease. While it is common for value to be allocated to intangible assets as a component of the larger assemblage of assets in a business acquisition, this allocation of value is rarely applicable to leasing arrangements. Moreover, paying

46 *United States ex rel. Singh v. Bradford Regional Medical Center*, 752 F. Supp. 2d 602 (W.D. Pa., 2010). *Editor's Note: The* Bradford *case is also discussed in Chapter 4.*

47 Report of Charles T. Day (attached as Exhibit 7 to Relators' Appendix), 752 F. Supp. 2d 602.

for intangible assets over time (through monthly lease payments) increases the risk that such payments may be linked to a continued expectation of referrals. When evaluating payments for intangible assets in acquisitions of physician-owned ancillary businesses, healthcare providers and their advisors should also keep in mind the general concept of commercial reasonableness that is embodied in the regulatory framework of the Stark Law and anti-kickback statute. In essence, the parties need to ask whether it is commercially reasonable for a purchaser to pay for intangible assets associated with a physician-owned ancillary business absent any expectation of referrals from the physician sellers. Facts to consider in this analysis are (a) whether the location and services of the acquired business are well suited for integration with the purchaser; (b) whether the purchaser will have to relocate or restructure the business; and (c) whether acquiring the business is more cost-effective than the alternative of independently developing a facility, buying or leasing equipment, recruiting staff, incurring start-up losses, and competing with the physicians.

Another issue highlighted in the *Bradford* case is the importance of making sure that payments for intangible assets do not take into account the volume or value of referrals from physician sellers, particularly when the fair market value of intangible assets is determined using discounted cash flows reflecting revenues from referrals by physician sellers under the income approach. Generally accepted valuation standards require consideration of all appropriate valuation approaches, including the asset approach, income approach, and market approach, and for a business that generates positive cash flows, the income approach is in many cases the preferred methodology.[48] When applying the income approach, it is extremely important that fair market value be determined using projected cash flows that reflect the ability of the business to generate cash flows in the absence of any obligation of physician sellers to continue referring to the business. The risk that physician sellers will no longer refer to the business should be accounted for by using appropriate growth assumptions and discount rates. This risk will be higher and the fair market value will be lower if physician sellers are the primary or only source of referrals to the business (which is often the case with physician-owned ancillary businesses). Assuming the income approach appropriately accounts for the risk that physician sellers will no longer refer to the business, arguably there will be no consideration tied to anticipated referrals from physician sellers. Conversely, disregarding the income approach when projected cash flows reflect referrals from physician sellers could actually lead to a purchase price that is below fair market value and may raise concerns under the anti-kickback statute. For example, if a physician-owned ancillary business is sold at below fair market value to a physician-owned hospital or

48 See National Association of Certified Valuation Analysts Professional Standards, Section 3.7; American Society of Appraisers Business Valuation Standards BSV-I, Section IV; American Institute of Certified Public Accountants Statement on Standards for Valuation Services No. 1, paragraph 31; Shannon P. Pratt, Robert F. Reilly & Robert P. Schweihs, *Valuing a Business: The Analysis and Appraisal of Closely Held Companies*, 40 (4th Ed., 2000)

surgery center in which the physician sellers are investors, the discounted purchase price could be viewed as consideration for anticipated referrals by other physician owners of the acquiring entity (which could result in higher distributions to the physicians sellers from such acquiring entity). Those involved in structuring transactions where such discounting assumptions are invoked to eliminate value attributable to future referrals from physician sellers should be alert to communications between the parties where, in pursuit of a higher valuation, selling physicians or their representatives may inappropriately attempt to argue that future referrals should be anticipated. Such communications may have a tendency to taint an otherwise appropriately structured transaction with evidence of improper intent.

Noncompete Agreements.[49] Like other types of intangible assets, valuation of noncompete agreements with healthcare providers requires careful consideration. Noncompete agreements may be attributed value to the extent the noncompete is an enforceable mechanism to preserve the value of an acquired business by prohibiting the detrimental effect of a seller from competing with the acquired business. Assessing the enforceability of the noncompete requires consideration of applicable state laws. The value of a noncompete is related to the avoidance of the potential negative impact on cash flows from allowing the seller to establish a competing business and should not be based on the anticipated volume or value of referrals from the seller because the seller could refer business to another entity regardless of the presence of a noncompete. The value of a noncompete should also take into account the reasonable ability of the seller to engage in competitive activity. For example, a physician might be able to establish an inexpensive surgery or imaging suite in his or her office relatively easily, but establishing a separately licensed surgery or imaging center may not be a realistic scenario.

The competitive business valuation method is a commonly accepted methodology for analyzing the value of a noncompete in the context of a larger assemblage of assets. However, as illustrated by the *Bradford* case discussed above, this methodology must be appropriately applied by assessing the present value of anticipated economic damage to the buyer if the seller were allowed to compete.[50] This requires an analysis of the realistic potential loss in earnings from the specific business being acquired by allowing the seller to compete with the business (in contrast, the accountant's report in the *Bradford* case included revenues associated with CT/MRI, inpatient, and outpatient services that were unrelated to the nuclear camera business). Moreover, the result of the competitive business valuation method should conform with or fit into the context of the overall purchase price for the business. For example, if the total enterprise value of the business is $100, the logical fair market value of the noncompete would be

49 *Editor's Note: The valuation of noncompete agreements is covered in Chapter 8.*

50 See Robert F. Reilly & Robert P. Schweihs, *Valuing Intangible Assets*, 400-09 (1999); IRS Coordinated Issue All Industries Covenants Not to Compete (February 19, 1996); *Ansan Tool v. Commissioner*, T.C. Memo 1992-121.

significantly less than $100 after accounting for the value of other identifiable assets included within the enterprise value.

When the enterprise value of a business is determined on a going concern basis, the value of a noncompete would be encompassed within the overall purchase price for the business (unless the noncompete was not factored into the enterprise value). However, when a business is valued using the cost approach, the value of a noncompete, if any, would have to be determined separately from the value of other identifiable assets based on the impact to projected cash flows of the business by allowing the seller to compete with the business in the future. In such case, valuators should carefully consider the reasonable ability of the seller to compete with the business. If the business is being valued on a cost approach because the sellers are losing money, then the sellers may have little ability to successfully compete with the business and the value of a noncompete may be may be minimal or nonexistent. In the context of noncompetes from physician sellers, it is important to remember that physician sellers cannot be prohibited from making referrals to competing businesses (i.e., they can only be prohibited from owning a competing business). Therefore, the value of a noncompete from a physician seller cannot be determined based on referrals made by the physician seller to the acquired business because they can make those referrals to a competing business regardless of the presence of a noncompete.

Noncompete agreements often arise in the context of physician practice acquisitions where the selling physicians agree not to compete with the purchaser under the terms of their employment agreements with the purchaser. In this case, the noncompete agreement is given in return for compensation provided under the employment agreement, rather than the purchase agreement. If the practice assets were valued using the cost approach, there would be no separate consideration for the noncompete as part of the purchase price.

Another situation that sometimes arises is when physicians desire to receive consideration for contributing a noncompete agreement in connection with their investment in a joint venture. If physicians are making a cash investment in a joint venture, then there is no associated business being acquired that they could adversely compete with and there would be no value to attribute to their noncompete agreement. In comparison, if physicians are contributing an existing business to a joint venture in return for investment interests in the joint venture, then the consideration for their noncompete would be encompassed within the fair market value purchase price paid for the business being contributed.

Investment in De Novo Joint Ventures. When valuing investment interests in de novo (new) joint ventures that include investors in a position to make referrals to the joint venture, the anti-kickback statute generally requires that anticipated referrals from such investors, which might otherwise be taken into account in a normal commercial setting, must be disregarded in determining the value of contributions to the joint venture or the value of the joint venture itself. In the context of a de novo joint venture, there is no existing business to be valued and the purchase price for investment interests should be based solely on the capital required to start up and operate the business. The purchase price for investment interests should not vary between individual investors, as such variance could give rise to an inference of improper remuneration in exchange for anticipated referrals and the OIG has indicated its concern when investors who are potential referral sources for the investment entity are permitted to obtain their investment interests at insider prices or at prices more favorable than those available to the general public.[51]

In contrast, if a party is contributing capital to a de novo joint venture in the form of assets related to an ongoing business, then it is important that such assets be fairly valued and that the contributing party receives fair market value investment interests in exchange. Additionally, investors may contribute capital in the form of pre-operational services or sweat equity, provided that the investment interests received in return are fair market value for actual services contributed.[52] However, it is important that the valuation of any assets or sweat equity contributed does not assign any value to anticipated referrals by the contributing party to the de novo joint venture.

Investment in Existing Joint Ventures. Just as with de novo joint ventures, the value of investment interests in existing joint ventures that include investors in a position to make referrals to the joint venture also should not attribute value to anticipated referrals from such investors. In contrast to a de novo joint venture, an existing joint venture typically has going concern value that may be affected by revenues stemming from referrals made by investors. Additionally, the inflow and outflow of investors actively involved in providing services in connection with a joint venture (which may actually be required to meet the anti-kickback statute safe harbor for ambulatory surgery centers) could potentially impact future revenues of the joint venture. In these circumstances, it is important that the value of investment interests is determined using projected cash flows based on the historical operations of the joint venture, as opposed to the projected future referrals by investors. When a business is valued using projected cash flows based on historical operations, the value of the business is based on the projected ability of the business to continue to operate in a profitable manner. Potential outflows of investors and losses in revenue would be reflected in the discount premium applied to the cash flows of the joint venture (reflecting a higher risk with respect to future

51 64 Fed. Reg. at 63522.
52 See 56 Fed. Reg. at 35970.

operations), however potential inflows of investors and additional revenues attributable to potential referrals from those investors should not be reflected in the purchase price because this could be construed as attributing value to anticipated referrals.

For example, if a physician owner of a surgery center is retiring and selling his or her ownership interests to a new physician and the new physician performs procedures that receive higher reimbursement than the retiring physician, the valuation of the ownership interests in the surgery center should not reflect any anticipated increase in reimbursement from the activity of the new physician at the surgery center because it would reflect the value of anticipated referrals. In contrast, if a surgery center invests in a new piece of high-technology equipment enabling it to perform certain cutting-edge procedures that receive higher reimbursement, the valuation of the surgery center should reflect the projected revenues from this new equipment. The important distinction here is that in the latter case, the valuation is appropriately based on the projected ability of the business to perform new procedures and is not based on projections of anticipated referrals from a new physician investor.

In valuing an existing joint venture, it is also important that an appropriate discount premium is applied so that the amount of capital invested by new investors is not disproportionately small compared to disproportionately large returns that an enforcement authority might assert to be "extraordinary returns" in comparison with the risk involved.[53] Assuming that a joint venture has a significant operating history and a relatively stable risk profile that allows for the application of an appropriate discount premium, the mere purchase of an investment interest should avoid any inference of improper remuneration to the purchaser, the seller, or other investors as long as the purchase is not targeted toward certain investors in return for their referrals and the purchase price is fair market value. The logical argument that can be made here is that if the price paid for an investment interest is fair market value, then the value of the purchase price consideration is equivalent to the value of the investment interest received and there is no additional remuneration that could be attributed to referrals.

Investment in Existing Joint Ventures With Limited Operating History. Sometimes investors may purchase ownership interests in an existing joint venture that has a limited operating history and minimal or no cash flow. This scenario presents unique challenges for valuators. The valuation of investment interests in an existing joint venture with a limited operating history should be careful to avoid (a) underestimating the value that has been created by the formation of the business; or (b) overestimating

53 Note that the OIG has stated that "a reasonable return can be appropriately measured only in light of the risk of the investment. An investor would surely expect a much higher return from an investment in an expensive piece of diagnostic equipment that might soon become obsolete than from an investment in a relatively inexpensive piece of equipment that can be expected to generate a steady profit stream for the foreseeable future." 56 Fed. Reg. at 35970.

the value that has been created by the formation of the business by ascribing value to anticipated referrals from physician investors.

To be sure, there is some value created by the syndication of ownership interests and the formation of a joint venture. This value is likely to increase as the business reaches additional milestones such as obtaining additional financing, constructing a facility, purchasing equipment, obtaining licenses and other regulatory approvals, and commencing operations because the related risk of future cash flows declines. Until those milestones are reached, the risk that they might not be met would warrant additional discounts to the value of the business. The attainment of certain milestones means that the purchase price for ownership units in the business likely is no longer based solely upon the equity capital required to start up the business. If, following syndication and formation of the joint venture, the fair market value of the business has increased, then it would no longer be appropriate to sell units to physician investors at the initial offering price if this price is less than the then-current fair market value of the business.

On the other hand, a joint venture with a limited operating history has significantly higher risks than an existing business with stable, continuing operations, and there is less certainty that a startup business will be able to meet projected cash flow levels. When there is no operating history upon which to base cash flow projections, valuators may be relying principally on their analysis of management's preliminary projections for future cash flows. Management's future cash flow projections, in an attempt to be more accurate, may incorporate an analysis of procedures expected to be performed by physician owners and other physicians in the community. This analysis might be particularly relevant in the context of surgery centers, where the anti-kickback statute safe harbor affirmatively requires that physician owners perform at least one-third of their procedures in the surgery center. To avoid attributing value to anticipated referrals from physician owners, the valuation of a business with a limited operating history should avoid ascribing certainty to any referrals from physician investors. Thus, a discounted cash flow analysis should include an appropriate discount rate to reflect, among the many other business risks, that physician owners are not required to make referrals to the facility (except to the extent to meet regulatory requirements under the anti-kickback statute safe harbor for surgery centers) and that there can be no assurance that the business will meet its cash flow projections.

Chapter 4

Bradford Regional Medical Center: Lessons for the Inexperienced

By Mark O. Dietrich, CPA/ABV

The federal whistleblower or qui tam law allows a private citizen (plaintiff) to bring a civil action[1] on behalf of the government against an alleged violator seeking damages, of which the qui tam plaintiff (or relator) may claim 15% to 35% of the total damages ultimately paid. The government may choose to join in the action against the alleged violator, bringing the enormous prosecutorial clout of the federal government to bear against the defendant. Thus, there are significant financial incentives to bring a qui tam action. This November 2010 case involved a whistleblower on whose behalf the government had intervened.

The facts of the case include the sublease of a nuclear medicine camera[2] by two physicians on the Bradford Regional Medical Center (BRMC) staff who were threatened with loss of hospital admitting privileges for competing with BRMC in the provision of nuclear medicine scans. Nuclear medicine scans represent the highest dollar cost to the Medicare Part B program performed by cardiologists. More importantly in the context of this guide, a valuation of a "noncompete" prepared by a CPA (referred to as CPA or [name] Redacted) is at the center of the case.

The background as summarized by the court is as follows:

1 There is a segment of the litigation bar that specializes in these cases.
2 SPECT, or single photon emission computed tomography, is the technical term. The fixed units look like a small CT or MRI unit, while the mobile units have a chair in which the patient sits and the camera rotates around that chair, generating an image of the heart.

> Before entering into a final sublease, BRMC had a fair market value assessment prepared by an accountant, Redacted. (Leonhardt[3] Dep. at 54; BRMC 30(b)(6) Dep. at 146-148.) BRMC sought this report to determine whether BRMC was paying fair market value under the proposed sublease arrangement. (Leonhardt Dep. at 54-55; BRMC 30(b)(6) Dep. at 148-149.) In September 2003, the board of BRMC received Mr. Redacted's report. The report concluded that the amounts to be paid pursuant to the proposed sublease were reasonable. (BRMC 30(b)(6) Dep. Appx., at 146-149.)
>
> In performing his fair market value analysis, Mr. Redacted compared the revenues BRMC expected to generate with the sublease in place to the revenues BRMC expected to receive without the sublease in place. (Report of Redacted, C.P.A.; Leonhardt Dep. at 55-56.) The projections were based on the expectation that V&S would refer such business to the hospital if the sublease arrangement was approved. (Id.) According to defendants, the basis of Mr. Redacted's report was what benefits BRMC would have lost had it terminated the medical staff appointment and clinical privileges of Drs. Vaccaro and Saleh pursuant to BRMC's policy. BRMC advised Drs. Vaccaro and Saleh that its valuation expert indicated that he could support the fair market value of the sublease, however neither Vaccaro nor Saleh received or reviewed a copy of Mr. Redacted's written valuation.

In denying, in part, both parties' cross-motions for summary judgment, the court concluded:

> Again, the record evidence is not strongly in favor of defendants [BRMC, et al.] as it tends to show that defendants entered into the equipment sublease fully aware that the arrangement, which had at its core a noncompete payment roughly equal to the referral business BRMC would gain from the doctors and the business V&S would lose from abandoning its own camera, may not be permitted under the Stark Act and Anti-Kickback Act. However, we are unable to conclude as a matter of law that defendants acted "knowingly" for purposes of the False Claims Act.
>
> For the foregoing reasons, we will deny defendants' motions for summary judgment and grant in part and deny in part relator's motion for summary judgment.[4]

As those of us trained in tax law[5] learn, court decisions are case-fact specific. The valuation report in this case was obtained through the federal court system's PACER service[6] since it was part of the public record. A review of that report indicates that it is not the typical valuation one would expect to see in a circumstance such as this; for example, the report states that the fair market value was tested against Section 482 of the Internal Revenue Code. As such, fewer risks might have been perceived from an initial reading

3 The hospital's CEO.
4 docs.justia.com/cases/federal/district-courts/pennsylvania/pawdce/1:2004cv00186/3406/145/
5 The author has a Masters in Taxation degree.
6 Thank you to Kathie Wilson, CPA/CVA one of the guide's contributing authors.

of the court's decision in those circumstances where the parties are relying upon the fair market value exception based upon an appropriately prepared report. At the same time, even a good report is never an absolute defense against an allegation under the Stark law or anti-kickback statute. Further, it is clear that in the court's view, factors cited in the valuation report were consistent with the purchase of referrals, e.g., "these statements, however, do not counter the record evidence that the analysis in the [CPA valuation] report was based on the assumption that the physicians would likely refer this business to the hospital" and that Mr. Leonhardt's summary presentation showed an expected profit for BRMC from entering into the lease agreement that was based on receiving business from V&S."

This suggests the court believed that the valuation had as an underlying assumption that all the nuclear scans done in the physicians' office would be referred post-transaction to the acquiring hospital. This, in turn, might indicate strategic value rather than fair market value, depending on how the valuation was performed. Given the requirement of the Stark regulations defining the modifications to fair market value, a compliant fair market value analysis would have considered the risk of the hospital (and other potential competitors) *not* receiving all of the referrals, to wit:

420 CFR 411.351 states: "Fair market value means the value in arm's-length transactions consistent with general market value. 'General market value' means the price that an asset would bring as the result of bona fide bargaining between well-informed buyers and sellers *who are not otherwise in a position to generate business for the other party.*" [Emphasis added]

And from Stark II-Phase 2: "Moreover, the definition of 'fair market value' in the statute and regulation is qualified in ways that do not necessarily comport with the usage of the term in standard valuation techniques and methodologies. For example, the methodology must exclude valuations where the parties to the transactions are at arm's length but in a position to refer to one another. In addition, the definition itself differs depending on the type of transaction: Leases or rentals of space and equipment cannot take into account the intended use of the rented item, and *in cases where the lessor is in a position to refer to the lessee, the valuation cannot be adjusted or reflect the value of proximity or convenience to the lessor.*" [Emphasis added]

Thus the cash flow analysis and the discount rate developed in connection with such a valuation would have to reflect something other than the actual relationship between purchaser and seller. The court clearly believed that the actual relationship was the basis for the valuation. And, it is clear from the court's opinion that the modifications to fair market value spelled out in the above two quotes from the Stark regulations were not taken into account.

The OIG's office has long expressed concern with the sale of ancillary designated health services ancillaries (DHS) owned by physicians to a hospital or other buyer when the DHS will remain in the selling physician's office and continue to be used by the physicians. Although it involved a surgery center, similar issues in the OIG's perspective can be seen in Advisory Opinion No. 07-05. [7]

The following section illuminates key issues in the case and then what fair market value in a regulatory context (should) mean to an appraiser and how the fundamental measure of an appropriate discount rate and measure of cash flows *should* avoid much of the inherent issue of "valuing referrals."[8]

The quotation below is one of the most damning elements of the fact pattern. Although the court does not mention it, fair market value includes a criterion that neither party is under duress.

> Drs. Vaccaro and Saleh had a history of referring patients to BRMC for nuclear imaging until they invested in their own General Electric nuclear camera. With their own camera, they no longer needed to refer patients to BRMC for imaging. BRMC threatened to revoke the doctors' hospital privileges, which led to lengthy negotiations.

Equally as problematic are the contents of the valuation report:

> Mr. [CPA] explained that his table is "based on the assumption that the physicians would likely refer this business to the hospital in the absence of a financial interest in their own facilities or services, although they are not required to do so by virtue of any of the covenants contained in the agreements or otherwise."
>
> Therefore, the report itself indicates that the analysis of whether the noncompetition agreement represents a fair market value is based, in part, on anticipated referrals from the doctors. BRMC affirmed that the report evaluated expected revenues based on the assumption that defendants would likely refer the business to BRMC.

Here is additional material along the same lines taken from the deposition of the hospital CEO and the portion of the court's opinion that followed the excerpt:

> Q. It's fair to say that the purpose of the noncompete agreement was to protect that revenue stream [referrals from Dr. Saleh and Dr. Vaccaro].

7 As I and other observers noted at the time, this advisory seemed to misconstrue fair market value, while emphasizing the focus on referrals. oig.hhs.gov/fraud/docs/advisoryopinions/2007/AdvOpn07-05C.pdf.

8 Note: Chapter 7 of the *BVR/AHLA Guide to Healthcare Valuation*, "The Anti-Kickback Statute and Stark Law," looks at many of the issues discussed in this case, including noncompete agreements, and Chapters 18 and 19 look at the mechanics of actually valuing a noncompete.

> A. The purpose of the noncompete, from my point of view, was to make sure that Drs. Vaccaro and Saleh didn't have a financial incentive to refer away from the hospital.
>
> Q. Because if they didn't have a financial incentive to refer away, they would refer it to you?
>
> A. We could hope that they would, yes.
>
> Q. You did more than hope. You expected they would refer to you?
>
> A. Expected they would refer a good bit of it to us, yeah.
>
> A compensation arrangement does not take into account the volume or value of referrals or other business generated between the parties if the compensation is fixed in advance and will result in fair market value compensation, and the compensation does not vary over the term of the arrangement in any manner that takes into account referrals or other business generated.
>
> While the value agreed upon by parties who are in a position to refer business to each other and who take into account anticipated referrals will be a fair value as between the parties, such an arrangement is not fair market value under the Stark Act. Here, the compensation arrangement between the parties is greater than what would be paid in the absence of the ability of Dr. Saleh and Dr. Vaccaro to provide referrals for BRMC's nuclear camera business.

As indicated above, the court concluded that the defendant hospital, et al., by their plain statements, considered the volume or value of referrals. Notwithstanding that, the court went on to say that even if that had not been the case, the defendants could not rely upon the fair market value exception because the *valuation itself* expressly considered referrals. Apparently key to this conclusion was the fact that the lease of the nuclear camera approximated $30,000 per month, of which nearly 80% was for a noncompete agreement. Further, a net present value analysis of the cost of the noncompete was compared to the revenues from inpatient and outpatient services the hospital expected to derive from the acquisition of the nuclear medicine camera.

Now, it would be foolhardy to suggest that a different valuation model might have caused the court to rule differently. However, assume for the sake of argument that none of the defendants or the valuation report was on record as stating that they considered referrals when negotiating or valuing the arrangements. What type of assumptions might an appraiser have put into a valuation model that would not take into account the volume of value of referrals from the seller to the buyer to conform to the requirement that "'general market value' means the price that an asset would bring as the result of bona fide bargaining between well-informed buyers and sellers *who are not otherwise in a position to generate business for the other party*" and "the definition itself differs depending on the type of transaction: Leases or rentals of space and equipment cannot take into account the intended use of the rented item, and *in cases where the lessor is in a position to refer to the lessee, the valuation cannot be adjusted or reflect the value of proximity or convenience to the lessor*." [Emphasis added]

Before going to the Stark modifications of fair market value, it is important to note that the use of an appropriate equity discount rate and weighted average cost of capital are designed to account for the investment risk inherent in owning a business. One of the many differences between fair market value and strategic, investment value, or value to the [existing] owner is the use of a market-based rate of return to discount future cash flows to present value. There is no discussion in the case about this at all. A value to the owner standard in the instant case might have resulted from the use of a risk-free rate, which in turn would have resulted in a much higher value than if a market-based rate of return[9] were utilized. At least from the standpoint of an appraiser undertaking an exercise of determining fair market value, the very use of a market-based rate of return will eliminate a significant portion of the value of referrals from the existing owners, because a hypothetical seller or buyer is substituted through the discount rate for the actual seller or buyer. The next part of the discussion focuses on the adjustment to the cash flows subject to discounting necessary to move from a value to the owner standard to a fair market standard that from an appraisal standpoint, does not consider referrals.

The subject nuclear medicine camera had been and remained post-transaction in the offices of the selling physicians for several years (through December 2006, about three years). During time, of course, most of the cases would come from the two selling physicians. It is not clear whether before or after the transaction, any patients came from other physicians on the hospital staff, though that would clearly be relevant to the determination of fair market value as well as to the hindsight required in the prosecution of the litigation. To meet the requirement that "the valuation cannot be adjusted or reflect the value of proximity or convenience to the lessor," an appraisal of a nuclear medicine camera lease would merely look to what the rent on the piece of equipment might be—and that would already have been clear from the GE lease, which the hospital assumed.

An appraiser valuing a nuclear medicine business—which is where a noncompete would become relevant—as opposed to simply a lease would have to base volume assumptions and resultant cash flows on what a freestanding nuclear camera owned, say, by an independent nonphysician vendor would expect to receive in referrals from the medical community assuming that the referring physicians had no financial interest in the

9 The report in this case actually used an 18% discount rate.

business. In a rural market such as that of BRMC, it is likely that before the physicians in the case acquired their nuclear camera, all of those cases had gone to the hospital and there was no competing provider. This would make the task challenging, indeed, but one would think the assumption would be two market competitors, the hospital and the independent vendor, and how that independent vendor might fare against the hospital— and not giving effect to the hospital's threat to revoke the staff privileges of physicians who did not refer to it.

A noncompete is part of the overall value of a business and represents the business that would be lost if the seller competed post-transaction, adjusted for the possibility that if allowed to compete, the seller would, in fact, do so, with the resultant cash flows discounted to present value at the discount rate used to determine the value of the business. This is referred to as the "with [the value with the noncompete in place] and without [the value without the noncompete in place] method." A noncompete is not in addition to the value of the business. In the instant case, there appears from the record to be confusion between the value of a lease, the value of a noncompete, and the value of a nuclear medicine business, among other things. Where that confusion originated is not clear.

One possible interpretation of the impact of the decision is that in circumstances such as this, the price paid for an operating business should be allocated to various component assets including the value of a noncompete to identify that portion of the value that is attributable to the sellers—assuming that noncompete value is based solely upon the sellers' DHS referrals. Such an approach would require some thinking about the traditional model of noncompete valuation. The two steps discussed above— an appropriate return to a hypothetical; buyer or seller and identifying cash flows available to a market participant not in a position to refer— need first to be considered in the noncompete analysis. Then, the appraiser also has to ask himself or herself how much business the buyer would lose if the sellers competed and what the likelihood of that competition is.

The larger question for the valuation community would seem to be whether an entire practice that owns DHS can be purchased *with* the valuation including the cash flows from DHS *and* the physicians being employed post-transaction by the purchaser. As suggested earlier, it has been clear to many for some time that purchasing DHS separately from a purchase of an entire practice and leaving the DHS physically present in the still independent practice is problematic from the government's standpoint.

It seems as well that a hospital buyer should be first guided not only by qualified legal counsel, but also by an opinion of fair market value from an appraiser with the requisite expertise to apply the regulatory standard to a valuation engagement *before* the hospital embarks on discussing price with a physician-seller in a position to refer DHS. This is a little different from retaining a neutral, subject to a confidentiality agreement, to evaluate financial terms in provider integration transactions subject to antitrust review before determining whether a memorandum of understanding is appropriate to move forward. Separately, the lack of statutory authority for the OIG to opine on fair market value is problematic and warrants extreme caution. Finally, threatening physicians in a position to refer DHS with loss of staff privileges if they compete is not a good idea.

Chapter 5

Assessing Intangible Value in a Physician Practice Acquisition

By Gregory D. Anderson, CPA/ABV, CVA; Carol W. Carden, CPA/ABV, ASA, CFE; Mark O. Dietrich, CPA/ABV; J. Gregory Endicott, CPA/ABV, ASA, MBA; W. James Lloyd, CPA/ABV, ASA, CBA, CFE; Todd J. Sorenson, MBA, AVA; Reed Tinsley, CPA, CVA, CFP, CHBC; and Kathie L. Wilson, CPA, CVA

Due in large part to concerns over healthcare reform and declining reimbursement rates, physicians are increasingly looking for opportunities to sell their practices to hospitals and work as employees. Similarly, hospital systems are interested in acquiring key practices to solidify or expand their provider networks. These transactions are clearly subject to the regulatory restrictions of commercial reasonableness and fair market value imposed by the Stark law[1] and the anti-kickback statute (AKS),[2] as well as the Internal Revenue Code Section 501(c) (3) regulations if the hospital is a not-for-profit entity. Many practices have very low or sometimes negative projected post-transaction earnings after adjusting for the physician's anticipated post-transaction compensation. Accordingly, an income approach valuation methodology, such as the discounted cash flow (DCF) method, will generally result in zero or a very low value for the practice. In such cases, the cost approach will be utilized instead. However, the problem arises when the cost approach results in substantial values being attributed to intangible assets,[3] such as physician workforce, that are not supported by an appropriate level of net cash flow needed to provide an economic return to the hypothetical buyer.

1 42 U.S.C. Sec. 1395nn.

2 42 U.S.C. Sec. 1320a-7b.

3 There are certain specifically identifiable assets (such as a certificate of need or electronic medical record systems) that may have value even in the absence of DCF value to the existing owner.

This chapter addresses the appropriateness of assigning substantial value to intangible assets, such as physician workforce, under the fair market value standard and going-concern premise of value, without such amounts being appropriately supported by net cash flow under the income approach.

The chapter first defines the key terms used and describes typical intangible assets, then looks at the theoretical underpinning of the cost approach as described in accepted valuation texts and court cases, then examines, critiques, and ultimately dismisses the sole use of the cost approach to value physician workforce as both a violation of professional standards and the regulatory structure for fair market value.

Key Concepts and Definitions

The following key concepts and definitions are important for understanding the analysis and conclusions expressed in this chapter.

Commercial reasonableness: Transactions between hospitals and physicians with the ability to refer designated health services (DHS) must be commercially reasonable. The Stark regulations explain commercial reasonableness as: "An arrangement will be considered commercially reasonable, in the absence of referrals, if the arrangement would make commercial sense if entered into by a reasonable entity of similar type and size and a reasonable physician of similar scope and specialty, even if there were no potential designated health services referrals."[4]

Accordingly, the commercial reasonableness requirement means the transaction must make good business sense *without* the potential of future referrals from either party.

Fair market value: The most widely used definition of fair market value is: "the price at which property or service would change hands between a willing buyer and a willing seller, neither being under a compulsion to buy or sell and both having reasonable knowledge of the relevant facts."[5]

The Stark regulations define fair market value similarly as "the value in arm's-length transactions, consistent with the general market value," and general market value is defined as "the price that an asset would bring as the result of bona fide bargaining between well-informed buyers and sellers who are not otherwise in a position to generate business for the other party or compensation that would be included in a service agreement as the result of bona fide bargaining between well-informed parties to the agreement who are not otherwise in a position to generate business for the other party on the date of the acquisition of the asset or at the time of the service agreement."[6]

4 69 *Fed. Reg.* 16093 (March 26, 2004).
5 Estate Tax Reg. 20.2031.1-1(b); Revenue Ruling 59-60, 1959-1, C.B. 237.
6 420 CFR 411.351. See also Section 1877(h)(3) of the Social Security Act.

Strategic value: In contrast to fair market value, strategic value is the value to a particular buyer rather than to a hypothetical buyer. There are a variety of strategic considerations that a specific buyer may employ in determining strategic value, some of which would likely not violate the Stark law and others of which almost certainly would. For example, a tax-exempt hospital would have access to tax-exempt bonds to acquire a practice, providing a low cost of capital and a correspondingly higher multiple of value. It would also not pay any income tax on income from the practice if the transaction were properly structured resulting in a higher cash flow and strategic value. Although they do not violate the Stark law, these two items likely violate the anti-inurement rules. When compared to a hypothetical nonhospital buyer, a hospital obtains various inpatient referrals from a physician practice, of course, but consideration of these referrals directly or indirectly is prohibited.

Income approach valuation methodology: The income approach is a general way of determining an indication of value based on the future income (benefits) expected to be generated by the asset. This approach is based on the fundamental valuation principle that an asset's worth is directly related to the present value of the future benefits of ownership. The most common income approach methodology is the DCF method, which discounts anticipated future net cash flow to present value by using a discount rate that reflects the time value of money and the risk associated with the asset.

The income approach is generally used to value operating companies that produce positive cash flow under the going concern premise of value.

Cost approach valuation methodology: The asset approach, which is also commonly referred to as the cost approach,[7] is a general way of determining an indication of value based on the entity's underlying assets and liabilities. This approach is based on the theory that an asset's worth is directly related to the amount that would be required to reproduce or replace it. The cost approach generally results in an upper limit of value for assets that can be easily replaced or reproduced, since no prudent investor would pay more for an asset than the cost to create a comparable one. Similarly, no prudent investor would pay to create an asset that would not generate an income return under the regulatory structure commensurate with the outlay that is allowed.

Intangible asset: Intangible assets are nonphysical assets, such as trademarks, patents, securities, contracts, and goodwill that have rights and provide economic benefits to the owner.[8]

7 The terms are used interchangeably.
8 Hitchner, James R., *Financial Valuation Applications and Models*, John Wiley & Sons Inc., 2003, p. 13.

Goodwill: Goodwill is a type of intangible asset that is related to the entity's name, reputation, customer loyalty, and similar factors not separately identified.[9] Assembled workforce is generally considered to be an integral part of goodwill and not identifiable as a separate asset.[10]

Typical Physician Practice Assets—Least Controversial to Most Controversial

- Furniture and equipment
- Accounts receivable
- Leasehold improvements
- Trade name
- Telephone numbers
- Patient charts
- Nonphysician workforce
- Physician workforce

The Context for Valuing Physician Workforce

While the proper premises of value to apply may be debated, there is little argument that tangible assets such as furniture and equipment and accounts receivable have some value in this context. Reasonable minds may differ on the proper treatment or value of intangible assets such as trade name and telephone numbers—intangible assets that may often be differentiated because they possess the potential for being both legally protectable and separately marketable.

Other intangible assets or economic phenomena that may not meet the definition of an intangible asset are of particular concern as you move further along in the list. Some appraisers make the mistake of not only assigning value to these items in the absence of cash flows, but also in attaching value to something that may not be an asset in the first place. In their book, *Valuing Intangible Assets,* Robert Reilly and Robert Schweihs note that, for an intangible asset to exist from a valuation perspective, it must include the following:

1. It should be subject to specific identification and recognizable description.

2. It should be subject to legal existence and protection.

9 Ibid.

10 See Statement of Financial Accounting Standards No. 164, Not-for-Profit Entities: Mergers and Acquisitions, paragraph A54; the IRS may recognize assembled workforce as a separate intangible when there is a DCF value to support it.

3. It should be subject to the right of private ownership, and the private ownership should be legally transferable.

4. There should be some tangible evidence or manifestation of the existence of the intangible asset (e.g., a contract, a license, a registration document, a computer diskette, a listing of customers, a set of financial statements, etc.).

5. It should have been created or have come into existence at an identifiable time or as the result of an identifiable event.

6. It should be subject to being destroyed or to a termination of existence at an identifiable time or as the result of an identifiable event.[11]

It is in this area that we see some valuations incorrectly assign value to phenomena such as a workforce in place when no legal right exists, such as in the case of a physician without an employment agreement or the nonphysician workforce of a physician practice in an at-will employment state.

The disparity of treatment and the rather large magnitude in associated value, however, approaches darker shades of gray as you approach the physician workforce in place. Our attempt here is not to minimize the need to properly treat each of the tangible and intangible asset classes, but the most controversial asset in this context also happens to be the item that some appraisers are attaching the greatest magnitude of value to—the physician workforce.

When practice acquisition valuations based on the cost approach imply intangible value attributable to physician workforce in the observed range of $50,000 to more than $400,000, there is cause for concern over the validity of the valuation analysis and the intentions of the parties.

Example

The argument for the attachment of significant value to the physician workforce in place arises out of a legitimate business consideration for hospitals in some scenarios. The scenario goes something like this:

Hospital X chief executive officer (CEO) in a two-hospital town relies almost exclusively on Heart Group, the only cardiology group of substance in the area, to generate volume (i.e., referrals) for Hospital X's cardiology line of business. Heart Group currently splits business between Hospital X and Hospital Y. Heart Group informs both Hospital X and Hospital Y that it wants to entertain the sale of its practice and employment. Faced with

11 *Valuing Intangible Assets.* Reilly, Robert F. and Schweihs, Robert P. McGraw-Hill (New York, 1999), p. 5.

the potential loss of the cardiologists that generate all of the volumes in the cardiology lines of business at his hospital, Hospital X CEO argues that if he doesn't buy Heart Group, he'll have to recruit and employ physicians to practice at Hospital X—absorbing recruiting costs and significant losses in the process. To further complicate the fact pattern, Hospital Y has retained a valuation firm that values these costs to re-create the physician workforce at $300,000 per physician despite that firm's analysis that there will be little to no cash flow from the cardiology practice after paying the cardiologists' salaries. Hospital X CEO is really left with no choice; he or she feels she or she must at least match Hospital Y's offer.

As is explained in more detail below, the sole reliance on the cost approach to value intangible assets is generally inappropriate. Whether the intangible assets are related to payments for physician workforce, noncompete agreements, or compensation, they must be viewed in the context of an even exchange between the parties with no benefit, *directly or indirectly,* ascribed to referrals. In the absence of an expectation of income from the acquired physician practice, the only source of income necessary to meet the fair market value standard is from future referrals associated with that practice.

A Review of the Significant Issues

Among the many problems with relying solely on the cost approach to value intangible assets related to an ongoing business enterprise is that it is inconsistent with valuation theory and the valuation guidance offered by the Stark regulations. While not necessarily exhaustive, the following is a list of the significant issues that would all need to be resolved favorably to attach significant value to the physician workforce in place.

1. Assuming a hospital can be considered the typical or likely buyer is inconsistent with both the classical and regulatory definitions of fair market value.

One argument often cited as a reason for hospitals paying for a physician workforce is the avoidance of costs related to recruiting and employing such physicians to meet their community need. The momentum of many of the concepts associated with healthcare reform such as bundled payments and accountable care organizations (ACOs) generates additional support for the business case for hospital employment of physicians. Given that hospitals will likely need to employ physicians and provided there are strong contractual relationships in place to secure it, there is little question or argument that securing a physician workforce in place brings *strategic value* (as distinguished earlier herein from fair market value) to a hospital in that it allows a hospital to forego the costs associated with recruiting and ramping up a physician workforce. However, this is inconsistent with both the classical and regulatory definitions of fair market value in the context of the acquisition of the assets of a physician practice since those assets must be shown to generate income and that income must not be proscribed by applicable regulations. For business appraisals performed in the context of hospitals purchasing physician practices, healthcare regulations and statutes require any transaction to occur at *fair market value (FMV).*

As stated earlier, FMV is classically defined as the price at which an asset would exchange between a willing buyer and a willing seller, neither being under compulsion to buy or sell, each having reasonable knowledge of all relevant facts, and with equity to both. Based on the guidelines established by the Stark II regulations, we typically expand our definition of FMV to encompass general market value (GMV), which is the price that an asset would bring as the result of bona fide bargaining between well-informed buyers and sellers who are not otherwise in a position to generate business for the other party or the compensation that would be included in a service agreement as the result of bona fide bargaining between well-informed parties to the agreement who are not otherwise in a position to generate business for the other party, on the date of acquisition of the asset or at the time of the service agreement (42 C.F.R. 411.351) and where the compensation has not been determined in any manner that takes into account the volume or value of anticipated or actual referrals and where the arrangement would be commercially reasonable even if no referrals were made to the employer (42 C.F.R. 411.351 and 42 C.F.R. 411.357(c)).

Given the definition of fair market value, the practice of simply assuming that a hospital is avoiding a significant cost by simply paying for a physician workforce or that a hospital should be considered the most likely buyer of the physician practice appears to be somewhat inconsistent with the classical definition of FMV in that there is some compulsion for hospitals to buy physician practices. Even if one is somehow able to get comfortable with being consistent with the classical definition of FMV, the assumption that a hospital is the only typical or likely buyer of a physician practice appears to be even more directly inconsistent with the further restrictions under Stark II that the assumed buyer not be in a position to benefit from the business generated by the seller.

2. Replication cost as a valuation methodology has significant weaknesses and its use to value the physician workforce is inconsistent with all premises of value other than going concern.

A book looked upon as an authoritative text in the valuation profession is *Valuing a Business: The Analysis and Appraisal of Closely Held Businesses.*[12] Chapter 6 provides guidance to appraisers in conducting the cost approach. According to the authors,

12 *Valuing a Business: The Analysis and Appraisal of Closely Held Businesses,* Shannon P. Pratt, 4th Edition.

conducting the cost approach requires the appraiser to not only choose the proper standard of value, but also to choose the proper premise of value. The four premises of value delineated include:

- Value in continued use as part of a going concern;
- Value in place as part of a mass assemblage of assets;
- Value in exchange, as part of an orderly disposition; and
- Value in exchange, as part of a forced liquidation.

Based on generally accepted interpretations of the guidance provided by this authoritative text, the only of the four premises of value above that would ultimately result in any significant value for the physician workforce in place is value in continued use as part of a going concern. According to the authors, "Under this premise, it is assumed that the subject assets are sold as a mass assemblage and as part of an *income producing* (emphasis added) business enterprise."[13] The assumption that the practice is income-producing is in complete contradiction to the reasoning used to rely exclusively on the cost approach. As previously discussed, relying exclusively on the cost approach is a function of the fact that considering the proposed compensation arrangement with the physicians, there is either no income or at least not enough income to justify any value over and above the value of the tangible assets.

The weaknesses of the cost approach in differentiating what has value and what does not have value are not limited to physician workforce. Michael Crain, CPA/ABV, ASA, CFA, a well-known and highly regarded member of the appraisal community, observes:

"Some criticize the cost approach by arguing that the evidence of a relationship between cost and price is weak, and thus, the cost approach is not a reliable way to estimate the value of something. One example of weak relationships is the decline in real estate prices in the late 2000s. It is conceivable that the costs of building some homes were higher than their market prices. Further, these downward price movements were weakly correlated with the costs of building a home. *A closely related argument is that the cost approach is overly simplistic and can violate the first principle of valuation that says the value of something is the expected future benefits expected from it, discounted to the present. This principle links value to future returns, whereas the cost approach has strictly a historical perspective."* (Emphasis added)

"Another argument criticizing the cost approach is that it assumes that if a firm develops something, it is valuable. We know from theory and observation that firm managers

13 Ibid., Chapter 6, page 176.

use trial and error in their operations. Simply put, some things managers do work and some do not. *The cost approach is unable to distinguish between the costs of successful and unsuccessful efforts*."[14] (Emphasis added)

The 2008 tax court case *Derby*[15] specifically addresses the cost approach issue for tax-exempt hospitals and related entities. Although the valuation in that case was a misuse[16] of the income approach, the principle that FMV constitutes an even exchange between hypothetical buyer and seller is the same.

"The Dutcher appraisal takes no account of the $35,000 'Physician Access Bonus' payable to each SWMG physician over the initial two years of the affiliation. Ignoring these payments when computing distributable earnings that SWMG would generate results in a overstatement of those earnings and a corresponding overstatement of the value of SWMG's intangible assets (since, under Mr. Dutcher's analysis, intangible asset value equals present value of future distributable earnings, less tangible assets and implied working capital)."

The point here, of course, is not limited to the physician access bonus. Any transaction involving the purchase of a medical practice must consider all the elements of that transfer in determining whether the transaction meets the FMV standard, as modified by the Stark law. This includes post-transaction compensation in addition to the purchase price and contractual terms.

"Petitioners have not shown that the value of what they transferred to SMF exceeded the value of the benefits they received in return. As noted above, those benefits included, in the first instance, employment that was compensated with shares of revenue (47% to 57.75%) that significantly exceeded the median share of revenue (45.18%) devoted to physician compensation in petitioners' specialties; a $35,000 'physician access bonus' for each SWMG physician, including petitioners; an absence of restrictions on establishing a competing medical practice in the event of cessation of employment with SMF; and greater economic security in the managed care environment."

3. Financial reporting, court cases, and other guidance point to *allocating* value to workforce in place *not* separately valuing it.

Similarly, it should be noted that while using replication costs to estimate the value of the workforce in place is widely accepted in valuation texts and other sources of guidance when allocating value, it is not necessarily sanctioned as proper for assigning

14 Michael A. Crain, "Study Guide, Business Valuation for Forensic Accountants" (working paper, School of Accounting, Florida Atlantic University, 2010) used with permission.
15 T.C. Memo. 2008-45.
16 Given the court's detailed rejection of the assumptions utilized.

value in the cost approach. Nowhere is this more clear than in the application of the Financial Accounting Standard Board's Statements on Financial Accounting Standards (SFAS). Citing SFAS 141, Valuation for Financial Reporting notes that "SFAS 141 specifically prohibits the recognition of assembled workforce as an intangible asset apart from goodwill." (Michael J. Mard, 2002). The Internal Revenue Service (IRS) has also offered several pieces of guidance regarding the valuation of physician practices. One of the often referenced pieces of guidance used for valuation of physician practices is *Valuing Physician Practices* (Charles F. Kaiser, 1996). It should be noted that while this article discusses at length the value of various tangible and intangible assets such as equipment, trade name, patient charts and workforce in place utilizing cost to re-create in an the cost approach, the context is clearly one *of allocating the value obtained from the income approach* (DCF method) and not one of using the cost approach in isolation.

4. Ability to terminate without cause may limit ability to protect value.

In the previous phase of physician practice transactions, many of the employment agreements included terms of five years or more without the ability for either party to terminate without cause. In addition, many of the employment agreements included trailing covenants not to compete that combined with inability to terminate without cause, made it not only virtually impossible for either party to terminate the agreement during the initial term, but also extremely difficult for the physicians to remain in a community following the initial term, absent employment with the hospital. One feature in the current phase of physician practice transactions that distinguishes it from the previous phase is that in many cases, the employment agreements permit either party to terminate the employment agreement without cause with only 90 to 180 days' notice, *with no restrictions on future competition*. This is certainly not always the case. However, if the subject employment agreements include the ability to terminate without cause and permit a physician to remain in the community, the potential inability to legally protect the physician workforce beyond the rolling 90-to-180-day virtual term of the employment agreements should be considered.

The tax court case *Derby* specifically addresses this issue for tax-exempt hospitals and related entities. Failure to follow these principles raises the specter of the intermediate sanctions provisions and anti-inurement provisions of the Internal Revenue Code, particularly with the post-reform emphasis on disclosure in Form 990—and the public access to those forms, including by potential qui tam plaintiffs and their attorneys.

> There is no adjustment for the fact that the SWMG physicians were not required to execute noncompete agreements. Mr. Dutcher treated each SWMG physician as transferring an allocable share of SWMG's intangibles, including goodwill, which was not treated as diminished in any way by the physicians' not having executed noncompete

> agreements with respect to SWMG or SMF. However, in *Norwalk v. Commissioner*, T.C. Memo. 1998-279, we found that there is no transferable or salable goodwill where a company's business depends on its employees' personal relationships with clients and the employees have not provided covenants not to compete.... *We also believe that, under the willing buyer-willing seller standard of fair market value enunciated in Rev. Proc. 59-60, 1959-1 C.B. 237, to which Mr. Dutcher purportedly adhered, a willing buyer of SWMG on the transaction date would have insisted on a significant discount with respect to the value of the entity's intangible assets*, precisely on account of the absence of noncompete agreements from the SWMG physicians. Indeed, the SWMG physicians not only did not execute noncompete agreements, but they also had the benefit of the 'free to compete' provision in the PSA that facilitated their reclaiming their patients in the event they decided to cease working for SWMG/SMF. Mr. Dutcher's failure to account for the risk to his estimated five-year stream of earnings posed by SWMG physicians' departing with their patients is contrary to well-established valuation principles and common sense and results in an inflated value for the SWMG physicians' goodwill. (Emphasis added)
>
> ... and (5) rather than a noncompete agreement, the 'free to compete' provision, which secured for each petitioner the express right, upon his or her termination of employment with SWMG/SMF, to have his or her patients as of the date of affiliation with SMF notified of the departure and given the option of having the patient's medical records transferred to the departing physician. In addition, when petitioners' circumstances before the transaction are considered, a second tier of benefits they secured in the transaction with SMF becomes apparent. First, petitioners solved their core economic problem arising from the advent of managed care; namely, the risk of loss from having patients requiring extraordinary care. After the transaction, by virtue of the minimum compensation guaranties, this risk was largely transferred to SMF, which could better manage it given SMF's greater patient population and resources. Second, as a result of their affiliation with a relatively large health care organization, petitioners secured the benefits of greater leverage in negotiating contracts with HMOs and greater efficiencies in providing care, with any resulting enhancement in revenues inuring to their benefit by virtue of SWMG's compensation being determined as a percentage of net revenues. In sum, by transferring their practices to SMF in the transaction at issue, petitioners ensured for themselves the continued ability to maintain or improve their accustomed level of earnings from the practice of medicine—something they had concluded was not likely to be possible had they continued to maintain solo or small group practices.

The example described earlier of a hospital relying upon a single heart group for admissions parallels to a large extent the recent qui tam case *Bradford Regional Medical Center* in which the Federal District Court for Western Pennsylvania granted summary judgment to the qui tam plaintiffs on violations of the Stark law. That case involved the "lease" of a Nuclear Medicine Camera from two internists who were responsible for a significant share of the hospital's high-tech imaging and inpatient and outpatient referrals. There, the hospital was confronted with the loss of the nuclear medicine scans that severely restricted its ability to recruit a cardiologist. Further risk apparently existed with respect to the possibility that the physicians might acquire their own MR or CT scanner, both of which have cardiac applications.

Part of the court's analysis was that the record indicated that the defendant hospital had clearly considered the volume and value of referrals in the price paid for the nuclear medicine camera sublease, *which price included a noncompete agreement.* As such, the valuation prepared in connection with that sublease was irrelevant, since the FMV exception could only be used if the sublease did not consider referrals in the first instance. Further, the valuation also discussed loss of referrals, and there the definition of FMV was not consistent with the modifications of the Stark law.

5. Lack of any evidence indicating hospitals could sell physician workforce back for any significant value.

Another key to valuing physician practices is consistent treatment of controversial items, regardless of which party is on the buyer side and which is on the seller side. We believe collectively performing hundreds of valuations for both potential purchases from physicians and sales to physicians provides a balanced perspective to approaching these issues. We are not aware of a single instance, even when enforceable employment agreements and covenants exist, that hospitals have successfully sold a physician workforce to the physicians. The accepted method for establishing the value of a noncompete covenant is to use the income approach.

6. Analyses typically include no consideration for physician age and need to amortize the asset.

Like Number 4, another concept that may often be ignored in assigning value to physician workforce is that of inevitability—it is inevitable that eventually the physician workforce must be replenished and the employer will incur the costs associated with recruitment and ramp up. In this sense, any cost to re-create the physician workforce is simply a present value exercise. Ignoring the other five factors or even assuming an appraiser is comfortable with his or her ability to successfully navigate the mine field, this must be considered.

Conclusion

Under the FMV standard of value, there is no basis for exclusive reliance on the cost approach in valuing intangible assets in general and physician workforce in particular when there is no expectation of income from the underlying assets of a going concern. The professional literature of valuation theory that serves as the basis for FMV provides no support. Additionally, the commercial reasonableness requirement under the Stark law that a transaction make sense in the absence of referrals would almost assuredly be violated by paying for physician workforce without such values being adequately supported by cash flows under the income approach. Given that both the economic value and the fair market value of an asset is the present value of expected future benefits of ownership, implicit in the use of the cost approach—and in our view, explicitly assumed—is income from the referrals to be received.

This chapter was originally published as a white paper by HORNE LLP in February 2011. The statements herein represent general principles of valuation. The specific circumstances present in a given engagement may affect the extent of their application.

Chapter 6

Choosing and Using the Right Valuation Methods for Physician Practices

By Mark O. Dietrich, CPA/ABV

The Market in 2011-2012

Healthcare industry transactions are in full swing, rivaling the volume of activity during the 1990s consolidation, although without the presence of significant public company players. The focus on cardiology practices common after the reductions in nuclear medicine's technical component in 2010 have been supplanted by a heavy emphasis on primary care practices as hospitals and integrated providers gear up for Medicare accountable care organizations (ACO) resulting from the reform legislation and the issuance of arguably more favorable final regulations in October 2011. Even if ACO participation proves to be small as many predict, the focus on primary care-oriented and the overall shortage of primary care physicians will drive the market.

Another notable difference between today's market and that of the 1990s is that there is recognition in most quarters, but certainly not all, of the need to carefully tie physician compensation to the forecast used to value the practice. Another is that physician compensation is typically linked to productivity—and increasingly as measured by work RVUs or wRVUs—and not fixed, the latter practice having led to low patient volumes and large operating losses. The importance of focusing on post-transaction compensation was re-emphasized in the 2008 Tax Court case *Derby*, cited in numerous places herein.

The consensus today, including that of many of the contributors to this guide, is that future physician compensation is typically a more significant element of a transaction than is the value of the practice. In many circumstances, hospitals and integrated delivery systems have superior contracts with insurers that in turn permit physicians to receive better compensation for the same amount of work, something published research in a variety of publications supports.[1] Over the course of five years or more, compensation is typically more valuable than sales proceeds to a physician, given the range of valuation multiples. Readers should note that it is not appropriate to value the practice using the buyer's better insurer contracts because that is inconsistent with fair market value although as described in the chapter on fair market compensation, those rate differences have become significant for evaluating post-transaction compensation.

As a final observation, practices with intensive investment in ancillaries are likely to be more valuable, all things being equal. Given the Stark laws restrictions or prohibition on post-transaction compensation with respect to the technical component of ancillary services in different employment and independent contractor settings, there is not the usual tradeoff between future compensation and current value.

Introduction

Simply stated, valuation models require two major components: future cash flows and a discount or capitalization rate. All valuation results are a function of the interaction between these two factors. Once the valuation analyst has gained a sufficient knowledge of the marketplace, regulatory environment, and the subject practice as described elsewhere in this guide, the actual measuring of value can begin.

Other chapters to review in this guide are:

- Healthcare Market Structure and Its Implication for Valuation of Privately Held Provider Entities—An Empirical Analysis
- Stark Law and the Anti-Kickback Statute: Avoiding Valuation of Referrals
- Critical Condition—A Coding Analysis for a Physician Practice Valuation[2]
- Understanding and Using the Technical and Professional Component of Ancillary Revenue When Valuing Medical Practices
- The CPA's Role in M&A Due Diligence Assistance to PPMCs and Private Equity Firms

Many experienced valuation analysts new to healthcare will be familiar and (perhaps) more comfortable with the market approach based upon databases such as those

1 See Chapter 9.
2 In my view, you cannot value a physician practice without doing a coding analysis.

maintained by the IBA or Pratt's Stats. When considering the merged and acquired company method, bear in mind that the historical data available regarding the "acquisition" of practices via management services agreements with physician practice management companies (PPMCs) are generally not relevant.[3] A PPMC transaction is fundamentally different from an outright purchase of the practice and therefore, should not be used for such a valuation without various adjustments, including those to cash-equivalent consideration and compensation. Finally, my experience is that physicians focus on cash returns in the form of additional compensation when they buy practices and regulators expect hospitals to focus on cash returns from within the practice.

This chapter is organized with a discussion of rules of thumb presented first, in the expectation that someone new to medical practice valuation will benefit from a frame of reference when studying the actual methods. Bear in mind that such rules are not methods and merely provide an oft-suspect means of a reality check.

A presentation of a discounted cash flow valuation is beyond the scope of the chapter but considerable detail about the differences in DCFs for physician practices is provided. A discussion of the build-up method for determining discount and capitalization rates then follows.

The chapter explains in detail the use of the excess earnings method and the capitalization of cash flows (CCF). The focus of this chapter is on asset purchases, not stock purchases, since the vast majority of physician practice transactions, aside from buy-ins, are assets only.

The excess earnings method is presented in its traditional physician-to-physician transaction approaches, using *pretax* excess earnings and a discount and capitalization rate applicable to *pretax* earnings for a hypothetical physician buyer.

Insight and Analysis

A notable aspect of valuing a physician practice is the need to get into the detail behind operating expenses for normalization purposes to identify discretionary expenses available to the owner of the practice in lieu of taking taxable compensation. A general ledger is a basic element of a data request—like it or not! Prior to commencing the actual quantitative valuation analysis, I review in detail the normalized operating results and compare them to statistical norms from the Medical Group Management Association (MGMA) or other sources.[4] You need to ask, "How would the practice look if operated

3 This guide's chapter on "The CPA's Role in M&A Due Diligence Assistance to PPMC's and Private Equity Firms" suggests there are limited circumstances such as anesthesia and pathology where these types of transactions remain relevant.

4 *The CPA's Role in Mergers and Acquisitions Due Diligence Assistance to PPMC's and Private Equity Firms* provides details and a checklist on how to approach gaining an understanding of a practice.

by the typical buyer or seller?" Bear in mind that the hypothetical buyer of a physician practice is interested primarily in what the cash return of the practice will be, not what anecdotal or "market" data say the practice might be bought or sold for.

For perhaps the best analysis of the general limitations of market data in valuation, see Business Valuation Resources' *The Comprehensive Guide to the Use and Application of the Transaction Databases* by Nancy Fannon, CPA/ABV and Heidi Walker, CPA/ABV.

Alleged Comparative Practice Sales Method

Medical practices, like most businesses, have rules of thumb for valuation. These are commonly expressed as a percentage of the practice's receipts. The most common source of such information is *The Goodwill Registry*, published annually by The Health Care Group of Plymouth Meeting, Pa. This consulting firm's figures are cited in such trade publications as *Medical Economics* and *Physicians Management*, which are widely read by physicians. The *Registry* contains information on practice sales, valuations, and divorce settlements accumulated by The Health Care Group from its own activities, as well as others who submit data to it. The data is usually (and abusedly) cited as an average percentage of revenues ostensibly paid for "goodwill."

Insight and Analysis

It is a commonplace principle of research in the scientific community that "the plural of anecdote is not data." Valuation analysts do well to remember this when using rules of thumb.

Rules of Thumb and Market Date: Understanding Comparatives

A comparative is only as useful as the underlying analysis of the subject practice. For example, if you decide to purchase a four-bedroom home, you cannot go to a realtor's office and get a standard price for a home. The price will vary with numerous factors, such as the age of the house, the size of the rooms, the number of bathrooms, the quality of the kitchen, the size of the lot, and so on. A medical practice is no different. It is not possible to value any practice by taking a percentage of its receipts. Further, just because Practice A is valued at 60% of receipts does not mean that Practice B is worth 60%. It may be worth 10%—or nothing.

Insight and Analysis

These "rules" originate from physician-to-physician transactions and have always been of limited use in a market area in which physician practice management companies operate or for purchases by hospitals or integrated delivery systems; in the latter circumstance, serious regulatory issues are raised from such use. In addition, during the buying frenzy of the mid-1990s, the market value (as reflected by actual transactions) often exceeded these levels. Like any rules of thumb, they need to be considered within the context of market conditions at the time a valuation is performed. I do not endorse use of such rules as valuation methods and caution against their use even as reality checks, especially where regulatory factors govern. Reconciliation of the results of a market approach with the income approach is critical, and the latter should be given preference. A weighting using a disparate result from a goodwill percentage with a disciplined income approach will simply dilute the meaningfulness of the income approach, not lead to a more accurate conclusion of value.

Use of the Goodwill Registry to Determine Intangible Value

If one were to accept the premise that the *Goodwill Registry* constitutes a valid source of market data on the intangible value of medical practices, it is necessary to understand precisely what that valuation method includes.

The *Goodwill Registry* contains the following definition of "goodwill:"

> As we see it, professional practice "goodwill" is a combination of practice intangibles varying, on a case-by-case basis, as to existence and value. That combination might include location, use of a practice's or an *individual's name*, patient information (embodied in the clinical record), a favorable leasehold, *a covenant not to compete, compensation for past (or future) management and entrepreneurial services, payments made for referral to an associate or recommendation of a successor*, patient lists, credit records, patient care and or employee contracts, as well as assignments of future income." (*Emphasis added* to identify those items denoting personal goodwill rather than practice goodwill and therefore not divisible property.)[5]

Thus, the reported values in the *Goodwill Registry* clearly *include*, for example, nondivisible personal goodwill via a noncompete, which is relevant in many jurisdictions for marital dissolution purposes. The entries also include *control* and *noncontrol* transactions, valuations which did not result in a transaction and final divorce settlements, which are court decisions, not transactions. For "market data" to be valid, they must represent actual transactions.

Valuation Community Professional Standards

Besides my own views of the limitations of rules of thumb, the broad valuation profession holds a similar view. A rule of thumb is a means of estimating what a transaction value might be, using a "deal" price rather than cash equivalents. Valuation analysts use rules of thumb to gauge or reality check the results of valuation methods under the three approaches to valuation. Rules of thumb are widely disparaged as valuation *methods* in the professional literature:

5 *Goodwill Registry*, Explanatory Notes.

> Formula values are not substitutes for careful consideration of other appropriate valuation methods that are applicable to the business being appraised.[6]
>
> Sometimes called "rules of thumb," the industry method can prove to be a valuable tool but should *never* be relied upon by itself for the valuation of an appraisal subject.... If enough transactions take place using a particular method, the end result is that *there are market data that will support the use of that method*. However, if these formulas are the only methods used, *an inappropriate valuation may result*.[7] (*Emphasis added*)
>
> Rule of thumb—a mathematical relationship between or among variables based on experience, observation, *hearsay*, or a combination of these, usually applicable to a specific industry.[8] (*Emphasis added*)

More importantly, rules of thumb do not represent *cash-equivalent values*, which are a key requirement of the definition of fair market value. Cash-equivalent value might well include proceeds attributable to a *stock* sale, not an *asset* sale. Rules of thumb represent the value of assets, not stock. There is a substantial difference between valuing the *stock* of an entity, which is sometimes the relevant task such as in marital dissolution, and valuing the *assets*. The purchaser of *assets* obtains *tax benefits* consisting of 1) the basis step-up in fixed assets (e.g., equipment and furniture) and the resultant additional depreciation deduction; and 2) the basis attributable to intangible assets and the resultant amortization deduction (IRC §197 allows the purchase price of intangibles to be written off over 15 years, generating substantial tax savings). Rules of thumb are "deal" prices representing the "value" of *assets*.

There are no data provided in the *Goodwill Registry* to determine whether or not the values reflected are cash-equivalent values, a necessary prerequisite for its use in determining fair market value.

Levin Associates' Health Care Acquisition Report

One source used widely during the consolidation era of the 1990s for "market" data was Irving Levin Associate's *Health Care Acquisition Report*. This report includes the following data points: location of the acquired practice, a brief description, the price paid (which may or may not represent cash-equivalent value, a prerequisite for fair market value), a brief summary of deal terms, the number of units (physicians) acquired, price paid divided by revenue and price paid divided by income. Few are actually reported, since the information is not publicly available. This report led to the questionable practice of valuing physicians based upon the number working for the

---

6 Glenn Desmond, *Handbook of Small Business Valuation Formulas*, as quoted in *The Lawyers' Business Valuation Handbook*, ibid, page 189.
7 *Understanding Business Valuation*, 2d Edition, Gary R. Trugman, American Institute of CPAs, 2002, page 255.
8 International Glossary of Business Valuation Terms.

acquired practice—something akin to the method during the stock market bubble of valuing software companies with large accumulated deficits based on the number of engineers and programmers.

Pratt's Stats[9]

Pratt's Stats, perhaps the most comprehensive and justifiably highly regarded of the databases, has data entry points for state, city, firm, and individual submitting the report of the transaction, 14 income statement items, 13 balance sheet items, actual transaction data based upon equity, market value of invested capital, allocation to noncompete agreement and other assets, and dozens of yes-or-no questions about the transaction as well as ratios computed from the core financial data. Often, however, not all of the data is submitted for each transaction, and there are very few medical practices. Regionalization is also critical to assessing the usefulness of this market data. For example, in November 2004, nearly 90% of 96 items identified as general dentistry were from three states: Pennsylvania, Arizona, and Oregon. Fifty of the entries were submitted by one brokerage firm and 20 by another. As the investigations of Wall Street investment bankers indicate, a few individuals' views of the market value of a business can distort the picture. Even broadly held views of market value, such as those that preceded the bursting of the stock market bubble in March 2000, can be based upon a *lack* of "reasonable knowledge of relevant facts."

A closer look at regional economics and the market data presents an even greater challenge. Managed care and its limitations on services and pricing are most prevalent in urban areas, where population density and employers make attractive insurance markets. Rural areas have less managed care and fewer patients per square mile. The profitability of a practice per unit of service is likely to be better in areas with less managed care. For example, an analysis of mean physician salaries from the Medical Group Management Association's (MGMA) *Physician Compensation and Production Survey* for 2011 indicates that incomes were greatest for both primary care and specialty care in the southern region, where population density is typically low (urban areas of Florida notwithstanding). The greater incomes are a function of several factors, including lower managed care, higher unit fees, and lower operating costs and in some areas, considerably higher utilization. This greatly limits the common use of goodwill percentage averages paid for all practices of a particular specialty from the *Goodwill Registry*. Valuation is, after all, a function of cash flow from profit not cash flow from revenue!

9 Edited portions of this discussion appeared in "Medical Practices: A BV Rx," *Journal of Accountancy*, November 2005 by the author.

Guideline Publicly Traded Companies

With very rare exception, a physician practice should not be valued based upon public company multiples. It is very difficult indeed to find a public company, even in SIC 801, which is comparable to a physician practice. Pediatrix Medical Group Inc. (NYSE: PDX), Mednax (NYSE: MD), and IntegraMed America Inc. (NASDAQ: INMD) could be relevant in limited circumstances depending upon the nature of the transaction.

Insight and Analysis

Always look at the underlying components of any SIC data to be certain you understand what the companies actually do. The result is often surprising.

Current Recruiting Data

Data on annual recruiting engagements from such firms as Merritt Hawkins[10] and Delta Medical indicate that the specialties in highest demand include internists, family medicine, orthopedic surgery, gastroenterology, dermatology, interventional and general radiology, and interventional cardiology. Hospitals or existing practices looking to recruit such physicians typically find the starting salary very high and the structure of a future buy-in on the table from the outset. It is not uncommon for a well-informed physician exiting residency to base his or her employment decision on competing buy-in opportunities—and the lower the better. For example, orthopedic surgeons are often looking for practices with ambulatory surgery centers, which offer significantly enhanced incomes and better working conditions, and the buy-in opportunity has to be affordable.

Recruiting data are another application of the market approach in that they represent market data on physician income. Income is what the investor in a physician practice is buying. There is a substantive question of whether a hypothetical buyer will pay for an asset that generates less income to that hypothetical buyer than a position as a noninvestor employee. Thus, it is important to compare the earnings available from the practice being valued to that offered in the recruiting market.

A serious shortage of physicians and particularly primary care (generalist) physicians is expected in the next several decades. This shortage will be dramatically increased as a result of the reform legislation and the attempt to bring some 40 million people or more into the primary care system. This has negative implications for practice value because new suppliers' ease of entry into the market is enhanced when there is unmet, excess demand for services.[11] It also puts a premium on midlevel providers as

10 www.merritthawkins.com/.

11 "Will Generalist Physician Supply Meet Demands of an Increasing and Aging Population?" Jack M. Colwill, James M. Cultice, and Robin L. Kruse; *Health Affairs*, 29 April 2008.

well as the renewed interest in so-called "minute clinics"[12] in chain pharmacies and supermarkets.

The ratio of physician to population varies quite significantly from state to state and from urban to suburban and rural areas. Medicare-participating physicians by specialty and region can be found in the publication *2010 CMS Statistics,*[13] shown in Exhibits 1 and 2. This in turn affects the value of practices as well as the incomes available in recruitment settings.

Exhibit 1. Number of Medicare-Participating Physicians by Specialty

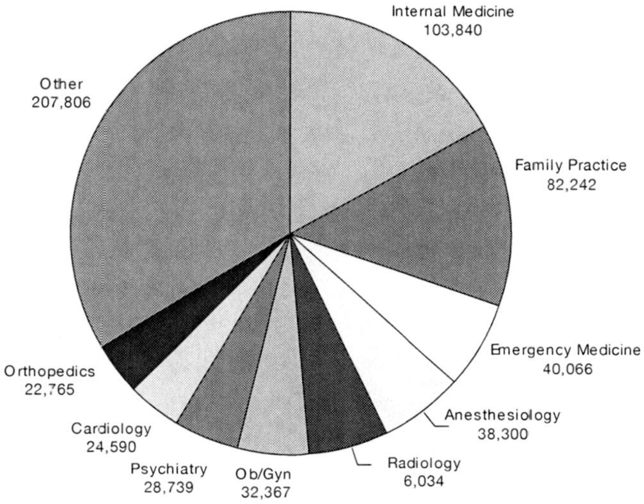

Exhibit 2. Number of Medicare Part B Providers by Region

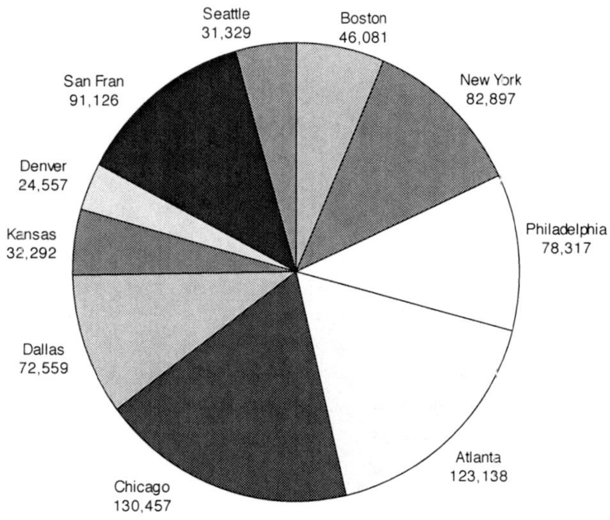

12 Known as walk-in medical centers, freestanding emergi-centers or "doc in the boxes" in the 1980s and 1990s.
13 www.cms.gov/ResearchGenInfo/02_CMSStatistics.asp.

Value of Transactions in Another Market Area

There are regional differences in what sellers will pay for physician practices, much of which are or were driven by the presence or lack of presence of for-profit buyers, as well as such items as the enforceability of noncompetes and enhanced income opportunities. These factors, along with the Stark regulations' requirement that data in a "particular market" be used for determining fair market value, make the data for one region of questionable relevance to another in the absence of appropriate correlation. What should drive price differentials on an economic level from market to market are differences in the availability of cash profits and ease of entry of competitors.[14]

Insight and Analysis

For those circumstances in which government regulations such as the Stark laws or the anti-kickback statute (AKS) are implicated, regionalized market data are further suspect. In recognition of the seeming abuses—intentional or unintentional—of market data, the Stark II regulations specifically define fair market value as "the price at which bona fide sales have been consummated for assets of like type, quality, and quantity in a particular market at the time of acquisition"[15] (emphasis added).

During the consolidation of the 1990s, the vast majority of purchases were in the South and Southwest, although the available market data were widely used in all regions. The Stark II regulations create a critical limitation on market data when the valuation is being undertaken for regulatory purposes, unless the valuation analyst can demonstrate that data from one region or state are somehow relevant to another.

The *IRS Exempt Organizations Continuing Professional Education Technical Instruction Program Textbook* for 1995[16] states the following in a section entitled "Establishing Comparability Under the Market Approach": "Factors affecting comparability include markets served; practice and specialty type; competitive position; profitability; growth prospects; risk perceptions; financial composition (capital structure); physician compensation; physician age, health and reputation; physician productivity; average revenues per physician; cost structure; and average revenue per visit or covered life to revenue to revenue mix (capitated versus fee for service)" citing *Financial Valuation: Businesses and Business Interests*. I know of no database with such information!

Empirical Study of Healthcare Markets

My chapter herein "Healthcare Market Structure and Its Implication for Valuation of Privately Held Provider Entities: An Empirical Analysis" was originally published in the Summer 2008 *Business Valuation Review*. The idea for that article came from a

14 See Chapter 2.
15 420 CFR 411.351.
16 www.irs.gov/pub/irs-tege/.

Government Accounting Office study of market share of health insurers in various states and my experience that pricing and profit differed significantly across the country. I reasoned that this insurer market share[17] and related market power would be one key element defining a market and set out to find out how it and other factors contributed. This, in turn, would define comparability for purposes of the market approach to valuation.

Here is a summary of my findings as to the key elements defining a market:

1. Total Medicare spending and Medicare spending per capita;
2. The presence and market strength of Blue Cross plans;
3. The degree of market strength of local nonprofit hospitals versus for-profit hospitals;
4. The degree of market strength of local nonprofit health insurers versus for-profit health insurers,
5. Certificate of need laws; and
6. Other local demographic and economic factors.

These factors contribute to the fact that most (certainly not all) larger for-profit healthcare providers are primarily located in Florida, Texas, California, and Tennessee. They also confirm the underlying rationale for the Stark Laws' restrictions on the use of out-of-market data as "comparable." The "Checklist of Factors to Consider When Evaluating the Significance of Out-of-Market Transactions" included in this guide provides a means for undertaking this analysis as well as links to Web sites where the underlying data are located.

As I observed with my friend Reed Tinsley in a 2006 article for the American Bar Association's Health Law Section:

> If the acquirer is a public company, an important dynamic is in effect. Public companies' stock prices or valuation multiples are heavily based upon their earnings growth. The higher the earnings growth, the higher the valuation multiple and the higher the value of the company. Thus, that growth needs to continue or the stock's price will decline. There is an arbitrage effect when the earnings of private companies are placed in the public equity markets through acquisition that can enable a public company to afford a higher price than a private company, all other things being equal.[18] Although fair market value in a given market area may be driven by the economics of public companies, the Stark requirement that comparable transactions

17 I am indebted to legendary health law attorney J.D. Epstein for his insights on this topic.
18 See, e.g., "Understanding the Difference Between Strategic and Fair Market Value in Consolidating Industries," *Business Valuation Review*, May 2002, by the author.

be in a particular market at the time of acquisition addresses this if public companies are not active acquirers in a given market area.[19]

Other Common Pitfalls in the Market Approach

Valuation analysts frequently prefer the market approach to valuing a business. As a colleague observed, "Appraisers are market observers, not market makers."[20] Trouble is, to observe, you have to have your eyes open and understand what you are looking at. Courts tend to understand easily that if businesses of a certain type sell for three times earnings, then a given business is likely worth three times earnings. Valuation analysts tend to be comfortable for the same reason; there is less judgment[21] in the market approach than in the income approach, if a good database of transactions for a type of business exists.

Medical practices present a unique challenge for proper use of the market approach. As we will see in the analysis that follows, the market data often do not contain sufficient data to determine precisely what the multiples in a given transaction were.

Example

Assume that a representative transaction in a database contains the following information:

Date of Transaction: July 1, 1997
Type of Practice: Ophthalmology
Subject Revenues: $1,000,000
Owner compensation: $450,000
Earnings after taxes: $2,000
Purchase Price: $540,000
Debts assumed: $0
Working Capital Included: Yes

Multiples:
Owner's Discretionary Comp: 1.20
Revenues: 0.54

What does this tell us about the value of this practice or about the practice we are trying to value today? Painfully little, unfortunately.

19 "Identifying Appropriate Business Valuation Approaches Under Stark and the AKS," the author with Reed Tinsley, CPA, CVA, *The Health Lawyer*, American Bar Association, December 2006.
20 Perhaps not the first to say it, but I heard it from Steve Bravo, CPA/ABV, ASA.
21 My opinion.

Analysis

The year 1997 represented the last "big year" of buying by the PPMC industry, which collapsed and died following the failed merger between MedPartners and Phycor at the end of that year. We do not know if the above transaction was a purchase by a PPMC, but it likely was, since very few other transactions in medical practices were disclosed.[22]

PPMC's purchased practices were based upon a multiple of earnings contracted to the PPMC. The contracted earnings typically were 15% to 20% of the earnings of the physician. In the above sample transaction, the purchase price of $540,000 could have been based upon a multiple applied to an earnings stream between $67,500 (15% of $450,000) and $90,000 (20% of $450,000). As such, the correct valuation multiple to be garnered from this transaction could be as little as six ($540,000 divided by $90,000) or as much as eight ($540,000 divided by $67,500). Generally, such multiples ranged between four and seven, but we cannot tell what the multiple was from the transaction. The purchase price included working capital, intangibles, and fixed assets. The illustrated multiples of 1.20 times owner's discretionary cash flow and 0.54 of revenues are not meaningful if this is a PPMC transaction. The PPMC was not buying 100% of the physician's earnings, nor was it buying the revenues—it was buying a portion of the practice's earnings before physician compensation.

If this was a physician-to-physician transaction, of course, the valuation multiples would be more meaningful. One clue that this is *not* a physician-to-physician transaction, however, is that accounts receivable were included—that is rarely the case in a physician-to-physician deal, while it was normally the case in a PPMC transaction. This, of course, is critical to the valuation analyst attempting to use the data to develop a market conclusion of value.

Particular Problems for Hospital Buyers

It is critical from a regulatory standpoint that the hospital receives an accurately determined fair market value for the practice. Using market data from the 1990s to establish trends that include a class of buyers (PPMCs) no longer present for most physicians, even if normally reasonable to general business valuation analysts, is a serious mistake from a regulatory standpoint. Besides the problems with using such data outlined above, equally important is the fact that the market conditions today are no longer what they were in 1990s.

Use of the *Goodwill Registry* rule of thumb based on a percentage of collected revenues is risky from a regulatory standpoint.

22 At least in my review of the databases, many if not most of the transactions predate 1998 and fall into the PPMC era.

> Using the *Goodwill Registry* to value a practice for purchase by a hospital would be a critical mistake as there would be no way of determining if the hospital was receiving an appropriate return on its investment without a disciplined application of the income approach described earlier. This is because an asset that has or will generate no cash flow has no value to the hypothetical buyer of the fair market value standard.[23]

When confronted with this type of valuation engagement, a valuation analyst can also consider a *replication cost* approach, looking at such intangible assets as workforce-in-place and going concern value, in addition to fixed assets, such as equipment and furniture. At a minimum, one might think the practice should be worth the cost to a physician buying it of establishing a similar practice, including the quantification of the reduced revenue during the start-up period. Nonetheless, there is a substantive question for a hospital as to whether replication cost is appropriate because a hypothetical investor will likely not invest in something that lacks cash return.

> The key question, of course, is whether or not the hypothetical buyer of the fair market value standard would incur a value based upon replication cost if there was no return on the investment. Most experienced healthcare appraisers would likely answer no in the absence of some additional mitigating factors. It is worth noting that, at least in this author's view, a hospital employing a physician post-transaction should evaluate the practice value differently than a physician buying a practice from another physician, where the seller retires or otherwise ceases to practice in the service area.
>
> Tax-exempt hospitals generally are subject to a standard of providing community benefit for the costs they expend. Thus, one potential mitigating factor in utilizing replication cost would be where the acquiring hospital met the community benefit standard. This might occur where the service area of the target physician was underserved and/or the physician serving that area planned to leave for a better opportunity.[24]

Note should be taken as well of any contractual relationships between the hospital and the physician in the proposed transaction documents, including a covenant not to compete held by the hospital and any guaranteed rights under an employment contract held by the physician. Valuing such contractual rights can be an important part of a proper fair market value determination when a transaction is being consummated or unwound. This was a critical issue in *Derby v. Commissioner*,[25] which involved valuation

23 "Identifying Appropriate Business Valuation Approaches Under Stark and the AKS," the author with Reed Tinsley, CPA, CVA, *The Health Lawyer*, American Bar Association, December 2006.
24 "Regulatory Issues in Using Replication Cost for Valuing Physician Practices," *Financial Valuation and Litigation Expert*, February/March 2007 by the author.
25 *Charles A. and Marian L. Derby, et al., Petitioners v. Commissioner, Respondent*, T.C. Memo. 2008-45, GALE, Judge.

issues associated with the donation of the intangible value of a medical practice to a tax-exempt hospital.[26]

Conclusion

Old market data in particular are only relevant if the market conditions today are the same as when the comparable transaction took place. We cannot sell 100 shares of a NASDAQ market index future today for the same price that we would have gotten in March 2000 or November 2007. Similarly, we cannot sell a physician practice today for the same market multiple, or even to the same class of buyers, as we could have from 1990 to 1997. Care needs to be taken to understand current market conditions and transaction terms when using databases of market transactions.

Understanding Physician Practice Discount and Capitalization Rates

Insight and Analysis

What is a discount rate? One of the most difficult concepts to grasp in valuation is the relationship between stock market returns and discount rates for businesses. A discount rate is the percentage of cash return an investor expects to receive for an investment of given risk. In the stock market—from where we derive discount rates used in all valuation engagements—the cash return consists of dividends plus capital appreciation on the stock. In a medical practice, the return consists of enhanced compensation and perhaps dividends, if the practice is an S corporation or limited liability company (LLC), or if the entity is an ambulatory surgery center or imaging center. There *may* also be capital appreciation at the time the practice is sold, although most physicians realize the bulk of the net present value of their investment through annual earnings, not from a business sale. When a business distributes all or most of its cash profits, it tends to have a lower rate of appreciation than a business that reinvests its cash.

The terms discount rate, expected rate of return, and cost of equity[27] all mean the same thing. It is important to note that the *actual* return in a given year is not likely to be equal to the *expected* return—that is what risk is all about! Over a long period of time, for investments in physician practices with the same risk profile, the actual return should equal the expected return—much the same way that stocks go up and down and have good years and bad years but are known to outperform bonds and money market funds over the long haul.[28]

26 "What Goes Around Comes Around: *Derby v. Commissioner*"; see Chapter 19 of this guide.

27 As seen later herein, the same terms can apply to debt or the cost of capital.

28 At least prior to the start of the recession in 2008.

A capitalization rate is obtained, of course, by subtracting the expected long-term (perpetual) growth rate in net cash flows from the discount rate. Growth rates are discussed in detail below.

Practice Risk Premium: Being Objective With the Subjective?

The actual unsystematic risk premium—RP_u— or the medical practice premium will depend upon whether your build-up method approach uses 1) the microcap premium or 2) the 10th decile premium.[29] For example, a portion of the unsystematic risk of the typical physician practice is accounted for in the 10th decile premium, considering that the healthcare industry is *less* risky than the broad market (S&P 500) from which the equity risk premium for large companies is derived. That said, many physician practices have dramatic additional risk, such as those that rely upon a single product and earn most or all their profits from a single insurer. This can be seen by examining the industry risk premium data for healthcare companies contained in the valuation edition of the *Morningstar Yearbook*, bearing in mind that excessive reliance on the industry risk premium leads to errors as well.[30] As I stated in a peer-reviewed 2007 article on the *Delaware Open MRI* case, better known for its S corporation tax-effecting scheme:

> Perhaps the most fundamental valuation mistake in the healthcare industry is failure to differentiate the risk of a small entity operating in a single state (Delaware) in a single line of business (MRI) with a few dominant health insurers from the risk of large public entities operating in multiple states in multiple lines of business with multiple health insurers paying for the cost of services. Use of the industry risk premium in the build-up method compounds this typical error.[31]

The risk premium for the medical practice being valued (i.e., unsystematic risk) is a highly subjective number and one that is heavily dependent upon the knowledge and skill of the valuation analyst. Some valuation analysts use a list of risk factors with a range of premium percentages assigned to each factor, while others use a single percentage and justify the additional premium in their written report. The following is a nonexhaustive listing of some of the factors that should be considered in developing the practice risk premium.

---

29 Or even the 10b risk premium, being the bottom half of the 10th percentile.

30 The single largest source of error is blindly relying on Morningstar data in any event.

31 See, e.g., "A Healthcare Appraiser Reviews a Judge-Appraiser's 'Report'" *Business Valuation Review*, Summer 2007, by the author.

1. Specialty;
2. Reliance on single product and service or payor;
3. Presence or lack of a repeat patient (customer) base;
4. Reliance upon individual skills and referrals from other physicians;
5. Profitability;
6. Total receipts;
7. Payor mix and quality of contracts;
8. Coding (!);
9. Age and gender of provider;
10. Quality of staff, particularly billing staff;
11. Longevity of staff;
12. Number of active patients;
13. Number of competitors;
14. Ease of entry into the market;
15. Current recruiting salaries;
16. Risk of reimbursement changes;
17. Available market strategies; and
18. Underwriting cycle for health insurance industry (see discussion below).

Additional risk factors for markets or practices with capitation are:

1. Likely transition to capitation;
2. Presence of Medicare capitation;
3. Experience with capitation;
4. Covered lives;
5. Reserves for capitated referrals or risk pools; and
6. The underwriting cycle for health insurance industry is particularly important here.

Exhibit 3 appeared in the article "Medical Practices: A BV Rx" in the November 2005 *Journal of Accountancy*.

Exhibit 3. Medical Practice Risk Premiums

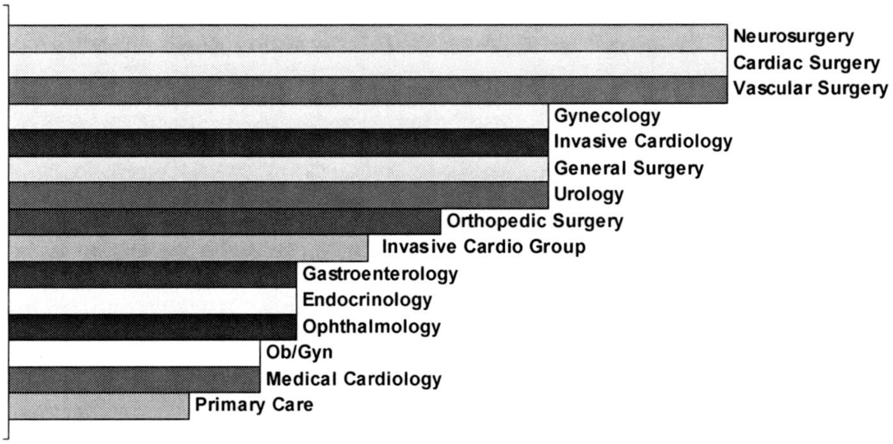

Weighted Average Cost of Capital (WACC)

Another commonly overlooked fact of valuation is the accounting equation, something that was emphasized by the Fifth Circuit Court of Appeals when overturning the Tax Court's decision in *Caracci*. If equity and long-term debt (including the current portion of long-term debt) are the *right side* of the accounting equation used in the market value of invested capital (MVIC), the *left side* of the equation includes tangible assets, such as furniture and equipment and working capital assets (such as accounts receivable and prepaid items), and intangible assets, such as personal and enterprise or practice goodwill, as well as the value of any noncompete agreement or enterprise value (EV). In computing the value of the business enterprise, working capital is reduced by accounts payable and accrued items to arrive at net working capital (NWC). Note that a valuation model that measures EV will include the entire value of the operating assets: tangible, intangible, and net working capital.

If the goal of a valuation engagement is to value MVIC/EV (the invested capital or operating assets of the practice, again, both equity and long-term debt), then use of the WACC is appropriate. If the goal of the valuation is to value a controlling interest in the practice, as is common for hospital buyers or transfers of solo practices to a new physician, the WACC can be used and the ratio of debt and equity can be based upon the optimum mix of debt and equity for any hypothetical willing buyer or seller. This is because a control buyer has the ability to alter the capital structure to the optimal ratio and debt is cheaper than equity, all things being equal. (The optimum capital structure of a specific buyer should not be used, as this is in the nature of a strategic adjustment inconsistent with fair market value.)

The discounted cash flow method when applied to an asset purchase and sale of a controlling interest should use a weighted average cost of capital, consisting of the result of the risk-adjusted equity rate above, and the after-tax cost of debt. If a control interest is being purchased, such as 100% of the practice, the percentage of debt utilized should, again, represent the optimum obtainable in the marketplace, and the cost of debt should reflect that of the hypothetical owner. If a minority interest is being valued, the percentage and cost of debt should generally be the present level in the practice since a minority owner cannot alter them—but be certain to read the discussion of excessive debt later in this chapter.

Insight and Analysis

The interest rate for debt used in computing this weighted average cost of capital, as well as the percentage of debt to equity available, must also consider those circumstances where a lender is looking to the personal guarantees of the owner(s), as well as the assets of the practice as collateral. In my view, a valuation analyst should consider adding a premium to the interest rate cost of debt for the value of the guarantees.

Valuation Tip

The percentage of debt should be a function of the underlying assets and the normal financing pattern for medical practices. Fixed assets are often financed, accounts receivable less frequently so. Equipment intensive practices such as radiology, dentistry, ophthalmology, or sports medicine (with physical therapy) have greater percentages of debt than, for example, primary care practices or general surgery.

We know as well from the capital asset pricing model (CAPM) that, all other things being equal, the more debt a company has versus an industry norm, the higher its cost of equity will be! The implications of this are profound because they demonstrate a *dynamic relationship* between the percentage of debt in the WACC and the cost of equity, which is part of the WACC. Therefore, although mathematically a valuation analyst can lower the WACC by increasing the percentage of debt in that computation, the CAPM—and relevering of beta—tells us that the cost of equity must be simultaneously adjusted. If the percentage of debt in the capital structure goes up, the cost of equity goes up as well. If the percentage of debt in the capital structure goes down, the cost of equity goes down as well. The example in this chapter's "In-Depth Review of the Excess Earnings Method" explores the impact of excessive debt as well. Medical practices with more debt than other practices of the same size and specialty have greater risk and therefore greater equity discount rates.

Growth Rate

As noted earlier, the cap rate is determined by subtracting the growth rate from the discount rate. The growth rate should reflect the long-term prospects for the practice's growth. The growth can come from increases in reimbursement for services, whether fee-for-service or capitation, or addition of providers or ancillary services, such as lab and imaging. Generally, this expansion is forecasted during the first five years. It is important to remember that the terminal growth rate is a growth rate into *perpetuity*[32] and must be sustainable. Very few businesses can sustain growth rates in excess of the inflation rate forever.

Insight and Analysis

There is a great opportunity for influencing the ultimate valuation conclusion via the growth rate, either deliberately or through an error of judgment. I recall one situation in a specialty practice where the independent valuation analyst used a cap rate on after-tax earnings of 13%, without first developing a discount rate, although this discount rate must have been at least 22%, implying a long-term growth rate into perpetuity of 9%—almost inconceivable!

I generally use the current estimate of the long-term rate of inflation as a ceiling on the growth rate; a reasonable range in my view in the absence of contradictory evidence is 2% to 2.5%. You can obtain the current rate of inflation estimate at the Philadelphia Federal Reserve Bank's Web site at www.philadelphiafed.org/research-and-data/real-time-center/survey-of-professional-forecasters/2011/survq311.cfm. I should emphasize that in my view, it is wholly inappropriate to use the nominal growth rate in the gross domestic product (GDP—real growth plus inflation) as a long-term growth rate.

General Price Per Unit of Service

What about increases in fees per unit of service? From 1994 to 2010, or 15 years, the compound rate of increase was only 1.96%, based on data from the Bureau of Labor Statistics' Producer Price Index for Physician Services, shown in Exhibit 4.

Medicare Price Per Unit of Service

Clearly, there is no evidence that unit reimbursement is growing at that GDP rate, and the capacity to provide units of service in a small practice is limited. Under federal law, Medicare expenditures for physician services are limited by a complex formula that considers the change in fees, the number of beneficiaries, growth in GDP per capita, and the impact of new laws. The Medicare sustainable growth rate, or SGR is then applied to the Medicare economic index (MEI), which measures the weighted average

32 As I am fond of saying, forever is a long time.

Exhibit 4. Medical Loss Ratio Trend

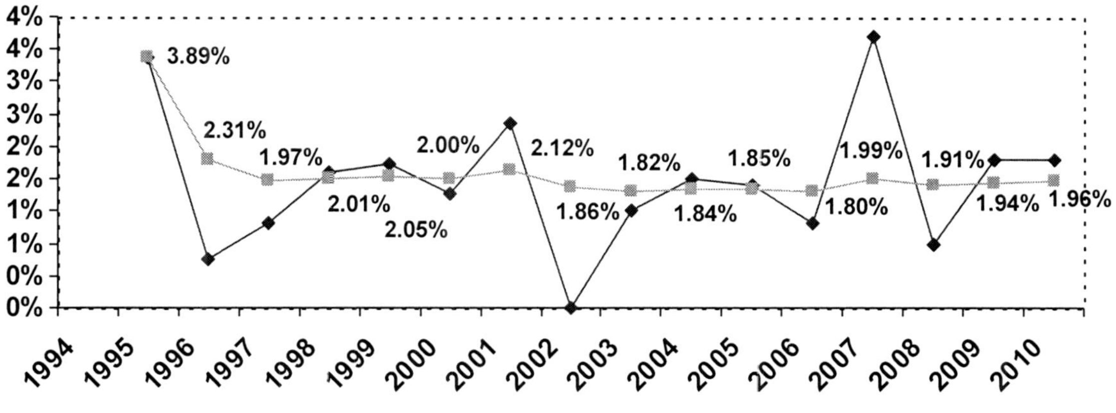

price change in physician services. The MEI[33] is a physician practice-specific measure of inflation and generally is less than 2.5%, absent recessions, when it is much lower. The Medicare Payment Advisory Commission or MedPAC Web site has the data each March (www.medpac.gov). For 2008, the scheduled increase of 0.5% (19 cents) was a result of legislation temporarily overturning the SGR methodology that would have resulted in a 10.5% decrease in the conversion factor used to set the fee schedule. The compound rate of increase from 1998 to 2009 amounted to only 0.43% and has since turned negative. (See Exhibit 5.)

Exhibit 5. History of Medicare Conversion Factor

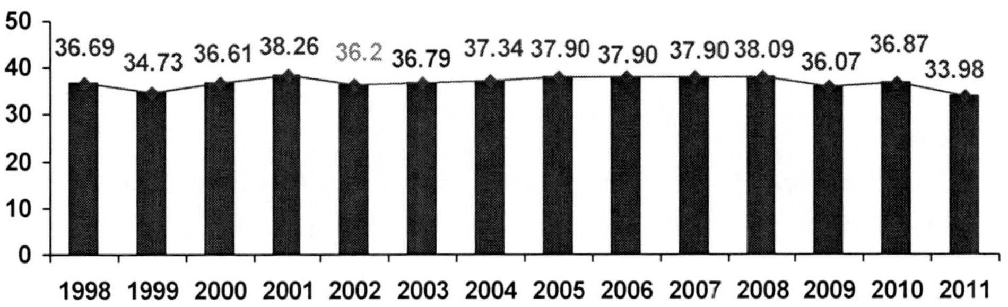

As I observed in the 2006 article for the American Bar Association's Health Law Section:

> In the valuation community, much of the potential inaccuracy in growth rates stems from a poor understanding of the impact of growth on value and of the limitations in the growth of per unit revenue under the current reimbursement system. For example, the Medicare Conversion Factor, which represents the value per Relative

33 This is similar to the market basket used for hospitals described in that chapter.

Value Unit (RVU), of services provided under Part B, has increased less than .5% in the last nine years; the compound rate of growth—which would be used to compare it to inflation, for example—is virtually zero, while annual inflation has been in the 3% range. What drives Part B revenue in general is utilization along with intensity of service as reflected in coding.[34]

Underwriting Cycle

One of the primary influences on the forecast of future cash flow is the underwriting cycle in the health insurance industry. Exhibit 6 reflects the historical cycle of premium increases and cost[35] increases. Note that in recent years, the rate of increase in premiums and costs has been equal. However, you can also see that at the end of the 1990s, a period of aggressive premium cutting in the face of mounting costs when the industry tried to buy market share. This led to the failure of many smaller insurers and the consolidation that affects the ability of providers to negotiate fees today.[36]

Exhibit 6. Premium and Cost Trends

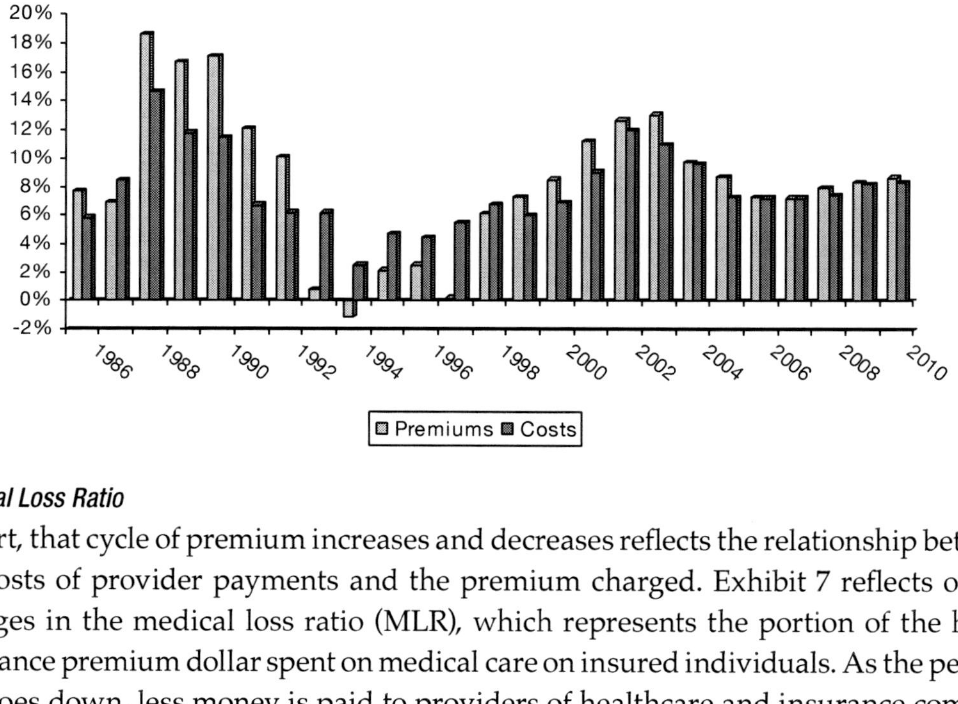

Medical Loss Ratio

In part, that cycle of premium increases and decreases reflects the relationship between the costs of provider payments and the premium charged. Exhibit 7 reflects overall changes in the medical loss ratio (MLR), which represents the portion of the health insurance premium dollar spent on medical care on insured individuals. As the percentage goes down, less money is paid to providers of healthcare and insurance company profits increase.[37]

34 "Identifying Appropriate Business Valuation Approaches Under Stark and the AKS," the author with Reed Tinsley, CPA, CVA, *The Health Lawyer*, American Bar Association, December 2006.

35 Cost here is the amount paid by the health insurers for the care of their insureds.

36 Based on *Health Care-Managed Care*, Jan. 7, 2010, Barclays Capital, sourced from Milliman, CMS, and company documents.

37 Based on *Health Care-Managed Care*, Jan. 7, 2010, Barclays Capital, sourced from Milliman, CMS and company documents.

Exhibit 7. Medical Loss Ratio Trend

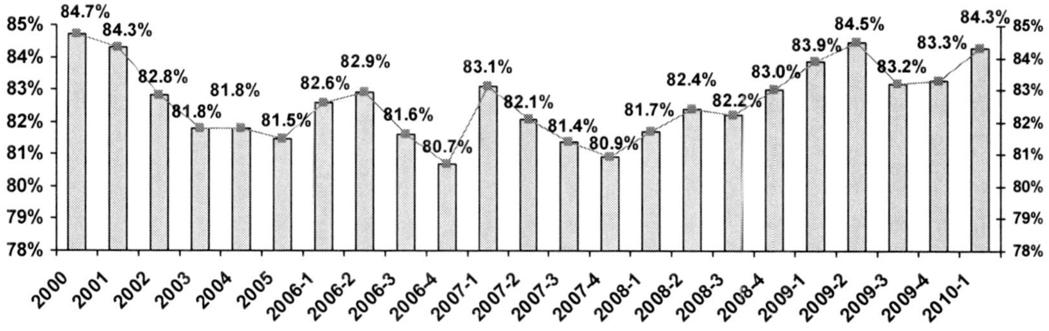

Growth in Units of Service

On a more practice-specific level, look at the impact of various units of service volume growth rates on a practice currently seeing 4,500 patients a year. (See Exhibit 8.)

Exhibit 8. Unit Growth

	Base Year	1	2	3	4	5	6	7	8
Visits	4,500								
Growth rate	4.00%	4,680	4,867	5,062	5,264	5,475	5,694	5,922	6,159
Growth rate	5.00	4,725	4,961	5,209	5,470	5,743	6,030	6,332	6,649
Growth rate	6.00	4,770	5,056	5,360	5,681	6,022	6,383	6,766	7,172
Growth rate	7.00	4,815	5,152	5,513	5,899	6,311	6,753	7,226	7,732
Growth rate	8.00	4,860	5,249	5,669	6,122	6,612	7,141	7,712	8,329
Growth rate	9.00	4,905	5,346	5,828	6,352	6,924	7,547	8,226	8,967
Growth rate	10.00	4,950	5,445	5,990	6,588	7,247	7,972	8,769	9,646

If this were a solo primary care practice, the maximum number of encounters is going to top out at between 4,500 and 5,500, depending upon whether it is adult, pediatric, or a mix of both![38]

Conclusion of Growth Rate Discussion

External evidence of the growth rate may be obtained by reviewing government data on the healthcare segment of the economy. Historically, this segment grows by well in excess of the inflation rate. However, the growth is driven in large part by the aging population and new technology and is generally spread over more physicians, not focused on existing physicians. Therefore, the long-term growth rate for a given practice is much less than that for the industry as a whole. Only very large entities involved in

38 See, e.g., "Computing the Growth Rate in Physician Practice Revenue," *CPA Expert*, Winter 2005 by the author.

a substantial cross section of the healthcare delivery system have an opportunity to match the industry growth rate.

> Perhaps the greatest risk of overestimating value and implicating Stark or the AKS stems from improper or unrealistic assumptions as to future growth in cash flow or profits.[39]

Discounted Cash Flow (DCF)

Development of Assumptions

Underlying the discounted cash flow method is the necessity of developing a five-year forecast of financial operations. The normalization of earnings process described above typically provides the base year for the financial forecast. Various assumptions about the increases in revenues, expenses, numbers of patients, penetration of capitation, and capitation rates then need to be made. The acquiring entity should play a crucial role in this process, as the ability to achieve the forecast will depend in large part on the actions taken by the acquirer's management after the acquisition. If the valuation is conducted by a CPA, a representation letter signed by the acquirer, and perhaps the seller, acknowledging development of the assumptions used in the model should be considered.

Where the capitalization of excess earnings methods tend to focus on normalized historical results and assumes those results will continue (often an incorrect assumption), the discounted cash flow method requires that future results be forecasted and the cash flows there from be discounted. The future results are forecasted, of course, based upon an analysis of the historical results. Future physician earnings must be forecasted as well. Note: This method is typically used in larger transactions and for regulatory purposes. It is rarely used in a buy-in or sale of a small practice.

Expense Growth

In addition to the discussion about growth rates in revenues in the previous section, as the number of patients and encounters increases, underlying operating costs must increase as well. Items such as nonphysician salaries and fringe benefits, supplies, and telephone will typically vary as a function of volume. Rent may be a function of the underlying lease, and depreciation will be a function of capital expenditures. The cash cost of purchases must be at least equal to the depreciation expense in the terminal period calculation— to continue to have deprecation expense, you have to continue to buy fixed assets!

An excellent source of expected increases in physician operating costs is the MedPAC Annual Report to Congress released each March. Exhibit 9 is from the 2009 report.

39 "Identifying Appropriate Business Valuation Approaches Under Stark and the AKS," the author with Reed Tinsley, CPA, CVA, *The Health Lawyer*, American Bar Association, December 2006.

Exhibit 9. Forecasted Input Price Increases and Weights for Physician Services for 2009

Input component	Price increases for 2009	Category weight
Total	**2.6%**	**100.0%**
Physician work	**2.7**	**52.5**
Wages and salaries	2.4	42.7
Fringe benefits (nonwage compensation)	3.5	9.7
Physician practice expense	**2.4**	**47.5**
Nonphysician employee compensation	2.9	18.7
Wages and salaries	2.9	13.8
Fringe benefits (nonwage compensation)	2.8	4.8
Office expense	2.1	12.2
Professional liability insurance	2.3	3.9
Medical equipment	0.7	2.1
Drugs and supplies	3.0	4.3
Pharmaceuticals	1.7	2.3
Medical materials and supplies	3.9	2.0
Other professional expense	2.1	6.4

In its March 2011 report, MedPAC stated the following with respect to price increases in physician practices:[40]

> CMS's 2012 forecast of the MEI—a measure of changes in the market basket of input prices for physician and other health professional services, adjusted for productivity growth in the national economy—is revised quarterly and has ranged from 1% (most recent) to 0.7%. For these forecasts, CMS collects pricing data from various data sets and surveys.

Of course, local economic conditions have to be considered as well.

Cash Flow Adjustments

This is a forecast of cash flow, not earnings! Valuation analysts unfamiliar with the deep discounts experienced by physicians from their usual charges for services frequently make major mistakes if they attempt to take accrual revenues and apply a bad-debt allowance. It is not uncommon for physicians to have a 40% or greater difference between gross revenues and net revenues. (See discussion of accounts receivable infra.) The various payors, such as Medicare or HMOs, determine what physicians are paid, and the physicians have little or no control. As a general rule, the discount rate applied to earnings is higher than that applied to cash flow due to the lag between generating earnings and collecting the cash.

Only the excess earnings method typically requires a separate measure of the value of tangible personal property, while the discounted cash flow method calculation includes both the tangible and intangible value of the practice in MVIC. Nonetheless, in a practice with large amounts of equipment such as that used in MR or CT imaging, radiation

40 The author observes that this is wholly inconsistent with his experience.

oncology or a blood chemistry lab, a separate measure of fixed assets is important to determine the depreciation expense that goes into the DCF and reduces income tax expense, thereby increasing value. Bear in mind that healthcare transactions are usually of assets, not equity, and therefore the basis step-up in the hands of the acquirer is relevant. The same rationale applies to amortizing any intangible value under IRC Section 197.

MVIC includes net working capital (NWC) as well, although NWC is often backed out of the valuation model as buyers typically do not acquire it in an asset purchase. The upshot is that it is very difficult to value the operating assets of a healthcare enterprise without allocating MVIC (the right hand side of the accounting equation) to the assets on the left-hand side.

Insight and Analysis

The reason NWC is not acquired is the difficulty of measuring the collectible value of accounts receivable, as well as a general desire not to assume liabilities. Even when it is acquired, retroactive adjustments to the purchase price are typically made based upon the ultimate receivable collections and actual payments of liabilities.

Physician Compensation

This is the most critical component of the model because it is generally the single largest expense. The compensation should be based upon some reasonable measure, *such as the employment agreement expected to be entered into as part of the transaction or some other measure consistent with the standard of value in the transaction, if the sellers will continue as employees post-acquisition.*[41] For example, if the physicians will have an incentive equal to 35% of any increase in net revenues, this should be reflected as part of the model. If additional providers will be added during the forecast period, the cost of salary and fringe benefits should be added.

Insight and Analysis

In fact, the valuation submitted in connection with the Friendly Hills transaction in 1991, cited in *Derby* and therefore relevant today, contains a letter signed by the managing partner stating that the partners recognized they were selling a portion of their earnings and that their future incomes would be less by virtue of that sale. In relevant part he states:

It has been clearly stated to the partners that, in the past, their compensation reflected not only the value of their medical services, but also the profits attributable to their ownership of the network; that the latter element will be replaced by a cash payment,

41 *Charles A. and Marian L. Derby, et al., Petitioners v. Commissioner, Respondent,* T.C. Memo. 2008-45, GALE, Judge

which they can invest ... that the medical group's income will thereafter be derived from arms-length contract for medical services; and that these rates will necessarily be significantly lower than the total historical income they have been receiving.... (Friendly Hills Valuation Report).

Relative Value Units

RVU-based compensation models are increasingly common when hospitals acquire physician practices. Medicare and other payors pay physicians under the Resource-Based Relative Value Scale (RBRVS) where each current procedural terminology code is assigned a certain number of relative value units (RVUs). These RVUs are then multiplied by a dollar-value conversion factor to set the fee Medicare pays.

The number of relative value units is based upon the consumption[42] of three types of resources in the delivery of physician services:

Physician Work

The principal factors comprising this component are time, technical skill and physical effort, mental effort and judgment, and the stress on the physician of certain patient risk factors.

Practice Costs

This component looks at the cost of delivering services by physician type, for example, family medicine versus cardiac surgery. Physician practice costs per dollar of revenue tend to be much higher in primary care than surgery.

Malpractice Insurance Cost

Surgical specialties, and particularly obstetrics, neurosurgery and cardiac surgery, tend to have the highest malpractice insurance. This is the least important of the three components.

Geographic Adjustment

There is an additional adjustment for the geographic location of the practice based upon various government studies, including the census, HUD data, and others.

Physician work RVUs or wRVUs are used in RVU-based models because they measure the work effort of the physician and avoid regulatory risks inherent in using broader measures of RVUs. For example, a cardiologist interpreting the result of a stress test ordered on a patient may be allocated the wRVU from the professional component

42 It is worth observing that the process of allocating RVUs is highly politicized; see www.medpac.gov for the Medicare Payment Advisory Commission discussion of this and related issues.

of the global fee in a productivity-based compensation system, but not the practice expense RVUs associated with the technical component of the global fee. To illustrate the impact of wRVUs, CPT code 93015—cardiac stress testing—has a wRVU weight of 0.75, whereas CPT code 33206—insertion of a cardiac pacemaker—has a weight of 7.31. Obviously, the work effort involved in the more invasive insertion of a pacemaker will be rewarded with a higher level of compensation in a wRVU based compensation model.

Insight and Analysis

This is one of the most difficult assumptions in a forecast because the acquirer may not have any idea what the incentive portion of a physician's compensation will be or what the outcome of a wRVU-based model will be. Although not advisable for a variety of regulatory reasons, the compensation arrangement is sometimes negotiated after the purchase price determined by the valuation has been agreed to by the parties to the transaction. My standard report advises the client that it should consider revisiting the valuation if the compensation ultimately negotiated differs from that in the valuation model. (See also *Derby v. Commissioner.*)[43] Whatever the amount used, bear in mind that "the accepted interpretation of reasonable compensation under the fair market value standard is the salary necessary to hire a nonowner replacement physician of equal experience."[44]

If the client does not specify a compensation formula (subject to its meeting an overall test of reasonableness for the valuation model), I will either work with it to develop a formula that meets the fair market value criteria I am opining on or suggest retention of an independent compensation consultant. Many acquirers now use work RVUs as a basis for measuring productivity, and compensation is a function of those RVUs and a payment rate. One of the many reasons I obtain data by CPT code when valuing a practice is that they are frequently not possible for the client to determine compensation without that data.

As a final observation, because compensation and value of the practice are opposite sides of the same coin—as compensation goes up, value goes down—the question often arises about changing compensation to make the value different, while maintaining the required mathematical relationship between the two. All valuation models are *dynamic*. You cannot properly change one assumption without considering the impact on all the others. One simple example: If you were to decrease compensation payable post-transaction to generate a higher value, you would have to consider the impact on the physician's productivity, which would then effect all the revenue and variable expense assumptions!

43 *Charles A. and Marian L. Derby, et al.,1 Petitioners v. Commissioner, Respondent*, T.C. Memo. 2008-45, GALE, Judge.
44 "Medical Practices: A BV Rx," *Journal of Accountancy*, November 2005 by the author.

Insight and Analysis

Notwithstanding the following discussion, I want to emphasize that I regard the MGMA data as the most useful in performing valuations. The key is to use it expertly.

Using the MGMA Compensation and Cost Data

As noted elsewhere herein, statistical data cannot be used blindly. The valuation analyst needs to understand the data to use them effectively in the valuation process. One of the most commonly used sources of data on compensation is the MGMA Compensation and Production Survey. The document contains numerous tables listing compensation, including means, medians, 75th percentile, single specialty, multispecialty, regional data, and a host of others. Which ones are relevant?

Table 1.1 in the MGMA data represents all physicians included in the survey by specialty. It is therefore the largest database, and arguably the means, medians, and other data items are the most representative: Without commenting on statistical science, the larger the population sampled, the more meaningful the data.[45]

There has been a marked shift over the last several years in the source of the MGMA data as well, with participating physicians increasingly shifting to hospital-employed and away from private practice-employed settings. Fully 47% of the physicians in the Compensation Report for 2011, based on 2010 data, were hospital employees versus 41% for physician-owned practices. In the 2009 report, based on 2008 data, the numbers were 37% and 51%, respectively. This shift of 10% of the underlying sample from private practice to hospital employment reflects the current trend in consolidation as well. (See Exhibit 10.)

Exhibit 10. Shifting Pattern of MGMA Survey Participants

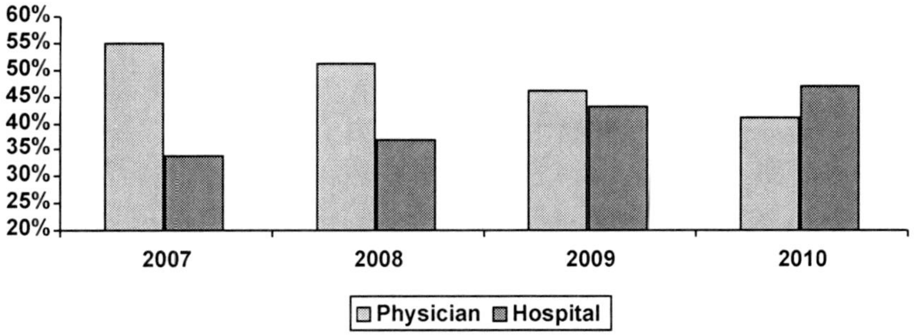

45 In a truly random sample, which the MGMA is not, a sample as small as 30 or 32 drawn from a population can be statistically relevant to one extent or another, depending upon the presence of outliers. What the MGMA *does* tell us is how the physician population included in that data fares from year to year.

The data are then broken down by single specialty and multispecialty practices. A single-specialty practice would represent a group practice reporting to MGMA that employs only physicians of a specific specialty, such as hematology and oncology or cardiology. The multispecialty groups include the physicians of more than one specialty—how many more, we do not know. Multispecialty practices could simply include cardiology and gastroenterology, for example. The combination of these two types of groups should equal the data contained in the combined data.

The data by geographic section or region breaks the combined data down into East, West, South, and Midwest. Looking at the tables, you should note that the sample size is, of course, smaller for each region than the total. The regional data are then broken down by single specialty and multispecialty practices, with even smaller sample sizes. There may be as few as only several dozen sample items, and perhaps fewer.

The problem is even more pronounced in the cost survey for specific physician practice specialties. The sample sizes for each of these practice types are quite small—and remember that those are number of physicians, not numbers of reporting practices. The data for multispecialty practices, which constitute a large sample size, are more meaningful. Nonetheless, this data are commonly cited and are the best available. They are most wisely used when their limitations are understood.

Accounts Receivable

In many valuation engagements, the valuation analyst may not need to be overly concerned with intangible value but may need to reach a conclusion of value on such assets as accounts receivable. Many small businesses and virtually all professional practices use the cash method of accounting. Under this method, accounts receivable are not reflected on the tax returns (or financial statements, if they exist), and the valuation analyst will need to obtain the necessary reports and compute the collectible value.

Introduction

In the absence of accrual accounting, measuring the accounts receivable becomes in large part the responsibility of the valuation analyst. (And even if accrual accounting is in place, the accounts receivable warrant careful attention.) In many medical practice valuation engagements, it may be the largest single asset. Some common examples include:

- A divorce where intangible assets such as goodwill are not marital property;
- A hospital-based practice where the patient base and other intangibles are owned by the hospital and not by the practice;

- A practice buy-in where goodwill is being excluded;
- Any practice where the intangible value is small; and
- In a liquidation scenario.

Like many aspects of valuation, valuing medical accounts receivable is perceived to be as much an art as it is a science. However, a number of key factors must be evaluated if the valuation analyst is to generate a meaningful estimate of value. The considerable expertise necessary to value this asset accurately is often greatly underestimated.

Characteristics of Medical Accounts Receivable

Unlike manufacturing or most service businesses, medical accounts receivable tend to consist of a large number of accounts with relatively small balances. Oil dealerships[46] are analogous in some ways, but they typically are selling a single product—oil—and perhaps some service and repair contracts.

Although some medical specialties, such as cardiac surgery, may have relatively large balances from a particular patient for procedures, there are typically additional smaller balances for office visits and similar services. In an internal medicine or family medicine practice, the typical charge may consist of a $100 office visit plus additional small charges such as $15 to draw blood and $20 for a rapid strep test. Each of the charges that originate with a single visit must be separately billed and accounted for. When (if) it is paid, the payment, if made by an insurer, will specify both the date the service was provided and the specific service that is being paid: There is a specific matching of service date and procedure with the payment. Not all of the services will necessarily be paid and the percentage that is paid will not necessarily be the same for each service—and it is a rare instance indeed where 100% of the charge for any service is paid. Note: If, in fact, 100% of an insured charge is being paid, it typically suggests the practice is charging less than the insurer is willing to pay!

The payment of medical charges raises another significant issue: The majority of such charges are not paid for by the patient individually, but rather by the third-party insurance company that provides the patient's insurance or by a government program, such as Medicare or Medicaid (hereinafter collectively referred to as payors). Further, these payors typically pay by a fee schedule that they set and that often bears little or no resemblance to the fee that the physician charges. As a result, each charge that is processed by the physician's billing department reflects both a payment and an *adjustment* or *contractual allowance*. There may be multiple payments for a particular service, such as when the patient has a deductible or co-pay due after the insurer pays its share

46 At least before the $145 a barrel prices seen in 2008!

or where the patient has a secondary insurance that covers any balance not paid by the primary insurance. The term "write-off" is generally limited to those situations involving a bad debt from an uninsured patient or where a payor refuses to pay for a service due to any of a host of reasons described below.

Situations in Which Write-Offs May Occur

The following is a nonexhaustive listing of the causes of write-offs or bad debts in a medical practice. These factors are also significant for normalizing revenue and determining the specific risk premium.

1. Uninsured patient fails to pay.
2. Office personnel fail to collect co-pays at the time of treatment.
3. Practice fails to meet payor's contractual deadline for submitting a "clean claim." A clean claim is one in which all of the necessary information appears on the claim, including the patient's name, insurance number, the procedure provided by Current Procedural Terminology (CPT) code, the diagnosis by International Classification of Disease (ICD) code, consistency of the CPT and ICD codes, the date of service, and other requirements specified by the payor. Typical periods for submission of clean claims are 45 to 60 days; thereafter, the payor is not obligated to pay the claim (although a denial can be appealed).
4. Failure to meet any requirements for preauthorization of the service by the insurer or a primary care physician, for example.
5. Failure to obtain correct insurance information from the patient.
6. Failure to submit additional information with the claims, such as operative reports for certain surgical procedures.
7. Failure to timely appeal denial of claims.
8. Billing for uncovered services (those that are not covered by the patient's insurance).
9. Billing incorrectly for services, which are considered part of a package or "bundle" of services, such as preoperative and post-operative visits considered part of the global fee paid for the surgery.

There are a host of others. One conclusion the valuation analyst should draw from this discussion is that the billing process in a medical practice is very complex, both in generating the charges and in recording the payment and adjustments for write-offs. This complexity leads to a variety of errors in all but the best-run practices. These errors result in otherwise collectible balances not being collected, uncollectible balances not being written off, uncovered services being paid, and the same service being paid more than once (a credit balance). Office staff involved in the process may be poorly educated, inadequately assisted or supervised, overwhelmed, or simply irresponsible.

The Process of Valuing Accounts Receivable

Generally speaking, the valuation of accounts receivable consists of two distinct components: identification of those charges that include *some* collectible amount and determination of the portion of those charges that is ultimately collectible. We will examine each of these two components in the paragraphs that follow.

Identification of (Partially) Collectible Balances Versus Uncollectible Balances

The first step is to obtain an aged accounts receivable by payor. This report typically consists of a listing of the various payors that the practice does business with and the total due from each of those payors by aging category: current, greater than 30 days, greater than 60 days, greater than 90 days, and greater than 120 days. The "# Days" is the number of days gross charges in accounts receivable. (See Exhibit 11.)

Exhibit 11. Total Due for Each Payer by Aging Category

Payor	Current	> 30	> 60	>90	>120	Total	# Days
A	$7,000	$8,000	$5,000	$5,000	$15,000	$40,000	72
B	1,000	4,000	5,000	10,000	20,000	40,000	144
Total	$8,000	$12,000	$10,000	$15,000	$35,000	$80,000	96
	10.0%	15.0%	12.5%	18.8%	43.7%	100.0%	

Analysis of this report provides the valuation analyst with a significant amount of the information necessary needed to determine what steps will be necessary to properly measure the accounts receivable. The first step is to compare the percentage of receivables in each aging category to statistical norms or to the valuation analyst's own experience. (Statistical norms are typically obtained from the Medical Group Management Association's Cost Survey). If the aging falls within accepted parameters, the valuation analyst may employ simple "short-cut" computations to estimate the collectible value. If not, a more complex computation may be required.

The most common indicator that a short-cut approach will not work is where the percentage of receivables in the greater than 90- or 120-day category is more than the expected level. The larger the variance, the more complex the computation required to determine the true collectible value.

Insight and Analysis

What is the expected level of receivables in the greater-than-120-day category, or in any category for that matter? One primary determinant is the whether or not and to what extent the practice uses electronic claims submission. This is the norm in most markets and can result in a clean claim being paid in less than 25 days. Depending upon the electronic sophistication of a given market and the practice, accounts receivable agings may be under 25 days or as low as 15 days! Another factor is the presence of a "prompt pay" statute in the state in which the practice operates. These statutes generally *require* an insurer to pay a clean claim within 30 to 45 days of receipt. Medicare generally requires all physicians except those with fewer than 10 full-time equivalent employees to bill electronically.

Example

Assume that the MGMA norm for the greater-than-120-days category is 20% and the valuation subject has 44% of its receivables in that category. This is an almost certain indication that uncollectible balances are not being written off. These balances more often than not consist of the unpaid portion of a charge representing the contractual allowance—that being the amount the payor is not obligated to pay under the terms of its contract with the physician. Another common component is uncollectible "self-pay," or uninsured balances. These balances accumulate because identifying such balances and getting approval for having them written off often take a lot of work. In the typical medical office, time tends to be spent on collecting collectible balances rather than on writing-off uncollectible ones.

The fact pattern of the example will require, at a minimum, that the valuation analyst separate the aged accounts receivable into two distinct groups: those greater than 90 or 120 days old and those less than 90 or 120 days old. Each of the two groups will then need to be valued separately.

The balances should be analyzed by payor if the data are available and the amount is material. For example, certain payors may have unusual aging distributions while others do not. Another common occurrence is where the practice's *largest* payor has an aging distribution different than that of the remaining payors.

Examples

In a valuation of a large healthcare facility where the cost approach was important, the entity's single largest payor was in serious financial difficulty. The aging of receivables from that payor was significantly worse than for the balance of the receivables. Although there was an audited financial statement, it was on the income tax method of accounting and therefore did not reflect an allowance for uncollectible accounts. A substantial reduction in the audited accounts receivable balance was required to reach fair market value of the receivables.

In a litigation matter, an opposing expert blindly accepted the calculation of collectible accounts receivable appearing in a practice consultant's report without undertaking a collectibility analysis. The consultant testified that the amount was, in fact, overstated by 20%. The error resulted in the expert's value of receivables being overstated and a working capital deficit being missed.

Measuring the Portion of Charges That Are Collectible

A standard analysis that should be done in any medical practice valuation is to compute charges, collections (payments), and adjustments for each of the practices principal insurers. Perform this analysis by payor is important because the contractual payment rate is likely to vary (and often significantly) for each payor that the practice contracts with.

Example

For simplicity, assume that a practice has contracts with two payors. Data from the billing system indicate that Payor A reimburses the practice at a rate equal to 50% of charges, while Payor B reimburses at a rate equal to 60% of charges, as shown in Exhibit 12.

Exhibit 12. Rate of Reimbursement by Payor

Payor	Charges	Payments	Adjustments	Collection Rate	Realization Rate
A	$200,000	$100,000	$100,000	50%	50%
B	$100,000	$60,000	$36,000	60%	62.5%

The collection rate *is equal to current payments divided by current charges.*

The realization rate *is equal to current payments divided by current payments plus current adjustments.*

If the billing system is working properly and adjustments are being recorded properly at the time payments are received, the realization rate is the best measure of the true collectible value. This is due to the fact that it reflects *both* elements of the charge relief activity: the payment and the contractual allowance or adjustment. If the adjustments are not being recorded properly however, the realization rate is inaccurate and the collection rate may be a better measure. The collection rate may understate collectibility when unpaid claims are inadequately reviewed and overstate collectibility when, for example, charges to a payor in the current period decline from prior periods.

A "short-cut" valuation of receivables would appear as follows (see Exhibit 13).

Exhibit 13. 'Short-Cut' Valuation of Receivables

Payor	Receivable	Collection Rate	Collectible
A	$40,000	50%	$20,000
B	$40,000	60%	$24,000
	$80,000	55%	$44,000

Or using the realization rate approach (see Exhibit 14).

Exhibit 14. Valuation Using the Realization Rate Approach

Payor	Receivable	Realization Rate	Collectible
A	$40,000	50.00%	$20,000
B	$40,000	62.50%	$25,000
	$80,000	56.25%	$45,000

The problem with either of these approaches should be obvious: Payor B constitutes only 33% of charges, while it constitutes 50% of receivables. This is a clear clue that something may be "wrong" with the Payor B receivables. A further analysis is likely to reveal one of several generic causes: Payor B pays more slowly than Payor A, there are completely uncollectible balances included in the Payor B receivables meeting one or more of the criteria discussed earlier, there has been a contract issue or termination, or an unusual decline in charges to Payor B patients.

If the valuation analyst suspects or determines that the collection rate and realization rate approach are inaccurate, the earlier approach described of dividing receivables into two distinct groups of those greater than 90 days old (the sum of the greater-than-90-days and greater-than-120-days categories) and those less than 90 days old should be followed. (Refer to this approach as the "detailed" method.) In Exhibit 15 below, the valuation analyst determines that the Payor B receivables greater than 90 days will yield only 40 cents on the dollar rather than the collection rate of 60 cents. (It should not be seen as unusual for insured receivables in the greater-than-90-day category to be worth substantially less than the historical collection rate for a particular payor.)

Exhibit 15. Yield on Receivables Great Than and Less Than 90 Days, by Payor

Payor	<90 Days	Factor	Collectible	>90 Days	Factor	Collectible	Total
A	$20,000	50%	$10,000	$20,000	50%	$10,000	$20,000
B	$10,000	60%	$6,000	$30,000	40%	$12,000	$18,000
	$30,000		$16,000	$50,000		$22,000	$38,000

Exhibit 16. Recap of Methodologies

	Collection Rate	Realization Rate	Detail
Value	$44,000	$45,000	$38,000

The recap in Exhibit 16 indicates that the choice of approach to valuing receivables can generate very different results. If you are not convinced, multiply each of the values in the recap by 10.

Gaining Insight Into the Aging

Depending upon the sophistication of the practice's billing software, the importance of the receivables to the overall valuation, and the budget for the engagement, it may be desirable to obtain a *detailed aging by individual account* of the greater-than-90-day balances.

Insight and Analysis

In a litigation engagement, the greater-than-90-day balances were 3.5 times the MGMA norm. My investigation indicated that a host of problems existed in the recording (or lack thereof) of contractual allowances. The review, for example, of several annual detailed agings demonstrated that the same balances appeared year after year and there was a clear failure to write them off. Inquiries of management disclosed that the largest payor had negotiated a fixed weekly payment (or capitated arrangement) for services and that the difference between the practice's charges to that payor and the capitated payment were never written off. The uncollectible balances in this case amounted to multiple seven figures and resulted in a dramatic reduction in the valuation.

Credit Balances

This is one of the most difficult potential problems to identify and resolve when valuing medical accounts receivables. Credit balances *may* represent overpayments on a particular account or they may be payments posted to an account that could not be matched with a particular service and service date. For example, assume that a patient has four distinct services recorded. A check is received from the patient's insurer that does not specify which services are being paid. The data entry person posts the payment to the patient's account but does not apply it to any particular service. The detailed aging will typically reflect the credit separately from the individual charges. In this case, the credit balance is not a true credit, but rather requires a journal entry. As another example, assume that the insurer mistakenly pays the claim twice, creating a true credit balance. Finally, a common source of credit balances exists where the patient has insurance, but the practice has not contracted to accept direct payment from the insurer. As a courtesy, the practice may submit a bill to the insurer for the patient but expects the patient to pay the bill directly. If the insurer subsequently pays the practice as well, a true credit balance will result.

Because credit balances are generally considered lost property under most states' law and must be "escheated"[47] back to the state, the seriousness of this problem should not be overlooked. Further, failure to refund overpayments from government programs may subject the practice to civil or criminal sanctions. Certain state laws may provide for civil or criminal sanctions for nongovernmental payors as well.

Tax Affecting

The question frequently arises whether "zero basis" accounts receivable (as they are known for tax purposes where the taxpayer uses the cash method) should be tax-affected, or reduced for the estimated income taxes that will be due when they are collected. If the standard of value is fair market, many valuation analysts believe the adjustment is appropriate; some jurisdictions would not allow tax-affecting if the tax would never, in fact, be paid. This is of particular significance if the ultimate value of the business will be offset against property received by the other spouse in a divorce. For example, if the spouse is to receive cash of $100,000 (previously taxed by definition) and the business owner is to receive a like amount of accounts receivable that have not yet been taxed, there will clearly be an inequitable result.

In valuing a corporate professional practice with zero basis receivables, they would typically be offset by a claim for future compensation due to the owner. Arguably, therefore, the balance sheet accounts receivable and liability for deferred compensation would offset and reflect no increase in equity. However, the deferred compensation would be an individual asset of the practice owner. This asset should, again arguably, be offset for the taxes expected to be paid when the receivables are paid out of the corporation as salary. In addition, it should be considered whether these same receivables, when collected, will be subject to a claim for alimony and whether there should not be some adjustment for this as well. Because receivables are the source of future income typically subject to alimony, counting them as both an asset and as income is seen as "double counting" in some courts and by some valuation experts.

Insight and Analysis

If the standard of value for divorce in your state is fair market value on a going concern basis, reducing the receivables by collection costs is likely an inappropriate modification to collectible value. Going concern means that after the valuation date (hypothetical sale date) the practice will continue to operate in the ordinary course. If the standard of value were liquidation value, collection costs would be considered.

47 The term is commonly believed to be based on the fact that the '**S**'tate ['**Es**'] "cheats" the consumer or business out of the money but actually is a term originating in feudal England and Wales when land was owned by the king and granted in "fiefs" to royalty and would revert to the king upon certain occurrences.

Conclusion

To properly measure accounts receivable of a medical practice, the valuation analyst requires a considerable knowledge of what information to request and how to interpret and use it. Even if relying primarily on an income approach or market approach, failure to properly estimate net working capital can expose the valuation to a serious possibility of overstatement. If the valuation engagement is to measure asset value, the individual components thereof—fixed assets, net working capital, and intangible value—must be known to compute the tax benefit from depreciation of fixed assets and amortization of the intangible value. It is difficult to escape the need to apply the cost approach in valuing a medical practice, at least as far as net working capital is concerned.

An In-Depth Review of the Correct Use of the Excess Earnings Method

Insight and Analysis

This section is based upon material I use in my continuing education courses for both basic business valuation and medical practice valuation. The premise is that the excess earnings method is a very useful tool, but one that has been maligned due to its misuse, rather than any inherent weakness in the method itself. Be certain to read this *entire* section to avoid drawing incorrect conclusions about the examples (the initial example contains a deliberate error). Bear in mind that "when weighted capitalization rates for tangible- and intangible-asset cash flows are used to derive a single capitalization rate for all cash flows, capitalized excess earnings (CEE) will generate the same result as capitalization of cash flows (CCF)."[48]

The appropriateness of the excess earnings method, notwithstanding the many valuation analysts who are apparently unfamiliar with the basic accounting equation, can be seen in that assets equals liabilities plus equity, the right-hand side of that equation being capital. As such, the weighted average cost of capital for assets must be equal to the WACC for capital, or else our valuation balance sheet will not balance! This was explored earlier in the chapter on WACC. The concept is presented visually in Exhibit 17.

Net Tangible Assets

Though there is no uniform agreement as to what the term "net tangible assets" means, it is important that the choice of a return on those net assets, however defined, is consistent (i.e., properly paired) with the definition being used—and there is no disagreement about that.

One definition of net tangible assets is the sum of net working capital and fixed assets (See Example 1. Historical Balance Sheet, Option 1). These values should be stated at fair

48 "Medical Practices: A BV Rx," *Journal of Accountancy*, November 2005 by the author.

Exhibit 17. Weighted Average Cost of Capital for Assets Equal WACC for Capital

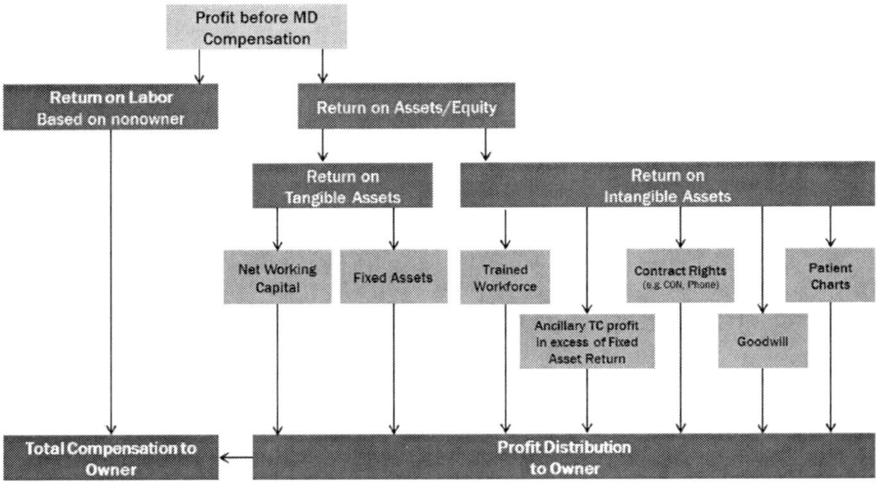

market value, although typically the book value of fixed assets is used unless the valuation analyst is comfortable *estimating* his or her fair market value or has a separate appraisal.

Example 1. Historical Balance Sheet	
Net working capital	$80,000
Fixed assets	$290,000
Net tangible assets—Option 1	$370,000
Long-term debt	$300,000
Equity or net tangible assets—Option 2	$70,000

The correct computation of the required return on net tangible assets using this definition is shown in Example 1: Weighted Average Cost of Capital. Here, we have assumed that the pretax cost of debt is 6%, based upon a borrowing rate of 9% less long-term growth rate of 3%. The cap rate for equity is 34%, determined by the 37% pretax discount rate less long-term growth rate of 3%. We know from the Historical Balance Sheet that there is $300,000 of debt and that the equity is equal to the net tangible assets of $70,000. Doing the calculations results in a required return on net tangible assets of 11.3%.

Valuation Tip

The components of the build-up of a discount rate below are hypotheticals for a valuation date. You need to use the correct components based upon the *actual* valuation date from Morningstar's SBBI Yearbook and other sources.

Long Treasury Bond	5.8%
Equity Risk Premium, S&P 500	7.5%
Base Equity Rate	13.3%
10th Decile Risk Premium, S&P 500	4.6%
Practice Risk Premium	5.5%
After-Tax Discount Rate	23.4%
Less: Growth Rate	-3.0%
Capitalization Rate, Subsequent Year	**20.4%**
Pre-Tax Cap Rate	**34.0%**
Plus: Growth Rate	**3.0%**
Pre-Tax Discount Rate	**37.0%**

Example 1. Cap Rate From the Weighted Average Cost of Capital				
Debt	6%	$300,000	81.08%	4.86%
Equity	34%	70,000	18.92	6.43
		$370,000	100.00%	11.30%

In the next portion of Example 1, we illustrate the calculation of the value of the business enterprise using the excess earnings method. Normalized 2002 earnings are based upon cash flows to invested capital (debt-free cash flows), which includes both long-term debt and equity, as should be clear from Example 1—Option 1.[49] The fair market value of the owner and employee physician's services is $270,000. For simplicity, we assume that the required return on intangibles is equivalent to the required return on equity of 34%. In an actual engagement, the valuation analyst should, of course, consider whether the intangibles require a higher rate of return than the "generic" return on equity.[50]

Example 1. Net Tangible Assets Based on Net Working Capital (NWC) Plus Fixed Assets			
Normalized 2002 earnings			$375,000
Fair market earnings			-270,000
Excess earnings			105,000
"Net tangible assets"	$370,000	11.3%	-41,800
Excess earnings attributable to intangibles			63,200
Capitalization rate			34%
Intangible Value			**$185,882**
Practice Tangibles			**$370,000**
Business Enterprise Value			**$555,882**

49 Read this two or three times. It is the key to understanding how to do the calculation correctly!

50 In fact, the return on equity of the entire business should be a separate weighted average of the required equity rates of return on tangibles partially financed by debt and intangibles financed by equity.

The second definition of net tangible assets (Example 2. Historical Balance Sheet, Option 2) is the sum of net working capital and fixed assets, less long-term debt. If book values are used for all of these factors, net tangible assets in this circumstance will equal stockholders' equity, unless there are excluded assets or liabilities.[51]

Example 2. Historical Balance Sheet	
Net working capital	$80,000
Fixed assets	$290,000
Net tangible assets—Option 1	**$370,000**
Long-term debt	$300,000
Equity or net tangible assets— Option 2	**$70,000**

Recall that normalized 2002 earnings are based upon cash flows to invested capital (debt-free cash flows), which includes both long-term debt and equity. There are two critical aspects of correctly performing the calculation when using this (Option 2) definition of net tangible assets. The first is to recognize that the return on the $300,000 of debt ($18,000) must be subtracted from the normalized 2002 earnings. This is necessary because the $18,000 is not available to equity.

The second critical aspect is that there is no need to compute a weighted average return because the net tangibles assets are equal to equity only. As such, the required return on the $70,000 is 34%, or $23,800.

Example 2. Net Tangible Assets Based on NWC Plus Fixed Assets Less Long-Term Debt			
Normalized 2002 earnings			$375,000
Interest on debt			-18,000
Fair market earnings			-270,000
Excess earnings			87,000
Net tangible assets	$70,000	34.0%	23,800
Excess earnings attributable to intangibles			63,200
Capitalization rate			34%
Intangible Value			**$185,882**
Practice Tangibles			**370,000**
Business Enterprise Value			**$555,882**

The proof that the two calculations have been handled correctly is that the valuation result—*$555,882*—is exactly the same in both options! I highly recommend that valuation analysts using the excess earnings method structure their spreadsheet models to

51 An example of excluded assets in valuing the business enterprise would be marketable securities not part of required working capital that are considered a nonoperating asset. Another example would typically be a loan receivable from an officer of the company.

perform the calculation using both Option 1 and Option 2. In this manner, you have an automatic proof of the correct application of the method.

The balance sheet based upon the fair market value calculation is shown below. The business enterprise value of $555,882 would be the price a buyer would pay for the assets, while the $255,883 would be the value of the equity (stock) of the company.[52]

Fair Market Balance Sheet			
	Historical Cost	Adjust	Fair Market
Net working capital	$80,000		$80,000
Fixed assets	290,000		290,000
	370,000		370,000
Intangibles		$185,882	185,882
Business enterprise value	370,000	185,882	555,882
Long-term debt	300,000		300,000
Equity	$70,000	$185,882	$255,882

Insight and Analysis

Bear in mind that the above example contains (what may be) a deliberate error in the concluded value. See the discussion under the caption Cost of Capital later in this chapter.

The Use of the Capitalization of Cash Flows in Conjunction With the Excess Earnings Method

A common user error is the failure to consider or properly assess whether the *overall* (weighted average) capitalization rate that results from the *separate* rates on tangibles and intangibles is reasonable. Computing the weighted average capitalization rate and using it to determine the practice's value under the capitalization of cash flows method can prevent this pitfall.

Exhibit 18 revisits the example from the previous section. In Exhibit 19, we have determined that the *pretax*[53] cost of debt is 6% and the pretax cost of equity is 34%. The cost of equity will apply to the tangibles not financed by debt as well as to the intangibles.[54]

52 If the goal of the valuation is to value assets, the valuator should consider adding the present value of the tax benefit of amortizing the intangible value under Internal Revenue Code 197.

53 We use pretax rates of return since that is what is commonly done for medical practices.

54 It is (also) correct to have a *higher* cost of equity for the intangibles and a *lower* cost of equity for the tangibles under the theory that intangibles are more risky and therefore, demand a higher rate of return.

Exhibit 18. Historical Balance Sheet

Net working capital	$80,000
Fixed assets	$290,000
Net tangible assets	$370,000
Long-term debt	$300,000
Equity or net tangible assets	$70,000

Exhibit 19. WACC Cap Rate for Tangible Assets

Debt	6%	$300,000	81.08%	4.86%
Equity	34%	70,000	18.92	6.43
		$370,000	100.00%	11.30%

Exhibit 20 is the calculation of the value of the practice using the excess earnings method from the previous section. The return on the tangibles of 11.3% is based upon the weighted average of the return on debt and the return on equity reflected in Exhibit 19 above.

Exhibit 20. Excess Earnings Method

Normalized 2002 earnings			$375,000
Fair market earnings			$(270,000)
Excess earnings			$105,000
"Net tangible assets"	$370,000	11.3%	$(41,800)
Excess earnings attributable to intangibles			$63,200
Capitalization rate			34%
Intangible value			**$185,882**
Practice tangibles			**$370,000**
Business enterprise value			**$555,882**

It is important to understand that the excess earnings method is nothing more (or less) than a *two-stage* capitalization of cash flows: The first stage is "reversed" in that we determine the value of the tangible assets *first*[55] and then apply a predetermined rate of return to that value. In the second stage, we determine the value of the intangible assets by capitalizing the remaining cash flow by the predetermined rate of return for

55 This is why the method is thought of as a hybrid method: In effect, you have to use the cost approach to determine the value of the tangibles.

intangibles. In effect, the excess earnings method says that there are two returns on equity to the owner of the practice: one on tangibles and one on intangibles. The reasonable compensation is a return on labor.

How do we know that the rate of return on the earnings after reasonable compensation—earnings attributable to both tangibles and intangibles—is itself reasonable? The only way to confirm this is to compute the weighted average return based upon the values determined in the excess earnings method and then apply it to the total earnings in excess of reasonable compensation. This computation is shown in Exhibit 21.

Exhibit 21. WACC Cap Rate for Entire Practice

Tangibles	$370,000	66.56%	11.30%	7.52%
Practice Intangibles	185,882	33.44	34.00	11.37
Weighted Average Cost Of Capital	$555,882	100.00%		18.89%

Thus, we see that the choice of a 6% pretax cap rate for debt and a 34% pretax cap rate for equity results in a WACC cap rate of 18.89% applied to the pretax earnings or cash flow of the practice, after the payment of reasonable compensation for labor. The analysis of whether or not this is reasonable requires the valuation analyst's assessment of the reasonableness of the separate costs of equity (34%) and debt (6%). It can also be viewed in the conventional fashion of the weights of equity and debt, rather than the weights of tangibles and intangibles, as shown in Exhibit 22.

Exhibit 22. Conventional WACC Cap Rate for Entire Practice

Debt	6%	$300,000	53.97%	3.24%
Equity	34%	255,882	46.03	15.65
		$555,882	100.00%	18.89%

What Exhibit 22 demonstrates is that the high percentage of debt is making the WACC quite low. The valuation analyst should consider whether this is a reasonable degree of debt for an engagement to value a controlling interest—the excess earnings method should only be used to value a controlling interest.

Finally, we can "prove" the computation of the WACC for the entire practice and the excess earnings method by valuing the practice using the traditional capitalization of cash flows method. This proof does not confirm the reasonableness of the 18.89% cap rate, only that it has been computed correctly.

Exhibit 23. Capitalization of Cash Flows

Normalized 2002 Earnings	$375,000
Fair Market Earnings	(270,000)
Cash Flow After Reasonable Compensation	$105,000
Capitalization Rate	18.89%
	$555,882

The value is exactly the same, as it should be!

Exhibit 24 indicates the most common mistake: assuming that all of the tangible assets can be financed with debt or at a low rate of return, based upon the IRS excess earnings method. Exhibit 25 is the calculation of the value under the excess earnings method. This silly result is based upon a case study presented in my course on business valuation.[56]

Exhibit 24. WACC Cap Rate for Tangible Assets

Debt	0%	$0	0%	0%
Equity—Tangibles	10%	1,000,000	100	10
		$1,000,000	100%	10%

Exhibit 25. Excess Earnings Method

Normalized 2002 earnings			$375,000
Fair market earnings			(270,000)
Excess earnings			105,000
Net tangible assets	$1,000,000	10%	(100,000)
Excess earnings attributable to intangibles			$5,000
Capitalization rate			34%
Intangible value			**$14,706**
Practice tangibles			**$1,000,000**
Business enterprise value			**$1,014,706**

Exhibit 26 will clue the valuation analyst in to the *fact* that a mistake has been made: A pretax return of 10.35% for a medical practice is not reasonable in any event! If we do a short-cut conversion of this rate to an after-tax rate by multiplying by 1 minus the tax rate (40%), or 60%, we get a return we can compare to standard costs of equity from

56 This is a case study based upon actual mistakes I have seen made by other "experts."

Morningstar. 10.35% times 60% equals 6.21% (a cap rate). Adding the growth rate of 3% gives us an after-tax discount rate of 9.21%. This is *less than* the required rate of return on the S&P 500, which represents the risk of an equity investment in the broad market, the standard of comparison. Simply put, it is ridiculous.

Exhibit 26. Conventional WACC Cap Rate for Entire Practice

Tangibles	$1,000,000	98.55%	10%	9.86%
Practice intangibles	14,706	1.45	34	0.49
Weighted average cost of capital	$1,014,706	100.00%		10.35%

Notwithstanding the mistake in the selection of the return on the $1 million of tangibles, Exhibit 27 demonstrates that this method agrees with Exhibit 23's excess earnings method.

Exhibit 27. Capitalization of Cash Flows

Normalized 2002 earnings	$375,000
Fair market earnings	(270,000)
Cash flow after reasonable compensation	$105,000
Capitalization rate	10.35%
	$1,014,706

Conclusion

Failure to test the reasonableness of the two rates of return used in the excess earnings method by computing a single rate of return for the cash flow attributable to both tangibles and intangibles (capitalization of cash flows method) can lead to serious mistakes, such as that shown in Exhibits 22 to 25. The valuation analyst should structure spreadsheets to perform this test *automatically*. The key element is whether the combined pretax cap rate (or the return in the practice's assets) is reasonable when compared to proper external benchmarks, such as those developed from Morningstar data under the capital asset pricing model or build-up method.

Control Adjustments to the Excess Earnings Valuation Model?

Introduction

The excess earnings method generally produces a control value. The technical reason for this is that the tangible asset measurement requires the cost approach, which always produces a control value. It *is* mathematically possible to adjust the assumptions in an excess earnings model to generate a noncontrol value, just as it is possible—and common—to vary the assumptions in a capitalization of cash flows model to produce a control or a noncontrol value. Medical practices are somewhat unusual in that the excess earnings method—properly applied, of course—could be used to determine a noncontrol value. This is in large part because the distribution of cash is generally governed by employment contracts and other ownership rights via a stockholders agreement and because the tangible assets are not typically material when compared to the intangible assets.

Control Adjustments

To apply control premiums to reach a control value, you must first have used a method that determines a *noncontrol* value. In addition, the valuation community has moved toward the position that most "control" premiums actually represent strategic considerations not consistent with fair market value. Use of control premiums when using the excess earnings method is therefore inappropriate, or stated more frankly, *wrong*.

Equally risky is use of the excess earnings method to determine a *non*control value. Lack of control or minority discounts should be *considered* when the excess earnings method is used to produce a noncontrol value. Better yet, *eliminate the control adjustments*. Perhaps the most frequently overlooked fact of medical practice valuation is that if all cash distribution is contractual, i.e., via a compensation plan and employment contracts, and the tangible value is low, using the excess earnings method for a physician practice buy-in is acceptable (and common), providing the noncontrol elements are properly considered.

Reasonable Compensation

In valuing medical practices using the excess earnings method, the most important adjustment is the one for reasonable compensation. As noted earlier in the chapter, determining the reasonable compensation for a physician requires more than merely looking at a statistical source and choosing the mean or median. The valuation analyst needs to first compare the physician's productivity or work effort to statistical norms and then base the reasonable compensation on that productivity. You cannot expect to pay a hypothetical buyer of the practice a 35-hour wage for 50 hours of work.[57]

It is equally important to focus on where the income in the practice is coming from. Practices that own laboratories or imaging equipment, e.g., x-ray, ultrasound, CT scan or MRI, may have significant profits from such operations. These profits need to be

57 See, e.g., "Medical Practices: A Bv Rx," *Journal of Accountancy*, November 2005 by the author. This is not to say that anomalous situations do not exist where P.T. Barnum's rule is in effect.

determined to correctly perform the valuation. They are not part of the physician work effort. Moreover, they may not be part of personal or professional goodwill in a divorce context and should be factored out of that debate in those jurisdictions where personal goodwill is not a divisible asset. Here is the same chart we looked at earlier in the chapter in the discussion of the weighted average cost of capital for the asset side of the balance sheet, now presented to show how the profit paid out as compensation in the typical physician practice consists both of a return on labor and a return on assets or capital.

The "compensation" needs to be considered in its broader sense of fringe benefits, retirement plan contributions and other perquisites. For example, the compensation in the MGMA data includes only W-2 (and equivalent[58]) compensation; retirement plan benefits are reported separately. As such, when figuring reasonable compensation in a valuation model, if the valuation analyst adds back the retirement plan contribution to available earnings, he or she then needs to add the MGMA retirement plan contribution to whatever (W-2) earnings are selected from the MGMA data.

Exhibit 28. Profit Paid Out as Compensation Consists of Return on Labor and a Return on Capital

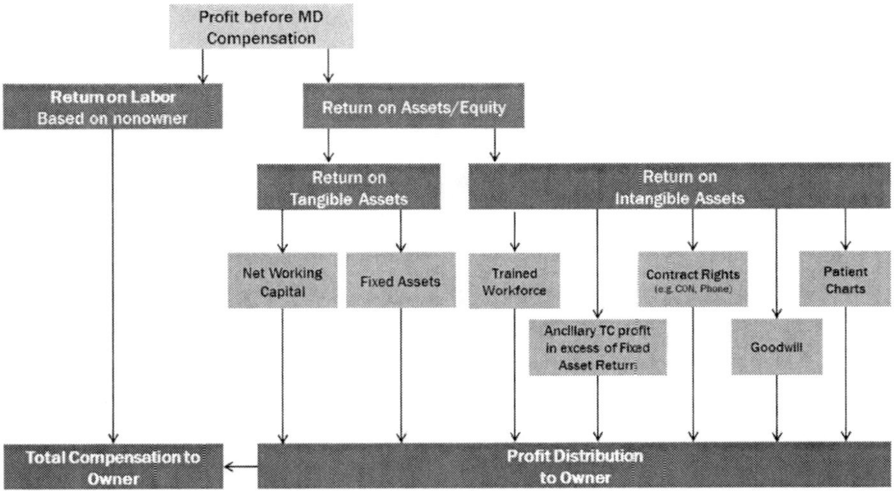

Insight and Analysis

In my experience, there is a cyclical pattern of the use of high contribution retirement plans by physicians and dentists with high incomes—typically solo practitioners or two- or three-partner practices. Defined benefit plans, target benefit plans and cash balance

58 Bonuses, a partner's or S stockholder's share of income, etc.

plans became highly attractive again during the George W. Bush administration due to a relaxation in the rules. Annual contributions for a high-income beneficiary over age 50 can be $150,000 per year or more, *plus* a 401(k) contribution and even a profit-sharing contribution of up to 6% of the Section 415 compensation limit. These add up to more than $200,000 per annum. Thus, it is critical to normalize compensation to take into account retirement contributions.

Cost of Capital

In the first part of this section, we saw that there was substantial debt in the practice used to finance tangible assets. This debt drove down the required rate of return on the tangibles, which in turn increased the amount of excess earnings available for intangible assets. This, of course, apparently increases the value of the practice. In short, the more debt one adds to the capital structure, the lower the cost of capital goes and the higher the value goes—*unless* one understands the CAPM and betas! This suggests that the analysis of the percentage of debt in the capital structure is critical to a correct valuation, although simply adding debt to lower the cost of capital is not acceptable since increased debt also increases the cost of equity.

Variations in the percentages of debt and equity that a hypothetical control owner of a practice would make need to be thought through carefully. In the real world, the debt of a medical practice is limited to some portion of the fixed assets and the accounts receivable in the practice. Rarely does one see the intangible value financed with debt. As such, it would generally be inaccurate to assume that the intangible value would be financed with debt in the absence of some peculiar set of circumstances.

Exhibit 29 is the computation of the pretax cap rate and discount rate for this example.

Exhibit 29. Computation of the Pretax Cap Rate and Discount Rate

Long Treasury Bond	5.8%
Equity Risk Premium, S&P 500	7.5%
Base Equity Rate	13.3%
10th Decile Risk Premium, S&P 500	4.6%
Practice Risk Premium	5.5%
After-Tax Discount Rate	23.4%
Less: Growth Rate	-3.0%
Capitalization Rate, Subsequent Year	**20.4%**
Pre-Tax Cap Rate	**34.0%**
Plus: Growth Rate	**3.0%**
Pre-Tax Discount Rate	**37.0%**

Insight and Analysis

The components of the build-up of a discount rate are *hypotheticals* for a valuation date. You need to use the correct components based upon the actual valuation date from Ibbotson's *Yearbook* and other sources.

Exhibit 30 highlights the hypothetical optimal mix of debt and equity used for the (same) practice that was presented in the first two parts of this article.

Exhibit 30. WACC Cap Rate for Tangible Assets

Pretax discount rate		37.00%	
Equity percentage		75.00%	
			27.75%
Cost of debt	9.00%		
Tax rate	0.00%		
After-tax cost of debt		9.00%	
Debt percentage		25.00%	
			2.25%
Weighted average cost of capital			30.00%
Less: growth rate			-3.00%
Cap rate, subsequent year			27.00%

Exhibit 31 is the calculation of the value of the practice using the excess earnings method from the previous section.

Exhibit 31. Excess Earnings Method

Normalized 2002 earnings			$375,000
Interest on debt			(5,550)
Fair market earnings			(270,000)
Excess earnings			99,450
Net tangible assets	$277,500	34.00%	(94,350)
Excess earnings attributable to intangibles			$5,100
Capitalization rate			34.00%
Intangible value			**$15,000**
Practice tangibles			**$370,000**
Business enterprise value			**$385,000**

Exhibit 32 is the cap rate determined in the earlier example, followed by the cap rate based on Exhibit 33.

Exhibit 32. WACC Cap Rate for Tangible Assets

Old Debt	6.%	$300,000	53.97%	3.24%
Equity	34%	255,882	46.03	15.65
		$555,882	100.00%	18.89%

Exhibit 33. WACC Cap Rate for Tangible Assets—New

Here, debt is 25% of the tangible assets of $385,000, or $92,500.				
Debt	6%	$92,500	24.03%	1.44%
Equity	34%	292,500	75.97	25.83
		$385,000	100.00%	27.27%

Insight and Analysis

Note the substantial difference in the weighted average cost of capital when the debt level is adjusted to 24% from the nearly 54% in the original example. Since "the lower the cap rate, the higher the value," we know that the value of the practice with 25% debt (Exhibit 34) will be much less than with 54% debt (Exhibit 35).

Exhibit 34. Capitalization of Cash Flows—New

Normalized 2002 earnings	$375,000
Fair market earnings	(270,000)
Cash flow after reasonable compensation	$105,000
Capitalization rate	27.27%
Asset value	$385,000
Less: long-term debt	300,000
Equity value	$85,000

Exhibit 35. Capitalization of Cash Flows—Old

Normalized 2002 earnings	$375,000
Fair market earnings	(270,000)
Cash flow after reasonable compensation	$105,000
Capitalization rate	18.89%
Asset value	$555,882
Less: long-term debt	$300,000
Equity value	$255,882

Which of these two answers is correct? This decision requires that most difficult of skills: judgment. Part of the answer lays in the conversion of the two cap rates to after-tax discounts rates (Exhibit 36) that can be compared to Morningstar's return on capital. Bear in mind that the cap rates are being applied to *invested capital* whereas the Morningstar data determine a cost of *equity* that then needs to be used in a computation of a weighted average cost of capital capitalization rate. The valuation analyst needs to ask the question: Is 19.36% (14.33%) a reasonable return[59] on invested capital for a medical practice? In point of fact, 14.33% would be quite low by both current and historical standards. At the peak of acquisition activity in the mid-1990s, when perceived risk was lowest, the weighted average cost of capital for the best physician practices was rarely less than 16%. Today, practices are considered much more risky. The 19.36% is a more reasonable rate of return.

Exhibit 36. Conversion of the Two Cap Rates to After-Tax Discounts Rates

Cap rate—pretax	27.27%	18.89%
1 less the tax rate	60.00	60.00
Cap rate—after-tax	16.36	11.33
Growth rate	3.00	3.00
Discount rate—after-tax	19.36%	14.33%

Insight and Analysis

One question I have often been asked: If using a hypothetical mix of debt and equity in the WACC, what is subtracted from the result to determine the actual equity of the practice, actual debt or hypothetical debt? The answer, of course, is the actual debt. The assumption is that the hypothetical owner would use an optimal mix of debt and equity, which in turn is what drives the enterprise value in the valuation. From the *seller's* standpoint, it gets the entire enterprise value and then pays off *whatever debt it has, if any.* Think about a scenario in which the optimal debt-equity mix is 25% to 75%, but the seller has 50% debt Clearly, the equity is less than if it had 25% debt. It is useful to prepare a pro forma FMV balance sheet[60]—allocating to working capital, fixed assets and intangibles—from the model so you can see what the actual assets, debt, and equity look like.

What About a Noncontrol Value?

Lawyers, judges, and some valuation analysts[61] like the excess earnings method for valuing physician practices. Many of the members of that subset of professionals do not

59 Net of growth.
60 And beware what you call it if subject to SSVS and SSARS.
61 Including the author for physician to physician transactions.

really understand how it works, however. The most frequent mistake in a transactional setting is using the excess earnings method to inappropriately value a *non*control interest.

For example, let's assume that the practice in Figures 3 and 6 consisted of one owner and one employee physician. The owner is paid $250,000 per year, and the employee is paid $125,000. The valuation analyst determines that reasonable compensation for the owner is $140,000 and for the employee, $130,000. The employee is going to buy 50% of the practice. Since the value is a control value and you do not get control with 50%, this should be your first clue that the value of the 50% interest is *not* one-half of $385,000, or $192,500. Since the employee does not get control, he or she cannot reduce the current owner's salary to $140,000 per year and therefore cannot get 50% of the excess earnings of $105,000. If he or she doesn't get that 50%, what is the practice worth? It is only worth the excess earnings that the employee receives, capitalized at 27.27%. If the owner continues to get paid $250,000, there are not any excess earnings *and the practice is worth nothing to the employee.*

In point of fact, valuing a practice for buy-in purposes really requires that the terms of the buy-in be known. The 2008 *Derby* tax court case indicates that the actual terms must be known for a sale to a hospital. As can be seen from the simple example above, *the value to the buyer depends upon what the buyer's income will be after the purchase.* If it doesn't change, there is no value. If the income does not change for a number of years, the excess earnings method (or CCF method) is not a correct choice, as both of these methods assume that there is level cash flow throughout the period of ownership that grows at a fixed rate each year. The correct method in such a circumstance is the discounted cash flow (DCF) method, which permits the valuation analyst to specifically match the year of the cash flow with the appropriate discount factor for that year.

A noncontrol owner could not alter the cost of capital, either. Therefore, one generally would not make this adjustment in determining a value for noncontrol purposes. However, if the capital structure contains *excessive* debt, the noncontrol buyer should not be willing to pay the inflated value resulting from the apparently lower WACC—since the lower WACC likely does not accurately reflect the true cost of equity. *Remember that fair market value will generally not exceed the amount determined on a control basis for the hypothetical buyer.* If the level of debt exceeds that hypothetical amount, the value will exceed fair market value. If fair market is the standard of value, then a lower level of debt would have to be assumed in the valuation model.

Chapter Summary

In this chapter, we reviewed the nuts and bolts of applying the commonly accepted valuation methods to physician practices. The key points for most readers are as follows.

The discount rate for a valuation measures the expected return on investment based upon the risk involved. The greater the risk, the higher the discount rate a hypothetical investor will demand. The discount rate consists of a risk-free rate, a large company equity risk premium, a small company equity risk premium plus a specific practice risk premium. The latter is subjective and highly contingent upon the skill, knowledge, and experience of the valuation analyst. The capitalization rate is derived from the discount rate by subtracting the expected growth rate in cash flows during the terminal period from the discount rate.

The discounted cash flow method is the most commonly accepted valuation method for physician practices subject to regulatory scrutiny and should be used with after-tax earnings. It measures enterprise value (EV), which includes tangible assets such as equipment and working capital plus intangible assets. Use of the method requires considerable effort and skill on the part of the valuation consultant.

Physician compensation expense in the valuation model should be based upon what is to be paid if the transaction takes place because a hypothetical investor would not pay for a cash flow return that was, in fact, being paid out to a physician employee. Valuation analysts may wish to advise clients that actual compensation negotiated in a transaction that differs from that used in the valuation suggests revisiting the valuation.

The excess earnings method is, in the author's opinion, the best method for small-scale transactions between physicians and can be performed using pretax or after-tax cash earnings, as long as the discount and capitalization rates are adjusted appropriately.

For experienced valuation consultants new to physician practice valuation, the factors for selecting the specific practice risk premium should be considered, along with the requirements of regulatory authority outlined in this chapter and throughout this guide.

This chapter was edited by Carol Carden, CPA/ABV, ASA of PYA.

The Thornton letter on the following pages is a 1992 response on valuing physician practices.

The Thornton Letter

This letter is one of the seminal events in physician practice valuation "lore and legend." Although it is generally accepted, nearly 20 years later, that a physician practice may be valued based upon its own internal revenue streams, there are still those who feel—or fear—that the letter is relevant.

November 2, 1993
John E. Steiner, Jr., Esquire
Assistant General Counsel
American Hospital Association
840 North Lake Shore Drive
Chicago, IL 60611

Dear John:

I am responding to your letter of July 20, 1993, requesting assistance in interpreting the scope of prohibited referrals under the Medicare and Medicaid anti-kickback statute with respect to the acquisition of physician practices. The focus of your inquiry was the position taken in my Dec. 22, 1992 letter to T. J. Sullivan at the Internal Revenue Service that payments for intangible assets or goodwill were open to question under the anti-kickback statute, and my subsequent oral comments on this issue.

In particular, in your letter you presented two specific situations involving the acquisition of a physician's practice. The first situation involved the purchase of a physician practice by another physician or a group practice. I have assumed the acquiring practice is not in a position to benefit from referrals by the acquired practice. After reaching agreement on the price for the hard assets, the parties proceed to value the remainder of the practice and assign a value for the expectation of future patronage by patients to the practice being acquired. The total price negotiated for the practice includes an amount for both the hard assets and the intangible assets. You described this situation as involving a "one-step" referral, a situation where the patients "self-refer" because of word of mouth about the physician or because another unrelated physician refers to the practice.

The second situation involves the acquisition of the same or a similar physician practice, except that the purchaser is a hospital, which is in a position to benefit from referrals by the acquired practice. The same valuation method is used to determine the purchase price. Even though the hospital can be expected to receive admissions and referrals from the practice, the value of these referrals are not used in the valuation of the practice. Only the expected future patronage to the practice is included and the hospital does not pay more for the practice than would another physician. This situation is described as involving a "two-step" referral process, one to the practice and a second one to the hospital.

You sought an opinion clarifying whether the payments made in either or both of these situations would be allowable under the anti-kickback statute. As you know, the Medicare and Medicaid anti-kickback statute, Section 1128B(b) of the Social Security Act, 42 U.S.C. 1320a-7b(b), makes it a criminal offense to knowingly and willfully offer, pay, solicit, or receive remuneration to induce, or in return for, the referral of business covered by Medicare or Medicaid.

For a number of reasons, we are not in a position to issue advisory or interpretive opinions on whether a particular practice or arrangement violates the anti-kickback statute. One reason is that since Section 1128B(b) is a criminal statute, the Department of Justice has exclusive authority to initiate a criminal prosecution or decline to do so under the statute. Another reason is that the statute requires proof of knowing and willful intent, and it is generally impossible to evaluate intent on the basis of a paper submission. Finally, in reviewing a particular arrangement, we cannot be sure that we have all the necessary information concerning the nature of the arrangement or practice and how it operates to make a proper decision concerning its legality or illegality.

I would like to emphasize that the position I articulated in the Dec. 22, 1992 letter to T. J. Sullivan remains the same. I did not state that payments for intangible assets are illegal per se. Nor have I indicated approval of any particular acquisition practices or valuation methodologies. Since payments for items other than the hard assets of a physician practice could be a payment to induce referrals or could be in return for future referrals, any such payments are subject to scrutiny to determine whether they violate the anti-kickback statute. The fact that the parties may identify the purpose of the payment as something other than a payment for referrals is not determinative.

Similarly, the fact that two different parties may offer to pay the same price for a particular or a comparable physician practice or may use a similar approach in "valuing" the practice does not mean that both will be afforded the same treatment under the anti-kickback statute. The intent of the parties is the critical element in the determination of a violation under the anti-kickback statute, and different parties may have different purposes and reasons for seeking to acquire a particular physician practice and for paying a particular price. Finally, the facts and circumstances involved in each situation are likely to be different as will be the nature of the relationship between the parties. Consequently, each particular situation must be judged on its own merits and based on its own facts and circumstances.

Turning to the two situations described above, we believe the first situation is far less problematic than the second. However, either situation could constitute a violation of the anti-kickback statute, depending on the intent of the parties, the nature of the intangible assets, the amounts paid for the intangible assets, and the past and future relationship of the parties, etc. One major factor is where the seller becomes or remains affiliated with the buyer. In such a case, the terms of that continued affiliation as well as the remuneration paid to the seller for services rendered would also need to be taken into account in determining whether a violation exists.

With respect to the second situation involving the purchase of the practice by a hospital, anytime an entity is acquiring a practice where the entity is in a position to benefit from referrals from the practice, there is always a question that a portion of the amount paid for the practice is attributable to the future referrals. As indicated above, it is the intent of the parties and the facts and circumstances of the particular acquisition that are relevant. Accordingly, the fact that a hospital purchases a physician practice for the same amount that another physician might pay does not insulate the hospital from liability under the anti-kickback statute. For example, another physician may offer a high price based on the savings in administrative costs and overhead which could be realized by combining practices. However, a hospital may not have that motivation at all; its offer of the same price could be motivated by a desire to pay for future referrals.

We hope this information is helpful and regret that we are unable to provide further guidance. Thank you for your interest in this matter.

Sincerely,

/s/
D. McCarty Thornton
Associate General Counsel
Inspector General Division

Chapter 7

Sample Table of Contents for a Physician Practice Valuation Report

TABLE OF CONTENTS

ANALYSIS AND SUMMARY OF OUTLOOK FOR THE PRACTICE AT THE VALUATION DATE

- Practice Positives
- Practice Risk Areas
- Summary

OVERVIEW OF VALUATION APPROACHES AND ISSUES

- Introduction
  - Income Approach
  - Market Approach
  - Asset Accumulation (Cost) Approach
  - Workforce-in-Place
  - Other Intangible Assets of a Business Enterprise
  - Revenue Ruling 59-60
- Discussion of Market Approach
  - Internal Revenue Service
  - Goodwill Registry
  - Pratt's Stats
  - Differences in Geographic Market Areas
  - Market Activity in General
  - Chosen Approaches

VALUATION DISCUSSION

- Income Statement Normalization Adjustments: For Valuation Purposes
  - Depreciation
  - Rent
- Balance Sheet Normalization Adjustments: For Valuation Purposes
  - Accounts Receivable
  - Prepaid Rent
  - Fixed Assets
  - Prepaids
  - S Corporation Distributions
  - Reasonable Compensation for Services

VALUATION METHODS UTILIZED

- Working Capital Assumption
- Capital Cost Assumption
- Working Capital
- Rates of increase
  - Fee-for-service Revenues
    - Figure 1, Physician PPI

Chapter 8

Valuation Solutions for Special Situations With Medical Practices

By Mark O. Dietrich, CPA/ABV

SECTION I: PRACTICE BUY-INS, BUYOUTS, AND MERGERS

One of the most common situations confronting a physician practice is the need to assign equity interests in a practice buy-in or merger. As the healthcare market experiences renewed consolidation, those practices that choose not to sell to hospitals or other buyers will invariably choose to merge into larger entities or expand through the addition of new owners via buy-ins. Many specialists, rarely afforded the opportunity of a hospital purchase, look to merging to maintain their competitive position in an era dominated by a focus on primary care. Many of these mergers do not involve the payment of cash by one of the merging parties to the other but accurately measuring the value of the merging units rationally is important in the allocation of equity. This segment of the chapter first addresses practice buy-ins, then mergers.

A Series of Group Practice Buy-In Considerations

Author's Insight and Analysis

Group practice buy-ins and mergers are typically a matter of negotiation between the parties, guided by professional advisors if necessary, and not necessarily a conventional exercise in "fair market value," as appraisers might see it. Notwithstanding what an appraiser without direct transaction experience might think when looking at a practice, large buy-in prices in an era of physician shortages, hospital recruitment alternatives, and high post-medical school debt are a barrier to obtaining good physician partners and a source of considerable friction in the practice. Supply and demand is critical in determining what the fair market value of an interest in a practice is, just as it is in any other industry's services or products. It is part of the market that needs to be understood to arrive at fair market value.

Overview of Transactional Valuation

In transactional valuation, it is critical that the appraiser look at the actual documents that will govern the transaction price. This is not strategic value! The documents determine the precise nature of the interests being transferred, which in turn, determines how much they are worth. "Terms make the deal" is a common cliché in transactions, but it is not an indicia of strategic value. As a simple example, consider the value of a noncompete agreement as part of the enterprise value of a given medical practice. Assume that the seller has the ability and intent to compete post-transaction absent a contractual provision precluding that competition. A hypothetical buyer would pay less for the business—if it pays anything at all—absent the noncompete, while a hypothetical seller expects to be paid for not competing in addition to the value of the other assets being sold. Thus, the noncompete has an identifiable value—that can be determined through a "with and without" analysis, as described elsewhere in this guide—and two different fair market value prices would be determined for the enterprise based upon the terms of the deal. The question is not whether the presence or lack of a covenant represents strategic value—it does not—but what purchase price the hypothetical buyer and seller would reach for the business with and without the noncompete.

The analysis doesn't end there. The terms of the noncompete itself determine its value. Thus, a noncompete with a geographic restriction of 10 miles might be expected to have a value less than one with a geographic restriction of 25 miles, assuming that the catchment area of the medical practice extended beyond 10 miles. The sale of the practice with a 10-mile noncompete provision versus one with a 25-mile noncompete provision would have two different fair market values! Nothing about the geographic range of the noncompete term represents strategic value as long as the appraiser focuses his or her attention on what a hypothetical buyer and seller would agree to as a transaction price.

One of the important lessons learned from the professional literature on FAS 141/142 and the focus on valuing the left—asset—side of the valuation equation is that the market value of invested capital (MVIC) is the aggregate of the assets of the business. If the transaction documents pull out certain of those assets—such as accounts receivable net of payables, which is a common exclusion in a medical practice sale—a hypothetical buyer and seller would and, in fact, must adjust the actual transaction price, notwithstanding any conclusion of MVIC.

The 2008 tax court case Derby makes it very clear that the appraiser of a practice for a hospital purchase must—read that must—review the actual transaction documents specifically with respect to the post-transaction compensation and terms of the noncompete to determine the value of what was transferred. If the actual documents are not available, key assumptions such as post-transaction compensation and noncompete terms must be obtained from the client, and they should be 1) specified in the report and 2) considered for a representation letter. This is a left-hand-side, or asset, approach to valuing transaction, which is in contrast to the simpler, default right-hand-side, or invested capital, approach. Assets have a fair market value just as invested capital does, and due to the terms of the deal, the two may not always be equivalent because either 1) some element of the invested capital is not transferred, such as working capital, or 2) the terms of the transaction transfer more or less value than what the appraiser's generic concept of the transaction might be, such as a noncompete with a 10-mile versus a 25-mile radius.

In healthcare transactions in general and medical practices in particular, we encounter these nuances more often than not. We are expected under the regulatory standard of practice to assign value to these nuances, otherwise the transacting parties and the appraiser risk regulatory review.

As a final thought, real estate appraisal and transaction are no different. If a hypothetical buyer makes an offer on a home and the building inspection determines that the heating system is about to fail and will cost $10,000 to replace, one expects that the hypothetical buyer and seller will make an adjustment to the offer price—or else a transaction will not take place. Simpler still, if there are two otherwise identical four-bedroom homes located in the same neighborhood and one has been recently renovated with new kitchen cabinets, bathroom fixtures, and a deck and the other requires updating, they will have two different prices. The reason is that the condition of the underlying component assets being transferred differs. The reduced utility and the present value of expected future outlays by the owner to maintain House 2 are greater than those for House 1, making House 1 more valuable today.

Documents to be Considered

Medical practices typically have at least two core documents that have a substantial impact on the value of the practice: the stockholders' agreement or other document establishing the arrangement amongst equity owners, such as an LLC Operating Agreement or Partnership Agreement, and the employment contract. The employment contract may—and should—contain or refer to a compensation plan that determines how the available income in the practice is divided among the owner-employees. That compensation plan represents the most critical document for the appraiser to be familiar with in most circumstances. As discussed later in the chapter in "Defending Against Unwarranted Damage Claims in a Practice Dissolution," income in productivity-based compensation schemes is not allocated based on equity, but rather according to who generated it. As such, the "excess earnings" available to one new owner may be very different than that to another new owner—and two owners may pay different prices for the same equity interest.

Minimum Buy-In

For an employee physician coming into a partner or shareholder status within a group, the minimum buy-in generally would consist of the accounts receivable resulting from services he or she performed through the date of buy-in along with those related to any ancillaries or other profit centers that might be shared, plus a pro-rated share of the fair value of fixed assets—what appraisers would call tangible assets. Fixed assets are typically valued by using adjusted book value, adjusting for any Section 179 deductions and considering extended useful lives as compared to tax lives. Salvage value may also be considered. As examples, a dental operatory or an ophthalmic "lane" (the chair and basic surrounding equipment) may be in service for 15 or 20 years if properly maintained and perhaps rehabbed at some point along the way. The same is true for basic X-ray machines.

The accounts receivable portion of this price is generally paid via reduction of the new partner's compensation otherwise payable, spread over a period of 12 to 36 months. The portion related to fixed assets may be paid in cash for shares of stock or other equity ownership position. Attention should be given to trade payables and outstanding loans for the purchase of fixed assets, of course.

Compensation-Shifting Strategies

Many practices accomplish buy-ins via compensation shifts. The rationale is that senior members contribute more in the way of compensable activity and that the value of an equity investment (dividends and capital appreciation) is comparatively minor. This is sometimes termed a "senior disparity" allocation. A simple form of this shift involves crediting a portion of the new partner's productivity in terms of receipts (or net income) to the existing partners, generally for a period not exceeding three years. Often, the new partner will have a minimum salary during this period, pegged to productivity in terms of number of hours or sessions worked,[1] charges generated, or some other standard to which the parties agree.

Sometimes, the use of a compensation shift in lieu of an outright stock purchase will be "grossed up" to account for the tax benefit to the buyer and tax detriment to the seller. Other times, it is not. It is important for the valuation analyst to determine this when looking at the practice's historical transactions under the market approach.

1 Pediatric practices often use sessions, such as a day session, afternoon session or evening session.

Author's Insight and Analysis

Internal buy-ins should be based upon the excess earnings the new partner or stockholder will receive by virtue of the buy-in, valued at some multiple or cap rate and adjusted for discounts for minority shares and marketability, if appropriate. For example, if an employee physician is earning $120,000 per year and will earn $150,000 per year after becoming a stockholder, the excess earnings are $30,000. This $30,000 would be capitalized or discounted to determine the value of the interest.

Deferred Compensation Approach

Another far less common version of a compensation-shifting strategy is to accrue a liability for deferred compensation to the seller equal to all or some portion of the intangible value. The normalized balance sheet would then include an intangible asset for the value of services contributed by the seller to the practice that have not yet been compensated, offset by a liability to pay for those services in the future. All things being equal, this enables a buyer to acquire an interest at a substantially lower price, but will likely obligate him or her to be responsible for what may be a significant payment to the seller when the deferred compensation obligation matures.

Among other downsides to this approach is that the Internal Revenue Code (§3121(v)) requires FICA and Medicare tax to be paid on deferred compensation at the time it is earned and becomes nonforfeitable. The amount subject to tax is based upon the present value of the deferred benefit; as such, if the amount is payable in the future and does not bear interest, the present value will be less than the total obligation. Of course, the accrual should be equal to the present value, not the total obligation, if the recording of the liability is handled consistently. Valuators should be aware that Section 409A of the Internal Revenue Code could also present an issue and any such arrangement should be carefully structured by an attorney or other individual with tax expertise in this area.

Exhibit 1. Compensation-Shifting Strategy: Deferred Compensation Equals Intangible Value

Tangibles	$20,000		Tangibles	$20,000
Intangibles	300,000		Intangibles	300,000
Total assets	320,000		Total assets	320,000
Deferred comp	-0-		Deferred comp	300,000
Net worth	$320,000		Net worth	$20,000

Economic-Equivalence When Buy-In Prices Are Significant

Substantial buy-in prices require, or should require, substantial buy-outs at the time of departure from the practice. Physicians who are ready to accept their share of buy-in proceeds may be reluctant to forgo income when it comes to buying out a retiring partner.

In terms of potential IRS attacks on unreasonable compensation and a lack of return on equity investment—a cyclical occurrence of which appraisers should be aware—large buy-ins represent a potential problem, especially in C corporations. If, for example, a physician pays $100,000 for a stock interest in a practice, basic economics, to say nothing of valuation theory, dictates that he or she should receive a market rate of return on that investment. Returns on equity investments are paid via either dividends or capital appreciation. The former, of course, are not tax deductible by C corporations—and are rarely paid for that reason. Equity returns are far less problematic in S corporations or LLCs, the latter having the greatest degree of flexibility since there is no one class of stock required if they are taxed as partnerships. Partnerships can use "guaranteed payments" under Section 707 to pay a return on capital. Capital appreciation should drive the need for an ever-increasing buy-out price over the term of the investment if dividends are not paid, since the present value of the future payment in retirement or redemption of the stock needs to be equal to the price paid today for that stock.

Purchasing a Retiring Equity Holder's Minority Interest

In the best of circumstances, a medical practice will have a stockholders' (or similar) agreement that provides a mechanism for buying out retiring members as well as a valuation method. Unfortunately, this is frequently not the case. If there has previously been a substantial buy-in price, a substantial buy-out at the time of departure from the practice is typically in order. Nonetheless, physicians who are ready to accept their share of buy-in proceeds may be reluctant to forgo income when it comes to buying out a retiring partner.

Author's Insight and Analysis

In my experience, one of two things happens at buy-out time when a large sum of money is involved: (1) The amount is paid to the first individual to retire and the remaining partners then realize the plan is unworkable and terminate it.—"first man out wins"or (2) the remaining partners cannot or will not pay it, and a lawsuit results.

Sale or Retirement Versus Continued Employment Post-Transaction

Another critical factor is the difference in transferability of goodwill between a sale or retirement and a sale with continued employment. In a retirement setting, the buyer has the opportunity to obtain the intangible value of the seller. In a setting where the seller continues in employment, typical of a practice management company, hospital, or integrated delivery system transaction, the buyer cannot separate the personal and professional goodwill from the practice goodwill, and therefore, an employment contract containing an enforceable covenant not to compete is necessary. One also needs to distinguish going-concern value to a physician-buyer from that of a hospital-buyer, which many valuators unfamiliar or deliberately ignorant of the Stark law and anti-kickback statute fail to do. A hospital-buyer that employs the selling physicians post-transaction at a rate of compensation that results in no positive cash flow from the practice would not be expected to pay for going concern value because to do so may, and likely does, implicate buying proscribed referrals.

Goodwill and Other Intangibles

A factor compounding buy-ins is the often apparent confusion in the business community at large between intangible value and goodwill. *Intangible value* includes, of course, a variety of assets beyond goodwill, including such things as workforce-in-place and going-concern value. Here, we use "going concern value" to describe an asset representing the value of the positive cash flow of an established business. (That term also, of course, refers to a premise of value.) In a medical practice, it can include patient charts, a phone number, payer contracts, and other items. *Goodwill* typically includes everything not separated out after all other intangibles have been measured. The residual allocation method under §338[2] of the Internal Revenue Code allocates to goodwill only that value left after all other assets have been identified and valued. Note that intangibles require a cash flow to demonstrate value to a buyer.

Personal Versus Practice Goodwill

In any professional practice, goodwill may be a significant asset. Goodwill is often a catchall term that encompasses a range of intangible assets that includes the income-generating ability of the underlying client or patient base and other items, including personal skills. This goodwill may be *personal* and nontransferable, *practice*-related and subject to transfer, or *both* personal and practice-related. A buy-out from a departing physician in excess of the tangible value of the underlying practice assets presumes the transferability of the goodwill. To accomplish this transfer to the buyer, buyers and sellers usually bargain at arm's length for a noncompetition agreement to prevent the seller from being paid for the *practice* goodwill and simultaneously taking that goodwill and using it in a competing practice. If the goodwill is both paid for and used in a competing practice, the "seller" is double-dipping.

An alternative argument might be made that a portion of the goodwill is personal and a portion of the transferable practice goodwill, with the latter representing the asset purchased by the buyer. However, the compelling transaction evidence is that practice goodwill cannot be purchased if the seller simultaneously competes. The two are inextricably linked, and the hypothetical informed buyer would not pay anything for goodwill without a noncompete. A good example of this transaction fact is the SEC filings and press releases for publicly traded physician practice management companies, such as Mednax, a buyer of anesthesia practices.

2 See Form 8594.

Impact of Noncompete Agreements

In addition to statutory prohibitions against physician noncompetes in some states such as Massachusetts and Delaware, there is a line of case law around the doctrine of "contravention of public policy." In medical practices, this doctrine provides that agreements among providers, or their employing entities, should not be permitted to interfere with the physician-patient relationship. In some states, agreements found to violate this doctrine, or otherwise found to be unconscionable, may be thrown out in their entirety by courts. More common is a modification by the court to something reasonable. The status of a noncompete in the state in which the practice is located is a factor to consider in the risk premium, the discount for lack of control or minority discount, and the lack of marketability—or as an intangible to be valued separately (see Chapter 5).

Example of a Noncompete's Impact on a Buyout Agreement

A noncompete agreement basically transfers some portion of a physician's personal goodwill to the employing entity, based upon the terms of that noncompete agreement, including duration and geographic scope. Not all goodwill in a practice will necessarily be personal, and some portion of it may therefore be a corporate asset.

At least if one follows the logic of the tax court in the *Martin Ice Cream* and *Norwalk* cases, along with the *Howard*[3] case, whether or not the stockholders have entered into a noncompete agreement with their employing entity determines to a large extent who owns the practice's goodwill. For tax purposes, the physician-stockholders selling their corporate practice can negotiate to have the buyer pay them directly for their *personal* goodwill, as properly valued, and then report it on their personal returns at favorable capital gain rates, avoiding double taxation if the practice is a C corporation. This tax-legal analysis is consistent with the underlying economics and should be considered in doing buyout and buy-in valuations.

To illustrate the concept for buy-in and buyout purposes, assume one stockholder-physician departs a corporation and opens another practice in the same area. It would seem irrefutable that if the goodwill is used in a new practice by the departing physician and also paid for by the stockholder's former colleagues in a buyout, the seller has been compensated twice for the same asset. Careful drafting of stockholder agreements should address this possibility.

3 *Larry E. Howard and Joan M. Howard, Plaintiffs v. United States of America, Defendant*, U.S. District Court, E.D. Washington, 2010-2 U.S.T.C.

Author's Insight and Analysis

Here are several cases that indicate the contravention of public policy trend in certain states in noncompetition agreements. Before valuing a practice, the valuation consultant should be aware of the status of the law in the state the practice is located in. If covenants are unenforceable, certain intangible assets can be acquired, but the risk associated with maintaining them will be higher.

Massachusetts: Ell Pond Medical Associates v. Lipski, MD

Massachusetts has a statute that makes unenforceable any contractual term that restricts the right of a physician to practice medicine in any geographic area after termination of employment. Several years ago in a case called *Abisla v. Falmouth Ob/ Gyn*, a Massachusetts trial court ruled that a financial penalty imposed on an employed physician who left a practice and opened a competing office was unenforceable. In 1998, Judge Hiller Zobel expended the interpretation of the statute to preclude an employer from limiting a former employee-physician's solicitation of patients, or suggesting that patients have their medical records transferred to the new practice.

Alabama: Michael B. Kline, MD v. Anniston Urologic Associates, PC

Alabama has a statute that voids any contractual provision that restrains the practice of a profession, citing contravention of public policy. In this case, Dr. Kline was a shareholder in Anniston Urologic (Anniston). The stock redemption agreement had two provisions that were the subject of the proceeding.

The first provision reduced the buyout price for the stock by $20,000 in the event the shareholder terminated employment voluntarily with less than nine months' notice. The second provision reduced the buyout price by $75,000 if the shareholder voluntarily terminated and engaged in a competing practice during the first year post-termination within a 25-mile radius of Anniston's office.

The Alabama Supreme Court, on appeal, ruled that the first provision did not restrict the physician's right to practice. The second provision, however, was found to violate the statute. Noting that a similar argument was made and rejected in *Associated Surgeons, PA v. Watwood*, where Associated argued that it was not a restraint of practice, but compensation for the benefit received by Watwood by his having been associated with Associated, the court rejected Anniston's argument that the provision did not restrict Kline's right to practice.

Tennessee: Murfreesboro Medical Clinic, P.A. v. Udom

Although a noncompete agreement between a physician and a hospital, for example, was then enforceable in Tennessee, in the above 2005 case, the Tennessee Supreme Court banned noncompete agreements between physicians and their private physician practice employers. The court cited the right of a patient to choose his or her physician in its decision.

The legislature followed in 2008 by almost entirely undoing the court's decision with Tenn. Code Ann. §63-1-148 and expanded the allowability of noncompetes beyond physicians to healthcare providers, such as chiropractors, dentists, optometrists, and psychologists. At that time, noncompetes effectively expired after the healthcare provider had been employed for six years. More significant from a valuation standpoint, Tenn. Code Ann. §63-1-148(a)(2) effectively exempts noncompetes in connection with a sale of a practice from the six-year term, allowing the noncompete to be enforced if it is otherwise reasonable.

In 2010, the legislature acted again to allow enforcement beyond six years but required that the noncompete be reaffirmed with consideration, amending TCA 63-1-148(a)(2) to read:

> The healthcare provider and the employing or contracting entity may agree to an unlimited number of extensions of the six (6) year period so long as the extension is in writing, is supported by consideration, and each extension does not exceed a term of six (6) years. Any agreement to extend the six (6) year time period must be accomplished through subsequent negotiations and cannot be extended by an automatic renewal provision in an employment contract. Refusal by either party to extend or enter into a new employment contract shall not be considered grounds for terminating an existing employment contract so long as the employment term of the contract then in effect is a term longer than month- to-month.

The legislature, yet again, modified the noncompete rules on May 20, 2011, effective Jan. 1, 2012, removing the above-described limitations on enforcing a noncompete that had been in place for more than six years.

Physicians who are employed as a result of their practice being acquired are subject to a different provision than physicians who are employed without a practice acquisition. A "reasonable"[4] geographic noncompete may be imposed that cannot exceed a 10-mile radius from the primary practice site; the noncompete cannot exceed two years in length unless the parties agree to a longer term, and that term cannot exceed five years. Further, the physician has to have the right to reacquire the practice at either the original purchase price or fair market value at the time it is repurchased. Finally, the physician need only give 30 days' notice to exercise the option to repurchase.

4 Tenn. Code Ann. § 63-1-148 (2011).

Texas: Valley Diagnostic Clinic, P.A. v. Dougherty

This Texas Court of Appeals case found a noncompete provision in a deferred compensation contract to be unenforceable The relevant provision contained a 50-mile radius around the practice location of Harlingen and lasted for four years. Texas law contains a Covenants Not to Compete Act (CNCA).

> Covenants not to compete are generally considered restraints of trade and are disfavored in law. See Tex. Bus. & Com. Code Ann. § 15.05(a) (Vernon Supp. 2008) ("Every contract, combination, or conspiracy in restraint of trade or commerce is unlawful."); see also *Travel Masters, Inc. v. Star Tours, Inc.*, 827 S.W.2d 830, 832 (Tex. 1991). However, the Covenants Not to Compete Act (CNCA) sets forth certain circumstances under which such covenants are enforceable.
>
> Notwithstanding Section 15.05 of this code, and subject to any applicable provision of Subsection (b), a covenant not to compete is enforceable if it is ancillary to or part of an otherwise enforceable agreement at the time the agreement is made to the extent that it contains limitations as to time, geographical area, and scope of activity to be restrained that are reasonable and does not impose a greater restraint than is necessary to protect the goodwill or other business interest of the promisee.
>
> Section 15.50(b) of the CNCA provides additional requirements for a covenant not to compete to be enforceable against a physician licensed by the Texas State Board of Medical Examiners. Specifically, the statute provides that:
>
> (1) the covenant must:
>
> (A) not deny the physician access to a list of his patients whom he had seen or treated within one year of termination of the contract or employment;
>
> (B) provide access to medical records of the physician's patients upon authorization of the patient and any copies of medical records for a reasonable fee as established by the Texas State Board of Medical Examiners under Section 159.008, Occupations Code; and
>
> (C) provide that any access to a list of patients or to patients' medical records after termination of the contract or employment shall not require such list or records to be provided in a format different than that by which such records are maintained except by mutual consent of the parties to the contract;
>
> (2) the covenant must provide for a buyout of the covenant by the physician at a reasonable price or, at the option of either party, as determined by a mutually agreed upon arbitrator or, in the case of an inability to agree, an arbitrator of the court whose decision shall be binding on the parties; and
>
> (3) the covenant must provide that the physician will not be prohibited from providing continuing care and treatment to a specific patient or patients during the course of an acute illness even after the contract or employment has been terminated.

To be enforceable, a covenant must comply with the terms of the statute, which require that any such covenant be "ancillary to or part of" another enforceable agreement, and as the court noted, "satisfy a two-pronged test: "(1) the consideration given by the employer in the otherwise enforceable agreement must give rise to the employer's interest in restraining the employee from competing and (2) the covenant must be designed to enforce the employee's consideration or return promise in the otherwise enforceable agreement."

The court concluded that the agreement failed to satisfy the second prong of the test:

> To satisfy the second prong, the forfeiture clause must have been "designed to enforce" Dr. Dougherty's "consideration or return promise" made in the deferred compensation provision. See id. Here, the only "consideration or return promise [s]" that Dr. Dougherty could be said to have provided under the deferred compensation provision were: (1) that he not compete with VDC after departing the practice, as detailed in the forfeiture provision, or (2) that he continue to practice with VDC. To the extent VDC claims that the consideration for its deferred compensation promise was a reciprocal promise by Dr. Dougherty not to compete, the forfeiture clause fails, because there would be no otherwise enforceable agreement—that is, there would be no agreement that is enforceable wholly separate from the covenant not to compete."

Indiana: Central Indiana Podiatry, P.C. v. Krueger

In Indiana, noncompetition agreements may be allowed to the extent deemed reasonable. Central Indiana was a multilocation podiatry practice that employed noncompete agreements with the providers staffing its various locations.

> To be geographically reasonable, the agreement may restrict only that area in which the physician developed patient relationships using the practice group's resources.

Dr. Krueger in this case worked for Central Indiana in Clinton, Marion, Howard, Tippecanoe, and Hamilton counties at one time or another during his nine-year relationship. His noncompete clause was described as follows:

> For two years after leaving CIP's employ, Krueger would be prohibited from divulging the names of patients, contacting patients to provide podiatric services, and soliciting CIP employees. Krueger also would be prohibited from practicing podiatry for two years within a geographic area defined as 14 listed central Indiana counties and "any other county where [CIP] maintained an office during the term of this contract or in any county adjacent to any of the foregoing counties.

The court observed that employer's have a protectable interest in their customer relationships:

> Indiana courts have held that "the advantageous familiarity and personal contact which employees derive from dealing with an employer's customers are elements of

> an employer's 'goodwill' and are a protectible interest which may justify a restraint...." E.g., Licocci, 445 N.E.2d at 561–62 (Ind. 1983) (citations omitted). CIP asserts that the noncompetition agreement serves its legitimate interest of protecting its goodwill and investment in developing its patient base."

After leaving Central Indiana, Krueger entered into an employment agreement with Meridian Health to work in Hamilton County, which was north of Marion County and subject to his noncompete clause. The court observed that:

> The record does not support any inference that Krueger used CIP's resources to establish relationships throughout the approximately 40 counties the agreement identifies by name or description. Because that is the area sought to be restricted by the agreement, the agreement is clearly overbroad. If a noncompetition agreement is overbroad and it is feasible to strike the unreasonable portions and leave only reasonable portions, the court may apply the blue pencil doctrine to permit enforcement of the reasonable portions.

In determining whether the geographic scope of the noncompete was reasonable, the court recorded the following analysis:

> "However, the geographic scope is unreasonable to the extent it reaches contiguous counties. The Nora office in northern Marion County is nearly 40 miles from parts of contiguous Johnson County.... Similarly, because CIP selected entire counties as the building blocks of its agreement, even more proximate Hamilton County includes an area too broad to be reasonable.... Accordingly, the contiguous county restriction is unreasonable, and the restriction applies only to Marion, Tippecanoe, and Howard counties.

When a Third-Party Sale Is Likely or Possible

In a circumstance where associate physicians are negotiating to become partners in a market where a sale of the entire practice to a third party is possible in the near future, additional consideration is necessary. For example, primary care physician groups may have significant value in an ACO setting as described elsewhere in this guide, whereas such values do not exist and are therefore not economically appropriate in a traditional buy-in.

States require at least a simple majority vote for approval of a corporate sale or liquidation, while many states require super-majorities. Corporate documents may also influence the required vote, so they need to be studied carefully before addressing discounts. Minority discounts are intended to reflect the *difference* in future economic benefit from a control interest. Such a discount may be appropriate in a market where there is third-party sales activity. If no sale is contemplated, then the future economic benefit will be governed by the compensation system used by the practice and the buy-out agreement, if any, among the partners or stockholders. If a third-party sale is a significant possibility, a new minority owner will not be able independently sell his or her interest; a discount for lack of marketability may also be indicated in such a circumstance.

Reality Checks

It is a basic principle of valuation that the valuator conduct "reality checks" on the value to ascertain whether it is reasonable. In a transaction between one physician and another, such as the sale of a solo practice or the purchase of a partial interest in a solo or group practice, a useful check is the debt service analysis below. This represents an actual proposal received by a client to buy a 50% interest in a subspecialty practice. The seller's representatives had valued the practice at $650,000 and asked for $325,000 for a 50% interest, payable over 36 months at 10% interest. The buyer had alternative income opportunities as an employee of $225,000 per year.

The monthly payment is $10,487 (see Exhibit 2) and, of course, nearly $110,000 of principal (on average) must be repaid in each of three years, leading to what proves to be impossible tax consequences resulting from paying off the debt with after-tax dollars. *Alternative earnings* are those available to the physician by remaining in his or her present circumstance as an employee. *Taxable debt service* is the annual payment, less interest and the amortization deduction for intangible value allowed. The amortization deduction is $325,000 divided by 15 years, or $21,667 per year, assuming that the entire purchase price is for intangible assets and that the entity structure permits the buyer to claim this deduction. The *disposable income* line indicates that the physician attempting to execute this transaction would be in an impossible circumstance. (The tax rate of 37% was estimated based upon federal, state, and Social Security taxes after a reasonable level of itemized deductions.)

Key Valuation Tip

Example 1: Buy-In to a Solo Practice

Exhibit 2. Compensation-Shifting Strategy: Deferred Compensation Equals Intangible Value

Purchase price	$325,000
Term	36
Rate	10%
Monthly payment	$10,487
Annual payment	$125,842
Total payments	$377,526
Total interest on debt	$52,526

		1	2	3	4	5	Totals
Earnings before taxes		$225,000	$225,000	$225,000	$225,000	$225,000	$1,125,000
Annual debt service		125,842	125,842	125,842	0	0	377,526
Net cash flow		99,158	99,158	99,158	225,000	225,000	747,474
Income taxes on principal		-28,148	-31,934	-36,118	8,017	8,017	-80,167
Earnings less tax on principal		71,010	67,223	63,040	233,017	233,017	677,307
Alternative earnings		150,000	160,000	170,000	185,000	200,000	865,000
Difference		-78,990	-92,777	-106,960	48,017	33,017	-197,693
Earnings before taxes		225,000	225,000	225,000	225,000	225,000	1,125,000
Interest on debt		28,101	17,866	6,559	0	0	52,526
Amortization deduction		21,667	21,667	21,667	21,667	21,667	108,333
Taxable adj. gross income		175,233	185,467	196,774	203,333	203,333	964,141
Income/FICA taxes	37%	64,836	68,623	72,806	75,233	75,233	356,732
Taxable debt service		76,075	86,309	97,616	-21,667	-21,667	216,667
Taxes on debt service	37%	28,148	31,934	36,118	-8,017	-8,017	80,167
Net cash flow		99,158	99,158	99,158	225,000	225,000	747,474
Income taxes		64,836	68,623	72,806	75,233	75,233	356,732
Disposable income		34,322	30,535	26,352	149,767	149,767	390,742

Author's Insight and Analysis

In this particular case, I found the practice seriously overvalued. Though it was a very profitable practice, the buyer was purchasing, in effect, only a right to "hang his hat" in a successful practice and would have to develop his own income stream—he was not purchasing the seller's income stream. The practice had been valued as a 100% controlling interest, with no thought given to the lack of control inherent in a 50-50 arrangement. In addition, the payment terms—as noted above—were draconian in their financial implication for the buyer, who had a family to support as well. The deal could be made viable by a combination of decreasing the purchase price and perhaps extending the payment period, though buy-ins extending beyond three years are problematic from an internal relations standpoint. Ultimately, the deal was done on a highly simplified basis, with the buyer agreeing to pay the seller a fixed percentage of his net from the practice for a period of years via an income reallocation. The transaction proved to be highly successful for both buyer and seller from a financial standpoint.

Example 2: Buyout of a Retiring Solo Practice by Management Company With Employed Physician

The second series of examples represents an actual offer for a specialty practice where the prospective buyer intended to hire a physician to work in the practice and (hoped to) earn a return from the investment. The valuation was prepared by a nonaccredited valuation consultant on a discounted free cash flow basis using what were wildly unrealistic growth assumptions, a marginal federal tax rate of 15%, and appeared to be designed to return a value of 100% of annual gross receipts or *$700,000*. The author suggested to the buyer that the maximum payable would be *$448,000*, based upon a cash flow break-even in the first five years (see Exhibit 3). The valuation model assumed that revenues would increase over the forecast period with a greater increase in the compensation paid to the employee physician, which accounts for the decline in *earnings before taxes*.

Author's Insight and Analysis

I thought the practice was worth no more than $350,000, however, due to the flaws in the valuation model.

Solving the Two-Person Practice Buyout Dilemma

Background

One of the most difficult engagements an advisor or appraiser can encounter is devising a plan for one physician (or dentist) of a two-physician practice to buy out the other. Generally speaking, if both physicians are busy, the continuing physician (or survivor) will be unable to absorb the workload of the retiree. This, in turn, leads to a circumstance in which the survivor is confronted with working long additional hours for no additional income, and perhaps less income, trying to generate the cash to fund the buyout.

Origin of the Problem

This problem is typically encountered either (1) when a sole proprietor is negotiating to bring in a new partner or (2) at or near the retirement of one partner. In the latter circumstance, there may be a buyout agreement in place with or without a formula or requirement of appraisal or there may be no prior agreement.

New Partner

Buying into a practice is complicated. There is often a dispute between buyer and seller as to whether or not any saleable goodwill (using the term broadly to encompass all intangibles) exists between physician-buyers and -sellers. Most small practices do, in fact, have some intangible value that is not attributable to the personal goodwill of the physicians, such as the value of a trained workforce, providing there is a positive cash flow from that goodwill. The following is a list of practice intangibles commonly present in a small practice, representing a list of tasks necessary to establish a practice:

1. Conduct a feasibility analysis;
2. Retain advisors;
3. Prepare a business plan;
4. Obtain financing;

Exhibit 3. Buyout Analysis

Purchase price	$700,000
Term	60
Rate	10.00%
Monthly payment	$14,873
Annual payment	$178,475
Total payments	$892,376

		1	2	3	4	5	Totals
Earnings before taxes		$180,000	$165,000	$155,000	4145,000	$125,000	$770,000
Annual debt service		178,475	178,475	178,475	178,475	178,475	892,376
Net cash flow		1,525	-13,475	-23,475	-33,475	-53,475	-122,376
Income taxes (next chart)		-27,378	-26,136	-27,392	-29,198	-27,612	-137,716
Cash out of pocket		-25,854	-39,611	-50,867	-62,673	-81,087	-260,092
Tax computation							
Earnings before taxes		180,000	165,000	155,000	145,000	125,000	770,000
Interest on debt		64,887	52,993	39,854	25,338	9,303	192,376
Amortization deduction		46,667	46,667	46,667	46,667	46,667	233,333
Taxable income		68,446	65,340	68,480	72,995	69,030	344,291
Income taxes	40%	27,378	26,136	27,392	29,198	27,612	137,716

Purchase price	$448,000
Term	60
Rate	10.00%
Monthly payment	$9,519
Annual payment	$114,224
Total payments	$571,121

		1	2	3	4	5	Totals
Earnings before paxes		$180,000	$165,000	$155,000	$145,000	$125,000	$770,000
Annual debt service		114,224	114,224	114,224	114,224	114,224	571,121
Net cash flow		65,776	50,776	40,776	30,776	10,776	198,879
Income taxes (next chart)		-43,442	-40,487	-39,851	-39,567	-35,672	-199,018
Cash out of pocket		22,334	10,289	925	-8,791	-24,896	-139
Earnings before taxes		180,000	165,000	155,000	145,000	125,000	770,000
Interest on debt		41,528	33,916	25,506	16,217	5,954	123,121
Amortization deduction		29,867	29,867	29,867	29,867	29,867	149,333
Taxable income		108,605	101,218	99,627	98,917	89,179	497,546
Income taxes	40%	43,442	40,487	39,851	39,567	35,672	199,018

5. Identify a location;
6. Negotiate the lease;
7. Choose and order furniture, equipment, billing system;
8. Hire employees;
9. Develop employment policies;
10. Develop a filing system;
11. Develop marketing materials;
12. Advertise for patients;
13. Develop coding and compliance policies;
14. Develop an encounter form;
15. Develop a general ledger system;
16. Develop a compensation system in a group practice;
17. Establish professional relationships;
18. Recruit patients;
19. Prepare patient charts; and
20. Register patients in the billing system (database).

In some circumstances, the advisor can move the transaction along by deemphasizing personal goodwill—which physicians are loath to pay for—and emphasizing the presence of practice intangibles. The use of the term "goodwill" should, in fact, be avoided.

Example

Dr. Smith has been working in Dr. Jones' ophthalmology practice for three years. He is paid 35% of his collections, and the practice has an overhead of about 50%, leaving Dr. Jones with a 15% profit. Dr. Smith is 41 years old, and Dr. Jones is 55 years old. If Dr. Smith does not buy into the practice, he plans on leaving and starting his own practice.

Dr. Jones has offered Dr. Smith an opportunity to buy an equal interest in the practice. After the elimination of various "senior doctor rights" that Dr. Jones wished to retain but which would have made Dr. Smith's "50%" share worth substantially less than 50%, the parties agree on a price to be paid over three years. Dr. Jones also wishes to come to an agreement on the amount he will be paid at retirement. When the buy-in is completed, he will be 58. He is reluctant to commit to waiting until age 65 to retire and may want to retire at age 62. In contrast, Dr. Smith is reluctant to finish his buy-in and have only four years of "full" earnings before he has to start working to pay Dr. Jones again. In addition, Dr. Smith does not see how he could possibly carry the workload of both physicians, even if he were inclined to do so—which he is not.

Analysis

All other things being equal, once the value of the 50% share being acquired by the new partner is established, it should serve as the measure of what the other 50% share is worth. The value is particularly important since it serves as a reference point for two transactions. If Dr. Smith is unwilling or unable to start his own practice—because of an enforceable covenant not to compete, for example—his options are limited and his negotiating position will be substantially undermined.

Physician buy-ins are often accomplished by income shifts, except for that portion of the buy-in related to fixed assets and existing cash balances. Using after-tax dollars to purchase the intangible value of a practice as part of the stock would make the cost prohibitive. In addition, in a small practice, it can be difficult to argue that there is a true return on investment from the intangibles as opposed to a return on labor, given that the physician must work in the practice to recognize the benefit.[5] After the buy-in period is complete, the physician expects to be earning a salary equivalent to what another partner in the practice would earn, based upon whatever compensation plan is in place.

Senior Doctor Rights

Senior doctor rights (SDRs) refer to a basket of special privileges that senior physicians try to retain when bringing in a new partner. From a valuation standpoint, these constitute factors leading to a minority discount or discount for lack of control for the buyer. It is quite common for individuals inexperienced with valuation to ignore SDRs, senior shareholder's protection, and similar restrictions on the ownership of stock that substantially diminishes its value.

Note: The presence of SDRs during the buy-in is not uncommon. The disposition of the payments made toward the buy-in if the seller terminates the deal needs to be negotiated, however. Following are some of the options:

1. If the buyer engages in a competing practice, the income shift payments are forfeited.
2. If the buyer engages in another practice outside the service area, a portion of the payments may be forfeited or they may all be returned.
3. If the buyer chooses to terminate, a portion or all of the payments may be forfeited.

5 Practices with profitable ancillary services and mid-level providers can have "profits" more in the nature of a return on capital or equity.

You should never pay 50% of the entire value of an entity if the interest you are acquiring does not have the same rights as the other 50% interest. For example, assume that the buyer's stock is subject to a repurchase option held by the seller. The seller can repurchase the buyer's stock if he or she (the seller) decides that the arrangement is not working out, using the original purchase price. Any payments made via the income shift are not returned. In addition, the seller retains all of the intangible practice assets, including the employees, phone number, location, and other items included in the list above. It should be easy to see that the buyer's "50% share" does not constitute anything close to 50%.

The most critical factor reflected in this discount is the difference in future economic benefit from that of a control interest. Particularly in a small practice, such as where an employee physician is buying into an existing solo practice, a minority discount can be considerable. Some common instances indicating a need for a minority discount include: where the interest acquired is less than 50%; where the present owner's spouse works in the practice; where certain SDRs are reserved to the seller; where the buyer has an inferior claim on certain practice assets in the event of a dissolution, such as the phone number, location, employment of staff, and possession of patient charts; and where the senior doctor has a tiebreaker vote or veto in a practice with more than two doctors. The following examples are intended to demonstrate that certain of these preferences can be directly valued, rather than being rolled up into an arbitrary percentage discount, which is frequently the subject of controversy. This chapter also considers techniques for valuing preferences within the context of a buy-in.

Key Valuation Tip

Examples: Valuing Senior Doctor Rights (SDRs)

Managing partner: As part of a buy-in, the senior doctor is granted managing partner status in the practice for a period of 10 years at an annual salary of $40,000 in a two-person practice. The true value of these services, assuming they are performed and performed competently, is $12,000. The difference of $28,000 can be discounted to a present value for the 10-year period of time. Assume that the 100% control value of the practice is $500,000, using a discount rate of 20% on pre-tax earnings. The present value of $28,000 at 20% for 10 years is $117,000, which must be subtracted from the $500,000 to reach a value of $383,000, since the salary strips out a portion of the value. One-half of $383,000 is $191,500, placing a ceiling on the value of the 50% interest considered for purchase. Additional discounts may apply, depending upon the compensation formula, stockholders' agreement, and other factors.

Call schedule preference: A frequent and very contentious SDR is reduced or "no call," the term used to describe evening and weekend coverage of the practice. As one would expect, one of the least desirable aspects of practicing medicine is getting called in the middle of the night or on a weekend afternoon. Exclusion from the call schedule has a significant value that should not be overlooked. Even if the physicians who must take the additional call get credited with the revenue for any services provided, they probably won't care (except in those specialties, such as plastic surgery, where taking an emergency room call is a common method for the young surgeon to demonstrate his or her skill in repairing injuries, particularly facial lacerations). In many specialties, the cost of coverage can be quantified by reference to market prices for locum tenens, or a per diem physician to provide the service. This is very common in radiology, for example, with costs in the vicinity of $1,200 to $1,500 for an overnight session where the radiologist is physically present (with residents receiving 20% to 30% less). Another reference source might be the cost of coverage from a company such as NightHawk/VRC that provides night and weekend coverage to practices via phone lines, now common in pediatrics (staffed with nurse practitioners) as well as radiology. (Imaging industry consulting expert Douglas Smith of the Barrington Lakes Group observes that many larger practices now provide their own night and weekend call as part of their schedule and that some practices hire radiologists solely to take night coverage.)

Assume that the senior doctor is taking a half-share of night call in a four-doctor pediatric practice, commencing at age 60 with expected retirement at age 65. There are 1,300 (52 weeks × five days × five years) nights in five years, with a value of $200 per night ($260,000 total). An equal share of night call would be worth $65,000, and half of that is $32,500, as computed in Exhibit 4. The half-share of weekend call would be worth another $26,000. This might be considered a pre-payment of any retirement benefit.

Exhibit 4

Number of Years in Preference	5
Weeks per Year	52
Call Nights per Week per M.D.	1.25
Total Days	325
Share of Call	50.00%
Preference Nights (rounded)	163
Value per Night	$200
Value	$32,600

Governance: It is much more difficult to quantify an SDR discount for practice governance. Clearly, having veto authority in one individual can impact the ultimate flow of cash, even if the compensation arrangement is specified in employment contracts and is otherwise fair. The veto could be used to block acquisition of a potentially profitable item of equipment; a move to a better and potentially more profitable location; hiring, retaining, or firing key, or more often nonkey, employees; or generally creating a nuisance. Each of these circumstances needs to be carefully evaluated, with the initial focus on the compensation allocation plan and the employment contract. The adviser has to identify those areas where the veto might influence the cash distributable to a prospective owner.

Author's Insight and Analysis

The medical world is full of these SDRs, some silent and some explicit. Advisers routinely overlook or ignore them, leading to preposterous results from a valuation standpoint. I recall one situation involving two surgeons where an overly aggressive (in polite terms) advocate on behalf of the seller loaded up the proposal deal with SDRs, including a one-way noncompete for the buyer, a permanent management salary for the seller, a job for the seller's spouse, and a deferred compensation plan for the seller that would have choked the proverbial horse—an annual accrual for the seller equal to about 40% of current earnings. To top it all off, the potential buyer was outproducing the seller by 40%, but net income was to be split equally. The buyer decided to open her own practice—and lived happily ever after.

Impact of Compensation and Stockholder Agreements

Many practices provide rules for distribution of income and resolution of conflicts through employment contracts or stockholder agreements that may substantially mitigate against a minority discount. The larger the number of shareholders and the more comprehensive the employment contracts and stockholder agreements, the less likely a minority discount is indicated. Centralized control via management is common in large group practices, as government by committee doesn't work well. Management, however, should serve at the discretion of ownership, just as in any other business.

Author's Insight and Analysis

General business valuators may not agree with the above discussion. In my experience, physician practices arrange for distribution of the net income of the practice via compensation formulas, eliminating the most significant factor—control over distribution of cash—indicating a minority discount. Historically, practices tend to have equal shareholders, with no one individual or few individuals controlling the majority of the stock. However, when there is disproportionate control, minority discounts should be considered.

Length of Service by Seller

The buyer's principal goal is to obtain an income stream commensurate with that of an owner in the practice. The longer the buy-in period lasts, the longer the period before that goal is reached. If the seller retires and expects a second wave of buy-out payments to begin, it may be many years before the buyer obtains the benefit of what he or she has bargained for.

Buyout

Once the parties have agreed on a buy-in price and terms, they can proceed to the buyout negotiation. It is difficult to reconcile the competing needs of buyer and seller in this regard. In addition to the buyer's legitimate concerns about becoming a full partner, the seller does not wish to be in a position where the new partner will be unable to fulfill the obligation of buying out the other half of the practice when the seller retires. Practically speaking, both buyer and seller need to cooperate to effectively arrange for the seller's retirement. One strategy is to develop the practice to the point where it will partially sustain a third individual and gradually transfer the senior physician's practice to that person. If the practice is inadequate in size, the replacement physician will need to be recruited no later than the year prior to the intended retirement. This may entail some loss of profit in the practice due to excess capacity, but this is a cost that must be incurred by the typical small practice to arrange for an orderly transition.

Sample Language

The following is not legal advice and should not be construed as same. Competent legal advice should be sought.

"A party to this agreement desiring to retire shall notify the corporation no later than September 1 of the second year preceding the July 1 on which he intends to retire. For illustrative purposes, if a party desires to retire on July 1, 2012, he shall notify the corporation in writing no later than Sept. 1, 2010. (These dates are consistent with the recruiting period for physicians leaving residency programs, and the parties recognize that these periods are critical to the ability of the practice to recruit a replacement.) Both parties agree to contribute their best efforts to identifying and recruiting a qualified individual to take the place of the retiring party."

Author's Insight and Analysis

There is a nearly two-year window in this version, which is probably more favorable to the buyer, although it may contribute to the ultimate success of the buyout for the seller.

"In the event that the recruited individual or some other appropriately qualified individual should be invited to purchase an interest in the practice, the parties agree that any compensation differential negotiated in connection therewith shall be allocated to the retiring party to the extent of the fair market value of the deferred compensation owing to that party. In the event that the parties cannot agree on the amount of deferred compensation, an appraisal shall be conducted by an individual qualified specializing in the healthcare industry and qualified in such matters and holding a valuation designation from one or more of the following: the American Institute of Certified Public Accountants, the American Society of Appraisers, the Institute of Business Appraisers, or the National Association of Certified Valuation Analysts. Notwithstanding the appraisal, the deferred compensation shall not exceed any compensation differential negotiated in connection with the purchase of an interest in the practice." (As a reminder, Section 409A has to be addressed in such an agreement.)

Author's Insight and Analysis

Buyouts are often structured in the form of deferred compensation payments.

"In the event that the retiring party retires due to death or disability, a qualified appraisal, if necessary, shall be conducted as described above to determine the deferred compensation liability. The continuing party shall promptly use his or her best efforts to identify and recruit a qualified individual to take the place of the retiring party, if the practice's existing staffing is insufficient to do so. The deferred compensation liability shall be paid as follows: The net income available for payment of deferred compensation shall be determined after providing for the compensation negotiated with any non-owner physician and an amount to any owner not to exceed his annual salary for the calendar year immediately preceding the death or disability of the retiring party. Practice income in excess of these amounts shall be applied in full to pay the deferred compensation liability, until it is reduced to zero."

Author's Insight and Analysis

It is also common to express the maximum payments as a percentage of net income before physician compensation, as a percentage of net collections, or as a maximum fixed dollar amount.

Summary

One of the most difficult tasks confronting an advisor is to develop a fair and rational approach to buying out one person of a two-person professional practice. Arrangements that place an unmanageable burden on the buyer often fail and lead to legal actions. The author has found the approach suggested in the sample language above to be a valuable tool in resolving this issue.

Strategies for Creating Merger Value

The healthcare industry is once again experiencing an historic period of consolidation. Many physicians are selling their practices outright to hospitals, integrated delivery systems, or for certain specialties such as anesthesia and practice management companies. Others are merging their practices with those of colleagues, hoping to stay independent and gain sufficient size to effectively compete in a marketplace of giants. Below, some of the strategies for successful formation of a group practice are explored.

Economies of Scale

One of the commonly cited synergies of a merger is cost reductions from economies of scale. The hoped-for reductions are in areas such as the billing function and information systems costs, including electronic medical records (EMR).[6] Often overlooked are the significant increases in costs resulting from the need for professional administration, a human resources department, and the cost of legal, accounting, and benefit plan consultants necessary to accomplish the transaction. Significant commitment of time is always required from the physicians as well. Many mergers simply result in a break-even scenario at best from a cost standpoint.

Author's Insight and Analysis

Mergers should not be undertaken unless both cost savings and significant revenue enhancement opportunities are available from capitation, accountable care organizations, expansion of services, or at least, conservation of existing revenues. Ideally, mergers should be offensive, not defensive, in nature, although for many specialists in an era focused on primary care, defense may be the most plausible strategy.

Valuation may be important in the allocation of equity among the physicians or if an opinion is desired as to the value of the post-merger entity to demonstrate the strategic value of the transaction. In general, value added or synergistic effects are expected from merger and acquisition transactions in industries, such as healthcare, undergoing consolidation. Appraisers need to differentiate strategic opportunities available to most or all merger candidates in a given timeframe versus those available to only a limited number of such candidates if the standard is a strict fair market value.

Actuarial Stability

Historically, capitation was used in the market as a means for creating financial incentives to control utilization of expensive services, such as ancillary testing and referrals to specialists. Actuarial factors create a significant issue for group practices looking to accept capitation. The eventual likelihood of one or more catastrophic cases, even when stop-loss insurance is in place, can have a severe adverse impact on the group's financial performance. Only if this risk is spread out among a large number of covered lives can the group have a reasonable expectation of successfully managing care. As an example, a client with approximately 1,000 patients in a full-risk commercial capitation contract had a catastrophic "out of area" case. The hospital where the patient was treated did not have a contract for allowed charges with the insurer, and as a result, 100% of the hospital charges were paid, with no discount. The patient developed severe complications and spent several months in the hospital. Even with a $100,000 stop loss,

6 Starting in 2015, physicians who fail to "meaningfully use" EMR are subject to a reduction in Medicare reimbursement that starts at 1% and increases to 5% in 2019 and beyond.

this one case increased costs by more than $4 per member, per month, in a total budget of under $200 per member, per month. This was an example of poor contract structure by the network with which the practice was affiliated. At least 10,000 lives are probably necessary (in this instance) for a reasonable balancing of actuarial risk, although the accountable care organization (ACO) regulations from the federal healthcare reform legislation start at 5,000—and that is a unmanaged system with substantial out-referral risk.

In another instance, a client with a panel of approximately 3,500 patients experienced six catastrophic cases in a single six-month period, each with a $50,000 stop loss. The insurer paying the capitation also had a marketplace strategy that tended to attract unhealthy patients and was suffering ongoing losses. This $300,000 of cost increased costs by more than $7 per member, per month in a budget of $110 per member, per month. In addition, this practice was located in an area with extremely unfavorable socioeconomics, including a high incidence of substance abuse among the insured population and a generally older, unhealthy population.

These two examples are intended to illustrate the serious risk inherent in taking capitation for small panels or more so, getting involved in a small ACO. Reducing or spreading this risk over a large number of lives is one of the principal goals of practice mergers. The latter example also illustrates the potential for "arbitrage" profits in a market where the competing insurance companies do not have uniform distribution of health status among their insureds. Arguably, the best place to begin a capitation strategy is with an insurer with positive rather than adverse selection.

(*Arbitrage* refers to the strategy of taking advantage of price differences in two different markets for the same thing. The insurer is presumed to set a price high enough to cover the costs [plus profit] of its insureds. Rates historically were typically only age and gender adjusted, not for severity of illness. A capitated group that succeeded in attracting healthy patients could obtain capitation rates based upon the higher costs of a sicker population.)

In markets employing capitation, premiums and, therefore, capitation rates will likely reflect health status differences in the underlying insured population. In early time periods, the insurers may have had less sophisticated approaches to health status determination. Further influencing this process is experience rating of (notably) the small employer and self-employed or individual markets and requiring community rating. These laws preclude insurers from increasing premiums to particular classes of insureds based upon prior claims experience. The ability of the insurer to selectively attract a healthier population through its marketing, advertising, and sales efforts historically created enormous differences in costs. Practices might be able to attract healthier patients through their own characteristics, such as location, age of providers, presence of female physicians, inclusion of pediatricians, and other factors. The 2010 federal healthcare reform legislation, however, has as one of its principal aims eliminating this type of arbitrage opportunity. Health status adjustments and uniform rating across a combination of the small group and individual markets will severely restrict this profit area and place a premium on medical management rather than demographic and health status selection.

A larger practice is more attractive to an insurer for negotiating purposes since a number of providers can be bound with a single contract, along with their underlying patient panels. Clinical protocols and medical management can be adopted more easily. Of course, the group obtains both efficiencies and leverage in its negotiations if it presents a plausible, integrated practice.

Addition of Ancillaries

This strategy can be successful in those increasingly fewer markets with little or no capitation or managed care and much fee-for-service reimbursement.

The Stark laws are critical in evaluating and executing this strategy and prohibit anything amounting to a payment in exchange for referrals among medical providers. Specifically, physician group practices must meet a qualifying definition under Stark to avoid liability for referrals among the members of the group.

As an example, assume a group practice of eight physicians includes the subspecialties of cardiology, invasive cardiology, and hematology. As a result, they own echocardiography equipment as well as a full lab with blood chemistry capability. Maintaining specialty referrals from primary care physicians becomes increasingly difficult. Certain insurers no longer permit the practice to perform laboratory tests on their patients but require the tests to be done by an outside reference lab with which the insurer has contracted. The practice will likely experience a steady decline in profitability.

This situation can be the foundation for a successful expansion of the group practice by adding primary care physicians and perhaps solo specialists who do not have the investment in equipment. A Stark qualifying group practice could provide laboratory and cardiac services to its new members' patients, as well as lock up the referrals that might otherwise go to specialists outside the group. The net income from the ancillary services would have to be allocated among the physicians in a manner permitted by Stark, basically one that does not reward a provider for the value or volume of referrals made. The simplest allocation would divide the ancillary profits up equally among the physician-owners of the group, but other methodologies are permitted.

Note that the two revenue strategies reviewed—gaining actuarial stability and negotiating leverage for capitation, and expansion of ancillary services—are enhancement or offensive strategies, not defensive strategies. Successfully executing either strategy is difficult, but more value is placed on growth and expansion than on operating efficiency in a practice of a given size. An expanding revenue base usually offers growing profit opportunities to the hypothetical buyer, where a fixed revenue base offers fixed profit once efficiencies are maximized. Nonetheless, revenue growth, in reality, does not always translate to profit growth due to such factors as payor pushback and poor management, but it remains the "Holy Grail" of value, since normalized profit assumes competent management.

Structures for Successful Mergers

There are a variety of issues besides value and allocation of equity involved in a merger of medical practices. Many of these issues, however, impact on the standard of value and the valuation approach chosen. *Failure to understand the nonvaluation issues can result in the valuation advisor killing, rather than aiding, a merger.*

Identifying Group Strategic Goals

With consolidation running rampant in the healthcare industry again, many physicians seek larger organizations simply because everyone else is doing it, without understanding the underlying market pressures or plotting a post-merger course. If the market dictates a larger physician practice for negotiating leverage and risk-taking, for example, the physicians then need to decide what they plan to do with the practice three, five, and 10 years out.

One Man, One Vote

Most physician groups historically developed around the concept that each equity holder should play an equal role in the governance of the entity, at least as far as voting power is concerned. In a small practice, quality physicians will not be subservient to other physicians with larger equity positions for extended periods; they will seek to establish their own practices instead. In larger practices, voting will lead to the creating of an executive committee, which then elects a managing physician and hires professional, nonphysician management.

The equality of voting can be established through a number of mechanisms without necessarily affecting the allocation of financial equity. Voting common stock can be allocated per physician, with individual physician equity in the practice—based upon general valuation principles—settled through preferred stock or a second class of common. Similarly, an LLC can have provisions that give the same result in conjunction with tax provisions under Section 704 of the code.

Financial Equity Versus Voting Equity

Financial, as opposed to voting, equity is a function of the market and the long-term strategies of the physicians. When physician practices are the target of third-party acquirers, resale in a control transaction of a recently acquired minority interest may be a very real possibility. Limited liability companies (LLCs) have thus increasingly become the vehicle of choice for accomplishing practice mergers since they are typically taxed as partnerships,[7] eliminating the double taxation problem of personal service corporations. From a federal tax standpoint, partnerships offer significant variability in the permitted manner of allocating income and expense, gains, and losses to the partners. It is perfectly acceptable for each partner to have an equal vote in practice governance, but very different shares in practice value. In contrast, a corporation with a single class of common stock would be compelled to have both voting and equity equivalent.

Due to the flexibility inherent in LLCs taxed as partnerships, it is possible to value each physician's interest *at the time of a third-party sale*, for example, rather than at the time the practice forms. Particularly for younger physicians, this mitigates the likelihood that the practice value will be determined by their success during the 15 or 20 years after a formation of a larger group by having that value allocated to another physician near retirement or, in fact, already retired. If the third-party sale does not occur during the career of the older physicians, they need to rely upon the buyout provisions in the agreement, coupled with the "lookback" provision described below.

Key Valuation Tip

The lookback provision: An active market for practice acquisition by physician practice management companies (such as now exists for anesthesia practices) or other buyers creates a substantial impediment to the orderly retirement of senior practice members who may fear being left out of the windfall that can result from such a sale. The character of a windfall generally accrues to those who will retire soon, while the burden associated with producing the future income stream necessary to support the value falls to the junior members who enter into long-term agreements for services with the acquirer. A common problem in group practices confronted with the "opportunity" for such a sale is the conflict between junior (in terms of age) and senior members. Due to income taxes and lack of capital, it will virtually never be practical or wise for the juniors to buy out the seniors at anything approaching third-party value—which may or may not represent fair market value in a physician-to-physician transaction. Experienced appraisers familiar with cost of capital will no doubt recognize that a public company will have a lower cost of capital and therefore a higher cap rate applied

7 See IRS Publication 541 for a simplified discussion of the workings of distributions between partnerships and partners.

to earnings—another example of arbitrage between the public and private sector that can drive consolidation transactions.

By the same token, junior members should not be in the position of vetoing a sale, forcing senior members to retire at less than third-party value, and then selling the practice thereafter and collecting the windfall for themselves, even if they must enter into the long-term agreements customarily required to consummate such a transaction.

The lookback provision basically phases out the equity ownership for a retiring member of the practice and provides that if the practice sells to a third party within, say, three years after the retirement, the retiree will be entitled to some portion of the sales proceeds. The following is a sample: "Assume Dr. Jones held 10% of the equity and retired. The group sells to a third party two years later. His 10% would phase down at the rate of 20% of the total (or 2%) per year, or have a value of 6% at the sale date."

SECTION II: OTHER SPECIAL CIRCUMSTANCES

Although much of the "action" in medical practice valuation is for "transactional" purposes, where a hospital is buying the practice, there continues to be a number of routine valuation scenarios involving medical practices. This segment will review the additional factors to be considered in a variety of valuation engagements.

Divorce

Divorce proceedings are a common source of valuations. The values of practices may vary from state to state, and even court to court within a state, based upon case law and the presence of *professional* versus *practice* goodwill (see Chapters 10 and 15 for detailed discussions). Although the standard of value is not the same in all jurisdictions, the valuation methods typically employed assume that a hypothetical seller will depart and leave the practice with the buyer. If the physician-spouse continues to work in the practice and the earnings are the subject of alimony or child support, a substantive question arises (or should arise) as to whether or not the practice has any value as marital property. The double-dip argument suggests that if an excess earnings method is employed, only the base earnings should be considered for alimony, while the excess earnings are considered property. The next paragraph looks at a common situation encountered by valuators.

Separating Professional From Practice Goodwill

Professional goodwill is that future income-producing capacity that attaches to the individual practitioner, while *practice goodwill* is that which attaches to location, workforce-in-place, phone number, and perhaps other intangibles that may be sold to a third party or considered an asset of the marital estate subject to division. Depending upon the jurisdiction, professional goodwill should be addressed in a marital dissolution through support payments based upon future income since the practitioner will be unable to sell it and maintain his or her income stream. Notwithstanding, state laws and local judges may have different views of which elements of intangible value are allocated to professional or practice goodwill.

It is common among dentists, for example, to find arrangements where a general dentist has excess office capacity and "rents" the space to one or more specialists who can provide services compatible with but not in conflict with his or her own; alternatively stated, the renter is a subcontractor to the general dentist or physician with the office and patient base. A typical arrangement would be to have the practice pay the "renter" specialist 40% to 50% of the receipts generated from such services. (Note: Valuators should be aware of the anti-kickback and Stark laws that regulate relationships among healthcare providers when applying this method to physician practices. Any affected rent or subcontractor payment has to meet a fair market value standard.) Several examples follow: a general dentist who rents space to a periodontist or endodontist, an ophthalmologist who rents space to another ophthalmologist who is a retina specialist, and a dermatologist who rents to a plastic surgeon who perhaps does liposuction or removes large skin growths outside the skill of the dermatologist.

Example

While it may be true that the ability to recruit other physicians into the office and then direct patients to them is tied to the professional's reputation, the rent payments represent a separate source of income not directly tied to the professional's services. How can this revenue stream be valued? Assume facts in Exhibit 5.

Exhibit 5

Owner receipts	$600,000	75.0%
Renter receipts	200,000	25.0
Total receipts	800,000	100.0
Variable expenses	240,000	30.0
Fixed expenses	60,000	7.5
Renter direct expense	100,000	12.5
Total expense	400,000	50.0
Owner's net income	400,000	50.0

Several approaches may be taken to determine the income attributable to the renter payments. The simplest approach on the surface would be to conclude that the income netted from the renter is $100,000 and that this is the income stream subject to valuation. This approach implies that all of the operating expenses would have existed without the renter and that the 50% of the renter's receipts retained is "pure" profit. Depending upon the risk associated with the future use of the location by the renter and with income for the particular specialty, a capitalization rate might range from 25% to 40%, or more. For the sake of illustration, assume that the cap rate is 33.3% and the value of this practice goodwill is therefore $300,000.

Another approach would be to argue that all the fixed costs are attributable to the owner and that the true profit from the renter is total revenue less variable cost less than the renter payment, as illustrated in Exhibit 6.

Exhibit 6

	Without	Renter	With
Owner receipts	$600,000	$200,000	$800,000
Fixed expenses	60,000		60,000
Variable expenses	180,000	60,000	240,000
Renter direct expense		100,000	100,000
Total expense	240,000	160,000	400,000
Net income	360,000	40,000	400,000

This clearly will yield a very different result. Using the same 33.3% cap rate from above, a value of $120,000 is generated.

The final approach to look at (although infinite variations are possible) is that of fully allocating costs to both the owner and the renter, as illustrated in Exhibit 7.

Exhibit 7

	Without	Renter	With
Owner receipts	$600,000	$200,000	$800,000
Fixed expenses	45,000	15,000	60,000
Variable expenses	180,000	60,000	240,000
Renter direct expense		100,000	100,000
Total expense	225,000	175,000	400,000
Net income	375,000	25,000	400,000

The difference is striking. Using the same 33.3% cap rate from above, a value of $75,000 is generated, one-fourth of the $300,000 derived from the "pure profit" approach.

Which method is most accurate, if any? The pure profit approach seems highly unlikely, unless the renter is bringing all the supplies, staff, and other items normally part of variable expense (which should, or course, be ascertained) and the owner has excess physical space that would be paid for in any event. The latter argument might be considered as being akin to strategic value since taking advantage of excess capacity in a buyer or seller is often seen as a synergistic adjustment. It is, of course, virtually impossible to perform additional services in any business with absolutely no increase in marginal costs.

Summary

The second approach is defensible on a contribution-margin basis, although some may find this to have synergistic overtones as well. An analysis of historical results may indicate that all fixed costs are, in fact, fixed for the indicated range of volumes with and without the renter, and the owner's compensation increased by $40,000 due to the rental arrangement. If the historical analysis points to a conclusion, it should be followed.

The third approach is the most conservative and reflects the normal view of fully allocating costs to income-producing divisions within a business. It can certainly be defended on conceptual grounds, although it seems unlikely that a historical analysis would support it unless the owner had expanded the physical plant to accommodate renters. As in all valuation engagement, the extent of the valuator's investigation is critical to reaching the correct valuation conclusion.

Valuing Independent Practice Associations (IPAs)

IPAs are commonplace in the practice of medicine. On the West Coast, they have been the norm for decades. Although they may not view it this way, physicians who join IPAs may create value in it that can then be sold to a third party. The value depends in large part on the ability of the IPA to bind the physicians to the insurer contracts it negotiates via the participating provider agreement the physicians sign when joining it. (IPAs may also be called or be analogous to physician networks, for example, and the discussion herein applies to both.)

Although fee arrangements for IPAs vary, the standard structure is a percentage of the budget, typically capitation (see Chapter 1, Section II), plus a share of profits if the IPA is investor-owned. Exhibit 8 illustrates this structure.

The annual budget for the IPA is generally fixed each year based upon the contract with the health plan. Since the IPA is allocated 5% of this budget, this portion of the revenue

Exhibit 8. Illustration of IPA Revenue

		PMPM	Total	
Insured members		20,000		
Months		12		
Member months		240,000		
Capitation rate PMPM		100		
Annual revenue			$24,000,000	
IPA fee	5%			
IPA share of revenue		5		$1,200,000

stream is predictable, or known in advance. It is necessary to carefully evaluate the trends in the market to know whether the current year's budget makes a reasonable basis for establishing a forecast to use the DCF model and whether subsequent budgets will increase or decrease.

IPA or Network Contracts With Payors

For anti-trust reasons, IPA contracts with HMOs and other payors are generally *risk-based,* meaning that a portion of the compensation in the contract is contingent upon the physicians in the IPA meeting certain defined performance standards, such as keeping the total cost of services within a predetermined budget. In limited instances, an IPA may have the exclusive right to provide services to an HMO's patients within its service area. An IPA may receive a higher budget from the HMO if it is exclusive with respect to that plan, meaning that it does not contract with any other HMO. This may occur when an HMO is attempting to develop market share or to keep other HMOs out of the market.

IPA or Network Contracts With Physicians

Contracts between an IPA and its participating physicians will generally fall into two categories: exclusive and nonexclusive. Under an exclusive contract, the IPA has the right to contract with HMOs and other payors on behalf of the physician, and the physician is generally bound to accept the contract and cannot contract directly with that HMO or via another entity, such as a physician hospital organization.

Under a nonexclusive contract, the physicians may accept or reject a proposal from the IPA. If rejected, the physician is generally free to contract with the HMO directly or through a different entity.

Within these two general categories, there are, predictably, infinite variations. A common example is an opt-out provision, where even though the contract is exclusive, the physician may choose not to participate. If the physician opts out, he or she may be permitted to maintain an existing relationship with that HMO, but not to enter into a new contract. Opt-outs may be structured to require the IPA to bring a "market best" contract to the physician to require participation.

Such contracts may also contain a "right of first opportunity" provision requiring a physician to bring any new proposals to the IPA for evaluation.

Author's Insight and Analysis

I have frequently used precisely this opt-out strategy in negotiating on behalf of IPA clients. Physician members need to expect that if they join an IPA and grant it exclusive contracting rights, they will be better off than if they did not join.

One method employed for potential IPA or network members or physicians considering joining another network is the so-called "black box" analysis. In this case, a neutral subject to a confidentiality agreement receives fee schedule information from each party and compares the fees for a number of CPT codes and payors deemed necessary to generate a meaningful conclusion to the neutral. The report back to the parties however, is very broad and contains only general statements, such as the new network fee schedule is 0% to 10% better than the physician's existing fee schedule.

Issues in Forecasting Revenue and Profit

The IPA's share of the profit shown above is much less predictable. Historical experience is critical to forecasting future profits, in addition to the market analysis. Profits in an IPA result from two general factors: the success of the physicians in controlling utilization of services by and on behalf of their patients and the IPA's success in negotiating good contracts, whether with an HMO or other insurer or for discounted prices for the services of non-IPA specialists or ancillary service providers the IPA utilizes. Experience in these areas is, in fact, one good predictor of future experience, but certainly not the only predictor. Utilization control is a learned skill. Obtaining good contracts is a function of negotiating skill and experience as well as market clout.

What cannot be forecasted with any certainty, particularly in small IPAs, is adverse actuarial experience, as is described elsewhere in this chapter.

Events Triggering a Need for Valuation

Although valuation of an IPA can arise at any time and for any reason, a common event triggering a valuation request is the need to decide whether to sell the IPA to a third party, perhaps a hospital network or a private equity firm, the latter of which would ultimately look to sell to a public entity or go public itself.

Defending Against Unwarranted Damage Claims in a Practice Dissolution[8]

Not all marriages are made in heaven, and neither are all business partnerships. Inevitably, the practitioner will encounter a breakup of a client medical practice or be asked to serve as an expert in assessing damage claims. This section highlights some of the typical goodwill and damage claim issues, how to identify their weaknesses, the importance of regulatory review, and how to defeat the claim in appropriate circumstances. It draws on information and facts presented in various sections of the book.

Loss of Goodwill

A typical damage claim involves a claim against one party for loss of goodwill by the other. One measure of this goodwill is accomplished through an "excess earnings" or capitalization of cash flows[9] approach, as illustrated below for simplicity, although a discounted cash flow methodology might be appropriate. Practitioners should also be aware of the relevant definition of "damages" as used in the statutes and the case law in the state in which the damage case is filed.

Exhibit 9. Three-person practice, one partner expelled

Earnings of entire practice	$900,000
Statistical earnings (e.g., from MGMA)	600,000
Excess earnings	300,000
Cap rate	20.00%
Claimed goodwill value	1,500,000
Plaintiff's interest	33.33%
Value to plaintiff	$500,000

When presented with such an "analysis," the first thing to ask is: "Who among the doctors was earning the $900,000?" (See Exhibit 9.) What was the compensation formula? What do the employment contracts say? How many services did each physician provide by CPT code (technical versus professional)? Did the practice provide any ancillary services? Were these services a source of profits? Were there any physician extenders? If so, were they profitable? What are values of the practice intangibles and related returns?

Is there a buy-sell agreement? Buy-sell agreements might treat accounts receivable as a compensation offset to permit entry and exit with much lower cash amounts than would be the case if accounts receivables were being purchased.

8 An earlier version of this material, co-authored by John J. Mayerhofer, CPA, FACHE, FHFMA, appeared in *CPA Expert*.

9 The EEM and CCF should generate equivalent results if the discount rates applied to assets and capital are equivalent—which they should be.

Author's Insight and Analysis

Whether partnership interests or stock shares, the practice should annually ratify the value of each unit of ownership, although few do, despite the old adage that "an ounce of prevention is worth a pound of cure."

Assume that the $900,000 of the income in the example was earned $400,000 by Dr. Allday, $300,000 by Dr. Begood, and $200,000 by Dr. DoLittle (see Exhibit 10). Dr. DoLittle is the plaintiff. The damage claim presented effectively redistributes $200,000 of Dr. Allday's "excess earnings" to the entire practice and accounts for $1 million of the valuation. If Dr. Allday is producing that income through a disproportionate number of total encounters, it will be difficult to convince a court that Dr. DoLittle is entitled to the fruits of Dr. Allday's labor. In fact, Dr. DoLittle is earning only $200,000 and contributing no excess earnings to the practice. Dr. Allday's counsel might ask Dr. DoLittle whether he was ever paid any portion of Dr. Allday's income or whether he ever expected to be paid a portion.

Exhibit 10

	Allday	Begood	DoLittle
Earnings	$400,000	$300,000	$200,000
MGMA norm	$200,000	$200,000	$200,000
Excess earnings	$200,000	$100,000	$0
Cap factor	20%	20%	20%
Value	$1,000,000	$500,000	$0

If the doctors in the example were, in fact, dividing income equally, Dr. DoLittle might have a better argument, since, as the lowest producer, he would be getting the fruits of someone else's labor. Whether the damages are for loss of equity or earnings would still be open to question. (See the discussion of Stark anti-referral issues, below, regarding the dangers of distributing the technical component of referred procedures on the basis of production.)

Wrongful Discharge

Another line of inquiry involves whether the damage claim is for loss of an asset—goodwill—or whether it is for loss of income due to wrongful discharge from employment. These are two different claims. If the plaintiff presents expert testimony as to the loss of an asset, it may be possible to defeat that claim, whereas an improper discharge claim may be more difficult to defeat.

It is important to analyze the underlying intent of the parties with respect to any excess earnings and whether the value of same was to be considered equity or a liability to the producer of that excess for compensation. Perhaps the first inquiry should be whether any prior buy-in transaction included accounts receivable (AR) as part of equity or whether the AR is reallocated via the compensation system and employment contracts.

The typical employment contract in a small practice will provide that upon retirement or other termination of employment for defined reasons the physician will be entitled to receive his or her share of AR as collected or over a period of time. (A cost of collection may be charged against the receivables to determine the amount due.) Paying the specific receivables of a physician to him or her at retirement or other termination clearly puts the offsetting credit on the right side of the balance sheet in the liability class, not equity. On the other hand, if the total AR were included in the buyback of stock under the shareholder's agreement, equity could clearly be indicated. If the retiring shareholder were entitled to a pro rata share of the AR regardless of who produced them, this would enhance Dr. DoLittle's claim of loss of equity if he did not get paid out.

Is there any (business) goodwill value in a practice that allocates all compensation on a productivity basis and at retirement pays receivables on the basis of who produced them? There may well be, but it will certainly not be determinable by lumping all the excess earnings into a single bucket. Some portion of the excess earnings may well be attributable to economies of scale resulting from the three doctors practicing together or return on enterprise intangibles such as workforce in place or going-concern value. This is where the "left-hand," or asset, side of the valuation balance sheet and related assignment of discount rates can be important. Note that the compensation values in common sources of data used to establish reasonable compensation such as MGMA likely include profit distributions as well as payment for services.

To measure economies of scale, the valuator might compare the overhead expense per physician in a hypothetical solo practice to that in the contested practice. For example, assume that overhead per physician in a hypothetical solo practice is $150,000 per physician. In the example above, it is $375,000, or $125,000 per physician, assuming expenses are shared equally. It may be possible for the plaintiff to successfully argue that $25,000 of each physician's earnings are attributable to being in a group, for a total of $75,000. Applying a 20% cap rate yields a total practice intangible value of $375,000. (We ignore a return on tangible assets for simplicity.)

Federal Anti-Referral Legislation

There are two principal statutes regulating the referral of Medicare and Medicaid patients for health services: the fraud and abuse law, also known as the anti-kickback statute (AKS), and the Stark laws (named for the California Congressman who introduced them). The fraud and abuse laws (criminal) are broad in scope and prohibit, generally, payments in exchange for referral of Medicare, Medicaid, and other patients covered by federal programs. The most feared penalty is to exclude offenders from participation in the Medicare and Medicaid programs, even in the absence of possible criminal conviction.

The Stark laws are civil statute and prohibit payments for referrals of designated health services. Basically, a referral is any request by a physician for designated health services that are reimbursable under Medicare Part A or B, whether or not Medicare actually pays for the service. Designated health services include clinical laboratory services, radiology and other diagnostic services, and inpatient hospital services, in addition to a number of others. A physician can violate the law and regulations by referring Medicare or Medicaid patients to their group practice for designated health services, unless the group meets the qualifying definition of a "group" and is excepted from the provision.

Any valuation must take these laws into account. It is conceivable that a settlement negotiated outside of a court with respect to damage claims may ignore these laws, leaving the parties with uncertain exposure, particularly if a whistleblower gets hold of the documents. A valuation methodology that takes into account referrals and allocates value upon dissolution in exchange for past referrals would appear to run a clear risk of violating the statutes.

In performing a valuation, the valuator must first assess the liability employment contracts imposed on the underlying net assets of the practice. Next, compliance of the compensation system with the various statutes and regulations must be determined, i.e., is the obligation valid under those laws? Assuming the system is found compliant, the valuator must utilize assumptions in constructing the valuation model that respect both the contracts and the regulatory environment.

Example

Assume the productivity-based compensation system in a multispecialty practice properly allocates certain income from cardiac echo exams to the cardiologist who performs the procedure, resulting in a disproportionately high income for the cardiologist. Many, but not all, of the referrals come from his partners in the practice, such as general internists, who do not perform such tests. One of these internists is forced out of the practice and seeks damages. Use of an excess earnings method with respect to the cardiologist's earnings to determine the value to the internist (1) contravenes the productivity-based compensation system and (2) may violate the prohibition against referral payments, depending upon whether the income is from designated health services (DHS). Generally, a test that has a technical component to the payment is subject to Stark, while the professional component to the physician for interpreting the test is *not* subject to Stark. An analysis of certain relevant provisions of the Stark law follows.

The prohibition on referrals set forth in §411.353 does not apply to the following types of services:

(a) Physician services.

(1) Physician services as defined in §410.20(a) of this chapter that are furnished -

(i) Personally by another physician who is a member of the referring physician's group practice or is a physician in the same group practice (as defined in §411.351) as the referring physician;[10]

Thus, one member of a group practice may refer patients for DHS to another member of the group practice.

> Referral does not include any designated health service personally performed or provided by the referring physician. A designated health service is not personally performed or provided by the referring physician if it is performed or provided by any other person, including, but not limited to, the referring physician's employees, independent contractors, or group practice members.'[11]

This is critical. A cardiac echo exam has both a professional component and a technical component. If the cardiologist both orders and does the test himself or herself (as opposed to having a tech do the test which is the norm), then all the *technical* component revenue can be allocated to him or her in the compensation plan.

> (i) Special rule for productivity bonuses and profit shares. (1) A physician in a group practice may be paid a share of overall profits of the group or a productivity bonus based on services that he or she has personally performed (including services "incident to" those personally performed services as defined in §411.351), provided that the share or bonus is not determined in any manner that is directly related to the volume or value of referrals of DHS by the physician."[12]

A group practice compensation plan must also meet specific requirements under Stark, including the distribution of income from the technical component of ancillary services. To the extent that other group practice members refer their patients to the cardiologist for echo exams, the technical component income is subject to Stark's rule that the compensation plan cannot incent the volume or value of services. Thus, for example, the referring internist could not be credited with a share of that technical component net income based upon how many referrals he made to the cardiologist. (See "Understanding and Using the Technical and Professional Component of Ancillary Revenue when Valuing Medical Practices.")

10 § 411.353.
11 § 411.352.
12 § 411.352.

Now, it should be clear that the use of an excess earnings method to compute damages, as described in the example of Dr. DoLittle, risks running afoul of the anti-referral rules. Remember that the valuator must first understand the existing compensation system and then assess the system's compliance with the regulatory environment. Obviously, the valuator must have some basis for assuming that the existing compensation arrangements among the parties are to be ignored for purposes of the valuation. Having passed that threshold, if the valuation method chosen for purposes of the damages calculation changes the allocation of compensation or earnings among the parties—as could be the case with the typical application of the excess earnings method—the valuator must (again) assess the compliance of his or her new compensation system with the regulations. If the procedure is also compensated with a facility fee, a separate and distinct analysis is required with respect to those fees. Clearly, performing this assessment requires the valuator to have an intimate knowledge of the various laws and regulations.

If the existing compensation system passed muster, the "valuator-installed" new compensation system for purposes of damages calculation must also pass muster and withstand the clear challenge that it is an attempt on behalf of the plaintiff (Dr. DoLittle) to obtain value for past referrals, which could also be a violation of the anti-referral legislation. Again, defendant's (respondent's) counsel might ask the valuation expert whether the changes to the compensation system are based on assumptions that attempt to reallocate historical results to compensate Dr. DoLittle for past referrals. It is not difficult to imagine the unfamiliar expert answering yes to that question.

Valuators should recognize as well that use of market approaches, such as actual control acquisitions of private group practices by publicly traded companies or private equity firms, may not be relevant to valuing a minority interest in a dissolution. There are separate considerations under the anti-referral laws when a third party controls the practice and sets or approves compensation agreements that may be irrelevant to the private control setting where the parties control compensation arrangements among themselves. There is the obvious difference between a nonmarketable minority interest in a private company and a nonmarketable controlling interest in a private company. There is also a valuation difference between a nonmarketable controlling interest in a private company and the marketable controlling interest represented by the acquisition of a practice by a publicly traded company.

More importantly, most of the practice management transactions provide that the acquirer will retain 15% to 20% of what would otherwise be physician compensation (or pre-distribution earnings), a typical structure used by the practice management industry, for example. Unless this same 15% to 20% of the earnings is reallocated in the valuation method applied to the group practice and such reallocation is valid under the regulations, it is easy to misuse the data. Given the structure of such transactions, it is multiples of earnings actually purchased from the physicians, and not revenue or other multiples, that are driving the value.

Ancillary Income

If a portion of the excess earnings arises from ancillary services (imaging, laboratory, and other testing), a going concern valuation analysis should be done, with the addition of the inquiry as to compliance with the Stark and Medicare fraud and abuse laws and regulations. The professional component of income from supervised tests—those requiring the presence and participation of the physician (e.g., colonoscopy and cardiac echoes)—should be considered separate from those that do not (e.g., blood chemistry panels). In fact, the final Stark II regulations recognize this distinction. Another important analysis is that of the professional and technical component in imaging studies, or the facility fee for certain outpatient procedures in a licensed facility setting. Supervised tests will tend to generate income more in line with personal goodwill if the compensation system is based on productivity (compliant with the Stark law as previously discussed), while unsupervised tests tend to generate income in line with business goodwill. Neither is an absolute. Under the anti-kickback statute, a wholly owned and controlled technical component is treated as an extension of the physician's office practice. If a single physician with a different specialty becomes a partner or stockholder, however, then the 60-40 rule described above may well be applicable.

In a radiology practice, the professional component of reimbursement is designed to compensate the radiologist for reading the film or study. The technical component compensates for the use of equipment, supplies, staff, and other costs to perform the study. If business goodwill exists, it will likely come from two sources: net income on the technical side and any profit from paying radiologists less than the professional component. The latter needs to be evaluated in light of the standard of value. Under fair market value, the hypothetical buyer or seller may not be able to sustain a pattern of paying less than the professional component for the services of radiologists.

Impact of Noncompete

The *Norwalk, Derby,* and *Howard* cases highlight the proposition that goodwill cannot exist at the entity level unless enforceable noncompetes are in place with the owner-employees, at least as far as the tax court is concerned. (This likely could extend to key nonowner employees' inclusion as part of the workforce in place.) Any damages measure should therefore make some assessment of the enforceability of noncompetes under local law and any relevant shareholder or employment agreements.

Conclusion

In a professional practice, much of the goodwill may attach to the individual professional, and excess earnings are often the result of longer hours, more procedures, and special skills. In a practice split-up or dissolution, valuation or damages methods that measure undifferentiated intangible value as part of business enterprise value are generally inaccurate with respect to the intangible value owned by the individual versus the entity. If an enforceable covenant not to compete exists between the individual professional and the entity, the professional may have assigned some portion of his or her goodwill to the entity. However, even in that case, only that portion of the individual's intangible value that inures to the benefit of the other professional in the entity should be the basis for valuation of damages. Practices in which the earnings are allocated on the basis of production—to whomever did the work—inherently have lower enterprise intangible value. Measuring intangibles value through non-earnings-based approaches, such as the going-concern analysis (really, a cost approach), seems to avoid the anti-referral problem. Treating a portion of the compensation received by each physician—an equal amount, if equal equity interests are held—as described in the earlier reduced-overhead scenario, also seems to avoid the issue.

Medical practices offer a unique valuation challenge since there is a federal statutory ban against paying for referrals of Medicare or Medicaid patients. Many states have analogous and more expansive statutes. Unlike a law firm or accounting firm, rainmaking (for others) may or may not legally be a direct factor in setting a physician's compensation. A number of common assumptions in methods used to compute damages, or goodwill for division in a breakup of a medical practice, may implicate federal anti-referral (Stark) and fraud and abuse law. The knowledgeable practitioner should be alert to point out these apparent violations and in so doing, assist legal counsel to appropriately limit claims for damages.

Chapter Summary

This chapter dealt with a variety of special circumstances that may arise in the context of a medical practice valuation.

The actual transaction documents in a medical practice purchase and sell determine precisely what is being bought and sold and therefore, need to be reviewed for consistency with the valuation. When a physician buys into an existing practice, the advisor and valuator should be certain that the economic return on the equity investment is reasonable. The greater the amount of the purchase price allocated to stock, the greater the direct return on that stock should be, either in the form of dividends or as a part of the buy*out* price. It is perhaps more common for buy-ins to be structured as some form of compensation shift to the existing owners.

Noncompetition agreements are typically included in a transfer of a physician practice and in buyout agreements among physicians. It is critical that the valuator understand the applicable state law with respect to the enforceability of such agreements when valuing a practice or testifying as an expert witness in a claim for damages. The author believes courts will increasingly be reluctant to enforce such agreements involving physicians as being in contravention of public policy—the right of the medical patient to have free access to the physician of his or her own choosing.

Any valuation result should be subject to a reality check. A reasonable standard for an internal buy-in is that the price must be payable in no more than five years, with the purchaser earning a reasonable after-tax income in excess of the purchase payments during the buy-in period.

Merger transactions, which may require valuations, should be evaluated based upon their potential for increased profitability, preferably from revenue enhancements, actuarial stability in capitated settings, negotiating leverage, and cost reductions. Strategic value plays an important role in such mergers, but valuators should assess whether the strategic opportunities are available to most market participants.

Damage claims among physicians and their acquirers are likely to increase as failed transactions start to unwind. Some damage concepts explored in this chapter include loss of workforce-in-place value, loss of goodwill, and loss of value from increased competition.

Chapter 9

Critical Condition—A Coding Analysis for a Physician Practice Valuation

By Mark O. Dietrich, CPA/ABV, and Frank Cohen, CMPA

At the outset, we should emphasize that a coding analysis is not always feasible. In a number of circumstances, the data may not be available because of poor information systems or a refusal to provide the data. Depending upon the nature of the engagement, the analyst may want to consider the implications of the lack of availability or a refusal to supply data. That said, this article focuses on the significance of a coding analysis. Basic coding analysis is within the reach of the valuation analyst using the approaches and tools described herein.

Established Patient Office Visits

The most commonly used codes in the Medicare database are the established patient office visits, which are designated 99211 through 99215. The codes are copyrighted by the American Medical Association (AMA). Of these five codes, 99212, 99213, and 99214 are the most frequently used; 99214 pays about 60% more than a 99213 and more than 220% of 99212. Clearly, incorrect or improper coding can dramatically affect the normalized revenues of a practice. For this reason alone, a coding analysis is critical.

In the last five years, there has been a steady, rightward shift of the historical bell curve coding pattern, with a decrease in 99212 codes and an increase in the 99214 codes. (See Exhibit 1.)

This shift has not gone unnoticed. The Department of Health and Human Services (DHHS), Office of Inspector General (OIG) produced Medicare fee for service (FFS) error rates from 1996 to 2002. This process, known as the comprehensive error rate

Exhibit 1. Internal Medicine Coding

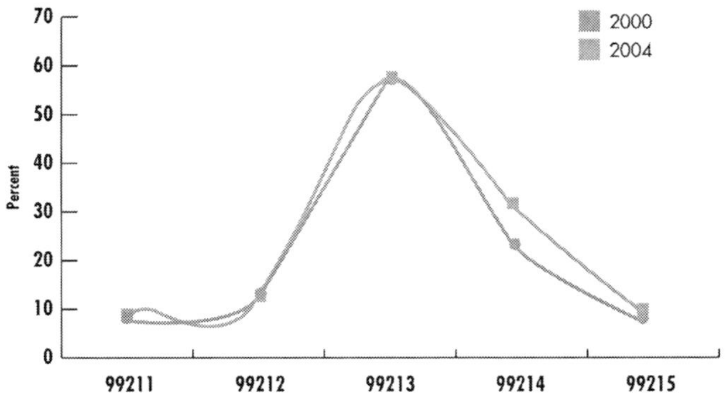

testing (CERT) program revealed that payers were reimbursing practices erroneously for procedures that were not documented properly and did not meet medical necessity tests. A focus of this study has been a select group of procedure codes that have historically had very high levels of improper payment, the least of which has been the aforementioned code 99214. Medical reviews of 4,436 lines for the period between Jan. 1, 2004, and Dec. 31, 2004, disclosed that 648 lines, or 14.6%, were in error. Based on the application of these results, Centers for Medicare & Medicaid Services (CMS) estimates that improper payments of $234,489,004 were made to physicians for this code alone. For medical practices, this means that these codes are under greater scrutiny from payers and other outside investigative agencies.

Evaluation and management (EM) coding in particular is dependent on a series of guidelines that require the physician to consider 1,600 unique decision points during a typical patient visit. In determining the code to be assigned, there are two major players with respect to validating the use of the EM code, namely, documentation and medical necessity.

Documentation is simply the process of recording or writing down a detailed summary of the visit, including the chief complaint, past family and social history, results of the physical exam, and information that would indicate the level of complexity of decision-making during the examination. This process is analogous to the working papers of the valuation analyst or certified public accountant (CPA).

Medical necessity is a process used by Medicare and private payers to determine whether they should pay for goods or services billed by the physician. Medical necessity is defined as including that which is reasonable and necessary to diagnose or treat illness or injury or improve the function of a malformed body member. Medicare has a number of policies, including national coverage determinations (NCDs) and local medical review policy (LMRP), also known as local coverage determinations (LCDs), that outline what is and is not covered. In a small number of cases, Medicare may even determine whether a method of treating a patient should be covered on a case-by-case basis. Even if a service is accepted as reasonable and necessary, coverage may be limited if the service is provided more frequently than allowed under standard policies or standards of care.

In almost every case, these two tests dominate the decision to reimburse the provider for the procedure submitted on the claim. It is a complicated process because there is no effective relationship between documentation and medical necessity even though both medical necessity and documentation are tied to the procedure code. Submitting a claim for a service or procedure binds the practice to a highly complex and complicated series of laws, policies, rules, and regulations, any violation of which could result in substantial civil and criminal penalties.

Other Examples

Many medical specialists, such as cardiologists, infectious disease specialists, and pulmonologists, earn a substantial amount of their income from consultations. A consultation is specifically defined as a request from another physician. The AMA's current procedural terminology defines a consultation as "a type of service provided by a physician whose opinion or advice regarding evaluation and management of a specific problem is requested by another physician or other appropriate source." There are four parts to a consultation, namely, a request for review and an opinion; the rendering of the opinion; the documentation in the patient's chart; and the report provided to the referring physician. A recent OIG study suggests that billions of dollars in improper consultations were being billed to Medicare, placing these procedures, along with established office visits and subsequent hospital visits, high on the OIG's hit list.

Sources Of Data

Certain data can be downloaded from the CMS Web site, at www.cms.hhs.gov/PhysicianFeeSched/01_Overview.asp#TopOfPage.

Copies of the CERT report, updated definitional information on consults, the physician fee schedule database (PFSDB), and other files related to this article may be downloaded for free by going to www.cpahealth.com and clicking on the download tab.

Identifying Problematic Coding

A major area of utilization analysis involves the use of the EM codes. This kind of analysis involves looking at the use of codes within specific categories and between specific categories and comparing the utilization of each category to the global use of EM codes. Performing a complete EM utilization analysis can be complex and time-consuming;

however, it is the category that most frequently accounts for the resource utilization and financial revenue of the practice. The use of EM codes is under considerable scrutiny from outside reviewers and special attention should be paid to this area.

In the valuation practice of Mark Dietrich, one of the co-authors of this article, the top 50 code spreadsheets by specialty are used extensively to identify potential issues that warrant further inquiry. (See Exhibit 2.) These data are extracted from the Medicare master database and summarized by CPT code and frequency of use. A complete set of tables for all specialties can be purchased by contacting info@cpahealth.com.

Exhibit 2. Ranking of Codes Within Top 50

Rank in Top 50	CPT Code	Service Description	Count	Percent of Inpatient Consults
7	99254	Initial inpatient consult	337,300	52.31%
13	99255	Initial inpatient consult	204,283	31.68%
21	99253	Initial inpatient consult	103,218	16.01%
				100.00%

Rank in Top 50	CPT Code	Service Description	Count	Percent of Top 50
35	99291	Critical care, first hour	37,849	0.68%
45	99238	Hospital discharge day	24,241	0.44%
26	99262	Followup inpatient consult	61,413	1.11%
34	99263	Followup inpatient consult	39,668	0.71%
39	99223	Initial hospital care	26,367	0.48%
7	99254	Initial inpatient consult	337,300	6.08%
13	99255	Initial inpatient consult	204,283	3.68%
21	99253	Initial inpatient consult	103,218	1.86%
33	99312	Nursing fac care, subsequent	40,830	0.74%
43	99311	Nursing fac care, subsequent	24,467	0.44%
46	99244	Office consultation	22,299	0.40%
6	99213	Office/outpatient visit, established	339,957	6.13%
10	99214	Office/outpatient visit, established	247,192	4.45%
24	99212	Office/outpatient visit, established	67,810	1.22%
29	99215	Office/outpatient visit, established	49,383	0.89%
31	99211	Office/outpatient visit, established	47,594	0.86%
2	99232	Subsequent hospital care	2,367,869	42.67%
3	99231	Subsequent hospital care	840,012	15.14%
4	99233	Subsequent hospital care	704,910	12.70%
			5,586,662	100.00%

For example, the spreadsheet for infectious disease (ID) indicates that the most frequently billed consult code is 99254, initial inpatient consult, which is 52% of all inpatient consults. The most frequently billed code is 99232, subsequent hospital care. The ratio of all consultations (both office and hospital) to all patient visits is 12%.

Note that the remaining Top 50 services in this subspecialty represent injections or tests. In reviewing the coding of an infectious diseases (ID) practice as part of a valuation, the Medicare data can easily be compared to those of the practice.

Another benchmark is to statistically analyze the incidence of related procedures, such as office visits and outpatient consults. In performing this intercategory analysis, we could take the total number of outpatient consults (99241 to 99245) compared to the total volume of new office visits (99201 to 99205). For example, the ratio of office consults to new office visits for cardiology is 4.3-to-1, meaning that for every new patient office visit, the average cardiovascular (CV) doctor or cardiologist reports about four consults. In our example, let's say that, for the practice, the ratio was 2-to-1. This might indicate that the practice is shifting what should be consults to new office visits. These kinds of aberrant practices could result in financial and compliance problems.

For example, significant excessive numbers of consults, no matter how they are measured, can help frame the interview questions used to assess whether there is something particular to the practice. The interview of an ID doctor might take place as follows:

Analyst:

Dr. Smith, I noted in my review of your coding data that the volume of office consultations you report is significantly higher than that of your peer group. I generally see physicians in your specialty seeing consults in the hospital. Can you tell me about the unique aspects of your practice that might explain the difference?

Dr. Smith:

Answer A: Since my office is here on campus, many patients simply come here rather than wait for me to see them in the hospital.

Answer B: You'll note that many of my patients have communicable diseases, and, in this area, I receive most of the referrals to confirm or rule out a particular diagnosis.

Answer C: I didn't realize there was a difference.

Answer D: When I see patients for the first time, I charge for a consult. It pays more than a new patient visit.

Analysis

Answer A would require the analyst to know whether a particular medical condition typically requires hospitalization before an ID consult. Answer B might be a perfectly acceptable answer if, for example, Dr. Smith practices in an inner city, where tuberculosis is often a public health problem. Answer D is a red flag and a tacit admission of incorrect coding. Obviously, Answer C is of no assistance to the analyst.

Modifiers

The same sort of analysis applies to the use of modifiers. Over- or underuse of certain modifiers may raise a flag with carriers, payers, and other outside reviewing agencies. For example, if modifier 25 (used to describe *separate, distinctly identifiable* services from other services or procedures rendered during the same visit) is used at a level greater than 10% of a particular EM category, it may cause a carrier to perform a review of the practice's billing and coding patterns. These flags are most often the source of focused reviews and audits. Most recently, OIG published two separate reports, one on modifier 59 and one on modifier 25. According to the reports, violations in the way these codes are reported by providers resulted in hundreds of millions of dollars in inappropriate payments. These reports are also available at www.cpahealth.com by clicking on the download tab.

Utilization of Tests

One process is the ranking of procedure codes within the practice compared to national averages. For example, we might rank the codes within our practice by frequency and dollar volume, and compare this result with the top 50 codes for that specific specialty based upon the national average. This analysis identifies areas in which there may be patterns of over- or underuse. A subset of this analysis is the utilization of tests in the physician's office, and many of the top 50 CPT codes consist of such tests. Some of this variation can be traced to the ancillary capabilities of the practice, such as whether it has a blood chemistry lab, X-ray, or other imaging technology. Comparisons between the practices with and without this equipment are not possible; therefore, it is important to ascertain the practice's capabilities before attempting a utilization analysis.

Surgical Practices

For surgical practices, the utilization of procedure codes is more complex and can involve a number of different kinds of analysis, many of which are likely beyond the purview of the valuation analyst. However, certain simple analyses can rule out or identify common problems. It may also be helpful to identify the revenue potential associated with procedures that are not being provided by the practice but that are being performed or reported by other practices within the same specialty. In specialty practices, such as ophthalmology, physicians trained in the most recently developed surgical techniques may have greater earning power than the current practitioners, who are relying on less-advanced techniques.

Another utilization issue concerns the use and reporting of the post-operative code 99024. Medicare pays for all surgery on the basis of a global fee that includes *both* pre-operative and post-operative care. For example, a practice reports 5,250 global surgical procedures that have either a 10- or 90-day follow-up period. In performing a utilization analysis, it is found that they reported the 99024 code (surgical follow-up) 1,025 times. The resulting ratio of 0.195-to-1 indicates that only one in five surgical procedures was followed! This conclusion could raise troubling questions about the quality of care, as well as compliance and *the potential for reimbursement.* Even though the relevant codes are considered bundled codes for Medicare, it is important to ensure that all post-operative visits that fall within the global period, i.e., are recorded for reasons relating to the global procedure, and accurately documented as such. For each global surgical code, there is a preservice, intraservice, and post-service component that represents both the resource consumption and fee allocation for that procedure. For example, for procedure code 28190 (the removal of a foreign body from the foot), the preoperative portion is 10%, the surgical portion is 80%, and the post-operative portion is 10%. If adequate follow-up is not reported, the insurer could reduce the post-service payment portion (by 10%), indicating that the follow-up portion was not satisfied based upon the utilization statistics.

The use of global fees for surgery is a critical consideration in valuation or litigation. For example, assume a surgeon has left the group practice and the geographic area and is seeking additional compensation or other benefits. The group practice has the responsibility and lost revenue associated with providing post-operative care, including the repair of complications, for any patients of that departed surgeon. This must be considered in any damages calculation.

Beware Changes in the Value of Codes

For example, in June 2006, CMS announced its intent to increase the relative values of EM services in 2007, following closely on the heels of a suggestion by MedPAC in its March 2006 report that these services had declined in value, in large part to the benefit of high-tech imaging services.

The work component for RVUs [Relative Value Units] associated with an intermediate office visit [99213], the most commonly billed physician's service, will increase by 37%. The work component for RVUs for an office visit requiring moderately complex decisionmaking and for a hospital visit also requiring moderately complex decisionmaking will increase by 29% and 31%, respectively. Both of these services rank in the top 10 most frequently billed physicians' services out of more than 7,000 types of services paid under the physician fee schedule.

The 99213 code presently has a fully implemented work RVU value of 0.67. Under this proposal, the value would rise to approximately 0.92 RVUs. With a conversion factor of $37.90, this would represent an increase in the fee of nearly $10, or 18%, to about $62.15 from the present level of $52.68 on the National Physician Fee Schedule.

Significantly, because of the budget-neutrality provisions of the existing Part B system, the increased cost associated with the increased RVUs has to come from a reduction in the value of other services and CMS proposes "to establish a budget-neutrality adjustor that would reduce all work RVUs by an estimated 10% to meet the budget-neutrality provisions." For example, CMS estimated that the proposed changes would increase reimbursement for internal medicine by 5% in 2007 while decreasing the reimbursement for radiologists by the same amount. The *Federal Register* notice contains the details of estimated changes for all specialties.

CMS is also proposing changes to the practice expense component of the RVUs to be phased in over four years through 2010, which will result in further revenue shifts.

Conclusion

Valuation analysts are not coding consultants. Nevertheless, given regulatory issues and the impact of coding on the future cash flow being valued, it is necessary that analysts have some basic knowledge of the subject and conduct a basic review. Relatively simple processes can be implemented using readily available data from the Internet or vendors such as MIT Solutions Inc. (www.mitsi.org) to incorporate a basic assessment of coding into the valuation process. This results in a valuation conclusion that reflects the risk, if any, of unusual coding patterns and may identify potential lost revenues available to a hypothetical or other owner of the practice. In the latter instance, the analyst can bring additional value to the valuation.

This article first appeared in the Fall 2006 Edition of CPA Expert. *Reprinted with permission.*

Chapter 10

Understanding and Using the Technical and Professional Component of Ancillary Revenue When Valuing Medical Practices

By Mark O. Dietrich, CPA/ABV, and Kathie L. Wilson, CPA, CVA

Valuing any business requires an understanding of how revenue is generated: what products or services are sold, how much revenue comes from each, competing products or services, and competing sellers. Valuing a medical practice is no different in that regard. It is important to understand that services sold by medical practices are commonly specified by current procedural terminology (CPT) codes and healthcare common coding procedure system (HCPCS or "Hickpicks") codes. For example, CPT code 99213 is a Level 3 office visit for an established patient. HCPCS codes can denote "products" such as certain injectible drugs or chemotherapy that are specified by J codes or services and procedures that are specified by G codes. The HCPCS codes are alphanumeric and start with a letter. For example, J0133 is the code for an acyclovir injection; G0202 is the code for screening mammography. Thus, considerable background is required by an appraiser to understand the revenue lines in the variety of medical practice specialties.

Many of the more common specialties require more expertise than simply being familiar with the codes for seeing patients in the office. Of particular note is the differentiation between the technical component and professional component of ancillary services for practices such as radiology, cardiology, neurology, and others. The technical component is paid in connection with ownership of equipment, provision of a technologist to operate the equipment, supplies, and general overhead. The professional component is paid to the physician specifically for interpreting the results of the test or study, e.g., an imaging study such as an X-ray or MRI. Revenue from the technical component, therefore, is related to the equipment investment of the practice, not the efforts of the physician.

This can be seen in the following quotes from the Centers for Medicare and Medicaid Services' Medicare Physician Fee Schedule 2010 Final Rule:[1]

> Services with technical components (TCs) and professional components (PCs). Diagnostic services are generally comprised of two components: a professional component (PC) and a technical component (TC), both of which may be performed independently or by different providers. When services have TCs, PCs, and global components that can be billed separately, the payment for the global component equals the sum of the payment for the TC and PC. This is a result of using a weighted average of the ratio of indirect to direct costs across all the specialties that furnish the global components, TCs, and PCs; that is, we apply the same weighted average indirect percentage factor to allocate indirect expenses to the global components, PCs, and TCs for a service. (The direct PE RVUs for the TC and PC sum to the global under the bottom-up methodology.)
>
> Modifier. A modifier is shown if there is a technical component (modifier TC) and a professional component (PC) (modifier -26) for the service. If there is a PC and a TC for the service, Addendum B contains three entries for the code. A code for: the global values (both professional and technical); modifier -26 (PC); and, modifier TC. The global service is not designated by a modifier, and physicians must bill using the code without a modifier if the physician furnishes both the PC and the TC of the service.

Within the relative value unit (RVU) allocations are components for physician work, practice expense, and malpractice insurance. As you might expect, the largest element in the TC is for practice expense, whereas the largest element in the PC is typically for physician work, known as wRVUs. In some circumstances, these can be important in measuring the productivity for reasonable compensation purposes as defined later herein.[2]

Some Common Mistakes

Most appraisers determine reasonable compensation when valuing a medical practice by reference to the physician's (or physicians' aggregate) productivity benchmarked against statistical norms such as those from the Medical Group Management Association (MGMA). The definition of collected revenue in the MGMA data is with the technical component of ancillary services excluded! MGMA does have some data that include the technical component and nonphysician providers at two levels, greater than 10% or less than 10%, but that differentiation is generally not specific enough to be useful for reasonable compensation purposes.[3] Thus, to use the data appropriately, it is necessary

1 CMS-1413-FC.

2 Not all, or even many, practices track wRVUs, however.

3 See the Rhode Island example later herein for an important exception.

for the appraiser to separate the revenues associated with the professional component (related to the efforts of the physician) from those of the ancillary or technical component (related to the equipment investment).

Example

While valuing a four-physician neurology practice with a single owner, the appraiser notes that the owner has collected revenue credited to him of more than twice the 90th percentile of MGMA. Upon investigation of the practice's reports of productivity by CPT (including HCPCS) code and the list of fixed assets, he determines that the practice owns an MRI unit in addition to other ancillary equipment. The technical component of the MRI services representing approximately 85% of the global (or total) collected revenue has been credited to the owner-physician as well as the professional component. To determine the owner's productivity consistent with the MGMA definition, the technical component of the MRI and other ancillaries will have to be backed out. This has a dramatic effect on the reasonable compensation determination: After the appropriate modifications are made, the owner-physician's collections are only at the 75th percentile of MGMA. Failure to identify and appropriately adjust for the technical component collected revenue would have resulted in a dramatic understatement of the practice's value due to an overstatement of reasonable compensation for the services of the owner-physician.

Jurisdictional Issues

Aside from the obvious effect on the reasonable compensation determination, the source of profit in a practice can be quite significant from a jurisdictional standpoint. For example, in marital dissolution valuation, many jurisdictions distinguish between personal goodwill and enterprise goodwill. In many circumstances, the revenue, profit, and value resulting from the technical component of ancillary services may be included in enterprise goodwill and therefore, considered marital property subject to division, again, because it is not related to the personal efforts of the physician, but to the investment in the equipment of the practice. In other circumstances, even the technical component element may be considered nondivisible if a noncompete agreement is required from the seller to maintain the related revenue and profit in the hands of a buyer. Absent a jurisdictional rule, that portion of the practice value connected to technical component revenue that would be present absent the seller is perhaps the clearest element of enterprise goodwill.

Transactions

In the current transaction market, differentiating reasonable compensation along with enterprise and personal goodwill can be equally important. After a physician practice is acquired by a hospital, a number of employment settings are possible, including employment by the hospital, a hospital-controlled group practice, or the physician practice itself, if the hospital purchases the stock. The Stark laws have different permitted compensation rules depending on the nature of the employment setting, which can impact how profits from the technical component of ancillaries are handled. This should, in turn, influence precisely what is being valued and how reasonable compensation is determined.

One of the most important practice types from a valuation and transaction standpoint in the present market is cardiology. Cardiologists employ a variety of ancillary testing equipment including single photon emission computed tomography (SPECT),[4] used for myocardial perfusion, ultrasound (echocardiogram as distinct from an electrocardiogram, or EKG), coronary computed tomography angiogram, and cardiac MRI. Despite some fairly dramatic cuts for SPECT and other nuclear medicine in the 2010 Medicare Physician Fee Schedule, these practices remain attractive for the technical component of tests as well as for the highly profitable admissions they generate for hospitals.

Example

CPT code 78465,[5] heart image (3rd) multiple, is a SPECT code for myocardial infusion and represented a staggering 10.3% ($2,072,176,147) of charges for cardiovascular physicians billing Medicare in 2007, the highest single code in terms of charges as well as frequency of billing. CPT code 78465 also represented 10.4% ($2,017,599,660) of charges in 2006 and 10.4% ($1,863,154,763) of charges in 2005. Exhibits 1 and 2 are taken from the indicated proposed and final rules and show the global, technical, and professional component breakdown by RVU.

Exhibit 1. 2010 Final Rule

CPT[1]/ HCPCS	Mod	Status	Description	Physician Work RVUs[2,3,4]	Fully Implemented Non-Facility PE RVUs[2,4]	Year 2010 Transitional Non-Facility PE RVUs[2,4]	Fully Implemented Facility PE RVUs[2,4]	Year 2010 Transitional Facility PE RVUs[2,4]	Mal-Practice RVUs[2,4]	CPT[1]/ HCPCS
78452		A	Ht muscle image spect, mult	1.62	8.84	8.84	NA	NA	0.06	XXX
78452	TC	A	Ht muscle image spect, mult	0.00	8.32	8.32	NA	NA	0.01	XXX
78452	26	A	Ht muscle image spect, mult	1.62	0.52	0.52	0.52	0.52	0.05	XXX

4 Due to its ability to generate true three-dimensional images, it is gradually replacing traditional gamma (ray) cameras.

5 Codes are Copyright, American Medical Association. This code was "cross-walked," or changed to 78452 in the period between the 2010 proposed and final rules. This illustrates one more complication that emphasizes the import of understanding CPT codes.

Exhibit 2. 2009 Final Rule

CPT[1]/ HCPCS	Mod	Status	Description	Physician Work RVUs[2]	Fully Implemented Non-Facility PE RVUs[2]	Year 2009 Transitional Non-Facility PE RVUs[2]	Fully Implemented Facility PE RVUs[2]	Year 2009 Transitional Facility PE RVUs[2]	Mal-Practice RVUs[2]	Global
78465		A	Heart image (3d), multiple	1.46	10.96	11.32	NA	NA	0.67	XXX
78465	TC	A	Heart image (3d), multiple	0.00	10.23	10.64	NA	NA	0.62	XXX
78465	26	A	Heart image (3d), multiple	1.46	0.73	0.68	0.73	0.68	0.05	XXX

Exhibit 3 is sample data from a cardiology group practice with numerous subspecialties (service codes in addition to those for SPECT also shown). Net revenue (expected collections) from SPECT nuclear medicine tests is $2.8 million. Assuming for the sake of illustration that all payors use an 85% TC and 15% PC split, nearly $2.4 million of net revenue has to be excluded from individual physician production to be comparable to MGMA data.

Exhibit 3. Sample Data From a Cardiology Group Practice With Numerous Subspecialties

STRESS LAB (P-K counted once)		UNITS	PERCENT	NET REVENUE	PERCENT
SPECT MYOCARDIAL PERF	78465	1,353	5.82%	1,488,000	24.00%
MYOCARDIAL PERFUSION	78478	1,143	4.92%	248,000	4.00%
MYOCARDIAL PERFUSION	78480-78481	517	2.22%	310,000	5.00%
MYOCARDIAL PERFUSION	78483	860	3.70%	744,000	12.00%
GENERATION AUTODATA-P	78490	1,240	5.33%	248,000	4.00%
INFUSION	90765	559	2.40%	248,000	4.00%
STRESS	93015	1,488	6.40%	372,000	6.00%
OTHER		4,960	21.33%	248,000	4.00%
SUBTOTAL		12,119	52.12%	3,906,000	63.00%

In some practices the professional component and technical component may be billed separately either because of payor rules or because the practice, in fact, only provides one or the other. In this case, a modifier is used for billing and should appear in the billing system reports: "26" is the modifier used for the professional component only and "TC" is the modifier used for the technical component only. If the billing is global (has no modifier), it is necessary to separate the professional component and technical component. The accompanying checklist provides detail on how to accomplish this.

Individual Market Idiosyncrasies

In some poorly reimbursed markets, it may, in fact, be necessary for the technical component income to supplement reasonable compensation for the physicians. For example, Rhode Island is notorious for the low levels of fees paid to physicians. This is due in large part to the fact that two insurers control nearly all of the health insurance market in that state and rates are artificially low as a result. As such, to attract and retain physicians, many practices have profitable ancillaries in place. In such a circumstance, it may be necessary to test the reasonable compensation analysis against an alternative

Professional and Technical Component Analysis Checklist

1. What is the practice's specialty?

   Note: Certain specialties may include technical component revenue (neurology, cardiology), while other specialties (family practice, pediatrics) would probably not include technical component revenue.

2. Does the practice own ancillary equipment that has a technical component?

   Note: Look through the depreciation schedule for expensive pieces of equipment. Technical equipment purchases typically stand out from the routine office equipment and furnishings.

3. Identify expected technical component CPT codes for equipment identified in Step 2.

   Discuss with provider and billing staff. Inquire as to whether ancillary revenues are billed globally separately for professional and technical component, or both; this may be payor-specific.

   Some practices may bill globally for in-office ancillary services and professional only for hospital-based services when the hospital owns the equipment. This is common for cardiology practices where the physician may interpret the result of hospital-based stress tests, for example.

4. Request production data by provider and CPT code for your period of analysis. If available, request both charges and receipts by CPT code.

   Review services by CPT code; professional component only income is denoted with a "26"; technical component income is typically denoted with "TC," but other acronyms may be used. Global is typically not specified, but assumed by default if no modifier is present.

5. Calculate production, by provider, preferably using receipts, excluding technical component receipts

   Receipts are used because best MGMA data is based upon collections. Because payment rates are set by insurers, the amount a practice charges has little significance except to an uninsured patient or noncontracted insurer.

   For globally billed ancillary tests, it is necessary to separate out the professional component. Download the Medicare Physician Fee Schedule for the years the data related to, state, and region in which the practice is located. www.cms.hhs.gov/PhysicianFeeSched/PFSCSF/list.asp#TopOfPage

measure of production, such as compensation per RVU, wRVUs, or annual encounters. This is an example where the productivity data *including* technical component revenue may need to be evaluated as well.

For example, these are codes for certain imaging procedures from the Massachusetts Medicare fee schedule, with the modifier:

Codes for Imaging Procedures From Massachusetts Medicare Fee Schedule

CPT Code	Modifier	Fee Nonfacility	Fee Facility	Percent
70490		$309.59	$309.59	100.0%
70490	26	70.80	70.80	22.9
70490	TC	238.79	238.79	77.1
70491		373.21	373.21	100.0
70491	26	76.19	76.19	20.4
70491	TC	297.02	297.02	79.6

Not all payors use the same split between professional and technical component, so make inquiries of the practice.

Consider alternative measures of productivity including wRVUs or collections including TC revenue depending upon data available from client.

For forecasting purposes, the values of CPT codes may change dramatically from year to year, particularly when ancillary testing is involved. You may want to look at the subsequent year's fee schedule, for example, if using 2009 data as a basis for forecasting 2010 results.

6. Compare calculated production to applicable statistical data to determine reasonable compensation.

   Subtract reasonable compensation from the practice's precompensation profit to determine cash flow to capital and equity.

   (Alternatively, add difference between actual compensation and reasonable compensation to the practice profit and loss.)

7. Isolate the cash flow attributable to the technical component production. Be sure to identify expenses associated with technical equipment.

   Note: Examples include billing and collection, technician wages and benefits, insurance, maintenance contracts, certifications, and so on.

8. Compare the cash flow profit in Step 7 to the practice's profit in Step 6.

   Consider Jurisdictional rules as to determination of personal and enterprise goodwill.

   E.g., if a noncompete agreement is nondivisible in a marital dissolution, calculate the impact on TC profit due to a noncompete.

Conclusion

Valuing medical practices requires an in-depth understanding of the individual practice and the healthcare industry. This article highlights just one aspect of a myriad of issues unique to medical practice valuation and the determination of reasonable compensation (see sidebar, What Is "Incident to" Billing?). The environment that physicians work in, dominated by the Medicare system, changes frequently. Some of these changes can be anticipated, such as the annual Medicare fee schedule modifications. Other changes are less predictable but can have a far greater impact, such as legislation. As any other highly regulated industry, it is critical that valuators remain current. The goal is always to have your valuation upheld, be it in court or in a settlement conference. Failure to understand the industry and its related terminology can undermine your authority as a valuation analyst and reduce the value of your opinion.

What Is 'Incident to' Billing?

Many medical practices increase revenue through the use of nonphysician providers (NPPs). These are employees who provide separately billable services to patients, but are not physicians. Physician assistants (PAs), nurse practitioners (NPs) and midwives are examples of NPPs.

Although they provide separately billable services, there are options for how to bill these services. The services can be billed directly and, because they are not physicians, the reimbursement for these services is a portion of the physician's fee schedule (Medicare sets the rate for many services at 85% of the rate for a physician; non-Medicare payors may have different rules). Another option is to bill the services as "incident to" the services of a physician. If the requirements for incident to billing are met, the services are billed under the physician's provider number and reimbursement is at the full physician's fee schedule. The physician is required to participate in the services provided by the NPP (e.g., supervision, chart review, physical presence in the office suite when the services are provided, among others), but the bulk of the effort is provided by the NPP.

This becomes an issue in valuation because, like the technical component billing, the productivity related to the nonphysician providers' services could be included in the physician's productivity. Without identifying and segregating the production unrelated to the efforts of the physician from the productivity related to the efforts of the physician, the valuation analyst can end up with an inconsistent reasonable compensation calculation.

In addition to understanding technical component revenue, understanding the use of nonphysician providers and the methodology for billing their services is important to developing reasoned valuation conclusions.

Chapter 11

Medical A/R: Top Issues That Impact Your Valuations

By Mark O. Dietrich, CPA/ABV

Like many aspects of valuation, valuing medical accounts receivable is as much an art as it is a science. Many small businesses and virtually all professional practices use the cash method of accounting. Under this method, accounts receivable are not reflected on the tax returns (or financial statements, if they exist), and the valuation analyst will need to reflect them.

In the absence of accrual accounting, measuring the accounts receivable becomes in large part the responsibility of the valuation analyst. And even if accrual accounting is in place, the accounts receivable warrant careful attention. In many medical practice valuation engagements, it may be the largest single asset. *Some common examples include:*

- A divorce when intangible assets such as goodwill are not marital property;
- A hospital-based practice when the patient base and other intangibles are owned by the hospital and not by the practice;
- A practice buy-in when goodwill is being excluded;
- Any practice where the intangible value is small; and
- In a liquidation scenario.

Analysts must evaluate a key number of factors to generate a meaningful estimate of value. Unlike manufacturing or most service businesses, medical accounts receivable tend to consist of a large number of accounts with relatively small balances. Although some medical specialties, such as cardiac surgery, may have relatively large balances from a particular patient for procedures, there are typically additional smaller balances for office visits and similar services.

In an internal medicine or family medicine practice, for instance, the typical charge may consist of a $75 office visit plus additional small charges, such as $15 to draw blood and $20 for a rapid strep test. Each of the charges that originate with a single visit must be separately billed and accounted for. When (or if) it is paid, the payment, if made by an insurer, will specify both the date the service was provided and the specific service that is being paid. Not all of the services will necessarily be paid and the percentage that is paid will not necessarily be the same for each service—and it is a rare instance indeed when 100% of the charge for any service is paid.

The payment of medical charges raises another significant issue. The majority of such charges are not paid for the patient individually, but rather by the third-party insurance company that provides his or her insurance or by a government program, such as Medicare or Medicaid (hereinafter collectively referred to as payors). Further, these payors typically pay by a fee schedule that they set that often bears little or no resemblance to the fee that the physician charges.

As a result, each charge that is processed by the physician's billing department reflects both a payment and an adjustment, or contractual allowance. There may be multiple payments for a particular service, such as when the patient has a deductible or co-pay due after the insurer pays its share or when the patient has a secondary insurance that covers any balance not paid by the primary insurance. The term "write-off" is generally limited to those situations involving a bad debt from an uninsured patient or when a payor refuses to pay for a service due to any of a host of reasons (see Exhibit 1 for insights on common causes for write-offs in a medical practice).

The valuation of accounts receivable generally consists of two distinct components:

1. *Identification of (partially) collectible balances versus uncollectible balances.* The first step is to obtain an aged accounts receivable by payor. This report typically consists of a listing of the various payors that the practice does business with and the total due from each of those payors by aging category: current, greater than 30 days, greater than 60 days, greater than 90 days, and greater than 120 days (see Exhibit 2). The "# Days" is the number of days' gross charges in accounts receivable.

Analysis of this report provides a significant amount of the information to determine what steps will be necessary to properly measure the accounts receivable. The first step is to compare the percentage of receivables in each aging category to statistical norms or to the valuation analyst's own experience. (Statistical norms are typically obtained

Exhibit 1. Write-Offs: Why They May Occur in a Medical Practice

Below is a nonexhaustive list of the causes of write-offs or "bad debts" in a medical practice. These factors are also significant for normalizing revenue and determining the specific risk premium.

1. Uninsured patient fails to pay.
2. Office personnel fails to collect co-pays at the time of treatment.
3. Practice fails to meet payor's contractual deadline for submitting a "clean claim." A clean claim is one in which all of the necessary information appears on the claim, including the patient's name, insurance number, the procedure provided by CPT (or current procedural terminology) code, the diagnosis by ICD (or international classification of disease) code, consistency of the CPT and ICD codes, the date of service, and other requirements specified by the payor. Typical periods for submission of clean claims are 60 days; thereafter, the payor is not obligated to pay the claim (although a denial can be appealed).
4. Failure to meet any requirements for preauthorization of the service by the insurer or a primary care physician, for example.
5. Failure to obtain correct insurance information from the patient.
6. Failure to submit additional information with the claims, such as operative reports for certain surgical procedures.
7. Failure to timely appeal denial of claims.
8. Billing for uncovered services (those that are not covered by the patient's insurance).
9. Billing incorrectly for services, which are considered part of a package or "bundle" of services, such as preoperative and post-operative visits considered part of the global fee paid for the surgery.

There are a host of others. The billing process in a medical practice is very complex, both in generating the charges and in recording the payment and adjustments for write-offs. This complexity leads to a variety of errors in all but the best-run practices. These errors result in otherwise collectible balances not being collected, uncollectible balances not being written off, uncovered services being paid, and the same service being paid more than once (a credit balance).

Exhibit 2. Total Due From Each Payor by Aging Category

Payor	Current	> 30	> 60	>90	>120	Total	# Days
A	$7,000	$8,000	$5,000	$5,000	$15,000	$40,000	72
B	1,000	4,000	5,000	10,000	20,000	40,000	144
Total	8,000	12,000	10,000	15,000	35,000	80,000	96
	10%	15%	12.5%	18.8%	43.7%	100%	

from the Medical Group Management Association's cost survey.) If the aging falls within accepted parameters, the valuation analyst may employ simple "short-cut" computations to estimate the collectible value. If not, a more complex computation may be required. The most common indicator that a short-cut approach will not work is when the percentage of receivables in the greater-than-120-days category is more than the expected level. The larger the variance, the more complex the computation required to determine the true collectible value.

Consider this example: Assume that the MGMA norm for the greater-than-120-days category is 20% and the valuation subject has 44% of its receivables in that category. This is an almost certain indication that uncollectible balances are not being written off. These balances more often than not consist of the unpaid portion of a charge representing the contractual allowance—that being the amount that the payor is not obligated to pay under the terms of its contract with the physician.

Another common component is uncollectible "self-pay" or uninsured balances. These balances accumulate because a lot of work is often needed to identify such balances and get approval for having them written off. In the typical medical office, time tends to be spent on collecting collectible balances rather than on writing off uncollectible ones.

The fact pattern of the example will require, at a minimum, that the valuation analyst separate the aged accounts receivable into two distinct groups: those greater than 120 days old and those fewer than 120 days old. Each of the two groups will then need to be valued separately. The balances should be analyzed by the payor. For example, certain payors may have unusual aging distributions, while others do not. Another common occurrence is when the practice's largest payor has an aging distribution different from that of the remaining payors.

2. *Determination of the portion of those charges that is ultimately collectible.* A standard analysis that should be done in any medical practice valuation is to compute charges, collections (payments), and adjustments for each of the practice's principal insurers. It is important to perform this analysis by payor because the contractual payment rate is likely to vary (and often significantly) for each payor with whom the practice contracts..

An example: For simplicity, assume that a practice has contracts with two payors. Data from the billing system indicate that Payor A reimburses the practice at a rate equal to 50% of charges, while Payor B reimburses at a rate equal to 60% of charges, as shown in Exhibit 3.

Exhibit 3. Collection and Realization Rates for Payer A and B

Payor	Charges	Payments	Adjustments	Collection Rate	Realization Rate
A	$200,000	$100,000	$100,000	50%	50.0%
B	100,000	60,000	36,000	60	62.5

The **collection rate** *is equal to current payments divided by current charges, and the* **realization rate** *is equal to current payments divided by current payments plus current adjustments.*

If the billing system is working properly and adjustments are being recorded properly at the time payments are received, the realization rate is the best measure of the true collectible value. This is due to the fact that it reflects *both* elements of the charge relief activity: the payment and the contractual allowance or adjustment.

If the adjustments are not being recorded properly, however, the realization rate is inaccurate and the collection rate may be a better measure. The collection rate may understate collectibility when unpaid claims are inadequately reviewed and overstate collectibility when, for example, charges to a payor in the current period decline from prior periods. A "short-cut" valuation of receivables appears in Exhibit 4.

Exhibit 4. 'Short-Cut' Valuation of Receivables

Payor	Receivable	Collection Rate	Collectible
A	$40,000	50%	$20,000
B	40,000	60	24,000
	80,000	55	44,000

Exhibit 5 uses the realization rate approach.

Exhibit 5. Using the Realization Rate Approach

Payor	Receivable	Collection Rate	Collectible
A	$40,000	50.00%	$20,000
B	40,000	62.50	25,000
	80,000	56.25	45,000

The problem with either of these approaches should be obvious. Payor B constitutes only 33% of charges, while it constitutes 50% of receivables. This is a clear clue that something may be "wrong" with the Payor B receivables. A further analysis is likely to reveal one of several generic causes: Payor B pays more slowly than Payor A, there are completely uncollectible balances included in the Payor B receivables meeting one or more of the criteria discussed earlier, or there has been a contract issue or termination or an unusual decline in charges to Payor B patients.

If there is a suspicion or determination that the collection rate and realization rate approach is inaccurate, the earlier approach described of dividing receivables into two distinct groups of those greater than 120 days old and those less than 120 days old should be followed. (Refer to this approach as the "detailed" method.) In Exhibit 6, the valuation analyst determines that the Payor B receivables greater than 120 days will yield only 40 cents on the dollar rather than the collection rate of 60 cents. (It should not be seen as unusual for insured receivables in the greater-than-120-days category to be worth substantially less than the historical collection rate for a particular payor.)

Exhibit 6. Receivables Versus Collection Rate Yields

Payor	<120 Days	Factor	Collectible	>120 Days	Factor	Collectible	Total
A	$30,000	50%	$15,000	$10,000	50%	$5,000	$20,000
B	20,000	60	12,000	20,000	40	8,000	20,000
	80,000		30,000			11,000	40,000

Exhibit 7. Recap of Methodologies

	Collection Rate	Realization Rate	Detail
Value	45,000	44,000	40,000

Exhibit 7 indicates that the choice of approach to valuing receivables can generate very different results. If you are not convinced, multiply each of the values in Exhibit 7 by 10. Depending upon the sophistication of the practice's billing software, the importance of the receivables to the overall valuation, and the budget for the engagement, it may be desirable to obtain a detailed aging by individual account of the greater than 120 days balances.

Credit balances are one of the most difficult potential problems to identify and resolve when valuing medical accounts receivables. Credit balances may represent overpayments on a particular account or they may be payments posted to an account that could not be matched with a particular service and service date. For example, a common source of credit balances exists when the patient has insurance, but the practice has not contracted to accept direct payment from the insurer. As a courtesy, the practice may submit a bill to the insurer for the patient, but expects the patient to pay the bill directly. If the insurer subsequently pays the practice as well, a true credit balance will result.

Because credit balances are generally considered lost property under most states' law and must be "escheated"[1] back to the state, the seriousness of this problem should not be overlooked. Further, failure to refund overpayments from government programs may subject the practice to civil or criminal sanctions. Certain state laws may provide for civil or criminal sanctions for nongovernmental payors as well.

1 The term is commonly believed to be based on the fact that the 'S'tate ["Es"] "cheats" the consumer or business out of the money, but actually the term originated in feudal England and Wales when land was owned by the king and granted in "fiefs" to royalty and would revert to the king upon certain occurrences.

The question frequently arises whether "zero basis" accounts receivable (as they are known for tax purposes when the taxpayer uses the cash method) should be tax-affected or reduced for the estimated income taxes that will be due when they are collected. If the standard of value is fair market value, many valuation analysts believe the adjustment is appropriate; some jurisdictions would not allow tax-affecting if the tax would never, in fact, be paid. This is of particular significance if the ultimate value of the business will be offset against property received by the other spouse in a divorce. For example, if the spouse is to receive $100,000 (previously taxed by definition) and the business owner is to receive a like amount of accounts receivable that have not yet been taxed, there will clearly be an inequitable result.

In valuing a corporate professional practice, zero basis receivables would typically be offset by a claim for future compensation due to the owner. Arguably, therefore, the balance sheet accounts receivable and liability for deferred compensation would offset and reflect no increase in equity. However, the deferred compensation would be an individual asset of the practice owner. This asset should, again, be offset for the taxes expected to be paid when the receivables are paid out of the corporation as salary. In addition, analysts should consider whether these same receivables, when collected, will be subject to a claim for alimony and whether there should not be some adjustment for this as well. Because receivables are the source of future income typically subject to alimony, counting them as both an asset and as income is seen as "double counting" in some courts and by some valuation experts.

To properly measure accounts receivable of a medical practice, the valuation analyst requires a considerable knowledge of what information to request and how to interpret and use it. Even if relying primarily on an income approach or market approach, failure to properly estimate net working capital can expose the valuation to a serious possibility of overstatement. If the engagement is to measure asset value, the individual components thereof—fixed assets, net working capital, and intangible value—must be known to compute the tax benefit from depreciation of fixed assets and amortization of the intangible value. It is difficult to escape the need to apply the cost approach in valuing a medical practice, at least as far as net working capital is concerned.

Chapter 12

Benchmarking Practice Performance

By Gregory S. Feltenberger, MBA, CACMPE, FACHE, CPHIMS, and David N. Gans, MSHA, FACMPE

Why benchmark? There are many reasons for benchmarking, and most are related to a specific purpose (usually improvement). For example, a practice may want to determine how the billing office performance or physician productivity compares to other like practices. But in general, practices benchmark to gain a deeper understanding of where they are, where they want to go, and how to get there.

However, benchmarking when used in conjunction with trending—comparison to a standard over time—can be a powerful tool for assessing the past and present. And although the past cannot predict the future, it can be used to "suggest" the future. Therefore, benchmarking and trending can provide numerical insights into the past, present, and future "value" of an organization. And since the current state of healthcare—constantly changing and growing in complexity—dictates more elaborate and accurate methods of measurement, analysis, comparison, and improvement, long-term success has become directly related to a practice's ability to identify, predict, and adjust for changes.

Two key principles of benchmarking are: (1) If you don't measure it, you can't manage it and (2) if you don't value it, you won't change it. These principles have been applied to nonhealthcare industries for many years and are ideally suited for use in healthcare. It has been said that healthcare is the only service industry that doesn't treat itself like one. And although the healthcare industry appears to have gone to great lengths to separate itself from other business sectors, there are many more similarities than differences.

If You Don't Measure It, You Can't Manage It

To manage something, it's necessary to know what it is (description), where it is (comparison), and how it got there (context). This can be accomplished through measurement and benchmarking. Proper practice management requires the use of subjective and objective measurement, analysis, comparison, and improvement.

If You Don't Value It, You Won't Change It

Driving change in a practice will affect every member of the organization and many will resist; therefore, the value (benefit) of instituting a change must outweigh the status quo, or leaving things as is. Measurement and benchmarking are not the final step in the process—they simply enable the process to evolve toward action. It is completely appropriate to measure and benchmark; however, this activity is in vain if something isn't done with the findings. Ideally, the results should be used to support change; however, they may be used to validate past changes or support the current status. And once a benchmarking process is finished, the practice can pick and choose the areas in which to focus its efforts, create buy-in (sell the change), and start the process of improvement (or repeat the entire benchmarking exercise—that is, continuous process improvement).

What can be done with the findings? There are many options: (1) drive and support change, (2) educate staff, (3) validate the past, (4) build buy-in, (5) conduct performance reviews, and (6) plan for the future.

When using the key benchmarking principles—"if you don't measure it, you can't manage it" and "if you don't value it, you won't change it," it is imperative to understand the interrelationship. First, proper management requires some degree of measurement to ensure the attribute of interest if fully understood (for example, is a full-time equivalent (FTE) clearly defined?). Second, once measurement has taken place, management must decide whether the value of pursuing change is worth disrupting the practice in the quest for improvement. And third, if management feels the measures dictate a need to change and value can be realized by making the change, the most important step is to instill a sense of value in making the change with physicians and staff—without buy-in, the value (benefit) of change will never be fully realized.

Of special note, processes can easily be changed, but it's only with the support and buy-in of physicians and staff that real improvement can be achieved. It has been said, "If you take care of your people, your people will take care of you, but if you don't take care of your people, your people will take care of you."

What is benchmarking? Simply put, benchmarking is measurement and comparison for the purpose of improvement. In particular, medical practice benchmarking is a systematic, logical, and common-sense approach to measurement, analysis, comparison, and improvement (see Exhibit 1). Therefore, benchmarking is comparison to a standard. Benchmarking improves understanding of processes and clinical and administrative characteristics at a single point in time (snapshot) or over time (trend).[1] In addition, benchmarking is the continuous process of measuring and comparing performance internally (over time) and externally (against other organizations and industries). And finally, benchmarking is determining how the best-in-class achieve their performance levels. This consists of analyzing and comparing best practices to uncover what they did, how they did it, and what must be done to adopt it for your practice (process benchmarking).

Exhibit 1. What Is Benchmarking?

- A systematic, logical, and common-sense approach to measurement, comparison, and improvement.
- Copying the best, closing gaps and differences, and achieving superiority.
- "A positive, proactive process to change operations in a structured fashion to achieve superior performance. The purpose is to gain a competitive advantage."
- Comparing organizational performance to the performance of other organizations.
- Continuous process of comparison with the best or "the toughest competitors or companies renowned as leaders."
- A method for identifying processes to new goals with full support of management.

The 'Value' of Benchmarking

Proper benchmarking consists of more than simple comparison of two numbers. The true value of benchmarking lies in the numbers and through an understanding of the current state of the practice, calculation of a difference between the current state and a new value or benchmark, knowing the context and background of the practice values when interpreting the results, deciding on a course of action and goal, and determining when the goal is achieved. For example, a comparison of average number of procedures per patient visit per physician to a known benchmark will only permit a mathematical analysis. However, what if one physician in the practice has been focusing on patients with simple medical issues that don't generate multiple procedures? The numbers alone would indicate this physician is underperforming and is below the others in procedural productivity; whereas, knowing the background, context, or other measures permit for a more detailed analysis. Perhaps this physician's focus is on acute care services and his or her average number of patient encounters per day is almost twice that of other physicians in the practice?

1 E.W. Woodcock, "Practice Benchmarking," in *Physician Practice Management: Essential Operations and Financial Knowledge* (Sudbury, MA: Jones and Bartlett Publishers, 2005).

How to Benchmark

There are several methods of benchmarking. A simple 10-step process might consist of the following:

1. Determine what is critical to your organization's success;
2. Identify metrics that measure the critical factors;
3. Identify a source for internal and external benchmarking data;
4. Measure your practice's performance;
5. Compare your practice's performance to the benchmark;
6. Determine whether action is necessary based on the comparison;
7. If action is needed, identify the best practice and process used to implement it;
8. Adapt the process used by others in the context of your practice;
9. Implement new process, reassess objectives, evaluate benchmarking standards, and recalibrate measures; and
10. Do it again—benchmarking is an ongoing process and tracking over time allows for continuous improvement.

Standardizing Data for Comparison

Since the primary purpose of benchmarking is comparison, it is necessary to standardize data so organizations of different sizes can be compared. A common method for standardizing data is to convert measures to percentages, per unit of input, or per unit of output. For example, per unit of input can be presented as per FTE physician, per FTE provider, or per square foot, whereas per unit of output can be presented on a per-patient, per-RBRVS unit, or per-procedure level.

What's Our Baseline?

Benchmarking, like any activity involving comparison, requires an understanding of "where you are"—this is known as your baseline. The baseline represents where you are today or where you've been and provides a point of origin or starting point. In addition, a baseline is an initial state that forms a logical basis for comparison. For example, to determine whether physicians have increased the average number of procedures per patient visit, it is necessary to have two measurements: the old value or baseline and the new value. To calculate the delta (or difference) between the two values, a simple formula can be used: new value minus old value. Without the baseline, it would not be possible to perform this or many other calculations like percentage change.

How Are We Doing?

This question can be answered by asking the question, "What is the difference between the baseline and current state (or where we are today)?" The baseline can be an internal benchmark (historical measure) from inside the practice, a benchmark across like practices from a Medical Group Management Association (MGMA) *Survey Report*, or a benchmark from outside the industries such as Disney or Wal-Mart. Additional insights can also be assessed by calculating the difference between current state and an established benchmark or industry average or median. To determine the difference, there are several methods and statistical tools. For instance, the mathematical difference, or delta, consists of subtracting the baseline value from the current value, whereas percentage change is a method for assessing changes over time or the proportion of one value in comparison to another. In addition to these methods, there are more statistically intense methods to determine difference that can be generalized across a group (see Exhibit 2).

Exhibit 2. What Is the Difference?

• Mathematical difference (delta) • New value minus old value • Current state minus Initial state	• Benchmark and industry value minus current state • Percentage change • Difference between three or more average

Interpretation of the difference is dependent on the method used. When using the delta, the difference will be a raw number, since the method consists of simple subtraction. Determining whether the difference is good or bad depends on the context, background, and what the values represent. For example, if medical revenue after operating cost per FTE family practice physician is $145,000 and the MGMA benchmark indicates a median of $214,377, then the delta is $69,377 ($214,377 minus $145,000). A delta of $69,377 may suggest poor practice performance, reduced physician productivity, a capital investment, or other practice deficiencies or large expenses, Whereas the percentage change method indicates this practice is only generating 67% of the median for similar types of practices (see Exhibit 3). Therefore, the result is different between delta and percentage change, and the interpretation may also be different.

Exhibit 3. Difference Between Delta and Percentage Change

Is the result positive or negative?	Delta	Percentage Change
Positive value	New value (or benchmark) is greater than the old value. For example, $214,377 minus $145,000 equals a delta of $69,377	New value has increased. For example, $145,000 divided by $214,377 equals 0.67. This when multiplied by 100 equals 67%.
Negative value	New value is less.	New value has decreased.

Methods and Checklists

Failing to plan, it has been said, is planning to fail. Therefore, an integral component of the benchmarking process is the proper use of systematic methods, checklists, scales, and comparable measures. Systematic methods consist of formulas and ratios as found in this chapter. Checklists are a planning tool to ensure all variables and methods are used and considered—checklists ensure attention to detail and minimize the chance of missing steps in a process (see Exhibit 4). Scales provide the measuring stick—meaning they indicate whether your measures are high or low, good or bad, or where they are in comparison to others. And comparable measures are key to the heart and soul of benchmarking and provide a means for determining how your practice compares to others.

Exhibit 4. Example Checklist[2]

The following checklist items can be used to increase the likelihood that a claim will be processed and paid when first submitted:

- ❐ Patient information is complete.
- ❐ Patient's name and address matches the insurer's records.
- ❐ Patient's group number and subscriber number is correct.
- ❐ Physician's Social Security number, provider number, or tax identification number is completed and correct.
- ❐ Claim is signed by the physician.
- ❐ All necessary dates are completed.
- ❐ Dates for care given are chronological and correct—for example, is the discharge date listed as before the admission date?
- ❐ Dates for care given are in agreement with the claims information from other providers, such as the hospital, etc.
- ❐ Diagnosis is complete.
- ❐ Diagnosis is correct for the services or procedures provided.
- ❐ Diagnostic codes are correct for the services or procedures provided.
- ❐ CPT and ICD-9 codes are accurate.
- ❐ Diagnosis is coded using ICD-9-CM to the highest level of specificity.
- ❐ Fee column is itemized and totaled.
- ❐ All necessary information about prescription drugs or durable medical equipment prescribed by the physician is included.
- ❐ The claim is legible.

Small and Solo Practice Benchmarking

Small and solo practices share many similarities with their larger counterparts; however, the benefits and risks associated with the differences can have significant impact on a small practice's longevity and financial success.

Similarities With Larger Practices

Small and solo practices share many similarities with larger organizations. For instance, all medical practices must operate in the same healthcare environment and deal with

2 DecisionHealth, "A/R Benchmarks," Part B News 20, no. 40 (Oct. 16, 2006).

the same healthcare legislation, malpractice insurance, payers, collection challenges, patient needs and expectations, delivery and standards of care, and processes—just to name a few.

Also, the benchmarking methods used by large organizations are identical to those used by small and solo practices (see Exhibit 5). And the use of normalized metrics permits comparison regardless of organizational size. Common examples available in most benchmarking datasets consist of measures per FTE physician or provider, per square foot, per patient, per procedure, and per RVU.

Exhibit 5. Similarities Regardless of Size or Type[3]

- Legislation can change payment (for example, Medicare and Medicaid reimbursement rates are determined through legislation).
- Costs are increasing greater than inflation (for example, medical supplies and equipment costs are increasing at a greater percentage than reimbursement rates).
- Expenses change.
- Increases in physician compensation are from production (for example, much of physician compensation is based on physician production or the number of patients seen and the procedures performed).
- Health savings accounts will change patient behavior (for example, patients will treat medical care more like a product or service they pay for using the funds in their account).
- Hospitals are purchasing physician practices (again).
- Advances in medical care are changing care delivery.
- Physicians are publicly rated for quality and outcomes.
- Physicians are publicly rated for patient satisfaction.

What's the Difference?

Small and solo practices are different from larger groups in several ways, some of which are beneficial, while others are not. For instance, smaller organizations are generally more flexible, can adapt or change quickly and in general, tend to be more efficient. However, small and solo practices are more sensitive to the risks associated with costly mistakes, lack of alternative revenue-generating methods, and the absence of (or antiquated condition of) robust information systems. For example, with only one or two physicians in a practice, what impact would a poor decision or loss of a physician (due to sickness or some other unforeseen event) have on the practice? Can a small practice afford to retain adequate earnings for contingencies? Does the existing information system compliment and add to the efficiency of the practice? And does it interface (communicate) with the information systems used by payers, hospitals, and other medical practices such as referring practices and physicians?

Ultimately, the goals of smaller practices mirror those of larger groups—to have more satisfied patients, more fulfilling work environments for physicians and staff, and better

3 E.J. Pavlock, *Financial Management for Medical Groups*, 2nd ed. (Englewood, Col.: MGMA, 2000).

economic outcomes. However, the additional sensitivities of small and solo practices must be considered to ensure surprise events don't adversely impact the practice.

Practice Measurement

Measurement is the collection and organization of data. In many cases, measurement is a method of converting an array, group, list, or set of data into a single variable that describes the entire dataset. A mean or average is a calculation that summarizes the central tendency or mathematical center of many data points, provided all data are of the same unit of measurement. In general, an average is the most common calculation used to analyze and compare data. It's the most common, since most people understand the concept of an average and how to calculate it. For example, if we count the number of patients seen per month for the last 10 months for an eight-provider family medical practice located in the suburbs, we have an array of data with 10 data points—one data point for each month (see Exhibit 6). If we also have a list with the number of patients seen per month for the last 10 months for an eight-provider family medical practice located in a rural community, how can we easily compare these two practices? We can line up and organize the data points in ascending order, but what does this tell us? We might conclude the suburban practice sees a greater number of patients per month, but we can't accurately describe the difference or make a comparison. All we've done so far is arrange the data and guessed there was a difference by looking at or "eyeballing" the data—not the most accurate method. However, by calculating the average number of patients seen per month for the last 10 months for each practice, a single and accurate measure can be used to describe and compare the two groups.

Exhibit 6. Example of Measurement: Number of Patients Seen Per Month

Month	Suburban Practice	Rural Practice
January	2,620	2,650
February	2,231	2,660
March	2,264	2,266
April	2,650	2,067
May	2,657	1,687
June	2,670	3,690
July	3,067	3,070
August	2,690	2,071
September	3,171	2,731
October	3,710	3,730
Sum of patients seen	**27,730**	**26,622**
Number of data points (months)	10	10
Average patients seen per month	**2,773**	**2,662**

Comparing these practices, the suburban practice, on average, sees more patients per month than the rural practice—111 more (average number of patients seen per month in the suburban practice minus average number of patients seen per month in the rural practice; 2,773 minus 2,662 equals 111).

Art and Science of Benchmarking

Benchmarking, as it's related to measurement, is the art and science of comparison. The "art" takes place during the data gathering and interpretation phases and requires a method with some common sense, whereas the "science" is the systematic and logical process of analysis. Once interpretation and analysis have occurred, data are considered transformed into information that can be used for comparison and decisionmaking. That is, it is possible to determine whether the data are similar or different and by how much. Exhibit 7 represents several examples of metrics and associated benchmarks.

Exhibit 7. Examples of Benchmarks

Encounters per FTE* physician	Mean	3,006	4,759	5,891	7,612	9,159
Total procedures per FTE physician	6,341	3,006	4,759	5,891	7,612	9,159
Physician work RVUs per FTE physician	4,751	4,412	7,506	5,123	5,622	6,809
Physician compensation	$4,751	$1,426	$3,684	$5,123	$5,622	$6,809

Other topics associated with benchmarking are: (1) continuous improvement and (2) evaluation and assessment. Continuous improvement refers to the need for repeated analysis using the same measures over time (trend). An evaluation is a subjective, personal judgment of the value (or worth) of something, whereas an assessment is objective and quantifiable (or assigned a numeric value).

Benchmarking Methods

Effective benchmarking consists of a systematic process; therefore, several methods have been developed to ensure the process is efficient (see Exhibit 8).

Proper measurement begins with selecting the right practice attribute, characteristic, property, dimension, or variable to be assessed. In other words, what do we want to measure? For example, encounters per FTE physician, total procedures per FTE physician, and physician work RVUs per FTE physician are common examples of benchmarks and practice measures. This book presents many practice attributes that have been operationally defined, that is, the attribute and measurement process have been clearly described in practice and literature as generally accepted. However, there may be practice attributes that are not typically measured or found in the literature. In these cases, it would be necessary to fully explore the characteristic before moving to the next step—this type of attribute could be called "homegrown." Of note, there are probably few instances when "homegrown" attributes are needed since the healthcare management field is sufficiently mature to have identified most, if not all, key practice characteristics.

Exhibit 8. Methods of Benchmarking

Transfer Model	Five Stages of Benchmarking	5 Steps of Benchmarking	10 Steps to Benchmarking
1. Identification and documentation of best practices. 2. Validation and consensus of what to focus on and what are true best practices. 3. Transfer and develop buy-in; sell ideas to management and get commitment to performance assessments, identify priorities, and establish a plan. 4. Implementation using team champions, selection of critical practices to support strategic initiatives.	1. Planning, selecting the processes to benchmark, and identifying customer expectations and critical success factors. 2. Form the benchmarking team from across the organization. 3. Collect the data from best practice organizations and identify own processes. 4. Analyze data for gaps. 5. Take action, identify what needs to be done to match best practice, and implement change.	1. Planning what to benchmark and what organization to benchmark against. 2. Analyze performance gaps and project future performance. 3. Set targets for change and communicate to all levels. 4. Develop action plans, implement plans, and adjust as necessary. 5. Achieve a state of maturity by integrating best practices into organization.	1. Determine what is critical to your organization's success. 2. Identify metrics that measure the critical factors. 3. Identify a source for internal and external benchmarking data. 4. Measure your practice's performance. 5. Compare your practice's performance to the benchmark. 6. Determine whether action is necessary based on the comparison. 7. If action is needed, identify the best practice and process to use to implement it. 8. Adapt the process used by others in the context of your practice. 9. Implement new process, reassess objectives, evaluate benchmarking standards, and recalibrate measures 10. Do it again—benchmarking is an ongoing process and tracking over time allows for continuous improvement.

Once a practice variable is selected, the next step is to decide on the appropriate method of measurement (or what metric should be used) and the intended purpose. There are two general categories of metrics: (1) informational and (2) actionable. Informational metrics provide a simple description and unlike actionable metrics, they don't clearly suggest ways of affecting change. For example, if we decide to measure the average number of patients seen per month in a suburban practice as a metric to describe monthly practice productivity, then this metric simply tells us the arithmetic mean—it doesn't suggest anything more, whereas, actionable metrics are usually more complex, require an understanding of the context, and are compared to a benchmark or baseline. For instance, the formula to calculate average number of patients seen per month (for the last 10 months) per provider for an eight-provider family medical practice is the sum of the number of patients seen per month for the last 10 months divided by the number of months divided by the number of providers. If we use this formula as a metric to assess monthly practice productivity per provider and want to improve productivity per provider, then this metric used in this context suggests, for example, we can affect change by working with individual providers whose average is below the practice's overall average to increase the number of patients seen per month by the provider of interest.

Several questions should be asked as part of preliminary measurement steps. For instance, what do you want to measure? Is it a generally accepted practice characteristic (typical practice factor) or is it a homegrown practice attribute (custom or self-defined factor or metric)? What metric should be used? What is the appropriate method for measurement? And finally, what type of metric do you want to use and what is your intended purpose (information or action)?

Interpretation Pitfalls

Reliability is defined as repeatability and consistency. If given the same dataset and using the same measure, someone else should be able to calculate, describe, and compare the data in the same way. For instance, if given the number of patients seen per month for the last 10 months in a suburban and rural practice and asked for the average number of patients seen per month for both practices, you would find the same average with the same comparison for each practice. Note that the same unit of measurement must be used, that is, all the data in your data set or data array should be the same unit of measurement (in the example above, all numbers are based on number of patients seen). Reliability cannot be achieved if the unit of measurement is different in any of the data used in the measurement. For example, you cannot calculate an average using 2,650 patients seen in January, 2,264 seen in February, 3,265 seen in March, 2,166 seen in April, 3,167 seen in May, 1,869 seen in June, 2,771 seen in July, and 3,171 appointments booked in August without first changing appointments booked to the number of patients seen in August.

Validity is meaningfulness within a generally accepted theoretical basis (see Exhibit 9). Or simply stated, does it really mean what it's expected to mean or is it being interpreted accurately? How you interpret your data and measurements are as important as ensuring you have used a highly reliable method. Understanding what a particular measure is meant to describe is paramount to using data properly to support good decisions. For instance, averages (means) represent the mathematical center of an array of data or central tendency, whereas the median is the 'actual' center of the array. In some cases, the average and median can be the same, but often, there is a difference. Therefore, knowing how a measure is used, collected, and calculated will assist in supporting your decisions, that is, your conclusions and analysis will be more valid and meaningful. This is particularly important when presenting your findings to others since the better you understand the measures, why you selected them, and how to explain them to others, the value and usefulness of your results will add significant credibility to your recommendations and decisions.

Exhibit 9. Example of Meaningfulness

It is important to understand the formulas used for measurement and how the measurement is collected and calculated. Using the data array from the previous example of number of patients seen per month [suburban practice: 2,620 (January), 2,231 (February), 2,264 (March), 2,650 (April), 2,657 (May), 2,670 (June), 3,067 (July), 2,690 (August), 3,171 (September), 3,710 (October)]:

- Average (mean) = Sum of all data divided by the number of data points
- Sum of all data = 27,730
- Number of data points = 10
- Average = 2,773
- Median = The data point in the center of the array (when arranged in order)
- Data array = 2,231, 2,264, 2,620, 2,650, 2,657, 2,670, 2,690, 3,067, 3,171, 3,710
- Center of array are two data points = 2,657 and 2,670
- Median = 2,657 + 2,670 divided by 2 = 2,664
- Note: If the data array consisted of an odd number of data points, the median would be the true center data point.

Another pitfall to avoid that is a common mistake is averaging averages, for example, which presents a danger during measurement. Since any array of data points can be averaged (or measured using other methods), it's important to understand the limitations or implications of measuring calculated measures. The validity of the interpretation may be suspect.

The extremely low and high values in all the practices are minimized or diluted (their effect is almost eliminated). The effects of the low- and high-productivity practices almost eliminate one another, which is why the average of the averages is near the average of the more balanced array (Family Practice 1).

Strength is related to validity and is the power, magnitude, or accuracy of your interpretation or how confident you are in your interpretation. For instance, if you want to describe the number of patients seen per month for three months (2,231, 2,264, and 2,620), a mean is an ideal descriptive statistic (mean = 2,372). This figure is somewhat descriptive of the lower months of 2,231 and 2,264, but a mean of 2,372 is not descriptive of the higher months when 2,620 patients were seen. Therefore, your confidence in a mean of 2,372 patients seen per month provides a less accurate description of the average number of patients seen per month. However, if this array consisted of a large number of months, that is, a large dataset with many data points, the accuracy of this metric and your confidence in the descriptive power of the mean is much higher.

A final interpretation issue is related to the mutually exclusive and exhaustive nature of data. Mutually exclusive refers to a data point fitting into only one category. For example, we decide months with 3,600 patients or more are categorized as high productivity, months with between 2,401 and 3,599 patients are medium or normal, and months with 2,400 patients or less are low. Therefore, each month fits into only one category—that's mutually exclusive—a single month cannot be categorized as "high" and "medium." If a single month could be assigned to multiple categories, it would be difficult to accurately describe each month or interpret your findings. Exhaustive refers to the description of the attribute, that is, does the definition encompass all collected attributes? For example, since all the measurements taken consisted of the number of patients seen per month, this attribute was defined to be actual patient encounters with a provider and all collected measures were based on this definition. That is, patients seen only by a nurse were not included since these encounters didn't fit the definition (or criteria).

Management can use numbers to diagnose and treat practice deficiencies, plan improvements, and examine practice activities and processes. And because numbers are less susceptible to the effects of human variation (feelings and emotions), they are more appropriate for decisionmaking. The beauty of numbers comes from their brevity, clarity, and precision. For example, using the example array (list) that shows the number of no-shows per day from last month, it is possible to quickly summarize the week or entire month regarding no-show activity. These averages and totals provide a brief, clear, and precise picture describing no-show activity during each week or the entire month. There's little room for misinterpretation or confusion, provided a no-show is clearly defined, that is, a no-show is a patient who fails to show up within 15 minutes of an appointment, rather than someone who fails to cancel 24 hours prior to his or her appointment.

Organizing a group of numbers is the cornerstone in the benchmarking process. An array or group of numbers only becomes valuable once it is organized, whereas statistical methods and proper interpretation of the findings are necessary to uncover the useful information behind the numbers. A systematic approach is necessary and has been established through the use of averages (or means), medians, standard deviations, percentiles, quartiles, and percentage change. These techniques can be used to measure and benchmark all practice attributes. In addition, these methods are easy to use, understand, and communicate—most people are familiar with some, if not all methods.

There are a handful of key financial performance indicators understood and used by the majority of practices to measure financial operations. Many of these formulas are presented in this chapter as a comprehensive "starter set" of key performance indicators and financial metrics for benchmarking.

Key Financial Indicators

Benchmarks for many of the following formulas are available in the MGMA *Cost Survey and Performance and Practices of Successful Medical Groups* reports.

Total net collections

Net fee-for-service revenue + capitation revenue – provision for bad debt

Gross (unadjusted) collection ratio

Definition: Indicates how much of what is being charged is actually collected.

Goal: The higher, the better

$$\frac{\text{Total net collections}}{\text{Total gross charges}}$$

Note: In general, the goal of this measure is "the higher, the better"; however, this metric will vary significantly depending on the fee schedule of the practice. For instance, a practice with a high fee schedule will have a lower gross collection ratio than a practice with a low fee schedule (setting a fee schedule too low can have a negative effect on net revenue). This metric is often used to measure billing office performance.

Gross collection ratio

Definition: Indicates a ratio of the amount of revenue "actually" collected over the amount charged.

Goal: The higher, the better

$$\frac{\text{Net FFS revenue or collections}}{\text{Gross FFS charges}}$$

Adjusted (net) collection ratio

Definition: Indicates how much of what is being charged (gross FFS charges) is actually collected after total adjustments to charges; does not include funds the practice should not receive (e.g., contractual allowances) and funds it will not receive (e.g., bad debt).

Goal: The higher, the better

$$\frac{\text{Net fee-for-service collections}}{\text{Net fee-for-service charges}}$$

Average adjusted revenue per day

Definition: Indicates the average amount of revenue generated per business day.

Goal: The higher, the better

$$\frac{\text{Adjusted charges for the last three months}}{\text{Number of business days for the same time period}}$$

Note: It isn't required that the time period be three months; rather, it should be a recent period of time.

Days revenue outstanding

Definition: Indicates how long it takes before claims and charges are paid.

Goal: The lower, the better

Step 1: Calculate "days revenue"

$$\frac{\text{Total revenue for the last three months}}{\text{Number of business days in the last three months}}$$

Step 2: Calculate "days revenue outstanding"

$$\frac{\text{Outstanding net AR}}{\text{Days revenue}}$$

Days in AR

Definition: Indicates how long it takes before claims and charges are paid.

Goal: A net collection ratio (NCR) of 96% to 99% and 40 to 50 days in AR (a days in AR of 45 or less is ideal) indicate your practice is functioning efficiently and doing very well. If NCR is 93% to 95% and 50 to 60 days in AR, there is some (little) room for improvement. And if 92% or less and 70 days or more in AR, there is significant room for improvement in billing operations.

$$\frac{\text{Outstanding AR}}{\text{(Average monthly charge/30)}}$$

Note: Include at least the last three months to calculate the average monthly charges

Days in AR (alternate calculation)

Definition: Indicates how long it takes before claims and charges are paid.

Goal: The lower, the better

$$\frac{\text{Outstanding net AR}}{\text{Average adjusted revenue per day}}$$

Months revenue in AR

Definition: Indicates the average number of months charges are outstanding for collection.

Goal: The lower, the better

$$\frac{\text{Total AR}}{\text{(Annual adjusted FFS charges * 1/12)}}$$

Expense to earnings

Definition: Indicates the ratio of overhead (expenses) to revenue (collections).

Goal: The lower, the better

$$\frac{\text{Total operating expenses}}{\text{Total collections}}$$

Average revenue per patient

Definition: Indicates the average amount of revenue generated per patient seen. In addition, it can be used to determine the number of patients that must be treated to receive a predetermined amount of revenue (collections).

Goal: The higher, the better

$$\frac{\text{Total monthly collections for last month}}{\text{Total patient visits last month}}$$

Average cost per patient

Definition: Indicates the average cost of providing treatment per patient visit.

Goal: The lower, the better

$$\frac{\text{Total operating expenses}}{\text{Total patient visits}}$$

Departmental or service ratio

Definition: Indicates the expenses to revenues ratio for a specific department or service.

Goal: The lower, the better

$$\frac{\text{Total expenses for ancillary service for the last three months}}{\text{Total net charges for all CPT codes related to ancillary service}}$$

Collections rate by payer

Definition: Indicates different rates of reimbursement by payer.

Goal: Depends on many practice factors; should be proportional to the percentage of patients covered by each payer.

$$\frac{\text{Net collections by payer}}{\text{Total gross charges by payer}}$$

Note: Reimbursement received from a payer is based on the specific fee schedule established with a payer and is on a per-procedure basis. Net collections is the sum of all reimbursement received from a payer, whereas gross charges is what the practice billed the payer.

Volume and reimbursement by service line

Definition: Indicates workload volume and revenue generated by service line; provides a method for identifying the relative contribution of each service line.

Goal: Depends on many practice factors; in most cases, volume should be directly related to revenue generated by service line.

Volume by service line:

$$\frac{\text{Volume measurement (encounters/visits, RVUs, etc.) by service line}}{\text{Volume measurement for total practice}}$$

Reimbursement by service line:

$$\frac{\text{Revenue by service line}}{\text{Total practice revenue}}$$

Surgical yield

Definition: Indicates relative contribution of revenue generated from surgical or procedural workload to total practice revenue.

Goal: Depends on many practice factors; in most cases, volume should be directly related to revenue generated by service line.

$$\frac{\text{Revenue derived from surgeries or procedures}}{\text{Total practice revenue}}$$

Reimbursement per procedure code

Definition: Indicates average amount of revenue generated from procedures provided to patients.

Goal: Depends on many practice factors; in general, it will be higher if the procedures provided to patients are higher RVU procedures.

$$\frac{\text{Net collections}}{\text{Total number of procedures}}$$

Note: This metric can be adapted to show average reimbursement per procedure by payer using net collections by payer divided by total number of procedures charged to a payer.

In conclusion, benchmarking provides a means to measure performance in relation to a standard like the odometer (total mileage) in a car is used as one of many measures to assess value (future performance). For example, a car with 100,000 miles is probably worth less than the same type of car with 50,000 miles. And this can be determined by comparison (benchmarking) against a standard like the Kelly Blue Book values for a car or the MGMA surveys for medical practice performance. Trending, as it's related to benchmarking, can be used to compare practice measures against a standard over a period of time—this increases the "value" benchmarking by displaying past and present performance. And once benchmarks are complimented with trended data, it is possible to extend the measures into the future, thereby predicting the future. However, like any measure of a complex system or organization, a single measure studied in a vacuum only provides a narrow view that's prone to error. Therefore, multiple benchmarks and trends should be evaluated to gain a richer, fuller, and more rewarding picture of the performance landscape and associated value of the organization.

Chapter 13

Designing a Chart of Accounts to Meet the Needs of Physician Practices

By David N. Gans, MSHA, FACMPE, and Steven Andes, Ph.D., CPA

The chart of accounts is the basis for an organization's accounting system. Whether the organization is a public entity or a private business, it needs a set of statements to record its financial condition. The chart of accounts is the starting point for every organization's financial records because it is the list of accounts used to record the organization's expenses and revenues as well as its assets and liabilities.

Businesses use accounting to record, monitor, and report their financial condition to managers, owners or shareholders, creditors, and governmental bodies. Accounting records describe an organization's current financial position as well as any changes. Managers require accurate and consistent financial information for both short-term and strategic decisionmaking. Creditors need the same information to decide the level of lending risk that is the basis for the amount of the loan and the interest rate that the organization is qualified to receive. Financial statements are also the basis for the tax return and other financial documents required by local, state, and federal agencies.

To be useful to all the various users, accounting records need to reliable, relevant, and consistent. Reliable means that the records are free from bias or error, faithfully represent the financial status of the organization, and must be verifiable, after the fact. Reliability means that financial records are neutral in their nature and can be verified by different accountants using the same objective data and measurement techniques. Accounting records must also be relevant, meaning that the records have the information that decisionmakers need and are sufficiently prepared and distributed in a timely manner. Additionally, accounting records should show consistency, meaning that there is comparability across organizations and with previous time periods.[1]

Financial accounting has standard rules, terms, and procedures that have been developed over time. These rules, terms, and procedures are classified as "generally accepted accounting practices," or GAAP. Until recently, a nongovernmental agency, the Financial Accounting Standards Board, was the ultimate authority for GAAP. Since the Sarbanes-Oxley Law of 2002 (Public Company Accounting and Investor Protection Act), the Public Company Accounting Oversight Board (PCAOB, www.pcaob.org) is now the final authority for GAAP, at least as it relates to publicly traded corporations. While the PCAOB is also technically not a government agency, the Securities and Exchange Commission, which is a government agency, appoints the chair and the members and approves the budget.

As stated before, the chart of accounts forms the basis for all accounting information recorded in the financial records. The chart of accounts lists each account with a corresponding number for the accounting system to track. The accounts in the chart of accounts determine the detail that financial transactions are recorded. Without a designated accounting code stated in the chart of accounts, it is impossible to track a revenue or expense item in the accounting records.

Therefore, the designation of an account code from the chart of accounts determines how an expense or revenue can be recorded into the financial records and from there, into the financial reports prepared for the organization.

All business and public entities have similar legal requirements to maintain accurate, representative accounting records that accurately show the financial status of the organization. All business and public entities have similar needs for reliable, relevant, and consistent accounting information for managerial decisionmaking. Healthcare organizations, in particular, have unique business requirements that dictate how financial information should be categorized. Healthcare entities need to understand their sources of revenue, how discounts and contracts are applied, how expenses are incurred and a detailed understanding of the costs incurred to provide services. These complexities make it necessary that healthcare organizations use a chart of accounts developed to meet their specific needs.

A healthcare manager must ensure that the chart of accounts has an account for every revenue and expense it needs to track. The number of separate accounts an organization needs in its chart of accounts depends somewhat on its size and organizational complexity.

1 Chart of Accounts for Health Care Organizations. Neill F. Piland, Dr. P.H. and Kathryn P. Glass, MBA, MSHA, Center for Research in Ambulatory Health Care Administration, Englewood, Colo. p. 2-3.

Generally, larger and more complex organizations need more accounts than smaller, less-sophisticated entities. Managers need input from their organization's financial and legal advisors, as well as their creditors, to identify particular revenues or expenses that must be tracked to meet specific legal and other reporting needs.

As stated earlier, a medical practice cannot track any revenue or expenses not listed in the chart of accounts. However, the more the accounts listed for recording various revenues and expenses, the more costly it is to maintain an accounting system. Additionally, if the accounting system records information in too much detail, the managerial uses of the information are handicapped by the inability to easily interpret financial records. The selection of the level of detail is an important aspect in the design of the organization's chart of accounts. Managers need to designate the accounts needed to generate the financial reports required for decisionmaking, for lenders, and to meet the legal reporting and tax filing requirements of government. In general, smaller organizations usually need fewer accounts than larger ones, and all organizations will usually expand the number of accounts they use as managers find the need for more detailed accounting and financial recordkeeping.

To set up a chart of accounts, a manager needs to define the various financial accounts the organization will need. Each account will be given a unique number, and similar financial activities should have numbers that have closely associated digits. Smaller, less-complex organizations may find that all of their accounting needs can be accommodated using only three digits (potentially yielding 999 separate accounts). However, more digits may be needed to simplify how accounts are categorized and provide room to add new accounts in the future. Complex organizations may have a chart of accounts with hundreds of categories with each category having multiple subclassifications. The chart of accounts for a large, complex organization can have thousands of different account numbers. Additionally, a chart of accounts can be set up to have multiple fields, allowing the organization to use the same accounting system for various legal entities and subordinates or to track the specific revenues or expenses for various responsibility centers within each entity.

Every chart of accounts is divided into five major categories:

1. assets,
2. liabilities,
3. equity, net assets, or fund balances,
4. revenues, and
5. expenses.

Each category will have a block of numbers assigned to it to show the general classification of each financial account and are generally presented in a standard order, beginning with the accounts presented in the balance sheet (also called the "statement of financial position") and then the accounts that build the "statement of income" for the organization.

Assets are resources owned by the organization such as accounts receivable, equipment, and property. Assets may be tangible, such as land, buildings, and equipment; a direct right to tangible property, such as amounts due from patient or insurance company payers, or assets can be intangible, such as goodwill, patents owned by the organization, licenses, and leaseholds. The chart of accounts will usually list assets in descending order of liquidity. Cash and other assets that are easily converted to cash are listed first, fixed assets such as property and equipment are listed next, and intangible assets are listed last. Asset accounts usually start with the number "1" and will be the first accounts listed in the chart of accounts.

Liabilities are debts or obligations owed by the organization to creditors, such as loans and accounts payable. These obligations come from the purchase of goods or services on credit or by obtaining a loan from a financial institution to finance the purchase of equipment or buildings. Current liabilities, the obligations that are due to be paid within one year, are generally listed first in the chart of accounts, with accounts payable, bank overdrafts payable, and payroll obligations (tax, insurance, and retirement plan withholdings and accrued payroll amounts) will be listed before other payables such as rent or insurance. Long-term liabilities, such as construction loans, long-term notes, and capital leases, follow current liabilities. Deferred revenue, deferred compensation, and severance plan obligations will be listed last. Liability accounts usually start with the number "2."

Equity accounts (sometimes called "fund balance" in some nonprofit organizations) reflect the financial worth of the organization and represent the residual value of an entity's assets after deducting its liabilities. In a for-profit business enterprise, the equity will be the ownership interest and in a not-for-profit, will represent the net financial worth of the organization. In for-profit organizations, equity generally is derived from two sources: contributed capital by the owners or shareholders and retained earnings, the accumulated value of income, less expenses and owner's withdrawals. Typical equity accounts are contributed capital, preferred and common stock, dividends and distributions (unique to for-profit corporations), and not-for-profit equity accounts, such as unrestricted assets, restricted assets, and endowments. Net asset accounts usually start with the number "3."

The accounts used to create the income statement accounts follow the statement of position accounts. While there is general agreement in the general numbering system for the accounts used to create the statement of position, there is no such convention for the income statement accounts. Generally the accounts used to describe revenue will precede the expense accounts and the last accounts will reflect nonoperating revenue, expenses, and income taxes paid. This sequence enables the chart of accounts to follow the same sequence as the statement of position, with account numbers that start with a "4" reflecting revenue, operating expenses will start with a "5," "6," "7," or "8," and nonoperating revenue and expenses starting with a "9."

In 1979, the Medical Group Management Association (MGMA) published a chart of accounts that was specifically designed to record the financial information needed to manage a medical group practice. The MGMA Chart of Accounts is structured to accurately describe the revenue and expenses associated with a healthcare organization, and its accounts flow logically into the financial statements a medical group practice has to produce. It classifies financial transactions into eight major categories and assigns a four-digit coding number to each.[2]

The eight major categories used by the MGMA Chart of Accounts are ordered in the way they appear on the practice's financial statements. The major categories and their corresponding codes appear in Exhibit 1.

Exhibit 1. Major Categories and Their Corresponding Codes That Appear on the MGMA Chart of Accounts

Account numbers	Description
1000	Assets
2000	Liabilities
3000	Owner's equity
4000	Revenues and adjustments to revenue
5000	Operating expenses—support staff salaries and fringe benefits
6000	Operating expenses—general and administrative
7000	Operating expenses—clinical and ancillary services
8000	Operating expenses—physician and nonphysician provider salaries and fringe benefits
9000	Nonoperating revenue and expenses

2 Chart of Accounts for Health Care Organizations. Neill F. Piland, Dr. P.H. and Kathryn P. Glass, MBA, MSHA, Center for Research in Ambulatory Health Care Administration, Englewood, Colo. p. 2.

The first three categories relate to the balance sheet, or statement of financial position. The remaining categories relate to the statement of income and to the order in which they appear on the statement of income.

Two unique aspects of the MGMA Chart of Accounts differ from most other charts of accounts. "Adjustments and allowances" is categorized as a 4000 series, the category for revenues, rather than a 6000 series expense, because allowances and adjustments must be treated as offsets to revenue rather than as expenses to understand the effect of the discounts required by government and insurance payers and to easily gauge the net revenue associated with operations. Another difference is to categorize provider salaries and fringe benefits as an 8000 series account. The majority of medical groups are owned and operated by the physicians who practice in the medical group. The compensation of the physicians-owners is based on the amount that remains from total net revenue after all expenses are subtracted. By organizing the MGMA Chart of Accounts with physician compensation and benefits as the last series of accounts, the logical flow of financial information is maintained. This sequence also allows management to logically present the financial situation of the practice in the same sequence as the chart of accounts.

The chart of accounts structure should allow the user to add subcategories in the future and to logically associate expenses with like costs. If the chart of accounts utilizes a four-digit accounting system, it can use the second digit of the account for a subcategories of the eight major categories and can use the last two digits of the coding number to reflect specific elements. Using this logic, a chart of accounts subdivides each major category into as many as nine subcategories. The subcategories can each have nine more minor classifications. Each category can be "rolled up" to equal the total for that category, usually reflecting the "0" account in the series. For example, if account 7000 is used to reflect "clinical expense," account 7100 can address "clinical Equipment, Supplies, and Services", account 7110 will record "Drugs and Medications," and 7111 will be "vaccines," and 7112 will be used for "chemotherapy drugs." In this example, the general ledger for the organization will provide both detailed information (71111 shows only the cost of vaccines). While 7110 shows the costs of all drugs and medications for the organization, 7100 is the sum of all the subaccounts related to clinical equipment, supplies, and services, and 7000 will have the total costs of all clinical expenses for the organization.

A chart of accounts can also establish codes for specific revenues and expenses that relate to more than one of the categories. For example, the employee benefits section can categorize payroll taxes paid for employees as 5710 and payroll taxes—state unemployment insurance—as 5713. The same chart of accounts can classify physician benefits as 8200 and nonphysician provider (nurse practitioner, physician assistants, and so on) benefits as 8400. In this organization, the cost of state unemployment insurance for physicians would be categorized as 8213 and the cost of state unemployment insurance for nonphysician-providers would be categorized as 8413.

Different business types need to structure their chart of accounts using different sequences that, ideally, will meet their individual needs. However, this may not always be the situation for healthcare organizations. Often a healthcare organization is a legal subset of a government entity, university, or private business. In these instances, the healthcare organization may be required to use the chart of accounts of its parent organization, so its financial performance can easily be aggregated into the parent organization's financial records.

When a healthcare organization has the flexibility to design a chart of accounts that can meet its specific information requirements, it has options well beyond the "basic field" of three or four digits that describe the specific asset, liability, revenue, or expense.

Through the use of additional single and multidigit fields, the chart of accounts can be expanded to allow the reporting of financial information from multiple legal entities, to track revenues or expenses to a specific responsibility center, or to identify the revenue or costs attributed to a specific physician or nonphysician provider. Using a multitiered chart of accounts enables the organization to easily customize the information collected in its financial information system to meet management's need for accurate information for its major units or to allow a medical group practice to track the productivity of each of its physicians.

A complex healthcare organization often has separate legal entities that integrate their functions in what externally appears to be a seamless organization but require separate financial statements. For example, an ambulatory care center may be part of a larger hospital-owned integrated delivery system, with a separate imaging center and ambulatory surgery center.[3] If each organization uses the same chart of accounts, expenses can be easily tracked for each organization as can patient revenues. Using an "entity field" as the first digit of the chart of accounts allows each entity to use the same "basic field" that describes the actual asset, liability, entity, revenue, and expense accounts, while keeping a separate set of financial records. The use of the same accounts with a different entity field allows the parent organization to easily roll up the financial performance of its subordinate organizations to evaluate the performance of the entire enterprise.

---

3 Management Accounting for Fee-for-Service/Prepaid Medical Groups, Eldon L. Schafer, Ph.D., CPA; Dwight J. Zulauf, Ph.D., CPA; Michael E. Gocke, MBA, CPA, Center for Research in Ambulatory Health Care Administration, Englewood, Colo., 1985, pp. 5-17.

Another often-used field allows the organization to track costs by responsibility center, organizational units within the organization that have responsibility to generate revenue and expenses. Such a "responsibility center field" simplifies the accumulation of revenue and expenses for a specific department or location. By tracking revenue and direct costs to each specific responsibility center, management can understand the relative contribution of the responsibility center to the organization. Additionally, if direct costs can be easily traced to a responsibility center, the organization can also allocate a fair share of the indirect costs incurred by other parts of the organization.

Some healthcare organizations need to track the amount of revenue produced by individual physicians and nonphysician providers or the expenses associated with their use of fringe benefits, such as continuing education tuition, travel, and lodging costs. Using a separate field that identifies each physician or nonphysician provider can enable the organization to easily prepare financial reports for each healthcare provider. Use of a provider field can be limited to recording only revenue or to record revenue and only certain expenses, such as fringe benefits.

The use of multiple tiers or fields allows the organization the greatest flexibility in its accounting records. Simultaneously, the organization can record revenue or expenses for specific locations or clinics (responsibility centers) and for each physician practicing in the location or clinic (provider field).

To decide what to include in a chart of accounts, a manager needs to evaluate several issues:

- What reports does the organization want to prepare?
- What financial decisions, evaluations, and assessments will be made regularly?
- What level of detail is required in the financial reports?
- Will the organization compare its financial performance to other organizations and therefore, need to collect financial data using agreed-upon definitions?
- Does the organization report financial performance to national, state, or local governmental agencies?
- Does the accounting software used by the organization limit the design?

Designing a chart of accounts that meets all the needs of a health organization can be a complex task. While complex, the task is not impossible, and the benefits that the organization will obtain from a well-designed chart of accounts and financial information system will far outweigh the costs associated with its design and implementation.

Chapter 14

Physician Compensation and Financial Statement Benchmarks: Using MGMA Data

By David Fein, MBA

Valuation of a medical practice, as with any valuation, consists of quantifying earnings and risk. The drivers of earnings and risk in a medical practice, however, are unique. There is a tremendous amount of diversity in medical practices, with over 700,000 physicians in the United States and over 470,000 working in over 40,000 group practices. There are single-specialty, multispecialty, hospital-affiliated, non-hospital-affiliated, for-profit, not-for-profit, and academic practices. Specifically, on the revenue side of a medical practice, the valuator must understand how encounters, procedures, and surgeries (physician production per RVUs) drive gross charges and billings and how the collection process (which can be complicated in a medical practice) drives gross revenue. In addition, many medical practices operate on a cash basis and pay out dollars to physician-owners before year-end earnings.

On the expenses side, a medical practice has significant physician and staff (e.g. business, front office, clinical, ancillary, contracted, and so on) costs as well as a number of unique general operating costs (e.g., medical supply, drug supply, lab, radiology and imaging, and so on). It's also very important to evaluate physician compensation in relationship to production, whereas in most businesses, the relationship between compensation and production is disregarded. A medical practice can be managed by physician owners, a hospital, a health maintenance organization (HMO) or management service organization (MSO). Medical practices also exist within a complex regulatory environment that must also be evaluated in relationship to revenue and risk.

Exhibit 1 shows some of the revenue and expense drivers in a medical practice.

To accurately value a medical practice, the valuator must understand these distinct characteristics. Medical Group Management Association's (MGMA) data provide excellent information professional valuators rely on to normalize physician compensation and benchmark financial performance. It is also important to understand that valuation of physician compensation arrangements (particularly when paid by tax-exempt hospitals) is becoming an increasing focus of the Internal Revenue Service (IRS) and the Office of Inspector General scrutiny.

Exhibit 1. Medical Practice Revenue and Expense Drivers

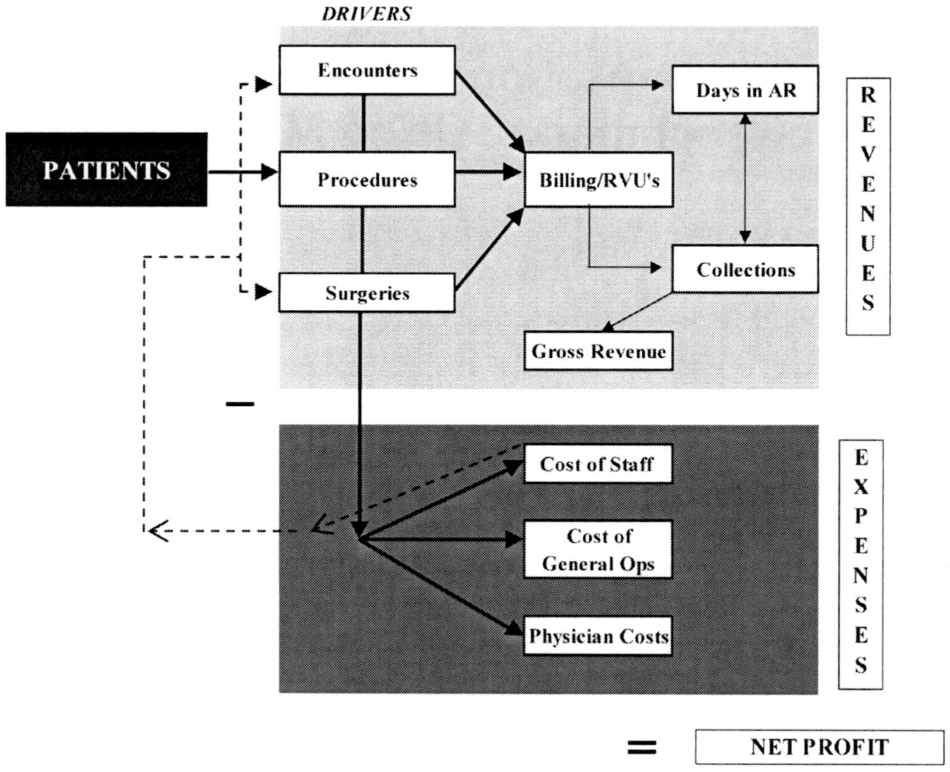

Founded in 1926, MGMA has nearly 21,000 members who manage and lead 12,500 practice organizations, representing 270,000 physicians. MGMA's survey *Interactive Reports* provides the valuator with statistically robust data, as well as sophisticated, easy-to-use tools.

The MGMA is a premier source of benchmarking data, but valuators should consider other sources, as well. You can find benchmarking data from the following:

- MGMA offers a number of benchmarking tools as well as the comparative data;

- The Centers for Medicare & Medicaid Services (CMS) and state governments can provide some external data, but they may be limited;

- Some specialty groups offer data, but they also may be limited;

- Physician Compensation and Production Survey reports that can be used include:

  - Medical Group Management Association's *Physician Compensation and Production Survey Report;*
  - Sullivan-Cotter & Associates' *Physician Compensation and Productivity Survey Report;*
  - Hay Group's *Physician's Compensation Survey Report;*
  - Hospital and Healthcare Compensation Services' *Physician Salary Survey Report;*
  - ECS Watson Wyatt's *Hospital and Health Care Management Compensation Report;*
  - American Medical Group Association's *Medical Group Compensation & Financial Survey; and*
  - American Medical Association's publications on physician statistics.

MGMA data are specifically useful for valuators because:

- MGMA has conducted physician practice surveys for over 50 years;

- Data are derived from group practices of all sizes, types, and specialties (with major reporting categories separately portrayed);

- The *2007 Report on Physician Compensation* observes more than 50,000 providers;

- Distinguishes private and academic physicians;

- The *2007 Cost Survey* observes more than 1,200 single- and multispecialty practices;

- Cost surveys are individualized for some of the larger specialties;

- Both tools use a census-style approach; and

- Built-in benchmarking tools are provided.

As with any data, MGMA data have limitations you should understand. One limitation is the data may not be representative of all practices. Because participation in MGMA surveys is voluntary and all practices do not complete and return the survey questionnaires, respondents represent only a sample of medical practices. It's difficult, therefore, to determine whether a sample is biased. Bias could occur if more professionally managed practices participate, with differences in region and size, with a lack of responses, and other characteristics.

It's important to use statistics correctly and understand both their strengths and weaknesses. There are a number of things to keep in mind when using statistics, including MGMA's:

- *Benjamin Disraeli* once said, *"Lies, damn lies, and statistics."* It's important to understand the data, how they were collected, what they truly represent, their strengths, limitations, and appropriate application to avoid both misusing and misinterpreting statistics.

- Understand medians versus means. Means include every data point; the median is the middle data point. Medians remove the impact of outliers and are a better representation of the midpoint than the mean.

- *Skewness.* The shape (or skewness) of sample can have a large impact on how you interpret the data. Understand not only the specific data points, but also the overall response curve, as well. The shape of the curve is represented by the standard deviation, but having a good visual picture of what this represents can be very useful.

- Exercise your judgment. Understand the limitations of the data and do not read more into them than is warranted.

- Talk to your peers. They can validate your thinking, and you can learn from them.

- Know the practice! Understand that MGMA data may not represent a particular practice due to specific characteristics of the practice.

- Consult other sources of information, such as specialty societies.

The Three Ps of Benchmarking

Before delving into the specifics of MGMA data, it's important to have a general feel for the kind of data the survey represents. MGMA data are best understood as a function of the three "Ps" of medical practice benchmarking. The three "Ps" are based on what the survey is observing or the "unit of observation." MGMA develops its survey products by sending out questionnaires to its members and asks questions about various aspects of physician and medical practice performance. The three major areas the surveys observe are the physician, the practice, and the procedure. MGMA produces surveys covering each of these areas.

The first "P" is for "physician." Individual physicians are the focus of MGMA's *Physician Compensation and Production Survey*, which has over 50,000 responses from more than 100 specialties. This survey includes compensation and productivity (compensation; relative value units, or RVUs; collections; gross charges; and so on). This survey, in other words, revolves around what the physician is paid and what he or she produces. As a valuator, it's crucial to understand the relationship between physician compensation and production and to normalize physician compensation in relationship to both of these metrics.

The second "P" represents the practice. Based on the entire practice, the MGMA *Cost Survey* measures more than 700 practicewide variables, such as revenue, costs, staffing, and accounts receivable (AR).

The third "P" is procedures. This survey is based on measuring individual procedures. Physicians can perform more than 10,000 procedures, and each has a unique current procedural terminology (CPT) code. Think of procedures as the unique (mostly billable) tasks a physician performs when he or she sees a patient. The CPT procedure codes are the basis for all medical practice billing and also are the basis for computing physician work RVUs (more information RVUs to follow). Although you can perform a great number of complex analyses using procedure-based data, one of the most useful is understanding how physicians are coding (i.e., what CPT code they assign) office visits (CPT codes 99201 to 99205 and 99211 to 99215). Although this advanced benchmarking topic will not be covered in this chapter, it's a very useful analysis we encourage valuators to understand. The survey pertaining to procedures is the MGMA *Coding Profiles Sourcebook*.

The data we are going to examine in this chapter come from two following MGMA interactive reports:

- *Physician Compensation and Production Survey;* and
- *Cost Survey.*

This chapter will cover both compensation normalization and financial statement benchmarking, and how each of the interactive reports data and tools can be used effectively. The chapter is organized around some of the important steps in the valuation process and concepts unique to medical practice valuation. As these topics are discussed, I will explain more about the available data and relevant tools that provide the valuator a strong quantitative approach.

Benchmarking Basics

It's important to understand benchmarking basics to best use the MGMA interactive reports. Benchmarking means comparing the data from a practice to either internal or external standards. Internal standards can be based on either comparing to physicians within the practice or comparing to data from a different time period (i.e., this quarter versus last quarter). This chapter will focus on external benchmarking using the MGMA data as the external standard.

Benchmarking Checklist

To understand the general concepts and steps in benchmarking, let's review the benchmarking checklist from Consulting Training Institute's "Health Care Boot Camp." This checklist applies to both the interactive reports as well as the printed reports. The checklist takes you step by step through the benchmarking process:

Step 1: Determine what you are benchmarking (i.e., RVUs, compensation, A/R aging, cost per full-time equivalent—FTE—and so on).

Step 2: Determine what is the benchmark (i.e., the specific number you are benchmarking against). For example, median RVUs for family practice would be 4,073).

Step 3: What is the practice data? (If you are benchmarking RVUs, determine the physician's RVU data.)

Step 4: Determine how you compare to the benchmark.

- Is your performance better than the benchmark? ❐ Yes ❐ No
- Is your performance in an acceptable range? ❐ Yes ❐ No
- Is your performance worse than the benchmark? ❐ Yes ❐ No
- Is there any action we need to take? ❐ Yes ❐ No (This step can be ignored for valuation.)

Step 5: If the benchmark is not acceptable, estimate the economic benefit derived if the benchmark were achievable and quantify best-case potential. (This is a very valuable step for valuators to take.)

Note: Steps 6 to 9 can be ignored for valuation but are included to provide the full benchmarking process.

Step 6: Assess potential changes if action needs to be taken.

Step 7: Quantify potential cost and estimate potential cost benefit of action and changes.

Step 8: What are the action items and responsibilities for the above action?

Step 9: How often will you review this benchmark and what progress do you expect?

Exhibit 2 is a diagram of the full benchmarking process. For the purposes of valuation, focus on the "assess" phase of the process. If you consult with medical practices as well, you can provide a tremendous service to your clients by understanding and using the full benchmarking process.

Exhibit 2. The Benchmarking Process

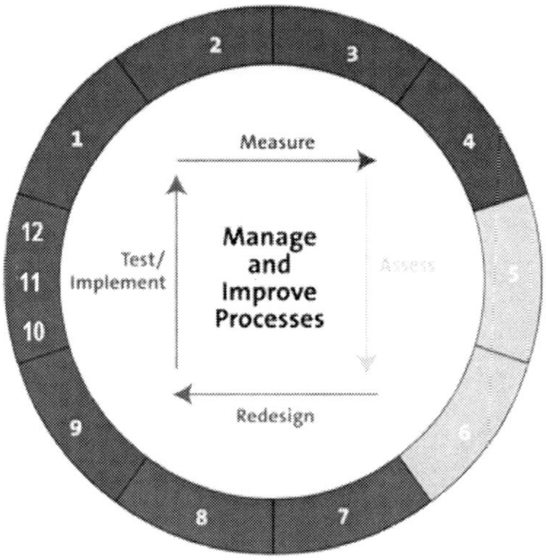

How MGMA Interactive Report Can Help You Benchmark More Precisely

One important concept to understand is the difference between benchmarking against medians and using rankings. Medians (also called the 50th percentile) represent the midpoint of the data and are commonly used as the key measure to benchmark against. For example, the median compensation for a family practice physician (without obstetrics) is $164,000. If the physician you are benchmarking is making $185,000, you would determine the difference as a percentage and use that as your benchmark. In this case, $185,000 is 13% greater than the median. If you have access to the entire curve of responses as you do in the interactive reports, however, you can quickly determine that $185,000 represents the 64th percentile. In other words, the compensation of $185,000 is larger than 64% of what the survey respondents reported as their compensation. Determining that your physician ranks at the 64th percentile is more precise than saying their compensation is 13% greater than the median.

Since response curves can have small or large standard deviations (i.e., be steep or shallow), it's difficult to quickly determine whether the magnitude of the variation from the median is significant. MGMA interactive reports allow you to easily understand the shape of the response curve and exactly where your data are ranked.

Exhibit 3 shows two different response curves: one with a standard deviation of one and the other with a standard deviation of two. You can see that the number "2" on the x-axis represents the 99th percentile for the curve with a standard deviation of one and the 62nd percentile for the curve with a standard deviation of two. The numerical difference from the median of zero is two for both curves, but this really represents vastly different situations. For the steeper curve, the data point 2 is extremely high, but for the flatter curve, the data point represents being slightly higher than the median.

Exhibit 3. Standard Deviation Curves

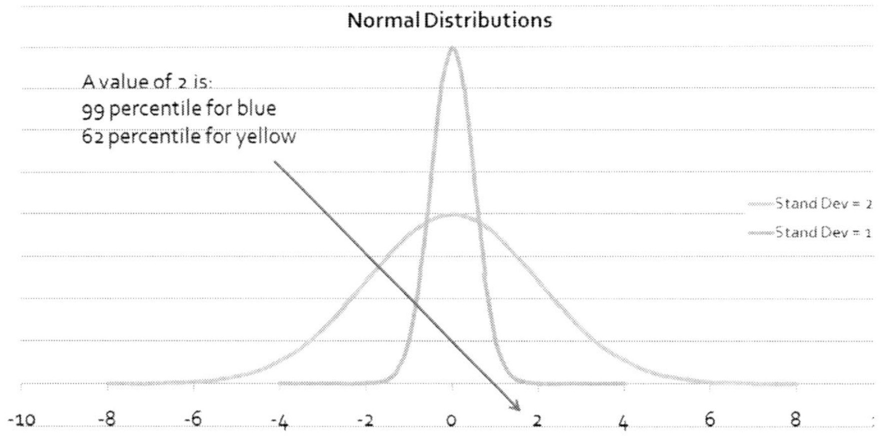

Normalizing Physician Compensation

MGMA's *Physician Compensation and Production Survey* interactive report provides a wide variety of data and tools to assist you in normalizing physician compensation for a medical practice valuation. The goal in normalizing physician compensation is to determine what is fair compensation for all owner-shareholder physicians and make an adjustment (normalize) for the excess compensation. For example, if there are three owner physicians in a family practice with each of them receiving more than fair compensation, you would make the following adjustments as shown in Exhibit 4.

Exhibit 4. Compensation Normalization Example

	Actual Compensation	Fair Compensation	Adjustment
Physician 1	190,000	174,000	16,000
Physician 2	209,000	174,000	35,000
Physician 3	234,000	174,000	60,000
Total	633,000	522,000	111,000

This example is simplified to show the concept of making adjustments for each physician based on fair compensation. However, in reality, each physician's "fair compensation" will probably be different based on a number of factors, including years in specialty, production, and so on.

Your task in normalizing compensation is to develop a practicewide compensation adjustment that will normalize the physician's compensation; it represents what owners would be earning if they were paid as nonowners. This means looking at each owner in a practice and determining the fair market compensation for each of them. To accomplish this, you will have to look at each individual physician, taking into account all the various conditions that impact fair compensation, including specialty, years in the practice, production levels, and so on.

It is possible to develop a practicewide compensation adjustment by using metrics, such as overall compensation, as a percentage of revenue or average compensation on a per-FTE basis. Using these practicewide adjustments, however, is just an approximation and not nearly as accurate as evaluating each physician and making individual adjustments. It is recommended you develop normalization adjustments for each individual physician.

To understand physician compensation, you have to understand physician production. To understand production, you have to understand specific production metrics, including:

- **RVUs:** relative value units, the value the Centers for Medicare and Medicaid Services (CMS) assigns to physician procedures;
- **Encounters:** number of patients the physician treats;
- **Procedures:** number of procedures the physician performs;
- **Gross charges:** how much the physician bills;
- **Collections:** how much the physician actually collects; and
- **Hours worked:** wow many hours per week the physician works.

Many valuators feel RVUs are the most appropriate measure for gauging production, but collections and charges are commonly used, as well. When using something other than RVUs as a productivity measure, you should compare RVU productivity to the measure being used. If both measures lead to the same conclusion about productivity, you can be more confident in the productivity measure. On the other hand, if RVUs provide a different productivity benchmark, you need to understand why. Collections can be used as a productivity measure, but a practice's billing procedures, payer mix, and other variables make it more challenging to isolate physician production from collections data. Encounters are a very weak indicator of production because they measure how many patients a doctor sees, rather than how much work they are performing. Therefore, attempting to gauge the amount of "work" a physician does based on encounters is not feasible. Gross charges can be a useful measure of productivity, but because there is wide variation in fee schedules, it's once again difficult to isolate physician productivity from the data.

The relationship between compensation and production is an area where medical practice valuation is significantly different from general business valuation. In general business valuation, there is no standardized method to gauge "productivity," therefore compensation is analyzed without regard to productivity. An easy way to think about this is to consider physician compensation as based on the amount of work performed. The more work a physician performs, the more he or she is compensated. A physician who is making 50% more than another physician may be fairly compensated if he or she is working twice as hard (however you measure "work"). That is why only looking at compensation data without considering production data is not recommended for normalizing physician compensation.

What is an RVU?

Now that we understand that an RVU is a good measure of physician productivity, let us review what an RVU is and how it is calculated. There are a number of complexities in understanding RVUs, but this chapter will provide only the basics so you can use them as productivity measures to normalize physician compensation. For a fuller understanding of RVUs, we recommend *RVUs: Applications for Medical Practice Success*, 2nd edition, by Kathryn P. Glass, MBA, MSHA, PMP, available through the MGMA store.

RVUs were developed by CMS to provide a standardized method to measure the work performed by physicians, as well as provide the basis to reimburse physicians. RVUs were constructed to represent the relative intensity of resources required to care for a broad range of diseases and conditions and are associated with CPT codes. An RVU contains three components: malpractice, physician work (work RVU, or wRVU), and practice expenses. For our purposes, we will only use wRVUs.

How are RVUs and CPT Codes Related?

When a physician provides any type of service to a patient, he or she must provide a billing code associated with that service to get paid. There are over 10,000 different CPT codes representing every possible service a physician can provide, from an office visit to brain surgery. Each CPT code has a corresponding RVU assigned to it; these values are the basis to determine how many RVUs a physician produces in a period of time.

Let's look at an example to see how this works. The CPT for a new patient office visit is 99201; the associated work RVU is 0.45. The CPT code for removal of a brain lesion (brain surgery) is 61510; the associated work RVU is 28.41. This makes sense, because brain surgery requires more "work" from a physician than an office visit. The beauty of the RVU system is that for most specialties, it is a very reliable indicator of how hard a physician is working. However, if you are working with radiologists, anesthesiologists, pathologists or emergency room physicians, you will need to find a different productivity measure than RVUs, because they do not accurately reflect the amount of work physicians in these specialties are performing.

For our neurosurgeon, let us take a very simple example calculating his RVU production for the year. We will assume he does only two procedures (new patient office visits and brain surgery). We need to determine how many of each of these procedures he performs, then calculate his total work RVU number for the year, shown in Exhibit 5.

Exhibit 5. Calculating RVU Production

CPT Code	Frequency	Description	RVU Value	Total
99201	500	New patient office visit	0.45	225
61510	100	Removal of brain lesion	28.41	2,841
Total				3,066

Although this is a simplified example, the concept is exactly how you would calculate a physician's total wRVUs for a period of time. Take every procedure (i.e., CPT code) he or she performs, how many times he or she performs the procedure, and multiply that frequency by the wRVU value. Do this for every procedure, add them up, and you have calculated the total number of work RVUs for the physician.

Remember, the MGMA data is based on annual data, so make sure your data also represent a full year. The MGMA data also represent a full-time physician, so make sure you normalize your physician data to one FTE. For example, if you have a physician that is working half-time (i.e., 0.5 FTE), you will need to multiply his or her wRVUs by two, to calculate a one FTE equivalent.

Luckily, most practice management systems have a built-in report that computes RVUs; just ask someone in the practice for the wRVU report. Make certain you specify "work RVUs" or you may get total RVUs, making your benchmarks meaningless because you will be comparing apples to oranges.

Using the Physicians Compensation and Production Interactive Report

The interactive report provides access to both data and tools to assist you in developing reasonable and defendable normalization adjustments for physician compensation. It also offers a wealth of data on more than 100 specialties and breaks the data down into a number of categories, including:

- By all providers;
- Group type;
- Region of the country;
- Method of compensation; and
- Ownership

The metrics the survey reports on are in Exhibit 6.

Exhibit 6. Metrics of Survey Reports

Compensation	Total compensation Retirement contribution
Productivity	Collections Gross charges Work RVUs Total RVUs Encounters Surgical cases Hours worked per week Weeks worked per year
Relationship of compensation to productivity	Compensation per $ of collections Compensation per $ of gross charges Compensation per work RVU Compensation per total RVU

The interactive report also includes data based on individual characteristics:

- Specialty;
- Years of experience;
- Gender; and
- Partner or shareholder status.

And organizational characteristics:

- Ownership;
- Geographic location;
- Percentage of capitation contracts;
- Compensation method; and
- Group type.

There are two basic tasks the interactive reports will be used for: opening tables and using the built-in benchmarking tools. When the interactive report starts, you'll see this startup dialog box in Exhibit 7.

Exhibit 7. Startup Dialog in the Interactive Report

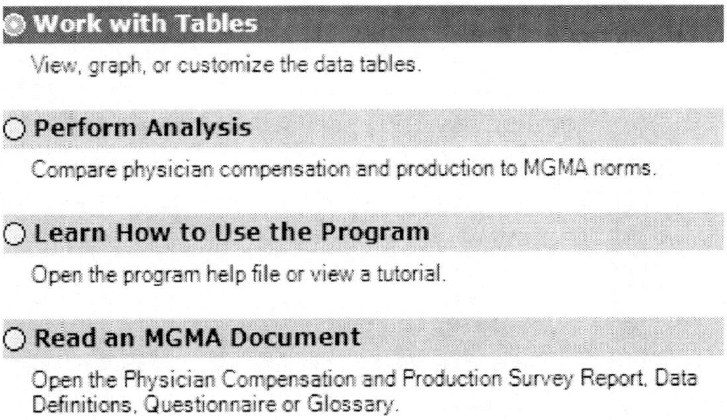

From this dialog, you can perform all the major functions of the interactive report. We encourage you to read the MGMA documentation, particularly the Survey Data Definitions, for a clear understanding of each metric in the survey. When you are collecting data from a practice, it is crucial you explain exactly what you are looking for. Otherwise, you may be provided data that do not match the MGMA definitions and your comparisons will be meaningless. For example, if you are seeking encounters, be sure the practice is not providing procedures.

To open a table, select the "Work with Tables" option or the "Open Tables" toolbar button from the main menu. You will see the following dialog (advanced mode is shown) in Exhibit 8.

Exhibit 8. Table Open Dialog in the Interactive Report

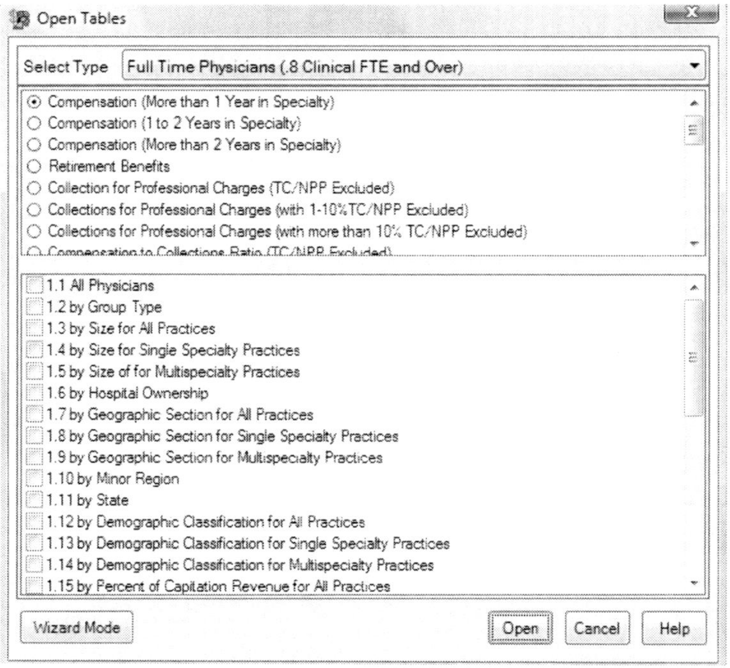

This dialog allows you to open any table on the interactive report. Note that for every metric (compensation, retirement benefits, collections, and so on) there are a number of tables available for view. Select the metric, then choose the table to open. For example, the Compensation for All Physicians appears in Exhibit 9.

Specialties are displayed on the left, with statistics shown in the columns. Be aware the interactive report will not display data unless there are at least 10 providers (physicians) and three unique practices. If you see blanks or stars in the data, it's because there are insufficient physicians or practices.

Since the interactive report contains every percentile from 10 to 90, you can customize the display to show more of the data. This is helpful to get a feel for what the entire MGMA curve looks like. The same table expanded to show deciles appears as below in Exhibit 10.

You can set the program defaults to always show more data so you do not have to customize each table. The interactive report allows you to open many tables at the same time to view multiple metrics or slices of the same table. All of the tables can be easily

Exhibit 9. Table 1.1

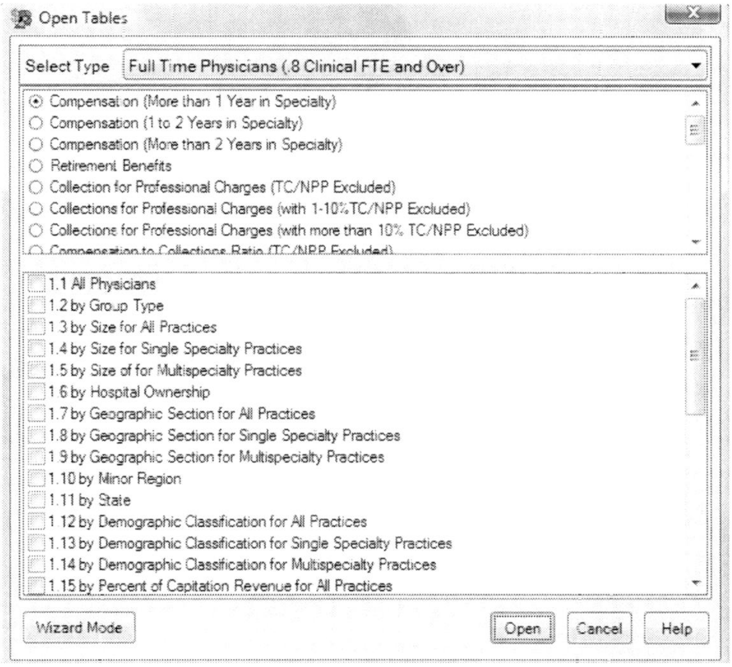

Exhibit 10. Table 1.1 Expanded to Show Deciles

Specialty	Providers	Practices	Mean	Std. Dev.	10th %tile	20th %tile	30th %tile	40th %tile	Median	60th %tile	70th %tile	80th %tile	90th %tile
Allergy/Immunology	175	85	$295,873	$136,255	$161,674	$196,748	$218,202	$239,055	$267,688	$284,229	$320,976	$374,534	$539,160
Anesthesiology	3,903	184	[illegible]	[illegible]	[illegible]	[illegible]	[illegible]	[illegible]	[illegible]	[illegible]	[illegible]	[illegible]	[illegible]
Anesthesiology: Pain Management	191	62	[illegible]	[illegible]	[illegible]	[illegible]	[illegible]	[illegible]	[illegible]	[illegible]	[illegible]	[illegible]	[illegible]
Anesthesiology: Pediatric	105	10	[illegible]	[illegible]	[illegible]	[illegible]	[illegible]	[illegible]	[illegible]	[illegible]	[illegible]	[illegible]	[illegible]
Cardiology: Electrophysiology	203	96	[illegible]	[illegible]	[illegible]	[illegible]	[illegible]	[illegible]	[illegible]	[illegible]	[illegible]	[illegible]	[illegible]
Cardiology: Invasive	528	139	[illegible]	[illegible]	[illegible]	[illegible]	[illegible]	[illegible]	[illegible]	[illegible]	[illegible]	[illegible]	[illegible]
Cardiology: Inv-Intvl	627	161	[illegible]	[illegible]	[illegible]	[illegible]	[illegible]	[illegible]	[illegible]	[illegible]	[illegible]	[illegible]	[illegible]
Cardiology: Noninvasive	516	138	[illegible]	[illegible]	[illegible]	[illegible]	[illegible]	[illegible]	[illegible]	[illegible]	[illegible]	[illegible]	[illegible]
Critical Care: Intensivist	97	20	[illegible]	[illegible]	[illegible]	[illegible]	[illegible]	[illegible]	[illegible]	[illegible]	[illegible]	[illegible]	[illegible]
Dentistry	58	18	[illegible]	[illegible]	[illegible]	[illegible]	[illegible]	[illegible]	[illegible]	[illegible]	[illegible]	[illegible]	[illegible]
Dermatology	361	128	[illegible]	[illegible]	[illegible]	[illegible]	[illegible]	[illegible]	[illegible]	[illegible]	[illegible]	[illegible]	[illegible]

exported to Excel for custom analysis and charting. You also can chart any table by selecting the chart toolbar buttons.

Benchmarking Tools

One of the most important functions of the interactive report is the seven built-in benchmarking tools, which allow you to input data from a practice and have the benchmarks performed automatically.

Physician Benchmarking Tool

This comprehensive benchmarking tool provides both internal (i.e., physician against physician) and external (i.e., against MGMA norms) benchmarking. You can input data monthly, quarterly, or annually. It provides a ranking report both in table and graphic formats. You can automatically load data from a practice's IT system into this tool, without having to manually input data. This tool also produces a number of tables and charts, including the ranking report below in Exhibit 11, which you can export to Excel for custom analysis. Note each physician is ranked for each metric benchmarked; the rankings show exactly where the physician lies on the curve.

Exhibit 11. Ranking Report Section of the Physician Benchmarking Tool

Physician Ranking Compared to MGMA Data for Specialty Cardiology: Invasive				
	MGMA	**Tyler Jones**	**Michael Cane**	**Sample Practice**
Compensation	Median	3 to 7 years in Specialty	8 to 17 years in Specialty	Practice Average
Physician Compensation	$431,533	<10th %tile	68th %tile	30th %tile
Physician Retirement Benefits	$29,500	18th %tile	70th %tile	32nd %tile
Production				
Physician Collection for Professional Charges	$629,195	42nd %tile	45th %tile	42nd %tile
Physician Gross Charges	$1,497,479	13th %tile	58th %tile	34th %tile
Physician Total RVUs	18,419	12th %tile	31st %tile	20th %tile
Physician Work RVUs	9,256	27th %tile	48th %tile	38th %tile
Physician Ambulatory Encounters	2,257	31st %tile	43rd %tile	36th %tile
Physician Hospital Encounters	1,264	34th %tile	52nd %tile	43rd %tile
Physician Surgery/Anesthesia Cases	82	61st %tile	82nd %tile	71st %tile
Physician Clinical Hours Worked per Week	40	54th %tile	23th %tile	53rd %tile
Physician Weeks Worked per Year	46	11th %tile	11th %tile	11th %tile

Physician Compensation Analysis Tool

This tool offers a quick method to determine compensation based on data from a number of tables. The output (see Exhibit 12) is a weighted average compensation that allows you to change the default weights and recalculate the weighted average compensation level.

Exhibit 12. Compensation Analysis Tool

Data Source	Compensation	Weight
Physician Compensation by All Physicians		
All Physicians	187,393	1
By Years in Specialty:		
1 to 2 years	-	0
By Method of Compensation:		
1-99% prod less allocated overhead	-	0
By Group Type:		
Single Specialty	187,396	1
By Geographic Location:		
Midwest	251,518	1
By Gender:		
Male	201,148	1
By Size of Practice:		
10 FTE or fewer	212,785	1
Weighted Average Compensation Level	$ 208,048	

Physician Compensation Estimator Tool

This tool provides a predictive statistical model based on the most significant compensation drivers. *Note: This tool should not be used to normalize physician compensation.*

Physician Pay-to-Production Plotter Tool

This is the single best (and statistically valid) method to get a comprehensive picture of how physician compensation and production (RVUs and collections) are related. You can input the compensation and production values for your physicians, and they are plotted against the MGMA data. This is the only tool that allows you to see individual MGMA responses rather than statistics based on the responses. The Pay-to-Production Plotter Tool offers a significant advantage to using compensation and production tables to correlate compensation and production, because the data are based on a sample population that responded to both the compensation and production questions. In this case, RVUs are along the x-axis, with compensation along the y-axis. You will see your physicians plotted as diamonds against the MGMA data (circles) in Exhibit 13.

Exhibit 13. Pay-to-Production Plotter

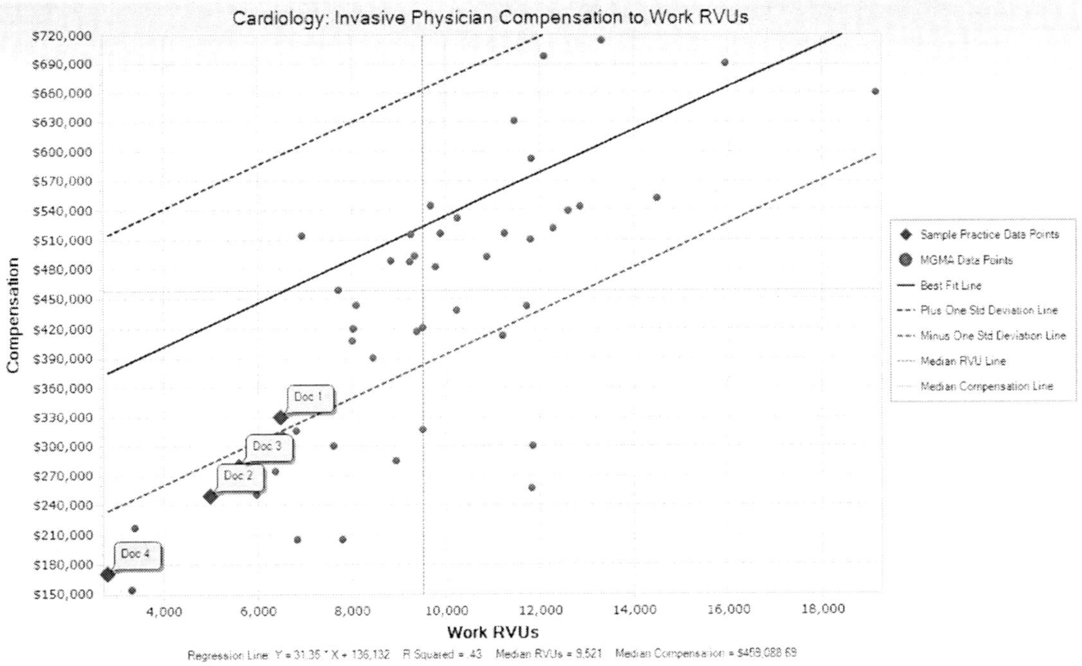

Physician Dashboard Report Tool

This tool provides a 50,000-foot view of physician compensation and production in a dashboard format. The dashboard gauges provide rankings for compensation, charges, collections, RVUs, ambulatory encounters, and hospital encounters. Because the dashboard presents the data in an easy-to-understand, green-yellow-red gauge format, the "benchmarking story" the gauges tell can be communicated to those who do not understand statistics, benchmarks, or MGMA data. Exhibit 14 shows the dashboard.

Exhibit 14. Physician Compensation and Production Dashboard

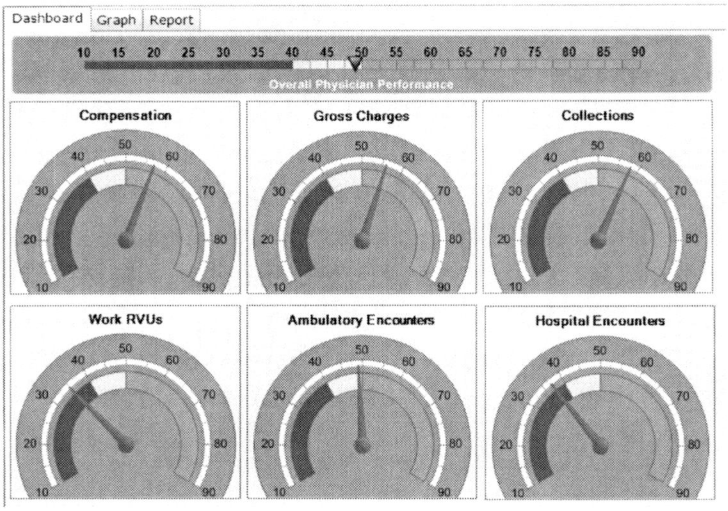

Management Summary Analysis Tables Tool

Provides summary tables for the management data that are included in an expanded version of the *Physicians Compensation* interactive report.

RVU 06-08 Conversion Utility Tool

This tool allows you to convert wRVUs from one year's values to another year's values. RVU values changed substantially between 2006 and 2007 and a little between 2007 and 2008. It's important that the data you input into the benchmarking tools and the comparisons you make are based on the same year's RVU scale.

Financial Statement Benchmarking

In the normal course of valuing a company, a financial statement benchmark often is performed to better understand how the company performs against industry norms. Performing this analysis assists the valuator in assessing ongoing cash flows, company risk, and sustainable growth. One of the challenges of financial statement benchmarking, however, is there is no direct correlation between the results of benchmarking and drivers of business value (cash flows, risk, and growth). In other words, there is no accepted valuation standard that allows the valuator to apply a formula or method to translate the results of financial statement benchmarking into something directly related to company value. Financial statement benchmarking will provide you a better understanding of the practice's financial and operational dynamics and give you a quantitative approach to assist you in developing and defending your assumptions relating to value drivers.

Finding Financial Statement Benchmarking Data

In looking for financial statement benchmarking data for medical practices, the industry has relied on sources such as Risk Management Association (RMA), Integra, and other general sources of benchmarking data. Although this general data provide some insight into how a medical practice is performing, a medical practice is substantially different from a general business. For example, in RMA data, you'll find common size statements and general financial ratios for physician practices, but the underlying financial and operational drivers that are unique to a medical practice are ignored.

This is where the MGMA data provide a far superior set of data and tools to benchmark a medical practice. RMA provides approximately 45 metrics (i.e., data points); MGMA's *Cost Survey* has more than 700.

Medical Practice Benchmarking Basics

To understand financial statement benchmarking for medical practices, you have to understand some of the value drivers in the practice. To understand these drivers, you have to understand the fundamental categories of group practice metrics including:

- **AR:** Accounts receivable should be broken down per physician, as well as a percentage of total medical revenue. You should also review a standard AR aging.

- **Gross charges by payer type:** A practice's revenue can be significantly impacted by its payer mix (i.e., insurance companies).

- **Charges and revenue:** Physician charges and revenue should be broken down per physician and as a percentage of total medical revenue.

- **Operating cost:** General operating costs should be broken down per physician, as well as a percentage of total medical revenue.

- **Provider cost:** Provider costs (i.e., cost for anyone providing billable services, including physicians, physician's assistants, registered nurses, and so on) should be broken down per physician, per provider along with as a percentage of total medical revenue.

- **Staff FTE levels and costs:** Staff costs should be broken down by FTE (i.e., how many FTEs per position) and their associated costs. The data should be also broken down on a per-FTE basis as well as a percentage of total medical revenue.

- **Procedures:** Procedures are broken down on a per-FTE basis.

This data, as you can see, delve deeper into the dynamics of value in a medical practice than a general data set such as RMA. As with the *Physician Compensation* data, it's important to understand the exact definition of each metric you use to obtain and interpret the data correctly. The *Cost Interactive Report* includes a definitions document we strongly encourage you read to be sure you are collecting data based on the same definitions that MGMA uses to collect it. There also are a number of complex formulas that go into calculating some of these metrics. By using the benchmarking tools in the interactive report, you are assured the calculations are performed correctly.

Using the Cost Interactive Report

The cost interactive report is based on observing organizations, not individuals. The data are presented in 30 tables that cover the 700-plus metrics. Each "slice" of data contains the exact same 30 tables. The 30 tables include the following:

Staffing and Practice Data

- AR data, collection percentages, and financial ratios;
- Breakout of total gross charges by type of payer;
- Staffing, RVUs, patients, procedures, and square footage per FTE physician;
- Charges and revenue per FTE physician;
- Operating cost per FTE physician;
- Provider cost per FTE physician;
- Net income or loss per FTE physician;
- Charges and revenue as a percentage of total medical revenue;
- Operating cost as a percentage of total medical revenue;
- Provider cost as a percentage of total medical revenue;
- Net income or loss as a percentage of total medical revenue;

- Staffing, RVUs, patients, procedures, and square footage per FTE provider;
- Charges, revenue, and cost per FTE provider;
- Staffing, RVUs, patients, and procedures per 10,000 square foot;
- Charges, revenue, and cost per square feet;
- Staffing, patients, procedures and square footage per 10,000 total RVU;
- Charges, revenue, and cost per total RVUs;
- Staffing, patients, procedures, and square footage per 10,000 wRVU;
- Charges, revenue, and cost per wRVUs;
- Staffing, patients, procedures, and square footage per 10,000 patients;
- Charges, revenue, and cost per patient;
- Activity charges to total gross charges ratios;
- Medical procedure data (inside the practice);
- Medical procedure data (outside the practice);
- Surgery and anesthesia procedure data (inside the practice);
- Surgery and anesthesia procedure data (outside the practice);
- Clinical laboratory and pathology procedure data;
- Diagnostic radiology and imaging procedure data; and
- Nonprocedural gross charge data.

The data is broken down by:

- Per FTE physician;
- Per FTE provider;
- Expense as a percentage of total medical revenue;
- Per square foot;
- Per total RVU;
- Per wRVU; and
- Per patient.

The key indicators for medical group are included in Exhibit 15.

Exhibit 15. Key Indicators for Medical Group Practices

Financial	Revenue - Medical revenue, ancillaries, other revenue Expense - Support staff, general operating and provider expense
Operational	Staffing Process efficiency and quality Resource utilization Contracting Relationship management – referrals/marketing
Clinical	Profile Quality – outcomes, adverse events Patient satisfaction Compliance
Individual	Productivity – work effort Income/Cost Clinical Profile – quality, procedure mix Job Performance
Environmental	Population Other Medical Groups – partners/competitors Payer Market Hospital Market Vendors

Depending on the nature of the engagement, you may have to understand and review one or more of these areas. The interactive report provides a robust benchmarking tool that allows you to quickly and easily perform a financial and operational benchmark.

The two basic tasks you will use the interactive report for are opening tables and using the built-in benchmarking tools. When the interactive report begins, you'll see the startup dialog box in Exhibit 16.

Exhibit 16. Startup Dialog in the Interactive Report

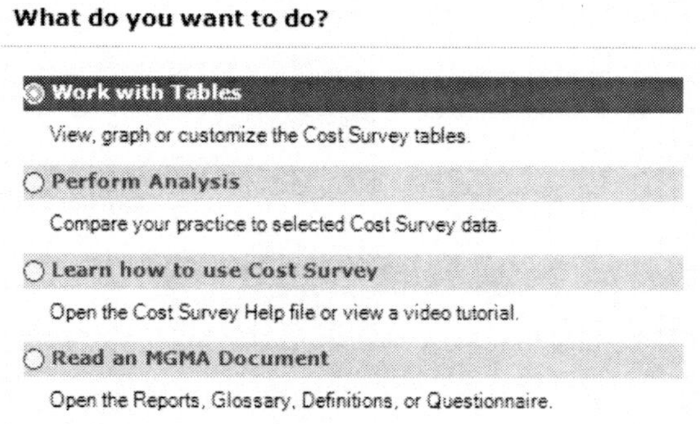

To open a table, select the "Work with Tables" option or the "Open Tables" toolbar button from the main menu. You will see the dialog (advanced mode is shown) in Exhibit 17.

Exhibit 17. Table Open Dialog in the Interactive Report

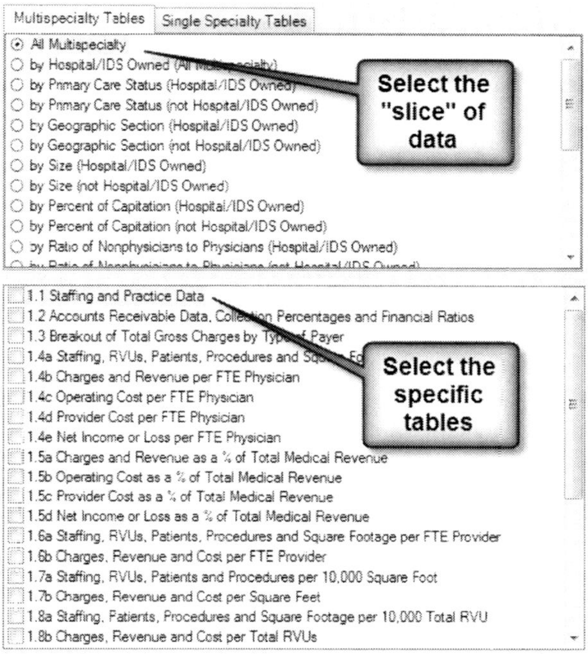

The interactive report consists of both multispecialty and single-specialty tables. In each of these categories, you may select from a number of different data "slices," including all, hospital-owned, geographic section, and so on. The next step is to pick one of the tables to display the specific data you are interested in. For all multispecialty, staffing, and practice data, the table appears in Exhibit 18.

Exhibit 18. Table 1.1

Staffing and Practice Data	Practice Type							
	All Multispecialty							
	Count	Mean	Std. Dev.	10th %tile	25th %tile	Median	75th %tile	90th %tile
Total provider FTE	**282**	**69.76**	**86.47**	**9.45**	**18.37**	**45.51**	**89.79**	**160.93**
Total physician FTE	325	52.90	[illegible]	[illegible]	[illegible]	[illegible]	[illegible]	[illegible]
Total nonphysician provider FTE	283	13.95	[illegible]	[illegible]	[illegible]	[illegible]	[illegible]	[illegible]
Total support staff FTE	**325**	**257.65**	[illegible]	[illegible]	[illegible]	[illegible]	[illegible]	[illegible]
Number of branch clinics	315	8.95	[illegible]	[illegible]	[illegible]	[illegible]	[illegible]	[illegible]
Square footage of all facilities	279	110,946	[illegible]	[illegible]	[illegible]	[illegible]	[illegible]	[illegible]

Metrics are on the left; statistics are shown in the columns. As with the *Physician Compensation and Production* interactive report, the program will not show data unless there are at least 10 providers (physicians) and three unique practices. If there are blanks or stars in the data, it is because there are insufficient physicians or practices.

Since the interactive report contains every percentile from 10 to 90, you can customize the display to show more data. This is helpful to get a feel for what the entire MGMA curve looks like. The same table expanded to show deciles appears in Exhibit 19.

Exhibit 19. Table 1.1 Expanded to Show Deciles

Staffing and Practice Data	Practice Type												
	All Multispecialty												
	Count	Mean	Std. Dev.	10th %tile	20th %tile	30th %tile	40th %tile	Median	60th %tile	70th %tile	80th %tile	90th %tile
Total provider FTE	**282**	**69.76**	**86.47**	**9.45**	**15.84**	**21.95**	**29.12**	**45.51**	**55.48**	**71.42**	**102.78**	**160.93**
Total physician FTE	325	52.90	[illegible]	[illegible]	[illegible]	[illegible]	[illegible]	[illegible]	[illegible]	[illegible]	[illegible]	[illegible]
Total nonphysician provider FTE	283	13.95	[illegible]	[illegible]	[illegible]	[illegible]	[illegible]	[illegible]	[illegible]	[illegible]	[illegible]	[illegible]
Total support staff FTE	**325**	**257.65**	[illegible]	[illegible]	[illegible]	[illegible]	[illegible]	[illegible]	[illegible]	[illegible]	[illegible]	[illegible]
Number of branch clinics	315	8.95	[illegible]	[illegible]	[illegible]	[illegible]	[illegible]	[illegible]	[illegible]	[illegible]	[illegible]	[illegible]
Square footage of all facilities	279	110,946	[illegible]	[illegible]	[illegible]	[illegible]	[illegible]	[illegible]	[illegible]	[illegible]	[illegible]	[illegible]

In the cost interactive report, data are available for multispecialty and 18 single-specialty practices. If your specialty is not provided, you will either have to use the multispecialty data or select a single specialty you feel is representative of the specialty.

Benchmarking Tools

One of the most important functions of the interactive report is three built-in benchmarking tools, which allow you to input practice data and have the benchmarks performed automatically.

Dashboard Report Tool

This tool provides a 50,000-foot view of a medical group in a dashboard format. The dashboard gauges provide rankings for total medical revenue per physician, total AR per physician, total operating cost per physician, total general operating cost per physician, total support staff cost per physician, and total medical revenue after operating cost per physician. Once again, because the dashboard presents the data in an easy-to-understand, green-yellow-red gauge format, the "benchmarking story" can be communicated to those who do not understand statistics, benchmarks, or MGMA data. The following screen shows the dashboard in Exhibit 20.

Exhibit 20. Cost Dashboard

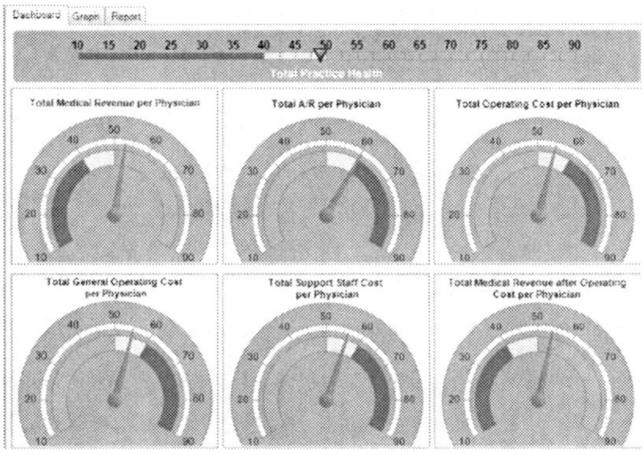

Practice Performance Report Tool

This is the tool you want to use if you are a valuator. Once data are collected, you can perform a comprehensive income statement, staffing, AR, and ratio analysis in under an hour. As with all benchmarking tools, select the areas you want to benchmark and ignore the rest. Unless you have the background to interpret staffing data (FTEs and costs), stick with the other sections of this tool. Staffing levels and costs, however, are a significant driver of value in a medical practice; we encourage you to learn how this area impacts both financial performance and value. This tool is Excel-based, so you can export the entire tool to perform detailed analysis, roll-ups, and other custom analyses. It is also possible to prepopulate the tool with data, so you do not have to type in each engagement's data. Exhibit 21 shows the first input screen from the tool.

Exhibit 21. Practice Performance Report Input Screen

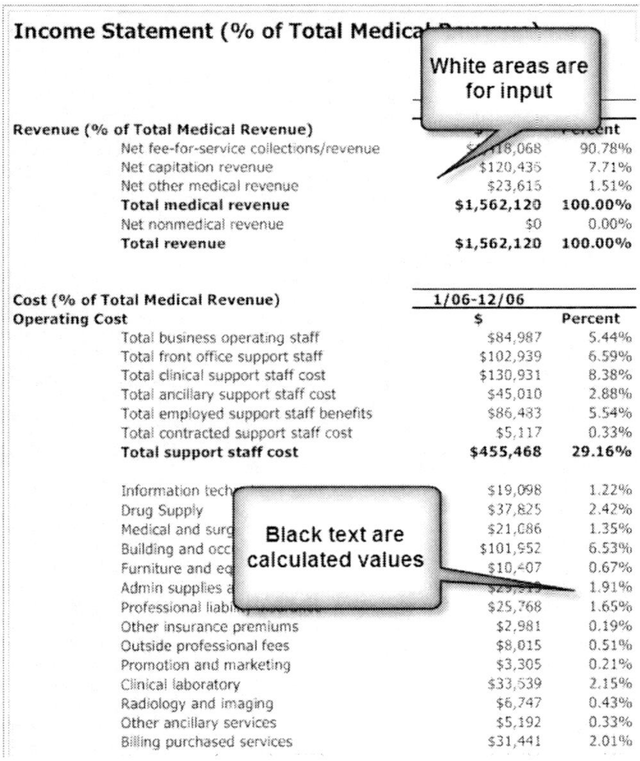

Income Statement (% of Total Medica

Revenue (% of Total Medical Revenue)		
Net fee-for-service collections/revenue	[illegible]18,068	90.78%
Net capitation revenue	$120,435	7.71%
Net other medical revenue	$23,615	1.51%
Total medical revenue	**$1,562,120**	**100.00%**
Net nonmedical revenue	$0	0.00%
Total revenue	**$1,562,120**	**100.00%**
Cost (% of Total Medical Revenue)	**1/06-12/06**	
Operating Cost	**$**	**Percent**
Total business operating staff	$84,987	5.44%
Total front office support staff	$102,939	6.59%
Total clinical support staff cost	$130,931	8.38%
Total ancillary support staff cost	$45,010	2.88%
Total employed support staff benefits	$86,483	5.54%
Total contracted support staff cost	$5,117	0.33%
Total support staff cost	**$455,468**	**29.16%**
Information tech	$19,098	1.22%
Drug Supply	$37,825	2.42%
Medical and surg	$21,086	1.35%
Building and occ	$101,952	6.53%
Furniture and eq	$10,407	0.67%
Admin supplies a	[illegible]	1.91%
Professional liabi	$25,768	1.65%
Other insurance premiums	$2,981	0.19%
Outside professional fees	$8,015	0.51%
Promotion and marketing	$3,305	0.21%
Clinical laboratory	$33,539	2.15%
Radiology and imaging	$6,747	0.43%
Other ancillary services	$5,192	0.33%
Billing purchased services	$31,441	2.01%

Once you input data, the tool performs the rest of the calculations and benchmarks, including a ranking report. The following schedule shows the revenue and cost as a percentage of total medical revenue, which is calculated based on the input screen. The last three columns show MGMA data, the differences between the practice and MGMA data, and the ranking of the practice. The ranking gives you a precise picture of how your practice compares to MGMA data, shown in Exhibit 22.

Exhibit 22. Practice Performance Report Benchmark Screen

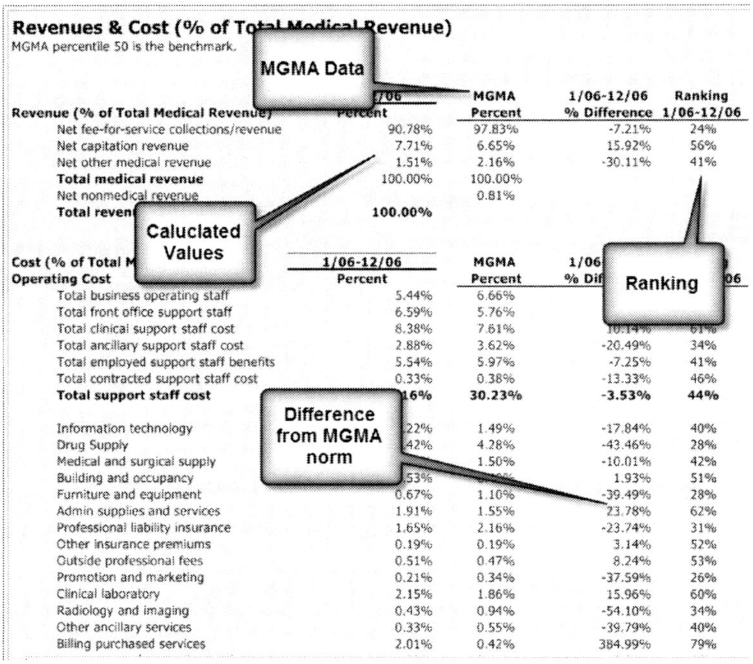

Revenues & Cost (% of Total Medical Revenue)
MGMA percentile 50 is the benchmark.

Revenue (% of Total Medical Revenue)	1/06-12/06 Percent	MGMA Percent	1/06-12/06 % Difference	Ranking 1/06-12/06
Net fee-for-service collections/revenue	90.78%	97.83%	-7.21%	24%
Net capitation revenue	7.71%	6.65%	15.92%	56%
Net other medical revenue	1.51%	2.16%	-30.11%	41%
Total medical revenue	100.00%	100.00%		
Net nonmedical revenue		0.81%		
Total revenue	**100.00%**			

Cost (% of Total Medical Revenue) Operating Cost	1/06-12/06 Percent	MGMA Percent	1/06-12/06 % Difference	Ranking 1/06-12/06
Total business operating staff	5.44%	6.66%	[illegible]	[illegible]
Total front office support staff	6.59%	5.76%	[illegible]	[illegible]
Total clinical support staff cost	8.38%	7.61%	[illegible]	[illegible]
Total ancillary support staff cost	2.88%	3.62%	-20.49%	34%
Total employed support staff benefits	5.54%	5.97%	-7.25%	41%
Total contracted support staff cost	0.33%	0.38%	-13.33%	46%
Total support staff cost	[illegible]	**30.23%**	**-3.53%**	**44%**
Information technology	[illegible]	1.49%	-17.84%	40%
Drug Supply	[illegible]	4.28%	-43.46%	28%
Medical and surgical supply	[illegible]	1.50%	-10.01%	42%
Building and occupancy	[illegible]	[illegible]	1.93%	51%
Furniture and equipment	0.67%	1.10%	-39.49%	28%
Admin supplies and services	1.91%	1.55%	23.78%	62%
Professional liability insurance	1.65%	2.16%	-23.74%	31%
Other insurance premiums	0.19%	0.19%	3.14%	52%
Outside professional fees	0.51%	0.47%	8.24%	53%
Promotion and marketing	0.21%	0.34%	-37.59%	26%
Clinical laboratory	2.15%	1.86%	15.96%	60%
Radiology and imaging	0.43%	0.94%	-54.10%	34%
Other ancillary services	0.33%	0.55%	-39.79%	40%
Billing purchased services	2.01%	0.42%	384.99%	79%

Advanced Benchmarking Report Tool

The practice performance report provides an easy-to-input financial statement format benchmark report. However, it only provides benchmarking for a subset of the *Cost Survey*'s 700-plus metrics. If you need to benchmark anything that is not contained in the practice performance report, use the advanced benchmarking report. This tool will allow you to customize the report for exactly the metrics you are interested in benchmarking.

Summary

Since medical practices are unique, using MGMA and other medically based data will help you understand the unique drivers of value in a medical practice. This chapter was developed as a brief look at using MGMA data for valuing a medical practice; it does not provide a comprehensive discussion of these topics. If you are interested in getting more detailed information, we encourage you to check out the following resources:

- Join the MGMA (www.mgma.com);
- MGMA *Physicians Compensation and Production Survey* interactive report;
- MGMA *Cost Survey* interactive report;
- *RVUs: Applications for Medical Practice Success*, 2nd edition by Kathryn P. Glass, MBA, MSHA, PMP;

- *Benchmarking Success: The Essential Guide for Group Practices* by Gregory Feltenberger, MBA, FACMPE, FACHE, CPHIMS, and David Gans, MHSA, FACMPE;

- Arrange a custom training session with ValuSource on these topics. You can reach ValuSource at 800-825-8763 or email sales@valusourcesoftware.com or visit its Web site at www.valusourcesoftware.com;

- Participate in the Consulting Training Institute's (CTI) five-day healthcare boot camp (www.nacva.com); and

- Read books and take webinars on these topics.

Thanks

I would like to thank the MGMA, Laurie Foote, Bill Sipes, and Robert Cimasi for their time, numerous conversations, and outstanding comments and suggestions regarding material in this chapter.

Chapter 15

Identifying and Measuring Personal Goodwill in a Professional Practice:[1] *Part I—Basic Concepts*

By Mark O. Dietrich, CPA/ABV

In many situations, most notably valuation for marital dissolution and allocation of purchase price for tax or financial reporting purposes, distinguishing personal goodwill from enterprise goodwill is a critical undertaking.

In the marital arena, personal goodwill is not a divisible asset in some jurisdictions, and the status is uncertain in many and therefore, cannot be awarded by the court. Given this norm, it is curious that many valuation analysts fail to provide evidence as to the separate values of personal and enterprise goodwill.

In tax planning, particularly for C corporations, allocating the proceeds of a sale of a business to personal goodwill and a noncompete agreement can reduce or eliminate the amount recognized as corporate gain and the related corporate-level tax. In valuation for purposes of a sale of a business, properly attributing value to different intangible assets may be critical to both buyer and seller in obtaining the proper measure of the bargain.

There are two fundamental issues in differentiating personal from enterprise goodwill:

1. Identifying which portions of cash flow are attributable directly to the individual's characteristics; and

1 Copyright 2005 by AICPA, reproduced with permission. Opinions of the authors are their own and do not necessarily reflect policies of the AICPA.

2. Identifying which cash flows attributable to otherwise enterprise-level tangibles and intangibles would be lost if the individual competed.

Illustrative Examples

1. Personal goodwill flowing from individual characteristics:

   - A physician at a renowned medical center is well-known for his skill in diagnosing complex diseases. His ability to do so is due to his intellectual skills, knowledge base, and experience in similar cases.

   - An attorney has won several high-profile cases because of her ability to relate to the jury and make complex issues understandable. In her current firm, she is also the principal "rainmaker."

2. Enterprise goodwill flowing from individual characteristics:

   - The same physician is part of a group practice. Subsequent to the diagnosis, other group physicians, some of whom are employed, may treat the patient. The employed physicians generate a profit in excess of their compensation that the practice owners share.

   - The same attorney has attracted dozens of new cases and is unable to handle most of them, which are assigned to other partners or members of the growing staff. The "points system" in the law firm allocates profits based in large part upon who generated the underlying business.

> *Observation: The second set of examples is perhaps subject to some dispute in jurisdictions that treat personal goodwill as a nondivisible asset in marital dissolution. Some judges may treat any profit resulting from the personal goodwill of a marital litigant as nondivisible. For example, in a Florida appellate case (*Weinstock *v.* Weinstock *634 So. 2d at 777), the court ruled that a dental practice had no divisible goodwill because the expert testified that a noncompete agreement would be required in any sale of the practice as well as the dentist's continued presence for a six-month patient transition period. Valuation analysts need to obtain a clear understanding from legal counsel as to the proper interpretation of state law or precedent.*

Personal goodwill, then, is the asset that generates cash profits of the enterprise that are attributed to the business generating characteristics of the individual, and may include any profits that would be lost if the individual were not present.[2] The value of a noncompete with that individual is the value of those cash profits, adjusted for the probability of the individual competing in each future year where the potential of competition exists. Thus, the noncompete is a portion of the value of personal goodwill and cannot exceed that value. Unless the probability of competition is 100%, the personal goodwill will always exceed the value of the noncompete.

Enforceability of Noncompetes

How much is an unenforceable promise to pay worth? Or, better yet, how much will the hypothetical buyer pay for an unenforceable contract with a hypothetical seller? "Not much" would seem to be the answer. To illustrate the concepts involved in factoring enforceability into the value of a noncompete, the following section looks at the statutes and precedents of several states.

> *Observation: The enforceability of noncompetes is a volatile area of law. Courts in many states have moved to restrict enforceability when public policy is an issue, such as noncompetes that by their nature restrict the free access of a patient to his or her physician. Other states have liberally interpreted noncompetes, finding that separate consideration is not necessary.*

Representative State: Texas

The Texas Business and Commercial Code §§15.50 provides that for a noncompete to be enforceable, it must be "ancillary to or part of an otherwise enforceable agreement at the time the agreement is made." If there is only an at-will employment relationship, the covenant is not enforceable. The term "at-will" appears to be interpreted as one in which the agreement has no specific term. If the relationship is other than at-will, the limitations of the covenant in time, scope, and geographic area must be no more than necessary to protect the goodwill of the employer or other entity.

Noncompetes among physicians are subject to a special set of provisions. To be enforceable, the agreement must conform to the statutory provisions, including not denying the physician access to a list of his or her patients whom he or she had seen or treated within one year of termination of the contract or employment and the covenant must provide for a buy out of the covenant by the physician at a reasonable price.

Therefore, the value of the covenant must exclude the value of that patient list.[3] The provision in subparagraph (C) would appear to require that the covenantor receive

2 Subject to jurisdictional precedents.
3 Always ask: Would the hypothetical buyer pay for something it already own?

an electronic copy of medical records if they are kept in that fashion. As a logical consequence, the enterprise value of a medical practice in Texas is different from an identical practice located in another state that has no limitations on the enforceability of a noncompete and does not require that the physician be given a patient list! When fair market value is the standard, hypothetical buyers and sellers must be assumed to be familiar with the law in the state in which the transaction takes place—as should valuation analysts.

Representative State: Pennsylvania

It is likely that a November 2002 Pennsylvania Supreme Court decision has significantly altered the law as it applies to the transfer of a business, including employment contracts. The case, *Hess v. Gebhard & Co., Inc.*, involved the sale of an insurance agency. As an employee of the agency, Hess' employment contract contained a covenant not to compete within a 25-mile radius for a five-year post-employment term. Significantly, the contract contained no language regarding the transferability of the contract.

The related purchase and sale agreement allocated no value to the Hess employment contract. Hess did not continue employment with the purchaser[4] and sought a position with another insurance agency. In the process, Hess solicited a customer of his former agency. As a result of threatened legal action, the new agency did not hire Hess. Hess then sued for interference with contractual relations.

The Pennsylvania Supreme Court ultimately held that the noncompete was not transferable to a subsequent purchaser absent a specific transferability provision: "We hold that a restrictive covenant not to compete, contained in an employment agreement, is not assignable to the purchasing business entity, in the absence of a specific assignability provision, where the covenant is included in a sale of assets." Perhaps a different result would have been reached if a sale of stock had been at issue.[5] It seems that, in Pennsylvania at least, when valuing the assets of a business, the analyst should read any employment contracts to see whether the noncompete is transferable.

Observation: Valuators should be aware that the various states might have one standard for enforcing covenants not to compete in an employment setting and another for enforcing a covenant in a purchase and sale of a business.

4 He was not offered a position he was interested in.

5 And may I further add that this is but one dramatic difference between asset sales and stock sales, suggesting that a hypothetical buyer should pay a different price for assets than for stock.

Reasonable Compensation

In the typical valuation of any professional practice or small business, the analyst's key assumption relates to reasonable compensation for services—there will not be any excess earnings to capitalize or any cash profit to discount if the professional does not earn more than "reasonable compensation." The higher the reasonable compensation relative to the total compensation earned, (of course) the lower the value of any goodwill.

Arguably, if there is no business or practice profit before normalization of the income statements, then some portion of the compensation earned must be coming from the return on tangible assets of the enterprise, namely net working capital and fixed assets. Later in this article, in the section titled "Mechanics of Valuation," we address the importance of this analysis. The analyst must understand not only how much compensation is earned, but also what the sources of that compensation are.

The other critical aspect of determining reasonable compensation is the work effort of the individual, typically referred to as "productivity." Many analysts determine reasonable compensation for their valuation models by taking the median or mean (average) compensation for a particular position, without considering the individual's productivity compared with the median or mean.

For example, the Medical Group Management Association (MGMA) data are commonly used for valuing physician practices. MGMA reports not only median and mean compensation, but also the 25th, 75th, and 90th percentiles of compensation. It reports the same percentiles for productivity, as to both charges and collections for professional services. The analyst should ask: "Can I hire a replacement physician for this practice at a median salary if the practice owner is producing at the 75th percentile?"[6] Given that most medical practices, as well as accounting and law practices, compensate their senior associates and partners at a percentage of production, the answer is almost surely *"no."* For those practices and businesses in which compensation is a function of piecework (patients seen, hours billed and collected, and so on), reasonable compensation must be a function of productivity.

Proper compensation analysis is critical to the overall quest to value goodwill because an understatement of reasonable compensation will result in an overstatement of goodwill. To the extent that reasonable compensation is understated, the amount of personal goodwill included in total goodwill will be greater. Alternatively stated, some portion of the personal goodwill issue can often be minimized by properly addressing reasonable compensation.

---

6 Certainly, if one looks at tax court cases involving reasonable compensation, the court always focuses on hours worked, responsibilities, and so on. Why should it be any different in "regular" valuation engagements?

Categories of Intangibles

Perhaps the most easily identified discreet intangible in a professional practice is the value of a trained workforce, or workforce-in-place. This asset is also one of the easiest to measure, typically being based upon a percentage of payroll reflecting longevity and skill, along with training and recruiting costs.[7] An initial analysis should be considered to determine whether the practice-owners can leverage junior or support staff, such as associates (as in a law firm) and staff (as in an accounting firm). For example, one of the reasons dental practices are readily saleable and at significant prices is that they afford the owner an opportunity to profit from providing cleaning (prophylaxis) through hygienists. Workforce-in-place should thus be divided into two components: one for direct revenue producers, such as dental hygienists or staff accountants, and another for support personnel, such as medical assistants, secretaries, and the like. Direct revenue producers can be valued similar to any other intangible using their associated profit stream, while support personnel can be valued in the conventional manner, based upon costs of recruiting and training, as a percentage of payroll.

A Simplified Example[8]

The analyst determines that $45,000 of annual free cash flow is derived from profits on nonpartner professional staff who are direct revenue producers and that this profit stream will continue to grow at a constant rate.

Free cash flow from direct revenue producers	45,000
Cap rate from weighted average cost of capital	16.17%
Value	278,336

Often missed in the analysis of personal goodwill is the potential impact of the presence or lack of a nonsolicitation provision. Such a provision would preclude the signer from seeking to employ the practice's personnel after terminating. As such, a portion of the value of workforce-in-place can be attributable to the noncompete if it contains a nonsolicitation provision and the analyst believes that certain employees would leave if the covenantor were no longer with the business. This could result from the covenantor operating a competing business or simply no longer being associated with the sold enterprise. A standard purchase and sales document would typically contain both a noncompete and a nonsolicitation provision. Nonsolicitation provisions may also apply to the business's clients, patients, and customers.

7 See, for example, "Financial Valuation," Hitchner, et al.; Medical Practice Valuation Guidebook, Mark O. Dietrich.

8 I use capitalization of cash flows here assuming the profit stream qualifies for capitalization.

Mechanics of Valuation

It is critical that the analyst consider the three principal categories of assets included in business enterprise value (BEV) when assessing the profits attributable to the seller: net working capital (NWC), fixed assets, and intangible assets. Just as the right-hand side of the BEV equation has a rate of return or discount rate for each of equity and debt, the left-hand side has a return on each of the assets. It does not seem reasonable for the return on NWC or fixed assets to be attributed in its entirety to a seller and therefore, the noncompete.

Once the BEV is known, it is typically possible to calculate the value of NWC using the historical balance sheets; certainly, if a discounted cash flow (DCF) is used, the working capital requirement needs to be estimated. Fixed assets can be valued by an appraisal. Once these two values are known, they are subtracted from the BEV to determine the aggregate value of the intangibles.

Constructing a noncompete DCF is best accomplished after estimating the value of each of the asset categories; it may also require calculating the value of certain individual components for each category, such as the workforce-in-place described above. This assists the analyst in gauging a reasonable total value for the noncompete. The analyst should also consider whether any portion of the value of fixed assets or working capital is attributable to the covenantor.

One approach to making this determination is to differentiate between the going concern value of these two categories of assets—which requires, to one degree or another, the continued presence or forbearance of the seller—and their liquidation or other value. For example, fixed assets are likely to have a significantly greater value in use as part of a going concern than as an assemblage not in a going concern or in liquidation. In liquidation, a buyer will not pay for the in-use value and is likely to consider the cost to transport and a markup to resell. The value of working capital may or may not be different in a going concern context depending upon the collectibility of receivables, for example.

Estimating that value may also require establishing a discount rate for each asset and allocating the cash flow based upon the discount rate.[9] The weighted average of those discount rates must, of course, be equal to the weighted average cost of capital (WACC) determined from the right-hand side of the BEV equation. Therefore, the analyst must also consider the portion of the value of each category that would be financed with debt.

9 This process is described in Financial Valuation as well as Valuation for Financial Reporting, Mark, Hitchner, Hyden, Zyla.

Observation: Notwithstanding the disdain with which some in the valuation community regard the excess earnings method, it is the classic example of a left-hand side of the equation approach to capitalization rates, and, by adding the appropriate long-term growth rate, deriving discount rates. Unfortunately, users of the method rarely calculate the capitalization rate derived by weighting the respective returns on tangibles and intangibles and comparing it to the traditional WACC approach for reasonableness.

Note: *The weighted average cap rate based on assets should then be used in the capitalization of cash flows method.*

Exhibit 1 shows the result of a DCF valuation along with an allocation of fair market to the three major categories of assets and their percentage of total BEV.

Exhibit 2 is the calculation of the WACC used in the DCF model; note that the WACC is based upon the fair market value of debt and equity, not book values.

Exhibit 1. Result of DCF Valuation

	Value	% of Value
Fixed assets	$975,000	34.97%
Net working capital	1,064,217	38.17
Intangible value	749,141	26.87
	2,788,358	100.00

Exhibit 2. Calculation of WACC

	Weight	Capital	Discount rate	WACC
Debt	25%	$697,089	3.54%	0.89%
Equity	75	2,091,268	23.71	17.78
		2,788,358		18.67

Exhibit 3 is the computation of the WACC, based on returns for the individual categories of assets. Fixed assets are financed with 50% debt (the pretax rate is 6%, the after-tax rate is 3.54%, using a 41% tax rate) and 50% equity; net working capital is financed with the remainder of the debt and the balance with equity. Intangible assets are financed entirely with equity.

Exhibit 3. Computation of WACC

Category (Cat)	Value	%	Debt	Cost of Debt	Equity	Cost of Equity	Cat WACC	Return	Total WACC
Fixed assets	$975,000	34.97%	$487,500	3.54%	$487,500	17.25%	10.40%	$101,351	3.63%
Net working capital	1,064,217	38.17	209,589	3.54%	854,628	17.50	14.75	156,979	5.63
Intangible Value	749,141	26.87			749,141	35.00	35.00	262,199	9.40
	2,788,358	100.00%	697,089		2,091,268			520,530	18.67

The analyst determines equity returns for each asset category. The aggregate weighting should agree with the WACC used in the original DCF.[10] The appropriate discount rates will vary from industry to industry and subject to subject. Bear in mind that intangible assets are generally the most risky and therefore, have the highest expected rates of return.

Exhibit 4 is a condensed version of the DCF from which the Exhibit 4 values are determined.[11] The analyst has concluded that a net of 55% of the free cash flow is attributable to the seller and would be lost to the buyer in the event of competition.[12] This is approximately equal to that percentage of the total return represented by the intangibles as reflected in Exhibit 4. This does not suggest, however, that only intangible value is relevant to the determination of cash flows attributable to the seller, since some of the workforce-in-place value might not be lost in the event of competition and some of the fixed asset value might be lost. For example, if the valuation subject was a medical practice using equipment for diagnostic testing, the departure of a physician might lower the volume of tests and therefore, the value in use of the equipment.[13] The analyst can also utilize these allocated cash flows to assess the reasonableness of the annual cash payment for a noncompete.

Exhibits 5, 6, and 7 show the calculation of the probability-adjusted lost cash profits assuming that competition begins in Year 1 (Exhibit 5), Year 2 (Exhibit 6), and Year 3

10 This is easier said than done using a DCF and individual WACCs for each asset category because discount rates (WACCs) are different for each category and there is not a linear relationship between discount rates and present value; the solution can only be found iteratively. It is comparatively easy to do using capitalization rates since the cash flow is fixed in the first period.

11 Note that the free cash flow in any year is not equal to the "return" shown in Exhibit 4. As noted earlier, an iterative process is required in the actual reconciliation of the individual WACCs with the entity WACC, in part because year-to-year cash flows are, in fact, variable, as shown in Exhibit 5.

12 As more fully explained in the original article, there may be a difference between the gross profits attributable to the sellers and what profits the buyer would lose if the sellers competed. This gives recognition to such intangibles as location.

13 The analyst could isolate the profit on the equipment and determine that profit's present value.

Exhibit 4. Discounted Cash Flow

Year		1	2	3	4	5	Terminal
Base valuation							
Free cash flow	$3,002,869	$489,819	$552,804	$580,024	$577,724	$450,838	$351,660
Present value	2,788,358	449,645	427,635	378,109	317,365	208,702	1,006,901
Gross % attributed to seller		50.00%	50.00%	50.00%	50.00%	50.00%	50.00%
Attributed to seller	1,394,179	224,822	213,818	189,054	158,683	104,351	503,451
Net % attributed to sellers		55.00%	55.00%	55.00%	55.00%	55.00%	55.00%
PV sellers free cash flow	766,798	123,652	117,600	103,980	87,275	57,393	276,898

(Exhibit 7). In this example, if competition does not commence before the end of Year 3, it is assumed never to commence.

At first glance, Exhibit 5, 6, and 7 may appear to count the same cash flows multiple times.[14] The way to be certain that there is no double counting is to check the joint probability table (see Exhibit 8). The probability of possible outcomes must total exactly 100%. For example, adding the probability-adjusted present value of lost profits for Year 3 from Exhibit 5, 6, and 7 totals $51,574, less than the total present value of Year 3's profits attributable to the sellers of $103,980. Assuming the rest of the model is properly constructed, the probability check assures that there is no double counting.[15]

If the probability of competing were 100% at the beginning of Year 1, the value of the noncompete (see Exhibit 4) would be $766,798, slightly more than the total intangible value. This value could be compared to the value of workforce-in-place and any other discretely measured intangibles while considering the probability that the sellers would

Exhibit 5. Competition Begins in Year 1

Year	1	2	3	4	5	Terminal
PV net profits attributed to sellers	$224,822	$213,818	$189,054	$158,683	$104,351	$503,451
Net % attributed to seller	55%	55%	55%	55%	55%	55%
Net profit attributed to seller	$123,652	$117,600	$103,980	$87,275	$57,393	$276,898
Probability of competing	10%	10%	10%	10%	10%	10%
PV of lost profits by year	$12,365	$11,760	$10,398	$8,728	$5,739	$27,690
PV of Year 1 lost profits	**$76,680**					

14 As noted by one reviewer, thereby prompting this explanation.

15 The second test, as discussed in the following paragraph, is to determine the value of the noncompete if the probability of competition is 100%; any probability less than 100% in Year 1 should result in a lower value for the noncompete.

take some portion of the value of those intangibles with them if they competed, as well as any diminution in the value in use of fixed assets. The $766,798 represents all of the present value of future profits attributable to the seller and is therefore also the value of personal goodwill.[16]

Exhibit 6. Competition Begins in Year 2

Year	1	2	3	4	5	Terminal
PV net profits attributed to sellers		$213,818	$189,054	$158,683	$104,351	$503,451
Net % attributed to seller		55%	55%	55%	55%	55%
Net profit attributed to seller		$117,600	$103,980	$87,275	$57,393	$276,898
Probability of competing		18%	18%	18%	18%	18%
PV of lost profits		**$21,168**	**$18,716**	**$15,710**	**$10,331**	**$49,842**
PV of Year 2 lost profits	**$115,766**					

Exhibit 7. Competition Begins in Year 3

Year	1	2	3	4	5	Terminal
PV net profits attributed to sellers			$189,054	$158,683	$104,351	$503,451
Net % attributed to seller			55%	55%	55%	55%
Net profit attributed to seller			$103,980	$87,275	$57,393	$276,898
Probability of competing			21.6%	21.6%	21.6%	21.6%
PV of lost profits			**$22,460**	**$18,851**	**$12,397**	**$59,810**
PV of Year 3 lost profits	**$113,518**					
Total: **$305,964**						

Exhibit 8. Joint Probability

	Year 1		Year 2		Year 3		
	Compete	Don't Compete	Compete	Don't Compete	Compete	Don't Compete	Joint Probability
Compete Year 1	10%						10.0%
Compete Year 2		90%	20%				18.0
Compete Year 3		90		80%	30%		21.6
Never compete		90		80		70%	50.4
							100.0

16 I caution that the example has personal goodwill in excess of total intangible value. I do not mean to imply or suggest that this is, or is not, the norm or that the analyst should not carefully note the implications.

The distinction between the value of personal goodwill and the value of a noncompete is less important in equitable distribution than for tax purposes. For the latter, the noncompete is ordinary income to the covenantor, while personal goodwill should be long-term capital gain.[17] It is prudent for the analyst to value both the noncompete and the personal goodwill when tax considerations are important.

In the following article, a single period capitalization model is explained and the author summarizes the key tasks for the valuation analyst.

The author expresses his gratitude to Kevin R. Yeanoplos, CPA/ABV, ASA, for his thoughtful critique of the concepts explored in this article, as well as for his corrections to my use of English language grammar.

17 With respect to tax issues, see, e.g., Martin Ice Cream 110 TC 189 (1998) and *Norwalk v. Commissioner* TC Memo 1998-279. The full-text court opinion of Martin is included online.

Chapter 16

Identifying and Measuring Personal Goodwill in a Professional Practice: *Part II—Using the Single Period Capitalization Model*[1]

By Mark O. Dietrich, CPA/ABV

As noted in the footnotes to the discounted cash flow (DCF) model used in Part I of this article, it is very difficult to devise a weighted average cost of capital (WACC) for each asset category, allocate the cash flow to each category, and get a net present value that agrees to the enterprise-level cash flow discounted to present value. Although a single-period capitalization model is not appropriate for those circumstances in which the future growth rate is not the same for all years, it is much easier to use and understand.

In this example, which might be representative of an approach in many jurisdictions for marital dissolution purposes, the data in Exhibit 1 were used.

The WACC cap rate[2] is based upon the fair market value (FMV) of the business enterprise. From the right-hand side of the balance sheet—debt and equity—the weighted average cap rate is based upon $30,000 of debt costing 4%, net of growth at 2.5%, with the balance of the capital structure consisting of equity. From the left-hand side of the balance sheet, the weighted average cap rate is based upon the pretax cap rates applicable to tangibles and intangibles. The result must be the same in both cases.

The capitalization of cash flows method reflects all pretax cash earnings in excess of reasonable compensation capitalized at the cap rate derived from the WACC of 39.36%.

1 Copyright 2005 by AICPA, reproduced with permission. Opinions of the authors are their own and do not necessarily reflect policies of the AICPA.
2 Technically, it is the capitalization rate derived from the WACC, the latter being the discount rate.

Exhibit 1. Calculation of WACC Cap Rate

	WACC	Equity Only
Discount rate	41.86%	49.04%
Growth rate	2.50	2.50%
Capitalization rate	**39.36**	**46.54**

		FMV	Percent	Return	Weighted
Debt	4.00%	$30,000	24.49%	0.98%	
Equity	46.54	92,500	75.51	35.14	
Cap rate: tangibles		**122,500**	**100.00**	**36.12**	
Practice intangibles		$55,341	31.12%	46.54%	14.48%
Practice tangibles		122,500	68.88	36.12	24.88
Cap rate—weighted average cost of capital		**177,841**	**100.00**		**39.36**
Debt		$30,000	16.87%	4.00%	0.67%
Equity		147,841	83.13	46.54	38.69

The excess earnings method capitalizes excess earnings on tangibles at the rates of return applicable to the portion financed with debt, $30,000, and the portion financed with equity, $92,500. These may be based upon the actual balance sheet of the valuation subject or upon optimal mix of debt and equity, depending upon the analyst's assessment. (See Exhibit 2.)

Exhibit 2. Capitalization of Cash Flows

Normalized 2002 earnings	$460,000
Fair market earnings	$390,000
Cash flow after reasonable compensation	$70,000
Capitalization rate	39.36%
Business enterprise value	$177,841

Note that the two methods produce exactly the same value. If used correctly, the WACC cap rate derived from either the left- or right-hand side of the balance sheet when applied to all enterprise cash flows will yield the same value as the excess earnings method, which splits those cash flows into two components. (See Exhibit 3.)

The excess earnings grow at a constant rate of 2.5% into perpetuity. Exhibit 4 values the noncompete assuming that the probability of competition is 100%, as it may be in many valuations for marital dissolution purposes. The base valuation reflects a DCF model with a uniform growth rate of 2.5%. Note that this DCF produces exactly the

Exhibit 3. Capitalization of Excess Earnings

Normalized 2002 earnings			$460,000
Fair market earnings			390,000
Excess earnings			70,000
Return on practice tangible value: debt capital	$30,000	4.00%	(1,200)
Return on practice tangible value: equity capital	92,500	46.54	(43,046)
	122,500		
Excess earnings attributable to intangibles			25,754
Capitalization rate			46.54%
Practice intangible value			55,341
Practice tangibles			122,500
Business enterprise value			177,841

same value as the capitalization of cash flows and capitalization of excess earnings method.[3]

The section of Exhibit 4 titled "Noncompete Valuation—Using WACC" values the cash flows attributable to the seller using the WACC of 41.86%. This is less than the cost of equity, of 49.04%, and therefore, results in a higher value. Use of the WACC would be appropriate if the analyst concludes that the cash flows attributable to the seller are a uniform blend of enterprise-level cash flows from both tangibles and intangibles. The section of Exhibit 4 titled "Noncompete Valuation–Using Equity Discount Rate" values the cash flows attributable to the seller using the equity discount rate of 49.04% and results in a lower value. This would be appropriate if the analyst concludes that the cash flows attributable to the seller are limited to those associated with intangibles. The value is identical to the value of intangibles previously determined. This is due to the probability of competition being 100%.

Probability of Competition

In addition to the factors discussed in the first part of this article, the analyst should consider how the noncompete is paid for. Payments are often made annually over the period of time that the covenant is in place as part of the inducement to the covenantor not to compete. Such a payment structure is likely to reduce the probability of competition.

Key Conclusions

Personal goodwill is the asset that generates cash profits of the enterprise that are attributed to the business generating characteristics of the individual and may include any profits that would be lost if the individual was not present.

3 Using end-of-period cash flows. It will not produce the same result if the midperiod convention is used, since that convention results in a higher value.

Exhibit 4. Valuation of Noncompete

		1	2	3	4	5	Terminal
Base valuation, constant growth							
Free cash flow		$70,000	$71,750	$73,544	$75,382	$77,267	$201,210
Present value	$177,841	$49,344	$35,653	$25,761	$18,613	$13,449	$35,021
Noncompete valuation—using WACC							
% profits attributed to seller		36.79%	36.79%	36.79%	36.79%	36.79%	36.79%
Free cash flow		$25,754	$26,397	$27,057	$27,734	$28,427	$74,027
PV sellers free cash flow	$65,429	$18,154	$13,117	$9,478	$6,848	$4,948	$12,885
Probability of competing		100.00%	100.00%	100.00%	100.00%	100.00%	100.00%
Present value	$65,429	$18,154	$13,117	$9,478	$6,848	$4,948	$12,885
Noncompete valuation—using equity discount rate							
Free cash flow—sellers		$25,754	$26,397	$27,057	$27,734	$28,427	$62,613
PV sellers free cash flow	$55,341	$17,280	$11,884	$8,173	$5,621	$3,866	$8,515
Probability of competing		100.00%	100.00%	100.00%	100.00%	100.00%	100.00%
Present value	$55,341	$17,280	$11,884	$8,173	$5,621	$3,866	$8,515

Tasks for the analyst:

- Identify which portions of cash flow are attributable directly to the individual's characteristics and which cash flows attributable to otherwise enterprise-level intangibles would be lost if the individual competed.

- Have a clear understanding from legal counsel of the proper interpretation of state law or precedent as to the value of a noncompete—and, therefore, the business itself. An unenforceable contract has little if any value. Even enforceable agreements are subject to "the hazards of litigation."[4] Similarly, the analyst should read all contracts between the valuation subject and its employees or others that may have a bearing on who owns what and obtain clarification from counsel as appropriate.

- Conduct a proper reasonable compensation analysis because an understatement of reasonable compensation will result in an overstatement of goodwill.

4 A term of art used to explain why unwinnable cases are won and unlosable cases are lost.

- Estimate the fair market value of the three principal categories of assets included in BEV: NWC, fixed assets, and intangible assets.

- Consider the need to value individual intangible assets, such as workforce in place. Recognize that a portion of the value of the workforce in place could be attributable to the noncompete if the agreement contains a nonsolicitation provision.

- Construct a joint probability table to be certain that the sum of the probability of competing and not competing is exactly 100%.

Chapter 17

Why Transaction Structure Affects Value and Other Nuances of Valuing Medical Practices

By Mark O. Dietrich, CPA/ABV

A Review of Complex Tax Issues

Defining the standard and premise of value, such as fair market value, on a going concern basis; the interest being valued, such as market value of invested vapital (MVIC) or equity; and the level of value, control or noncontrol, is not the end of the story. Substantial differences in the concluded value of an interest should result when the transaction contemplated by the engagement is an asset transaction or a stock transaction. Further, some apparent stock transactions should be treated as if they were asset transactions due to requirements of the Internal Revenue Code, and a variety of other code provisions influence the ultimate valuation result. Finally, the cost approach for the valuation of intangible assets is not appropriate for the valuation of a medical practice for transfer to a tax-exempt hospital if the intangible have less or no value under the income approach.

Fair Market Value?

Many times, appraisers feel that the specifics of a transaction are outside the scope of their assignment, citing the "hypothetical" buyer and seller as a rationale such that looking at the specific terms of the transaction would represent strategic value. This represents a misunderstanding of the term "hypothetical" within the context of an actual transaction. The hypothetical refers to the buyer and seller and their price motivations being consistent with fair market value. It does *not* refer to the specific interest being valued. For example, a hypothetical buyer and seller would pay two different prices for a business where one contemplated transaction included a noncompete from a seller capable of competing post-transaction and the other excluded such a noncompete. Thus, the specific transaction terms for a business result in different values under the fair market value standard.

In healthcare appraisal and transaction, fair market value is modified by the statutory and regulatory constraints of the Stark laws, the anti-kickback statute, anti-inurement provisions of the Internal Revenue Code, and, as described below, other tax statutes and regulations. Proper application of the government restrictions on the underlying motivations of the buyer and seller and the resultant price that can be paid for a business must of necessity be part of the consideration of Fair Market Value; the law always trumps *perceived* differences with appraisal standards. Certainly, a hypothetical buyer subject to fair market value would not pay anything for an illegal cocaine dealership, recognizing that law enforcement officials could confiscate not only all the assets of the business but also any assets acquired from income generated by the business—to say nothing of sending the owner to prison. The anti-kickback statute, coupled with the False Claims Act, works in much the same way.

Stock and Asset Transactions

The principal difference between an asset transaction and a stock transaction, of course, is that in an asset transaction, the buyer obtains a basis step-up in fixed assets and if intangible value is present, a code section 197 asset that can be amortized over 15 years. These added depreciation and amortization deductions create additional value[1] in an asset transaction because they reduce future taxable income and taxes, thus making after-tax cash flow higher. In contrast, when valuing an equity interest, only the pre-existing basis of depreciable and any intangible assets is used for purposes of computing future depreciation and amortization deductions. Thus, after-tax cash flow and value are lower.

Unlike the generic market value of invested capital, or right-hand side of the balance sheet approach to valuation, medical practices and other healthcare enterprises should also be viewed from the asset, or left-hand, side.[2] In structuring a discounted cash flow model for an asset transaction, it is advisable for the appraiser to, at least, estimate the value of underlying assets using the residual method of allocation under Section 338; otherwise, the necessary depreciation and amortization deductions cannot be incorporated into the valuation model. This method first allocates value to cash, then receivables and inventory, fixed assets, various intangibles, and finally, goodwill. It is

1 Generally, pretax proceeds are higher to both buyer and seller, but not after-tax for the seller; for the buyer, individual asset components must be analyzed to determine the difference between pre- and after-tax value.

2 See the 5th Circuit of Appeals decision in *Caracci/Sta-Home* for a good explanation of why.

comparatively easy to estimate the value of cash and receivables, of course. An appraiser with industry experience can often obtain sufficient knowledge of the fixed assets from studying the depreciation schedule and other records of historic acquisitions and inquiries of management to estimate that value. Good examples of where this is possible include ophthalmology and optometry practices, imaging centers, and dental practices.

For tax purposes, code section 1060 requires buyer and seller to file a statement with their tax returns for the year of sale (Form 8594) indicating the allocation of the transaction value to the underlying assets. Many times this may seem outside the scope of the typical asset transaction appraisal, but to reiterate, the depreciation and amortization deductions directly affect the concluded value, creating the equivalent of an algebraic simultaneous equation: The total value of the assets cannot be known until allocation of that value to each class of assets is known.

Healthcare Transactions, in Particular

"Where ignorance is bliss, 'tis folly to be wise"[3] seemingly defines the state of appraisal engagements in the healthcare industry, with methodologies debunked in the 1990s reappearing and lessons learned then forgotten or overlooked.

Cash-Basis Taxpayers

One advantage that CPAs often have over competing appraisers is their familiarity with tax law as a result of providing tax services in addition to performing business valuations. Medical practices are a peculiar beast in this regard.

IRC section 441 permits "qualified personal service corporations" (PSCs) of practically any size to utilize the cash method of accounting. The price paid for this flexibility is that PSCs are subject to a flat 35% federal corporate tax rate and cannot use the graduated rates available to other (small) businesses. For CPAs or other appraisers unfamiliar with cash-basis taxpayers, the cash method creates some interesting issues to be addressed in valuation, particularly when addressing "normal" working capital.

Year-End Tax Planning

Many valuations take place at the end of a company's fiscal year. For a closely held accrual method taxpayer, IRC section 267 may require any bonuses to stockholder-management and family members, as well as related entity transaction, to be settled via a cash payment, but unrelated trade payables and (many[4]) accrued expenses can be deducted irrespective of whether they have been paid in cash.

3 *Ode on a Distant Prospect of Eton College,* Thomas Gray's poem, 1742

4 Accruals treated as "deferred compensation" such as those for uncompensated absences are one troublesome aspect.

For a cash-method taxpayer, virtually all expenses have to have been paid in cash by the end of the year to be deducted in computing taxable income for that year. The primary exception is the deduction for qualified retirement plan contributions, which can be deducted for a given year if paid over to the plan before the due date (including extensions) of the tax return—which is the 15th day of the third month after the tax year closes, or if a valid extension is filed, the 15th day of the ninth month after the tax year closes.

As a result of the differences in tax planning between a cash-method and accrual-method taxpayer, there may be significant differences in the historical working capital levels for a cash-basis taxpayer at the end of a taxable year versus an accrual-method taxpayer. One thing that is common to cash-basis medical practices is paying all available trade payables at year end, before paying out "bonuses" as part of "zeroing out" taxable income. Many practices, in fact, pay bonuses only once a year at year-end such that during the year, there may be significant accumulations of cash—resulting in *apparent* excess working capital when looking at a cash-basis balance sheet since accrued bonuses will not be reflected. Depending upon the reason for the valuation, this excess can be addressed in several different ways.

1. Treat as excess working capital and add back to operating asset value.
2. Accrue a bonus to extent of apparent excess cash less outstanding trade payables, based upon historic practice.
3. Normalize working capital to industry levels for an accrual taxpayer and reassess the presence of excess working capital.

Observation

When preparing a discounted cashflow method valuation under the income approach, there is likely to be a significant difference between the historical working capital and the "normal" working capital for a hypothetical nonphysician practice buyer. As such, if possible, a thorough analysis of current and prior years' balance sheets should be made, and each year should be converted to a "full" accrual basis. Besides obvious accruals that are typically made for accounts receivable, there may be inventories and prepaid items on the asset side that the valuation analyst or appraiser will have to identify through inquiry or analysis.[5] On the liability side, there are often little readily available historical data for payables or accruals. The lack of historical data can make conversion of prior-year balance sheets problematic.

5 Privately held companies typically focus on tax minimization in their bookkeeping and tax filings. As such, "product" inventories, such as chemotherapy drugs, could be understated, and supplies inventories, such as X-ray film or MRI and CT contrast, may not even be recorded.

Working capital is, of course, equal to current assets less current liabilities. If accruals for inventories and prepaids are not made, current assets will be understated and existing working capital understated.[6] This could, in turn, lead to a failure to properly calculate any excess working capital. Similarly, if accounts payable or accrued items are not reflected—considered in light of cash balances not reduced by early payment of these items—working capital could be overstated along with any excess working capital—or a deficit in working capital could be understated. In the assessment of normal working capital, cash balances and accounts payable are closely tied for the typical medical practice.

Section 448

Less well-known than the nuances of cash-basis tax planning and working capital is the requirement under section 448 that the acquisition of 80% or more of the stock of a cash-method taxpayer by an accrual method taxpayer requires the cash-method taxpayer to convert to the accrual method as of the transaction date if the combined entities' receipts exceed $5 million. For purposes of section 448, the two entities are treated as one under Section 448(c)(2)'s aggregation rules. This typically occurs because the acquirer (a hospital or related entity, private equity entity, or public company) is not eligible for PSC status, and the cash-basis of accounting is only available generally to entities with less than $5 million in gross receipts.

Section 337

Prior to the Tax Reform Act of 1986, C corporations could liquidate and not incur a tax at the corporate level on any appreciated assets distributed in the liquidation. Since that legislation, any liquidation of a C corporation generally subjects the liquidating corporation to tax on the difference between the fair market value of its assets and their tax basis. An election is available to avoid any tax by the acquiring entity electing to take a carryover tax basis in the assets.

Since many hospital-buyers of physician practices are tax-exempt, this may appear not to be an issue. However, hospital buyers of the stock of a physician practice in jurisdictions where the corporate practice of medicine doctrine[7] permits same often plan to convert the for-profit practice to tax exempt status. *Section 337(d)(4) specifically treats the conversion to tax-exempt status as if an asset sale had taken place, resulting in a gain at the corporate level.* The IRS has long taken[8] two significant positions with respect to acquisi-

6 This also has implications for the net asset value or asset accumulation approach.

7 An excellent if perhaps dated discussion is in the IRS Exempt Organizations CPE Text *Corporate Practice of Medicine* by Charles Kaiser III and Marvin Friedlander; another source is *Corporate Practice of Medicine Doctrine 50 State Survey Summary* by the firm Boerner Van Deuren s.c. in conjunction with the National Hospice and Palliative Care Organization (NHPCO) and the Center to Advance Palliative Care (CAPC)

8 2000 Exempt Organizations CPE Text *Treas. Reg. Section 1.337(d)-4 and Exempt Organizations* by Charles Kaiser III and Thomas Miller

tion of a taxable healthcare corporation's stock by a tax-exempt entity: 1) that continuing to operate the acquired corporation as a taxable entity is not an efficient use of the acquirer's tax-exempt status and 2) that the conversion tax must be taken into account by the appraiser in opining on the fair market value of the stock. It is directly analogous to the built-in gains tax in valuing S corporations. Whether and to what extent the tax can be discounted may be open to question in the appraisal community, but it is not clear that the IRS would entertain such a discount if the conversion is contemplated at the time of the sale of the stock.

> If the hospital purchases the C corporation's stock, the corporate level tax is borne while the corporation is owned by the exempt hospital, and does not reduce the proceeds available to the selling physician-shareholders. However, in an arm's-length purchase, the buyer would pay less for the stock than it would for the net assets because the buyer assumes the burden of the corporate level tax on the assets built-in appreciation. Thus, the hospital's failure to make a downward adjustment to the fair market value of the stock, as determined by an independent appraisal, to reflect the corporate level tax might be viewed as a private benefit to the selling physicians.
>
> Under Reg. 1.337(d)-4, a taxable corporation that transfers substantially all its assets to a tax-exempt organization must recognize gain or loss at the time of the transaction. The corporate tax is imposed on the taxable corporation. The act of transferring is referred to as the Asset Sale Rule under Reg. 1.337(d)-4(a)(1). It is very important to understand that transferring assets includes liquidating the corporation's assets, which was previously a taxable event to the taxable corporation, *as well as transferring the taxable corporation's stock, which is considered an asset under IRC 1.337(d)-4.*" [to wit, Reg. 1.337(d)-4(a)(2) states: "For example, if a state, a political subdivision thereof, or an entity any portion of whose income is excluded from gross income under section 115 acquires the stock of a taxable corporation and thereafter any of the taxable corporation's income is excluded from gross income under section 115, the taxable corporation will be treated as if it transferred all of its assets to a tax-exempt entity immediately before the stock acquisition." (Note: The meaning of the italicized portion of this statement is not clear; however, it appears that the statement would be incorrect if the intent was to make the mere transfer of the stock an asset gain recognition event in the selling corporation. It is possible it refers to a subsequent transfer of the stock by the acquirer.)
>
> Under Reg. 1.337(d)-4, if a taxable corporation converts to a tax-exempt organization, the taxable corporation must pay the corporate taxes. The act of conversion is referred to as the Change in Status Rule under Reg. 1.337(d)-4(a)(2). Thus, the corporate level tax is borne while the taxable corporation's stock is owned by the selling physician/stockholders, which ultimately reduces their available proceeds.

Reg. 1.337(d)-4(a)(4)(b) provides that if an asset will be used partly or wholly in an exempt entity's IRC 511(a) activity, the taxable corporation will recognize an amount of gain or loss that bears the same ratio to the asset's built-in gain or loss as 100% reduced by the percentage of use in the IRC 511(a) activity bears to 100%.

A taxable professional medical corporation, C, merges with a tax-exempt affiliate of hospital A or medical foundation B, created by A to operate C. After Jan. 28, 1999, this A reorganization is subject to gain or loss recognition by C, and payment of corporate tax on gain by C.[9]

When valuing a medical practice for acquisition by an exempt entity, it is wise to consider whether section 337 has an impact similar to that of the rules for estate tax valuation (Chapter 6) and ESOP valuations. If, however, one ignores the statutory and regulatory construct, this raises two issues for the appraiser:

- Would the hypothetical buyer of the subject—whether it be a C corporation, a tax-exempt, or some other form of business enterprise—liquidate the target to obtain a basis step-up in the underlying assets to fair market value; and

- Would that hypothetical buyer insist on a discount equal to the tax incurred on liquidation.

If the answer to the first question is yes, then the expected basis step-up to be obtained in the liquidation has to be taken into account in the appraisal via the higher depreciation and amortization deductions described above! This will result in higher sales proceeds to the seller, partially compensating it for the loss of capital gains treatment. Thus, employing the proper approach to the appraisal—assets versus stock—is necessary.

If the answer to the first question is an unqualified no, the second question may be evaluated in the more traditional built-in gains tax approach. Typically, one would not expect a hypothetical buyer of a going concern operating company to insist on any built-in gain discount for the underlying operating assets inside a corporation. By the same token, a properly undertaken appraisal would not reflect any of the value associated with an asset acquisition, effectively building the discount into the price.

If the specific tax-exempt buyer does, in fact, intend to convert the target corporation to exempt status, buyer and seller may have an issue independent of the appraisal, depending upon the appraiser's assessment of the hypothetical buyer and seller. This requires a more complex assessment of hypothetical buyer and seller driven by local market conditions and jurisdictional rules. For example, if a medical practice transaction takes

9 *Treas. Reg. Section 1.337(d)-4 and Exempt Organizations*, ibid.

place in a state where only a licensed physician or another professional corporation can own the stock, an asset transaction may effectively be the only way to consummate the sale. A variant on this circumstance may occur if the state permits the stock to be held through a so-called friendly PC, where a physician employed by the acquiring entity is the nominal owner of the stock, but all the rights of that stock are effectively held by the acquirer. This suggests that an asset transaction is not mandated.

Another consideration for the appraiser is the use of the cost approach or asset accumulation method to determine net asset value and the impact on the conclusion of value. If net asset value is the concluded value, the appraiser will have to evaluate whether the hypothetical buyer would liquidate the target to acquire the assets or is motivated by avoiding replication cost on a going-concern basis. This may involve consideration of the premise of value and highest and best use of the assets.

Use of the Cost Approach

As enumerated in the CPE texts cited above, the long-standing IRS position is that the use of the cost approach in valuing *intangible* assets of a medical practice is only appropriate if intangible value is first found to be present under the income approach. The 1996 CPE Text explains:

> The value of goodwill can be allocated to specific intangible assets; the value of the latter is limited to the value of the former, as calculated under the income approach. For example, if the total value of the individual intangible assets exceeds the total value of the medical practice net of the aggregate fair market value of the tangible assets, the amount of value that can be allocated among the intangible assets is more limited. Also, it is important to note that intangible value may not always be present in a medical practice. Thus, ascribing value to intangible assets is a matter of allocating value derived using the income approach to specific intangible assets.[10]

In other words, the total value of the individual intangible assets cannot exceed the total value of the medical practice under the income approach, net of the aggregate fair market value of the tangible assets.

The 2008 Tax Court case *Derby*[11] specifically mentions the 1994 CPE Text having to do with integrated delivery systems and how institutions might acquire the assets of a physician practice, including outright purchase, donation, or a combination of both. Irrespective of the means of transfer, the entire transaction is subject to fair market value. Thus, the court's commentary in the *Derby* opinion applies to fair market value in

10 Charles F. Kaiser and Amy Henchey, IRS Exempt Organizations Continuing Professional Education Text for FY 1996, Topic Q, "Valuation of Medical Practices" (1996 EO CPE Text), available at www.irs.gov/pub/irs-tege/eotopicq96.pdf

11 *Derby et al v. Commissioner*, T.C. Memo. 2008-45

general, not solely to the specific means of transfer present in the *Derby* matter, namely a charitable donation.

In the following extracts from the opinion, the court highlights what are general principles of transactions: Specific contractual rights are obtained in the exchange, and those rights are subject to valuation.

> More fundamentally, the Dutcher appraisal takes no account of the various contractual rights and other intangible benefits that petitioners and the other SWMG physicians sought and obtained in the transaction with SMF, such as avoiding signing noncompete agreements and obtaining preferred working conditions. Because it does not fully account for the benefits that petitioners received in the transaction with SMF, the Dutcher appraisal does not establish that petitioners contributed property to SMF that exceeded the values of the benefits they received in return.
>
> But when petitioners were offered the opportunity to affiliate with foundation (and receive an outright cash payment for their intangibles), they collectively rejected the prospect in favor of an acquirer that offered them working conditions they preferred, greater economic security through multiple sources of payment, a "free to compete" provision whereby any of them could essentially "unwind" the transaction and retrieve his or her patients if he or she desired to terminate the relationship with the acquirer, a role in management, and other intangible benefits that were negotiated between the SWMG physicians and SMF. Viewed in this light, it is apparent that the intangible benefits that petitioners received in the transaction with SMF were of substantial value to them. Petitioners spurned a cash payment for their medical practice intangibles in order to obtain these benefits in a different transaction.[12]

Where the *Derby* court states ". . . the Dutcher appraisal does not establish that petitioners contributed property to SMF that exceeded the values of the benefits they received in return," it is easy to foresee a circumstance in which a court would similarly state: "The cost approach appraisal of intangible assets does not establish that the sellers transferred property to the buyer that exceeded the value of the tangible assets transferred by the sellers and the contractual employment benefits that the sellers received."

Conclusion

The wave of transactions in healthcare today mirrors that which took place during the 1990s, providing evidence that my late mentor, Jim Rigby, CPA/ABV, ASA was correct when he advised that consolidation trends are cyclical every 10 years or so. It is wise for those new to healthcare appraisal as well as those who have been practicing in the sector since the last consolidation to review the lessons and rules learned in the 1900s.

A version of this material originally appeared in the Spring 2010 (final) edition of the AICPA's CPA Expert.

12 Ibid.

Chapter 18

Supply & Demand: Assessing the Impact of the Shortage of Physicians on Value

By Mark O. Dietrich, CPA/ABV

Introduction

The healthcare delivery system in the United States is in a persistent state of turmoil due to, in order of importance, political, financial, social, and now geopolitical factors representing a healthcare equivalent of the Four Horsemen of the Apocalypse. The next 20 years may well represent the proverbial "perfect storm," with a shortfall of physicians driving the negatives associated with those Four Horsemen ever higher.

Global Factors

Much is made of the fact that the economy is now global with the recent chaos in the financial markets being but one indication that when an investment bank fails in New York, people may starve in the Third World.[1] Not catching any particular attention outside the healthcare community, the rapid economic growth in places such as Pakistan, India, and, to a lesser extent, China has led to a decline in the retention of international medical graduates (IMGs) who fill many positions in the U.S. healthcare delivery system. IMGs often attend medical school overseas and then train in U.S.-based residency programs in teaching hospitals and their affiliates.

With increasing wealth and opportunity at home, many IMGs are returning to their home countries after training here, and many experienced physicians are returning to their foreign homelands as well. Where incomes and lifestyle previously drove the

1 Or, as chaos theory suggests, a butterfly flapping its wings in Florida may cause a volcano to erupt in Polynesia.

decision to practice in the U.S., the ability to export accumulated wealth and then earn a decent living overseas has created a financial incentive for IMGs to leave.

Even "medical tourism" to overseas hospitals that charge significantly less than in the U.S. has become popular. Thus, the U.S. finds itself funding the training of physicians who will practice here for only the short time required to meet their post-training commitment.

Domestic Factors

Virtually all residency training programs are funded by Medicare through supplemental payments to teaching hospitals for direct medical education (DME) and indirect medical education (IME). This is one factor in IMGs' decision to train here. Budgetary pressure on Medicare has led to a failure in funding to keep pace with demand for physician training and services. In fact, the first cutbacks in specialist training date back to the Balanced Budget Act of 1997, during the Clinton Administration, when the drive to managed care demanded more primary care training programs. The number of all residency programs was frozen then and has changed little in nearly 20 years, despite the rapid growth in total population and the average age of that population. A further complication is that aging physicians who retire are not being replaced by new physicians at the same rate. Thus, each new physician graduate of a training program is confronted with a higher per capita patient load.

The distribution of physicians in the U.S. is by no means equal. Exhibit 1, taken from CMS 2007 Medicare and Medicaid Statistics, displays wide disparities in the locations where physicians choose to practice. This disparity is sometimes driven by the tendency to stay in the area where one trains. Other factors include standard of living, lifestyle, and significant differences in income opportunities and levels of reimbursement from health insurers, among others.

Financial Effects

Basic economic theory would suggest that as the demand for a service provider rises and the supply of that provider remains fixed or falls, the price of retaining that provider will increase. In fact, this is what is happening. However, the reimbursement system in the form of health insurers and government programs does not respond to the physician shortage for reasons that would be inexplicable were it not for political and legislative factors.

The compound growth rate in the payment by the Medicare program for the last 11 years is in the vicinity of 0.4% (four-tenths), while inflation has averaged 2.5% to 3.5% per annum in physician office operating costs. Congress has continually declined to fix

Exhibit 1. Part B practitioners / CMS region

	Active practitioners	Practitioners per 100,000 population
All regions[1]	1,226,327	414
Boston	95,316	669
New York	145,680	457
Philadelphia	130,492	453
Atlanta	218,627	381
Chicago	208,189	406
Dallas	116,451	327
Kansas City	61,934	467
Denver	45,527	456
San Francisco	149,235	326
Seattle	54,876	456

[1]Nonfederal physicians only. Includes limited licensed, nonphysician practitioners.
Unduplicated count (may include practitioners practicing in multiple sites or states).
Unknown provider states distributed. Notes:
Physicians as of March 2007. Civilian population as of July 1, 2005. Resident population for outlying areas and the Virgin Islands are not available.
Sources: CMS, ORDI, and the Bureau of the Census.

the underlying formula that limits increases. The compound growth rate in the Producer Price Index for physician services reflecting annual rate increases in the broader health insurance world is 1.9% in this same period. Some of this mismatch has been offset by "intensity of service," where the physician bills for a higher level of service than might otherwise be expected and therefore, receives a higher payment.

The rapid expansion of physician-based high-tech imaging, such as ultrasound, CT, and MRI, has allowed selected specialties, such as orthopedics and cardiology, to maintain and enhance their incomes, but such opportunities are outside the reach of most primary care physicians, who will be one focus of the remainder of this chapter.

As can be expected from the historical pattern of responses with respect to excessive utilization, the payment per unit of service side of high-tech imaging was reined in by the Deficit Reduction Act of 2005. The outright availability of physician office-based imaging as an option was significantly constrained by new regulations in the summer of 2008 prohibiting so-called "per-click" leases of equipment. New proposed regulations, if adopted, will likely require physician-based imaging operations to register under Medicare's Independent Diagnostic Testing Facility (IDTF) rules, which are far more restrictive. Further, existing IDTFs are now precluded from sharing their facilities with third-party users under lease arrangements. Finally, it is possible that an IDTF may be required to have a radiologist (or even an employed radiologist) on-site when services are provided, which would force many physician-based imaging facilities to close.

Despite numerous attempts over the years, physicians have been denied legislatively and administratively the ability to jointly negotiate for fees due to both federal and state antitrust policy. In fact, the federal government policy is quite explicit, if perhaps inexplicable, in this regard:

> Indeed, even if we assume physicians confront a monopsonist health plan that neither unlawfully acquired nor unlawfully exercised that power, authorizing physicians to engage in collusive conduct will not serve the interests of consumers. A health insurer with monopsony power is likely to impose quantity restrictions that will increase prices for consumers. If providers were to acquire countervailing market power, the result is likely to be further quantity restrictions—increasing the prices paid by consumers above those already imposed by the monopsonist.[2]

**A monopsonist refers to a situation in which there is a single buyer in a market, similar to a monopolist, which refers to a single seller in a market.*

Thus, there are nearly insurmountable barriers to the ability of physicians to increase their income as might otherwise be expected in any unregulated sector of the economy where the forces of supply and demand are allowed to operate freely. Hospitals, which rely upon physicians to provide the patients that they generate revenue from, have stepped into this void by recruiting and employing physicians at salaries in excess of what they might otherwise earn. This, in turn, has led to both increased regulatory risk—because federal law precludes paying for patient referrals—and a drain on the financial resources of the hospitals.

Primary Care Physicians

Perhaps the most dramatic physician shortage will be among primary care physicians, including general internal medicine, family medicine, and others collectively referred to as "generalists." Managed care relied upon these physicians to serve as "gatekeepers," controlling access to specialists and others. That burdensome task has become increasingly untenable as the volume of patients per generalist increases.

The Association of American Medical Colleges (AAMC) now recommends increasing medical school class sizes by 30 percent, based on the above factors as well as on the rising demand historically associated with economic growth and concern that U.S. overdependence on international medical graduates (IMGs) is causing a physician "brain drain" from third-world countries....

2 "Improving Health Care: A Dose of Competition," July 2004, DOJ and FTC.

The U.S. population is expected to increase 18 percent between 2005 and 2025, to 349 million. During the same period, the population above age 65 will increase 73 percent. This group seeks care from generalists almost three times per year—twice the rate of those under age 65....

If the 2002-2005 rate of decline continues through 2008, the supply of generalists to provide adult care in 2025 will be only 2 percent above 2005 levels.... In the face of a 29 percent increase in workload, the adjusted supply figures point to a 20 percent shortage of adult care generalists in 2025, or 27 percent if graduate declines continue through 2008. These translate into shortfalls of 35,000-44,000 adult care generalists, assuming that generalists maintain current numbers of visits.[3]

Effect on Value

The increase in the price (salary) of physician-employees relative to physicianowners has implications for the value of existing medical practices. Often unable to earn a salary commensurate with employment plus a return on investment, physicians are increasingly disinclined to buy practices. When there is a shortage of buyers for a product, price drops to meet available demand!

Value is also driven by factors such as ease of entry into the market. A high demand for services and few providers leads to long patient waits and eases market-entry barriers because developing a patient base is easier. High recruiting salaries and incentives decrease the potential "profit," or added earnings, from buying a practice. Value is the risk-adjusted present value of future cash flow. Even though the risk associated with the income stream of a practice may be low due to high demand, the income spread between owners and nonowners is declining and value is declining along with it.

Of course, it is important to observe that notwithstanding the overall national conditions described herein, many localized anomalies exist, such as the physician distribution in Exhibit 1. Healthcare markets are unique and are defined by a variety of economic, demographic, and sociopolitical factors, including:

- total Medicare and Medicare spending per capita,
- the presence and market strength of Blue Cross plans,
- the degree of market strength of local nonprofit hospitals versus for-profit hospitals,

3 "Will Generalist Physician Supply Meet Demands of an Increasing and Aging Population?" Jack M. Colwill, James M. Cultice, and Robin L. Kruse; *Health Affairs*, 29 April 2008.

- the degree of market strength of local nonprofit health insurers versus for-profit health insurers and their concentration of market power (the monopsony described earlier),
- Certificate of Need laws, and
- other local demographic and economic factors.[4]

As such, it would be inaccurate to conclude that physician practices are being devalued in every market. A good place to start with the evaluation is the "market prices" (salaries) offered to new and established physicians to relocate as reflected in annual surveys such as that by the recruiting firm Merritt Hawkins. When a coherent database of physician practice sale transactions does not exist, the data on physician incomes is more readily available.

Practices will continue to exist with unique income earning opportunities,, including those able to maintain ancillary income streams, operate surgery centers for surgical specialties, and possess superior contracts from health insurers resulting in better rates of pay per service. It will, therefore, be incumbent on the valuation analyst to focus on the data associated with those unique opportunities in the data collection and interview process. In addition, assessment of the prospects for continuation of those unique income streams at a given level and the underlying risk associated with them will be critical to the valuation conclusion. As observed above, the crackdown on high-tech imaging is part of a long-term pattern of governmental response to excessive healthcare spending, with physicians and other Medicare Part B providers a primary target.

4 "Healthcare Market Structure and Its Implication for Valuation of Privately Held Provider Entities: An Empirical Analysis," *Business Valuation Review*, Summer 2008 by Mark Dietrich.

Chapter 19

What Goes Around Comes Around: *Derby v. Commissioner*

By Mark O. Dietrich, CPA/ABV

Established healthcare valuation principles from the 1990s remain in full force and effect.

The tax court case *Derby, et al. v. Commissioner*[1] is important for a variety of reasons, not the least of which is its instructive value as today's consolidation in the healthcare industry mirrors that in the early and mid-1990s when the *Derby* case originated. Key factors in the case include those which this author has repeatedly cited in numerous articles over the last 10 years in *CPA Expert* and the *Journal of Accountancy,* among others. Those factors are as follows:

1. The use of expected post-transaction physician compensation in the discounted cash flow model based on the transaction documents *rather than* use of some arbitrary compensation figure, such as the median, for a given physician specialty.
2. Allocating enterprise or invested capital value among working capital, fixed assets, and intangible assets.
3. Carefully studying transaction documents to discern the character and extent of any intangibles being transferred or not being transferred.
4. The critical import of allocating between personal and professional goodwill and enterprise goodwill when valuing a medical practice for acquisition by a hospital.

1 *Charles A. and Marian L. Derby, et al.,1 Petitioners v. Commissioner,* Respondent, T.C. Memo. 2008-45, Gale, Judge.

5. The importance of any noncompete agreement in determining the value of the medical practice and the import of *Norwalk v. Commissioner.*

6. The need for "donative intent" when claiming a deduction for the value of a medical practice or other enterprise allegedly donated to a tax-exempt entity.

7. The relevance of the Friendly Hills private letter ruling and the 1994 Exempt Organizations Continuing Professional Education Technical Instruction Program manuals.

8. The citation of the anti-kickback statute (AKS).

9. The issue of the timeliness of the valuation versus the date of the transaction.

This is a well-written decision that highlights the typical issues in the valuation of a physician practice for sale or other transfer to a hospital or integrated delivery system. As such, Judge Gale's words are frequently quoted.

Case Summary

The case arose out of a claimed charitable deduction for the intangible value of the medical practices of more than a dozen physicians who sold their medical practices to Sutter Medical Foundation (Sutter) in 1994. The purchase agreements contained payments for fixed assets, while the selling physicians retained their accounts receivable.

The transaction took place during the period of consolidation of the healthcare industry associated with the rise of managed care and capitation on the West Coast in the early 1990s, which later spread across the country. Although restrictive managed care and capitation have fallen into disfavor and lost market share over the last six or seven years, consolidation is once again the rage in healthcare. Although some markets, such as Boston, are reconsidering the use of capitation, much of the present consolidation is driven by the more typical revenue concerns associated with fee for service medicine. Major hospital and ancillary testing revenue sources, such as cardiology, orthopedics, and high-tech imaging, are driving many of today's transactions.

The key decisions for the court were whether there had, in fact, been a *donative* transfer of intangible value, what the value was, and *if* the claimed value of the donation was overstated, whether the donor-physicians were subject to understatement of overvaluation penalties. As such, the valuations submitted by the taxpayers in connection with the donation received careful scrutiny from the court.

Critical in the ultimate resolution of the donation issue was a review of the history of the transaction with Sutter, which had declined to *pay* anything for intangible value, citing the AKS and the "famous" Thornton Letter in which the then Deputy Counsel of the Office of the Inspector General stated that a sale of goodwill by a physician to a hospital was problematic. Peter Grant, legal counsel in the seminal integrated delivery system transaction of the 1990s, represented the *Derby* physicians known as the Davis Medical Group (DMG).

> Unlike Foundation, Sutter Health was unwilling to pay anything for the intangible assets, or goodwill, that might be associated with petitioners' medical practices ... first, and principally, because Sutter Health's management believed that doing so might constitute a crime under the Medicare and Medicaid antikickback statute, 42 U.S.C. Sec. 1320a-7b(b), prohibiting payments for referrals of patients eligible for Medicare or Medicaid; and second, because Sutter Health's management believed, on the basis of their projections of the financial performance of the UHMG physicians' group after acquisition, that any additional payment for intangibles would have rendered the deal financially nonviable for Sutter Health.
>
> Mr. Grant recommended that petitioners structure the transfers of the intangibles as donations because that technique had been used in connection with an acquisition of a group medical practice by a nonprofit medical foundation (*Friendly Hills Healthcare Foundation*), for which Mr. Grant had served as an adviser. Mr. Grant was familiar with the annual *Exempt Organizations Continuing Professional Education Technical Instruction Program manuals*, including the manual for 1994.... *[Emphasis added]*

Transaction Overview

The parties retained Houlihan Lokey (Houlihan), the valuation firm in the Friendly Hills transaction, and arranged for an appraisal of the "business enterprise value" defined below. Note the emphasized items.

> The fair market value of the aggregate assets of [the Davis Medical Group] *exclusive of any benefit or element of value conferred upon Sutter* [Health] as a consequence of its current or proposed relationship with.... [Davis Medical Group], and *with consideration of proposed post-transaction compensation and benefits to the physician group.*

Houlihan also agreed to "allocate the appraised value ... to each of its physician/shareholders" using a method to be agreed upon in consultation [physician] steering committee, but the agreed-upon method "[had to] be acceptable to Houlihan." *[Emphasis added]*

SWMG (Davis Medical Group later changed its name to Sutter West Medical Group, or SWMG) entered into a professional services agreement (PSA) or employment contract with Sutter as part of the transaction.[2] The court spelled out the key economic terms of the PSA, which included a very limited noncompete—the terms of which are critical in this valuation and, for that matter, any such valuation—and a complex revenue sharing formula that included a minimum compensation guaranty. The PSA also contained what amounted to a signing bonus that the court would see as in part a payment for goodwill.

> The PSA contained a noncompete provision, under which SWMG and its physician shareholder/employees were prohibited from participating in the ownership, management, operation, or control of any business or person providing healthcare services within the service area covered by the agreement. However, specifically exempted from this prohibition was any SWMG physician who left the employment of SWMG.... Departing physician may give written notice to the departing physician's patients named in the departing physician's patient list furnished to SMF on or before the ... effective date ... announcing the departing physician's separation from ... SWMG and his or her new practice location, and offering the patient an opportunity to choose whether his or her patient records should remain with SMF or be transferred to the departing physician.
>
> To provide an incentive to SWMG to form and sustain a group, SMF will pay SWMG a physician access bonus.... The "physician access bonus" was $35,000 for each of SWMG's full-time physicians.

The transaction documents stated that the seller and buyer believed the purchase price was less than the fair market value and that the difference was being donated. Significantly, the document contained a provision requiring the appraisal be completed within 60 days—designed to avoid a "stale" valuation. Finally, a discounted cashflow model was used. All of the factors outlined in the case closely track the Friendly Hills private letter ruling and the *1994 Exempt Organizations Continuing Professional Education Technical Instruction Program* manual.

As discussed above, the donation was to be allocated among 29 physicians who formed the group practice based on the valuation. In actuality, the donation was allocated using a formula designed by one of the physicians that attributed "(i) 50% of the aggregate value on the basis of each physician's share of gross revenues generated in the year preceding the transfer to SMF; (ii) 25% on the basis of each physician's 'years in the community,' with up to a maximum of five years being counted; and (iii) 25% on the basis of each physician's share of the aggregate fixed assets transferred to SMF by the SWMG physicians." Although the physicians attached a Form 8283 to their tax returns, Sutter never reflected the donation in its tax return—despite the transaction documents obligating it to do so.

2 This is a standard feature of purchase transactions.

Taxpayers' Valuation for Trial

For healthcare industry appraisers and valuation analysts, the issues surrounding the appraisal submitted for trial are the most important. Perhaps the most significant feature of the appraisal prepared for the trial was the use of median compensation for the physician-sellers rather than the actual compensation negotiated in the transaction! This remains an item of ill-considered debate and frequently results in mistaken assumptions in physician practice and other professional practice valuation, despite being long-settled and in direct conflict with fair market value.[3] The question can be stated as follows: Would the hypothetical buyer pay a price for the practice based on a *lower* compensation than he or she intended to pay post-transaction, thereby paying twice to the extent of the extra compensation.[4]

> ... the national median for the "Western Region" for a weighted average of the medical specialties comprising SWMG, or 45.18%" in determining the physician compensation expense for the discounted cashflow model.[5] *However, the actual negotiated compensation negotiated in the transaction "provided for compensation to SWMG equal to 57.75% of fee-for-service revenue, 47% to 53% of capitation revenue, and at least 55% of risk pool revenue. [Emphasis added]*

The Dutcher Appraisal contained other significant weaknesses in the view of the court. There was no allocation of any intangible value to the professional goodwill of the physicians[6] as opposed to enterprise goodwill, which the court differentiated as follows:

> ... no allocation of any value to the professional goodwill of the SWMG physicians despite the fact that Mr. Dutcher distinguishes, in the case of the goodwill of a professional practice, between "practice" goodwill and "professional" goodwill, the former attributable to characteristics of the practice entity such as patient records, provider contracts, and workforce in place; and the latter attributable to the personal attributes of the individual practitioner, such as charisma, skill, and reputation and he acknowledge[d] that professional goodwill is not transferable.

Dutcher's testimony that professional goodwill is not transferable would have been one of many fatal blows to the taxpayers' position. The court went on to discuss the lack of noncompete agreements and importantly emphasized the continuing viability of *Norwalk v. Commissioner*,[7] perhaps the seminal case on the ownership and valuation

3 See, e.g., "Medical Practices: A BV RX," *Journal of Accountancy*, November 2005.

4 Besides the inurement risk under the Internal Revenue Code, this error creates risk under the AKS and Stark laws.

5 The phrase "national median for the 'Western Region'" appears to be a misnomer. The data were taken from the MGMA *Physician Compensation Survey* 1994 report based on 1993 data.

6 "Identifying And Measuring Personal Goodwill in a Professional Practice," *CPA Expert*, Spring 2005 and Summer 2005.

7 T.C. Memo. 1998-279; See "Goodwill Requires Enforceable Covenant Not to Compete," *CPA Expert*, Spring 1999.

of personal goodwill and noncompetes. A noncompete is the contractual basis for transferring personal or professional goodwill to an employer. The court also observed that the willing buyer would have insisted on "a significant discount" due to the lack of a noncompete!

> There is no adjustment for the fact that the SWMG physicians were not required to execute noncompete agreements. Mr. Dutcher treated each SWMG physician as transferring an allocable share of SWMG's intangibles, including goodwill, which was not treated as diminished in any way by the physicians' not having executed noncompete agreements with respect to SWMG or SMF. However, in *Norwalk v. Commissioner*, T.C. Memo. 1998-279, we found that there is no transferable or salable goodwill where a company's business depends on its employees' personal relationships with clients and the employees have not provided covenants not to compete.... We also believe that, under the willing buyer/willing seller standard of fair market value ... a willing buyer of SWMG on the transaction date would have insisted on a significant discount with respect to the value of the entity's intangible assets, precisely on account of the absence of noncompete agreements from the SWMG physicians.

Other problems cited by the court included the taxpayers' use of an intangible value allocation model developed by one of the taxpayers rather than one based upon sound appraisal techniques and failure to include in the valuation any consideration of the $35,000 signing bonus described above.

The Donation

There is a fundamental requirement in a charitable transfer that the contributor have "donative intent" to receive a tax deduction. Donative intent contemplates a disinterested gift to a charitable organization without the donor receiving any corresponding benefit. It remains commonplace to attempt to structure physician practice transfers as part-sale, part-donation in the current environment.

> In its analysis of the transaction, the court found that the taxpayers received significant benefits from the transaction that belied any intent to make a disinterested donation with no consideration in return. The court cited the advantages of patient retention, negotiating leverage as part of a larger system, compensation based upon a percentage of net revenue, all of which was embodied in an employment contract with "carefully delineated terms."

Conclusion

Consolidation trends are cyclical and the wave that collapsed 10 years ago in the healthcare industry is back yet again. *Derby* reminds us that the old adage "those who fail to learn from history are doomed to repeat it" remains in full force and effect. From the standpoint of the hypothetical buyer, the court reiterated old guidance with respect to the common sense requirement that the value of the practice be based on expected post-transaction compensation. Equally important, the court restated the principles espoused in the *Norwalk* case that contracts—in this case the purchase and sale and professional services agreement—be part of the analysis of intangible value due to the impact of (any) noncompete agreements. Thus, when valuing a medical practice for purposes of an actual transaction, the appraiser must be familiar with the terms of that transaction if the buyer and seller are to rely upon it for regulatory purposes. As the court seemed to suggest of the appraisal submitted by the taxpayers in this case, something other than that which the parties transacted was valued. Transactional valuation *requires* understanding the terms of the transaction to opine on fair market value.

Chapter 20

Converting Physician Practices to Tax-Exempt Status: Is There an Upside to the Downturn?

By Mark O. Dietrich, CPA/ABV

Historically, hospitals and physician practices have integrated for a variety of non-tax-related reasons. Integrated delivery systems provide hospitals with immediate direct revenues from an expanded patient base and offer the potential for substantial indirect revenues flowing from inpatient referrals. The physicians who sell their practice may benefit from having access to an established hospital and its attendant perks, such as superior managed care contracts and the ability to offer patients a wider range of services. Another particularly significant consideration, given the long-standing opposition of the Federal Trade Commission (FTC) and Department of Justice (DOJ) to physician joint-contracting efforts, includes qualification under the *Copperweld* doctrine,[1] where common legal control permits the negotiation of nonrisk contracts in addition to risk-based and quality-based contracts.

Tax benefits play a role, however. When the acquiring hospital is tax-exempt, another benefit is the ability to operate the acquired physician practice on a tax-exempt basis. The obvious incentive is the ability to retain the practice's profits free of income tax, but this strategy presents a variety of issues.

This article is concerned with the tax aspects of a physician practice's acquisition and conversion to tax-exempt status. Basis tax principles of the transaction are discussed first. The article then explains how to reduce the tax cost of the transaction through proper valuation techniques. The article concludes with a comment on how the current

1 *See Copperweld v. Independence Tube*, 467 U.S. 752 (1984).

economic downturn may benefit acquiring hospitals and selling physicians by reducing their tax cost.

Basic Tax Consequences

A Section 501(c)(3)[2] hospital seeking to acquire a for-profit physician practice to operate on a tax-exempt basis typically structures the acquisition through a newly formed nonprofit corporation, of which the hospital is the sole member and ultimate governing authority. The newly formed entity purchases the practice's assets or stock if the practice is in corporate form. When the physician practice is organized as a Subchapter C corporation, the selling physicians face an unavoidable "double tax" if they sell the corporation's assets to the hospital. First, the corporation pays tax on any gain realized from the sale of its assets,[3] leaving only the after-tax proceeds available for distribution to the physician shareholders. The shareholders are then individually taxed on any distributions received from the corporation.[4] Reversing the two steps does not change the result; double taxation similarly applies if the corporation first distributes its assets to its shareholders, who then sell them to the hospital. The Internal Revenue Service (IRS) illustrated these principles in the following example in its 2000 Exempt Organizations Continuing Professional Education Text (EO CPE Text):

> In 1990, 10 physicians invested $50,000 each ($500,000 in total) in a C corporation to purchase land and construct a freestanding ambulatory surgery center. The ambulatory surgery center was constructed and has thrived. In 1999, the physician-owners decided to sell the center to a local hospital. The hospital wanted to purchase the corporate assets instead of the stock because of liability concerns and to operate as a tax-exempt organization. Assume for this example that the C corporation's basis in its assets is $1 million and it has no liabilities. If it sells its assets to the hospital for $6 million, it will be taxed on its gain (35% × $5 million = $1.75 million), leaving $4.25 million for the physician-shareholders in liquidation. They will net about $2.57 million on the sale after paying individual tax (39.6% × $4.25 million = $1.68 million).[5]

The physician-shareholders can avoid double taxation, however, by instead selling their stock in the C corporation. In a taxable stock purchase, the selling shareholders are still subject to one level of tax on the gain realized from the sale of their stock, but there is no corporate-level tax on the sale. The above example continues:

2 Unless otherwise specified, all section references are to the Internal Revenue Code of 1986, as amended (Code).

3 Code Section 1001.

4 Code Sections 301 and 311.

5 Charles F. Kaiser III and Thomas Miller, *IRS Exempt Organizations Continuing Professional Education Text for FY 2000*, Topic U, Treas. Reg. Section 1.337(d)-4 and Exempt Organizations (2000 EO CPE Text), at p. 3 of the PDF, *available at* www.irs.gov/pub/irs-tege/eotopicu00.pdf.

> In contrast, if the hospital buys the C corporation stock from the physicians, the physicians will be taxed $1.68 million on their gain on the stock, but the corporate tax, $1.75 million, will be deferred.[6]

The preceding example illustrates that the selling shareholders are theoretically able to increase their after-tax proceeds by $1.75 million by selling their stock in the C corporation rather than selling the corporation's assets. But the 2000 EO CPE Text importantly points out that corporate-level tax is not eliminated; it merely shifts to the purchaser. Although the hospital could continue to defer the corporate-level tax as long as it operates the C corporation as a for-profit subsidiary, this is not an effective use of its tax-exempt status. If the hospital wishes to operate the physician practice on a tax-exempt basis, it must either convert the subsidiary to a tax-exempt organization or distribute the subsidiary's assets to itself—both options trigger taxable gain to the hospital.[7]

A hospital engaging in an arm's-length stock purchase should adjust the purchase price to account for the corporate-level tax it would eventually incur on the built-in gain. The failure to consider the tax could constitute a private benefit to the selling shareholders and implicate the anti-inurement or intermediate sanctions provisions of the code.[8] Thus, the shareholders in the preceding example have not necessarily increased their after-tax proceeds by $1.75 million by selling stock rather than assets. An appraisal prepared in connection with such a stock transaction must consider this tax.

Valuing Intangible Assets

An arm's-length acquisition of a physician practice requires an independent appraisal, and thus a 1996 EO CPE Text discussing the valuation of medical practices has become a staple in the healthcare appraisal community.[9] Although instructional on the use of the discounted cash-flow method under the income approach, the document importantly establishes criteria for the allocation of intangible asset value that while basic to valuation theory, are often overlooked in valuing medical practices.

For example, the 1996 EO CPE Text explains that although the value of goodwill can be allocated to specific intangible assets, "the value of the latter is limited to the value of the former, as calculated under the income approach."[10] In other words, the total value of the individual intangible assets cannot exceed the total value of the medical practice net of the aggregate fair market value of the tangible assets.

6 *Id.* at p. 3 of the PDF.

7 Code Sections 311 and 337(b)(2); see Treas. Reg. Section 1.337(d)-4.

8 See 2000 EO CPE Text, supra note 5, at p. 2 of the PDF.

9 Charles F. Kaiser and Amy Henchey, *IRS Exempt Organizations Continuing Professional Education Text for FY 1996*, Topic Q, "Valuation of Medical Practices" (1996 EO CPE Text), *available at* www.irs.gov/pub/irs-tege/eotopicq96.pdf.

10 *Id.* at p. 22 of the PDF.

The authors of the 1996 EO CPE Text also point out that intangible value is not always present in a medical practice, a fact appraisers all too frequently overlook. Rather, they mistakenly attribute value to certain intangible assets even when the discounted cash-flow method shows that the medical practice has no overall intangible value. This error often occurs with intangible assets that are typically valued using the cost method, such as medical records, assembled workforce, and trade name. Appraisers forget that using the cost method to value such intangible assets is only appropriate if the income approach first finds the presence of intangible value.

Personal Versus Enterprise Goodwill

Well-defined tax principles, originally enunciated by the United States Tax Court in *Martin Ice Cream*[11] and *Norwalk*[12] and recently re-emphasized in *Derby*,[13] establish a framework for potentially reducing the value of corporate-level intangible assets, thus reducing the tax cost of converting a physician practice to tax-exempt status. These cases illustrate how to distinguish between personal goodwill, i.e., goodwill owned personally by the business' owners or employees, and goodwill owned by the corporation.

In *Derby*, a group of independent physicians decided to affiliate with a larger healthcare organization and sold the tangible assets of their practices to a tax-exempt medical foundation that was affiliated with multiple hospitals in an integrated delivery system. The acquiring organization, however, refused to purchase the goodwill or similar intangible assets associated with the physicians' practices, citing, in part, potential violation of the Medicare and Medicaid anti-kickback statute. Instead, the physicians donated their intangibles to the tax-exempt foundation and claimed charitable contribution deductions. The tax court, however, denied the physicians' deductions, finding that the physicians received consideration for their intangible assets in the form of future employment with the medical foundation.

The *Derby* court observed that the terms of employment contracts—and particularly noncompetition provisions—are a crucial factor in determining whether enterprise goodwill is present and whether a physician has assigned his or her professional goodwill to the practice, thereby making it a practice asset. However, many appraisers incorrectly believe that fair market value contemplates or requires the sellers agreeing to provide the buyers with a noncompete agreement. This assumption is often blindly included in the valuation without confirmation, as was the case in *Derby*.

11 *Martin Ice Cream v. Commissioner*, 110 T.C. 189 (1998).
12 *Norwalk v. Commissioner*, T.C. Memo. 1998-279; *see "Goodwill Requires Enforceable Covenant Not to Compete," CPA Expert* (Spring 1999).
13 *Derby v. Commissioner*, T.C. Memo. 2008-45.

Appraisers must keep in mind that noncompete agreements can be independently valued, and that such agreements do not contain standard provisions. The nature of the included (or excluded) provisions drives the value of noncompete agreements. Moreover, different states have different statutory and judicial precedents on what is and what is not enforceable in such an agreement, and these also may have a consequential effect on value. It is more accurate to state that fair market value contemplates understanding the terms of the transaction and the laws that govern it before attempting to assign value to the whole or its component parts.

Derby also emphasized the necessity of using negotiated post-transaction compensation in the valuation model. Reasonable compensation is a critical aspect of determining whether and to what extent any enterprise goodwill (as distinct from personal goodwill) is present and how much of that enterprise goodwill would be allocable to a noncompete agreement. A November 2005 article in the *Journal of Accountancy* articulated why an accurate valuation must incorporate compensation:

> If the selling physician(s) still will be employed by the practice after the sale, the cash flow the buyer is purchasing—the subject of the valuation—can't be known without including a realistic amount of post-sale compensation in the valuation model.[14]

The threshold question in such a valuation is relatively easy to state, if difficult to appraise or value: How much of the practice's value would be lost if the physicians competed or were able to compete with the practice following conversion. Importantly, this question applies *whether or not* the physicians have a pre-existing noncompete agreement, because it is the basis for the methodology used to value that noncompete agreements.

The valuation method's mechanics are beyond the scope of this article but can be summarized as follows:

1. Determine reasonable compensation under the fair market value standard for the physicians post-conversion;
2. Determine the value of the entity assuming that noncompete agreements are in place based on historical and forecasted entity cash-flows using the discounted cash-flow method;
3. Allocate that value first to working capital assets (cash, receivables, inventory), then to property and equipment, and finally any remainder to intangible assets in the manner contemplated by the residual method of allocation described in the regulations under Section 338;

14 *"Medical Practices: A BV Rx, J".* Accountancy (Nov. 2005).

4. Allocate that intangible value first to any readily identifiable intangible assets, such as a below-market lease on real property assumable by a purchaser, trade name, trained workforce, patient charts, or others that the buyer could retain if the sellers competed. (Trained workforce contemplates an enforceable nonsolicitation provision; patient chart valuation requires an understanding of the extent to which a patient requesting transfer of his or her personal health information to a new practice entity could be charged);
5. Any remaining value is attributable to the sellers' noncompete agreement (an ordinary income component) and personal goodwill (a capital asset component);
6. Assess and quantify the entity cash flows that would be lost if the sellers competed post-transaction;
7. Revisit any allocation in Step 3 above to identifiable intangible assets;
8. Assess and quantify the probability that the sellers would, in fact, compete post-transaction;[15]
9. The quantified probability is applied to the forecasted cash flow expected to be lost as a result of competition then discounted to present value to determine the noncompete's value. This step must consider the enforceability of a noncompete in the applicable jurisdiction; and
10. The balance is a capital asset in the nature of personal goodwill of the sellers.

Hypothetical Sale

Appraisers are often confused by the concept of the hypothetical buyer and seller in the fair market value standard. They mistakenly believe that it requires the use of hypothetical assumptions such as an enforceable noncompete agreement, even when the interest being valued has no such agreements in place.

Appraisers must understand that a valuation in an actual transaction is significantly different than a valuation based upon a hypothetical sale. Valuations accompanying an estate and gift tax reporting, litigation, or a property division for marital dissolution, unlike a business acquisition, lack transactional documents and do require the appraiser to make a variety of assumptions.

An interest in the assets or equity of a private company is a specific basket of legal and contractual rights and obligations and economic risks and rewards. Each of that basket's characteristics must be evaluated to determine at what price a member of the

15 For litigation, alternative damage causation theories may be relevant such as violation of fiduciary obligations or intent to defraud via the sale, among others.

universe of hypothetical buyers and sellers would transact. The "hypothetical" aspect of the valuation in a real transaction is what buyer and seller would pay for the specific business or business interest being transacted *as reflected in the transaction documents.*

Understanding this difference is critical in a healthcare transaction because failure to do so may implicate the anti-kickback statute, Stark law, or other civil and criminal penalty provisions. It is perhaps easier to understand within the concept of post-closing adjustments in an actual transaction. A typical post-closing adjustment in the purchase of the stock or equity of a business would be an increase or decrease in the sales price based upon the actual measure of the liabilities assumed and paid; in an asset transaction, those liabilities would typically not be assumed. Another adjustment would be for any difference in the value of accounts receivable purchased versus ultimately collected, if they are purchased at all. Certainly, a hospital purchasing a physician practice for a value that includes the accounts receivable when they are not transferred would be placed in significant jeopardy. Paying an amount that assumes a noncompete is in place without obtaining one as part of the transaction should be viewed no differently.

Advantages of a Down Economy

The current troubled economic times may offer an unforeseen and counterintuitive benefit to hospitals and physicians seeking to integrate. Namely, the depressed economy may produce depressed valuations of physician practices. This might not sound like a reward, but lower valuations translate to reduced tax costs in converting physician practices to tax-exempt status.

One cause for lower valuations is that perceived risk is significantly higher in the current environment than at any other time in recent memory. Risk and value are inversely related. Another factor is that access to capital is significantly more difficult. Despite heretofore unforeseen low interest rates, many entities are unable to borrow money at any rate. Inability to access debt capital in turn requires increasing amounts of more-expensive equity capital. But as the stock market indicates, that well has been reduced to a trickle.

An appraiser typically captures these factors in the valuation multiple through development of the discount rate or cost of capital. Traditional methods of developing that multiple, however, do not capture the current combination of increased risk and decreased availability of capital.

In addition to lower enterprise values, increased marketability discounts—including consideration of liquidity factors—may be available for conversions taking place now. As the economic depression reduces the pool of potential buyers, it is becoming more difficult to find a suitable acquirer. A smaller market thus warrants consideration of a larger valuation discount for lack of marketability.

Conclusion

The contractual agreements a physician practice entity has in place with its owner- and nonowner-physicians determine how much of the goodwill or intangible value is owned by the practice and how much is owned personally by the physicians. To the extent that the enforceability of a noncompete, nonsolicitation, trade secrets, or other provision is limited or barred by state law, that portion of the agreement will have less or conceivably no value. A practice owned by physicians that has no post-termination noncompete agreements does not contractually own the personal goodwill of those physicians and therefore, should not recognize a taxable gain on that personal goodwill in a conversion to tax-exempt status.

Chapter 21

A Healthcare Appraiser Reviews a Judge-Appraiser's 'Report'

By Mark O. Dietrich, CPA/ABV

The decision in *Delaware Open MRI Radiology Associates, PA (majority) v. Kessler, et al. (minority)*[1] has created a great deal of commotion in the valuation community for a variety of reasons. Not the least of these is that Vice Chancellor Strine (Judge) of the Delaware Chancery Court adopted an S corporation tax-effecting scheme based on the difference between the after-tax dividend cash flow in the hands of an S shareholder versus that of a C shareholder, the latter taxed at 15%. There is also a replication of a discounted cash flow (DCF) model based upon the Judge's changes in the underlying assumptions and an often scathing critique of the majority's valuation expert. This article does not focus on those issues but rather on the failures in the application of the income approach, including a discussion of the use of the industry risk premium in lieu of the *capital asset pricing model*'s (CAPM) beta in the buildup method.

When using the income approach in any business valuation engagement, the appraiser's most critical task is to perform a reasoned analysis of the future revenue and profit prospects for the valuation subject. Industry expertise is required for many valuation engagements in various industries. In the valuation of healthcare entities in general and the MRI facilities that were the subject of this case in particular, studying industry trends commonly used by the peer group of healthcare industry valuation specialists is required. As will be seen from the analysis that follows, either the experts failed to address known industry trends in their reports, legal counsel failed to bring them out in testimony, or the Judge ignored it. Healthcare industry knowledge can be readily

1 Since the case involved suit and countersuit, "majority" and "minority" is more descriptive than plaintiff and defendant.

obtained from sources such as the Medicare Payment Advisory Commission (MedPAC) described below.

Time Line of the Case

The merger giving rise to the lawsuit in this matter occurred in January 2004. This date is critical because the MedPAC had already identified high-tech imaging such as MRI as a problem spending area in 2003. The first lawsuit was filed in February 2004.

The court's findings on revenue growth are directly contradictory to foreseeable changes—foreseen by the majority expert (Mr. Reed), whose testimony was dismissed in the following extract from the opinion. If, in fact, Mr. Reed failed to cite external sources to give his revenue reduction forecast credibility, it is indeed unfortunate since he had it right.

> I also find that Mitchell (minority expert) made reasonable assumptions regarding the revenues that Delaware Radiology would receive for doing scans. Mitchell began by using the same base reimbursement rates as Reed for Delaware I ($601 per scan) and Delaware II ($571 per scan). Mitchell used those reimbursement rates because they were the numbers the Broder Group provided to Reed for the purpose of performing a valuation, and Mitchell found them reasonable. *Mitchell held these rates constant throughout his projection period.* Reed, by contrast, assumed reductions in reimbursement rates of 9% for Delaware I and II in Year 2, or 2005, and then increased them at 3%, the rate of inflation, annually. Essentially, the basis for Reed's reduction was speculation by Carr and Reed's own opinion that Delaware reimbursement rates were high relative to neighboring states and that they were likely to fall. But the record is devoid of information from more objective sources to substantiate that viewpoint, which, like other elements of Reed and Carr's testimony, fits within the self-interest of the Broder Group.

History of MedPAC's Identification of High-Tech Imaging Expense Trends

"The Medicare Payment Advisory Commission (MedPAC) is an independent federal body established by the Balanced Budget Act of 1997 to advise the U.S. Congress on issues affecting the Medicare program."[2] This is the most easily identifiable and readily obtainable source of insight into future healthcare industry reimbursement. Although it applies specifically to Medicare payments to healthcare providers, many health insurers link their payment levels to Medicare.

Revenue, of course, is a function of the number of units of service provided and the rate per unit paid. Consider the following from the March 2003 MedPAC Report to

2 2003 Report to Congress.

Congress, highlighting the rapid growth in MRI services provided to the Medicare population.

> Relatively high growth rates for imaging services were concentrated in several specific categories, all of which involve technology of one kind or another. For instance, nuclear medicine grew by 13%, computerized automated tomography (CAT) of parts of the body other than the head grew by 15.3%, *magnetic resonance imaging (MRI) of parts of the body other than the brain grew by 15.9%, and MRI of the brain grew by 14.6%.* It is noteworthy, however, that none of these technologies are new. Instead, *it appears that use of well-established technologies is increasing.* CAT, for example, was introduced in the 1970s. MRI began to diffuse as a new technology in the 1980s. Thus, the indications for use of these technologies may be changing. (*Emphasis added*)

The March 2004 MedPAC Report to Congress repeated the observation.

> Among broad categories of services—major procedures, evaluation and management, other procedures, imaging, and tests—growth rates vary, but all are positive. Imaging and tests grew the most. *From 2001 to 2002, the imaging growth rate was 9.4%,* and the growth rate for tests was 11.1%.
>
> Within these categories, some services grew much faster than others (see Exhibit 1). From 2001 to 2002, we see the highest growth in volume—*approaching 20%*—of nuclear medicine, computed tomography, *magnetic resonance imaging*, laboratory tests, and minor procedures, which include outpatient rehabilitation. (*Emphasis added*)

And yet again the observation was repeated in the March 2005 MedPAC Report to Congress (see Exhibit 2) At this time, MedPAC formally advised Congress to implement strategies for reducing the volume of MRI and other high-tech imaging. These reductions were announced in August 2005 by CMS[3] and were scheduled to be implemented over two years starting in January 2006. The Deficit Reduction Act, signed in 2006, brought further dramatic reductions to MRI reimbursement in 2007.

> Imaging services have been growing much more rapidly than other services paid under the physician fee schedule. We examined per-beneficiary growth in the volume and intensity, or complexity, of fee schedule services. Between 1999 and 2002, the per-beneficiary average annual growth rate in the use of fee schedule imaging services was twice as high as the growth rate for all fee schedule services (10.1% versus 5.2%) (See Exhibit 3). Use of the following types of imaging services increased by 15% to 20% per year: MRI of parts of the body other than the brain, nuclear medicine, computed tomography (CT) of parts of the body other than the head, and MRI of the brain.

3 Centers for Medicare and Medicaid Services of the Department of Health and Human Services.

Exhibit 1. Change in Per Capita Use of Physician Services by Beneficiaries in Traditional Medicare, by Selected Type of Service, 1999-2002

	Per capita service use						
					Average annual percent change		
Type of service	1999	2000	2001	2002	1999-2001	2001-2002	Percent of total service use
All services	663.4	691.8	707.9	738.5	3.3%	4.3%	100.0%
Evaluation and management	353.6	359.4	361.9	372.5	1.2	2.9	50.4
Office visits—established patient	127.6	131.2	130.3	133.3	1.1	2.3	18.1
Hospital visit—subsequent	65.0	64.6	64.7	66.7	-0.2	3.1	9.0
Consultations	39.8	41.5	42.6	44.5	3.5	4.4	6.0
Emergency room visit	18.1	19.0	20.1	21.4	5.3	6.5	2.9
Specialist—psychiatry	18.5	18.3	18.2	18.5	-1.0	2.1	2.5
Specialist—ophthalmology	15.9	16.8	17.5	18.1	4.9	3.5	2.4
Hospital visit—initial	17.6	17.4	17.2	17.2	-1.2	0.3	2.3
Office visits—new patient	15.4	15.5	14.9	14.9	-1.4	-0.2	2.0
Imaging	81.1	88.2	96.1	105.1	8.9	9.4	14.2
Echography—heart	12.6	13.8	14.9	16.5	8.8	10.8	2.2
Standard—nuclear medicine	10.0	11.7	13.6	15.4	16.5	13.0	2.1
Advanced—CAT: other	9.3	10.7	12.3	14.1	14.8	15.3	1.9
Advanced—MRI: other	6.4	7.9	9.4	10.9	21.3	15.9	1.5
Standard—musculoskeletal	8.5	8.8	9.2	9.5	3.9	2.9	1.3
Advanced—MRI: brain	5.1	5.8	6.5	7.4	12.6	14.6	1.0
Standard—chest	6.7	6.5	6.3	6.3	-3.3	0.4	0.9
Advanced—CAT: head	2.7	2.8	2.9	3.0	3.2	4.5	0.4
Imaging/procedure—heart, including cardiac catheterization	1.9	2.1	2.4	2.4	10.4	-0.4	0.3

Exhibit 2. Use of Physician Services in Fee-for-Service Medicare, for Selected Services, 1999-2002

	Percent change in units of service per beneficiary		Percent change in volume per beneficiary		
Type of service	Average annual 1999-2001	2001-2002	Average annual 1999-2001	2001-2002	Percent of total volume
All services	3.8%	5.1%	4.9%	5.6%	100.0%
Evaluation and management					
Office visit—established patient	2.2	2.8	2.7	4.0	18.3
Hospital visit—subsequent	1.9	2.6	2.1	4.0	8.5
Consultation	4.6	4.2	5.8	6.0	5.9
Emergency room visit	4.1	2.8	6.9	6.6	2.7
Hospital visit—initial	0.3	1.1	0.4	1.8	2.2
Office visit—new patient	0.4	1.2	0.1	0.9	2.1
Nursing home visit	-0.8	1.2	0.3	3.5	1.8
Imaging					
Echography—heart	9.2	9.8	11.0	13.1	2.0
Standard—nuclear medicine	14.7	12.1	18.0	17.1	1.9
Advanced—CT: other	14.5	13.8	16.4	16.5	1.8
Advanced—MRI: other	18.5	15.3	22.3	17.4	1.5
Standard—musculoskeletal	3.5	3.7	5.5	6.5	1.2
Advanced—MRI: brain	19.2	12.3	16.1	13.8	1.0
Standard—chest	-0.4	1.9	-1.1	1.2	0.8
Advanced—CT: head	5.6	5.6	4.9	5.3	0.4
Imaging and procedure—heart, including cardiac catheterization	6.9	3.2	8.8	6.4	0.3

Exhibit 3. Use of Selected Physician Services Per Beneficiary in Fee-for-Service Medicare, 1999-2003

	Percent change in units of service per beneficiary		Percent change in volume per beneficiary*		
Type of service	Average annual 1999–2002	2002–2003	Average annual 1999–2002	2002–2003	Percent of total volume*
All services	4.3%	3.6%	5.2%	4.9%	100.0%
Evaluation and management	**2.3**	**2.2**	**3.4**	**3.9**	**42.1**
Office visit—established patient	2.4	2.5	3.2	3.9	18.1
Hospital visit—subsequent	2.2	1.8	2.8	3.5	8.4
Consultation	4.5	3.3	5.9	5.0	5.9
Emergency room visit	3.7	1.9	6.8	4.8	2.7
Hospital visit—initial	0.6	1.3	0.9	2.1	2.1
Office visit—new patient	0.7	-1.9	0.4	-1.2	2.0
Nursing home visit	-0.1	1.8	1.4	4.0	1.8
Imaging	**5.4**	**4.2**	**10.1**	**8.6**	**14.8**
Echography—heart	9.4	6.2	11.8	7.6	2.1
Standard—nuclear medicine	13.8	9.1	17.8	13.2	2.2
Advanced—CT: other	14.3	12.9	16.6	14.6	2.0
Advanced—MRI: other	17.4	15.9	19.5	16.5	1.6
Standard—musculoskeletal	3.6	3.6	5.9	4.5	1.3
Advanced—MRI: brain	16.9	8.0	15.5	8.6	1.0
Standard—chest	0.4	0.5	-0.3	0.1	0.7
Advanced—CT: head	5.6	4.6	5.1	4.2	0.4
Imaging/procedure—heart, including cardiac catheterization	5.6	1.6	8.0	4.6	0.3

> Between 2002 and 2003, the per-beneficiary growth rate for imaging services moderated to 8.6% but was still much higher than the growth rate of all fee schedule services (4.9%). Although imaging services paid under the fee schedule have been shifting from facilities, such as hospitals, to physician offices, about 80% of the increase in the volume and intensity of these services between 1999 and 2002 was unrelated to this shift in setting (MedPAC 2004a).
>
> The secretary should improve Medicare's coding edits that detect unbundled diagnostic imaging services *and reduce the technical component payment for multiple imaging services performed on contiguous body parts. (Emphasis added)*

To reiterate, *one place valuation analysts are sure to find insight into future changes in Medicare reimbursement is in the annual MedPAC report released in March of each year.*

The Medicare Conversion Factor

Valuation firms have work codes and rates per hour (unit of service) for their services. Similarly, healthcare providers have work codes (current procedural terminology,[4] or CPT, codes) for their services. The Medicare program and most health insurers pay for services included in Medicare Part B based upon a unit of service called a relative

4 Copyrighted by the American Medical Association.

value unit, or RVU (see discussion later herein) assigned to services under the resource-based relative value scale (RBRVS). The rate per RVU from Medicare is known as the Medicare conversion factor.

The lack of growth in the Medicare conversion factor is separate and distinct from this foreseeable response to the enormous growth in imaging utilization and expenditures, which has risen from $36.69 in 1998 to $37.90 in 2007—a compound growth rate of virtually zero. For non-Medicare services, the compound rate of growth for the last 11 years based upon the Bureau of Labor Statistics' producer price index for physician services is 1.85%.

The Gordon growth model used in the discounted cash flow models of the two experts and the Judge assumed perpetual growth in cash flow to equity (3% for one the majority expert and 4% for the minority expert, the Judge choosing 4%). Cash flow to equity is revenue *less* expenses! There is no evidence in available industry data to suggest that a 4% perpetual growth rate could be sustained.

The recent history of the relationship between physician practice expenses and the physician producer price index demonstrates that practice expenses are rising much more rapidly than fees (Centers for Medicare & Medicaid Services, or CMS, data).

As the facts demonstrate, expenses were and are rising more rapidly than per unit costs. This is called an eroding profit margin. The only way to maintain an overall profit would be to do more services at a lower margin—*precisely* what the MedPAC analysis from 2003 forward indicated was happening and precisely what the government moved to put an end to in 2005!

Exhibit 4 shows the recent history of Medicare payments for an MRI scan of the chest (CPT code 71552), one of the most frequently performed MRI services. Note that the bottom drops out in 2007. No future increases could be expected to offset such a dramatic drop so as to generate a 4% terminal growth rate.

The decreases in another common MRI procedure were less dramatic, but nonetheless wholly inconsistent with a 4% terminal growth rate.

Exhibits 4 and 5 are the *per unit* of service payments only. They do *not* illustrate the effect of the implemented recommendation from MedPAC in its 2005 report that the *"payment for multiple imaging services performed on contiguous body parts"* be reduced, which had a dramatic effect on many MRI providers.[5]

5 Medicare estimated the cuts at 8% of revenue for the affected scanning procedures.

Exhibit 4. Medicare Payment for Chest MRI

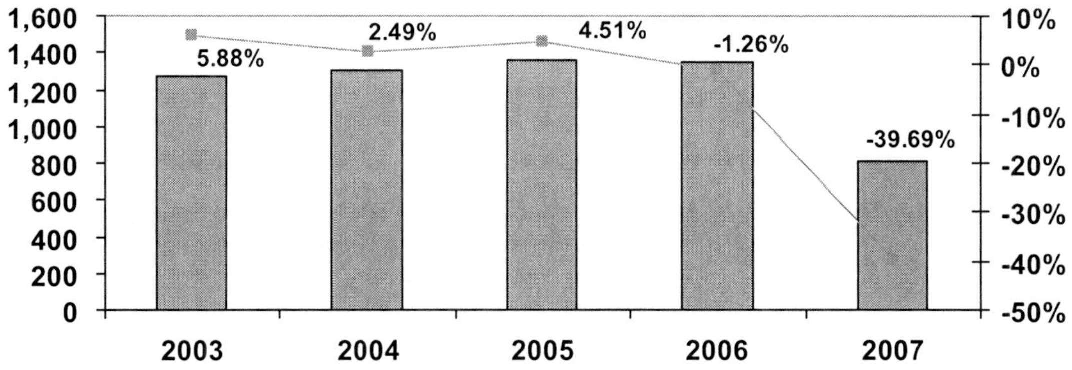

Exhibit 5. Medicare Payment for Brain MRI

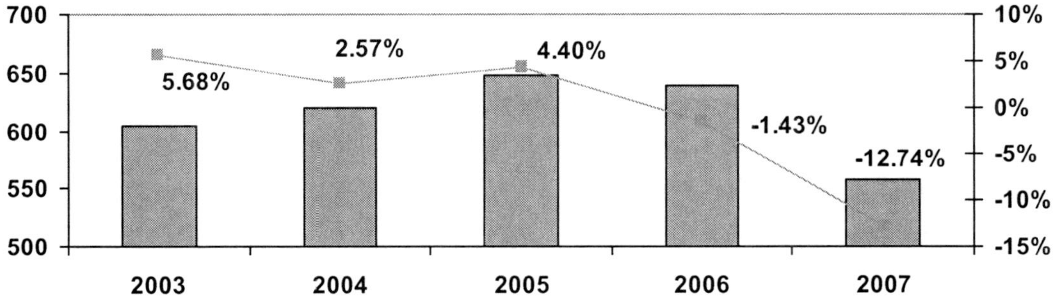

Reduction in the Relative Value of MRI Services

As if this is not compelling enough evidence that explosive growth in service volume leads to forceful counter-measures, on June 29, 2006, CMS published in the *Federal Register* notice of a plan to revalue physician services under the resource-based relative value scale; the plan was adopted in August 2006. Less one think this only affects Medicare, many insurers follow Medicare's lead—particularly when it gives them an excuse to cut expenses. The changes followed closely on the heels of a suggestion by MedPAC in its March 2006 report that evaluation and management services (typically, face-to-face physician-patient encounters) had declined in value, in large part to the benefit of high-tech imaging services. The changes would cut radiology reimbursement 5% as of January 2007.

A Quantitative Analysis of the Court's Excessive Terminal Growth Rate

Returning to the court's conclusion that the terminal growth in cash flow (profit) should be pegged at 4%, the following sort of quantitative analysis must have been missing from the experts' reports.

Exhibit 6 presents a "base case" scenario with no growth in volume of services. A "profit margin" of 44% (close to that determined by the court) is used in the illustration. Note that the compound growth rate in cash flow continues to decline at an ever increasing amount.

Exhibit 6. 'Base Case' Scenario With No Growth in Volume of Services

Year	0	1	2	3	4	5
Revenue	$100	$101	$102	$103	$104	105
Expense	56	58	60	62	64	67
Cash flow	44	43	42	41	40	39
Compound growth in cash flow		-2.18%	-2.27%	-2.37%	-2.48%	-2.59%
Revenue growth		1.00%	1.00%	1.00%	1.00%	1.00%
Expense growth		3.50%	3.50%	3.50%	3.50%	3.50%

Exhibit 7 presents what the growth in annual volume would have had to have been to maintain the constant 4% growth rate in cash flow through the fifth year as determined by the court. The key assumption is that total unit expenses grow as rapidly as the units provided. The lower the profit margin, the greater the annual growth in units of service to maintain the 4% cash flow growth rate. By Year 5, growth in units of service would have to be 7.26%. By Year 15, to maintain a constant growth rate of 4%, the units of service would have to grow more than 13% per annum—and that rate would *increase* in each subsequent year *into perpetuity*. Clearly, this is an unrealistic assumption that violates professional standards as well as common sense.

Exhibit 7. Annual Volume With Constant 4% Growth Rate

Year	0	1	2	3	4	5
Revenue	$100	$107	$116	$125	$135	$146
Expense	56	62	68	75	83	92
Cash flow	44	46	48	49	51	54
Compound growth in cash flow		4.00%	4.00%	4.00%	4.00%	4.00%
Revenue growth per unit		1.00%	1.00%	1.00%	1.00%	1.00%
Revenue growth units		6.32%	6.52%	6.74%	6.99%	7.26%
Expense growth per unit		3.50%	3.50%	3.50%	3.50%	3.50%
Expense growth units		6.32%	6.52%	6.74%	6.99%	7.26%
Constant growth per court		4.00%	4.00%	4.00%	4.00%	4.00%
Target growth in cash flow		46	48	49	51	54

The Broader Revenue Picture in the Healthcare Industry

The cutback in imaging is not an isolated occurrence. The same thing happened with outpatient physical, occupational, and speech therapy, on which Medicare has imposed an annual limitation per beneficiary of only $1,790 (with some limited exceptions). This was done to rein in explosive growth in the cost of outpatient physical therapy in particular, as noted in this quote from a Dec. 30, 2004 MedPAC letter to the vice president of the United States.

> **Amount of medically unnecessary PT services**
>
> The Office of Inspector General (OIG) of the Department of Health and Human Services examined the provision of outpatient physical and occupational therapy services provided in skilled nursing facilities (SNFs) and found considerable and widely varying shares of medically unnecessary services. One study found that from 5% to 26% of services was unnecessary, depending on the patient diagnosis. Another OIG study found that three-quarters of the contractors hired to review and process claims for payment commonly found medically unnecessary and excessive therapy claims. The services were medically unnecessary because:
>
> - the services were not skilled,
> - the treatment goals were too ambitious for the patient's condition, and
> - the frequency of the service provision was excessive given the patient's condition.
>
> The appropriateness of care provided at CORFs[6] and ORFs[7] has also prompted examination. In its study of ORFs, the OIG found that about 40% of the claims reviewed were for services that were not reasonable and medically necessary for the conditions of the patient. The Government Accountability Office (GAO) examined CORFs in Florida and found that on a per-patient basis, Florida CORFs' payments were two to three times higher than payments to other facility-based therapy providers and that the differences were not explained by patient characteristics, such as diagnosis. These studies indicate that unnecessary therapy is frequently provided and that the current requirements alone do not eliminate unnecessary service provision, even in settings supervised by physicians, such as SNFs and CORFs. The studies may also reflect low levels of physician oversight provided in some institutional settings. It is possible that unnecessary services are provided more frequently in settings where there even less physician supervision. Finally, the findings may illustrate a poor understanding of Medicare coverage by physicians and physical therapists.

Another recent case of significance in the healthcare valuation arena—*Caracci*—found the Fifth Circuit[8] throwing out the tax court's decision that a home healthcare agency

6 Comprehensive outpatient rehabilitation facility.
7 Outpatient rehabilitation facility.
8 Correctly in the author's view.

that had never made a profit had an asset value well in excess of its liabilities. The tax court had acknowledged that the government was planning a changeover to a prospective payment system (PPS)[9] at the time the *Caracci* case arose, but rather than focusing on the income approach to value the taxpayer, the tax court used the IRS's expert's *market* approach, primarily based upon guideline public companies that were in dissimilar lines of business. The changeover to the PPS resulted in total Medicare spending on home health falling by 52% in two years! It is difficult indeed to see how a business losing money (i.e., expenses in excess of revenues) could make more money if revenues dropped by 52%.

There are numerous examples across all sectors of the healthcare industry to conclusively prove that the government and private insurers will move to defeat excessive utilization and cost. In the hospital sector, outlier payments for inpatient services—those where the patient's length of stay exceeded a defined limit for the underlying diagnosis-related group (DRG)—were a major cost problem for the government. In a June 29, 2006 press release, the Department of Justice Civil Division and U.S. Attorney for the Central District of California in Los Angeles announced that Tenet Healthcare Corporation, the nation's second largest hospital chain, had agreed to pay a fine of more than $900 million for "alleged unlawful billing practices." "Of the $900 million settlement amount, the agreement requires Tenet to pay more than $788 million to resolve claims arising from Tenet's receipt of excessive "outlier" payments (payments that are intended to be limited to situations involving extraordinarily costly episodes of care) resulting from the hospitals' inflating their charges substantially in excess of any increase in the costs." A fine of nearly $250 million was levied against the University of Medicine and Dentistry in New Jersey for similar outlier issues—and that is a tax-exempt, state-owned institution.

An Observation on the Industry Risk Premium

An analysis of *Ibbotson Stocks Bonds Bill and Inflation Industry Premia Company List Report for 2003* would indicate that the companies used in the determination of the industry risk premium are not comparable to an MRI operator. The Standard Industrial Classification (SIC) codes of some of these companies were likely assigned at a point in their history when they were engaged in some other line of business (see Exhibit 8).

An analysis of *Ibbotson Stocks Bonds Bill and Inflation Industry Premia Company List Report for 2004*[10] in SIC Code 807 would indicate that only three of the companies (Alliance,

9 Simply stated, a PPS establishes a standard fee schedule for services, rather than basing the fee on a retrospective settlement, such as one based upon the actual cost of providing those services.

10 The only match for the -4.51% negative risk premium cited in the case is SIC 807 in Ibbotson's 2004 yearbook, which post-dates the merger-valuation date of January 2004.

Exhibit 8. SIC Code 801

Amsurg Corp.	Surgery center operator
Coventry Health Care	Managed care products
Health Grades Inc.	Provides ratings of hospitals, physicians, etc.
Integramed America	National network of fertility/infertility clinics
Metropolitan Hlth Ntwrks Inc.	Provides healthcare benefits to Medicare Advantage members in Florida
Novamed Eyecare Inc.	Surgery center operator
Sight Resource Corp.	Manufactures, distributes, sells eyewear and related products

Primedex, and Miracor) used in the determination of the industry risk premium is arguably comparable to an MRI operator (see Exhibit 9). The betas of these stocks would have been a better indicator of industry risk.[11]

Exhibit 9. SIC Code 807

Alliance Imaging Inc.	Medical diagnostic imaging
Array Biopharma Inc.	Biopharmaceutical company
Bio Imaging Technologies Inc.	Medical image management for clinical trials
Bio Reference Labs	Clinical laboratory in the greater New York
Enzo Biochem Inc.	R&D, MFR, biotechnology, and molecular biology
Labone Inc.	Medical laboratory operator (now part of Quest)
Laboratory Cp. of Amer.	Medical laboratory operator
Medcath Corp.	Cardiac hospital operator
Medtox Scientific Inc.	Specialty laboratory testing services
Miracor Diagnostics Inc.	Medical diagnostic imaging
National Dentex Corp.	Dental laboratory operator
Orchid Biosciences Inc.	DNA testing
Primedex Health Systems Inc.	(Now part of Radnet: diagnostic imaging services)
Psychemedics Corp.	Detection of abused substances
Quest Diagnostics Inc.	Medical laboratory operator
Sagemark Companies Ltd.*	Management and operation of PET imaging
Specialty Laboratories Inc.	Medical laboratory (now part of Ameripath)
*Unlike MRI, positron emission tomography (PET) was not covered by the Stark laws at this time (although it now is) giving it a much different cash flow profile.	

Outside the community of healthcare appraisers, there seems to be an assumption that all providers are paid in a similar fashion. Nothing could be more factually inaccurate.

11 An interesting exercise is to plot the prices of these stocks against the S&P 500 in this time period; they are quite volatile!

This leads to such errors as the use of inappropriate and irrelevant comparables for obtaining betas and market transactions. Physicians, nonhospital-based imaging providers, such as Delaware Open MRI, podiatrists, and a host of others, for example, are paid from Medicare Care Part B using the RBRVS as described above. Hospitals are paid from Medicare Part A using a methodology based upon DRGs, which bundle hospital services based upon an expected length of stay for the patient's diagnosis. Home healthcare agencies are paid in yet another fashion, as are surgery centers and skilled nursing facilities. Most private health insurers follow a similar construct, but the rates of payments vary radically from state to state and even market areas within states.

Perhaps the most fundamental valuation mistake in the healthcare industry is failure to differentiate the risk of a small entity operating in a single state (Delaware) in a single line of business (MRI) with a few dominant health insurers[12] from the risk of large public entities operating in multiple states in multiple lines of business with multiple health insurers paying for the cost of services. Use of the industry risk premium in the buildup method compounds this typical error.

Conclusions

As valuation experts, we can only fault the court if a) we do not provide adequate compelling evidence, b) legal counsel does a poor job on direct and cross-examination, or c) the court decides to ignore the evidence and rule on some other basis, the expert testimony notwithstanding. Like newspaper reporters trying to write stories on complex economic matters without adequate research, judges need lots of input in understandable terms that must be coupled with a desire and willingness to be educated when making decisions on healthcare valuation. Most of the traditional valuation rules fail in healthcare because of the substantive and repetitive interference by government regulators that make historical performance nothing more than yesterday's news.

A unit growth analysis is a critical part of the determination of the reasonableness of a perpetual growth rate for a healthcare entity. Due to the statutory construct of Medicare Part B reimbursement, providers drawing revenue from that program face fixed or declining per-unit revenue even as costs increase more rapidly than the generic rate of inflation. Entities limited to a single service line—such as *Delaware Open MRI*—have no ability to respond by expanding services, unlike large healthcare entities, which operate in multiple lines of business. Even those large entities face numerous problems, as witnessed by the fines levied against Tenet.

This article first appeared in the Summer 2007 Edition of Business Valuation Review. *Reprinted with permission.*

12 See, e.g., Government Accounting Office *Private Health Insurance: Number and Market Share of Carriers in the Small Group Health Insurance Market.*

Chapter 22

The CPA's Role in M&A Due Diligence Assistance to PPMCs and Private Equity Firms

By Ronald D. Finkelstein, CPA/ABV, and Lydia M. Glatz, CPA

Editor's Note: Many of the approaches and techniques described in this chapter are appropriate to a regular valuation engagement as opposed to a due diligence engagement. The discussion of the reports to obtain from the medical practice's billing system, how to use them, and the nuances thereof is of particular value. Portions of the checklist can be adapted for a standard valuation engagement.

Caveat emptor—let the buyer beware—and the term "due diligence" go hand in hand. Due diligence, or the process of investigating and providing financial analysis and assistance, can prove to be an invaluable tool during mergers and acquisitions (M&A) when planned and carried out properly. CPAs can assist their physician practice management company (PPMC) and private equity firm (PEF) clients to properly structure M&A transactions to reach optimum financial results for both the acquiring and acquirer entity. This chapter will address the various types of due diligence assistance the CPA can provide as well as provide insightful information and guidance on carrying out the engagement.

Professional Reporting Standards

The first step in the M&A due diligence assistance process is for the CPA to determine the scope of the work and the type of reporting desired by the PPMC/PEF. Due diligence services performed by the CPA generally fall under the following professional engagement and reporting standards promulgated by the American Institute of Certified Public Accountants (AICPA) and the Financial Accounting Standards Board (FASB):

- Audit of financial statements—rendering an independent audit opinion in accordance with the Statement on Auditing Standards (SAS) by adhering to generally accepted auditing standards (GAAS) and applying generally accepted accounting principles (GAAP);

- Agreed-upon procedures—performing specific analytical testing agreed upon by the PPMC/PEF and the CPA and rendering a findings report in accordance with the Statement on Standards for Attestation Engagements (SSAE);

- Forecasts and projections—reporting on an entity's forecasted or projected financial position and operating results in accordance with the SSAE;

- Pro forma financial information—reporting on the effects a M&A transaction (proposed or consummated) would have on the historical financial information of an entity in accordance with the SSAE;

- Financial analytics—review and analysis of key financial areas of a target entity that PPMC/PEF requests the CPA to perform in accordance with the Statement on Standards for Consulting Services (SSCS);

- Calculating the value of intangible assets—rendering a report on the calculated value of the intangible assets in an M&A transaction in accordance with the Statement on Standards for Valuation Services (SSVS).

Engagement Planning

After the PPMC/PEF and CPA have agreed upon the scope and extent of the M&A work, the next important step is to develop a due diligence assistance program and related detailed document request list. The document request list is a very useful tool in planning any due diligence engagement; it should be tailored to request sufficient information that the PPMC/PEF needs for the M&A transaction. The document request list should include requests for documentation that can be utilized to perform analytical procedures on the operational statistics of the target practice. The list should be sent to the target practice well in advance of any due diligence field work to provide the target practice ample time to gather the requested information.

A sample document request list is attached in Appendix A.

For larger transactions that require a significant exchange of documents, the latest trend in due diligence document management is for the PPMC/PEF to set up a Web-based data site, where designated parties to the M&A transaction can access and share stored information.

A critical step the CPA must perform at the initial stage of engagement planning is to obtain and read the memorandum of understanding or, as it is commonly referred to, the letter of intent (LOI). The LOI will provide the CPA with information on the purchase price, the type of purchase for tax purposes (stock or asset purchase), the calculation of the purchase price, and any related purchase price adjustments agreed upon by the parties. To the extent the purchase price is based on a multiple of earnings before interest, taxes, depreciation, and amortization (EBITDA), the CPA may be required to report on EBITDA and calculate an adjusted or normalized EBITDA, as defined in the LOI.

Operating Statistics

Physician practices maintain a plethora of historical data that can assist the CPA in analyzing the operational statistics of the practice. Historical data containing operational statistics may consist of:

- Reports produced from electronic databases containing patient billing information;
- Insurance company contracts;
- Contracts for the provision of professional medical services with hospitals, ambulatory facilities, diagnostic facilities, and third-party and related party contracts;
- Audited, compiled, and internally produced financial statements;
- Filed tax returns; and
- Monthly bank statements.

Historical data from these sources can be utilized to extract and analyze various operational aspects of target practices, such as information relative to the number of patient encounters, types of procedures performed, charges billed, charges collected, accounts receivable, and reimbursement rates. Further, historical productivity data can be utilized to compare and analyze the operational results of the target practice with the operational results of other practices of similar specialty and size in the same geographic area. The target's historical performance measures can also be benchmarked to performance measures contained in published industrywide data, and various analytics and pro forma calculations can be performed to compare the target's productivity to the performance measures of the PPMC/PEF.

The information gathered can prove to be invaluable in yielding answers to past and future trends, which in turn may be utilized by the acquiring and selling practices to arrive at mutually agreeable buy and sell transactions.

Patient Volume

When comparing a practice's operational results, patient volume is by far one of the leading indicators of revenue trends. Patient volume can be measured in terms of the number of patients seen by the physician providers in the office, inpatient hospital consults, and in the number of cases and procedures performed at outpatient diagnostic testing facilities. Patient volume also bears a direct relationship to practice size, number of physicians in the practice, number of midlevel providers, employees, and number of practice locations. In other words, when comparing patient volume, the CPA should not just look at medical billing reports but should compare the medical billing reports with other practice variables to verify the accuracy and reliability of the reports.

The CPA should request that billing reports be generated, by date of service, and, at the very least, for two concurrent periods, such as for the immediate and previous calendar year. Comparing similar reports of differing periods can also prove to be invaluable at yielding answers to past and future trends.

Some sample patient volume comparisons may include comparing the number of patients seen in total by the practice and by the individual providers in the office, hospitals, diagnostic centers, and outpatient facilities during the current and prior year. Testing the reliability of the billing reports may include comparing the number of patients listed on the billing reports to the patient sign-in sheets and hospital admission or operating room case records.

Trends generated through this exercise can assist and provide the PPMC/PEF with an understanding of the productivity of the practice and of individual physicians within the group. It will also assist in addressing areas for improvement, pinpointing profitable and nonprofitable practice centers, and determining the size of the personnel pool required to run and maintain the practice efficiently. Further inquiry into this flux analysis will most certainly generate answers to questions that could improve physician productivity post-acquisition and assist in crafting an incentive-based productivity compensation arrangement. A sample table comparing daily and weekly patient volume by provider could be fashioned as follows:

Patient Volume Analysis

	Average Number of Office Visits		Average Number of Surgeries	
Physician	**Daily**	**Weekly**	**Daily**	**Weekly**
Dr. 1	13	38	3	12
Dr. 2	31	94	4	12
Dr. 3	21	41	3	14
Dr. 4	38	76	6	19
Dr. 5	20	61	5	15
Dr. 6	20	61	3	11
Dr. 7	9	19	2	7
Total	**152**	**390**	**26**	**90**

Charges and Collections

Medical billing reports can be generated to provide historical physician practice productivity data related to charges billed and collections received. These reports can be customized to include numerous variables, such as total charges billed and collections received by provider, CPT code, payor source, and practice location. And, as a caveat, the CPA should be cognizant during this exercise that medical billing systems have the capability of producing reports that match collections to actual charges based on date of service (accrual basis reporting)[1] or, in the alternative, that simply track collections received in a period to charges posted in the same period (cash basis reporting). Reports that match collections to actual charges by date of service are comparable to accrual financial statements, and reports that match collections to charges posted in a period are comparable to cash basis financial statements. Both types of reports contain valuable information, but must be read with caution, as the data contained in each of the two reports may be misleading when not interpreted and applied to analytical procedures correctly.

The PPMC/PEF would be interested in the historical information these medical billing reports contain. For instance, the PPMC/PEF would want to know information such as the types of procedures the physicians perform, reimbursement rates, total charges and collections during specific periods, and the productivity of the various practice

1 Editor's note: When looking at charges and matched collections for a fixed period, such as 12 months, the collections will reflect *less than* 12 months' volume, because of the lag between billing a charge and collecting it. To see the total collections against charges specified by date of service, it is necessary to use what auditors call a cutoff period, of at least 90 days and perhaps 180 days, depending upon the efficiency of the billing and collection effort, state prompt-pay statutes, and similar factors.

locations. Numerous analytical procedures can be performed utilizing the data contained in the medical billing reports. Analytical procedures may include summarizing and comparing total charges and collections received by procedure (CPT) code during the current year and comparing them to the previous year's total charges and collections, calculating gross and net collection percentages, calculating average charge and average collections by type of practice specialty, and determining the significance the practice's fee schedule plays on these calculations.

This type of information can be presented in the form of a table that highlights total charges and collections by CPT code, location, and provider. The table could also be expanded to include information relative to gross and net collection percentages. The CPA should utilize the "accrual"-type billing reports for this exercise to compare actual collections applied to actual charges. Utilizing the "cash"-type billing reports could skew the true collection percentage results.

Physician fee schedules play an important role in comparing a physician practice collection ratio to another practice of similar size and specialty. Since fee schedules can be fashioned utilizing numerous variables, prior to calculating a practice's gross and net collection percentages, the CPA should obtain the group's fee schedule and inquire about how the fee schedule was developed and whether there were any changes to the fee schedule during the reporting periods. Was it based on Medicare allowable rates, a multiple of Medicare allowable, or some other benchmark? Lower fee schedules will produce higher gross collection percentages than will higher fee schedules. Preparing a chart that compares the practice's fee schedule to other fee schedules will assist the PPMC/PEF with its gross and net collection analysis. The table that follows demonstrates the role a practice fee schedule plays when calculating gross and net collection percentages.

Assuming a Medicare reimbursement rate of $50, the following gross collection percentages can be calculated.

Fee Schedule Comparison

	Physician Fee Schedule	CPT Code 99242	Gross %
Medicare x 2	100	50	50%
Medicare x 3	150	50	33%

Total collections during specific periods can be verified to the total deposits per the bank statements. Further inquiry and analysis can be performed utilizing the "cash" basis billing reports to verify the validity of the receipts by tracing a sample of individual deposits from the bank statement to the supporting back-up documentation. This exercise could be taken one step further by reconciling the previous year's net collections to financial statements and to the net revenues reported on the federal income tax returns.

Appendix B contains a list of the more commonly used ratios, including formulas for calculating gross collection and net collection ratios.

Payor Mix

A payor mix analysis can provide valuable insight into understanding the target practice's reimbursement rates and who its key payors are. This type of analysis will highlight profitable and nonprofitable payors. A payor mix analysis will assist the PPMC/PEF in planning and projecting future revenue growth trends and highlighting nonprofitable payors whose contracts the PPMC/PEF may want to renegotiate.

Medical billing reports generated on the "accrual" basis to include total charges, collections and adjustments by payor will contain the information required to perform this analysis. Most medical billing software can export reports into Excel-formatted files, which allow data to be sorted to achieve various results. The data should be sorted by total charges in descending order to segregate payor billings from largest to smallest. This type of analysis can be presented in the form of a table that highlights the top 10 payors, along with charges, collections, adjustments, and gross and net collection percentages by payor.

A payor mix analysis could also be utilized by the PPMC/PEF to compare the practice's collection percentages with those of published industrywide benchmarks and with its own collection percentages.

CPT Code Analysis

A practice's total charges and collections are a function of the number and type of procedures performed. CPT codes can be compared with payor reimbursement rates. For instance, a payor reimbursement matrix could be prepared to compare the fee charged by the practice for its top 10 procedures to the reimbursement rate of its top 10 payors.

A sample matrix of five payors is presented in Exhibit 1.

Exhibit 1. Payor Reimbursement Matrix

Top CPT Code	Fee Schedule	Payor 1	Payor 2	Payor 3	Payor 4	Payor 5
64483	$ 374	$ 77	$130	$104	$ 86	$271
64484	267	50	135	69	94	149
77003	120	27	19	40	23	21
99214	220	43	62	64	72	64
99215	355	73	92	95	97	91
	$ 1,336	$ 270	$438	$372	$372	$596
Collection %		20%	33%	28%	28%	45%

This type of analysis highlights reimbursement and collection percentages by payor and can lead to PPMC/PEF contract renegotiation and follow-up.

Accounts Receivable

Accounts receivable play a vital role in the determination of a practice's cash flow. How quickly charges are collected is determined by the efficiency and accuracy with which the practice's billing and collection department processes claims and makes subsequent timely collection follow-up. The practice's accounts receivable can be benchmarked with the Medical Group Management Association (MGMA) annual publications, which provide statistical comparisons for different specialty and size practices by geographic regions. Ratio analysis can also be performed to calculate the number of days the practice takes to collect its receivables. Accounts receivable at the beginning of a period can be compared to those at the end of the period, and cash collections can be analyzed to determine whether significant differences have occurred as a result of increases or decreases in accounts receivable.

Cash to Accrual Conversion

Generally, most medical practices and other healthcare providers maintain their accounting records and financial statements on the cash basis of accounting. The PPMC/PEF usually requests the CPA to convert the financial statements from the cash to the accrual basis of accounting. This conversion process requires revenue and expense cutoff information for both the beginning and ending reporting periods to properly measure EBITDA under GAAP.

The following financial information can assist the CPA in preparing cash to accrual accounting conversion adjustments:

- Accounts receivable aging reports;
- Charges, adjustments, and collections—by date of service;
- Accounts payable and accruals;
- Cash disbursements cutoff data;
- Payroll register for payroll period ending reporting; and
- For risk based providers—IBNR lag analysis.

EBITDA Measurement

The LOI may define how the purchase price is calculated and specify certain agreed-upon purchase price adjustments to EBITDA. The PPMC/PEF may request the CPA to report on EBITDA as of a certain period. The period(s) can be as of the most recent year and a subsequent stub period through the closing date of the transaction or a trailing 12-month period. EBITDA measurements for purposes of the LOI are generally calculated as follows:

GAAP EBITDA

Purchase price adjustments for:

- Nonrecurring revenue and expenses;
- Owner compensation and fringe benefits;
- Assumption of certain debt;
- Related party transactions; and
- Other agreed-upon post-acquisition expenses.

Acquisition Accounting

The PPMC/PEF may also require assistance early in the due diligence process to properly account for the fair value of the assets acquired and liabilities assumed as part of a business combination in accordance with ASC Topic 805, Accounting for Business Combinations (formerly FASB 141R). Identifying and understanding the target's operations can assist in addressing some of the post-deal accounting impacts and decrease the risk of restating financial statements.

A challenging area in meeting the requirements of ASC 805 is measuring the fair value and reporting contingent consideration or "earnouts" paid as part of the M&A. ASC 805 requires contingent consideration be reported at fair value as part of the acquisition or be expensed as part compensation expense. Assistance with projections and forecasts may be helpful in forecasting future earnings, structuring post-acquisition incentives by tying payouts to future performance, and avoiding earnings volatility.

Tax Matters

Depending upon the type of M&A tax structure, the PPMC/PEF may request the CPA to assist in computing the tax consequences to both the buyer and seller. Typically the PPMC/PEF buyer prefers an asset purchase: The purchased assets are allocated on a tax basis equal to the purchase price, and there is no assumption of seller-related liabilities. Conversely, the selling entity owners prefer a sale of stock because this form of transaction maximizes the after-tax sale proceeds by taking advantage of the lower capital gains tax rates, eliminates the 35% built-in gain (BIG) tax for S corporations with unrecognized built-in gain still within the recognition period, and avoids sales tax on the sale of tangible personal property for corporations residing in states imposing such tax.

Whether structured as an asset sale or a stock sale, the recognized total net gain may be the same.[2] However, the character of the gain is different. An asset sale will trigger ordinary income while a stock sale will trigger capital gain. A common tax strategy that may be agreed upon by both the buyer and seller is the Internal Revenue Code Section 338(h)(10) election. This code section is intended to make the tax benefits neutral with respect to acquisitions of corporate assets and acquisitions of corporate stock. Following a qualified stock purchase and depending on the circumstances, the purchasing corporation could elect under Section 338(g) to step up the basis of the underlying acquired assets to their adjusted grossed-up basis (generally equal to FMV). In this scenario, the buyer obtains a tax benefit on depreciation and amortization deductions on the acquired tangible and intangible assets. To the extent the seller recognizes an incremental tax liability on the difference between the tax liability incurred on the sale of stock versus the tax liability incurred on the theoretical sale of assets, the CPA can assist the parties by computing the incremental gross up in income taxes required to be reported in the purchase agreement.

Since this is only a deemed sale of assets for tax purposes, a Section 338(h)(10) election does not relieve the buyer of the target's corporate liabilities (known and unknown). Buyers should obtain legal advice from an attorney specializing in this area so a thorough due diligence is performed.

2 *Editor's Note:* There are circumstances where the "inside" and "outside" basis of a stock interest differ from the underlying basis of the corporate assets; this in turn can lead to a difference in the gain realized between a stock and an asset sale. One example is where are previous purchase of stock by a current holder of same reflected a higher value than the amount paid by stockholders at the time the corporation was formed.

Reverse Triangular Merger

Unique structural considerations relating to healthcare entity buyouts include those designed to minimize the possibility that the transactions will constitute a change in ownership (CHOW) for licensure or certification purposes or trigger anti-assignment provisions in professional service or managed care contracts (which should be avoided, if possible, because the counterparties often use the consent process to renegotiate or extract additional consideration).

One way to minimize the regulatory and contractual approvals required is through a reverse triangular merger structure under Internal Revenue Code Section 368(a)(2)(D) in which a newly formed subsidiary of the acquirer merges with and into the parent of the target holding company. Often the providers and facilities are organized as subsidiaries of the target holding company, and in many cases, CHOW approvals will not be required using this approach. Similarly, this structure may limit (but not eliminate) the managed care and provider contract consents required. See Exhibit 2.

Exhibit 2. Reverse Triangular Merger Code Section 368(a) (2) (D)

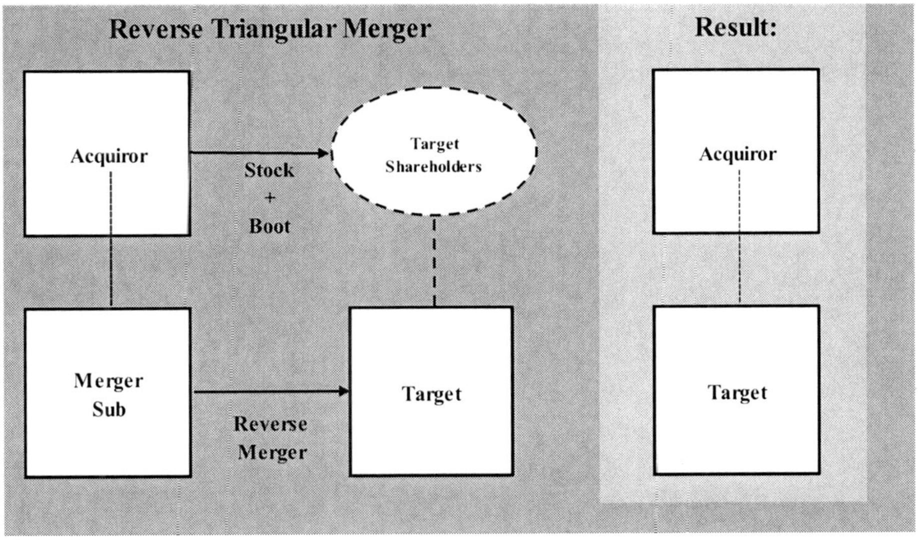

Conclusion

The CPA's role in providing M&A assistance should be guided by the professional standards promulgated by the AICPA and the FASB. The professional standard hierarchy to be utilized will be dependent on the scope and type of reporting required. Understanding the transaction and properly planning the engagement will lead to efficiencies during the process.

A wide range of information, documentation, reports, and other data is available to physician practices to assist the CPA in quantifying results and performing numerous analytics. The information obtained can be utilized to obtain insight into the practice's operational aspects (historical and future), benchmark the target's performance to similar targets, and obtain information about the target's historical and future revenue streams.

Most physician practices maintain their accounting records on the cash basis of accounting, and the CPA may be requested to provide assistance in converting cash-basis financial statements to accrual-basis financial statements. This type of assistance can provide the PPMC/PEF with a full understanding of the target's economic cash flow and a more accurate measurement of EBITDA.

The due diligence assistance engagement plays an important role in M&A transactions and can assist not only the PPMC/PEF prospective buyer, but also the selling target entity in reaching optimum financial results.

Appendix A: Sample Document Request

Due Diligence and Document Request

For the Acquisition of: ______________________________

If you feel that any of the requested information does not apply or exist, please provide a statement to that effect for the applicable section.

Financial Data: **Comments**

_____ 1. Audited or compiled financial statements for six months ended June 30, 200_ and for the year ended December 31, 200_ and supporting detailed general ledger reports for both periods. _____________

_____ 2. Accounts receivable aging report run at June 30, 200_ month-end closing and at December 31, 200_ month-end closing by patient and payor source, detailing charges, payments, adjustments, and credit balances. _____________

_____ 3. All bank statements for the six month period ended June 30, 200_ and for the 12 months ended 200_. _____________

_____ 4. Description of intercompany transactions, if any. _____________

_____ 5. List of related parties and transactions with related parties. _____________

_____ 6. List of suppliers and vendors and copies of any written purchase agreements or other contractual agreements. _____________

_____ 7. Copies of debt or line of credit arrangements. _____________

_____ 8. Copy of any operating budgets or forecasts of the Companies. _____________

_____ 9. Income tax returns filed for federal, state, city and county for prior 3 years. _____________

_____ 10. Copies of 200_ Form 940—Employer Annual Federal Unemployment Tax Return, Forms W-2 and W-3, and most recent federal and state quarterly payroll tax filings, Form 941. _____________

_____ 11. Tangible personal property tax returns for prior three years. _____________

Corporate Documents:

_____ 1. Articles of Incorporation of the entities. _____________

_____ 2. Bylaws of the entities and any other shareholder/partnership agreements. _____________

______ 3. Minutes of Board of Directors. ______

______ 4. Copies of stock certificates including both sides and copy of stock transfer ledger. ______

______ 5. Copies of any D/B/A and fictitious name filings. ______

______ 6. Corporate organizational chart of entities and ownership. ______

______ 7. List of states in which Company is qualified to do business and evidence that Company is qualified to do business in each state. ______

Physical Plant, Real Property and Other Property:

______ 1. List of all real estate (owned and leased). ______

______ 2. Instruments evidencing title to such real estate (e.g., deeds, title papers, title insurance policies and binders, title opinions, appraisals, and surveys). ______

______ 3. Real property office leases. ______

______ 4. Personal property leases, for example; copier lease, telephone equipment lease, computer equipment and software, etc. ______

______ 5. Description of any property which is collateral under financing arrangements. ______

______ 6. Detailed listing of furniture, fixtures, and medical equipment, and a general description of condition. ______

Environmental Matters:

______ 1. Biomedical hazardous waste permits. ______

______ 2. Description of the Company's generation, storage, handling, and disposal of all hazardous and infectious waste, including asbestos, chlordane, medical related waste and radioactive materials. ______

______ 3. Copy of written agreement with any contracted waste disposal service. ______

Risk Management:

______ 1. Complete copies of professional liability insurance policies (malpractice) and commercial liability policies (property and office). Malpractice insurance policy and loss history (loss runs) as provided by malpractice insurance carrier, including claims status reports from the insurance carrier. Include status on any physicians for which there are no claims. Description of any claims or events which have not been reported to the insurance carrier. ______

______ 2. Copies of letters from Company's outside legal counsel to independent accountants for the past three years regarding litigation in which the Company or an employed physician was involved. ______

______ 3. Copies of correspondence relating to any federal or state governmental investigations or proceedings before any federal, state, or municipal department, board, bureau, agency, or other instrumentality and any citations received. ______

______ 4. Copies of any documents related to payment denials, appeals, or other payment controversies between the Company and a nongovernmental third-party payor. ______

______ 5. A description of any settled, pending, or threatened claim or action against the Company arising from its participation in a government program, including, without limitation, investigations or legal action arising under the federal healthcare program fraud and abuse laws. ______

______ 6. Copies of internal investigation memoranda, assessment or audit reports, correspondence, review letters, or other documents relating to healthcare regulatory compliance audits and other activities. ______

______ 7. Any correspondence regarding employees or personnel policies from any regulatory agency such as: ______
The Department of Immigration and Naturalization
Department of Labor
National Labor Relations Board
Internal Revenue Service ______

______ 8. Identify any employment related claims, lawsuits, arbitrations, or other proceedings (including administrative and arbitrage proceedings and government agency investigations) which are pending or threatened. Furnish copies of any related documentation. ______

______ 9. List all discrimination complaints against the Company or any predecessor during the last 5 years. Show date of claims, persons involved and actual or expected outcome. ______

______ 10. Description of workers' compensation program and copies of certificates of insurance. ______

Human Resources:

______ 1. Copies of all employment or employment-related contracts, agreements, or understandings with current employees (inclusive of officers, directors, managers, physicians, nurses, technicians and any other allied healthcare professionals). Include agreements with former employees if employment-related commitments exist. ______

______ 2. Listing of all current personnel, including title, date of hire, site location, classification (full-time, part-time, per diem), experience, certifications and education, compensation, bonus targets, and accrued benefits. Description of any special compensation arrangements or incentive programs and accrued but unpaid benefits. ______

______ 3. Copies of all consulting agreements currently in effect. ______

______ 4. Most recent payroll register. ______

______ 5. Current internal organizational chart of officers and key management. ______

______ 6. Provide a description of any of the following programs: bonus, company car or auto expense allowances, cellular phone, housing and relocation, deferred compensation arrangements, jury duty, bereavement leave, personal time off, educational assistance, tuition reimbursement, employee recognition, community service programs, service awards, and executive perquisites. Provide copies of all relevant documentation, including plan documents/ communication to employees. If you have programs other than those listed above, please include. ______

______ 7. Copies of employer policy manuals or statements. ______

______ 8. To the extent not provided above, describe all vacation, sick pay, paid time off, and holidays. ______

______ 9. Description of any employee loans or loans to directors or officers. ______

______ 10. Description of group employee benefit plans, for example: (i) group health, (ii) pension and profit sharing, (iii) disability, (iv) life insurance, and (v) cafeteria plan and copies of invoices. ______

______ 11. Employee benefit plan documents for the above and 5500 filings for 200_ and 200_ for both 401k, money purchase pension plans, and cafeteria plans. The original adoption agreements, the plan document and any amendments, the summary plan descriptions, copies of fidelity bonds, most recent nondiscrimination testing results, external audit report if required, trust agreements, recent plan statements, any cafeteria plan documents, and IRS determination letters. ______

Contractual:

______ 1. All hospital, ambulatory facility, diagnostic facility, or other contracts related to the provision of professional services. ______

______ 2. Copies of operating policy and procedure manuals. ______

______ 3. All written contracts and agreements, for example; postal meter agreements, biomedical waste agreements, maintenance agreements, telephone equipment, etc. ______

Billing and Collections:

______ 1. Copies of current billing fee schedules. ______

______ 2. Schedule of major payor contract rates. ______

______ 3. All contracts, agreements and understandings with any party regarding the provision of medical services to patients, including all provider agreements with HMOs, PPOs, third party payors, IPAs, PHOs, MSOs, etc. Include all supporting schedules, amendments, addendums, referenced documents, etc. ______________

______ 4. Describe global or special arrangements with facility/providers (written and verbal). Provide copies of agreements. ______________

______ 5. Describe self-pay arrangements (written and verbal). ______________

______ 6. Description of any outsourced billing services and copies of agreements. ______________

______ 7. Medical Billing Systems generated reports (by date of service) for the six months ended June 30, 200_ and for the year ended December 31, 200_ detailing unit volume, charges, adjustments, and collections by:
a.CPT Code
b.CPT Code for major managed care providers
c.Provider
d.Location
e.Payor source ______________

Credentialing:

______ 1. Licensing and credentialing information for all physicians, other allied healthcare providers, and the P.A. These include medical licensure, curriculum vitae, occupational licenses, radiological licenses, bio-medical hazardous waste permits, and CLIA licenses. Note: Please see grid provided (Provider Information). ______________

______ 2. Listing of health care facilities in which good standing staff memberships are maintained by physicians ('privileges'). Note: This should be indicated on the grid above. ______________

______ 3. Listing of Medicare and Medicaid group and individual provider numbers and any other billing numbers pertinent to claim submission. Note: Please see grid provided (Government Plan Information). ______________

Other:

______ 1. Software and computer hardware licenses and agreements for services (please specify function software is used for, i.e. accounting, billing, payroll, etc). ______________

______ 2. Listing of other business interests of any owners, partners, or employees that represent a potential conflict of interest. ______________

______ 3. Provide copies of all government permits, clearances, and approvals for each clinic(s) held by the Company or its employees necessary to conduct business (e.g. HCC Clinic License for the State of ______). ______________

Appendix B: Commonly Used Physician Practice Ratios

$$\text{Gross Collection Ratio} = \frac{\text{Gross Collections}}{\text{Gross Charges}}$$

$$\text{Net Collection Ratio} = \frac{\text{Gross Collections}}{\text{Gross Charges} - \text{Adjustments} + \text{Refunds}}$$

$$\text{Days in Accounts Receivable} = \frac{\text{Average AR for the year x 365 days}}{\text{Net Collections for the year}}$$

$$\text{Overhead Expense \%} = \frac{\text{Operational (nonphysician expenses)}}{\text{Net Collections}}$$

$$\text{Current Ratio} = \frac{\text{Current Assets}}{\text{Current Liabilities}}$$

$$\text{Debt Ratio} = \frac{\text{Total Liabilities}}{\text{Total Assets}}$$

$$\text{Total Asset Turnover} = \frac{\text{Total Net Medical Revenue}}{\text{Total Assets}}$$

Chapter 23

When the Marriage Is Over, What Is the Practice Worth?

By Stacey D. Udell, CPA/ABV/CFF, ASA, CVA

When a physician gets divorced, the value of his or her ownership interest in the practice is likely to be included as an asset for property distribution purposes. Additionally, the income generated from the practice is likely to be utilized in the determination of support.

Valuation is an art, not a science, which makes the task of valuing a medical practice more difficult (and more likely to be disputed) than valuing the marital residence or a spouse's retirement plan. The value of a practice is based on the valuator's judgment applied to the specific facts and circumstances. Different assumptions lead to different conclusions of value, any of which may be reasonable.

Some of the major issues that must be considered are:

- Standard of value;
- Premise of value;
- Valuation dates;
- Buy and sell agreements;
- Goodwill; and
- Double dip.

Standard of value

The valuator must determine the appropriate standard of value applicable in the state or jurisdiction of the divorce. Standards of value differ among the various states and jurisdictions. Often, the family law attorney can inform the valuator of the appropriate standard of value. This standard may be based on state statute or case law. Reliance on an incorrect standard of value could lead to an incorrect value conclusion, your report and testimony being excluded as evidence and more significantly, becoming the basis of a malpractice suit.

Arkansas[1] and Louisiana[2] have statutes precisely defining the standard of value to be used in divorce. In other states, the standard of value is often left undefined. To confuse matters even more, many state statutes refer to "value" or "net value" without any further clarification or definition. To take it even further, many states inconsistently apply standards of value to arrive at an equitable result. We are not aware of any case law or statutes in Alabama or Georgia discussing the standard of value to be used in matrimonial litigation. Therefore, determining the appropriate standard of value can be a perplexing problem for the valuation expert to resolve.

The standards of value utilized in the valuation arena are fair market value, fair value, intrinsic value, and investment value.

Fair market value, which is used for estate and gift tax purposes, is defined as:

> the price, expressed in terms of cash equivalents, at which property would change hands between a *hypothetical* [emphasis added] willing and able buyer and a *hypothetical* [emphasis added] willing and able seller, acting at arms length in an open and unrestricted market, when neither is under compulsion to buy or sell and when both have reasonable knowledge of the relevant facts.[3]

While the foundation of fair market value considers a hypothetical sale, fair market value could be viewed as not contemplating one sale but a blend of potential sales.

In a marital dissolution, an actual sale of the practice is not usually contemplated. Often in divorce, the term "fair market value" is used but the court's definition may not conform to the definition for tax purposes as quoted above. Frequently, in application, a different standard of value is actually used, even though it is termed fair market value.

One derivation of fair market value is "net value," which is defined as the fair market value of the business minus any debts, liens, liabilities, or encumbrances. Net value is

1 Arkansas Statute § 9-12-315 (4).
2 La. R.S. 9:2801.
3 *International Glossary of Business Valuation Terms,* 2001.

the standard of value used in Alaska,[4] Michigan,[5] Nevada,[6] North Carolina,[7] and West Virginia.[8]

Exhibit 1 reflects the states that are considered fair market value states, either explicitly or by application. States that have utilized fair market value in addition to another standard of value are reflected in Exhibit 2.

Discounts. As part of the determination of fair market value, it may be appropriate to apply discounts for lack of control and marketability. These discounts have historically been allowed in Alaska, Arkansas, Connecticut, Iowa, New Hampshire, New York, Oregon, Vermont, West Virginia, and Wisconsin.[9]

Fair value is a statutorily or judicially defined standard of value. Frequently used in oppressed minority shareholder actions, this standard assumes one owner is an unwilling participant in the transaction, generally the seller. To compensate, discounts (for lack of control and marketability) are often not applied or applied only under extraordinary circumstances.

As reflected in the New Jersey case of *Brown v. Brown*, 348 N.J. Super. 466 (App. Div. 2002), New Jersey's standard of value for divorce purposes is fair value. In New Jersey, fair value reflects fair market value without discounts (for lack of control or marketability), barring extraordinary circumstances.[10] Unfortunately, what constitutes an extraordinary circumstance is undefined. Case law indicates that Indiana,[11] North Dakota,[12] Virginia,[13] and Massachusetts[14] are also considered fair value states. North Dakota has also utilized fair market value, as reflected in *Heggen v. Heggen*, 452 N.W.2d 96, 99 (1990).

Intrinsic value is defined in the *International Glossary of Business Valuation Terms* as "the value that an investor considers, on the basis of an evaluation or available facts, to be the 'true' or 'real' value that will become the market value when other investors reach the same conclusion." In other words, for valuation purposes, intrinsic value represents the value that a securities analyst places on the investment based on his or her perception of the risk and returns inherent in the investment.

4 *McQueary v. McQueary* , 902 P.2d 1326, 1327 (Alaska 1995).
5 *Kowaleski v. Kowaleski* , 148 Mich. App. 151; 384 N.W.2d 112; 1986 Mich. App. LEXIS 2380.
6 *Robison v. Robison* , 691 P.2d 451, 455 (Nev. 1984).
7 *Walker v. Walker* , No. COA03-998, 2004 LEXIS 1319, at 7-9 (N.C. Ct. App. July 20, 2004) (unpublished).
8 *Alley v. Alley*, No. COA02-594, 2003 LEXIS 1986, at 8-10; *Durnell v. Durnell*, 460 S.E.2d 710, 717-18 (W. Va. 1995).
9 Fishman, Jay *Standards of Value: Theory and Applications* (Hoboken, NJ: John Wiley & Sons, Inc., 2007), 218.
10 *Brown v. Brown* , 348 N.J. Super. 466 (App. Div. 2002).
11 *Bobrow v. Bobrow* , 711 N.E.2d 1265:1999.
12 *Fisher v. Fisher* , 568 N.W.2d 728, 732-33 (N.D. 1997).
13 *Gardner v. Gardner* , No. 0468-04-03, 2005 LEXIS 10, at *15 (Va. Ct. App. Jan. 11, 2005) (unpublished).
14 *Judith E. Bernier v. Stephen A. Bernier* , SJC-09836, Sept. 14, 2007.

Exhibit 1. Fair Market Value States—Explicitly or by Application

Arizona	*Sample v. Sample*, 731 P.2d 604, 606 (Ariz. Ct. App. 1986)
Arkansas	Ark. Code Ann. § 9-12-315 (2005)
Connecticut	*Eslami v. Eslami*, 591 A.2d 411, 416 (Conn. 1991)
Delaware	*E.E.C. v. E.J.C.*, 457 A.2d 688, 694 (Del. 1983);
District of Columbia	*McDiarmid v. McDiarmid*, App. D.C., 649 A.2d 810 (1994)
Florida	*Thompson v. Thompson*, 576 So. 2d 267 (Fla. 1991)
Hawaii	*Antolik v. Harvey*, 761 P.2d 305, 319 (Haw. Ct. App. 1988);
Idaho	*McAffee v. McAffee*, 971 P.2d 734, 740 (Idaho Ct. App. 1994);
Illinois	*In re Marriage of Grunsten*, 709 N.E.2d 597, 602 (Ill. App. Ct. 1999);
Indiana	*Trost-Steffen v. Steffen*, 772 N.E.2d 500 (Ind. Ct. App. 2002);
Iowa	*In re Marriage of Frett*, No. 4-083/03-1305, 2004 LEXIS 694, at 7 (Iowa Ct. App. May 14, 2004) (unpublished);
Kansas	*Bohl v. Bohl*, 232 Kan. 557; 657 P.2d 1106; 1983 Kan. LEXIS 236
Maine	*Dargie v. Dargie*, 778 A.2d 353, 357 (Me. 2001);
Maryland	*Long v. Long*, 743 A.2d 281, 291 (Md. Ct. Spec. App. 2000);
Massachusetts	*Champion v. Champion*, 764 N.E.2d 898, 901 (Mass. App. Ct. 2002); now replaced by *Bernier*
Minnesota	*In re the Marriage of Berenberg*, 474 N.W.2d 843 (Minn. Ct. App. 1991);
Mississippi	*Singley v. Singley*, No. 1999-CT-00754-SCT, 2003 LEXIS 283, at 20 (Miss. June 12, 2003);
Missouri	*L.R.M v. R.K.M.*, 46 S.W.3d 24, 29 (Mo. Ct. App. 2001);
Montana	*In re Marriage of Ortiz*, 938 P.2d 1308, 1310 (Mont. 1997);
Nebraska	*Gohl v. Gohl*, 13 Neb. App. 685 (Ct. App. 2005), No. A-03-1102, 2005 LEXIS 143, at 30-31 (Neb. Ct. App. July 5, 2005);
New Hampshire	*Rattee v. Rattee*, 767 A.2d 415, 421 (N.H. 2001).
New Mexico	*Trego v. Scott*, 961 P.2d 168, 172-73 (N.M. Ct. App. 1998);
Oklahoma	*Bond v. Bond*, 916 P.2d 272, 275 (Okla. Ct. App. 1996);
Oregon	*I/M/O the Marriage of Hanson*, 86 P.3d 94, 98 (Or. Ct. App. 2004);
Pennsylvania	*Traczyk v. Traczyk*, No. 78435. 891 P.2d 1277. 1995 OK 22
Rhode Island	*Moretti v. Moretti*, 766 A.2d 925, 928 (R.I. 2001);
South Carolina	*Dixon v. Dixon*, 512 S.E.2d 539, 549 (S.C. Ct. App. 1999);
South Dakota	*Fausch v. Fausch*, 697 N.W.2d 748 (S.D. 2005), No. 23316, 2005 LEXIS 63, at 11, 13-14 (S.D. May 18, 2005);
Tennessee	*Barbara Lee Bunce Kerce v. Stephen Paul Kerce*, No. M2002-01744-COA-R3-CV (Tenn. Ct. App. August 29, 2003)
Texas	*Zeptner v. Zeptner*, 111 S.W.3d 727, 738 (Tex. Ct. App. 2003);
Utah	*Sorenson v. Sorenson*, 769 P.2d 820 (Utah App. 1989)
Vermont	*Goodrich v. Goodrich*, 613 A.2d 203 (Vt. 1992), 158 Vt. 587, 591-92 (1992);
Wisconsin	*Frawley v. Frawley*, 693 N.W.2d 146 (Wis. Ct. App. 2005), No. 03-2550, 2005 LEXIS 7, at 4 (Wis. Ct. App. Jan. 6, 2005);
Wyoming	*Neuman v. Neuman*, 842 P.2d 575, 581-82 (Wyo. 1992).
Primary source of data: Vuotto, Charles F., Jr., Esquire. "Fair Market Value— Everyone Else Is Doing It, So Why Can't We?" *New Jersey Law Journal: Family Law Supplement* (2005), www.vuotto.com/new-jersey-divorce-articles/fairmarket-value.htm	

Exhibit 2. States Utilizing More Than One Standard of Value

State	Fair Market Value Case Law	Additional Standard of Value	Additional Standard Case Law
California	*In re Cream*, 16 Cal. Rptr. 2d 575, 579 (Ct. App. 1993)	Investment value	*In re Marriage of Hewitson*, 142 Cal. App. 3d 874 (Ct. App. 1983).
Michigan	*Golden v. Golden*, No. 218106, 2001 LEXIS 1057 (Mich. Ct. App. Mar. 20, 2001) (unpublished)	Investment value	*Sutherland v. Sutherland*, No. 240158, 2004 LEXIS 174, at 9 (Mich. Ct. App. Jan. 20, 2004) (unpublished)
New York	*Morse v. Morse*, 784 N.Y.S.2d 590, 591 (App. Div. 2004);	Investment value	*O'Brien v. O'Brien*, 66 N.Y.2d 576; 489 N.E.2d 712; 498 N.Y.S.2d 743
North Dakota	*Heggen v. Heggen*, 452 N.W.2d 96, 99 (N.D. 1990),	Fair Value	*In Fisher v. Fisher*, 568 N.W.2d 728, 732-33 (N.D. 1997).
Ohio	*Cronin v. Cronin*, 2005 Ohio 301 (Ct. App. 2005), No. 02-CA-110, 03-CA75, 2005 LEXIS 268, at 5-6 (Ohio Ct. App. Jan. 28, 2005).	Intrinsic Value	*Brookhart v Brookhart*, No. 93 CA 1569, 1993 LEXIS 5586 (Ohio Ct. app. Nov. 18, 1003) (unpublished)
Primary source of data: Vuotto, Charles F., Jr., Esquire. "Fair Market Value—Everyone Else Is Doing It, So Why Can't We?" *New Jersey Law Journal: Family Law Supplement* (2005), www.vuotto.com/new-jersey-divorce-articles/fairmarket-value.htm			

The term "intrinsic value" has been used rather liberally by the courts and appears to be defined by the facts and circumstances of the particular case. The only state specifically requiring the use of the intrinsic value standard is Virginia. In the Virginia case of *Howell v. Howell*, 31 Va. App. 332, 345-46, 523 S.E. 2d 514, 521 (2000), Mr. Howell was an owner in a family business started by his father. Mr. Howell's two sons worked in the business, with one likely to operate the business after him. The court determined that since the sale of the business to a third party was not contemplated, no discount for lack of marketability should be taken from the value of the stock. In its decision, the court defined intrinsic value as "the value of the business interest to its current owner given the owner's current use of the interest, current resources, and current capabilities for economically exploiting the business interest." By application, this appears to be a fair value standard even though it is specifically identified as intrinsic value by the Virginia court.

Investment value represents the value to a specific buyer, as opposed to the hypothetical buyer contemplated in the fair market standard of value. In his book *Standards of Value: Theory and Applications*, Jay Fishman aptly states that "fair market value is impersonal, but investment value reflects the unique situation of a particular person or company."[15]

This standard of value allows the consideration of synergies available to the potential buyer. In the California case of *Golden v. Golden*, 270 Cal. App. 2d 401, 75 Cal. Rptr. 735, 1969 Cal. App. LEXIS 1538, the court recognized the similarities between value to the

15 Fishman, Jay *Standards of Value: Theory and Applications* (Hoboken, NJ: John Wiley & Sons, Inc., 2007), 218.

holder and investment value. [Editor's note: California divorce cases are discussed in Chapter 24 of this guide.]

Particularly in divorce matters, investment value is often referred to as "value to the holder" or "divorce value" because it recognizes that, in the context of a divorce, there is no hypothetical or actual sale of the practice and the physician owner will continue to receive benefits based on his or her ownership in the practice. Courts in California, Colorado,[16] Michigan, New York, and Washington[17] have adopted the investment value standard of value for marital dissolution purposes.

Premise of value

The *International Glossary of Business Valuation Terms* defines premise of value as "an assumption regarding the most likely set of transactional circumstances that may be applicable to the subject valuation."[18] The two recognized premises of value are going concern and liquidation.

The going concern value assumes the business will continue operating into the future. This results from having such things as "a trained work force, an operational plant, and the necessary licenses, systems, and procedures in place."[19] Unless otherwise excluded from the marital estate (by statute, for example), goodwill is included under the going concern premise of value.

Liquidation value can be defined as the amount that would be realized if the business were terminated. Liquidation can be either "orderly" or "forced." An orderly liquidation would generate higher proceeds and results when the business is terminated and the assets are sold piecemeal. In a forced liquidation, the assets are sold as quickly as possible and lower proceeds are usually generated. Liquidation value is applicable when a controlling interest is being valued because a minority (noncontrolling) owner may not compel the sale of the business. Furthermore, the liquidation value would be pertinent only if it is greater than the value determined by an income or market approach.

In the North Dakota case of *Sommers v. Sommers* , 2003 N.D. 77, 660 N.W. 2d 586 (2003), when valuing an orthodontics practice, the court stated "liquidation value is the least favored method of valuing any type of marital property in a divorce."

16 *In re marriage of Huff* , 834 P.2d 244, 254 (Colo. 1992).
17 *Matter of Marriage of Fleege* , 588 P.2d 1136 (1979).
18 *International Glossary of Business Valuation Terms*, 2001.
19 *International Glossary of Business Valuation Terms*, 2001.

Valuation date

State law reflects the appropriate date to value the practice for divorce purposes. Fourteen states require the use of a date as close as possible to the date of trial. Fifteen states and the District of Columbia require the use of the date of complaint. Nineteen states suggest using the date of divorce. Two states mandate the use of the date of separation. When the use of a trial date or dissolution date is required, often the state laws suggest the use of a current date. Exhibit 3 reflects each state's requirement.

Exhibit 3. Property Valuation Date

Trial	Complaint	Divorce	Separation
Alabama	Arizona	Arkansas	Hawaii
Alaska	Dist. of Columbia	Connecticut	North Carolina
California	Florida	Georgia	
Colorado	Indiana	Idaho	
Delaware	Kansas	Illinois	
Iowa	Maine	Kentucky	
Missouri	Michigan	Louisiana	
North Dakota	Mississippi	Maryland	
Oregon	New Hampshire	Massachusetts	
Pennsylvania	New Jersey	Minnesota	
Rhode Island	New York	Montana	
Tennessee	Ohio	Nebraska	
Vermont	Oklahoma	Nevada	
Virginia	South Carolina	New Mexico	
	West Virginia	South Dakota	
	Wyoming	Texas	
		Utah	
		Washington	
		Wisconsin	

Appreciation

What happens when a physician gets married and then divorced, all while owning a medical practice? Depending on the state, the appreciation in the value of the practice during the marriage may need to be determined. The appraiser must determine the value of the practice at the date of marriage and the date of complaint.

In re Marriage of Ackerman, 146 Cal. App. 4th 191 (Cal. App. 2006), the husband was board certified in plastic and reconstructive surgery. He began his practice in 1987 and was married in 1991. The husband and wife signed a premarital agreement in which they stipulated to a value of the practice as of the date of marriage. In 2001, the couple separated. Therefore, only the increase in value from the date of marriage to the date of complaint was deemed community property subject to equitable distribution.

Clearly, when a value is not determined at the beginning of the marriage, the valuator has a difficult task ahead because often a significant amount of time has passed and records may not be available.

Buy and Sell Agreements

Often physicians are party to a buy or sell agreement. These agreements are typically utilized in situations of death, disability, retirement, or withdrawal of a partner. While these agreements may set a value and be binding for transfers of an ownership interest, disagreements exist as to the use of these values or formulas in the context of marital dissolution because the nonphysician spouse is not party to the agreement and no change in ownership is occurring.

The courts have recognized that often values included in these agreements contain artificially low values. However, some states consider the agreement value the sole indicator of value, concluding that the amount in the agreement is the only amount the owner will ever receive and it would be inequitable for the nonowner-spouse to receive more than the owner-spouse.

In the New Mexico case of *Hertz v. Hertz*, 99 N.M. 320, 325, 657 P.2d 1169, 1174 (N.M. 1983), the spouse was bound by the $1 value contained in the attorney husband's Restrictive Stock Agreement because, as the court stated, "We hold that a nonshareholder spouse is bound to the same terms of a shareholder valuation agreement, which affects the shareholder spouse. This insures that the nonshareholder spouse does not receive a *greater* value than that of the shareholder." The State Supreme Court, overturning the local district court's decision, noted that if the husband terminated his employment with the law firm, he would never realize the value of the goodwill that was awarded to the wife by the district court.

The New York case of *McDiarmid v. McDiarmid*, 649 A.2d 810, 815 (D.C. App. 1994) referenced the *Hertz* case and stated that goodwill of the medical practice was not includable as marital property since the buy or sell agreement specifically excluded it.

In *Weaver v. Weaver*, 72 N.C. App. 409, 324 S.E.2d 915 (1985) and *Stern v. Stern*, 66 N.J. 340, 331 A.2d 257 (1975), the courts indicated that when the terms of a partnership agreement are followed, the value of the interest calculated is only a presumptive value, which can be attacked by either plaintiff or defendant as not reflective of the true value. In

Stern v. Stern, the Supreme Court of New Jersey stated that the value of a partnership interest determined by use of the partnership agreement should only be used "once it is established that the books of the firm are well-kept and that the value of the partners' interests are in fact periodically and carefully reviewed . . ."

The majority of states follow West Virginia's ruling in the case of *Bettinger v. Bettinger*, 396 S.E.2d 709, 714 (W.Va. 1990), wherein the court opined that the value pursuant to the buy or sell Agreement should be considered along with any other relevant evidence regarding the value and weighted accordingly.

Additionally, the physician's age may be a consideration. A value set by an agreement may be more relevant in the case of a 58-year-old physician subject to mandatory retirement at age 60 who is nearing the end of his professional career than the case of a 38-year-old physician subject to the same agreement when sale or retirement is not imminent.

Valuation approaches. Generally, the preferred approach for valuing a medical practice, like any other service business, is an income approach. This method considers the expected long-term earnings stream that the physician can reasonably expect to receive until retirement.

In valuing medical practices, asset approaches are generally not favored because there is often value beyond the physical assets.

The market approaches, particularly the comparable transactions method, are often utilized, but many times sufficient details regarding the transactions are unknown, and the valuator may not be comparing apples to apples. Specifically, a valuator would not be aware of any synergies or other investment value characteristics that influenced the transaction.

There are situations where the market approach may be considered an indicator of value. For example, in recent years, AmSurg, a publicly traded hospital management company, has purchased a number of ambulatory surgical centers. The multiples used by AmSurg have been relatively consistent, so their application to the subject practice may be appropriate. The weakness in this approach, of course, is knowledge of the underlying characteristics of the comparable companies and the subject company. [Editor's note: See Chapter 2, "Healthcare Market Structure and Its Implication for Valuation of Privately Held Provider Entities."]

The question arises as to whether it is fair to use a market approach when a transaction is not likely to occur. A market approach is often better used as a reasonableness check, rather than a primary or even secondary indicator of value.

Goodwill

In addition to the value of the tangible assets owned by a medical practice, the value is also comprised of intangible assets such as goodwill, patient lists, medical records, and covenants not to compete. The value of the intangible component is often greater than the value of the tangible component.

Goodwill is defined as "that intangible asset arising as a result of name, reputation, customer loyalty, location, products, and similar factors not separately identified."[20] It can be viewed as the ability to earn a return over and above the return earned on the tangible assets.

Once it has been determined that goodwill exists, it must be valued. Goodwill is often valued to compensate the nonphysician spouse for his or her marital contribution.

Two types of goodwill may be associated with the value of a medical practice. Personal (or professional) goodwill is attached to the individual and his or her unique abilities and characteristics. Practice (or entity) goodwill is attached to the medical practice and is not associated with the physician's unique abilities and characteristics.

Personal goodwill presumes that a practice has a higher value as a result of the particular professional's knowledge, experience, and reputation. "Personal goodwill is that which would make a doctor's patients follow him even if he changed his location, staff, and phone number."[21] As such, personal goodwill is difficult to transfer, but it may be done with advance planning and cooperation between the buyer and the seller. However, would a hypothetical buyer pay anything for personal goodwill (under the fair market value standard of value)?

Practice goodwill is associated with the practice as a unit, including its location, systems, operating procedures and policies, staff, an established client base, and patient records. Another indicator of practice goodwill is a telephone number. Assume a family practice has a telephone number of 808-555-1212. As a patient of that practice needing an appointment, you will call that number and ask for an appointment with Dr. A. If Dr. A is not there, you still are likely to see whatever doctor is available at that telephone number.

A distinction must be made between personal goodwill and practice goodwill because the majority of states do not consider personal goodwill a marital asset (Exhibit 4).

A minority of states have ruled that goodwill is never marital property, whether it is personal goodwill or practice goodwill (Exhibit 5). Then, there are states that have ruled that all goodwill is marital property (Exhibit 6). These three exhibits reflect cases

20 *International Glossary of Business Valuation Terms*, 2001.

21 Fishman, Jay E. *Standards of Value: Theory and Applications* (Hoboken, NJ: John Wiley & Sons, Inc., 2007), 203.

Exhibit 4. Practice Goodwill is a Divisible Marital Asset
Personal Goodwill is not a Divisible Marital Asset

Alaska	*Fortson v. Fortson*, 131 P.3d 451 (Alaska 2006)
Arkansas	*Wilson v. Wilson*, 294 Ark. 194 (1987)
Connecticut	*Eslami v. Eslami*, 218 Conn. 801, 591 A.2d 411 (1991)
Delaware	*E.E.C. v. E.J.C.*, 457 A.2d 688 (Del. 1983) (Law Practice)
District Of Columbia	*McDiarmid v. McDiarmid*, 594 A.2d 79 (D.C. 1991 (Law practice)
Florida	*Young v. Young*, 600 So.2d 1140 (Fla. App. 5 Dist. 1992).
Georgia	*Miller v. Miller*, 2010 WL 4704326(Ga.)(Nov. 22, 2010)
Hawaii	*Antolik v. Harvey*, 761 P.2d 305, 319 (Haw. Ct. App. 1988)
Illinois	*In re Marriage of Head*, 273 Ill. App.3d 404, 652 N.E.2d 1246, 210 Ill. Dec. 270 (1995)
Indiana	*Yoon v. Yoon*, 711 N.E.2d 1265 (Ind. 1999)
Kentucky	*Gaskill v.Robbins*, 2009 WL 425619 (Ky.) (Feb 19, 2009)
Maine	*Ahern v. Ahern*, 2008 ME 1, (January 3, 2008)
Maryland	*Skrabak v. Strabak*, 108 Md. App. 633, 673 A.2d 732, 1996 Md. App. LEXIS 39
Massachusetts*	*Goldman v. Goldman*, 28 Mass. App. Ct. 603, 554 N.E.2d 860 (1990)
Minnesota	*In re Marriage of Baker*, 2007 Minn. App. A06-1252
Missouri	*Hanson v. Hanson*, 738 S.W.2d 429 (Mo. 1987)
Nebraska	*Taylor v. Taylor*, 222 Neb. 721, 386 N.W.2d 851 (1986)
New Hampshire	*In re Watterworth*, 149 N.H. 442, 821 A.2d 1107 (2003)
Oklahoma	*Traczyk v. Traczyk*, No. 78435. 891 P.2d 1277, 1995 OK 22
Oregon	*Matter of the Dissolution of the Marriage of Goger*, 27 Or. App. 729 (1976)
Pennsylvania	*Gaydos v. Gaydos*, 693 A.2d 1368 (Pa. Super. 1997)
Rhode Island	*Gibbons v. Gibbons*, 619 A.2d 432 (R.I. 1993))
Texas	*Nail v. Nail*, 486 S.W.2d 761 (Tex. 1972)
Utah	*Sorenson v. Sorenson*, 769 P.2d 820 (Utah Ct. App. 1989)
Vermont	*Mills v. Mills*, 167 Vt. 567 (1997)
Virginia	*Hoebelheinrich v. Hoebelheinrich*, 2004 Va. App. LEXIS 376
West Virginia	May v. May, 214 W.Va. 394, 589 S.E.2d 536 (2003)
Wisconsin	Holbrook v. Holbrook, 103 Wis.2d 327, 309 N.W.2d 343 (1981)
Wyoming	Root v. Root, 2003 WY 36, 65 P.3d 41 (2003)
*Although *Goldman* is oft-cited as suggesting that personal goodwill is nondivisible, it has little sway in that it involved a neurosurgery practice where transferable enterprise goodwill would be hard to find. The sole statement in this Appellate decision is "The judge was warranted in accepting the husband's accountant's opinion that there was no goodwill in this one-man professional corporation." As a result of *Sampson* (62 Mass . App. Ct. 366 (2004), Massachusetts now considers the extent of any "Double Dip" in what is equitable; Double Dipping is not precluded, however, as it may be in other jurisdictions.	

Exhibit 5. Goodwill is a Divisible Marital Asset - Whether Personal or Practice

Arizona*	*Wisner v. Wisner*, 129 Ariz. 333, 631 P.2d 115 (Ariz. Ap. 1981)
California*	*In re Marriage of Foster*, 42 Cal.App.3d 577 (1974)
Colorado	*In re Marriage of Nichols*, 43 Colo. App. 383 (1979)
Kentucky	*Clark v. Clark*, Ky. App., 782 S.W.2d 56 (1990)
Michigan	*Kowalesky v. Kowalesky*, 148 Mich. App. 151, 384 N.W.2d 12 (1986)
Montana	*Marriage of Hull*, 219 Mont. 480 (1986)
Nevada*	*Ford v. Ford*, 105 Nev. 672, 782 P.2d 1304 (1989)
New Jersey	*Stern v. Stern*, 66 N.J. 340, 331 A.2d 257 (1975) (Law practice)
New Mexico*	*Hurley v. Hurley*, 94 N.M. 641, 615 P. 2d 256 (1980)
New York	*Nehorayoff v. Nehorayoff*, 08 Misc. 2d 311; 437 N.Y.S.2d 584 (1981)
North Carolina	*Poore v. Poore*, 75 N.C. App. 414, 331 S.E.2d 266 (1985)
North Dakota	*Sommers v. Sommers*, 2003 ND 77, 660 N.W.2d 596 (2003)
Ohio	*Kahn v. Kahn*, 42 Ohio App.3d 61 (1987)
Washington*	*In re Marriage of Fleege*, 91 Wn.2d 324 (1979)
* Community Property State	

Exhibit 6. Goodwill is Never a Divisible Marital Asset

Kansas	*Powell v. Powell*, 231 Kan. 456, 648 P.2d 218 (1982)
Louisiana	*Chance v. Chance*, 694 So. 2d 613 (La. App. 1997)
Mississippi	*Singley v. Singley*, 1999-CT-00754-SCT (Miss. 6-12-2003)
South Carolina	*Donahue v. Donahue*, 299 S.C. 353, 384 S.E.2d 741 (1989)
Tennessee	*Hazard v. Hazard*, 833 S.W.2d 911 (Tenn.App. 1991)

specifically related to medical practices, unless noted otherwise. Of course, there are some states (Alabama, Idaho, Iowa, and South Dakota) that are undecided in this matter.

In Indiana, enterprise goodwill is marital; personal goodwill *may* be. The party wishing to exclude personal goodwill must submit evidence of its value to the trial court.[22]

Many court cases have detailed factors to consider in determining professional goodwill. *In re Marriage of Lopez*, 38 Cal.App.3d 93 (1974) identifies the following factors:

1. Practitioner's age and health;
2. Demonstrated earning power;
3. Reputation for judgment, skill, and knowledge;
4. Comparative professional success;
5. Nature and duration of practice, either as sole practitioner or as a contributing member of a partnership or professional corporation.

22 *Balicki v. Balicki*, 837N.E.2d 532 (Ind. App. 2005)

The Pennsylvania case *Fexa v. Fexa*, 396 Pa. Super. 481, 578 A.2d 1314 (1990) addressed the distinction between personal goodwill and practice goodwill. The court reasoned that since:

> partners have bought in and been bought out and the practice has been maintained, there is a clear basis upon which to determine that the goodwill enjoyed by the practice was not entirely personal to the individual professionals involved. Likewise, where the professionals share clients within the corporation or partnership, there is a basis upon which to conclude that the goodwill is not purely personal.

In valuing a medical practice, many factors, such as those described below, must be evaluated that contribute to goodwill, whether it is personal or practice goodwill.

Age and health of practitioner. There is likely less goodwill in the case of an older or unhealthy practitioner, since expected future earnings are not expected to continue for a long period of time.

Ancillary services. A medical practice that has a laboratory attached or is in close proximity is likely to have greater practice goodwill and receive a greater return on its investment. Alternatively, however, a primary care physician with a single X-ray machine is not likely to earn excess profits by having that single machine.

Area of specialization. A cardiologist or neurologist is likely to have personal goodwill, while a radiologist is more likely to have practice goodwill, particularly because the patient may not even see the radiologist.

Cash flow and earnings ability. A physician's cash flow or earnings ability as compared to his or her partners is likely an indicator of personal goodwill, while the earning ability of the practice compared to its peers is likely an indicator of practice goodwill.

Changes in ownership. When physicians are entering and leaving the practice regularly and there is little or no impact on the practice, it likely is an indicator of practice goodwill. On the other hand, if the practice disbands or suffers economically upon the termination of an individual, it was likely personal goodwill creating the value.

Location and competition. If the subject is the only local practice, it is likely that practice goodwill exists. However, if there are many physicians in town, personal goodwill is likely the driver.

Patient base. Where a practice has a large, established patient base that requires recurring care, practice goodwill is likely to exist. This could be the case with practices specializing in primary care, internal medicine, pediatrics, and family medicine, for example.

Patient visits. If a patient is shared among practice physicians, it likely represents the existence of practice goodwill. For example, in a group obstetrics practice, a pregnant woman is likely to visit various physicians. If she returns to the practice, she is likely continuing due to practice goodwill.

Referral base. Referrals made to the individual physician would likely indicate personal goodwill, while referrals to the practice in general would indicate practice goodwill. Some examples are that a patient is likely to get a referral to a specific cardiologist (personal goodwill) or may be referred to a certain radiology practice for X-rays (practice goodwill).

Relationships. Example: A pulmonologist is an owner of a group medical practice that provides inpatient services to various hospitals under contract. The physician also sees patients in the office one or two days per week, which are primarily follow-up visits from hospital patients. This pulmonologist is likely to have practice goodwill because the practice receives the majority of its patients due to the follow-up visits required as a result of the physician's relationship with the hospital, rather than the physician's individual reputation. However, one could argue that if a patient continues to visit this same pulmonologist after the initial follow-up visit, then personal goodwill exists. [Editor's note: Appraisers should also consider the underlying contracts with the hospitals as part of this practice and personal goodwill analysis.]

Tangible assets and equipment owned. A practice with a significant investment in equipment is likely to have more practice goodwill than a physician, such as a family practitioner, that does not require the use of highly technical and expensive equipment.

Work habits. When comparing two physicians working the same amount of hours in the same specialty, for example, the physician that works more efficiently is likely to have more personal goodwill. Increased time spent per patient is also likely an indicator of personal goodwill.

Years in profession. The longer a physician has been in practice, the more likely he or she is to have personal goodwill.

Double dip

The "double dip" dilemma exists when the same income stream is used for multiple purposes—for example, when the income stream of a business is utilized to value a practice and that same earnings stream is used as the basis for support.

Normalized compensation is utilized in determining the value of a practice. It represents what the owner physician would have to pay another physician to come in and perform the same function as the owner-physician, distinguishing between the return on labor and the return on equity.This is the key task for the appraiser of a professional practice. Often, the determination of reasonable compensation is the most disputed part of the valuation. Further discussion of reasonable compensation is located at the end of this chapter.

The actual compensation, which is usually greater than the normalized compensation, often includes discretionary personal expenses that are paid by the business, such as automobile expenses, dues and subscriptions, household expenses, meals and entertainment, retirement plan contributions, telephone, and travel. The use of normalized compensation for valuation purposes increases the value of the practice. At the same time, actual compensation is often used as the basis for support.

For example, assume the information in Exhibit 7 for Dr. A.

Exhibit 7. Information for Dr. A

	Actual	Normalized
Revenue	$800,000	$800,000
Operating expenses	300,000	300,000
Operating Income before physician compensation	500,000	500,000
Physician compensation	490,000	200,000
Pretax income	10,000	300,000
Income taxes	4,000	120,000
Net income	$6,000	$180,000

Assuming a capitalization rate for net income of 20%, the value of the practice using normalized compensation is $900,000. The spouse's alimony is going to be calculated based on the physician's compensation of $490,000. Therefore, the spouse is receiving the double benefit from the normalized earnings utilized in determining the value of the practice and the actual compensation taken by the physician.

As is the case with determining the applicable standard of value, the states' treatment of the double dip varies.

Michigan[23] and New Jersey have implied that the double dip dilemma does not exist. In 2005, the New Jersey Supreme Court ruled in *Steneken v. Steneken*, 183 N.J. 290 (App. Div. 2005):

23 *McGregor v. McGregor*, 2004 Mich. App. Lexis 2560.

> The interplay between an alimony award and equitable distribution is subject to an overarching concept of fairness.... The goal of a proper alimony award is to assist the supported spouse in achieving a lifestyle reasonably comparable to the one enjoyed during the marriage.... Much of the controversy inherent in this appeal stems from the unspoken premise that because alimony and equitable distribution are interrelated, a credit on one side of the ledger must perforce require a debit on the other side; otherwise, defendant claims, the interplay between alimony and equitable distribution results in "double counting." We disagree....

In other words, in Michigan and New Jersey, it is acceptable to use a normalized compensation for purposes of valuing the business but actual compensation for determining support.

On the other side of the coin, in *Holbrook v. Holbrook*, 103 Wis. 2d 327, 309 N.W. 2nd 343 (Ct. App. 1981), a Wisconsin Appellate Court disallowed the double dip and stated that Mr. Holbrook's actual earnings could not be utilized for purposes of determining the value of the practice's goodwill.

New Hampshire[24] and New York have taken it a step further, by stating that the double dip is not allowed for alimony but is allowable for child support. In *Holterman v. Holterman*, 3 N.Y. 3d 1; 814 N.E. 2d 765; 781 N.Y.S. 2d 458 (2004), the state reiterated that there is a value to a physician's medical license (or other advanced degrees, certifications, or celebrity status) for equitable distribution purposes. The court also opined that the income stream utilized in valuing the license may not be used to determine spousal support but is allowed to be used in the determination of child support.

Reasonable compensation. The reasonable compensation adjustment is likely the biggest bone of contention in marital litigation because it is often the largest adjustment in terms of dollars. While this section is not designed to discuss the topic in its entirety, this discussion will provide an overview specifically for the purposes of medical practice valuation.

Often, surveys provide the best data for use in determining reasonable compensation, also called normalized compensation. Some of the most commonly referenced surveys are the following:

- American Medical Association's *Physician's Socioeconomic Statistics* surveys;
- Medical Group Management Association *Physician Compensation and Production Survey;*

24 *Rattee v. Rattee*, 767 A.2d, 415 (Sup. Ct. New Hampshire 2001).

- Merritt Hawkins *Physician Compensation* surveys; and
- Sullivan Cotter and Associates Inc. *Physician Compensation Survey.*

Additionally, the Economic Research Institute has a database that provides compensation figures based on numerous classifications.

Rather than relying on any of the survey data blindly, as the appraiser or valuation analyst, you must know and understand how and where the data are obtained. While the data themselves may be reliable, common sense must also be utilized. In the California case of *In re Marriage of Ackerman* (2006), Cal. App. 4th, at issue was the reasonable compensation of a plastic surgeon located in Newport Beach. The experts utilized information contained in the Medical Group Management Association surveys and the American Medical Association surveys. The court requested the husband's expert survey local plastic surgeons. In this particular case, the survey of local practitioners was given the greatest weight by the court. The court reasoned that plastic surgery used discretionary income, which is more available in Newport Beach than other areas that would have been included in the survey data. [Editor's note: See also Chapter 10.]

In addition to the specialty and geographic area of a physician, the appraiser must consider, at a minimum, the duties, experience, efficiency, productivity, and hours worked. Often, the size of the practice has an impact on compensation, as does the profit distribution method. In addition to a physician's patient care duties, any administrative duties or hospital board duties should be evaluated.

Summation

Successful valuation engagements require sound judgment. You must be confident that the conclusions reached are reasonable based on the unique facts and circumstances of the case and that your value is reasonably defensible. With the majority of the issues discussed in this chapter, the courts have looked to previous decisions not only in their own state, but also in other states. As valuators, knowledge of the relevant case law would likely increase the value of your services to referring attorneys.

Chapter 24

Jurisdictional Issues in Physician Practice Divorce Valuation: California

By Kathie Wilson, CPA, CVA, and Tracy Farryl Katz, Esq., CPA

Family law courts are "courts of equity," and as such, they can define and redefine concepts to achieve just results. The result in California has been a very fluid body of family law. A significant amount of the medical practice valuation methodology is not found in the Family Code or prior court cases but is entirely up to the discretion of the court. In recognition of this, the organization of this chapter is based upon the stability of the concepts. It starts with some concepts right from the Family Code and ends with an analysis of four recent court cases involving professional practice valuation issues. The discussion here is limited to concepts that appear to be unique to California. As you read through this chapter, you will get a flavor for the concepts that are routinely accepted by the courts and those that are more situationally accepted. The fluidity of family law means that the effects of the four recent significant court cases are still not completely known.

Family Code §771, Earnings and accumulations after date of separation are separate property

It is a relatively simple concept: What you earn after the date of separation, you get to keep. Once the community is irreparably broken, it no longer has an interest in either spouse's earned income or accumulations related to that earned income. This general rule impacts physician practice valuations in two key ways: date of value and permissible valuation methods.

Family Code §2552, Valuation date of assets and liabilities

The valuation date for the assets and liabilities of the community, under Family Code §2552, is "as near as practicable to the time of trial." As a general rule, this makes sense; the community retains its interest in the assets and liabilities until they are legally divided. Certainly a clear example of this is the valuation of a brokerage or retirement account that has no activity subsequent to the date of separation and nothing affecting its value other than market forces. In this instance, the community either bears the risk or shares in the reward when the asset is ultimately divided at the time of trial.

It is the reconciliation of these two code sections that can affect the date of value of a physician's practice because the value of the practice is typically impacted by the efforts of the physician. If he or she is working less after the date of separation, all things being equal, the value of the practice would be expected to decrease. By the same token, an increase in efforts after the date of separation, all things being equal, should result in an increase in practice value. In both of these examples, the rise or fall in value after the date of separation is due to the efforts of the doctor. When post-separation efforts affect the practice value, an alternate valuation date (i.e., date of separation) may be available. An alternate valuation date is only available if it is requested and approved by the court. It does not apply automatically.

It follows that the community's interest in the physician practice is correctly determined at the date of separation as earnings and *accumulations* after the date of separation are separate property. This is not to say that all physician practices are greatly impacted by the efforts of the individual doctor. A large group practice or one with significant ancillary income, nonphysician providers, large capital investment, and a compensation system less determined by individual productivity could arguably be correctly valued near the time of trial as an individual physician's efforts may not have a great impact on the practice value. In the case of *Aufmuth v. Aufmuth*, 89 Cal.App.3d 446 (1979), valuation at the date of separation was denied because the court determined that the efforts of the spouse, a young attorney with a 5% ownership interest in his firm, were not the reason for the increase in the value of the law firm between date of separation and time of trial. The court concluded that the increase in the value of the law firm was related to the increase in the accounts receivable and that Mr. Aufmuth's efforts were not responsible for the increase in the accounts receivable.

The concept that earnings after the date of separation are separate property can also impact the valuation methodology. In the case of *Foster v. Foster*, 42 Cal.App.3d 577 (1974), the court summarized permissible valuation methods for goodwill as follows:

> In sum, we conclude the applicable rule in evaluating community goodwill to be that such goodwill *may not be valued by any method that takes into account the post-marital efforts of either spouse* but that a proper means of arriving at the value of such goodwill contemplates any legitimate method of evaluation that measures its present value by taking into account some past result. Insofar as the professional practice is concerned, it is assumed that it will continue in the future. [emphasis added]

The above quote seems to prohibit the use of any method of valuation that involves projecting income or cash flow into future periods, such as a discounted cash flow model. In practice, although discounted cash flow models are not used, capitalized excess earnings models are permitted (see Exhibit 1). The growth rate used in a capitalization rate buildup would seem to violate the prohibition against looking into the future. One can only surmise that the courts accept this form of projection because the long-term growth rate is often presented and defended based on the expected rate of inflation, not actual practice growth, and the efforts of the physician could hardly be deemed to influence rates of inflation. That being said, the use of buildup models to achieve capitalization rates for medical practice valuations is less common in California than the use of rounded capitalization rates, such as 40% or 50% (or the reciprocal multipliers, 2.5 or 2), which have not been built up.

Premise of value

Investment value seems to be the premise of value for medical practice valuations in marital dissolutions in California. Investment value here means "value to the holder," as contrasted with fair market value, which is the "willing buyer" standard. This principle does not come directly from the Family Code but has been accepted and reaffirmed throughout the years. Numerous cases have used investment value rather than fair market value for professional practices, each making the statement slightly differently. For example, in 1962, *Brawman v. Brawman*, 199 Cal.App.2d 876 (1962), the court said:

> In considering this value, consideration must be given to the fact that, on divorce and dissolution of the community, a professional practice goes automatically to the spouse licensed to practice it. He or she is not selling out or liquidating but continuing the business. Effectually, it is the case of a silent partner withdrawing from a going business. And if such partner is to receive fair compensation for his or her share on his or her enforced retirement, it should be evaluated.

Another California case, *Golden v. Golden*, 270 Cal.App.2d 401 (1969), stated it slightly differently and contrasted divorce with the dissolution of a partnership:

> We believe the better rule is that, in a divorce case, the goodwill of the husband's professional practice as a sole practitioner should be taken into consideration in

> determining the award to the wife. Where as in *Lyon* (*Lyon v. Lyon*, 246 Cal.App.2d 519 (1966)), the firm is being dissolved, it is understandable that a court cannot determine what, if any, of the goodwill of the firm will go to either partner. But, in a matrimonial matter, the practice of the sole practitioner husband will continue, with the same intangible value as it had during the marriage. (case citation added)

In 1974, in *Foster*, the court confirmed again:

> The value of community goodwill is not necessarily the specified amount of money that a willing buyer would pay for such goodwill. In view of exigencies that are ordinarily attendant in a marriage dissolution, the amount obtainable in the marketplace might well be less than the true value of the goodwill. Community goodwill is a portion of the community value of the professional practice as a going concern on the date of dissolution of the marriage.

Property can be characterized as separate, community, quasi-community, or a combination

California is a community property state. The rebuttable presumption is that property acquired during marriage is community. This means that the court presumes that all property acquired during marriage is community property unless that presumption is contested and proven otherwise. In the case of a medical practice started or joined during marriage, the value of the practice on the date of separation (or trial depending on whether the factors discussed above exist) is generally the value that will be divided. An interesting issue regarding the character of the practice arises when a practice is started or joined *before* marriage. Arguably, this practice would be both community and separate in nature. A portion of the value of the medical practice is the separate property of the spouse that owned it prior to marriage, and it therefore, is not subject to division by the community. The portion of the practice fostered during marriage belongs to the community. Remember that earnings and accumulations after the date of separation are separate. Family Code §760 states: "Except as otherwise provided by statute, all property, real or personal, wherever situated, acquired by a married person during the marriage while domiciled in this state is community property." The physician's efforts during marriage that increase the value of the practice benefit the community via his or her earned income and the increase in practice value.

How to apportion value between separate and community estates is the subject of two very old, yet very significant, court cases, *Pereira v. Pereira*, 156 Ca.1, 103 (1909) and *Van Camp v. Van Camp*, 53 Cal.App 17 (1921). In the case of a typical medical practice, *Pereira*, decided in 1909, is the case most applicable. Under the *Pereira* methodology, as applied to a medical practice, valuations are performed as of the date of marriage and the date of separation. The value calculated as of date of marriage, which is the value of the separate property interest, is treated as if it had been "invested" during the marriage and earning interest. That value, grown by the interest factor, represents the separate property component of the valuation as of either the date of separation or trial. To derive the community's interest in the practice, the value as of date of marriage, grown by the interest factor, is subtracted from the value calculated as of either the date of separation or trial. The court described this concept as follows:

> It appears, however, that the decision of the court was made upon the theory that all of his or her gains received after marriage, from whatever sources, were to be classed as community property and that no allowance was made in favor of his or her separate estate on account of interest or profit on the$15, 500 invested in the business at the time of the marriage. This capital was undoubtedly his separate estate. The fund remained in the business after marriage and was used by him in carrying it on. The separate property should have been credited with some amount as profit on this capital.

Conversely, the *Van Camp* decision, in 1921, typically applies when the efforts of the spouse are farther removed from the overall success of a business. In other words, the business grew in value, but it did so as a result of the capital invested rather than the efforts of the owner-spouse. The types of businesses that would be vulnerable to a *Van Camp* argument would be capital-intensive with more than one investor, perhaps manufacturing concerns or very large companies. This is usually not an arguable case with medical practices, even large medical practices.

You can compare the courts' statements in *Pereira* and *Van Camp* to understand the different views of the circumstances. In *Pereira*, where the husband owned and operated a saloon and cigar business, the court states:

> It is true that it is very clearly shown that the principal part of the large income was due to the personal character, energy, ability, and capacity of the husband. This share of the earnings was, of course, community property. But without capital he could have not carried on the business.

In *Van Camp*, where the husband was president of Van Camp Sea Food Co., the court states:

> While it may be true that the success of the corporation of which the defendant was president and manager was to a large extent due to his capacity and ability, nevertheless without the investment of his and other capital in the corporation, he could not have conducted the business, and while he devoted his energies and personal efforts to making it a success, he was by the corporation paid what the evidence shows was an adequate salary, and for which another than himself with equal capacity could have been secured.

The significant difference between *Pereira* and *Van Camp* is that *Pereira* allows the community to obtain an interest in an otherwise separate property business. *Van Camp* does not. Even if the spouse in a *Van Camp*-type business receives inadequate compensation (i.e., below-market salary), all that the community can get is the value of the services provided. The community does not gain an interest in the separate property business.

Current Case Analysis

Rosen v. Rosen, 105 Cal.App.4th 808 (2002)

In 2002, in the *Rosen* case, the court once again affirmed the use of excess earnings in the calculation of professional goodwill, but also concluded that Mr. Rosen did not have any professional goodwill. The court had interesting discussions about a variety of issues surrounding goodwill calculations in the context of divorce. One of the primary issues was that Mrs. Rosen's expert used one year's net income to calculate goodwill. That single year was the most recent full calendar year at the time the valuation was performed, but it was also a high income year. The court said:

> Further, it is obvious that using one year's net income (not coincidentally a high-income year) is not illustrative of Bruce's volatile income over a period of several years.... Picking one year's net income, where income rises or falls from year to year, is not a reasonable basis for determining value.... Pat's expert admitted that had he averaged Bruce's income over any period of years he considered, goodwill value would be nominal or nothing.

The court was also displeased with Mrs. Rosen's expert's use of national surveys for the calculation of reasonable compensation without applying the survey results against some kind of local measure:

> Pat's expert testified he did not have any particular knowledge of lawyer compensation, other than what he had learned from valuations he had performed. He admitted he was not familiar with a law practice such as Bruce's. He did not conduct a survey or perform any kind of study of lawyer compensation in Southern California. Rather, he relied entirely upon two surveys of compensation (the Altman Weil survey and the Robert Morris survey), neither of which dealt with a sole-practitioner lawyer handling state-funded criminal appeals. The expert did not attempt to relate the information in the surveys to Bruce's law practice.

The surveys were deemed, by the court, not representative of law practices such as Mr. Rosen's. The court also disliked the fact that Mrs. Rosen's expert used his own judgment in determining which reasonable compensation numbers to use. Her expert stated that he had no experience in the area of attorney reasonable compensation outside of preparing law practice valuations in the context of divorce.

> Pat's expert then used his own judgment to come up with a compensation figure based upon the numbers in these two surveys, even though he admitted he did not have any particular knowledge about lawyer compensation and did not know of any attorney with a law practice such as Bruce's. In essence, Pat's expert did nothing more than pick $100,000 because it was about halfway between $125,000 and $67,000. Those two numbers bear no particular materiality to the issue of reasonable compensation in this case.
>
> Our concern is that the surveys relied upon by Pat's expert were not relevant to Bruce's law practice and therefore were not useful in establishing compensation under either the "average salaried person" standard of *In re Marriage of Garrity* and *Bishton* (181 Cal. App.3d 675) or the "similarly situated professional" standard. We are also troubled by the fact that Pat's expert ultimately reached his determination of compensation by exercising his judgment when the expert admitted he did not have any knowledge of a law practice such as Bruce's (citation added).

In the end, the court determined that Mr. Rosen's law practice had no goodwill without any expert testimony being offered by Mr. Rosen.

Iredale v. Cates, 121 Cal.App.4th 321 (2004)

Two years later, the court affirmed and expanded a concept used in *Nichols v. Nichols,* 27 Cal.App.4th 661 (1994) that allowed a stock purchase agreement to determine the value of the community's interest in a corporate law firm. In *Nichols,* the court allowed the limited use of the stock purchase agreement where the stockholder did not purchase accounts receivable or work in process upon joining and did not own any accounts receivable or work in process upon withdrawing. The court was persuaded because the agreement was arm's length: was entered into for an independent business purpose, not entered into in contemplation of divorce: and resulted in a value similar to the value derived from other approaches. Although the stock purchase agreement also addressed the value of goodwill, the court did not discuss goodwill valuation in the context of goodwill in the law firm as opposed to personal goodwill of the attorney, but ultimately decided that the attorney had personal goodwill. In *Iredale,* the court followed the partnership agreement, which stated that the partner (and therefore, the community) had no interest in certain assets (e.g., accounts receivable, work in progress, and goodwill of the firm). The *Iredale* court, while using *Nichols* as a basis to accept the values from the partnership agreement, took it one step further by discussing the partnership agreement's limitation on Ms. Iredale's interest in the firm's goodwill. The court opined:

> Thus, the trial court was not evaluating Iredale's interest in PHJW at liquidation value rather than as a going concern as Cates claims, but instead was looking at the specific interest that Iredale holds in PHJW. That interest does not include an entitlement, at

> any time, to collect a portion of the accounts receivable, work in progress, or goodwill of the law firm. The trial court reasonably concluded that Iredale's interest was limited to the value of her capital account, which reflected the value of her interest in the hard assets of the firm, but not the firm's accounts receivable, work in progress, or goodwill.

The court did find goodwill for Ms. Iredale—not goodwill in her law firm, but personal goodwill.

> After concluding that Iredale did not have an interest in a proportionate share of the goodwill of her law firm, the court determined that Iredale herself possessed goodwill and accepted the value of that goodwill offered by her expert, $42,318, finding her goodwill to be "partially a community asset."

In reviewing the goodwill calculation, the court revisited the reasonable compensation issue. It adopted the "similarly situated professional" standard over the "average salaried person" standard. The court stated:

> We conclude that the trial court's use of the "similarly situated professional" standard to calculate goodwill was entirely reasonable and supported by substantial evidence. Cates' own expert had to concede that his method of comparing Iredale's compensation number to what it would cost to hire an associate (actually 1.4 associates) did not account for the nonbillable hours expended by Iredale, nor would an associate be likely to have a client base comparable to Iredale's. Comparing Iredale's compensation to that of similarly situated professionals, rather than to a salaried employee, was indeed a more rational and reasonable method by which to calculate the value of Iredale's goodwill in this case.

Iredale marks the end of using an "average salaried employee" in the calculation of reasonable compensation in favor of the "similarly situated professional." Use of the "similarly situated professional" usually means a lesser value for goodwill; e.g., there are zero excess earnings when reasonable compensation mirrors actual compensation. Further, when relying on national surveys to obtain reasonable compensation, the valuator must consider adjustments to the compensation of the "similarly situated professional" that make the national survey data more relevant and applicable to their subject—i.e., for excessive hours worked. It also solidifies the use of agreements to limit the community's interest in a law firm's (or, logically, medical practice's) goodwill in certain situations.

McTiernan v. Dubrow, 133 Cal.App.4th 1090 (2005)

California's celebrity goodwill case was *McTiernan,* and, unlike New Jersey, it was decided that celebrities do not generate divisible goodwill. The court focused on the definition of goodwill found in the Business and Professions Code at §14102: "The goodwill of a business is property and is transferable." The court also focused on the definition of a business, determining that it is "... professional commercial or industrial enterprise with assets, i.e., an entity other than a natural person." The court stated:

> Endowing "a person doing business" with the capacity to create goodwill, as opposed to limiting goodwill to "a business," has wide ramifications ... all such persons who would have the "expectation of continued public patronage" would possess goodwill. This would create a substantial liability, as in this case, without a guaranty that the liability would be funded. It is clear that, from an economic perspective, the goodwill in this case is based on earnings and that goodwill is an expression of a husband's earning capacity.[1] However, there is no guaranty, especially in the arts that earnings will not decline or even dry up, even though expectations were to the contrary. In such an event, a person would find himself or herself saddled with a massive liability without the means of satisfying it. Putting it another way, endowing directly persons with the ability to create goodwill would create an "asset" predicated on nothing more than predictions about earning capacity.

The court makes the observation, more than once, that Mr. McTiernan's business activity is unlike doctors' or lawyers' practices.

> The fact that the husband's "elite professional standing" is not transferable effectively refutes the trial court's conclusion that the husband's practice as a motion picture director is like the practice of an attorney or physician. The practice of an attorney, physician, dentist, or accountant is transferable, but the husband's "elite professional standing" is his alone, and not susceptible to being transferred or sold.

McTiernan opened the door for all professionals to craft arguments grounded in the case's dicta to try to subvert the traditional calculations of goodwill. Although the case specifically states that a film director is different from a doctor or lawyer, in stating that "'elite professional standing' is not a property interest," it has opened the door for any professional to make a claim of "elite professional standing." If a medical practice has to be transferable to generate goodwill, what about psychiatrists' practices? The characteristics of a physician that would allow the generation of significant excess earnings are the same characteristics that would allow a claim of "elite professional standing" and the corresponding claim that the practice is not transferable.

1 While we acknowledge that the "excess earning" method of valuing goodwill in a professional corporation is generally accepted, it is true that this method is not far removed from a prediction about future earnings. For good and sufficient reasons, the expectancy of future earnings may not be considered in determining goodwill. (See generally 11 Sitkin, Summary of Cal.Law, Community Property, §71.) Whether categorized as "excess earnings" or "future earnings," the point is that this type of goodwill is an expression of earnings that have not yet been paid. Thus, when, as here, a person doing business is found to have goodwill and it is measured by the excess earnings approach, the "asset" that is credited is a prediction, not a fact. This is quite a distance from an established business enterprise with assets, and a clientele, that has generated goodwill in the traditional sense.

Judge Cooper concurred with the court on all issues except the determination of goodwill. In his concurring and dissenting opinion, he states:

> The lead opinion's effort to limit goodwill to a business as opposed to an individual is semantic. Any professional who independently practices his or her profession, for profit—be it lawyer, doctor, computer consultant, or film director—thereby conducts a business, with the lead opinion's own unattributed definition, as well as more traditional ones.

In discussing the issue of transferability, he says:

> As for whether this goodwill is transferable and therefore qualifies as property, the short answer is that the law has determined both question. Business and Professional Code Section 14102 establishes, as a matter of law, that "the goodwill of a business is property and is transferable." That includes the goodwill of the husband's business as a director. Whether or not a third party is willing to buy it is not material.

Judge Cooper's final statement on the case:

> In this case, the trial court properly determined the existence and extent of the husband's goodwill, in accord with substantial evidence and with California law, as consistently expounded for half a century. Even under the majority's refashioning of that law, those determinations remain sustainable. I respectfully dissent.

The ramifications will become clear when *McTiernan*-type arguments wind their way through the courts. So far, California has not distinguished between personal or professional goodwill and enterprise (practice) goodwill. *McTiernan* appears to identify a type of personal goodwill that is not owned by the community. If McTiernan's excluded personal goodwill is combined with an *Iredale* agreement that excludes enterprise goodwill, it leads to a conclusion that the "court of equity" might not favor.

Ackerman v. Ackerman, 146 Cal.App.4th 191 (2006)

Ackerman follows *Rosen* regarding the use of national surveys and their applicability locally to determine reasonable compensation. The addition in *Ackerman* was that Dr. Ackerman's attorney compared survey data from the American Medical Association to an informal local survey that he performed. In the end, the court determined the reasonable compensation for Dr. Ackerman, using neither expert's numbers, and applied the excess earnings method to determine goodwill.

The trial court once again rejected the "average salaried person" for the "similarly situated professional" standard saying:

> ... it just boggles the mind to think anyone making as much money as the husband would work for an employer and receive a third of what he is actually making.

The above quote seems to indicate that using compensation statistics that do not correspond to productivity statistics would generate incorrect reasonable compensation assumptions.

Although *Ackerman* was decided after *McTiernan*, its proximity in date to *McTiernan*, meant that Dr. Ackerman, a plastic surgeon, would not have been able to make a claim of "elite professional standing." Future cases involving professional practices will be important in determining where California goes from here.

Conclusion

California's family law principles come from both the Family Code and court cases, but court decisions are the primary sources for most of the business valuation issues (see Exhibit 1 on the next page). The concrete concepts, such as earnings after date of separation are separate, fairly easily understood and have an impact on both the date of valuation and the methodology allowed. California, over the years, has recognized practice value using the "value to the holder" or investment value premise, rather than the "willing buyer" or fair market value premise, although the *McTiernan* case could possibly signal a change in this area. A medical practice can consist of both community and separate property, necessitating multiple valuations. The date of marriage and date of separation are two of the most important pieces of information that are needed for any case. Finally, the valuation case decisions over the last few years signal that the court may be changing its direction in the future. We await the first professional practice valuation case in the post-*McTiernan* period to see what that future holds.

Exhibit 1. Selected California Dissolution Cases Timeline

Year	Case Name and Citation	Valuation Issues
1909	*Pereira v. Pereira* 156 Ca. 1, 103	Cigar store owner, separate and community property valuation and apportionment; theory based on efforts.
1921	*Van Camp v. Van Camp* 53 Cal.App 17	President of large seafood company, separate and community property valuation and apportionment; theory based on capital.
1969	*Golden v. Golden* 270 Cal.App.2d 401	Physician, goodwill exists in professional practice, valuation methodology not addressed.
1974	*Lopez v. Lopez* 38 Cal.App3d 93	Attorney, trial court erred in not determining the value of any goodwill in law practice. Discusses factors to be considered in determination of goodwill.
1974	*Foster v. Foster* 42 Cal.App.3d 577	Physician, goodwill value upheld, valuation methodology not specifically identified.

continued

Exhibit 1. Selected California Dissolution Cases Timeline, Continued

1976	*Fonstein v. Fonstein* 17 Cal.3d 738	Attorney, value determined by partnership agreement that called for compensation payments upon withdrawal from firm. Improper to take into account tax consequences in determining value unless the taxable event occurred during marriage or will occur as a result of the division of property. To be taken into account, a tax liability must be "immediate and specific," not speculative.
1979	*Aufmuth v. Aufmuth* 89 Cal.App.3d 446	Attorney, date of valuation should be date of trial because spouse's efforts were not responsible for increase in value after date of separation.
1986	*Garrity v. Bishton* 181 Cal.App.3d 675	Attorney, excess earnings method not sufficient to calculate practice value if it fails to take into account fixed assets, accounts receivable, costs advanced, and work in process.
1986	*Slivka v. Slivka* 183 Cal.App.3d 159	Physician, no goodwill in case of partnership that services only Kaiser patients. Situation deemed similar to an employee with no ownership interest.
2002	*Rosen v. Rosen* 105 Cal.App.4th 808	Attorney, use of a single year's income in the excess earning method to calculate goodwill when historical income is highly volatile is incorrect. Reasonable compensation based on national surveys is incorrect unless related to local data.
2004	*Iredale v. Cates* 121 Cal.App.4th 321	Attorney, upheld use of partnership agreement to limit value of accounts receivable, work in process, and partnership goodwill. Calculated personal goodwill using excess earnings.
2005	*McTiernan v. Dubrow* 133 Cal.App.4th 1090	Movie director, no goodwill, despite excess earnings. Elite professional standing deemed not transferable and therefore could not generate divisible goodwill.
2006	*Ackerman v. Ackerman* 146 Cal.App.4th 191	Physician, goodwill calculated using excess earnings method. Discussion of national surveys to determine reasonable compensation.

Chapter 25

Lost Profits for Physician Practices

By Mark O. Dietrich, CPA/ABV

Unlike lost profits pertaining to other businesses, claims for lost profits in connection with physician practices are typically defined in terms of loss of compensation. As such, for the typical small practice, a lost profits analysis might look much the same as a physician's claim for lost earnings in a personal injury case, although the loss period is likely to be different.

Larger practices and those with ancillary testing capability, such as imaging and laboratory services, may have more traditional lost profits damages claims, as might those practices with greater leverage over nonowner physicians or physician extenders such as nurse practitioners and physician assistants. A good example would be a medical practice's claim for damages resulting from the alleged violation of a noncompete or nonsolicitation agreement by a former employee. In this situation, the practice could lose profits related to ancillary testing revenues and from losing the violator's patients. It could also incur recruiting and training costs for replacing the lost employees and losses due to the unabsorbed overhead that revenues from the violator formerly covered.[1]

Basic Factors to Consider

Basic compensation analysis

Physician profits and compensation are in large part driven by individual productivity and the rate-per-unit-of-service paid for the various services. Thus, any claim for lost profits should consider the historical pattern of work by the physicians and the local

1 Note: Financial aspects of medical and physician practices involve unique terms and statutory regulations; for the reader's convenience, a glossary of such terms and legislative references is set forth in the final section (*Section G*) of this chapter.

market area. A proper analysis would require, at a minimum, consideration of the following factors:

- Plaintiff's work hours in the office, hospital, or other venue;
- Number of patients seen, surgeries performed, images read, and so on;
- Use of physician billing codes;
- Trends in reimbursement rates for the services provided;
- Staffing and overhead rates for the practice;
- Age of the physicians;
- Historical earnings of the physicians;
- Presence of physician extenders;
- Ancillary testing income, if any;
- Ancillary-driven differences in physician compensation;
- Regional, localized, or practice-specific differences in payments by insurers for physician services;
- Regional differences in physician compensation due to:
  - Supply and demand effects of a surplus (unlikely) or shortage of physicians;
  - Cost of living;
  - Utilization (clinical practice styles);[2]
- Collection rate for services performed versus charges for those services;
- Payor mix; e.g., percentage of revenue generated from Medicare, Medicaid, private insurance plans, self-pay, and so on;
- Training and skill of the physician, such as surgical skills for a surgeon;[3]
- Malpractice claim history;
- Activities in developing the practice; and
- Competing practices.

Of course, undertaking the analysis requires that the financial expert (through efforts by the attorney) successfully obtains the necessary data during the discovery process. Thus, it is wise to retain an expert early in such litigation to be certain the document request contains the appropriate information. Furthermore, review of *initial* documents produced

2 For example, certain areas of the country have high incidences of Caesarean deliveries, use of advanced imaging such as MRI, or surgical versus interventional treatment of coronary artery disease.

3 A decline in physician's income could be traced to failure to train in current surgical or clinical techniques, for example.

invariably leads to additional requests for other documents, making early retention in the discovery phase even more critical.

Example

A member of a hospital medical staff brings a claim for lost income against the hospital after it terminated her staff privileges. In valuing her claim, the plaintiff's financial expert uses Medical Group Management Association (MGMA)[4] national data for median physician earnings as a basis for the "but-for" earnings calculation (the income the physician would have earned, but for the defendant's alleged wrongful termination). The following are the particular areas that the expert should review for purposes of analyzing potential lost earnings.

General measures of productivity

Productivity measures in a physician practice include hours worked, patients seen, physician extenders (such as nurse practitioners and physician assistants) supervised, as well as charges and collections for services.

Hours worked is an important element to assess in conjunction with the number of patients seen during those hours. Industry sources such as MGMA, for example, provide data on the number of patients seen and hours worked. Looking at the relationship between the two can offer insight into the efficiency of the practice, an important driver of income.

Nurse practitioners and physician assistants (referred to as nonphysician providers, or NPPs, in the MGMA data) are frequently billed under the physician's provider number if the physician supervises their services, including reviewing the charts of patients seen.[5] In some instances, these extenders can also bill directly for their services without physician supervision. If extenders are included in the individual physician's productivity, then the analyst will need to separately identify the work that the particular physician actually performed versus the work that extenders did when using the MGMA benchmark data. *Tip*: All the MGMA data exclude the productivity associated with physician extenders. Thus, one all-too-frequent misuse of MGMA data is failing to adjust for physician extender revenues.

Physician Billing Codes

One of the most challenging aspects of measuring damages relative to a physician practice is to understand the revenue cycle, including CPT[6] codes for billing. These

4 Medical Group Management Association; www.mgma.com.

5 Medicare allows this under the so-called "incident to" rules; other insurers may or may not follow Medicare guidelines.

6 Current Procedural Terminology, trademarked by the American Medical Association.

are a series of five-digit billing codes used for the vast majority of physician services, although there are also HCPCS (Healthcare Common Procedure Coding System) codes for certain testing, G[7] codes and J[8] codes, and a host of other esoteric terms that may be relevant in a particular engagement.

Example 1

An orthopedic surgeon specializing in knee and shoulder arthroscopy brings a claim for lost wages against a practice for wrongful discharge. During his employment, the CPT™ codes associated with arthroscopy permitted the practice to use multiple codes to bill for certain procedures, resulting in enhanced payments. Subsequent to the alleged discharge and damaging event, these codes were combined into a required G code for billing, resulting in significantly lower payment levels for the same arthroscopic services. As a result, part of the physician's decline in income could be traced to specific reductions in payment for the services he provided, and the expected "but for" earnings could be lower.

Example 2

A primary care physician brings a claim for loss of income due to unlawful discharge from a medical practice. Prior to the discharge, she was earning $150,000 per year and her use of billing codes was subject to review by the practice manager and compliance officer before their submission to insurance companies for payment; the physician did not properly educate herself in the use of codes.

Exhibit 1. Coding Distribution

Code Level	Distribution	Visits	Fee	Revenue
99211	5%	250	$20	$5,000
99212	10.	500	40	20,000
99213	50	2,500	60	150,000
99214	30	1,500	80	120,000
99215	5	250	110	27,500
	100	5,000		322,500

In her new practice, an inexperienced individual who does not understand physician codes manages the billing, and is concerned that patients may be overcharged. Although the physician sees the same number of patients with a similar set of clinical problems in the new practice as in the old, her income has dropped to $100,000.

7 G codes apply to professional healthcare procedures and services that would be coded as CPT but for which no CPT code exists; insurers sometimes combine services that have separate CPT codes into a single G code resulting in reduced payment. See, e.g., www.reimbursementcodes.com/hcpcs_codes_d.html.

8 J codes are used for injections and pharmaceuticals.

Exhibit 2. Drop in Income Due to Incorrect Coding of Services

Code Level	Distribution	Visits	Fee	Revenue
1	15%	750	$20	$15,000
2	20	1,000	40	40,000
3	50	2,500	60	150,000
4	10	500	80	40,000
5	5	250	110	27,500
	100	5,000		272,500

As Exhibits 1 and 2 indicate, the entire $50,000 drop in income *could* be due to incorrect coding of services.

Physician Supply and Demand

The relevance of local-versus-national data on physician compensation depends on many factors, including supply and demand and the recruiting market. A nationwide shortage of a particular specialty can lead to relative equivalence in compensation expectation from one area to the next. Other factors are rates paid by particular insurers for services, cost of living differentials, and local factors such as the relationship between a physician with significant influence and his or her hospital. The latter is a particularly important factor in hospital-based practice, such as radiology, pathology, and anesthesia.

Ancillary Testing Income

This item refers to physician practice profits or compensation contributed by testing equipment owned or leased by the practice. (The MGMA data refer to this revenue as "TC," or the technical component.[9] Clearly, if the practice does not have such equipment, the physician cannot partake in any such profits or compensation.

Collections for Services

Charges are generally considered a poor measure of productivity because the payment system controlled by health insurers is often indifferent to charges. Charges may be relevant as *one* productivity measure in a practice with little or no insured patients, such as a cosmetic plastic surgery practice or a walk-in clinic that does not accept insurance.

Exhibit 3 shows the representative data for collections available from the MGMA survey. Note that "NPP Excluded" is part of each subset of the sample data. Collections for practices with over 10% TC are significantly higher than those with less than 10% TC. The sample sizes also vary significantly.[10]

9 For an excellent discussion of technical component revenue and its implications in physician compensation see BVR's *Guide to Physician Practice Valuation*.

10 MGMA bases its data on a survey of medical group members as opposed to a random sample from a

Exhibit 3. Data for Collections

	Providers	Practices	Mean	Std. Dev.	25th %tile	Median	75th %tile	90th %tile
Overall TC/NPP excluded	1,569	182	$345,779	$140,449	$258,320	$329,767	$403,896	$501,279
Eastern region TC/NPP excluded	369	40	354,056	133,686	275,169	346,302	421,846	514,994
Overall NPP excluded, with 1%-10% TC	601	85	410,983	166,632	313,776	386,401	476,962	564,883
Overall NPP excluded, with over 10% TC	164	38	474,743	212,399	344,813	441,338	582,429	727,105

Data from Eastern Region are representative; other regions are reported[11]

Payor mix

Perhaps the most critical factor affecting a physician's income after productivity and coding is the practice's revenue per procedure, which is significantly influenced by the underlying payor mix. There is no uniformity among the ways that various government and private insurers pay for services. Although Medicare[12] might pay 60% of a particular charge, Medicaid[13] might pay only 25% and Blue Cross might pay 70%. Data from a Medicaid plan in one state will usually have no relationship to data from another, and the many Blue Cross and Blue Shield plans in the United States do not value physician services the same way. Medicare actually adjusts the fee schedule for each state to account for geographic differentials such as cost of living and wages.

The payor mix therefore constitutes a limitation on using national data, and an analysis of the mix is critical to assessing a plaintiff's future income prospects in a "but-for" earnings analysis. Financial experts should also bear in mind that the payor mix may have changed during the loss period, which could impact the "but-for" damages analysis. In a given circumstance, assessing the payor mix over several years should be considered to see how any changes may impact the measurement of damages.

Example

A financial expert reviews the physician's productivity in terms of hours worked, patient encounters, and gross charges and finds that each figure is at or near the MGMA mean value. In examining the collections, however, the value is near the 25th percentile. Analysis of the payor mix indicates that the practice has a large Medicaid patient base

population; it includes more private practice groups than other surveys, something to consider.

11 *Medical Group Management Association Physician Compensation and Production Survey*, 2006 Report Based on 2005 Data.

12 A federal program primarily for the elderly with a generally uniform benefit package but vastly different pay rates from area to area. Local coverage determinations by Medicare intermediaries can affect the benefit package.

13 A state-specific program of benefits that is funded partially by each of the state and federal government; which government pays what depends in part on state decisions as to benefits.

and Medicaid is paying only 30% of the practice's charges. Conclusion: The "but-for" earnings prospects of this practice are not comparable to a mean MGMA value.

Compensation

One of the difficulties with MGMA compensation surveys is that they do not present the data in the same categories as the collections data, i.e., there are no categories for compensation with NPP excluded or for TC included. Therefore, the financial expert must exercise judgment and adjust the compensation data as necessary to account for differences in the degree of NPP and TC (ancillary) revenues.

Competition

The financial expert should also assess the extent to which the alleged damages might be due to some factor other than the cause alleged by the plaintiff. This prescription applies regardless of which party, plaintiff or defendant, engages the expert.

Physicians compete on many factors. An adage among doctors says that practice success is driven by "availability, affability, and ability," in that order. Although the saying may be trite, this discussion has already identified hours as a key element in compensation. If at the time the alleged damages occurred, a competing practice extended its hours to evenings and weekends, this might have been a contributing factor in the plaintiff's loss of income. A financial expert would have to consider and measure the impact of this and other factors, since the plaintiff must prove that the defendant's actions proximately caused the damages.

Affability may be difficult to assess other than from a personal interview, which an expert for the defendant may not have access to; a change in affability contributing to a decline in the physician's income is also difficult to assess, if not altogether unusual. To the extent possible, legal counsel should make inquiries about the plaintiff's reputation with patients and colleagues as well as personal difficulties contributing to demeanor, such as a divorce or death in the family. Financial experts should expect cross-examination questions such as, "If Dr. Smith were known to raise his voice with employees, how would this affect your conclusion?" or "If patients had lodged complaints about Dr. Smith's hostile attitude during examinations, how would this affect your conclusion?" Defense counsel may very well depose various fact witnesses to assess a physician's comportment and professional as well as patient relationships. In addition to the physician's affability, that of the office staff, particularly the front desk and reception personnel, may also be critical. If a key employee was replaced at or near the time of the alleged damages, the financial expert should also consider its potential impact on the claimed damages. Public records, such as the state Boards of Registration in Medicine, are generally good sources of information regarding prior complaints or disciplinary action involving the physician.

Ability is another factor that the attorney and financial expert should consider, particularly when the case involves specialists such as surgeons; however, assessing a physician's ability may require another expert with clinical expertise. Medicine is a dynamic practice area and new techniques and procedures are always being developed. These technical and procedural innovations can have consequences on the physician's income. If competing surgeons at a hospital, for example, have trained in a new, less invasive procedure with a lower complications rate and the plaintiff-surgeon failed to train in it, then this lapse could lead to a gradual decline in referrals from other physicians, with a concomitant loss of income. An excellent example is the current rise of using interventional radiology in breast cancer biopsy. Certain gynecological surgeries versus traditional surgical intervention are another. Another example is the shifting tide of opinion about the effectiveness of coronary stents[14] placed by interventional cardiologists versus traditional coronary bypass surgery done by cardiac surgeons. The advent of drug-eluting coronary stents[15] and their approval by Medicare led to dramatic declines in cardiac surgeon incomes and dramatic increases in interventional cardiologists incomes.

Other factors that financial experts may commonly overlook in their lost profits analysis include:

- An increase in the number of physicians practicing a particular specialty in a service area (known as a "catchment" area), resulting in decreased volume for existing physicians;
- A decline or increase in population;
- Poor economic conditions contributing to a rise in bad debts and a drop in patient insurance coverage, such as those present in 2008 through 2010;
- Changes in health insurance that reduce a patient's benefits;[16]
- Decreases (or increases) in the fee schedule paid by health insurers to the physician;
- Competition among hospitals that affect the incomes of physicians on the staff of those hospitals, particularly when a hospital system is able to negotiate contracts superior to that of competing hospitals (common in many market areas);

14 Another area under current debate is drug-eluting stents versus standard stents.

15 See 67 *Fed. Reg.* 49,983, 50,004 (Aug. 1, 2002) for advance approval of drug-eluting stents by CMS even before its approval by the FDA.

16 This factor will be exacerbated by the 2010 federal healthcare reform, for example, which increases the economic burden of healthcare on insured patients, thereby discouraging utilization even as it expands coverage to the uninsured, trying to make room for them in the system.

- Failure of the physician practice billing department to collect all otherwise collectible amounts (an absolute must-review in any damages analysis); and Poor quality medical billing software or a failed attempt at changing to a new software program.

In short, dozens of factors can contribute to an observed change in physician income that both parties' financial experts should consider in assessing causality.

In-Depth Look at Special Issues in Identifying Damages

Physician compensation systems

Unallocated Overhead

A physician who quits a group practice in violation of a noncompete agreement or a fiduciary responsibility may leave his former colleagues with a large amount of fixed overhead to pay out of what otherwise would have been their income. Physicians often share variable expenses based upon productivity; e.g., if one doctor produces 30% of the revenues, then he or she will be allocated 30% of the variable expenses.

Example 1: fixed expense

A two-owner medical practice with four physicians relocates to new office space designed for the four physicians. But the two employed physicians leave the practice in violation of their noncompete agreements and open a competing practice nearby. Each physician's share of the rent was $50,000 per year, such that the remaining two physician-owners now face an additional out-of-pocket cost of $50,000 a piece. The expert's "but-for" lost profits analysis should consider fixed and variable expenses projected separately for the relevant period of time, depending upon the circumstances. Generally, one would expect variable expenses to trend down sooner as part of the mitigation process, and the fixed expenses to remain fairly constant for a longer period of time. Experts should, however, consider that even for fixed expenses, plaintiffs will likely be expected to mitigate their losses within a reasonable period of time.

Example 2: variable expense

Assume further that this same practice spends $800,000 per year on staff wages and benefits, representing 25% of annual revenues of $3.2 million. The competing physicians recruited staff with a cost of $200,000. As part of their attempt to mitigate damages, the owners reduced staff by an additional $100,000. On a per-capita basis, the two owners now have $50,000 of additional payroll costs to contend with, but depending on the compensation system, each may suffer a different degree of harm.

For example, if Owner 1 generates 55% of the collections and Owner 2 generates 45%, Owner 1 suffers a loss of $55,000, while Owner 2 suffers a loss of $45,000. This can be important if the financial expert is required to allocate the damages among the injured parties.

Large practices and integrated providers

Depending on the type of entity claiming the damages—e.g., a hospital or a large, integrated group practice with significant ancillary capability—the magnitude of the loss-types can be substantial. One ready source for assessing the magnitude of these potential revenue losses is the survey by Merritt Hawkins & Associates of hospital chief financial officers (CFOs), although data specific to the litigation should be used in a damages calculation, if available:

> The 2010 survey indicates that average net inpatient and outpatient revenue generated by physicians for their affiliated hospitals differed from the 2007 survey based upon specialty. Average revenue generated by primary care physicians declined from $1,433,532 in 2007 to $1,385,775 in 2010. Specialist physician revenue increased from $1,509,910 in 2007 to $1,577,764 in 2010. Neurosurgery was the single largest contributor followed by invasive [invasive is generally considered a cardiologist who performs cardiac catheterization, while interventional is a cardiologist who inserts coronary stents] cardiology, orthopedics, and general surgery.[17]

Surgical specialties tend to generate the largest revenues. The largest and most profitable lines of business in the typical acute care hospital are cardiology and orthopedics. For example, an orthopedic surgeon who leaves a hospital position in violation of a noncompete and goes to work for a competing organization may cause the hospital to lose significant inpatient and outpatient surgery revenues. Orthopedic surgeons are large users of MRI and CT scans, both of which represent significant revenue sources. Similarly, if the orthopedic surgeon leaves a position with a medical practice that provides an outpatient surgery center along with MRI and CT services, damages well in excess of the surgeon's annual income can result.

Growth rates in "but-for" and future earnings calculations

In the author's experience, this is the most common and serious error that occurs in physician damages calculations. In general, there are a variety of broad economic and Medicare-specific limitations on physician incomes.

General price per-unit of service[18]

What about increases in fees per-unit of service? From 1994 to 2009—or for 15 years, the compound rate of increase for all physician services was only 1.94%, based on data

17 *2010 Physician Inpatient/Outpatient Revenue Survey*, Merritt Hawkins & Associates (Irving, Texas); www.merritthawkins.com.

18 Mark Dietrich, "Choosing and Using the Right Valuation Methods for Physician Practices," BVR's *Guide to Healthcare Valuation*, Business Valuation Resources (2009).

from the Bureau of Labor Statistics Producer Price Index for Physician Services (see Exhibit 4).

Exhibit 4. BLS PPI-Physician Services, Annual

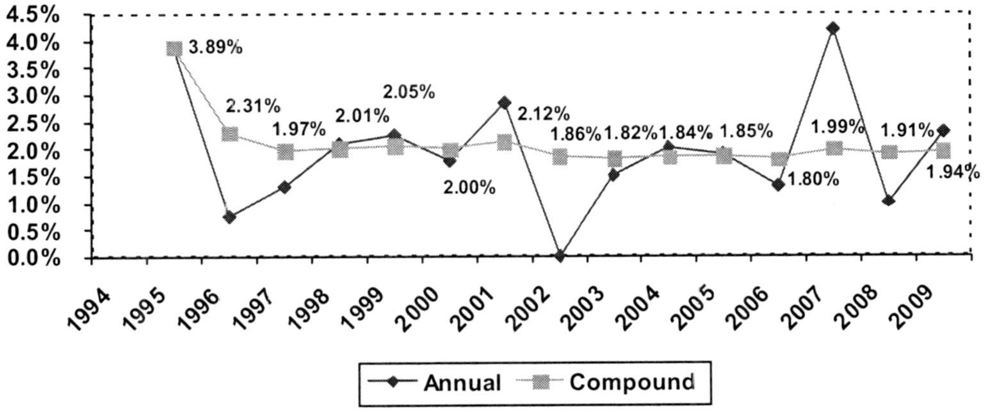

Medicare Price Per Unit of Service[19]

Clearly, there is no evidence that per-unit reimbursement rates are growing at the gross domestic product (GDP) rate or the Consumer Price Index rate, and a small practice's capacity to provide units of service is limited. Under the federal Medicare sustainable growth rate (SGR) formula, Medicare expenditures for physician services are limited by a complex formula that considers the change in fees, the number of beneficiaries, growth in GDP per capita, and the impact of new laws. The SGR is then applied to the Medicare Economic Index (MEI), which measures the weighted average price change in physician services. The MEI is a physician practice-specific measure of inflation and generally is in the range of 3.5%. The Medicare Payment Advisory Commission (MedPAC) Web site publishes the updated, annual data each March.[20]

The pattern since 2006 has been for Congress belatedly to suspend the statutory cutbacks in the conversion factor. The 2007 conversion factor of $35.9848 initially reflected a decrease of 5% and was subsequently overturned by Congress and left equal to the 2006 factor. The 2008 factor was scheduled to drop by 10.1% until the end of December 2007, when the Medicare, Medicaid, and SCHIP Extension Act of 2007 legislation updated the conversion factor by 0.5%, to $38.0870. In July 2008, Congress extended the $38.09 conversion factor for the balance of 2008 over the president's veto and put a 1.1% increase in place for 2009. Since November 2009, Congress has acted several times to delay the scheduled cut for 2010 to $28.41, having failed to include a fix in the healthcare reform legislation. *Note*: The 2009 Medicare physician fee schedule final rule on

19 Ibid.
20 www.medpac.gov.

Oct. 30, 2008 provided for the statutorily mandated 1.1% update for calendar year 2009; *however*, the budget-neutrality adjustment to the conversion factor associated with the review and reallocation of relative value units (RVUs) was a negative 6.41%, resulting in a rate of *$36.07*. The budget-neutrality adjustment is now included in the conversion factor where historically it was applied to a reduction of RVUs for each CPT code. As such, the 2009 rate and the precipitous drop in the 2010 rate shown in Exhibit 5 are not entirely comparable to the prior years.

Exhibit 5. Medicare Conversion Factor

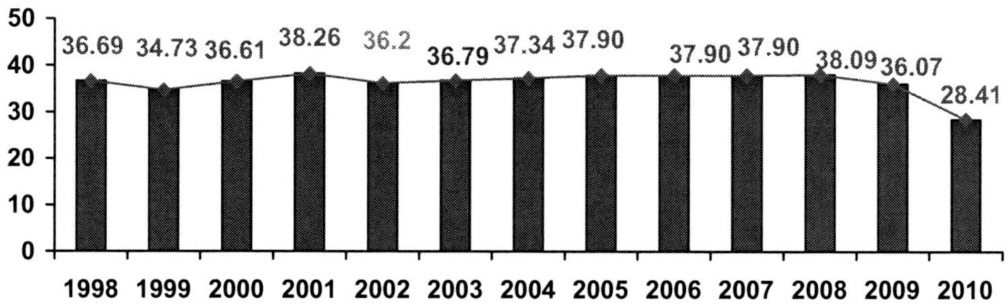

These two items represent the broad picture for physician practices in general. For a physician practice of a specific specialty, an in-depth analysis of that particular specialty's income growth opportunities is necessary.

Example

Larger physician practices including cardiology, neurology, and orthopedics as well as multispecialty practices frequently invest in high-tech imaging equipment, such as MRI and CT scanners. A lost profits analysis that involves a practice with such equipment should account for the impact of the Deficit Reduction Act of 2005 on the payment for these services;[21] the changes in independent diagnostic testing facilities qualification;[22] and the Stark IV regulations adopted as part of the 2009 inpatient payment system final rule.[23] MRI, CT, and PET were all further negatively impacted by provisions of the federal 2010 healthcare reform legislation, with the utilization assumption[24] increased

21 Pub.L. 109-171, 120 Stat. 4, Feb. 8, 2006; see, e.g., Mark Dietrich, "A Healthcare Appraiser Reviews a Judge-Appraiser's 'Report,'" *Business Valuation Review* (Summer 2007); Douglas Smith, "Valuation Considerations Specific to Diagnostic Imaging Entities," BVR's *Guide to Healthcare Valuation* (2009).

22 See generally 42 CFR 410.33, Independent Diagnostic Testing Facility (December 2005); cfr.vlex.com/vid/410-independent-diagnostic-testing-19805522.

23 42 CFR Part 412, Medicare Program; Inpatient Rehabilitation Facility Prospective Payment System for Federal Fiscal Year 2009; Final Rule, *Federal Register*, Vol. 73, No. 154 (Friday, Aug. 8, 2008); edocket.access.gpo.gov/2008/pdf/E8-17797.pdf.

24 The utilization assumption determines the expected number of units of service over which fixed expenses of operation are spread in establishing the fee that Medicare will pay. The higher the utilization assumption, the lower the expected fixed expense per unit of service and as a result, the lower the fee Medicare will pay.

from 50% to 75% for diagnostic imaging equipment, costing more than $1 million. This significantly reduces the technical component of Medicare revenue and will spread to other payors.

Regulatory considerations

Healthcare may well be the most regulated industry in the country. Since it also represents the largest sector of the economy (+/-17%) and drives federal and state budget concerns, regulatory and other government agencies conduct extensive enforcement activities in the healthcare sector. Many of the more common claims for damages may, in fact, be irrelevant in a physician practice analysis because the underlying rationale for the claim violates one or more federal or state laws. As such, the financial expert should make a threshold determination whether the conduct of the allegedly damaged entity is consistent with the law. Cases in which the plaintiff and defense counsel may be experienced in civil litigation but unfamiliar with healthcare law can create considerable challenges for the expert.

Violations of noncompete agreements are one area that results in frequent litigation. In these cases, financial experts must carefully scrutinize the assumptions related to expected profit contributions from the covenanter.

Example

Assume that a hospital claims lost profits against a former physician employee (cardiologist) who violated a noncompete agreement by joining a competing practice. During the course of his former employment, the physician referred patients to the hospital for services such as catheterization and angioplasty as well as lab tests, CT scans, stress testing, and cardiac ultrasound (collectively considered "ancillaries" for this example). After leaving the hospital, the physician's new practice has the same testing capabilities, so he refers his patients there. The physician also joins the medical staff of a competing hospital to admit his patients.

Because federal law prohibits payment for patient referrals, there could be some concern that the hospital could not claim damages against the physician based on his historic referrals. Although this appears unlikely.[25] the financial expert needs to carefully examine the physician's historical utilization patterns for compliance with applicable laws before using these as the basis for the damages calculation. Even if otherwise permissible, the type of "hockey stick" assumptions seen in many damage claims are unlikely to

25 "A requirement to refer to a specific provider is different from an agreement not to establish a competing business. In other words, a covenant not to compete might prevent a physician from setting up a private practice or offering services that compete with the entity that purchases his or her practice. If an agreement also included the requirement that the physician refer business to the purchaser, it would be suspect under the anti-kickback statute." 66 Fed. Reg. 879 (Jan. 4, 2001).

pass regulatory muster, because they will likely be difficult to construct a permissible rationale for the physician referring ever-increasing amounts of business to the hospital.

Another common but perhaps fatal approach to calculating damages in this example would be to use the physician's *post*-employment utilization in his new practice as a basis for measuring the hospital's losses. If the physician becomes an owner in his new practice and shares in the profits generated by ancillary referrals, then utilization is likely to be higher than the physician historically incurred as an employee in the hospital, where the Stark laws precluded him from receiving a part of the ancillary profit.[26] A proper analysis would differentiate between growth in referrals due to an increase in the number of patients seen by the physician, which might have been foreseeable had he remained with the hospital, as opposed to growth motivated by his ability to profit from those referrals. Plaintiff's counsel could use the latter, of course, to attack the credibility of the defendant and his motives to violate the noncompete.

From the standpoint of the physician-defendant, the scrutiny of the previous relationship may yield potential defenses and counterclaims. So-called *qui tam* or whistleblower cases in healthcare, along with their astounding fines—in which the whistleblowers often share—frequently result from wrongful termination or other lawsuits that the informants may have instigated against the *qui tam* defendants.[27] Surprisingly, perhaps, informants often escape penalties for whatever part they played in the alleged schemes because the government has a vested interest in whistleblowers coming forward.[28]

From the standpoint of the plaintiff, the discovery process directed against the new practice unit could uncover regulatory violations that would lead to settlement.

Typical physician practice claims that do not 'fly'

A typical claim for lost profits generally arises from the proximity of the parties to one another in a business relationship and the resulting strategic advantages that they each enjoyed prior to a breach. For example, a small donut store located in a strip mall next to a major consumer retailer such as Home Depot or Loews would benefit from the customer flow to those stores. If the donut shop brings a claim against the landlord for failure to deliver the lease, for example, then a financial expert would certainly look at both the historical and future customer traffic flow to the home goods retailer as one basis for measuring the donut shop's lost profits.

26 See generally 420 CFR 411.

27 The University of Medicine and Dentistry in New Jersey (UMDNJ) investigation is an excellent case in point. In December 2005, the DOJ entered into an agreement with UMDNJ, by which UMDNJ paid back nearly $5 million in double-billings to Medicaid and undertook certain operational reforms in return for deferred charges of healthcare fraud; see www.usdoj.gov/usao/nj/press/files/pdffiles/UMDNJFINALDPA.pdf.

28 *McLeod Regional Medical Center to Pay U.S. Over $15 Million to Resolve False Claims Act Allegations*, DOJ Press Release (Nov. 1, 2002); www.usdoj.gov/opa/pr/2002/November/02_civ_634.htm.

By contrast, the Stark laws specifically prohibit market value from being based on the ability of strategic parties to refer patients to one another; similarly, the anti-kickback statute prohibits payment for referrals.[29] Assume that the physician-owners of a medical office building lease space to a tenant who plans to construct an imaging center; assume further that the physicians-owners decide to construct their own center and force out the tenant. If one accepts the premise that claimed damages cannot be based on a possible violation of the law, then it would be incorrect to base the tenant's future profits on the potential referrals that would have been available from all physicians in the building. Further, with respect to referrals from the physician-owners, although they likely would have referred all of their business to their own center, they likely would not have referred all of their business to a tenant's independent center. Of course, the tenant may have alternative damages claims available, to preclude the physician-owners from unjustly profiting from their actions.

Conclusion

After reading this chapter, one might conclude that it focused primarily on factors that tend to reduce potential claims for lost profits related to physician practices. In fact, a host of potential damages theories can apply to these and related cases, but because physician practices are one of the economy's most heavily regulated sectors, calculating damages based on these damages theories requires a body of knowledge that the typical damages expert may not generally have. More importantly, in litigation of this type, the opposing party is more likely to retain an expert to refute any damages claim, and any plaintiff's expert who does not appropriately consider the factors discussed in this chapter will likely be subject to attack. Accordingly, it is critical that any financial expert retained in this area of practice consider the following *areas of inquiry and evaluation for potential damage claims:*

1. Loss of physician income in general;
2. Loss of nonphysician support staff;
3. Loss of nonphysician provider staff who perform billable services;
4. Loss of physician staff (e.g., to a hospital);
5. Loss of practice value;
6. Loss of ancillary revenue from laboratory, imaging, and cardiac testing;

29 Arguably, even if the standard of value in physician lost profits is not fair market value, the outright prohibition on paying for referrals likely precludes the use of "strategic value" assumptions.

7. Loss of inpatient admissions;

8. Loss of skilled nursing facility admissions;

9. Loss of outpatient surgical facility fees;

10. Loss of home health agency revenue; and

11. Loss of durable medical equipment revenue.

In an era when hospitals and larger practice entities are fiercely competing for physician specialties—including cardiology, cardiac surgery, and orthopedics—events giving rise to potential damages claims are on the increase. Analysis of the expansive revenue and profit opportunities that plaintiffs have lost in such circumstances is where financial and damages experts should focus their attention.

Glossary of Terms

In many ways, the financial aspects of medical practices have a unique vocabulary. The following definitions will be helpful to financial experts and attorneys who may be new to the area.

- Ancillary—refers to a collection of testing equipment such as imaging (CT, MRI, ultrasound, stress testing, and so on).
- Payor—An industry term for the source of payment for services, such as Blue Cross, Medicare, Medicaid, an HMO, and so on.
- Payor mix—the percentage of business done with various payors.
- Stark laws—Federal civil legislation comprised of three separate statutory provisions governing physician self-referral for Medicare and Medicaid patients.[30] Stark regulations contain an outright prohibition on physicians referring certain services to entities in which they have defined financial interests, for example. The statute is enforced with draconian fines.
- Anti-kickback statute—Federal criminal legislation that prohibits payment of anything of value to a healthcare provider for referring services provided to beneficiaries of federal programs including Medicare, Medicaid, and Civilian Health and Medical Program of the Uniformed Services (CHAMPUS).[31]

30 Stark legislation is codified at 42 U.S.C.S. §1395nn (§1877 of the Social Security Act) and 42 C.F.R. §411.350 through §411.389.

31 See Criminal Penalties for Acts Involving Federal Health Care Programs, 42 U.S.C. § 1320a-7b(b)(2000).

- Integrated provider—An entity that engages in a variety of services in the "continuum of care." For example, a large physician practice may have both primary care and specialist physicians, broad-based radiology and imaging capability, a freestanding ambulatory surgery center, and a laboratory.

- Integrated delivery system—An entity with hospital and physician components, usually both primary care and specialist care, in addition to such services as radiology and imaging, laboratory, skilled nursing facility, and home health care.

- Professional component (PC or "26")—The portion of a payment for a test or imaging (e.g., cardiac stress or a CT scan) that compensates the physician for interpreting the results of the test.

- Revenue cycle—the process commencing with the preparation of a charge or bill (claim) for a service through the collection of all the payments for it. In healthcare, the process is complicated by different rates for the same service by different payors, partial payments by one or more payors for the same service, and the need to collect from the patient after all insurance and government payors have weighed in on a claim. There are also complex documentation and coding rules as well as retrospective review of charges for claims already paid.

- Technical component (TC)—The portion of a payment for a test or imaging (e.g., a cardiac stress test or a CT scan) that compensates the physician practice for owning the equipment, employing the technician (if any), providing supplies, and so on (See also Professional Component, above).

- Global—The combination of the PC and TC for a service.

CPSIA information can be obtained at www.ICGtesting.com
Printed in the USA
BVOW060023300513

321872BV00007B/333/P

9 781621 500018